STALIN'S EAGLES

★ ★ ★

STALIN'S EAGLES

★★★

An Illustrated Study of the Soviet Aces of World War II and Korea

Hans D. Seidl

Forewords by Günther Rall & Vitalij Popkov

Schiffer Military History
Atglen, PA

Aircraft profile artwork by John C. Valo.
Dust jacket artwork by Steve Ferguson.

RED SKY OVER THE DNYEPR RIVER
In the coral light of morning, 1st Eskadrilya leader Vitalij Popkov pulls away in his La-5FN, "Yellow 01," from his latest victim in the 1944 spring offensive fought in the Dnyepr River valley of southern Ukraine.

Dedication
Meinen Eltern, Jean Sebastian und Dorothee

Book Design by Robert Biondi.

Library of Congress Catalog Number: 98-84259.

Printed in the United States of America.
ISBN: 0-7643-0476-3

We are interested in hearing from authors with book ideas on related topics.

Published by Schiffer Publishing Ltd.
4880 Lower Valley Road
Atglen, PA 19310 USA
Phone: (610) 593-1777
FAX: (610) 593-2002
E-mail: Schifferbk@aol.com.
Please write for a free catalog.
This book may be purchased from the publisher.
Please include $3.95 postage.
Try your bookstore first.

CONTENTS

FOREWORD I

At the beginning of the 1940s there were apparently already many who knew and spoke about the coming war with Hitler's Germany, nevertheless like every disaster it came over our land unexpectedly. At dawn on June 22, 1941 fascist Germany invaded the territory of the USSR, violating the non-aggression pact between the two countries, and plunged the Soviet people into a difficult and bloody war. At the time of the invasion Hitler's Germany enjoyed a significant advantage in military forces. What is more, our nation was behind in the production of modern military technologies, to say nothing of equipping and training the troops with the new equipment. This had extremely serious consequences for the effectiveness of our fighting units in the first days and months of the war.

Even fifty years after the war, the older generation cannot forget the terrible suffering, the many victims and the destruction that the war brought with it. I remember the young fighter pilots who came to the front at the start of the war after an accelerated training program of only sixty-five hours flying time. In spite of their inadequate training, these airmen often engaged a numerically superior enemy and emerged victorious. They demonstrated the utmost fighting spirit and psychological strength, as well as loyal fulfillment of duty, unconditional loyalty to the ideals of justice, a true willingness to perform feats of heroism in the pursuit of sacred goals, international brotherhood, and comradeship. During the course of the war I was able to convince myself of this firsthand over and over again.

It is not without reason that the aviation units make up the bulk of the first rank of Heroes of the Soviet Union. A total of 2,420 airmen received this title during the war. Our air forces were responsible for 62% of all aircraft lost by the enemy in the war as well as 74% of the losses on the German-Soviet front – proof of the degree of skill achieved by our pilots during the war and of the increased capabilities of our aircraft. Equipped with modern planes and led by experienced commanders, by mid-1943 Soviet airmen had achieved strategic air superiority, which they maintained until the end of the war.

We must also not forget the assistance rendered by our allies; the approximately 14,000 aircraft provided by them was equivalent to almost 23% of Soviet aircraft production.

It is regrettable that in recent times repeated attempts have been made to absolutize the dramatic pages of Soviet history and simultaneously reevaluate our victory and everything that is associated with it. In evaluating history the idealization of the past and the ignoring of the complete and harsh truth about the tragedy of those days and the attempt to negate everything really great and worthwhile achieved by previous generations – including the victory have proved equally dangerous.

With each year the events of the Great Patriotic War retreat further into the pages of history. But for those who fought, who emptied the bitter cup of the retreat to the bottom and experienced the joy of our victory, these events will always be remembered, always remain near and vivid.

This is actually all that I wanted to say after first reading this manuscript. But it is not just simple episodes from the biographies of my wartime comrades. In many respects our postwar fates were probably similar. Most combat pilots remained in the ranks. They became familiar with the new technologies, studied at military academies. For us, simple youths from families of modest means, a broad road into the future opened itself. And now, when I look back on the path that I took, I remember with gratitude the men with whom I knew good as well as bad during the difficult years of war and especially with whom I learned to understand the souls of men and their secrets. I remember the time when I came to love a tough but very necessary profession. Later this proved helpful in telling about my experiences fulfilling the difficult tasks of an airman of the fatherland. We are therefore pleased to see every sentence dedicated to our dear friends. I wish them luck and health and to the author of this extraordinary work – continued success.

V.I. POPKOV
Twice Hero of the Soviet Union
Lieutenant-General of the Air Forces
Distinguished Military Pilot of the USSR

FOREWORD II

Whether an act of aggression or a preemptive strike, on June 22, 1941 the Germans stormed into Russia, and the Russians were called upon to defend their nation. Ideologically motivated, the war was waged by both sides with extreme harshness. A mutual offsetting of action against reaction will not bring a one-sided justification.

Involved from the beginning as a fighter pilot, I was surprised by the Russians' numerical superiority, but their inferior training, their inadequate tactics in the air, and their obsolete aircraft gave us sufficient self-confidence in aerial combat. Consequently the Russian losses during the first three months were tremendously high; however, their unbroken morale earned our highest respect. The Russians succeeded in setting up new production lines on the other side of the Urals, beyond the range of German bombers, and beginning in mid-1942 they introduced new, better and more modern aircraft into front-line service in large numbers. As well through the Lend-Lease Treaty they were helped by their allies with deliveries of large numbers of fighters such as the P-39, P-40 and Spitfire, as well as the Douglas Boston and other bomber types. Now our opponents were Red Banner Guards Regiments with well-trained, experienced ace pilots in modern aircraft – the picture had changed.

The air forces played a major role in the great battle of Moscow and the battles of encirclement at Stalingrad and Kursk. Their military successes and the experience they had gained in many encounters strengthened the self-confidence of the Russians, while on the German side after Kursk there were only retreats and a defensive morale prevailed. The Russians ended the eastern campaign with a victorious march into Berlin.

Fifty years later we fighter pilots from both sides have met and talked dispassionately about our experiences. Free from historical or political judgments, but with great respect for the actions, the victims, and the victories on both sides, we all share the same conviction: never again! This sentiment is best expressed in the words:

"Yesterday's enemy, today's friend"

GÜNTHER RALL
Lieutenant General (Rtd.)

INTRODUCTION

This is the story of Soviet fighter aces whose electrifying exploits have long been shrouded in mystery. These young men sharpened their skills in a furious war of attrition against a tried and tested foe and eventually formed the bulk and guts of the Soviet Air Force.

I have tried to present a factual account allowing the records to speak for themselves. More than an outline was necessary here. I have produced this book as a result of decades of research in the course of which I have gained access to much previously unpublished material along with enjoying valuable connections in Russia in my aim to make it the last word on Soviet aces.

Every effort has been made to arrive at the fullest detail and greatest authenticity. *Stalin's Eagles* contains hundreds of biographical sketches of the operational careers of the aces. These are the most detailed writings ever published on the subject.

During my frequent visits to Russia I was able to unearth much valuable material in anonymous files and private collections enabling me to illustrate this study with a wealth of photographs.

The book has taken a lot of blood, sweat and tears as Soviet military publications of the past have tended to leave much in obscurity, dealing in generalities or rendering highly polemical accounts only.

I am grateful to all those individuals and organizations who have generously helped me over the years to finish a long cherished project. It would be impossible to list and thank all of them here.

Thank you to my old friends Dr. Yurij Mikhajlov, Sasha Negriyenko and Viktor Kulikov. A very special thank you is due to Herr Horst Amberg of the Gemeinschaft der Jagdflieger, who introduced me to some of the leading German aces; further thanks are due to General Major P.F. Vyalikov, director of the Central House of Aviation and Cosmonautics in Moscow, who provided much original material and to John C. Valo for preparing the color profiles included in the book.

Acknowledgment is due to the Department of the Air Force, Air Force Historical Research Agency, Maxwell Air Force Base, Alabama, for access to USAAF records relating to a November 7, 1944 air encounter between Soviet and American aircraft, and to the Bundesarchiv in Koblenz for providing me with a number of photographs.

I would like to extend my warmest thanks to Vitalij Ivanovich Popkov and Günther Rall for very kindly writing the forewords and who gave freely of their time in interviews, correspondence and general discussion of their experience.

Finally, the deepest gratitude is due to my wife Dorothee and our son Jean Sebastian for allowing me to spend many nights and holidays on research.

It is my goal to continually add new material, and if any reader can supply data or correct any inaccuracies, they are welcomed to write me at the following address. Please give a reference to the source of your information.

HANS D. SEIDL
Am Bichlberg 8
82237 Wörthsee
Germany
March, 1998

1

THE EASTERN FRONT AIR WAR

When Operation Barbarossa struck the Soviet Union on the fateful June 22, 1941 the Red air forces were caught in the midst of an extensive rearmament program. The units were made up of large numbers of ill-trained fledglings who had never fired their guns in anger and were flying obsolescent aircraft that were no match for the standard German fighter, the Messerschmitt Bf 109, under normal circumstances. What was more, the political purges of the late 1930s had rendered the command levels with many incapable, inexperienced officers. There was a nucleus of veterans available – Soviet pilots had fought in Spain and against the Finns during the embarrassing Winter War of 1939/40 while the fighter arm in particular had done well fighting the Japanese in Mongolia in 1939 (claims totaled 646 enemy planes destroyed at the cost of 207 of their number), but the lessons of these battles had been largely ignored.

On the eve of war, the VVS enjoyed a crushing numerical superiority over the Luftwaffe with 35 air divisions being deployed in the five major districts in European Soviet Russia as follows:

Leningrad Military District	eight divisions numbering 1,270 aircraft
Baltic Military District	five divisions/1,140 aircraft
Western Military District	11 divisions/1,560 aircraft (or eight divisions numbering 1,825 aircraft according to other sources)
Kiev Military District	10 divisions/1,672 aircraft
Odessa Military District	four divisions/950 aircraft

But this force was a paper tiger. It primarily consisted of aircraft with manifest obsolescence. The fighter arm, which was in the process of rebuilding with a new generation of excellent designs such as the MiG-3, LaGG-3 and Yak-1, could field only 980 modern planes including 886 MiG-3s to confront the tried and tested Luftwaffe. By June 22, 1941 only eight of 106 fighter regiments were mounted on advanced machines. They were not capable of playing a prominent role in the darkest hours of the 1941 air war many being destroyed on the ground on airfields along the front. A large number of pilots was not sufficiently familiar with the new types of aircraft to be able to get optimum performance from them. Ground control methods were rather rudimentary and fighter tactics equally immature. Leading Luftwaffe pilots generally agree on the basis of their experience that the Russian fighters in 1941 were often rather amateurishly led in combat. The results were catastrophic. When night fell on June 22, the Luftwaffe had struck at 66 major airfields where Baltic, Western, Kiev and Odessa Military Districts had deployed 70% of the strength to hand, causing great damage.

Amongst the hardest hit was Western Military District which at that time contained the 12 and 13 BADs, 43, 59 and 60 IADs of Frontal Aviation along with the 9, 10 and 11 SADs which were attached to combined arms armies. Additionally there was the 3 DBAK of the High Command being made up of the 42 and 52 BADs and 61 IAD. In all, the district could call on 1,560 aircraft at the outset of the war consisting of 377 SB-2s, 42 Pe-2s, 22 Ar-2s, 24 Yak-4s, 75 Su-2s, 424 I-16s, 262 I-153s, 73 I-15s, 233 MiG-3s, 20 Yak-1s and 8 Il-2s. A relatively large number of fighter units was much too close to the frontier with the result that heavy losses were incurred in preemptive bombardments of German artillery. Devastation was tremendous as the hammer blows of the Luftwaffe were completing the destruction. Western Military District alone lost 47% of the strength to hand not including the long-range bomber forces, i.e. 387 bombers and 351 fighters were destroyed, 210 of them in air combat. Before the day was out, 9 SAD had lost 347 of its 409 aircraft, while 10 SAD had lost 188 of 231 and 11 SAD 127 of 188. Total Soviet losses that day are estimated to have exceeded 1,200, 300+ of which were shot down in combat.

Quality of training fell rapidly in the weeks that followed. Novices were sent into the struggle after an all too brief training period scarcely able to control their aircraft. 249 Il-2s that had been supplied before the outbreak of war were harshly treated by German fighters as they frequently had to operate without escort.

The well-known series of staggering Soviet defeats has been covered in detail so often that they do not require further elaboration here. Battle-hardened Luftwaffe pilots were taking a terrible toll of Soviet aircraft in adding to their prowess. The story of German aces achieving tremendous scores on the Eastern Front has led to much speculation and misunderstanding while views of the battles fought over Soviet Russia tend to generalities. The characteristic features of the Soviet forces and pilots which had been badly mauled and disorganized during the first months of the fighting, are seen as an innate sluggishness and lack of initiative. Nothing could be farther from the truth.

Individual life was not precious, and no one was allowed to give up. The Russians were putting up a surprisingly ferocious resistance. What average Soviet pilots initially lacked in skill, they made up for with incredible bravery and determination, ready to sacrifice themselves. In this desperate situation they were beginning to display a propensity for deliberate ramming, which later was becoming a commonplace on all sectors of the front. Successful pilots were celebrated by propaganda glorifying the last-ditch efforts of individuals in the collective battle for mother Russia, the Great Patriotic War, as this vast conflict came to be called.

Amongst airmen, the aerial ramming (vozdushnyj taran) became more popularly known as the "falcon attack" (sokolnyj udar). Almost 600 aerial taran were performed during the war including 558 by fighters, 19 by Shturmovik and 18 by bomber aircrews. 28-victory ace B.I. Kovzan was the leading exponent of the taran attack. He survived no fewer than four successful rammings although his left eye was destroyed while achieving his fourth such victory. Following his recovery, Kovzan returned to combat duty adding six air victories (some 10 according to another source) to his tally.

They fought with what they had . . . thrown into the fray against the all-conquering Luftwaffe in substantial numbers, the I-153 fighters offered spirited resistance during the early months of the war but suffered terrible losses. Some Russian high-scorers were able to built up respectable tallies on this machine owing to its extraordinary maneuverability. (Author's collection)

The months of 1941 were black with disaster for the Russians. Admitted losses included 1,777 aircraft during the desperate defensive battles in Byelorussia (June 22 – July 9, 1941), 990 in the Baltic (same time frame) and 1,218 in the Western Ukraine (June 22 – July 6, 1941). (Bundesarchiv)

This unidentified VVS Lejtenant fell into German hands south of Smolensk and is being taken to the dispensary by his guards. Summer 1941. (Bundesarchiv)

First heroes. On July 8, 1941 three Mladshij Lejtenanti of the 158 IAP – M.P. Zhukov, S.I. Zdorovtsev and P.T. Kharitonov (from left) – received acclaim as the first pilots to gain the title of Hero of the Soviet Union in the Patriotic War. In all, this coveted title was to be bestowed upon 2,271 pilots, 65 of them receiving it twice, and two three times. (Author's collection)

Fortune favors the brave! Starshij Serzhant I.M. Chumbarev of 237 IAP poses with the wreckage of a Ju 88 that he successfully rammed at Stalingrad on September 14, 1942. He managed to safely nurse his aircraft back to his own airfield. (Author's collection)

A.S. Khlobystov and N.V. Terekhin both received credit for three successful rammings each while a total of 34 pilots accomplished this feat twice; Mladshij Lejtenant Leonid Borisov of the 43 IAP also performed three taran but only two of his opponents were actually destroyed. Twenty fighter pilots achieved the remarkable exploit of two successful rammings in one sortie. If the attack was carried out at sufficient altitude, the pilot stood a fair chance of parachuting to safety or struggling back to base. During the air battles over Kursk in 1943 Soviet pilots reportedly performed 47 successful taran. 15 of them either returned to their own airfields or carried out a forced-landing. Nine abandoned their aircraft, 17 were killed, while six were reported missing or failed to return.

Tactics were devised under combat conditions. This vital development though suffered some drawbacks of which the redoubtable Aleksandr Pokryshkin gives an illuminating account:

> "Innovations, for instance new forms of attack, almost invariably encountered obstacles one way or the other. The air division commanders much too often demanded strict observance of service regulations which were also prescribing forms of attack. Veteran pilots thus were unable to convey their combat experience to the beginners. This, however, did not prevent them from utilizing their personal formula in air combat!" Tireless Pokryshkin not only finished as the second ranking Allied ace of World War II, but also became the acknowledged innovator of Soviet fighter tactics, a great tutor of green pilots many of whom were to emerge as distinguished fighters. He recalls the following unusual mission with novices of a fledgling outfit:

"We were making for the Manych which the enemy had forced at Vesseloye. Contrary to my orders the young pilots stayed close to me, maintaining an unsteady formation without varying altitude. After strafing we were headed for home when a flight of Messerschmitts turned up to

Right: Period postcard depicting the feat performed by Mladshij Lejtenant I.S. Chernykh of the 125 BAP (gunner – S.K. Kosipov, radio operator – N.P. Gubin) near Chudovo, Novgorod area, on December 16, 1941. Upon being hit by flak, Chernykh deliberately crashed his stricken bomber into advancing enemy columns. Known as "ognennyj taran" (fiery ramming attack), this form of attack was to become commonplace, 503 being accomplished throughout the war, including 98 by fighters. (Author's collection)

make things hot for us. I ordered the attack and turned into them. My comrades though only moved closer and raced away for home. The Messerschmitts turned after them disregarding me. I opened fire at close range and shot one of them down. The three remaining fighters now swept down on me and I hardly escaped their attacks."

In an all-out effort the Soviets were able to make up for their horrendous losses in relatively short time by skillfully preserving their facilities for the production of aircraft and the training of pilots. While strength to hand had fallen to 2,495 planes in the field by December, 1941, the air forces could already call on a substantial fleet of 3,164 aircraft as of May, 1942. During the same time frame, Soviet-constructed aircraft were increasingly supplemented by substantial numbers of Lend-Lease fighters such as Hurricanes, Spitfires, Tomahawks, Kittyhawks and Airacobras. With the exception of the latter, all types were to wind up as more or less controversial among Soviet pilots. Most felt, that these machines were inadequately armed and did not have any attribute that was outstanding. The P-39 Airacobra though was destined to become the favorite mount of many legendary fighter aces developing its best performance at low to medium altitudes where most of the action took place while possessing tremendous firepower. Major G.V. Zimin, who commanded the 485 IAP and 240 IAD in World War II, provides the following recollection, which is shared by many VVS command personnel:

"The pilots flying Hurricanes showed a particularly pessimistic outlook. They bluntly stated that they would never stand a chance against the Messerschmitts which had a distinctively superior performance, could leave them standing and handle them roughly with ease."

In consonance with this development, the organizational structures were subjected to drastic consolidation measures. The early battles had proven most dramatically the ineffectiveness of unwieldy air units which were attached to combined arms armies and subordinate to the army commander.

The Soviet Command focused on building up its air power to permit the concentration of forces at points of main effort. Learning from the disastrous setbacks, the commitment of air power was no longer to be performed in a piece-meal manner.

Right above: This photo shows Kapitan Mariya Ivanovna Dolina, a deputy squadron leader in the 125 GBAP. On August 18, 1945 she was awarded the highest Soviet distinction, the title of Hero of the Soviet Union for making a brilliant record at Stalingrad, Yelnya, Smolensk, and over Byelorussia, the Baltic and East Prussia. As of January, 1945 she totaled 63 sorties in Pe-2s combining forces with comrades to destroy three German fighters in air combat. As the situation for Russia aggravated, women were allowed into combat many fighting with great distinction as snipers, aircrew members and tankers. 28 women were awarded the title of Hero of the Soviet Union as aircrew of nightbombers, two titles went to Shturmovik pilots while L.V. Litvyak seemingly was the only female fighter pilot to win the award – posthumously. (Author's collection)

Right: Podpolkovnik Bershanskaya of an unknown unit. (Frunze House)

The idea was to swiftly maneuver strong forces between front sectors within the framework of ground operations.

Thus on May 5, 1942 the first of an eventual eighteen air armies was established by order of the People's Comissariat, abandoning the front and combined arms armies' air services. The 1st Air Army (Vozdushnaya Armiya) was built around the air units of West Front, 2nd Air Army around those of Bryansk Front. By November, Soviet Frontal Aviation was no longer subordinate to the combined arms armies, which were left with one composite air regiment only for reconnaissance and liaison duties.

Strength ratios at the front now were rapidly developing in favor of Soviet forces. Late in 1942 powerful air corps were activated as Supreme High Command General Headquarters (STAVKA) air reserves. These units usually consisted of two or more divisions with strength ranging from 120 to 270 planes to be committed to action according to STAVKA directives so as to achieve numerical superiority at points of main effort; upon completion of their mission, the air corps were withdrawn for possible transfer to another front sector. In order to develop this numerical superiority, adjacent areas frequently had to be stripped of fighter support. Strength of the air armies continued to gain as the war dragged on according to the needs of the campaign or theater of operations. The order of battle thus ranged from six to twelve divisions and 900-1,000 aircraft in 1942/43, 1,500 aircraft in 1944 and 2,500-3,000 during the final stages of the war.

Right and below: Two shots of Ju 52s that were forced down by Red fighters in the Stalingrad area in December, 1942. VVS fighter air regiments that were put in the path of Luftwaffe transport aircraft trying to supply the troops in the pocket frequently encountered unescorted formations of these sluggish machines, and great slaughter was done. (Author's collection)

Below: Typical scene during the infamous Russian winter. With temperatures dropping like a stone in a well, everything froze, soldiers losing their digits or limbs to the cold or even froze to death while relieving nature. (Author's collection)

Representative VVS Air Armies Orders of Battle

Date	Total on hand	Bombers	Shturmoviks	Fighters
1-1-1943				
7 VA	384	43	144	179
13 VA	285	57	57	141
14 VA	192	29	90	40
15 VA	376	23	132	175
3 VA	535	-	182	322
1 VA	941	324	386	186
16 VA	651	182	77	377
2 VA	562	81	222	229
5 VA	635	141	166	304
17 VA	421	91	148	125
8 VA	746	92	221	389
1-1-1944				
7 VA	715	47	246	395
13 VA	429	91	139	165
14 VA	170	39	73	48
15 VA	388	-	148	192
3 VA	600	-	204	356
1 VA	952	387	309	199
4 VA	418	-	133	253
6 VA	281	-	101	146
16 VA	1,388	322	267	742
2 VA	1,306	249	448	557
5 VA	1,172	261	435	457
17 VA	979	115	342	487
1-1-1945				
13 VA	481	12	57	357
15 VA	415	73	166	139
3 VA	1,172	298	338	495
1 VA	1,286	220	456	500
4 VA	1,481	199	543	640
16 VA	2,396	388	750	1,172
2 VA	2,273	419	771	990
8 VA	499	80	184	194
5 VA	645	66	227	316
17 VA	882	102	353	381

In 1944 Soviet forces were conducting a series of powerful blows that would decisively smash German Army Group Center in Byelorussia and carry them to the eastern borders of the Third Reich. The Soviet Union now could muster 6,165,000 men in the field, 88,900 guns and mortars, 4,900 tanks and self-propelled guns and 8,500 planes. Atrophied Luftwaffe formations that rose to oppose these armadas no longer compared with the crack units of the Blitzkrieg campaigns, they were plagued by degenerating pilot training, lack of fuel. Although the Experten continued to run up big scores, their success no longer constituted a serious hazard to Soviet aerial supremacy.

1944 saw a further reorganization of the air divisions. They were organized into three to four regiments each with Shturmovik and fighter regiments containing 40 aircraft.

Soviet tactics and techniques improved immeasurably as the war progressed, first slowly then with increasing rapidity. As the airmen were gaining combat experience, success increasing their self-confidence, they contributed to the rehabilitation of Soviet airpower through their personal effort. Numerous stellar performers were to survive the ordeals of continuous fighting from the earliest days of the war to acquire an expertise that would make them the equal of their adversaries in every respect. It is interesting to note that the majority of leading Russian aces survived the war.

If Luftwaffe pilots sometimes were contemptuous of their Russian opponents – although there is a wide disparity of opinions – the notion that the air war on the Eastern Front was easy cannot be sustained.

"The claim that the Russians were poor flyers is false. The beginners among the German fighter pilots were just as awkward as the Russian beginners," was the view of Helmut Lipfert, one of the great aces of World War II. Lipfert ran up a staggering total of 203 kills fighting with the legendary JG 52 mostly over Soviet Russia, and in the process was shot down 15 times.

In endorsing this comment, Walter Krupinski, another JG 52 luminary, who tallied 197 aerial victories, adds the following assessment to the author:

> "I feel that the Russian fighter pilots were of equal ability at the time of my transfer into the Reichs-

Right and below: State Aircraft Factory No.18 (GAZ-18) at Kujbyshev. After evacuation from Voronezh in October, 1941 production was resumed in a roofless and unheated building, and with the advent of winter, temperature dropped below 30 degrees centigrade. On December 23, 1941 Stalin telegraphed emphatically: "You are leaving our country and our Red Army in the lurch . . . Our Red Army needs Il-2 aircraft as it needs air and bread . . . If factory 18 considers to neglect our country by rendering one Il-2 per day it is making an awful mistake that would be punished. I am demanding that you produce more Il-2s!" The motto translates: "Everything for the front, everything for victory." (Author's collection)

verteidigung in the spring of 1944. The Guards regiments certainly played a special role, of which we only had partial knowledge then. For instance, I once had a fifteen minute battle with a hot pilot. Only the two of us. I shot him down as he was turning for home apparently with fuel getting low."

Walter Krupinski, a brilliant JG 52 ace, who tallied 177 victories in the east and 20 more in the west including two with the Me 262. This photo is dated May, 1944 when he was Gruppenkommandeur of II./JG 11. (Author's collection courtesy of W. Krupinski)

On December 6, 1941 the Soviet government awarded the honorary title of Guards for the first time to air regiments for making a significant contribution to the fighting – the 29, 129, 155 and 526 IAPs. The units thus decorated were presented with a special Guards banner while officers' ranks were prefixed Guards. Like battle decorations and honors, the latter being awarded for distinguished combat duty at particular locations, the epithet Guards became part of the unit's official title. By the close of war, a total of 346 Soviet Air Force units had been designated Guards: 12 air corps, 48 divisions, 204 regiments and 82 eskadrili. Outstanding pilots sometimes were posted to Guards regiments to achieve a concentration of fighting skill. A case in point was the famous 9 GIAP which had won the Guards title on March 7, 1942 for excelling in the hell of Odessa. In the fall of 1942, during the bloody fighting for Stalingrad, Soviet High Command ordered the concentration of successful pilots in the 9 GIAP so as to establish an outfit capable of doing battle with the best of the enemy. The air aces, however, usually stayed with their original units or were assigned to inexperienced or battered ones to get these into operational trim.

Also, on September 14, 1942 each fighter division was to form a special "okhota" (hunting) unit composed of volunteers who were skillful and experienced pilots. These units were tasked with penetrating into the German rear with attacks on airfields and searching out enemy planes, particularly reconnaissance aircraft. Simultaneously, the Luftwaffe Schwarm (flight) consisting of two elements each was adopted to replace the existing three-plane formation for increased flexibility and effectiveness. During the war 31,330 "svobodnaya okhota" (free hunt) sorties were successfully carried out by fighters. According to Soviet sources, the success rate was one enemy plane

Four of the most famous Soviet fighter pilots of the war are seen here together in front of Moscow's Red Square. From left, they are: N.D. Gulayev (57 kills), A.I. Pokryshkin (59), G.A. Rechkalov (56), and A.I. Trud (24). They all flew the P-39 Aeracobra with noteworthy success, gaining all or most of their scores on this type. (Author's collection)

The fast Petlyakov Pe-2 multi-role aircraft played a vital role in attacks on tactical targets. It was one of the outstanding aircraft of the war and proved very difficult to intercept. It was used throughout the war in large numbers, production eventually totaling 11,202. This photo is dated 1943. (Author's collection)

destroyed for every 3-4 sorties flown. The most successful exponents of free hunt missions were Major I.N. Kozhedub, the Allied ace of aces, Major A.I. Koldunov, Kapitan N.M. Skomorokhov and others.

The Soviet air forces produced a very large number of air aces, many having gained valuable combat experience in Spain, Mongolia or against Finland. The VVS top aces frequently were in continuous action from the first until the last days of the war and developed into exceptionally capable fighter pilots. As a consequence, fourteen Soviet aces amassed higher victory totals than the ranking Anglo-American ace, Major R.I. Bong, who tallied 40 kills against the Japanese. Official estimates indicate that nearly 800 aces scored in excess of 15 personal victories each, and about 200 were credited with 20 or more victories. It is little wonder that the majority of these men came from the elite Guards regiments, which almost invariably were committed wherever the struggle was hard thus giving them great opportunities to add to their records. But there was also a striking number of fine pilots who came into prominence fighting with regiments that hardly became known. This reflects the enormous recuperating powers of the Soviet air forces which gradually had created a corps of highly qualified, versatile and aggressive personnel under the most appalling of circumstances.

When hostilities ceased, 43,000 enemy planes had been claimed shot down in air combat, 19,000 by antiaircraft fire plus 13,000 more that were destroyed in ground attacks. (According to Soviet military analyses, a massive 75% of all fighter victories were gained on the first pass at 150-50 meters range.) In contrast, USAAF fighters claimed 11,000 air victories in the ETO and MTO throughout the war.

The highest scoring period came in 1943 when the Russians started their major offensives with 28.5% of the overall claims being reported. The bulk of victories came from the powerful fighter arm of the Red Army Air Force. This information reveals that the long-accepted notion of easy victories against a second-rate adversary on the Eastern Front violates the facts. What is more, it would appear that about three quarters of all Luftwaffe losses in fact were sustained in the grueling battles of attrition over the German-Soviet front. It seems that the air forces in the east were eventually much more closely matched technically and psychologically than had been previously thought.

Owing to the Soviet fighters' principal mission of providing protection for the attack armies, Shturmovik and bomber formations, they were to achieve only relatively modest results against enemy airfields. Because of these requirements, only 58,446 sorties were afforded in this role or 2% of the overall Soviet fighter sorties with the following results:

1941	1,116 enemy planes destroyed on the ground
1942	1,452
1943	1,247
1944	1,027
1945	2,148

Highest ground scorer probably was Kapitan I.A. Avekov of the 519 IAP who was credited with destroying 19 enemy planes in the air plus 23 on the ground before being killed in action on April 17, 1943; Avekov's bag though almost paled into insignificance when compared with Kapitan I.I. Zinovyev's record, who ranks as the top Shturmovik strafer with 87 ground and nine air.

The final statistical figures for the other Soviet air forces were as follows:

PVO air defense: 7,313 enemy planes air/ground including victories claimed by antiaircraft units; fighters only accounted for 3,930 air and 238 ground during 269,465 sorties.

KBF Baltic Fleet: 58,050 sorties, 2,418 enemy planes air/ground, 843 tanks destroyed, 185 ships and 184 transport vessels sunk.

ChF Black Sea Fleet: 131,637 sorties, 2,149 enemy planes air/ ground, 680 tanks destroyed, some 500 ships and vessels sunk or damaged.

SF Northern Fleet: 57,203 sorties, 1,045 enemy planes destroyed, including 933 air, 178 ships and vessels sunk.

When Moscow was counting the cost, losses had long passed the limits of imagination. Although cold statistics cannot adequately picture the scope of destruction, some idea of the horrendous losses suffered by the Soviet Union may be gained from the following figures:

While official figures vary from source to source, the total number of enemy aircraft destroyed by the Soviet naval air forces probably is 5,509, including 4,495 in air combat. This Luftwaffe plane fell foul of Northern Fleet's fighters. (Author's collection)

Aircraft	106,400 (46,100 of which were attributed to enemy action)
Tanks	83,500
Self-propelled guns	13,000
Armored cars	37,600
Guns and mortars	317,500

A breakdown of aircraft losses reveals that the fighter arm incurred the heaviest numerical losses but proportionally less than the ground attack forces (36.8% of strength to hand) and the bomber forces (36.2%).

Summary of Soviet Fighter Aircraft Losses in World War II

YEAR	OVERALL LOSSES	LOSSES TO ENEMY ACTION ONLY	% OF STRENGTH TO HAND
1941 (6-22/12-31)	9,600	5,100	29.1
1942	7,000	4,400	23.7
1943	11,700	5,600	19.6
1944	12,700	4,100	11.1
1945 (1-1/5-10)	5,800	1,500	4.5
TOTAL	**46,800**	**20,700**	**27.9**

The "losses to enemy action" category covers aircraft known lost to enemy action either in air combat or shot down by flak but conceivably is not including the missing in action figures.

Fittingly perhaps, the last words should be from the men who had done it all. Aleksandr Yakovlev, whose design bureau gave birth to a family of excellent fighter aircraft, expresses the following evaluation of Soviet and enemy aces:

"The aces of the bourgeois armies tend to be individualists who are fighting for the benefit of their personal glory and thus are resembling movie stars. They are presumptuous, haughty and look upon themselves as a chosen caste. The leading Soviet pilots are completely different. In spite of their remarkable skills they in no way contrast with their fellow pilots. The spirit of team work in which the Soviet people are raised also embosses the Soviet fighter hero. He not only goes off on free hunt missions to search out and destroy the best of the enemy, but also enters into group combats leading his comrades."

VVS notables pose for a group portrait wearing the new parade dress. From left, they are: D.B. Glinka (100 GIAP), V.I. Popkov (5 GIAP), I.N. Kozhedub (176 GIAP), A.Ye. Borovykh (728 IAP) and P.Ya. Golovachyov (9 GIAP). Back row: the top tank killer of the war, A.N. Yefimov (62 ShAP), A.K. Nedbajlo (75 GShAP) and V.I. Mykhlik (566 ShAP). (Author's collection)

Twice Hero of the Soviet Union Arsenij Vorozhejkin who scored 52 aerial victories, six of them against the Japanese in Mongolia, made the following comment on German fighters:

> "German fighters excelled in hit and run attacks from altitude. It was their favorite tactic, and they achieved fairly good results."

Georgij Zimin was the brilliant commander of the 485 IAP and 240 IAD and finished with 19 personal victories together with 20 fractional credits. He battled one of Luftwaffe's most accomplished fighter outfits about which he remembered:

> "Later, as encounters were becoming more frequent, we established that we were fighting against the pilots of the famous German Jagdgeschwader 51 "Mölders." By the spring of 1945 this unit, which erstwhile had boasted the cream of the German fighter arm, had already lost many of its famous aces, but nonetheless they remained dangerous until the close of war. One can say that after the battles of 1943 the majority of our pilots was superior to the Germans, but in spite of this fighting against Geschwader "Mölders" demanded increased circumspection."

Polkovnik V.A. Kitayev who commanded the 283 IAD and faced the Luftwaffe at Stalingrad remarked:

> "Our aircraft, with the exception of the Yak-1, were not only approximately equal to the enemy fighters but had advantages in terms of maneuverability and rate of climb below 2,500 meters altitude."

The knightly traditions of World War I air warfare had not survived on Eastern Front. Air fighting rather was a ruthless cat and mouse type of combat, and although it usually made pilots feel sick when one of their comrades was strafed in his parachute by enemy fighters, it seems that pilots on both sides who knew no better were doing it. Aleksandr Pokryshkin, who commanded the crack 9 GIAD later in the war and emerged as the second ranking Allied ace with 59 kills, recalls at least one occasion a fellow pilot was strafed after abandoning his aircraft:

> "In the morning we received a phone call telling us that the pilot Ostrovskij of the 16 Guards Fighter Regiment was interred near a hamlet on the Kuban. Enemy fighters had shot him down while he was returning home. Ostrovskij managed to get out of his burning aircraft but

3rd Air Army pilots and Heroes of the Soviet Union, who paraded in Moscow on June 21, 1945 to celebrate the victory over Germany. They are wearing the new parade dress introduced at the end of the war. They are, left to right: P.A. Yermilov (766 ShAP), A.D. Panov (766 ShAP), T.A. Sayevich (11 ORAP), V.F. Sirotin (17 IAP), A.S. Smirnov (28 GIAP), I.D. Likhobabin (72 GIAP), S.G. Yankovskij (6 GShAP), Ya.N. Orlov (11 ORAP). (Author's collection)

> was killed by a burst of fire. I was upset. How many times had I shot down a Messerschmitt and seen the pilot bail out. But never had I thought of shooting him."

F.S. Gnezdilov, who was serving in the 18 GIAP as chief of staff at Kursk, over Byelorussia and East Prussia, summarizes his opinion on the enemy:

> "Many pilots of Hitler's Germany admittedly were competent airmen and gunners, who skillfully exploited the tactics of air fighting such as surprise, altitude, attacks from the sun. Among their ranks there were true aces – "hunters" – and fighting it out with them was no easy thing. Each victory thus was the result of formidable skill, courage and valor, the concentration of all mental and physical vigor."

Podpolkovnik (Rtd.) V. Alekseyenko, former chief engineer of the NII VVS (Nauchno-issledovatelskij institut VVS – Scientific Research Institute of the VVS), provides the following thoughtful and revealing recollections:

> "If one of our pilots was shot down over enemy held territory, evaded capture and managed to reach the Soviet lines he was exposed to serious investigation by SMERSH. Sometimes neither merit, nor intercession was a safeguard against suspicion, accusation and punishment."

A.F. Kovachevich, who served with great distinction with the 9 GIAP, gives a very pertinent comment as to the harsh conditions prevailing:

> "Prikaz no.227: Yes, there was this order. The reasons for its existence are known. I reason that this was a factor in all fighting armies. In respect of aviation, I am aware of so-called shtrafnye eskadrili (penal squadrons). Pilots were passed to these units for various offenses: cowardice, refusal to obey an order, lack of discipline and others. I happened to meet with one of these squadrons in the middle of the war. The pilots were flying the I-16, and it occurred to me 'They are all doomed.' It happened that pilots were put in the infantry from where they too seldom returned."

2

THE ACES

ABDRASHITOV, Shamil Munasypovich

Combat record: 12 personal victories, 155 sorties, 17 engagements.

Decorations: Gold Star of Hero of the Soviet Union on August 2, 1944; the Orders of Lenin, the Red Banner, Aleksandr Nevskij, the Patriotic War 1st Class, the Red Star.

Abdrashitov was born in Orenburg on May 19,1921 and completed his flight training at Orenburg military flying school in December, 1941. He was assigned to the Far East prior to being posted to the 402 IAP in April, 1943. He saw a great deal of action over the Kuban and the Crimea but on May 4, 1944 fell victim to airdrome flak near Khersones (S Sevastopol) and crashed to his death. He was a Lejtenant and deputy squadron leader at the time of his death.

ABRAMCHUK, Nikolaj Ivanovich

Combat record: 16 personal victories, 300 sorties.

Decorations: Gold Star of Hero of the Soviet Union on October 9, 1943 for 11 victories, 239 sorties of which 114 were ground attacks as of June, 1943; the Orders of Lenin, the Red Banner (2), the Red Star.

Abramchuk was born on November 20, 1912 and entered the Soviet Army for flight training in 1932. He received his wings at Engels military flying school in 1936 and fought from the very start of the Patriotic War. He saw considerable fighting on Southwest, West, Stalingrad and 1st Ukrainian Fronts while serving with the 894 IAP. He was a Kapitan and squadron leader when awarded the Gold Star for his efforts. Abramchuk left active duty with the rank of Podpolkovnik in 1954 and died on February 1, 1974.

ABRAMOV, Vladimir Fyodorovich

Combat record: 5 personal victories, 15 fractional credits, 287 sorties, 135 of which were armed reconnaissance and 94 escorts, 57 encounters.

Decorations: Gold Star of Hero of the Soviet Union on July 22, 1944; the Orders of Lenin, the Red Banner (4), the Patriotic War 1st Class, the Red Star (2).

Abramov was born in the Penzen area on June 14, 1921 and enrolled for service in the VMF in 1939. He completed his training at Yejsk military flying school a year later and was posted to the 71 IAP of the Baltic Fleet's air service before the war. In June, 1941 he commenced his combat duty flying I-16s in the defense of Tallin, Kronshtadt and Lavansaari. Between June, 1941 and June, 1942 he was credited with two personal victories along with fractional credits in seven more to rank him among the regiment's more successful pilots of the period. He subsequently was occupied with armed reconnaissance and in early 1944 reequipped with the La-5 fighter. On March 19, 1944 Abramov managed to score one of the unit's initial victories on the new mount when he was leading five fighters against a formation of 27 enemy planes personally downing one of them. Abramov served with the postwar VVS until 1974 when he retired with the rank of General Major. He died on May 23, 1985.

ACHKASOV, Sergej Vasilyevich

Combat record: 8 personal victories, 2 fractional credits, 160 sorties, 17 encounters.

Decorations: Gold Star of Hero of the Soviet Union on February 4, 1943; the Orders of Lenin (2).

Achkasov was born in the Tambov area on July 18, 1919 and entered military service in 1940. He graduated from Kacha military flying school and in January, 1941 received orders to the 16 IAP in the Moscow area as a Serzhant. On October 10, 1941 he got into his first encounter with the Luftwaffe while flying a nocturnal air patrol in the vicinity of Rybinsk. He spotted four Ju 88s and made a determined attack from astern, destroying one and forcing the others to jettison their bombs. He successfully rammed an He 111 on October 17 after running out of ammunition and parachuted to safety near Yaroslavl. In recognition of this feat he was decorated with the Order of Lenin returning to his unit shortly afterward. In 1942 he was posted to Voronezh Front joining with the 176 IAP as a Lejtenant and flight leader. On August 13, 1942 he became involved in a melee NW Voronezh and blasted a Bf 109 but ran out of ammunition in doing so. Observing a second German fighter as it was working over Lejtenant A. Ozhe, Achkasov dove down and in willful disregard for his own personal safety deliberately rammed the enemy plane which fell out of control. He was badly injured hardly being able to bail out of his own blazing aircraft. Upon his recovery he returned to combat operations in January, 1943 and was promoted to squadron leader a short time later. On March 14, 1943 the regiment's base near Kursk was struck by a Luftwaffe attack with Achkasov being killed by bomb splinters. He was buried in a common grave in the village of Khalino.

The Bell P-39 Aeracobra, an aircraft that was instrumental in early Soviet air victories. 4,924 P-39s and 2,421 P-63s were shipped to the USSR between 1941-45. This Cobra of an unknown unit shows well the aircraft's "car door" entrance for the pilot. (Author's collection)

ADONKIN, Vasilij Semyonovich

Combat record: 16 personal victories, 13 of which were single-engined fighters, 365 sorties, 42 encounters.

Decorations: Gold Star of Hero of the Soviet Union on January 22, 1944; the Orders of Lenin, the Red Banner (3).

Adonkin was born in the Byelgorod area on April 7, 1913 and entered the VMF in 1937. Upon receiving his wings at Yejsk military flying school in 1941 Adonkin was posted to the 78 IAP-SF as a Mladshij Lejtenant. He got his initial success on June 22, 1941, the day the Wehrmacht knifed into Soviet Russia, when he bagged a Ju 88 with an I-16 fighter. He managed to get another of these seven days later when four Red fighters fought a pitched battle with a superior enemy force claiming four kills. Adonkin put up a good performance in 1942 after the regiment had converted to Hurricanes achieving three air victories in some 30 sorties and nine encounters. He added two victories to his score on June 2 while carrying out three patrols in the Murmansk area and on June 19 took eight Hurricanes on an Il-2 escort with enemy aircraft being engaged over the Varanger Fyord. In all, they destroyed four of them for no losses. A short time later six Hurricanes with Adonkin in the lead were off to escort a formation of I-16s tasked with strafing Luostori airfield. In the target area Luftwaffe resistance appeared in the form of 10 Bf 109s and Fw 190s but these reportedly fared badly, the Hurricanes claiming five Bf 109s without loss while the I-16s shot up two planes on the ground. Adonkin quickly rose to squadron leader and in 1944 was given

Right: V.S. Adonkin of the Northern Fleet's 78 IAP. While others lamented the British Hurricane fighter, Adonkin was able to build up a good score over Murmansk in 1942 while flying this machine. (Author's collection)

command of the Airacobra equipped 255 IAP-SF. He fell foul of German fighters in a violent combat near Ekkere (Finland) on March 17, 1944.

ALEKSANDRYUK, Viktor Ilyich
Combat record: 15 personal victories, 4 fractional credits, 252 sorties, 69 engagements.
Decorations: Gold Star of Hero of the Soviet Union (no. 7696) on June 29, 1945; the Orders of Lenin (no. 52255), the Red Banner (2), the Patriotic War 1st Class.

Starshij Lejtenant V.I. Aleksandryuk, one of 176 GIAP's leading personalities. (Author's collection)

Aleksandryuk was born in Kursk on September 30, 1921 and entered military service in 1940. He was graduated at Chuguyev military flying school a year later and was posted to the 17 IAP. He fought from the very start of the war, and subsequently was in continuous action on Bryansk, Voronezh, 1st Ukrainian, 3rd Baltic and 1st Byelorussian Fronts, winning the Orders the Red Banner in 1943 and 1944 and the medal "For Valor" in 1942. Serving with the 171 IAP on Bryansk Front between March, 1942 and October, 1942, Aleksandryuk gained two kills with one each Bf 109 and Ju 88 along with four fractional credits in the course of 98 sorties and 30 aerial encounters. He next was involved in the fighting on Voronezh Front from December 27, 1942 until March 17, 1943 bagging two Bf 110s in 55 sorties and 10 engagements. He took part in the big air battles above Kharkov and then enjoyed considerable success after being posted to the crack 176 GIAP flying La-5s. Aleksandryuk next required but 29 encounters and 99 sorties to chalk up a string of 11 kills on 1st Byelorussian Front during the period of January 20, 1944 to April 1, 1945. Of his victims seven were Fw 190s, two were Bf 109s with one each Ju 88 and Hs 126. On July 21 he was flying free hunt with seven La-5s between Krasnoye-Rejovets when combat occurred with six Fw 190s and an Hs 126. Aleksandryuk bounced the Hs 126 and started to pour fire into him at 50m range. The enemy plane crashed South of Rejovets. While flying another free hunt on September 23 he dispatched a Fw 190 which spun into the ground some 10 km north of Valmiera (NE Riga) and then got a Ju 88 East of Warsaw on December 22. He downed a Fw 190 in the vicinity of Freienwalde (E Stettin, Pomerania) on February 10, 1945 and added another of these later that day while flying free hunt 120 km Northwest of Küstrin. On March 8 he was off on another free hunt in the Gollnow area (NW Stettin) when he spotted two Rotten of Bf 109s fitted with bombs. He flew in to 80m with all guns blazing whereupon the enemy aircraft went down in flames and crashed some 5 km east of Köschitz. On March 22 he was sweeping the Müncheberg area with his wingman when they became embroiled in a dogfight with eight Fw 190s. Aleksandryuk blasted one of them on his first pass, the 190 crashing 3 km north of Obersdorf, and then closed in on the lead enemy plane from 45 degree astern causing him to burst into flames and spin into the ground in a solid sheet of flames. The following day Aleksandryuk and his wingman returned to the Müncheberg area where they ran into eight Fw 190s which evaded combat and tried to escape utilizing cloud cover at 7,500m altitude. He picked a 190 and hit him from behind and below at close range, following which the fighter crashed in flames. He closed out his scoring on March 27 when a Bf 109 fell to his guns in a scrap near Zehden (NE Berlin), the German plane crashing close to a lake in the Alt Rüdnitz area. During the course of his combat career Aleksandryuk never was touched by an enemy bullet; he had demonstrated outstanding leadership and tactical skill, his flight being credited with 30 enemy planes in the air while putting up 600 sorties between January, 1944 and April 1, 1945. Aleksandryuk's aerial victories by type were:

The remains of a KG 53 "Legion Condor" Ju 88, knocked down by Aleksandryuk on Bryansk Front. The date is August 28, 1942. (Author's collection)

Fw 190s 7
Bf 109s 4
Bf 110s 2
Ju 88s 1
Hs 126s 1

He remained in the VVS following World War II and left active duty as a Kapitan in 1953. He lives in Kursk.

ALEKSEYEV, Konstantin Stepanovich
Combat record: 10 personal victories, 272 sorties, 110 encounters.
Decorations: Gold Star of Hero of the Soviet Union (no. 857) on June 14, 1942; the Orders of Lenin (no. 8861), the Red Banner (4), Suvorov 3rd Class, the Patriotic War 1st Class, the Red Star, the British Empire.

Alekseyev was born in the Mozhajsk area on October 7, 1914 and enrolled for service in the VMF in 1936. Two years later he completed his training at Yejsk military flying school and was in action from the earliest days of war. He was serving in the 6 GIAP of the Black Sea Fleet's air service (the former 8 IAP-ChF) and managed to put up a good performance in the contested air space above Sevastopol in 1942, acquiring a string of seven confirmed victories against great odds within a few weeks. His success led to his promotion to Major and commanding officer of the 25 IAP-ChF, and in this capacity was to see considerable action at Kerch in late 1943 while flying the LaGG-3. The regiment had a field day on November 2, 1943 when 13 enemy planes were shot down while being engaged in covering the Eltigen landings. Alekseyev stayed in the service after the close of war and graduated from the naval academy in 1948. He came off active duty as a Polkovnik in 1970 and passed away on February 24, 1971.

Kapitan K.S. Alekseyev of the Black Sea Fleet's air service is shown after receiving his Gold Star of Hero of the Soviet Union for his exploits in the skies above Sevastopol. (Author's collection)

ALEKSEYEV, Nikolaj Mikhajlovich
Combat record: 21 personal victories, 102 sorties, 35 encounters.
Decorations: Gold Star of Hero of the Soviet Union posthumously on August 24, 1943 for 12 kills, 6 fractional credits, 84 sorties, 28 engagements as of June, 1943; the Orders of Lenin, the Red Banner (after five personal victories and four fractional credits), the Patriotic War 1st Class (for scoring three victories in a day), the Red Star (for two kills and two fractional credits).

Alekseyev was born in the Groznyj area on June 26, 1919 and enlisted in the VVS in 1939. He received full flight training at Batajsk military flying school prior to receiving his wings in 1941. He was posted to the 271 IAP entering combat with the Luftwaffe in the vicinity of Velikiye Luki on September 18, 1942. He gained his initial success on December 1, 1942 while flying free hunt with a fellow pilot. They spotted three Ju 88s and went after them. Alekseyev took a bomber but had to make three passes to destroy it and then teamed with his comrade to send down a second. All of a sudden they were then bounced by two Bf 109s from out of some clouds. Alekseyev broke into them and attacked one that blew up, and crashed with the other enemy fighter breaking off and racing away just above the ground. He then began a remarkable run of success, scoring his next victories on December 30, when eight Yak-7s were engaged in escorting a formation of Il-2s between Gromovo-Butitino. In the target area they engaged a formation of 20 bombers covered by eight Bf 109s forming up for an attack on Soviet ground forces. In the ensuing action, Alekseyev personally accounted for two Bf 109s and shared in the destruction of two bombers. He added a Fw 190 in the Ramushevo-Kobylkino area on March 16, 1943 when eight Yaks tackled with 10 German fighters, seven of these being shot down. Later that day he became involved in two further combats with enemy fighters in the Lovat River area claiming two more Fw 190s. Another of these fell to his guns in the vicinity of Orel on June 8, and he was then nominated for the Gold Star for his efforts by Podpolkovnik Razsudkov six days later. At this stage his record stood at 84 sorties, consisting of 29 escorts, 2 armed reconnaissance, 53 ground force cover, and 12 personal victories along with six fractional credits; ground observers had confirmed eight of his kills while fellow pilots had verified four more claims over enemy-held territory. His personal victories by type were:

Bf 109Fs 6
Fw 190s 5
Ju 88s 1

In addition, he was awarded fractional credits for four Ju 88s and one each Ju 87 and Fw 189. Alekseyev continued to chalk up victories at a formidable pace in the subsequent air battles above Kursk. On July 12 he became involved in a dogfight near Novosil (E Orel) and blasted two fighters out of the sky but was then killed deliberately ramming a third, having expended the ammunition of his Yak.

A.V. Alelyukhin, whose operational career covered almost four arduous years and some 600 missions. Here, he is pictured in the cockpit of his La-7. The legend beneath the cockpit – Alekseyu Alelyukhin ot kollektiva tresta No.41 N.K.A.P. – translates: "To Aleksej Alelyukhin from the collective of factory No.41 of the People's Komissariat of Aviation Industry." (Author's collection)

ALELYUKHIN, Aleksej Vasilyevich

Combat record: 40 personal victories, 17 fractional credits, 601 sorties, 258 encounters.

Decorations: 1st Gold Star of Hero of the Soviet Union on August 24, 1943 for 11 victories, 6 fractional credits, 265 sorties, 65 combats; 2nd Gold Star on November 1, 1943 for 26 victories, 410 sorties, 114 encounters; the Orders of Lenin (2), the Red Banner (3), Suvorov 3rd Class, Aleksandr Nevskij, the Patriotic War 1st Class, the Red Star (2).

Alelyukhin, the fourteenth ranking Soviet ace, was born in the Kalinin area on March 30, 1920 and entered military service in 1938. A year later he completed his training at V.P. Chkalov military flying school and began his brilliant combat career right after the German attack on Soviet Russia in June, 1941. He was serving with the 69 IAP at Odessa, on which fell the full weight of the enemy onslaught. He quickly proved his out standing attributes, teaming with Mladshij Lejtenants Zhilin and Livenkov on June 25 to destroy an He 111 over their own airfield. A short time later he managed to gain his first personal victory which entitled him to the award of the Order of the Red Banner. Alelyukhin subsequently enjoyed above-average success in the great aerial campaigns against the Luftwaffe over Kharkov, Stalingrad, Rostov, Taganrog, Melitopol, Sevastopol, Odessa, East Prussia and Berlin. He displayed exceptional skill in the big air battles above Stalingrad, claiming four bombers in the Kalach area and two Ju 87s and a Bf 109 at Kotelnikovo (SW Stalingrad). His efforts earned him the Order of Lenin and a second Red Banner award. In time he was promoted to command the regiment's 1st Eskadrilya and on February 2, 1943 led eight Yak-1s in a head-on attack against a formation of 10 German fighters, two Bf 109s and a Bf 110 being shot down. Alelyukhin really came into his own after converting to Airacobras in April and then had his best day on

Major Alelyukhin with his Lavochkin La-5. He commanded a MiG-15 unit in Korea but further details are not available. (Author's collection)

July 17 with a triple as the regiment was having a field day with 21 kills. In a fierce series of dogfights at Taganrog he led the squadron to run up 24 kills in a four day period. He personally accounted for five and went on to become the top-scoring pilot of the whole battle downing 12 enemy planes. The fury of the Donbas air engagements saw Alelyukhin's fighters cut a swath through unescorted Luftwaffe dive-bomber Geschwader, the Junkers Ju 87s suffering heavily when intercepted by fighters. In the course of 249 encounters no fewer than 51 Stukas were destroyed with Alelyukhin being credited with downing 14 (possibly including fractional credits). When he was decorated with his second Gold Star of Hero of the Soviet Union for 26 kills, his score actually already stood at 32 after getting five Bf 109s in quick succession. He accomplished one of the regiment's last victories over East Prussia when he bagged a Fw 190 on April 12, 1945 and finished the war in command of the regiment. He was 9 GIAP's first ranking ace and had gained his victories on I-16s, LaGG-3s, Yak-1s, Hurricanes, Airacobras, La-5s and La-7s. Following the close of war he continued on active duty with the VVS assuming many command assignments. In 1948 he graduated from Frunze military academy and from the General Staff Academy six years later. He wound up his military career with the rank of General Major in 1985 and died in October, 1990.

V.Ya. Alkidov spent his World War II career with the 434 and 529 IAPs. He won a Gold Star for his efforts during the epic Battle of Stalingrad on August 12, 1942. His final score was at least 10 personal kills during 300+ sorties. (Author's collection)

AMELIN, Aleksej Stepanovich
Combat record: 15 personal victories, 216 sorties, 70 encounters.
Decorations: Gold Star of Hero of the Soviet Union on October 26, 1944; the Orders of Lenin, the Red Banner (4), the Patriotic War 1st Class and 2nd Class, the Red Star (3).

Amelin was born in the Moscow area on March 12, 1921 and joined the VVS for flight training in 1939. He won his pilot wings at Chuguyev military flying school two years later and was posted to the crack 240 IAP flying La-5s in March, 1943. During his time with the regiment he rapidly rose to command his own squadron after giving a good account of himself in the big air battles above Byelgorod-Kharkov. His specialty reportedly were close-in high-g combats. While leading a patrol of four La-5s in the vicinity of Mishurin Rog on October 2, 1943, they became embroiled in a dogfight with eight Bf 109s, five of these being shot down. Three days later he led his squadron against a large force of Luftwaffe fighters between Borodayevka-Tarasovka-Pogrebnaya and personally accounted for one of the five Bf 109s claimed destroyed. He added another of these on a further mission later that day. He continued to fly with great distinction in the fighting above the Dnyestr and Prut Rivers winning two Orders of the Red Banner along with the Order of the Patriotic War 2nd Class for his efforts in 1943. Amelin stayed in the service after the war advancing to Polkovnik. He concluded his active duty in 1960.

AMET-KHAN, Sultan
Combat record: 30 personal victories, 19 fractional credits, 603 sorties, 130 encounters.
Decorations: 1st Gold Star of Hero of the Soviet Union on August 24, 1943 for 11 kills, 19 fractional credits; 2nd Gold Star on June 29, 1945; the Orders of Lenin (3), the Red Banner (5), Aleksandr Nevskij, the Patriotic War 1st Class, the Red Star.

Amet-Khan was born in the Crimea on October 25, 1920 and enlisted in the VVS in 1939. He had his flight training at Kacha military flying school and received his pilot wings in 1940. He was serving in the 4 IAP in the Odessa area at the outbreak of the war with the rank of Mladshij Lejtenant. He managed to put up a good performance with the I-16 fighter in the dark months to follow, logging 130 sorties mostly in support of the battered Soviet ground forces at Kishinyov, Tiraspol, Nikolayev, Odessa and Kherson up to October, 1941. For his efforts he was promoted to flight leader and in late 1941 began flying Hurricanes. He deliberately destroyed a Ju 88 by ramming near Yaroslavl on May 31, 1942 when he found his guns had jammed, entitling him to the award of the Order of Lenin. Although Soviet pilots received much acclaim for successful ramming attacks, Amet-Khan personally took a different view of this form of attack: "I fully acknowledge that air fighting always is this way, that is to say, there is the need to resort to the extreme and risk everything, the aircraft, the pilot. But those days, when our aircraft were outnumbered four to one, a successful ramming was no victory. Ramming consequently was not the best possible method of attack but rather the ultimate one . . ." In June, 1942 he was greatly involved in the fighting above Chornaya Kalitva and Svinukha Rivers with 5-6 sorties daily being commonplace. In July he claimed at least two Bf 109s, and then the regiment began to reequip with Yak-1s in the vicinity of Voronezh. Shortly afterward he bagged a Ju 88 while flying the new mount and was well qualified for a second Order of the Red Banner after gaining seven kills in a fierce series of air battles above Kastornoye (E Kursk) and Voronezh. In August he moved with the regiment to Stalingrad to provide Il-2 escort while being based at Verkhnij Akhtuba (E Stalingrad). He was shot up in an encounter with Bf 109s SE Verkhnij Akhtuba and made a forced landing. The regiment suffered very heavy losses, and by orders of General Khryukin the most experienced pilots of the 8th Air Army were to be concentrated in the 9 GIAP in October, 1942 so as to establish a fighter outfit capable of meeting the enemy on equal terms. Amet-Khan was appointed to lead 1st Eskadrilya and in a burst of energy and skill ran up a string of six kills along with shares in seven more to raise his score to 13 while flying 110 sorties. After the annihilation of the beleaguered German forces at Stalingrad he saw considerable fighting over Rostov, Batajsk and the Mius. He claimed a double with an He 111 and a Bf 109 near Rostov on March 25, 1943 as the regiment shot down 16 Luftwaffe planes. 9 GIAP then converted to Airacobras and made a significant contribution to the fighting over the Kuban. Amet-Khan was successful in blasting two He 111s and a Ju 88 out of the sky over the Mius River in a single engagement. He subsequently excelled at Taganrog in August scoring 11 kills in an impressive display of combat skill, including a double on the 21. There is a strong possibility that this tally also consists of fractional credits, but unfortunately the records here are vague. He was decorated with a further Order of the Red

Famous Soviet pair: Major Amet-Khan Sultan and Kapitan Borisov pose in front of Amet-Khan's La-7. His eagle logo is prominent in this shot. The date is February, 1945. (Author's collection)

Amet-Khan with his LaGG-3 "28." (Author's collection)

Major Amet-Khan, widely regarded as one of the best of all Soviet fighter pilots. (Author's collection)

Banner following which he flew in the battles over Melitopol, Dnyepropetrovsk, the Crimea acquiring doubles each in clashes at Odessa and Sevastopol. He got a Fw 190 still with the Airacobra in the final affray over Sevastopol in May, 1944 prior to converting to La-7s and deploying with the regiment to Latvia. Combat duty over East Prussian soil was begun in autumn of 1944 and saw Amet-Khan add at least two further Fw 190s in the Gumbinnen area. For displaying exceptional leadership and scoring six air victories over East Prussia he was awarded the Orders of Aleksandr Nevskij, the Patriotic War 1st Class and the Red Banner. On January 18, 1945 he led six La-7s against 25 Fw 190s in the Gumbinnen area, five of these being shot down with Amet-Khan personally accounting for a single. He had by now become a Major and was to see a great deal of action against the Luftwaffe in its dying months. The regiment moved forward to the Posen (Poznan) area to participate in the battles for Berlin and then deployed to Berlin-Schönefeld in April. On the 25th he bagged a Bf 109 right over his own base. The German pilot was captured and reportedly was an Oberst and Knight's Cross holder, but unfortunately his identity has not been established. He did not further add to his score, and following World War II became a very proficient test pilot joining with the LII (letno-ispytatelnyj institut), the aviation test institute in Moscow, in March, 1946. The following year he was decorated with the coveted title "Test Pilot First Class" and eventually rose to Podpolkovnik. He was killed in a flying accident in a Tu-16 on February 1, 1971. Throughout his career Amet-Khan had flown some 100 types of aircraft logging approximately 2,000 hours test flying production prototypes.

ANDRIANOV, Ilya Filippovich

Combat record: 23 personal victories.
Decorations: Gold Star of Hero of the Soviet Union (award number 4276) on August 19, 1944 for 17 personal victories, 303 sorties, 65 encounters as of June, 1944; the Order of Lenin (award number 18160), Aleksandr Nevskij, the Patriotic War 1st Class (2), the Red Star.

Andrianov was born in the Ryazan area on August 3, 1918 and entered military service in 1940. He completed his training at Batajsk military flying school a year later and joined the 516 IAP on November 4, 1941 to fly I-16s on South Front. On one early occasion he met a single Ju 88 near Novorossijsk, but the bomber gradually pulled away from him after dropping its cargo into the sea below and escaped. While flying air patrol in the Taganrog area on November 22 a number of He 111s were encountered, one of these being shot down by Andrianov, which crashed in flames at Kojsul. The regiment then was beginning to reequip with LaGG-3s, and on March 17, 1942 three of these were escorting a formation of nine Il-2s when combat occurred with six Bf 109s. In the ensuing melee Andrianov got one of the enemy fighters which crashed into the ground in the vicinity of Slavyansk. He later converted to Yak-1s and deployed with the regiment to Voronezh Front on March 27, 1943. On July 6 six Yak-1s were engaged in escorting nine Il-2s when at 1700 hours flying at 2,000m they were attacked by eight Fw 190s. Andrianov pulled in behind one of them and after a few bursts the fighter plunged earthward crashing in the vicinity of Dragunskoye. Two days later eight Yak-1s were ordered off to provide ground force cover and became embroiled in a dogfight with 12 Bf 109s and six Fw 190s, one claim for a Fw 190 shot down being made by Andrianov in the Ryazanovka area. On July 25 the regiment again was posted, this time to Steppe Front and on August 3 he bagged a Bf 109 while escorting two Il-2s, the enemy aircraft diving into the ground near Shopino. Andrianov then began to establish a reputation for aggressiveness and air combat skill in a fierce series of encounters, destroying another Bf 109 in the Lukyanin area on August 9. The following day 12 Yaks were assigned to providing cover for an equal number of Il-2s when they ran into a Ju 88 escorted by Bf 109s. Andrianov attacked the bomber from dead astern, whereupon it burst into flames and crashed in the vicinity of Tsirkuny. He next received credit for a Fw 190 on August 23 near Lyuboshin and then destroyed a Bf 109 at Sokolovka on September 6 when four Yaks tackled with three Bf 109s while escorting 12 Shturmoviks. He bagged another of these in the Borodayevka area on September 28 and shot down one on October 7, which blew up and crashed near Michiurin. A Ju 87 fell to his guns in the Chernyakovka area on October 29 when eight Yak-1s engaged a formation of 20 Stukas covered by six Fw 190s at 755 hours while engaged in escorting 27 Il-2s. His success led to his promotion to squadron leader in December, 1943, and in the course of the next 136 sorties his Eskadrilya was credited with downing 12 enemy planes in 14 combats. Andrianov next scored a double with two Bf 109s in a fighter battle near Blagodatnoye on January 7, 1944 at 1015 hours. He got a Ju 87 on January 29 when three Yaks were off to reconnoiter the Lebedin-Shpola areas where combat action took place with two large formations of Luftwaffe dive-bombers at 1455 hours, his victim crashing in flames south of Mizhigovka. He got another Ju 87 two hours later when four Yak-1s were engaged in air patrol in the area of Shpola where they spotted nine enemy planes with Andrianov accounting for one southeast of Nechayevka. He was nominated for the Gold Star award on February 25, 1944 by which time he had brought his score to 17 in 65 encounters. The author was able to trace 16 of his aerial victories by type as follows:

Bf 109s	8
Fw 190s	3
Ju 87s	3
He 111s	1
Ju 88s	1

Andrianov went on to wind up as the regiment's second highest scoring ace. He remained in the VVS following World War

II assuming command of an air regiment. He left active duty with the rank of Polkovnik in 1955.

ANISKIN, Aleksandr Dmitriyevich
Combat record: 10 personal victories, 295 sorties, 105 encounters.
Decorations: Gold Star of Hero of the Soviet Union on February 22, 1943; the Orders of Lenin, the Red Banner (2).

Aniskin was born in Dnyepropetrovsk on November 24, 1918 and enrolled for service in 1938. Two years later he completed his flight training at Kacha military flying school and was in action from the very start of the war. He was serving in the 434 IAP and by the end of 1941 had claimed three air victories and engaged in 40 ground-attack missions on West Front. He became greatly involved in the Battle of Stalingrad during the course of which he scored at least one victory, this occurring on September 21, 1942 when 12 Yaks led by Kapitan A.I. Yakimov attacked a force of 15 Ju 87s escorted by 10 Bf 109s, seven of the enemy planes being shot down. Aniskin was shot down and killed in the Staraya Russa area on February 20, 1943.

Lejtenant A.D. Aniskin, an outstanding pilot of the darkest hours of the 1941/42 air war, who fought with the 434 IAP. (Author's collection)

ANKUDINOV, Yegor Yefremovich
Combat record: 15 personal victories, 4 enemy planes on the ground, 250 sorties, of which 80 were ground-attack missions.
Decorations: Gold Star of Hero of the Soviet Union on May 15, 1946; the Orders of Lenin, the Red Banner (3), Aleksandr Nevskij, the Patriotic War 1st Class (2), the Patriotic War 2nd Class, the Red Star.

Ankudinov was born in the Kalinin area on April 10, 1910 and entered the Soviet Army in 1932. He completed his training at Orenburg military flying school but did not commence his combat duty before 1943, when he was posted to the 812 IAP. On October 25, 1943 he led eight fighters in an encounter with 60 enemy bombers in the area of the Molochnaya River, eight of these being shot down with Ankudinov personally accounting for one. He claimed another single in the vicinity of Müncheberg on March 24, 1945. He wound up his military career with the rank of Major in 1954.

ANTONENKO, Aleksej Kasyanovich
Combat record: 10 personal victories.
Decorations: Gold Star of Hero of the Soviet Union on July 14, 1941; two Orders of Lenin.

Antonenko was born in the Mogilov area on February 23, 1911 and enrolled for service in 1929. He had his flight training at Yejsk military flying school and was a pilot instructor for a while prior to cutting his teeth against the Japanese at the Khalkhin Gol in 1939. He was early in the public eye for winning six fractional credits in the course of 40 air encounters. He next won the Order of Lenin and the medal "For Valor" (Za otvagu) for his efforts against the Finns during the Russo-Finnish Winter War of 1939/40 but unfortunately, no further details have emerged. By June, 1941 he was serving as a Kapitan with the 13 IAP-KBF flying I-16s. On June 23, 1941 he earned the distinction of gaining Baltic Fleet's first air victory of the Patriotic War period by downing a Ju 88 in the Tallin area. He next teamed with his friend and comrade Pyotr Brinko to destroy another of these near the Soviet base of Hanko (Hango, SW Helsinki) on July 3, 1941 with both pilots expending but eight resp. 11 rounds in the process. Antonenko then was bounced by two fighters without further notice but managed to outturn them and got in a good burst, whereupon one of them crashed in flames. A few days later they were both off again together running into two Finnish Fiat G.50 fighters over the Hanko Peninsula and received credit for both of them although these claims are not substantiated by Finnish records. Antonenko had by now become a national hero and was decorated with a Gold Star with five victories to his credit, all scored in a 20 day period while operating in appalling conditions against great odds. On July 23 Antonenko and Brinko were tasked with strafing a seaplane base where they managed to share two aircraft between them. Returning to the same target area the following day with two fellow pilots, five more were destroyed on the water. This time opposition appeared in the form of six Fokkers, but these reportedly fared badly, losing five of their number without inflicting any damage. Once again, Finnish sources do not record these losses and it seems likely however that the dates are in error. Antonenko was shot down in air combat on July 26, 1941 crashing to his death. He was buried on the Hanko Peninsula. Soviet records are not entirely clear as to his final score, some suggesting 11 aerial victories.

ARKHIPENKO, Fyodor Fyodorovich

Combat record: 30 personal victories, 14 fractional credits, 467 sorties, 102 encounters; two tanks, 10 antiaircraft guns, 20 motor vehicles, some 450 soldiers on the ground.

Decorations: Gold Star of Hero of the Soviet Union on June 27, 1945; the Orders of Lenin, the Red Banner (3), the Patriotic War 1st Class, the Patriotic War 2nd Class, the Red Star.

Arkhipenko was born in the Mogilyov area on October 30, 1921 and commenced his brilliant military career in 1938. He won his wings at Odessa military flying school two years later and was in the forefront of action from the earliest days of the war serving in the 27 IAP (later designated the 129 GIAP). He gained his first combat experience on Southwest Front, gaining two air victories while flying 70 sorties and entering into 10 encounters between June 26, 1941 and January 1, 1942. He managed to achieve his initial success on August 17, identifying his victim as an "He 113", and added a Ju 88 three days later. On September 14 he shared in the destruction of an He 111 with fellow pilots. He next was posted with the regiment to Bryansk Front and logged 30 more missions up to July 7, 1942, being awarded a fractional credit for a Ju 87 on June 7. In July the regiment deployed to Voronezh Front where he shot down a Bf 109 on the 20th and teamed with fellow pilots to dispatch a Do 215 on October 5. He was well qualified for his first award of the Order of the Red Banner on January 20, 1943, by which time his score was three kills along with three fractional credits. During the period of December 11, 1942 and March 10, 1943 he logged an additional 49 sorties becoming involved in three combats with the Luftwaffe. He was successful in bagging another Bf 109 on January 9, 1943 and then converted to Airacobras to begin a rather spectacular run of success. In an action over Verkhopenye on July 7 he got a single

A.K. Antonenko of the 13 IAP-KBF, a veteran of the Khalkhin Gol and the Russo-Finnish Winter War, smiles for the camera. With his loss on July 26, 1941 the VVS was deprived of one of its finest pilots from the early days of the war. (Author's collection)

Aeracobra ace. Major F.F. Arkhipenko of the 129 GIAP enjoyed above-average success fighting on Bryansk, Voronezh and 2nd Ukrainian Fronts. (Author's collection)

Ju 87 and also teamed with fellow pilots to destroy four more. The following day another of these fell to his guns in the vicinity of Sukhosolotino while sharing in the destruction of two more Ju 87s, a Bf 109 and a He 111. In October, 1943 the unit was posted again, this time to 2nd Ukrainian Front where Arkhipenko chalked up seven kills in a fierce series of dogfights until February 10, 1944. On October 24, 1943 he led six P-39s to attack a large force of enemy dive-bombers near Chechelivka, personally accounting for a Ju 87 while Starshij Lejtenant N.D. Gulayev, soon to be a leading ace, blasted one each Ju 87 and Bf 109 out of the sky. Six days later he shot down another Stuka in a clash over Starodub (SW Bryansk) while leading four Cobras to gain three kills. He next claimed a double with two Ju 87s between Batyzman-Ingulo Kamenka (SE Kirovograd) on December 15 and downed a Bf 109 5 km south of Vishnyakovka on January 8, 1944. Two days later six fighters under his leadership tackled with 40 Ju 87s and 6-8 Bf 109s in the Kirovograd-Lelekovka-Balashovka areas, two Ju 87s and two Bf 109s being shot down for no losses. Arkhipenko personally got one of the Stukas while Lejtenant Burunov shot one fighter off his tail. On the 17th Arkhipenko and six Cobras caught eight Ju 88s, five He 111s and eight escorting fighters near Kirovograd with two Ju 88s and two Bf 109s being shot down in running battles to the deck while ground fire sent one P-39 down out of control. In the action Arkhipenko added a Bf 109 to his score, the enemy plane crashing in flames between Yeleno-Kosogorovka. He continued his streak during subsequent aerial campaigns between February 10 and March 30 and shot down four more Ju 87s and a Fw 190 while also sharing in the destruction of a second in the next 48 sorties. On March 19 he and Lejtenant Karlov were sweeping the Yampol area and encountered two He 111s and two Fw 190s. While the bombers escaped in a cloud layer, Arkhipenko managed to latch onto the tail of a Fw 190 and pulled in to 25m range scoring many strikes. Simultaneously Karlov was making a head-on pass whereupon the enemy aircraft crashed southwest of Yampol and exploded. Returning to the Yampol area later that day Arkhipenko personally dispatched another of these and then destroyed two Ju 87s in the same area two days later. On March 26 a further dive-bomber fell to his guns near Beltsy while he added another over Pyrlitsa-Korneshti four days later while leading four Cobras to bounce nine Ju 87s, four of these being shot down. He flew with great distinction during the period of March 30 to August 12, 1944 running up nine kills in 52 missions and 17 encounters. On April 15 he knocked down a PZL-24 and then bagged a Bf 109 south of Yassy two days later. On May 4 he took six P-39s on a sweep of the Dumbrovitsy-Tyrgu-Frumos areas where an action with 30 Fw 190s took place. The enemy fighters were intent on their ground targets when the Cobras hit them losing five of their number, including a single to Arkhipenko, the aircraft crashing 5km northwest of Tyrgu-Frumos. On May 7 he got a Bf 109 in the Blyndeshti area and another of these near Vulturul on the 30th. He claimed another Bf 109 in an encounter near Skulany (N Yassy) on

Arkhipenko continued on active duty with the VVS following World War II. He was a Polkovnik when this photo was taken. (Author's collection)

May 31 and then destroyed a Hs 129 ground-attack plane in the same area on June 1. He shot down a Ju 87 near Movileni the following day and on the 6th was successful in downing a Bf 109 in the vicinity of Kharleshti. Between August 10, 1944 and February 7, 1945 he logged another 32 sorties, 18 of which were ground force cover, four strafing missions, three escorts and seven free hunts. He entered into five engagements and was credited with downing three Fw 190s. He scored a single on August 11 and another one six days later when eight P-39s mixed it with 18 Fw 190s in the Opatuv area, five of these being shot down for no losses. Arkhipenko closed out his scoring on January 17, 1945 with another such fighter in the vicinity of Tschenstochau (Czestochowa) and came out of World War II as deputy regiment commander and the unit's second highest scoring ace. His aerial victories by type of enemy aircraft destroyed were as follows:

Bf 109s	9
Ju 88s	1
He 113s	1
Fw 190s	5
Ju 87s	12
PZL-24s	1
Hs 129s	1

In addition, he was awarded fractional credits for three He 111s, seven Ju 87s, one Fw 190, two Bf 109s, one Do 215. In the course of his combat duty Arkhipenko was slightly wounded twice, once in January, 1943 and once in June, 1943. He is remembered by Podpolkovnik Figichev, the regiment commander, as a capable and deadly fighter pilot. Following World War II he graduated from the Air Force Academy in 1951 and wound up his military career as a Polkovnik in 1959.

Major N.A. Arkhipov, whose distinguished combat career with the 32 and 265 IAPs extended from the first to the last days of the war. (Author's collection)

ARKHIPOV, Nikolaj Arsentyevich

Combat record: 11 personal victories, 8 fractional credits, 275 sorties, 134 encounters.

Decorations: Gold Star of Hero of the Soviet Union (award number 1251) on September 28, 1943; the Order of Lenin (award number 15564), the Red Banner (2), the Patriotic War 1st Class (2), the Red Star (2).

Arkhipov was born in the Yaroslavl area on October 23, 1918 and enlisted in the Soviet Army in 1939. He qualified as a pilot at Stalingrad military flying school a year later and commenced his combat duty as a member of the 32 IAP at the very start of the war. He later advanced to deputy commander of the 265 IAP and during his combat career he was to see a great deal of action on West, North Caucasus and Voronezh Fronts. He managed to put up a good performance in the skies above Byelgorod, by which time he had become a squadron leader. Within two weeks he acquired five personal victories while his squadron was credited with destroying 19 enemy planes. In an action on July 16, 1943 five Hs 123s and two Bf 109s were shot down with Arkhipov accounting for a double in the Novoselovka area (SE Izyum). He served with the postwar VVS until 1973 when he came off active duty with the rank of Polkovnik.

Kapitan N.S. Artamonov, who flew with the 193 IAP making a big name for himself in the big air battles over 1st Ukrainian Front. He scored 18 personal victories before he fell victim to flak on March 26, 1945. (Author's collection)

ARTAMONOV, Nikolaj Semyonovich

Combat record: 18 personal victories, 8 fractional credits, 19 enemy planes on the ground, 165 sorties, 42 encounters.

Decorations: Gold Star of Hero of the Soviet Union (award number 1469) on August 19, 1944; the Orders of Lenin (award number 16804), the Red Banner (3), the Patriotic War 1st Class (2).

Artamonov was born in the Penza area on May 21, 1920 and entered military service in 1941 for flight training. He won his wings a year later and gained his first combat experience while serving in the 32 IAP. In 1943 he was posted to the 193 IAP and subsequently was greatly involved in the big air battles above Byelgorod-Kharkov, Kremenchug and Borodayevka. By mid-1944 he had become a Kapitan and deputy commanding officer of the unit taking part in the aerial operations against the Luftwaffe during the Yassy-Kishinyov campaign. In the course of the battle he was credited with downing at least one Fw 190 on August 20, 1944 pulling in to 50 meters range before firing. He scored a double with two Ju 87s on October 6 while leading six fighters in an encounter with a large enemy formation near Sokodor, Hungary, seven of the Stukas being shot down. On November 1 six La-5s with Artamonov in the lead tangled with a number of enemy fighters in the Tertel area claiming the destruction of two Fw 190s. On March 26, 1945 he was hit by ground fire while strafing and crashed to his death.

Avdeyev poses for a photograph in front of a Yak fighter. He was recognized as one of the ablest leaders in the Black Sea Fleet, commanding the 6 GIAP. (Author's collection)

ASTAKHOV, Ivan Mikhajlovich
Combat record: 12 personal victories, 7 fractional credits, 283 sorties, 63 encounters.
Decorations: Gold Star of Hero of the Soviet Union posthumously on July 1, 1944; the Orders of Lenin, the Red Banner, the Patriotic War 1st Class, the Red Star.

Astakhov was born in the Tula area on May 15, 1921 and entered the Soviet Army in 1939. He had his flight training at Borisoglebsk military flying school and was serving in the 49 IAP at the outbreak of the war. A short time later he was posted to the 168 IAP flying LaGG-3s, and on March 7, 1942 claimed a Ju 87 near Yukhnov. He was shot down and killed on March 3, 1944 and was buried in the hamlet of Perevolochye, Smolensk area.

AVDEYEV, Mikhail Vasilyevich
Combat record: 17 personal victories, 498 sorties, 141 encounters.
Decorations: Gold Star of Hero of the Soviet Union (award number 858) on June 14, 1942 for 9 personal victories, 302 sorties, of which 31 were at night, 83 combats as of June, 1942; the Orders of Lenin (award number 8862), the Red Banner (6), Suvorov 3rd Class, the Red Star (2).

Avdeyev, great Soviet fighter leader, was born in the Mogilyov area on September 15, 1913 and enrolled for service in 1932. He completed his flight training at Voroshilovgrad military flying school prior to being assigned to the VMF in 1934. He joined with the 32 IAP of the Black Sea Fleet's air service before the war and achieved fame for his efforts during the bloody months of 1941. During the period of June, 1941 to June, 1942 he was credited with nine enemy planes in the air, some 300 missions and 83 air engagements (other sources suggest only 63). He rapidly rose to Kapitan and squadron leader, his Eskadrilya achieving a high level of success during the epic defense of the Crimea with a total of 80 kills, of which 31 occurred in the Sevastopol area, all while flying I-16s. In November, 1941 he was posted with 5th Eskadrilya to the 8 IAP-ChF, where it was reformed as the 1st Eskadrilya. On April 26,

Right: M.V. Avdeyev prepares to take to the air wearing a British Irvin jacket. (Author's collection)

1943 he assumed command of the 6 GIAP-ChF by which time he was a Major. The unit subsequently was to do yeoman service under his leadership in the contested skies above the Caucasus, the Crimea, Rumania and Bulgaria. At the close of hostilities the regiment had 300 air victories, 54 enemy planes on the ground, 21,600 sorties and 2,219 encounters to its credit. Avdeyev stayed in the service after the war and graduated from the General Staff Academy assuming various assignments. He left active duty as a General Major in 1964 and died on June 22, 1979.

AVEKOV, Ivan Avdeyevich
Combat record: 19 personal victories, 6 fractional credits, 23 aircraft on the ground, 178 sorties.
Decorations: Gold Star of Hero of the Soviet Union on August 24, 1943; the Order of Lenin.

Avekov was born in the Vitebsk area on May 19, 1919 and started his military career in 1937. He qualified as an air observer at Kharkov military flying school in 1939 and won his wings at Odessa military flying school a year later. He commenced his combat duty in June, 1941 and throughout his combat career took part in air operations on Southwest, West and Central Fronts while serving in the 519 IAP. His most memorable mission came on March 20, 1942 when he tackled with seven enemy planes near Gzhatsk (Smolensk area), downing two and ramming a third in his crippled plane while being wounded in the process. He was shot down near Lipetsk on April 17, 1943, and while making a forced landing in a pasture his aircraft cartwheeled, and he was flung from the cockpit and killed.

AZAROV, Yevgenij Aleksandrovich
Combat record: 15 personal victories, 339 sorties, 101 encounters.
Decorations: Gold Star of Hero of the Soviet Union on August 19, 1944; the Orders of Lenin, the Red Banner (3), Suvorov 3rd Class, the Red Star.

Azarov was born in the Kursk area on November 20, 1914 and entered military service in 1935. He received his pilot wings in 1938 and then cut his teeth during the Russo-Finnish Winter War of 1939/40. By June, 1941 he had become a member of the 19 IAP and was to make a brilliant war record in the dark months to follow. Between June, 1941 and October 29, 1941 he was credited with downing three Bf 109s and two Bf 110s while completing 251 missions for 256 combat hours and entering into 60 aerial encounters, all on Leningrad Front. What was more, he also accounted for 100 motor vehicles and four artillery batteries while beating up ground targets. On August 15, 1941 six MiG-3s bounced a formation of 60 Ju 88s and escorting fighters near Sivoritsa with Azarov singling one Bf 109 out for attack, driving right up his tail to within 50m, and after a few bursts the enemy plane blew up and plunged earthward. While returning from a mission ten days later he intercepted four Bf 110s that were making passes across his field and in a brief combat shot down one, which crashed on the perimeter. He got another of these near Moluksinskoye Lake on August 29, and then was posted with the regiment to Volkhov Front in early 1942. He flew 15 sorties in LaGG-3s between February 26 and April 17 and knocked down a Ju 88 and also damaged a second in the vicinity of Glabochka on March 13 being wounded by return fire. He had become a squadron leader when he was posted again on December 27, 1942, this time to Voronezh Front. He became engaged in 44 missions on La-5s and was credited with downing three Ju 88s, a Fw 189, a Hs 126 and a "Me 100" while becoming involved in 32 air combats. On January 20, 1944 he entered combat on 1st Ukrainian Front and subsequently saw a good deal of action on 1st Byelorussian Front, adding two Fw 190s and a Bf 109 to his score in the course of 39 missions and eight encounters. When hostilities ceased, his aerial victories by type of aircraft destroyed were:

19 IAP fighter ace Major Ye.A. Azarov, who achieved a high level of success during the darkest hours of 1941. (Author's collection)

Ju 88s 4
Fw 189s 1
Bf 110s.................... 3
Bf 109s 3
Fw 190s 2
"Me 100s" 1
Hs 126s 1

He wound up his military career in 1946 and died on January 26, 1957.

Starshij Lejtenant I.I. Babak of the 100 GIAP began to come into prominence on South Front once the regiment had converted to Aeracobras in 1943. His biggest day came on July 16, 1944 when he bagged four Fw 190s in one sortie. (Author's collection)

BABAK, Ivan Ilyich
Combat record: 37 personal victories, 4 fractional credits, 330 sorties, 103 encounters.
Decorations: Gold Star of Hero of the Soviet Union on November 1, 1943 for 18 kills, 4 fractional credits as of September, 1943; the Orders of Lenin, the Red Banner (2), the Patriotic War 1st Class, the Red Star.

Babak, the seventeenth ranking Soviet ace of World War II, was born in the Dnyepropetrovsk area on July 26, 1919 and enlisted in the VVS in 1940. Two years later he completed his flight training at Stalingrad military flying school following which he was posted to the 45 IAP on North Caucasus Front in May, 1942. Flying wing to the redoubtable Dmitrij Glinka, Babak achieved his first success by downing a Bf 109 near Mozdok. He really came into his own after the regiment had converted to Airacobras in early 1943 being rushed to the Kuban theater. During the fury of the fighting Babak excelled, running his score to six in April. He next achieved a string of four kills in 31 sorties and 11 encounters over Melitopol and enjoyed considerable success during the Lemberg (Lvov)-Sandomierz campaign, chalking up 10 more air victories in a very short time. His big day was July 16, 1944 when four Fw 190s fell to his guns still while flying the P-39. He was appointed commanding officer of the glorious 16 GIAP in early 1945 but on March 16, 1945 was hit by ground fire while being engaged in a free hunt near Lauban (Luban), between Dresden and Breslau. He bailed out and was captured, enduring the hardships of prison camps until liberated by American tank forces on April 24. Babak concluded his active duty as a Kapitan in 1949.

Babak seen here as a Lejtenant. On the left breast he is wearing the Gold Star – Hero of the Soviet Union – the Orders of Lenin (second pattern with suspender) and the Red Banner. On the right breast there is the Order of the Red Star and the Guards badge. (Author's collection)

Hurricane IIBs on a Karelian airfield in 1942. Northern Russia saw the introduction of the first Hurricanes in September, 1941 when 151 Wing (RAF) was sent to Russia to convert Soviet pilots to the aircraft. During its inconspicuous service career on the Soviet-German front the British fighter caused endless problems while units were suffering inordinate losses. In consequence, their morale was below the zero point. Amongst regiments performing creditably was the 485 IAP under the leadership of Major G.V. Zimin. On June 19, 1942 its pilots reported the destruction of 10 Luftwaffe planes at the cost of one of their number. (Author's collection)

BABKOV, Vasilij Petrovich

Combat record: 23 personal victories, 450 sorties.

Decorations: Gold Star of Hero of the Soviet Union on November 23, 1942 for 11 victories, 9 fractional credits, 287 sorties, 68 encounters as of August, 1942; the Orders of Lenin (2), the Red Banner (2), Aleksandr Nevskij, the Patriotic War 1st Class (2), the Red Star (2).

Babkov was born in the Zaporozhye area on April 14, 1918 and entered the Soviet Army in 1937 and qualified as a pilot at Borisoglebsk military flying school the same year. He started flying combat at the outbreak of the war and wrote a distinguished record at Stalingrad in 1942, by which time he had become a Major in the 434 IAP. He got a single on September 16 and then bagged two Ju 87s four days later while leading seven Yaks to attack a superior enemy force, four German bombers being shot down. Soon after he was appointed commanding officer of the regiment and in December was posted with this to the Velikiye Luki area. January 6, 1943 was a field day for the unit with 17 kills in air-to-air combat in a series of dogfights near Iskusstvennoye Lake. Babkov subsequently displayed exceptional leadership and tactical skill in air operations above Demyansk and personally added a string of seven victories in the wild air battles above Kursk and Kharkov. On July 17, 1943 he relinquished command to Podpolkovnik V.I. Davidkov to take over an air division. Following World War II Babkov graduated from the Air Force Academy in 1950 and the General Staff Academy in 1956. He retired with the rank of General Polkovnik in 1986.

BALANDIN, Vladimir Aleksandrovich

Combat record: 15 personal victories, 1 fractional credit, 228 sorties, 30 engagements.

Decorations: Gold Star of Hero of the Soviet Union posthumously on April 19, 1945; the Orders of Lenin, the Red Banner (2), the Patriotic War 2nd Class (2).

Balandin was born in Baku in February, 1923 and entered the Soviet Army in 1941. He completed his training at Stalingrad military flying school a year later and was posted to the 18 GIAP in May, 1942. He flew in the Battle of Kursk in July, 1943 and managed to put up a good performance in the heavy air battles above Smolensk between August-September, 1943, scoring seven kills to lead the regiment. He blasted a Fw 190 out of the sky near Vitebsk on October 12 and accounted for another of these in the vicinity of Borisov on June 26, 1944. Flying the new Yak-3 fighter, he added a further Fw 190 over East Prussia on October 17. On December 30 Balandin attacked a Ju 88 reconnaissance plane but was hit by return fire and was seen to spin down and crash to his death. He was buried in Kapsukas, SW Kaunas (Lithuania).

BALYUK, Ivan Fyodorovich

Combat record: 22 personal victories, 16 fractional credits, 247 sorties, 98 combats.

Decorations: Gold Star of Hero of the Soviet Union on August 24, 1943 for 14 victories, 3 fractional credits as of June, 1943; the Orders of Lenin, the Red Banner (2), Aleksandr Nevskij, the Patriotic War 1st Class (2), the Red Star.

G.S. Balashov with his Yak-3 fighter. Balashov went to war with the 402 IAP in April, 1943 and won the title of Hero of the Soviet Union for his efforts on 4th Ukrainian Front on July 1, 1944. He tallied at least 15 kills during 103 sorties and 37 combats (Author's collection)

Balyuk was born in the Sumy area on April 30, 1919 and started his military career in 1937. He won his pilot wings at Chuguyev military flying school in 1940 and by the outbreak of war had become a member of the 38 IAP. He saw a great deal of action on Northwest Front and was mainly occupied with ground targets in desperate attempts to stem the German drive in the area. He logged 95 sorties and was credited with 15 tanks, four aircraft and 30 motor vehicles destroyed on the ground. He was then posted with the unit to Leningrad Front claiming five air victories prior to joining with the 237 IAP on Stalingrad Front. He was given command of the 1st Eskadrilya in August, 1942 and under his leadership this was to run up 32 kills during the course of the battle. Balyuk personally added nine victories to his score and by May, 1943 had raised his tally to 16 along with three fractional credits. His record of missions and aerial encounters as of this stage is uncertain, one source suggesting 300 sorties and 135 air combats. He fought in the Battle of Kursk and shot down a Fw 189 on July 3 to further his score to 18. Balyuk subsequently saw considerable fighting over Byelorussia, Poland, the Reich and finally, Berlin, finishing as deputy commanding officer of the 54 GIAP. He stayed in the service after the war and graduated from the Air Force Academy in 1951, coming off active duty as a Polkovnik in 1973.

BARANOV, Mikhail Dmitriyevich

Combat record: 24 personal victories, 28 fractional credits, 6 aircraft in ground attacks, 285 sorties, 85 encounters.

Decorations: Gold Star of Hero of the Soviet Union on August 12, 1942; the Orders of Lenin, the Red Banner (2).

Baranov was born in the Leningrad area on October 21, 1921 and enrolled for service in 1939. He completed his training at Chuguyev military flying school the following year and began his brilliant combat career in the VVS right after the German attack in June, 1941. Serving with the 183 IAP he gained a triple with one each Bf 109, Ju 88 and Hs 126 in the Novomoskovsk area on October 30, 1941. His next score possibly did not come until several months later after the unit had deployed to the Stalingrad area. In the fury of the Stalingrad air battles Baranov was to develop into a fighter pilot of formidable skill whose courage and exploits have become legend to the Russians. Throughout of his combat duty he flew the Yak-1, a sturdy, highly maneuverable fighter that was easily maintained in the field. On one occasion he was leading a strafing mission and personally accounted for three antiaircraft guns and three planes on the ground while also catching a fighter that was trying to takeoff knocking him down in one straight pass. Baranov's big day was August 6, 1942 while leading his flight in escorting 226 ShAD Il-2s to the Abganerovo area (SW Stalingrad). There was considerable action with Bf 109s in the target area. The Yaks instantly broke up and went after the enemy planes. Baranov made a firing pass at one "Messer" head-on and managed to score many strikes whereupon it hit the ground in a splash of flames while a second was destroyed by St.Lej. A.S. Yudin. He was then bounced by two others but shook them off spotting six Ju 87s to starboard. He knocked one of them down in a straight pass from astern and pulled away to see several Bf 109s driving up on some Il-2s low on the deck. He dove down and pulled in to point-blank range with all guns blazing. One enemy plane burst into flames and pieces barely missed him as he broke away. He was in the process of finishing off another when he ran out of ammunition and resorted to ramming. The German fighter spun down and crashed while Baranov managed to bail out, badly wounded. He was rushed to hospital and required until January, 1943 to recuperate. He was assigned to the 9 GIAP but was not allowed to fly combat sorties right away. On January 15 (or 17 as suggested by another source), he went off on flight practicing but crashed and was killed as was recalled by twice Hero of the Soviet Union, Amet-Khan Sultan. Not all Soviet sources agree on this version, some reporting he was lost while ramming an enemy aircraft, but there would seem little likelihood that this has any substance.

BARSUKOV, Vasilij Nikolayevich
Combat record: 22 personal victories, 6 fractional credits, 360 sorties, 70 encounters.
Decorations: Gold Star of Hero of the Soviet Union on April 19, 1945 for 20 victories, 2 fractional credits, 286 sorties, 44 engagements as of March, 1945; the Orders of Lenin, the Red Banner (2), Aleksandr Nevskij, the Patriotic War 1st and 2nd Class.

Barsukov was born in the Kalinin area on August 6, 1922 and entered military service in 1941. He received his pilot wings at Chernigov military flying school a year later and was posted to the 18 GIAP commencing his combat duty in July, 1942. He destroyed an He 111 in the vicinity of Yelnya on August 28, 1943 and in a burst of energy and skill was credited with downing six enemy planes in the air battles above Smolensk. One of his victims was a German fighter that he caught as it was trying to takeoff at Borovskoye airfield on September 14. He next claimed doubles near Mogilev and Vitebsk on October 12 resp. 15, 1943. He bagged another Bf 109 in the Vitebsk area on January 12 while leading a flight of Yak-9s on an Il-2 escort mission. A short time later he was promoted Kapitan and squadron leader and then managed to put up a good performance over East Prussia, gaining a string of seven kills with the new Yak-3 fighter. A Fw 190 fell to his guns on October 16, 1944 while he shot down another of these two days later and then added a Bf 109 near Heiligenbeil on February 15, 1945. He dispatched a further Fw 190 on April 8 and closed out his scoring four days later when he received credit for two Bf 109s. Barsukov concluded his active duty with the rank of Polkovnik in 1958.

BASHKIROV, Viktor Andreyevich
Combat record: 19 personal victories, 281 sorties, 35 encounters.
Decorations: Gold Star of Hero of the Soviet Union on February 4, 1944. for 14 kills, 233 sorties, 31 encounters as of December, 1943. the Orders of Lenin, the Red Banner (3), Aleksandr Nevskij, the Patriotic War 1st and 2nd Class.

Bashkirov was born in the Vladimir area on November 27, 1920 and enrolled for service in 1940. He completed his flight training at Stalingrad military flying school in May, 1941 and was assigned to the 519 IAP entering combat with the Luftwaffe in September. He claimed a Bf 109 while flying the Yak-7 in an action in the Kursk area on May 22, 1943 and had his best

Lavochkin La-5FN "57" of an unknown regiment. This formidable fighter was introduced into aerial combat at Stalingrad and was flown during the war by a very large number of aces, either throughout or for a part of their service career. Crack fighter outfits such as the 5 GIAP or 240 IAP became permanently identified with this aircraft. On the machine's debit side was the lack of ventilation in the cockpit which might cause high temperatures of up to 55 degrees centigrade during cockpit readiness and the development of carbon monoxide under combat conditions. (Author's collection)

day on November 3, 1943 bagging three Fw 190s and a Ju 88 while on a free hunt. Bashkirov later scored on a regular basis during the air operations on Byelorussian Front. He fought in the final battles over the Reich and destroyed another Fw 190 on the outskirts of Berlin on April 16, 1945 to raise his score to 19 and finish as a Major and the regiment's top-scoring ace. He wound up his military career as a Polkovnik in 1960.

BASHKIROV, Vyacheslav Filippovich

Combat record: 18 personal victories, 312 sorties.
Decorations: Gold Star of Hero of the Soviet Union on February 8, 1943; the Orders of Lenin, the Red Banner (2), the Patriotic War 1st Class (2), the Red Star.

Bashkirov was born in the Kursk area on April 22, 1915 and enlisted in the Soviet Army in 1940. He completed his training at Chuguyev military flying school a year later and was posted as a Politruk to the 788 IAP. He started flying combat in 1941 but it was during the epic Battle of Stalingrad that he proved his attributes. In August, 1942 he shot down six enemy planes consisting of four Ju 88s and two Bf 109s and was to complete a total of 130 sorties throughout the battle. In September he was shot down by Bf 109s and reportedly strafed in his parachute, sustaining leg wounds. He was picked up by Soviet armored forces and rushed to a field hospital. Upon his recovery he was assigned to the 907 IAP in early 1943 when the unit was being activated at Tula comprising of two squadrons equipped with La-5s and one with Yaks. He won the Orders of the Red Banner and the Patriotic War 1st Class for his efforts at Kursk. Participating in periods of intense activity in the skies of Byelorussia in 1944, he was seriously wounded and did not return to combat operations. Following World War II he served with the PVO and graduated from the Air Force Academy in 1955. He was released from active duty with the rank of General Major in 1966.

BASKOV, Vladimir Sergeyevich

Combat record: 15 personal victories, 293 sorties of which 175 were armed reconnaissance, 88 encounters.
Decorations: Gold Star of Hero of the Soviet Union on February 23, 1948; the Orders of Lenin, the Red Banner (3), the Patriotic War 1st Class and 2nd Class.

Baskov was born in the Murmansk area on September 8, 1913 and entered military service in 1933. The following year he won his wings at Odessa military flying school following which he was a pilot instructor at Odessa and Voroshilovgrad prior to being posted to the 291 IAP in 1939. He was in the forefront of action from the earliest days of the war and during his combat career fought on West, South, 3rd and 1st Byelorussian Fronts. In all he was shot down four times and badly wounded five times and managed to evade capture on two occasions after bailing out behind the enemy lines. He did well in the wild air battles above Minsk, Rostov, and during the Vistula-Oder campaign in January, 1945. He became greatly involved in the fighting over the Oder bridgehead at Küstrin scoring at least a single victory in early March, 1945. He left active duty as a Major in 1945 and became a director of Petrozavodsk civil airport.

Kapitan Ye.D. Basulin of the 239 IAP, the strain and fatigue of action etched in his face. He entered combat in 1942 and was in the center of action on Voronezh Front, winning the title of Hero of the Soviet Union on September 28, 1943. He tallied a string of at least 13 air victories during just 88 sorties. (Author's collection)

BATURIN, Aleksandr Gerasimovich

Combat record: 18 personal victories, 12 fractional credits, 543 sorties, 84 encounters.
Decorations: Gold Star of Hero of the Soviet Union on October 23, 1942 for 9 personal victories, 421 sorties of which 67 were reconnaissance and 75 ground-attack as of June, 1942; the Orders of Lenin, the Red Banner (3), the Patriotic War 1st Class.

Baturin was born in the Aktyubinsk area on July 21, 1915 and entered military service with the VMF in 1938. He completed his training at Yejsk military flying school two years later and was posted to the 71 IAP of the Baltic Fleet's air service, starting flying combat in June, 1941. He gained his first victory, a Ju 88, on August 21, 1941, when his flight was fighting a pitched battle with 20 enemy planes in the Tallin area. He continued to score on a regular basis and by mid-1942 had developed into one of the unit's more noted fighter pilots. He had the rare distinction of scoring a victory with a salvo of RS-82 rockets, mounted on racks attached to the lower wing of his I-153. He had a big day on April 3, 1942 when he downed four enemy aircraft in two sorties. On April 4, 1944 he was almost finished off by German fighters when Baturin and his wingman, Mikhail Machabeli, became involved in a dogfight with 16 Fw 190s. Baturin claimed two of them and Machabeli a third, but the latter was then shot down and became a prisoner. Baturin was badly hit in his face but his fighter still flew. He dove away and was able to stagger back to his own airfield. Soviet records are lacking in unanimity with regard to his final tally, one source suggesting a combined total of 38 personal victories and fractional credits. Baturin wound up his military career as a Major in 1948.

BATYAEV, Vasilij Sergeyevich

Combat record: 19 personal victories, 7 fractional credits, 639 sorties, 234 encounters.

Decorations: Gold Star of Hero of the Soviet Union on May 15, 1946; the Orders of Lenin, the Red Banner (4), Aleksandr Nevskij, the Red Star.

Batyaev was born in the Penzen area on February 11, 1920 and enlisted in the Soviet Army in 1939. He qualified as a pilot at Kacha military flying school a year later joining with the 88 IAP in March, 1940. He saw a lot of action in the North Caucasus winning three Orders of the Red Banner in this theater while flying I-16s. He was credited with his fourth kill over the Terek River in September, 1942 by which time he had logged some 400 sorties. He later became a member of the 54 GIAP and managed to put up a good performance on 1st Byelorussian Front, advancing to Kapitan and squadron leader. He served with the postwar VVS and graduated from the Air Force Academy in 1956. He came off active duty with the rank of Polkovnik five years later and died on May 28, 1970.

BAYEVSKIJ, Georgij Arturovich

Combat record: 19 personal victories, 232 sorties, 52 encounters.

Decorations: Gold Star of Hero of the Soviet Union on February 4, 1944 for 16 victories, 144 sorties, 45 combats as of late 1943; the Orders of Lenin, the Red Banner (2), Aleksandr Nevskij, the Patriotic War 1st and 2nd Class, the Red Star (4).

Bayevskij was born in Rostov-on-Don on July 11, 1921. His father being a diplomat, Bayevskij also grew up in Berlin, where he became acquainted with Wilhelm Batz, one of the Luftwaffe's future luminaries while attending the same school. He entered the VVS for flight training in 1940 and won his pilot wings at Serpukhov military flying school a year later. He was posted to the 5 GIAP and commenced combat duty in April, 1943 flying La-5s. He proved his skills at blasting enemy aircraft in the wild air battles above Byelgorod, Kharkov and Izyum and is credited with at least a single victory during this campaign on August 29. He bagged a Bf 109 also damaging a second on October 11, 1943 and then saw considerable fighting at Zaporozhye claiming another "Messer" on the 15th. Bayevskij participated in the air battles over Dnyepropetrovsk and destroyed a Fw 189 during a free hunt between Nikopol-Krivoj Rog but was hit and wounded by return fire. His engine cut and he came down short of a Luftwaffe base and 80 km from the Soviet lines. His wingman, Pyotr Kalsin, landed his Lavochkin in a nearby pasture to attempt a rescue. Bayevskij squeezed into the accumulator compartment with his legs dangling out, and in spite of marshy ground and snow they managed to takeoff successfully and fly back to safety. This exploit earned both of them the award of the Order of the Red Banner. He later took part in the operations against the Luftwaffe in the vicinity of Kovel, over the Oder River and in the final air battles over the Reich. While leading six La-5s assigned to beat up ground targets on the outskirts of Guben on February 28, 1945

The Yakovlev Yak-l, one of the outstanding fighter aircraft of World War II. Although under-armed, it was a superb dogfighter with excellent controls. A total of 8,720 were built between 1940/44. This Yak was captured intact by the Germans and was soon put through its paces. (Author's collection)

they spotted eight Fw 190s below and tied into them. In the action that followed seven German fighters were shot down for the loss of Aleksandr Buzunkin, a young pilot. Most successful pilot in this affray was Bayevskij with two kills. He remained in the service following the close of hostilities and graduated from the Air Force Engineering Academy in 1951 and from the General Staff Academy in 1962. He advanced to General Major two years later.

BAZANOV, Pyotr Vasilyevich

Combat record: 22 personal victories, 6 fractional credits, 320 sorties, 60 encounters.

Decorations: Gold Star of Hero of the Soviet Union on October 26, 1944 for 19 victories, 3 fractional credits, 219 sorties as of February, 1944; the Orders of Lenin, the Red Banner (2), the Patriotic War 1st Class (3), the Red Star (3).

Bazanov was born in the Moscow area on January 10, 1923 and entered military service in 1941. Upon graduating at Kacha military flying school he was assigned to the 3 GIAP flying La-5s in September, 1942. He entered combat with the Luftwaffe at Stalingrad and destroyed his first enemy aircraft in the air in December. The following day he became engaged in two missions scoring a double with one each Ju 88 and Ju 52. Bazanov later wrote a distinguished record in the fury of the Caucasus air engagements and during the Korsun-Shevchenkovskij campaign between January 24 and February 17, 1944. He closed out his scoring over Berlin and finished as the regiment's second ranking ace. Bazanov assumed various assignments after the war and graduated from the Air Force Academy in 1958. He wound up his military career as a General Lejtenant in 1985 with 44 years service.

BAZAROV, Ivan Fyodorovich

Combat record: 12 personal victories, 342 sorties, 69 encounters.

Decorations: Gold Star of Hero of the Soviet Union posthumously on September 2, 1943; the Orders of Lenin, the Red Banner (3).

Bazarov was born in the Volgograd area on December 31, 1916 and began his military career in 1938. He qualified as a pilot at Stalingrad military flying school two years later and was in continuous action from the beginning of the war. He gained his first combat experience on South Front and rapidly rose to Kapitan and squadron leader in the 247 IAP. In an outstanding effort he personally gained five victories in the air battles above Byelgorod-Kharkov while his squadron was credited with downing 37 enemy planes over a two months period to lead the regiment. On November 22, 1943 he led four Yak-1s against a mixed gaggle of Fw 190s and Bf 109s and personally accounted for two of them before he was shot down and killed by

P.V. Bazanov, seen here as Polkovnik. He downed 22 enemy planes while flying with the crack 3 GIA. : (Author's collection)

four Fw 190s. He was buried in Lozovatka, Dnyepropetrovsk area.

BEKASHONOK, Mikhail Vasilyevich

Combat record: 18 personal victories, 4 fractional credits, 170 sorties, 50 encounters.

Decorations: Gold Star of Hero of the Soviet Union on June 27, 1945; the Orders of Lenin, the Red Banner (3), the Patriotic War 1st and 2nd Class.

Bekashonok was born in the Smolensk area on September 5, 1915 and enrolled for service in 1935. He graduated from flight training at Stalingrad military flying school in 1938 and gained his first combat experience against the Finns during the ill-fated Winter War of 1939/40. He commenced combat duty against the Luftwaffe in May, 1943 flying Airacobras with the 129 GIAP and quickly gave a good account of himself. He shot down a Ju 87 on May 14, 1943 as the regiment successfully broke up an enemy attack against its base at Grushka. On October 20, 1943 he claimed two more of these when six P-39s with Podpolkovnik V.I. Bobrov in the lead bounced 18 dive-bombers between Chervona Kamenka-Pyatikhatka-Popelnastoye. He served with the postwar VVS and left active duty with the rank of Major in 1949. Bekashonok died on February 17, 1964.

BELIKOV, Oleg Stepanovich
Combat record: 15 personal victories, 14 fractional credits, 635 sorties, 114 encounters.
Decorations: Gold Star of Hero of the Soviet Union on August 19, 1944; the Orders of Lenin, The Red Banner (3), Suvorov 3rd Class.

Belikov was born in the Dnyepropetrovsk area on August 22, 1918 and joined the VVS for flight training in 1937. He completed his training at Kacha military flying school two years later and was serving as a squadron leader in the 19 IAP at the outbreak of the war. Belikov subsequently saw a lot of action on Southwest, North Caucasus, Steppe, 1st Ukrainian, 1st Byelorussian and Far East Fronts. During his combat career he was seriously wounded once. On July 20, 1942 he was leading nine fighters on a patrol when they intercepted a force of 30 bombers headed for Rostov, six of these being shot down. He blasted a Bf 109 out of the sky on February 9, 1943 and had his best day on July 5, 1943 when he was credited with four kills while flying Il-2 escort in the Byelgorod area. Six La-5s under his leadership chalked up six victories on a free hunt between Gorodenka-Kolomiya (NW Chernovtsy) on May 3, 1944 when they got into two separate scraps with some 20 Ju 87s. Belikov's share: one Stuka destroyed as well as four damaged. He rose to Kapitan and was greatly involved in the fighting surrounding the Vistula-Oder bridgeheads in early 1945. On January 17, 1945 he led a free hunt that claimed six enemy planes on the ground at Lowicz airfield, West of Warsaw. Following World War II he returned to civilian life and died on February 28, 1982.

BELOZEROV, Ivan Pavlovich
Combat record: 8 personal victories, 300 sorties, 34 encounters; 10 motor vehicles, 2 heavy guns on the ground.
Decorations: Gold Star of Hero of the Soviet Union on May 16, 1944; the Orders of Lenin, the Red Banner (2), the Patriotic War 1st Class (2), the Red Star.

Belozerov was born in the Kharkov area on September 1, 1918 and entered military service in 1939. He won his wings at Chuguyev military flying school a year later and was in action from the beginning of the war. He fought with the 6 GIAP of the Black Sea Fleet's air service in the skies above Odessa, Sevastopol and the Caucasus. He made a big name for himself as a flight leader during the dark months of 1941 his fighters being credited with downing 18 enemy planes in the course of 865 sorties and 94 air combats. On December 28, 1941 he led four I-16s in a determined attack on eight Ju 87s in the vicinity of Mekenziyevikh Gor (N Sevastopol) and personally accounted for one of them. He remained in the VMF after the war winding up his military career as a Podpolkovnik in 1964.

The remains of a Luftwaffe aircraft after it had been bounced by Soviet fighters. Photo dated July 22, 1944. (Author's collection)

BELYASNIK, Pyotr Nikiforovich
Combat record: 9 personal victories, 17 fractional credits, 250 sorties, 78 engagements as of February, 1943.
Decorations: Gold Star of Hero of the Soviet Union April 28, 1943; the Orders of Lenin, the Red Banner, the Patriotic War 1st Class, the Red Star (2).

Belyasnik was born in the Sumy area on December 21, 1917 and enlisted in the VVS in 1939. He completed his flight training at Kacha military flying school a year later and had joined with the 126 IAP when the Germans initiated Operation Barbarossa in June, 1941. The regiment suffered inordinate losses on the ground and was withdrawn to the Moscow area. He converted to Tomahawks and scored a string of seven victories in the epic defense of Moscow. He was posted with the unit to Stalingrad and was able to claim three more kills including fractional credits. His most memorable mission came on August 31, 1942 when he was leading four Tomahawks and they ran into a force of 22 enemy aircraft, his flight claiming the destruction of six Bf 109s. It has not been possible to ascertain Belyasnik's final score. He stayed in the service after the close of hostilities and retired with the rank of Polkovnik in 1964.

BENDELIANI, Chichiko Kajsarovich
Combat record: 12 personal victories, 20 fractional credits, 400+ sorties, 72 encounters.
Decorations: Gold Star of Hero of the Soviet Union on August 24, 1943 for 7 victories, 12 fractional credits, 385 sorties as of June, 1943; the Orders of Lenin (2), the Red Banner, the Patriotic War 1st and 2nd Class.

Bendeliani was born in the village of Chokhatauri, Georgian SSR, on January 29, 1913 and started his military career in 1935. He was entered into flight training at Kacha military flying school on September 8, 1935 and upon receiving his wings was posted to a unit in the Ukraine. By June, 1941 he had become a Lejtenant and flight leader in the 43 IAP. He was early in the public eye when with fellow pilots Borisov, Melnikov and Shishkin he intercepted a Luftwaffe force headed for Kiev in their I-16s piling up a score of six Ju 88s between them. A month later he had the distinction of successfully ramming a Bf 109, a feat that earned him the award of a first Order of Lenin. He had become a Major and shturman when he deployed with the regiment to Stalingrad. Over the Volga he developed into a thoroughly competent air fighter becoming famous for his propensity for head-on attacks. He chalked up five kills in the brutal fighting over Stalingrad and then fought in the Battle of Kursk flying Airacobras. On July 20, 1944 he was engaged in an Il-2 escort with Major V.D. Verkhovskij when Luftwaffe fighters bore in on the Shturmoviks. Bendeliani broke into them dispatching a Fw 190 in a head-on pass and scoring strikes on a second. He then spotted four more fighters working over some Il-2s and splashed another 190 before hits sent him crashing down to his death. He was buried in the village of Biten near Kovel.

BEREZUTSKIJ, Ivan Mikhajlovich
Combat record: 15 personal victories, 223 sorties, 73 encounters.
Decorations: Gold Star of Hero of the Soviet Union on February 23, 1945; the Orders of Lenin, the Red Banner (3), the Patriotic War 1st Class (2) and 2nd Class, the Red Star.

Berezutskij was born in the Volchikha area on November 13, 1918 and enlisted in the VVS for flight training in 1940. He qualified as a pilot at Chkalov military flying school and commenced his combat duty in July, 1942. During his time with the 63 GIAP Berezutskij successfully fought on Stalingrad, Kalinin, Northwest, Bryansk, 2nd and 1st Baltic and 3rd Byelorussian Fronts. For displaying exceptional combat skill he was promoted to lead his own squadron following which he put up a good performance at Vitebsk and Polotsk. He finished the war as a Major. Following the close of hostilities he continued on active duty and graduated from the Air Force Academy in 1955. He rose to Polkovnik and retired in 1969.

BERKUTOV, Aleksandr Maksimovich
Combat record: 15 personal victories, 332 sorties, 68 encounters.
Decorations: Gold Star of Hero of the Soviet Union on August 2, 1944; the Orders of Lenin, the Red Banner (3), Aleksandr Nevskij, the Patriotic War 1st and 2nd Class, the Red Star.

Berkutov was born in the Kujbyshev area on November 11, 1911 and commenced military service in 1931. He gained his wings at Voroshilovgrad military flying school in 1935 and first fired his guns in anger against the Japanese at the Khalkhin Gol in 1939 prior to his assignment against the Finns in 1939/40 but Soviet sources unfortunately are lacking in detail. He entered combat with the Luftwaffe in August, 1942 when he was posted to the 84 IAP, flying I-153s. The unit was mostly occupied with ground targets and ground support duties at the Kuban until 1943 when it had accomplished transition to Airacobras. He found the new mount much to his liking, run-

The Russians lost no time in improving the Yak-1. Initially conceived as a two-seat trainer, the first small batches of the Yak-7 were employed by the VVS in late 1941. It soon proved to be able to hold its own against German fighters, outclassing them in maneuverability although its acceleration in a dive was inferior. Shown here is a Yak-7B, serial number 22-03, which was built at Novosibirsk State Aircraft Factory No.153. An outstanding exponent of this type was twice Hero of the Soviet Union A.V. Vorozhejkin. (Author's collection)

ning up a string of 10 kills in the course of 67 sorties and 25 air-to -air combats over the Crimea in December, 1943. On one occasion he was leading a fighter sweep of the Kerch area when they were jumped by six Bf 109s. Berkutov sent one of them down in flames in a head-on encounter and wound up with two more on his tail. He allowed a "Messer" to get close and cut back on the throttle the pursuing 109 passing right across his sights. He gave him a short burst and the enemy aircraft blew up right in his face. Berkutov subsequently performed well in the air operations on 4th Ukrainian Front becoming commanding officer of the regiment and leading it through the final campaigns in Poland and over the Reich. He came off active duty as a Podpolkovnik in 1946 and passed away on January 26, 1962.

Kapitan A.D. Bilyukin, top-scoring ace of the 196 IAP, in the cockpit of his Aeracobra "Aleksandr Nevskij." (Author's collection)

BILYUKIN, Aleksandr Dmitriyevich
Combat record: 22 personal victories, 1 fractional credit, 418 sorties, 35 encounters.
Decorations: Gold Star of Hero of the Soviet Union November 2, 1944; the Orders of Lenin, the Red Banner, Aleksandr Nevskij, the Patriotic War 1st Class, the Red Star (3).

Bilyukin was born in the Smolensk area on September 11, 1920 and enlisted in the VVS in 1939. He completed his training at Borisoglebsk military flying school a year later and was in the forefront of action from the very first days of the war. He enjoyed considerable success while serving in the 196 IAP on Karelian Front and had a big day on August 1, 1943 when he knocked down four enemy planes on the outskirts of Leningrad, consisting of at least three Fw 190s. He advanced to Kapitan and squadron leader and by early 1944 his score had risen to 12 personal kills. Bilyukin graduated from the Air Force Academy in 1957 and wound up his military career in 1966, by which time he was a Polkovnik. He died on October 24, 1966.

BLAGOVESHCHENSKIJ, Aleksej Sergeyevich
Combat record: 12 personal victories, 25 fractional credits, 73 sorties.
Decorations: Gold Star of Hero of the Soviet Union on November 14, 1938; the Orders of Lenin (2), the Red Banner (3), Suvorov 2nd Class, Kutozov 2nd Class, Bogdan Khmelnitskij 2nd Class, the Patriotic War 1st Class (2), the Red Star (2).

Blagoveshchenskij was born in Brest on October 18, 1909 and entered military service in 1927. He completed his training at Borisoglebsk military flying school two years later and did well during his first combat assignment to the Khasan Lake in China between December, 1937 and August, 1938. While leading a squadron of I-16s with the rank of Kapitan he was credited with downing 12 Japanese planes with 25 fractional credits in the course of 73 missions to emerge as one of the top-scoring aces of the conflict. He had become a Polkovnik and commanding officer of the 27 AD when he was awarded the Gold Star for his efforts. He next saw action during the Russo-Finnish Winter War of 1939/40 following which he made a significant contribution to the fighting against the Luftwaffe. He took over the 2 IAK as a General Major on October 10, 1942. Blagoveshchenskij was promoted to General Lejtenant on April 30, 1943 and continued to lead the unit with above-average success in the aerial campaigns on Kalinin, 1st Baltic, 1st Ukrainian and 3rd Byelorussian Fronts. On February 10, 1945 his aircraft struck a mine on Luben airfield (NW Breslau) and he was seriously injured, his place being taken by General V.M. Zabaluyev. He served with the postwar VVS assuming various assignments and concluded his active duty with the rank of General Lejtenant in 1960.

BOBKOV, Valentin Vasilyevich
Combat record: 13 personal victories, 4 fractional credits, 400 sorties of which 126 were armed reconnaissance, 80 encounters.
Decorations: Gold Star of Hero of the Soviet Union on June 27, 1945; the Orders of Lenin, the Red Banner (3), the Patriotic War 1st Class (2), the Red Star (2).

Bobkov was born in the Vladimir area on July 29, 1920 and joined the Soviet Army in 1937. He qualified as a pilot at Kacha military flying school in 1940. The German assault on Soviet Russia found him as a Mladshij Lejtenant with the 88 IAP flying I-16s. In a short time he was able to claim four air victories and also damaged two more for which he was decorated with the Order of the Red Banner on December 1, 1941. He was posted to the 814 IAP and began to score on a regular basis while flying Yak-1s. In May, 1943 he was given command of his own squadron, which was to achieve a high level of success with 117 kills in the skies above Kharkov, Dnyepropetrovsk, Krivoj Rog, Poland and the Reich. By the time hostilities ceased, he was a Kapitan. During his postwar career Bobkov graduated from the Air Force Academy in 1955 returning to civilian life with the rank of Polkovnik two years later.

BOBROV, Vladimir Ivanovich
Combat record: 43 personal victories, 24 fractional credits, 112 encounters

Bobrov, master air fighter and outstanding leader, finished as the 11th ranking Soviet and Allied ace of the war. In spite of his rather spectacular combat career he neither won his country's highest award, the coveted title Hero of the Soviet Union, nor did his exploits receive the proper historical attention. I was told in Moscow that Bobrov "had problems with his character", which invariably is suggesting he was difficult, outspoken, did not exemplify the best type of Soviet officer. There is a very strong possibility that he fell from favor with his seniors and any recommendation for such an award would in consequence not have passed beyond them. Bobrov early demonstrated his potential as a fighter pilot by gaining 13 kills along with 4 fractional credits during the Spanish Civil War. When the Germans launched their assault on Soviet Russia in June, 1941 he was a squadron leader and scored for the first time against the Luftwaffe on the 22nd. Because of his success in the heavy air battles during the early stages of the war he rose to command the crack 129 GIAP, which was to develop into one of the hottest fighter outfits on the Eastern Front with 549 kills to its credit at the end of the war. He seems to have acquired a large number of his victories whilst flying the Airacobra. His wingman on many occasions was Mikhail Devyatayev. On May 14, 1943 when the regiment intercepted a strike against its own base at Grushka Bobrov personally accounted for one of the nine Ju 87s that were shot down in the melee while two P-39s were lost. The 129 GIAP then achieved a high level of success during the wild air battles above Kursk running up 55 kills in a 13 day period up to July 18, 1943. The unit had a big day on July 6 when 10 Airacobras with Bobrov in the lead tackled with 27 Ju 87s and 12 Bf 109s, 10 of the enemy planes being destroyed for no losses. Bobrov bagged a double on October 20, 1943 leading six Airacobras against a formation of 18 Ju 87s between Chervonaya Kamenka-Pyatikhatka-Popelnastoye (Kirovograd area) with four of these being shot down. He added three more air victories to his tally while taking part in the Lemberg-Sandomierz campaign in July, 1944 following which he participated in periods of intense activity over the Reich. On April 18, 1945 he destroyed two Me 262s on the ground at Alt Lönnewitz closing out his scoring over Czechoslovakia on May 9, 1945. Following World War II Bobrov was a lecturer at Kharkov State University.

BOCHKOV, Ivan Vasilyevich
Combat record: 8 personal victories, 31 fractional credits, 308 sorties, 45 encounters.

V.I. Bobrov, a tough veteran of the Spanish Civil War, who later made a brilliant war record as a pilot and leader against the Luftwaffe on the Eastern Front. However, he fell from favor of his superiors and never received his country's highest award, the title of Hero of the Soviet Union. (Author's collection)

Decorations: Gold Star of Hero of the Soviet Union posthumously on May 1, 1943; the Orders of Lenin (2), the Red Banner, the Patriotic War 1st Class.

Bochkov was born in the Kaluga area on September 17, 1915 and entered the Soviet Army in 1937. He completed his training at Borisoglebsk military flying school two years later and won the medal "Za Otvagu" (For Valor) for his efforts during the Russo-Finnish Winter War of 1939/40. He became a member of the 145 IAP before the Patriotic War but did not get an opportunity to score before the regiment had converted to Airacobras. On May 15, 1942 he was leading a sweep of four P-39s when they engaged a formation of 12 Bf 109s and eight Bf 110s, two of these being shot down. Bochkov personally accounted for one. He claimed another Bf 109 the following day and then dispatched a Ju 88 near Olenya on May 21. On June 15 six Cobras with Bochkov in the lead attacked 30 Luftwaffe planes headed for Murmansk. In breaking up the formation, eight enemy aircraft were destroyed without loss with Bochkov receiving credit for one each Bf 110 and Ju 88. On April 4, 1943 he was bounced by fighters and crashed to his death. He was buried in a common grave in Shonguj (S Murmansk).

BOKIJ, Nikolaj Andreyevich

Combat record: 13 personal victories, 400 sorties, 40 encounters.
Decorations: Gold Star of Hero of the Soviet Union on July 24, 1943; the Orders of Lenin, the Red Banner (3), the Patriotic War 1st Class, the Red Star.

Bokij was born in the Krasnodar area on November 22, 1918 and started his military career in the VMF in 1939. He completed his training at Yejsk military flying school two years later whereupon he was posted to the 72 IAP of the Northern Fleet's air service as a Starshij Serzhant on August 18, 1941. A short time later he shot down his first enemy aircraft in an I-16 and converted to Hurricanes in early 1942. From then on he was in continuous action in the Murmansk area his exploits against great odds leading to an almost legendary reputation. He got a single on April 15, 1942 when 2nd Eskadrilya led by Kapitan I.I. Kovalenko badly mauled a formation of 26 enemy aircraft claiming the destruction of eight Ju 87s. He added a Bf 109 on May 8 and another on June 12 prior to reequipping with Airacobras. His most memorable mission probably came on April 19, 1943 when he shot down Ofw. Rudolf Müller, one of the successful pilots of JG 5 with 94 kills on the Eastern Front. The action started when the standing patrol of four Hurricanes and Kapitan P.D. Klimov in his Cobra called in three swarms of enemy fighters consisting of four to eight Bf 109s and Fw 190s each enroute to Vayenga (Severomorsk), northeast of Murmansk. The alert flight of six Airacobras was scrambled and a terrific battle commenced when Mladshij Lejtenant Bokij's flight attained 7,500m several minutes later, spotting eight Bf 109s flying in pairs and approaching Vayenga. Soon after four more Bf 109s and two Fw 190s streaked in. These aircraft dive-bombed the airfield below scoring some hits on a line of fighters while most bombs fell wide. In the same time frame two Bf 109s peeled off and closed on Mladshij Lejtenant Romanov and his wingman. Postwar investigation has suggested that it was Ofw. Rudolf Müller who carried out this attack. Bokij dived to the rescue and fired a long burst from astern closing in to 200m. The German fighters immediately broke away with Müller going into a steep dive while the second zoomed up into a layer of clouds. Bokij followed Müller down to tree-top level where he got in several good bursts forcing the 109 down to a wheels-up landing 8km East of Malyarvi Lake. Müller set out for the German lines on snow-shoes but was captured a short time later. Following his interrogation Müller was sent to a POW camp but his fate after 1944 has remained a mystery. Bokij shot down another Bf 109 near Murmansk on April 29 to raise his tally to eight. His final score is unclear, one source suggesting a record of 14 personal victories, 1 fractional credit, 385 missions and 30 air combats as of May, 1943 qualifying him for the Gold Star award. He served with the postwar VVS and attended the Air Force Academy. He was a Polkovnik when he wound up his military career in 1965.

Rudi Müller was one of the great aces of JG 5 "Eismeer" in the north. On April 19, 1943 he lost his last battle against Nikolaj Bokij in his P-39. (Bundesarchiv)

Although not the best quality shot, this photo shows Ofw. Rudi Müller's Bf 109G-2/R6 "Yellow 3" after he had effected a forced landing eight kilometers east of Malyarvi Lake. The aircraft visible in the background is a Po-2. (Author's collection courtesy of Yu.V. Rybin)

BORISENKO, Ivan Ivanovich

Combat record: 23 personal victories, 2 fractional credits, 245 sorties, 63 encounters.
Decorations: Gold Star of Hero of the Soviet Union on May 15, 1946; the Orders of Lenin, the Red Banner (3), Bogdan Khmelnitskij 3rd Class, the Patriotic War 1st Class, the Red Star (2).

Borisenko was born in Zaporozhye on September 28, 1923 and enlisted in the Soviet Army in 1940. He won his wings at Kacha military flying school two years later and commenced his combat duty in September, 1942. He flew with great distinction on 2nd Ukrainian Front while serving in the 73 GIAP (formerly the 296 IAP). He advanced to Kapitan and deputy squadron leader and came out of the war as the regiment's top-scoring ace. On March 12, 1945 he was leading a flight of Yak-1s on a fighter sweep when they became involved in a melee with four Bf 109s north of Budapest. Two "Messers" went down in flames while Borisenko was able to force another to land at the Soviet airfield of Tekel. He stayed in the VVS after the close of war and was a Polkovnik when leaving active duty in 1975 with 35 years service.

BORISOV, Ivan Grigoryevich
Combat record: 25 personal victories, 8 fractional credits, 4 enemy aircraft destroyed in ground attacks.
Decorations: Gold Star of Hero of the Soviet Union on November 1, 1943 for 10 victories, 210 sorties, 80 encounters as of late 1943; the Orders of Lenin, the Red Banner (5), Aleksandr Nevskij, the Patriotic War 1st Class.

Borisov was born in the Moscow area on September 28, 1921 and entered the VVS for flight training in 1940. He won his wings a year later at Ostafyev military flying school being posted to the 4 IAP in October. He saw a great deal of action in the skies above Kishinyov, Tiraspol, Nikolayev, Odessa, Kherson and in late 1941 converted to Hurricanes. He later fought with the regiment over Voronezh and in August, 1942 was assigned with the unit to Stalingrad flying Yak-1s. In late 1942 he was posted to the crack 9 GIAP and subsequently was to make a big name for himself in the great aerial campaigns over the Kuban, Sevastopol, East Prussia and the Reich while flying Airacobras and finally La-7s. He came off active duty with the rank of Major in 1949 and died on August 10, 1954.

BORODACHYOV, Viktor Ivanovich
Combat record: 26 personal victories, 5 fractional credits, 552 sorties, 116 encounters.
Decorations: Gold Star of Hero of the Soviet Union on July 1, 1944 for 19 victories, 5 fractional credits, 364 sorties and 91 engagements as of February 1, 1944; the Orders of Lenin, the Red Banner (4), Aleksandr Nevskij, the Patriotic War 1st Class (2), the Red Star (2).

Borodachyov was born in the Volgograd area on August 23, 1918 and started his military career in 1936. He qualified as a pilot two years later and first saw combat against the Finns during the Winter War of 1939/40. He was with the 131 IAP through World War II displaying his great skill and courage in the heavy air battles above Tiraspol, Dnyepropetrovsk, Taganrog and Kursk-Orel. On July 9, 1943 he led six La-5s to bounce a large formation of Ju 87s escorted by Bf 109s in the vicinity of Kochetovka (NE Lipetsk) and personally accounted for one of the six dive-bombers that were shot down in the encounter. He later performed well while serving with the regiment on 1st Ukrainian Front and rose to Kapitan and squadron leader. He remained in the service following World War II and graduated from the Air Force Academy in 1950 and the General Staff Academy in 1960. He was promoted to General Major but "tragically died" on July 11, 1968, the circumstances of his death not being recorded.

Five 9 GIAP top-hands in front of a La-7. From the left they are: S. Amet-Khan, I.G. Borisov, V.D. Lavrinenkov, I.G. Korolyov, and P.Ya. Golovachyov. Their combined victories came to 139. Korolyov wears an A-2 jacket supplied by the American allies while all the others are evidently finding comfort in the warmth of their British Irvin jackets. (Author's collection)

BOROVYKH, Andrej Yegorovich
Combat record: 32 personal victories, 14 fractional credits, 424 sorties, 104 encounters.
Decorations: 1st Gold Star of Hero of the Soviet Union on August 24, 1943 for 12 victories, 14 fractional credits, 341 sorties as of June, 1943; 2nd Gold Star on February 23, 1945 after 19 more kills and 132 missions as of December, 1944; the Orders of Lenin (2), the Red Banner (5), Aleksandr Nevskij, the Patriotic War 1st Class, the Red Star (3).

Major V.I. Borodachyov, high-scoring 40 GIAP ace. (Author's collection)

Borovykh was born in Kursk on October 30, 1921 and began his brilliant career in the VVS in 1940. He completed his pilot training at Chuguyev military flying school prior to being posted to the 728 IAP on Kalinin Front in December, 1941. He subsequently proved his skills at blasting enemy aircraft over Kholm, Rzhev, Kursk, Gomel, during the Lemberg-Sandomierz campaign, over Warsaw and finally, Berlin. He eventually was promoted to Kapitan and squadron leader and had developed into an exceptionally capable fighter pilot. Borovykh was able to gain his initial success early in the war when he shot down a Ju 88 near Kholm with the I-16. Shortly afterward he got two more of these in the vicinity of Toropets. By the time he was assigned to the 157 IAP in September, 1942 his tally stood at 10 kills including fractional credits, ranking him among the unit's stellar performers. On July 11, 1942 he led 10 Hurricanes in a pitched battle with a superior Luftwaffe formation with seven enemy planes being blasted out of the sky. He personally got a double with two Bf 109s near Rzhev a short time later when his flight became embroiled in a dogfight with 12 fighters. Borovykh then gave a good account of himself by downing eight enemy planes at Kursk within a month and was put in command of his own squadron. Huge aerial melees became the order of the day during the period of October, 1944 to February, 1945 and saw his fighters chalk up 51 kills in the course of 73 encounters. He participated in periods of intense activity during the Vistula-Oder campaign in January, 1945 and at the Küstrin bridgehead in February, by which time he had become a Kapitan. He is rated as one of the best Soviet fighters and credited with some 600 sorties by one source. He remained active following World War II and graduated from the Air Force Academy in 1951 and from the General Staff Academy in 1957. He assumed various assignments in the Moscow PVO, DVO and KVO between 1958 and 1977. He was promoted to General Polkovnik in 1968 and a year later was appointed commander of the PVO fighter forces.

Major A.Ye. Borovykh, the aggressive young ace who ran up strings of victories on Central and 1st Byelorussian Fronts. His 32 kills made him the 31st ranking Soviet ace of World War II. (Author's collection)

Starshij Lejtenant Ivan Petrovich Borodin, deputy squadron leader in the 21 IAP, with his Lavochkin La-5 fighter. The date is June 18, 1944 at which time his bag was 10 personal kills along with two fractional credits during some 350 sorties. Final total not available. (Author's collection)

BRINKO, Pyotr Antonovich

Combat record: 15 personal victories.

Decorations: Gold Star of Hero of the Soviet Union on July 14, 1941; the Orders of Lenin, the Red Banner, the Red Star.

Brinko was born in the Donetsk area on September 17, 1915 and commenced his legendary career in the VMF in 1935. Upon receiving his wings at Yejsk military flying school he took part in the operations against the Japanese at Khasan Lake in 1938 and over the Khalkhin Gol in 1939 following which he became involved in the Russo-Finnish Winter War of 1939/40. He already was an accomplished pilot when entering combat with the 13 IAP of the Baltic Fleet's air service in June, 1941. He wrote an indelible combat record during the early months of the war when the regiment was engaged in the desperate fighting at Dago, Tallin and Leningrad. In July he successfully rammed a bomber on the outskirts of Leningrad and on the 23rd claimed a double with two Fokker D.XXIs during a fighter battle in the Hanko area, the Finnish port leased to Russia after the Winter War. All told, the Finns reportedly lost five fighters in this scrap. He brought his score to seven in late July and then shot down another Fokker on August 2. On September 5 Brinko was bounced by four Bf 110s which were taking turns making passes at him. By skillfully hauling back into tight turns which the faster and less maneuverable enemy fighters could not follow he was dodging their attacks. At a point when he had expended most of his ammunition and the engine was beginning to give trouble, Brinko managed to get on the tail of one "Messer" slicing off part of its rudder with the propeller of his I-16 and sending it crashing down. He staggered back to his own airfield with great gaping holes in the fuselage of his fighter and landed safely. For this feat he was decorated with the Order of the Red Banner and was back in the air four days later claiming a Fw 189. On September 11 he bagged a Hs 126 but on the 14th was shot down and killed while attacking a Ju 88.

One of the more successful pilots of the 21 IAP was Starshij Lejtenant Leonid Arsfyevich Bryzhko shown here on October 10, 1944. He totaled 150 sorties with 8 victories in air combat. (Author's collection)

BRYZGALOV, Pavel Aleksandrovich
Combat record: 19 personal victories, 1 enemy aircraft on the ground, 243 sorties, 61 encounters.
Decorations: Gold Star of Hero of the Soviet Union on May 15, 1946; the Orders of Lenin, the Red Banner (2), Aleksandr Nevskij, the Patriotic War 1st and 2nd Class, the Red Star (2).

Bryzgalov was born in the Perm area on September 8, 1922 and enlisted in the VVS for flight training in 1941. He completed his pilot training at Rustavi military flying school a year later and started flying combat with the crack 178 GIAP on Voronezh Front in June, 1943. He gained his first combat experience on Steppe and 2nd Ukrainian Fronts completing 56 sorties until August, 1943. He then scored a string of five air victories in a fierce series of dogfights over the Dnyepr River in October, 1943 and performed brilliantly in subsequent operations over Hungary. He was credited with a double on October 6, 1944 and on the 20th gained a single while leading his flight in an engagement with a mixed gaggle of eight Bf 109s and Fw 190s between Terescht-Miklosch. On January 3, 1945 12 Bf 109s chose to do battle with 10 La-5s, but the Red fighters quickly turned the tables claiming six kills with Bryzgalov accounting for one of them. He added another single on February 17 when his flight became embroiled in a dogfight with eight Fw 190s, five of these being shot down for no losses. He ended the war as a Starshij Lejtenant and the regiment's third highest scoring ace. Bryzgalov served with the postwar VVS and graduated from the Air Force Academy in 1953. He retired as a Polkovnik in 1959.

BULGAKOV, Andrej Panteleyevich
Combat record: 18 personal victories, 182 sorties, 39 encounters.
Decorations: Gold Star of Hero of the Soviet Union on August 18, 1945; the Orders of Lenin, the Red Banner (3), Aleksandr Nevskij, the Patriotic War 1st Class.

Bulgakov was born in the Byelgorod area on September 20, 1920 and entered the Soviet Army in 1940. He completed his training at Chuguyev military flying school a year later and then attended flight leader classes. He commenced his combat duty in August, 1943 and from then on was in continuous action on 1st Byelorussian, 3rd and 1st Baltic Fronts. Bulgakov eventually rose to command his own squadron in the 265 IAP, and under his leadership this was credited with downing 60 enemy planes in the course of 1,000 sorties and 43 air combats. He had a big day on July 20, 1944 when combat with 12 Bf 109s occurred in the vicinity of Doroguska. One Bf 109 went down before his guns as it was working over Mladshij Lejtenant Tutko, an inexperienced pilot. A moment later, he went to the rescue of another comrade and got a second 109 at 50m range. He stayed in the service following World War II and wound up his military career with the rank of Podpolkovnik in 1954. He died on April 24, 1981.

BURMATOV, Vladimir Aleksandrovich
Combat record: 12 personal victories, 1 fractional credit, 191 sorties, 43 encounters.
Decorations: Gold Star of Hero of the Soviet Union on May 31, 1944; the Orders of Lenin, the Red Banner (3), the Patriotic War 1st Class, the Red Star (2).

Burmatov was born in the Vladimir area on July 15, 1921 and entered the Soviet Navy in 1940. Upon completion of pilot training at Saransk military flying school he was posted to the 255 IAP of the Northern Fleet's air service. He immediately found his range and soon had established a reputation for aggressiveness and air combat skill. On June 23, 1943 eight Cobras were assigned providing cover for Il-2s of 46 ShAP tasked with striking shipping off Cape Kibergnes. In the target area eight Bf 110s were intercepted with three of them being shot down by Lejtenants Burmatov, Semyonov and Strelnikov. On July 16, 1943 he was able to shoot down 65-victory ace Leutnant Hans Döbrich of 6./JG 5 to run his score to 10. Döbrich was seriously injured and did not return to combat operations. Burmatov remained in the VMF after the war and graduated from the Soviet Air Force Academy in 1952. He left active duty as a Polkovnik in 1957 and passed away on October 27, 1986.

Knights Cross Holder Oberleutnant Hans Döbrich of 6./JG 5 chalked up 65 kills, all but one against fighters, before he was shot down and wounded by Lejtenant V.A. Burmatov over Pechenga (Petsamo) Bay on July 16, 1943. (Bundesarchiv)

BURNAZYAN, Sergej Avdeyevich
Combat record: 22 personal victories, 2 fractional credits, 224 sorties.
Decorations: Gold Star of Hero of the Soviet Union posthumously on August 2, 1944; the Orders of Lenin, the Red Banner, the Patriotic War 1st Class.

Burnazyan was born in the Rostov area on May 28, 1918 and enrolled for service in 1938. He received his wings at Kherson military flying school two years later. In January, 1942 he was posted to the 629 IAP on Stalingrad Front commencing his combat duty on June 17. He scored on a regular basis and by October 22 his tally had risen to five including fractional credits in the course of 23 engagements. On September 7 he was credited with two fractional credits while leading his flight against a superior force of 12 Ju 88s and eight Bf 109s. He then was assigned to the 866 IAP on Southwest Front to achieve aerial victories at a formidable pace. He gained a string of 17 kills in only 76 missions, 22 of which were air patrol, 20 escorts, 17 scrambles and 7 ground-attacks while entering into 29 encounters. His big day was January 1, 1943 when six-Yak-1s engaged a formation of 10 Ju 87s and eight Bf 109s, nine of these being shot down. Most successful pilot in this affray was Burnazyan with a triple. He got a double with two Hs 129 ground-attack planes on January 31 while leading his flight to attack 12 of these and six escorting Bf 109s. In all, they destroyed six Henschels for no losses. He was appointed squadron leader and quickly displayed remarkable leadership and tactical skill, the Eskadrilya chalking up 62 kills in the course of 815 sorties. On April 15, 1943 He 111s hit the Duginka-Khrenovaya railroad station and Burnazyan, who was confined to the ground that day, was killed by bomb fragments.

Luftwaffe echelon in Kiev, the "pearl of the Ukraine." The city was liberated by forces of the 1st Ukrainian Front on November 6, 1943. (Author's collection)

BYKOVETS, Leonid Aleksandrovich
Combat record: 19 personal victories, 274 sorties, 50 encounters.
Decorations: Gold Star of Hero of the Soviet Union on August 18, 1945 for 16 victories, 4 fractional credits, 200 sorties as of March, 1945; the Orders of Lenin, the Red Banner (4), Aleksandr Nevskij, the Patriotic War 1st Class (2), the Red Star (2).

Bykovets was born in the Moscow area on December 14, 1921 and enlisted in the VVS in 1940. He received his wings at Kacha military flying school a year later and was posted to the 28 GIAP entering combat in December, 1942. He subsequently flew with the regiment on Northwest, Kalinin, 2nd and 1st Baltic Fronts and managed to put up a good performance during the Soviet summer offensive of 1944 in Byelorussia, that was to smash German Army Group Center. On July 3 he was able to dispatch one of the two Bf 109s that tried to interfere with an Il-2 strike and added another of these twelve days later. Bykovets stayed in the service after the close of war rising to Polkovnik. He left active duty in 1960.

BYKOVSKIJ, Yevgenij Vlasovich
Combat record: 9 personal victories, 100 sorties of which 18 were ground-attack.
Decorations: Gold Star of Hero of the Soviet Union posthumously on May 14, 1965; the Orders of Lenin and the Red Banner.

Bykovskij was born in Apostolovo, Dnyepropetrovsk area, in 1921 and started his military career in 1940. He completed his pilot training at Batajak military flying school two years later joining with the 5 GIAP as a Serzhant in May, 1942. He saw a lot of action while flying LaGG-3s on Il-2 and Pe-2 escorts in the Rzhev and Velikiye Luki areas and while operating on

19-victory ace L.A. Bykovets, a flight leader in the 28 GIAP, on the wing of his Aeracobra. The date is June 20, 1944 when his bag was 7 personal kills plus one fractional credit. (Author's collection)

Mladshij Lejtenant Yurij Mikhajlovich Chapliyev, a very capable 28 GIAP pilot, photographed with his P-39 on June 20, 1944. By this time his tally stood at nine personal kills, four fractional credits and five balloons. It seems likely that he added to this later but details are not available. (Author's collection)

ground-support duties between Kholm-Byelyj. On April 27, 1943 he became involved in a battle with 26 Luftwaffe bombers and eight fighters near Starobyelsk (Voronezh area) but was shot down crashing to his death.

CHASNYK, Nikolaj Leontyevich
Combat record: 19 personal victories, 8 fractional credits, 685 sorties, 46 encounters.
Decorations: Gold Star of Hero of the Soviet Union on August 22, 1944 for 16 victories, 3 fractional credits, 39 air combats as of April, 1944; the Orders of Lenin (2), the Red Banner (2), Aleksandr Nevskij, the Patriotic War 1st Class, the Red Star.

Chasnyk was born in Orsha on October 26, 1921 and enrolled for service in 1940. He was graduated at Borisoglebsk military flying school a year later and in October, 1941 became a member of the 630 IAP as a Serzhant flying I-16s. He was successful in scoring his first victory by downing a Ju 88 in February, 1942. He later was posted to the 148 GIAP in August, 1942 and won the Order of the Red Banner for his efforts a short time later. He received a second such award in 1943 and was promoted to command a squadron of Yak-9s. The squadron made a significant contribution to the fighting at Kursk with 19 kills being acquired in a single day. On April 2, 1944 he deliberately rammed an He 111 which fell out of control near Sarny to earn the rare distinction of performing a successful taran attack at night. On July 7 he was hit by the return fire of a Ju 88 and crash-landed his Yak in a pasture becoming a prisoner. He was liberated by U.S. forces in 1945 after he had been in various prison camps including Pinsk, Brest, Siemiatycze (NW Brest), Blonie (Warsaw area), Lodz, Königsberg-Neumark (N Berlin) and Buchenwald. He stayed in the service after the war and graduated from the Air Force Academy in 1952 winding up his military career as a Polkovnik in 1958.

CHIRKOV, Andrej Vasilyevich
Combat record: 29 personal victories, 9 fractional credits, some 400 sorties, 78 encounters.
Decorations: Gold Star of Hero of the Soviet Union on February 4, 1944 for 18 victories, 9 fractional credits, 389 sorties, 60 encounters as of June, 1943; the Orders of Lenin (2), the Red Banner (2), the Patriotic War 1st Class.

Chirkov was born in Dnyepropetrovsk on October 10, 1917 and joined the VVS for flight training in 1937. He received his wings at Kacha military flying school a year later and cut his teeth against the Finns during the Winter War of 1939/40. When the Germans initiated Operation Barbarossa in June, 1941 Chirkov was serving as a Lejtenant in the 158 IAP on Leningrad Front. He was early in the public eye scoring the Front's first aerial victory on the 23rd by downing an He 111 near Pskov with the Yak-1 fighter. From then on Chirkov was in the forefront of action and his exploits soon earned him a reputation for toughness and air combat skill but was wounded in action twice during the year. While sweeping the same area around Pskov on June 25 Chirkov spotted two He 111s and shot one down and damaged the other. Unfortunately he was then badly hit and wounded by return fire but was able to nurse his crippled fighter in safely at his own airfield. After a short stay in hospital he was back in action running up a string of seven kills in August. His feats qualified him for one of the first Red Banner awards on Leningrad Front. On one occasion he was then almost finished off by Bf 109s while flying bomber escort and with complete disregard for his injuries and personal safety maintained formation scoring a number of victories before breaking off and turning for home. He was posted to the 154 IAP a short time later and converted to Tomahawks in November, 1941. He seems to have been successful while flying this aircraft and on January 20 (or 21 as suggested by one source) he successfully rammed an He 111 in the Pogostya area. He parachuted and landed in enemy territory but was able to evade capture and returned to his unit two days later. He later rose to Major and deputy regiment commander and eventually assumed command of the 196 IAP. Chirkov wound up his military career in 1949 and died on September 10, 1956.

Major A.V. Chirkov came out of World War II as one of the leading aces with a confirmed score of 29. He cut his teeth against the Finns and later took part in the ferocious fighting on Leningrad Front. (Author's collection)

CHISLOV, Aleksandr Mikhajlovich

Combat record: 21 personal victories, 13 fractional credits, 333 sorties.

Decorations: Gold Star of Hero of the Soviet Union on August 24, 1943 for 15 kills, 300 sorties as of July, 1943; the Orders of Lenin (2), the Red Banner (2), Aleksandr Nevskij, the Patriotic War 1st Class (2), the Red Star.

Chislov was born in the Volgograd area on March 14, 1915 and joined the Soviet Army in 1938. He received his wings at Borisoglebsk military flying school and fought from the very start of the war. Chislov enjoyed considerable success while flying La-5s with the 63 GIAP on Bryansk Front scoring heavily at Demyansk and in a fierce series of dogfights over Velikiye Luki. Because of his success he rapidly was promoted to Kapitan and squadron leader and then continued his streak during the Battles of Kursk and Orel with 7-8 sorties daily being commonplace. His Eskadrilya was credited with destroying 41 aircraft in the air following which he took over command of the regiment and was promoted to Podpolkovnik. In this capacity he took part in the great aerial campaigns against the Luftwaffe over Byelorussia, the Baltic and the Reich. The regiment's final score was 400 kills. Chislov remained in the VVS after the war retiring with the rank of Polkovnik in 1956.

CHUBUKOV, Fyodor Mikhajlovich

Combat record: 34 personal victories, 5 fractional credits, 300+ sorties.

Decorations: Gold Star of Hero of the Soviet Union on August 19, 1944 for 17 victories, 5 fractional credits, 296 sorties, 52 encounters as of May, 1944; the Orders of Lenin, the Red Banner, Aleksandr Nevskij, the Patriotic War 1st and 2nd Class, the Red Star (2).

Chubukov was born in the Voronezh area on June 21, 1920 and enlisted in the VVS for flight training in 1939. He completed his pilot training at Borisoglebsk military flying school a year later and began his brilliant combat career at the outbreak of the war. He was serving in the 154 IAP on Leningrad Front and gave a good account of himself after the unit had reequipped with Tomahawks in late 1941. He was wounded during a fighter battle on March 15, 1942 but was back in the air shortly afterward and on July 11, 1942 got a double with Bf 109s when six Tomahawks tackled with 20 Luftwaffe fighters. He shot down a Ju 88 on September 3 and another of these eleven days later. On the 26th two Bf 109s fell to his guns when Chubukov and five fellow pilots fought a pitched battle with 32 enemy aircraft. In January, 1943 he converted to Yak-7Bs and in late 1943 began flying Yak-9s. He was promoted Kapitan and became a squadron leader and had his best day in September, 1944 when he bagged four Fw 190s in one mission. He went on to become one of the deadliest fighters of Leningrad Front. Following World War II Chubukov continued on active duty and graduated from the Soviet Air Force Academy in 1952. He retired as a Polkovnik in 1962 and later

F.M. Chubukov by the business end of his fighter. He won fame on the Leningrad Front tallying 34 kills together with five fractional credits. The date of this photo is February, 1944. (Author's collection)

became an executive of the Riga Engineering Institute of Civil Aviation.

CHUPIKOV, Pavel Fyodorovich

Combat record: 14 personal victories, 6 fractional credits, 400+ sorties, 77 encounters.

Decorations: Gold Star of Hero of the Soviet Union on August 19, 1944 for 11 victories, 8 fractional credits, 388 sorties, 72 engagements as of June, 1944; the Orders of Lenin (4), the October Revolution, the Red Banner (5), Suvorov 3rd Class, the Patriotic War 1st Class (2), the Red Star (4).

Chupikov was born in Tashkent on December 21, 1913 and enrolled for service in 1931. He completed training at Volsk aircraft mechanics school a year later and first saw action against the Japanese at Lake Khasan in 1938. He later applied for pilot training and was sent to Kacha military flying school, receiving his wings in 1940. He was in the thick of the fighting from the earliest days of the Patriotic War and assumed command of the 40 IAP with the rank of Major in 1942. He demonstrated his potential as a fighter leader in the heavy air battles above the Caucasus. In March, 1944 he was appointed as regiment commander of the 19 IAP, and under his leadership the unit was to produce some of the most outstanding Russian aces of the war finishing with a confirmed total of 398 enemy planes in the air and 56 on the ground. The regiment scored heavily in the air operations over Proskurov, Bobrujsk, Warsaw, during the Vistula-Oder campaign and finally, over Berlin. Chupikov continued to go off on combat missions whenever possible and on March 11, 1945 claimed a single. The regiment's big day came on April 16, 1945 when its La-7s forced down 16 Fw 190 fighter-bombers without loss to themselves. Chupikov advanced to Polkovnik in August, 1944 and closed out his scoring on April 23, 1945 during the fighting for Berlin. During his postwar career he held various assignments including as a commander of the air services of a military district and general-inspektor of the Soviet Ministry of Defense. He graduated from the General Staff Academy in 1954 and had become a General Polkovnik when winding up his military career in 1976 with 45 years service.

CHURILIN, Aleksej Pavlovich

Combat record: 17 personal victories plus 21 enemy planes on the ground, 273 sorties, 83 encounters.

Decorations: Gold Star of Hero of the Soviet Union on August 18, 1945; the Orders of Lenin, the Red Banner (2), Aleksandr Nevskij, the Patriotic War 2nd Class, the Red Star (4).

Churilin was born in Kamensk-Uralskij on December 26, 1916 and entered military service in 1940. A year later he won his wings at Stalingrad military flying school and was assigned to the 611 IAP to start flying combat in December, 1942. He enjoyed considerable success in a series of tough encounters over Krasnodar, the Mius River and at Akhtyrka. In the course of his combat duty Churilin was wounded in action twice and took over as leader of a fighter squadron with the rank of Major. He made a specialty of beating up enemy planes on their airfields and came out of World War II as one of the top Soviet strafers. Most of his air victories were achieved against single-engined fighters, the most difficult opponents:

Airborne portrait of a P-39 Aeracobra. Although lacking altitude performance because it had no turbocharger, the sleek Cobra proved a low to medium altitude fighter and "ace maker" par excellence. In the hands of pilots of the standing of Pokryshkin, Rechkalov and Gulayev it helped to stem the tide of Luftwaffe victory. (Author's collection)

Bf 109s 12
Fw 190s 2
Ju 87s 3

He remained in the VVS following the close of war and rose to Polkovnik retiring in 1972. He passed away on August 23, 1982.

DANILENKO, Nikolaj Nikitovich
Combat record: 16 personal victories, 1 fractional credit, 256 sorties, 49 encounters.
Decorations: Gold Star of Hero of the Soviet Union on April 19, 1945; the Orders of Lenin, the Red Banner (2), the Patriotic War 1st Class (2), the Red Star.

Danilenko was born in the Byelgorod area on October 24, 1921 and enlisted in the Soviet Army in 1940. He completed his pilot training at Kacha military flying school two years later and was posted to the crack 18 GIAP commencing his combat duty in April, 1942. On August 28, 1943 he was able to shoot down an He 111 near Yelnya. He scored heavily during the big air battles above Smolensk in September, 1943 adding five kills to his tally. One of his victims was a fighter that he dispatched as it was scrambling for takeoff at Borovskoye airfield on September 14. He claimed a double with one each He 111 and Fw 190 on October 15 and hardly managed to struggle back to base in his crippled Yak-9 before running out of gas. Danilenko continued his streak into the East Prussian campaign while flying the new Yak-3 fighter. On October 17, 1944 he bagged a Fw 190 in the Insterburg area and damaged another of these six days later while flying escort for Il-2s. He got another double on April 13 when two Fw 190s fell to his guns in an encounter near Gross-Hubniken airfield. Danilenko served with the postwar VVS and returned to civilian life in 1954 by which time he had become a Podpolkovnik.

DANILOV, Stepan Pavlovich
Combat record: 11 personal victories, 172+ sorties.
Decorations: Gold Star of Hero of the Soviet Union on November 17, 1939; the Orders of Lenin, the Red Banner, Suvorov 2nd Class, Kutuzov 2nd Class, the Patriotic War 1st Class.

Danilov was born in the Vologda area on December 15, 1909 and entered the VVS for flight training in June, 1931. He received his wings at 7th military flying school two years later and served as a Mladshij Lejtenant and flight leader prior to entering combat in Spain in January, 1937. He met the requirements for the award of the Red Banner and went home eight months later to take over as commander of the 44 IAP. He was promoted Major and was posted again this time assuming command of the 56 IAP. He deployed with the regiment to the Khalkhin Gol and started flying combat there on July 17, 1939. The unit took a heavy toll of opposing Japanese aircraft by chalking up 80 kills in a 25 day period with Danilov personally accounting for six fighters and two bombers. He next took part in the Russo-Finnish Winter War of 1939/40 and in 1940 advanced to Polkovnik. When German forces knifed into Soviet Russia in June, 1941 he had become commander of the 7 IAK-PVO and in this capacity was to see a lot of action during the dramatic defense of Leningrad. Successive assignments saw him lead the 5 SAD, 287 IAD and 14 IAK on Northwest, Leningrad, Bryansk and 2nd Baltic Fronts. He displayed outstanding leadership as commander of the 14 IAK the unit being credited with destroying 196 enemy planes in the air during 6,475 sorties. Danilov was successful in adding three kills in 23 air-to-air combats during the course of the Patriotic War. He rose to General Major but was killed in the Far East on May, 24, 1945 the circumstances not being known.

DAVIDKOV, Viktor Iosifovich
Combat record: 20 personal victories, 2 fractional credits, 434 sorties.
Decorations: Gold Star of Hero of the Soviet Union on June 6, 1942 for 6 kills, 2 fractional credits, 186 sorties as of September, 1941; the Orders of Lenin (2), the Red Banner (4), Suvorov 2nd Class, Kutuzov 2nd Class, Aleksandr Nevskij, the Patriotic War 1st Class, the Red Star (2).

Davidkov was born in the Zaporozhye area on August 17, 1913 and began his military career in 1932. He qualified as a pilot at Engels military flying school following which he gained his first combat experience at Lake Khasan against the Japanese in 1938. There followed his assignment against the Finns during the Winter War of 1939/40 and next was posted to the 131 IAP in the vicinity of Zaporozhye in 1940. By June, 1941 the regiment had deployed to South Front following which he was in the forefront of action from the earliest days of the war. Davidkov had by now become deputy regiment commander and was to achieve fame for his exploits in the big air battles above Rostov and Taganrog. While flying the LaGG-3 fighter he ran up a string of 13 kills there and rapidly rose to commanding officer. With Davidkov in the lead the unit racked up 90 air victories in the skies above Rostov and Izyum-Barvenkovo. His most memorable mission was a fighter sweep with M.S. Tokarev. Soon after takeoff they became engaged in a tough battle with 16 Bf 109s and using mutual support tactics they reportedly were able to destroy three fighters between them before breaking clear and turning for home. He subsequently saw considerable fighting over the North Caucasus and at Kursk and eventually assumed command of the crack 8 GIAD finishing the war at Berlin. He remained in the VVS following the close of war and in 1951 graduated from the General Staff Academy. Davidkov wound up his military career with the rank of General Polkovnik in 1977.

DEKHTYARENKO, Andrej Nikolayevich

Combat record: 10 personal victories, 2 enemy planes on the ground, 39 sorties.

Decorations: Gold Star of Hero of the Soviet Union posthumously on July 21, 1942; the Orders of Lenin, the Red Banner (2).

Dekhtyarenko was born in the Sumy area on May 17, 1909 and entered the Soviet Army in 1931. He commenced his combat duty against the Japanese at the Khalkhin Gol in 1939 and was posted to the 580 IAP as a squadron leader in March, 1942. It was not long before he started knocking enemy aircraft out of the sky. In an impressive display of combat skill he ran up a string of 10 kills in but 39 sorties while his squadron made a significant contribution by gaining 41 victories during 220 sorties to lead the regiment. On May 8 six Yak-1s with Dekhtyarenko in the lead were flying escort for Il-2s when they spotted four He 111s south of Ilmen Lake, two of these being blasted by Dekhtyarenko and his wingman. All of a sudden they were then bounced by four Bf 109s. Dekhtyarenko executed a hard 180 degree turn to meet them head-on and poured a stream of fire into one of them which exploded before it could take any evasive action. He bagged another Bf 109 a few days later when he was headed out alone searching for Aleksej Maresyev, who had gone down in enemy territory. He ran into two enemy fighters and was able to destroy one of them in a head-on encounter. Following this combat he finally succeeded in finding the badly wounded Maresyev and returned in a U-2 to pick him up. On July 11, 1942 he failed to return from a sortie in the Novgorod area.

Bombing up a Chajka ("gull"). Although being completely outclassed by the enemy fighters it met, the I-153 soldiered on in some fighter regiments such as the 40 and 84 IAPs until well into 1943. By 1941 the last of 3,437 examples of the I-153 had been delivered to the VVS. (Author's collection)

This Henschel Hs 129 antitank aircraft has been forced down somewhere in Hungary and is being examined by curious Soviet soldiers. 2nd Ukrainian Front. (Author's collection)

DEMA, Leonid Vasilyevich

Combat record: 17 personal victories, 5 fractional credits, 273 sorties, 38 engagements.

Decorations: Gold Star of Hero of the Soviet Union on October 26, 1944; the Orders of Lenin, the Red Banner (2), the Patriotic War 1st and 2nd Class, the Red Star.

Dema was born in Mikhajlovka, Bashkir ASSR, on June 18, 1916 and enlisted in the VVS in July, 1941. He was posted to a newly formed night bomber regiment but applied for transfer to a fighter unit. He joined with the 236 IAP and started flying Yak-1s in the epic Battle of Stalingrad. He was promoted to squadron leader in time and next saw a good deal of action in the skies above the Kuban. On May 18, 1943 he was in the public eye for successfully ramming a Luftwaffe bomber in the Krymskaya area. Unfortunately he was wounded in the process but returned to his unit three weeks later. He later was greatly involved in the fighting along the Dnyepr and over Kiev and on one particular day in September, 1943 led six Yaks to attack a large force of Ju 88s, six of these being shot down. Dema personally accounted for two of the victories and in turn was awarded the Order of the Red Banner. He finished the war as a deputy regiment commander in Czechoslovakia. He served with the postwar VVS and came off active duty in 1946, by which time he was a Major.

DEMENKOV, Sergej Vasilyevich

Combat record: 15 personal victories, 358 sorties, of which 20 were strafing ground targets, 78 air encounters.

Decorations: Gold Star of Hero of the Soviet Union on September 28, 1943 for 11 victories, 313 sorties, 51 encounters as of August, 1943; the Orders of Lenin, the Red Banner (2), the Patriotic War 1st and 2nd Class, the Red Star (2).

Demenkov was born in the Zaporozhye area on December 25, 1919 and started his military career in 1939. He qualified as a pilot at Kacha military flying school a year later and was in continuous action from the very first days of the war. He spent his combat career with the 103 GIAP of the PVO forces and was seriously wounded in action on January 7, 1942 when he tackled with four enemy aircraft alone. He required two months to recuperate and on May 29 was leading his flight of Airacobras on a sweep of the Volkhov area when they became embroiled in a tough battle with 30 Luftwaffe bombers and 12 escorts. Demenkov was attacked by two Bf 109s but was able to out turn them, pulled in behind one and destroyed it with a well aimed burst at point-blank range. He then dove away and came up behind a number of Ju 88s and destroyed one of them in spite of heavy return fire. He was wounded in arms and legs and broke clear setting course for home. He later converted to Yak-9s and bagged a Fw 190 near Dubrovka on January 13, 1943 and a Bf 109 in the Krasnaya Bor area on March 23. Demenkov remained in the VVS following World War II and concluded his active duty as a General Major in 1975.

DENISOV, Konstantin Dmitriyevich
Combat record: 13 personal victories, 6 fractional credits, 536 sorties.
Decorations: Gold Star of Hero of the Soviet Union on October 23, 1942 for 7 kills, 6 fractional credits, 233 sorties as of October, 1942; the Orders of Lenin, the Red Banner (4), Suvorov 3rd Class, Ushakov 3rd Class, the Patriotic War 1st Class, the Red Star.

Denisov was born in the Mozhajsk area on August 27, 1915 and entered the VMF in 1934. He completed his training at Yejsk military flying school in 1936 and during his first combat assignment fought against the Japanese at Lake Khasan two years later. He then was posted to the 7 IAP of the Black Sea Fleet's air service before the Patriotic War first meeting the Luftwaffe in the skies above Sevastopol. He saw a great deal of action during the dramatic siege of the city and for his efforts was appointed squadron leader in time. He flew his last sortie over Sevastopol on June 29, 1942 leading a sweep of eight Yak-1s. He took over as commanding officer of the regiment in July and subsequently took part in the air operations over Novorossijsk, Anapa and Taman. Early in 1943 he began flying Kittyhawks and recalls on the American fighter's attributes as follows: "Whilst the Kittyhawk was a reliable aircraft with easy handling qualities, it did not have adequate top speed and rate of climb. There only was its solid armament – six heavy machine guns. As for the Spitfire, this plane had good ailerons control and a reasonable top speed being aerodynamically superior to the Kittyhawk. It was armed with eight 7.62mm guns in the wings." On April 23 he splashed a Ju 88 25km North of Poti with the new mount, the bomber crashing into the Black Sea close to the shore. On October 3, 1943 he assumed command of the crack 11 GIAP-ChF flying Airacobras. He participated in the fighting over Kerch and at Eltigen in November and on the 6th of this month Denisov and B.M. Litvinchuk between them destroyed two Bf 109s as they were working over some LaGG-3s of the 25 IAP. On November 22 he teamed with Lejtenant V.V. Prozor to force down an Ar 195 over the Crimea. The regiment had a big day on March 10, 1944 when 11 Luftwaffe planes were blasted out of the sky during a strike against Kulbakino airfield (E. Nikolayev) for the loss of three P-39s. The unit finished the war as the Black Sea Fleet's top-scoring fighter regiment with 304 air victories. Denisov remained in the VMF after the war and graduated from the General Staff Academy in 1950. He wound up his military career as a General Major in 1976.

N.F. Denchik of the 64 GIAP with his steed of war sporting 13 kills. Denchik ran up a high score on Bryansk Front earning him the title of Hero of the Soviet Union on February 4, 1944. (Author's collection)

DERGACH (also spelled DERKACH), Aleksej Nikolayevich
Combat record: 11 personal victories, 14 fractional credits, 273 sorties, 24 encounters (as of July, 1943).
Decorations: Gold Star of Hero of the Soviet Union on February 4, 1944; the Orders of Lenin, the Red Banner (2), Aleksandr Nevskij, the Patriotic War 1st Class, the Red Star (4).

Dergach was born in the Novosibirsk area on March 23, 1916 and entered military service in June, 1941. Six months later he started flying combat and was to give a good account of himself in 1943 when he was serving as a Starshij Lejtenant in the 86 GIAP on Northwest Front. He claimed a Fw 190 in the Volkhov area on May 27, 1943 and was able to nurse his badly damaged Yak-7B safely back to base. On June 5 he was leading six fighters on a patrol when they engaged a formation of 30 German bombers in the vicinity of Zhikharevo (Volkhov area). He ordered the attack but they were bounced by eight enemy fighters and broke into them. In the ensuing melee three Fw 190s and Bf 109s were sent down in flames. By June, 1943 Dergach's score had risen to eight and shortly after he met the conditions for the award of the Gold Star. In 1944 he took an active part in the air battles over Orsha, Borisov and Minsk, and had by now become a Major. On June 26 he destroyed a Fw 190 at 100m range while flying an Il-2 escort and got another of these 3km southeast of Gumbinnen in East Prussia on October 20. He stayed in the service after the war rising to the rank of Polkovnik. He wound up his military career in 1971 and died on September 17, 1983. His final score is uncertain, but is over 13.

DEVYATAYEV, Mikhail Petrovich
Combat record: 9 personal victories, 180 sorties, 35 encounters.
Decorations: Gold Star of Hero of the Soviet Union on August 15, 1957; the Orders of Lenin, the Red Banner, the Patriotic War 1st and 2nd Class.

Devyatayev was born in the Mordovskaya ASSR on July 8, 1917 and entered the Soviet Army in 1938. Two years later he received his wings at Chkalov military flying school and fought from the very start of the war serving with a fighter unit in the Minsk area. He got his first victory near Mogilov shortly afterward but in September, 1941 came within a hair of getting lost when he collided with a "Messer" he had just shot down. By some miracle he was able to bail out of his flaming aircraft but was so badly wounded that the medical battle took months. He resumed combat in April, 1944 joining with the 104 GIAP as a Starshij Lejtenant and flying Airacobras. He saw considerable action in the big air battles over Moldavia but on July 13 his aircraft was badly shot up in a pitched battle near Gorokhov (Lemberg) causing him to bail out. He was captured and sent to Klein-Königsberg. After failing in an escape attempt he was moved to Sachsenhausen and with other prisoners was committed to maintaining the landing ground at Usedom. In early February, 1945 Devyatayev and several other pilots including Starshij Lejtenant A. Voronchuk and Lejtenant A. Fedirko of the 5 GIAP, who had been shot down on June 26, 1944, overwhelmed the guards, seized one of the He 111s that was warming up its engines. Fortune favors the brave, and with Devyatayev at the controls, they managed to takeoff smoothly reaching Soviet lines on the 8th. This exploit won him the Gold Star after the war but he did not return to combat and left active duty in November, 1945. In all, Devyatayev was wounded in action four times.

DILIGEJ (also spelled DELEGEJ), Nikolaj Kupriyanovich
Combat record: 16 personal victories, 3 fractional credits, 200 sorties, 30 encounters.
Decorations: Gold Star of Hero of the Soviet Union on July 1, 1944 for 15 victories, 3 fractional credits, 172 sorties as of February, 1944; the Orders of Lenin, the Red Banner (2), the Red Star.

Diligej was born in the Khmelnitskij area on October 24, 1911 and entered military service in 1932. He completed pilot training at Kharkov military flying school in 1937 and gained his first combat experience while serving in the 9 IAP early in the war. On December 17, 1941 he achieved his initial success by downing a Bf 110 near Kashin (NE Kalinin). He later rose to Major and assumed command of the 508 IAP. In this capacity he took part in the operations against the enemy on 2nd Ukrainian Front and participated in periods of intense activity at Kirovograd in early 1944. He served with the postwar VVS but was killed on October 3, 1945, the circumstances of his death unknown.

DMITRIYEV, Nikolaj Pavlovich
Combat record: 15 personal victories, 415 sorties, 75 encounters.
Decorations: Gold Star of Hero of the Soviet Union on August 24, 1943; the Orders of Lenin, the Red Banner (2), the Patriotic War 1st Class.

Dmitriyev was born in the Nikolayev area on November 25, 1917 and enlisted in the VVS in 1938. He qualified as a pilot at Odessa military flying school two years later and when the Germans initiated Operation Barbarossa in June, 1941 he was serving in the 129 IAP. On August 20, 1941 he claimed a Ju 88 when five MiG-3s ran into 10 bombers escorted by nine Bf

Hurricane pilots sitting ready in their cockpits, awaiting orders to take off on a mission. (Author's collection)

109s in the Dukhovshchina area (NE Smolensk), four of the enemy planes being shot down. He got another of these on December 5 when the regiment intercepted an attack against Kalinin and added a Ju 87 two days later. For his efforts he was appointed squadron leader in November, 1942 and subsequently became involved in violent combat over the Don River, at Slavyansk, Starobyelsk, Kharkov and Izyum while flying the La-5. He was credited with one of three Fw 189 reconnaissance planes that were destroyed between Yarovaya-Bannovskij-Prishib on March 10, 1943 and then caught a Ju 52 that was taking off at Rogan and forced it down with a long burst. On August 15 he was shot down by antiaircraft fire near Izyum and bailed out, badly wounded. After an extended stay in a Moscow hospital he was back in action but was killed on August 1, 1945 details not being available. He was buried in Prague, Czechoslovakia.

DMITRYUK, Grigorij Fedoseyevich

Combat record: 18 personal victories, 206 sorties, 37 encounters.
Decorations: Gold Star of Hero of the Soviet Union on November 2, 1944; the Orders of Lenin (2), the Red Banner (2), the Patriotic War 1st Class, the Red Star.

Dmitryuk was born in Vladivostok on March 12, 1920 and enlisted in the Soviet Army in 1938. Upon receiving his wings at Batajsk military flying school two years later he was posted to a unit in the Far East prior to joining the 145 IAP to commence combat duty in May, 1942. Dmitryuk subsequently did well in the air fighting over Murmansk, Tula, Kirov and Petrozavodsk. He appears to have accomplished all or most of his success while flying Tomahawks and Airacobras. In 1944 he advanced to Kapitan and squadron leader and was able to run up a string of four air victories on Karelian Front in October. In 1942 he met the requirements for the award of the Red Banner and a year later was decorated with the Order of the Patriotic War 1st Class. He remained in the VVS after the war and graduated from the Air Force Academy in 1956. He retired with the rank of General Major in 1969 and died on April 27, 1982.

DOLGARYOV, Pavel Mikhajlovich

Combat record: 21 personal victories, 7 fractional credits, 1 enemy plane on the ground, 152 sorties, 42 encounters.
Decorations: Gold Star of Hero of the Soviet Union on June 29, 1945; the Orders of Lenin, the Red Banner (5), the Patriotic War 1st Class (2), the Red Star.

Dolgaryov was born in the Byelgorod area on June 22, 1923 and enrolled for service in the VVS in July, 1941. He qualified as a pilot at Armavir military flying school in July, 1942 and at Batajsk a year later. He entered combat with the Luftwaffe in August, 1943 and flying La-5s with the 116 IAP he quickly proved his outstanding attributes and began to achieve victories at a formidable pace. In an outstanding effort he was credited with downing six Bf 109s, five Fw 190s and one Ju 88 over Hungary to emerge as one of the top-scorers of the campaign, all in a few weeks. He stayed in the service after the war and graduated from the Air Force Academy in 1956. He had been promoted to General Major when he left active duty in 1974.

DOLGUSHIN, Sergej Fyodorovich

Combat record: 17 personal victories, 11 fractional credits, 500 sorties of which 120 were strafing ground targets and 86 reconnaissance.
Decorations: Gold Star of Hero of the Soviet Union on May 5, 1942 for 7 victories, 4 fractional credits, 185 sorties, 29 air combats as of February, 1942; the Orders of Lenin (2), the Red Banner (4), Aleksandr Nevskij, the Patriotic War 1st Class (2), the Red Star (2).

Dolgushin was born in the Tula area on September 25, 1920 and enlisted in the VVS in 1939. He completed his pilot training at Kacha military flying school a year later and at the outbreak of the Patriotic War was serving as a Mladshij Lejtenant in the 122 IAP flying I-16s. He was successful in scoring his initial victory on June 22, 1941 – the first day of the German assault on Russia – by downing a Bf 109 but the following day his aircraft was shot up by strafing Bf 110s on Lida airfield. He converted to MiG-3s in late July and was appointed flight leader. In August Dolgushin joined with the 180 IAP South of Rzhev continuing to score on a regular basis. In January, 1942 he advanced to squadron leader and by early February his tally had risen to seven kills, comprising of five Bf 109s and one each Ju 87 and Ju 88. The following month he began flying Hurricanes and between June and July saw a good deal of action at Kharkov. In spite of considering it a failure he gained a total of 4 or 5 kills with the British fighter prior to being posted again in August, this time to the Yak-7B equipped 434 IAP. During the fury of the Stalingrad air engagements he added a number of victories including a Ju 87 on September 16 and a Bf 109 the following day. On the 19th he was shot down by the gunner of a Ju 88 and force landed in Russian territory. He bagged a further Ju 87 two days later and was assigned as a fighter inspector during the period of November and December, 1942. He rejoined the 32 GIAP (the former 434 IAP) in January, 1943 moving with the unit to the Demyansk area on Kalinin Front. While flying Yak-9s he claimed a string of six kills in this theater and was then assigned to the 30 GIAP (the former 180 IAP) on July 5, 1943. He took part in the clashes at Kursk achieving two further victories with the Airacobra. In September, 1943 he was appointed as commander of the 156 IAP and served in this capacity until 1946. During the final stages of the war he successively flew La-5s, La-5FNs and La-7s taking

Rare shot of a Yak-3 belonging to an unknown Guards unit on a German airfield, possibly Berlin-Tempelhof airport, shortly after the Russian occupation – the pilot is A. Shataryev. Many Luftwaffe notables such as 203 victory ace Helmut Lipfert of JG 52 determined from their experience that the nimble and fast Yak-3 was more dangerous than the famed P-51 Mustang. (Author's collection)

part in the air operations over Bobrujsk and Poland. In February, 1945 he was hit by groundfire, and was obliged to carry out a force-landing. He flew his last mission on May 6, 1945 by which time he had become a Podpolkovnik. Following World War II Dolgushin attended Lipetsk higher tactical fighter school between 1946/47 and continued to command the 156 IAP flying Yak-3s, Yak-9s and La-9s. In 1949 he took over the 196 IAP and later was put in command of the 32 GIAP. In 1951 he was appointed commander of an Il-28 bomber division at Kalinin and was promoted General Lejtenant in 1967. He came off active duty in 1976 with 37 years service.

DOLNIKOV, Grigorij Ustinovich
Combat record: 15 personal victories, 1 fractional credit, 160 sorties, 42 encounters.
Decorations: Gold Star of Hero of the Soviet Union on February 21, 1978; the Orders of Lenin (2), the October Revolution, the Red Banner (2), the Patriotic War 1st Class, the Red Star.

Dolnikov was born in the Mogilyov area on May 8, 1923 and joined the Soviet Army in 1940. He qualified as a pilot at Batajsk military flying school in 1943 and started flying combat in July. He made a brilliant war record as a member of the crack 100 GIAP and proved his gunnery skills in the skies above Yassy by downing five enemy planes within a week. His personal aircraft was "White 01", an olive drab/neutral gray P-39N, no. 29033, with blue spinner. He stayed in the service after the war and graduated from the Air Force Academy in 1955. In 1967 he was assigned as a tactical advisor to the Egyptian Air Force and in 1981 was appointed deputy commander of the VVS educational institutions.

DRANKO, Pyotr Aleksandrovich
Combat record: 15 personal victories, 271 sorties, 59 encounters.
Decorations: Gold Star of Hero of the Soviet Union on September 2, 1943 for 10 victories, 2 fractional credits, 198 sorties as of July, 1943; the Orders of Lenin, the Red Banner (3), the Patriotic War 1st Class, the Red Star (2).

Dranko was born in the Volgograd area on September 9, 1913 and entered military service in 1934. He was graduated at Engels military flying school three years later and cut his teeth during the Russo-Finnish Winter War of 1939/40. By June, 1941 he had been posted to the 29 IAP as a Komissar and then was in the forefront of action from the first days of the war seeing a great deal of action at Grodno and during the battle for Moscow. He next fought in the big air battles over Bryansk, Leningrad and Kursk-Orel chalking up 10 kills comprising of five bombers and five fighters. He gained all or most of his score flying the Hurricane to rank him among the top-scorers on this machine. He was then posted as a Major to the 89 GIAP and took over as leader of a squadron. He ended the war as commander of a fighter regiment remaining in the VVS until 1956, when he retired with the rank of Polkovnik.

DUDNICHENKO, Viktor Markovich

Combat record: 22 personal victories, 180 sorties, 64 encounters.

Decorations: Gold Star of Hero of the Soviet Union on July 1, 1944 for 16 victories, 120 missions of which 58 were air patrols and 50 escorts, 26 encounters as of January, 1944; the Orders of Lenin (2), the Red Banner, the Patriotic War 1st Class (2).

Dudnichenko was born in the Dnyepropetrovsk area on May 25, 1923 and enrolled for service in 1941. He completed his pilot training at Chuguyev military flying school a year later and in April, 1943 started flying combat after joining the 239 IAP on North Caucasus Front. He began his remarkable career with the Lavochkin La-5 fighter and did not have to wait long for action. In August, 1943 Dudnichenko bagged four kills with two bombers and two fighters within five days and next enjoyed considerable success after the unit had deployed to 1st Ukrainian Front. On one occasion in January, 1944 he claimed two Bf 109s in one sortie and was then promoted to deputy squadron leader. He went on to wind up as the regiment's highest scoring ace. He served with the postwar VVS and left active duty with the rank of Podpolkovnik in 1955.

DUGIN, Nikolaj Dmitriyevich

Combat record: 14 personal victories, six enemy aircraft, three locomotives and 14 motor vehicles on the ground, 325 sorties, 77 encounters.

Decorations: Gold Star of Hero of the Soviet Union posthumously on May 15, 1946; the Orders of Lenin, the Red Banner (2), Aleksandr Nevskij, the Patriotic War 2nd Class, the Red Star.

Dugin was born in the Moscow area on April 26, 1921 and entered the VVS for flight training in April, 1940. Upon receiving his wings at Kacha military flying school a year later he was posted to a fighter air regiment in the Far East tasked with guarding the Manchurian border. In early 1943 he joined with the 402 IAP and moved with this to the Kuban, entering combat with the Luftwaffe in April. He took off on his first sortie on the 20th, an Il-2 escort to the Myskhako area (S. Novorossijsk), and soon found himself in a fierce dogfight with German fighters. He closed in on one 109 while it was busy firing at an Il-2 and after several bursts the enemy plane fell from the sky in flames. This qualified him for the award of the Order of the Patriotic War 2nd Class. On September 18 he was flying free hunt with Major Balashov when they saw 15 He 111s and six Bf 109s approaching the Gulyaj Polya area (also spelled Gulyajpolye, SE Zaporozhye). They immediately dove on the enemy formation with Dugin destroying one of the "Messers" while Balashov got a bomber. He subsequently distinguished himself in the Crimea, above Byelorussia, Lithuania and Poland. By early 1945 he had advanced to Kapitan and deputy squadron leader and next participated in a series of encounters during the Vistula-Oder campaign (January 12/February 2, 1945) and over the Oder bridgehead at Küstrin. He added a single victory in early March but on May 2, 1945 was fatally hit by antiaircraft fire while strafing German forces as they were sallying out of the Berlin pocket at Spandau. Although he managed to stagger back to his own airfield near Dallgow (W. Berlin), he had passed away as a result of his injuries before Russian soldiers hurrying to the scene could pull him from the aircraft. He was buried in Falkensee close to the regiment's base.

DUNAYEV, Nikolaj Panteleyevich

Combat record: 24 personal victories, 9 fractional credits, 500 sorties.

Decorations: Gold Star of Hero of the Soviet Union on September 2, 1943 for 13 kills, 7 fractional credits, 337 sorties and 38 air engagements as of August, 1943; the Orders of Lenin, the Red Banner (3), Aleksandr Nevskij, the Patriotic War 1st Class, the Red Star.

Dunayev was born in the Voronezh area on May 5, 1918 and enlisted in the Soviet Army in 1938. He completed his pilot training at Borisoglebsk military flying school two years later and was in continuous action from the very first days of the Patriotic War. He gained his first combat experience while flying Yak-1s and MiG-3s with the 16 IAP-PVO and began his rise to fame during the dramatic battle for Moscow. On September 15, 1941 he took off leading eight fighters to bounce 12 Ju 87s escorted by 20 Bf 109s. In all they claimed four kills without loss, with Dunayev teaming to destroy one of the Stukas with Lejtenant N.A. Semyonov. On December 17 he was off with seven Yaks to make things hot for 36 Ju 87s and 12 Bf 109s approaching the Soviet front, and a running battle developed in the course of which seven German planes fell from the sky in flames. Dunayev personally accounted for a bomber the following day and was then promoted Kapitan and squadron leader being occupied with close air support and strafing duties until January, 1942. Shortly afterward he was posted to the veteran 270 IAP and was to spend the remainder of his World War II career with this. He was wingman to the redoubtable Sergej Luganskij on many occasions and then excelled during the big air battles above Byelgorod-Kharkov in 1943. He achieved singles near Byelgorod on July 6, over Tamarovka on the 8th and again in the vicinity of Byelgorod three days later. While leading a mission of four Yak-7Bs on the 13th

Dunayev claimed a double with a bomber and a fighter when they became embroiled in a tough melee with two large gaggles totaling 26 Ju 88s and 17 Bf 109s. In this action his aircraft sustained 16 cannon strikes. During the fighting at Byelgorod he was credited with downing a total of six enemy planes in 56 sorties and 19 air-to-air combats. Dunayev subsequently put up a good performance over Poltava, Cherkassy and during the Lemberg-Sandomierz campaign (July 13/August 29, 1944) closing out his scoring in the skies of Berlin on April 30, 1945. He stayed in the service after the war and concluded his active duty as a Polkovnik in 1960.

DYACHKOV, Aleksandr Alekseyevich
Combat record: 27 personal victories, 1 fractional credit, 217 sorties, 54 encounters.
Decorations: Gold Star of Hero of the Soviet Union posthumously on May 15, 1946; the Orders of Lenin, the Red Banner (2), the Patriotic War 2nd Class.

Dyachkov was born in the Tambov area in 1923 and entered military service in 1941. He received his wings at Borisoglebsk military flying school a year later and was posted to the 297 IAP in June, 1943 to begin his remarkable combat career. Triumph followed triumph during the Soviet Yassy-Kishinyov offensive (August 20-29, 1944) and in the contested air space above Hungary. He scored a single on October 6, 1944 when six La-5s led by Kapitan N.S. Artamonov dove down on a formation of Ju 87 dive-bombers near Sokodor, seven of these being shot down. On March 31, 1945 Dyachkov was shot down crashing to his death in the vicinity of Budapest. He was the regiment's top-scoring ace.

DZUSOV, Ibragim Magometovich
Combat record: 6 personal victories, 89 sorties, 11 encounters.
Decorations: Gold Star of Hero of the Soviet Union on May 29, 1945; the Orders of Lenin (3), the Red Banner (3), Suvorov 2nd Class (2).

Dzusov was born in the North Ossetian ASSR on March 16, 1905 and commenced his military career in 1924. After serving with the cavalry for three years he was sent to Borisoglebsk military flying school where he was graduated as an aerial observer in 1932. He was put in command of a fighter unit in 1937 and already was a well-seasoned pilot when entering combat in January, 1942. He proved his potentials in the dramatic fighting for Sevastopol (October, 1941/July, 1942) and then fought with above-average success in the great aerial campaigns on West, Caucasus, North Caucasus, Central and 1st Byelorussian Fronts. He advanced to General Major in 1944 and took over the 6 IAK on May 20. The unit enjoyed considerable success at Bobrujsk and Minsk and participated in heavy fighting over Warsaw, the Vistula bridgeheads and finally Berlin. In the course of these operations it was credited with 832 enemy planes in the air – of which 219 were claimed over Berlin – in 18,654 sorties and 1,243 encounters. Dzusov remained in the ranks following the close of war and graduated from the General Staff Academy in 1955. He died on October 28, 1980.

V.I. Fadeyev served with the glorious 16 GIAP to make an illustrious record on North Caucasus Front flying Aeracobras. He was killed in a scrap with Bf 109s on May 5, 1943. (Author's collection)

FADEYEV, Vadim Ivanovich
Combat record: 21 personal victories, 1 fractional credit, 394 sorties, 48 engagements.
Decorations: Gold Star of Hero of the Soviet Union posthumously on May 24, 1943; the Order of Lenin, the Red Banner (2).

Fadeyev was born in the Ulyanovsk area on December 25, 1917 and enlisted in the VVS in 1940. He won his wings at Chkalov military flying school later in the year and was posted to the 446 SAP in the Rostov area in July, 1941 flying I-16s. He did not claim any victories while flying with this and was then assigned to the 630 IAP. He downed a Bf 109 in January, 1942 to open up his score and subsequently gave a good account of himself in the big air battles above Rostov, Slavyansk and

Kramatorsk by chalking up five more kills. In late 1942 he was posted again, this time to the crack 16 GIAP. Fadeyev was promoted leader of the 3rd Eskadrilya and in April, 1943 introduced the Airacobra into combat over the Kuban. His exploits in this theater earned him an almost legendary reputation for courage and air combat skill. Surprise attacks were his forte. Instead of turning with the enemy he would fight his combats at full throttle or would dive down on his prey from above and climb back up to a safe altitude using his excessive speed. On April 13 while leading his flight on a free hunt two Bf 109s were spotted and shot down in quick succession by Fadeyev and Lejtenant Trud, the former's victim crashing 10 km southwest of Petrovskaya. Three days later 10 Cobras (Fadeyev/Trud, Rechkalov/Tabachenko, Fyodorov/Gorokhov, Sutyrin/Nikitin and Pokryshkin/Stepanov) were prowling around between Kholmskaya-Abinskaya-Krymskaya and ran into 12 Luftwaffe fighters, seven of these being forced down for no losses. Most successful pilot in this tussle was Fadeyev with a double. He began running up air victories at a formidable pace and by early May his tally had risen to 19 personal kills, recommending him for the Gold Star award. On May 5 five Airacobras fought a pitched battle with eight Bf 109s near Krymskaya. During the wild dogfight Fadeyev managed to dispatch two fighters but was in turn attacked by the number two of the German he had just shot down and never had a chance. He was buried in the center park of Kievskaya. While flying the Aeracobra, Fadeyev bagged 14 Bf 109s and one Ju 87 between April 9 and May 5. His wingman was Lej. A.I. Trud, who was to finish the war as an ace with 24 kills.

FEDORETS, Semyon Alekseyevich

Combat record: 7 personal victories, 1 unconfirmed, 98 sorties, 40+ encounters (all Korea 1950/53).

Decorations: The Order of Lenin, the Order of the Red Banner.

Fedorets completed his pilot training at Odessa military flying school in March, 1944 following which he was posted to the 403 IAP-PVO on Leningrad Front flying Airacobras. He did not encounter the enemy during this war only catching a glance of reconnaissance aircraft in the distance twice. In 1946 he joined the 26 GIAP and in September was posted again, this time to the 913 IAP at Voskresenka in the Far East. He was a flight leader when he deployed with the regiment to China in April, 1952 where it passed under command of the 64 IAK. In late August the unit moved to Antung from where it was to commence combat duty the following month. Fedorets destroyed his first enemy aircraft in the air on December 17 when he claimed an F-86. He added another of these on February 19, 1953 and a further one two days later. On March 3 he was successful in getting his fourth Sabre and then forced down the USAF fighter ace Captain Joseph McConnell in his F-86E "Beautious Butch" on April 12. McConnell ejected over the Yellow Sea and was picked out by an Air-Sea Rescue helicopter. In the same time frame Fedoret's MiG was fatally damaged by other American fighters causing him to bail out. As the gun-camera film was lost, his claim was never officially allowed. He returned to his regiment after a month off operations and bagged further Sabres on June 10 and July 19 during 20 sorties his final victory occurring over Dapu airfield. He finished as 32 IAD's highest scoring ace.

FEDOSEYEV, Mikhail Andreyevich

Combat record: 20 personal victories, 329 sorties, 67 encounters.

Decorations: Gold Star of Hero of the Soviet Union posthumously on June 6, 1942; two Orders of Lenin.

Fedoseyev was born in Kazan on September 20, 1912 and enlisted in the VVS for flight training in 1933. He completed his pilot training at Orenburg military flying school later in the year and volunteered for service in Spain. He was not slow to get started scoring his initial victory while flying the I-16 on August 4, 1938. He then achieved victories on a regular basis and when returning to Russia in autumn he had been credited with downing 7 enemy aircraft in 160 sorties and 40 air-to-air combats to emerge as one of the outstanding pilots of the conflict. His efforts won him the Order of Lenin and he was then appointed commander of the 6 OAE. When the 88 IAP was activated in 1940 from a nucleus of pilots of the 6 OAE, Fedoseyev became its deputy commander. He next took over as leader of the newly formed 247 IAP and led this with consummate skill during the hellish inferno of the first stages of the Patriotic War. In a fierce series of fighting the regiment chalked up 42 kills until March, 1942 with Fedoseyev personally accounting for 13 victories in 169 missions and 27 air engagements during the period of September, 1941 to March, 1942. He was lost in a running battle on March 22, 1942 by which time he had become a Podpolkovnik. He was buried in Semisotka, Leninskoye area (Crimea).

FEDOTOV, Andrej Andreyevich

Combat record: 22 personal victories.

Decorations: Gold Star of Hero of the Soviet Union on May 1, 1943 for 15 victories in 160 sorties as of March, 1943; the Orders of Lenin (2), the Red Banner, Aleksandr Nevskij, the Patriotic War 1st Class (2).

Fedotov was born in Sverdlovsk on October 16, 1914 and joined the Soviet Army in 1935. Three years later he was graduated at Orenburg military flying school and first fired his guns in anger in 1939 during the Russo-Finnish Winter War. He commenced his combat duty against the Luftwaffe right after the German attack in June, 1941. He really came into his own when he began flying La-5s with the 169 IAP in 1942. On December 29 he had a big day scoring a triple and on March 5, 1943 was off with six fellow pilots, and soon they found themselves in a

LaGG-3 refueling on Kalinin Front in May, 1943. (Author's collection)

tussle with six Stukas escorted by four Bf 109s. Three of the dive-bombers fell from the sky in flames with Fedotov accounting for one of them. He subsequently built up a good score in the big air battles above Volkhov, Kalinin and Demyansk being recommended for the Gold Star award after 15 kills. He gained a number of victories at Kursk including a single Fw 190 on July 20, 1943. He then was put in command of the regiment with the rank of Major but fell foul of German fighters while leading 11 La-5s against a formation of 18 Ju 87s and six Fw 190s on December 15, 1943. The unit thus lost one of its most accomplished pilots and top-scoring ace.

FIGICHEV, Valentin Alekseyevich
Combat record: 21 personal victories.
Decorations: Gold Star of Hero of the Soviet Union on November 23, 1942 after 7 kills in the air, 5 enemy aircraft on the ground, 339 sorties, 26 encounters as of July, 1942; the Orders of Lenin (2), the Red Banner (3), Aleksandr Nevskij, the Patriotic War 1st Class, the Red Star.

Figichev was born in the Altajsk area on February 12, 1917 and entered military service in 1936. Two years later he received his wings at Voroshilovgrad military flying school and started flying combat early in the war. He was one of the best fighter pilots passing through the glorious 16 GIAP in 1941/42 managing to put up a good performance while flying MiG-3s on South Front. He was promoted to Kapitan and squadron leader and later displayed his skills at blasting enemy aircraft with the Airacobra in the skies above the Kuban, the Crimea, Moldavia, Poland and the Reich. He served with the postwar VVS and left active duty as a Polkovnik in 1957.

FOMCHENKOV, Konstantin Fyodorovich
Combat record: 8 personal victories, 26 fractional credits, 320 sorties, 37 encounters.
Decorations: Gold Star of Hero of the Soviet Union on August 24, 1943; the Orders of Lenin, the Red Banner, Aleksandr Nevskij, the Patriotic War 2nd Class, the Red Star (2).

Fomchenkov was born in the Smolensk area on October 20, 1918 and started his military career in 1937. He completed his pilot training at Borisoglebsk military flying school two years later and first saw action during the Russo-Finnish Winter War of 1939/40, and for his efforts during the conflict was awarded the medal "For Valor" (Za Otvagu). He was serving as a flight leader in the 145 IAP when German forces knifed into Russia in June, 1941 and was soon greatly involved in the bitter fighting in the north. Fomchenkov gained a large number of his victories flying the Bell P-39. His most memorable mission occurred on June 15, 1942 when six Airacobras were headed out to intercept a force of 30 enemy planes enroute to Murmansk. He pulled in behind a Bf 109 and after a few bursts it blew up and plunged earthward. He then slid over to team with Kapitan Bochkov to destroy one each Ju 88 and Bf 110. Three days later the regiment's alert flight became embroiled in a dogfight with an equal number of German fighters. Fomchenkov hit one "Messer" from a range of 100 meters and continued firing until it exploded with large pieces of wreckage plunging down like blazing torches. For his exploits he was promoted to Kapitan and deputy squadron leader but on February 24, 1944 he was badly hit and reportedly steered his blazing aircraft into an enemy service station. He was a Major at the time of his death.

FROLOV, Aleksandr Pavlovich
Combat Record: 13 personal victories, 7 fractional credits, 475 sorties.
Decorations: Gold Star of Hero of the Soviet Union on May 6, 1965; the Orders of Lenin, the Red Banner (3), Aleksandr Nevskij, the Patriotic War 1st Class.

Frolov was born in the Tambov area on September 27, 1921 and entered military service in 1940. He received his pilot wings at Chuguyev military flying school the following year and was posted to the 659 IAP, starting flying combat in September, 1942. Frolov saw a great deal of action at Stalingrad, Kharkov, Odessa and over Rumania and Hungary. On one occasion he was shot down behind the enemy lines but managed to evade capture returning to his combat unit shortly afterward. He completed his 475th mission, an air patrol to the Szekesfehervar area (Stuhlweissenburg, SW Budapest) on February 19, 1945. 205 of his missions were armed reconnaissance, 103 escorts and 78 strafing sorties. Frolov returned to civilian life with the rank of Major after the close of war.

FYEDORCHUK, Igor Aleksandrovich
Combat record: 15 personal victories, 136 sorties.
Decorations: Gold Star of Hero of the Soviet Union on February 4, 1944; the Orders of Lenin, the Red Banner (2), the Patriotic War 1st Class, the Red Star (2).

Fyedorchuk was born in Slavyansk on December 26, 1919 and joined the VVS for flight training in 1940. A year later he received his wings at Chuguyev military flying school and was posted to the 191 IAP on Kalinin Front in March, 1942. He deployed with the unit to Southwest Front in July becoming involved in very heavy combat at Stalingrad. In this theater he was able to score three kills with the Hurricane and next added two victories in two air encounters during 43 sorties in the skies above Demyansk. Shortly afterward he was assigned as a flight leader to the 67 GIAP and was to built up a good score during subsequent operations on Central Front. On August 2, 1943 he led his flight to jump a force of 60 enemy aircraft in the Orel area, two Ju 88s being shot down. The following day Fyedorchuk personally accounted for one each Ju 87 and Fw 190 but a few days later sustained such serious injuries in a fighter battle that he did not return to combat after his recovery. Eight of his victories were against bomber aircraft. He served with the postwar VVS and graduated from the Soviet Air Force Academy in 1951. He retired with the rank of Polkovnik in 1973.

FYODOROV, Aleksandr Yakovlevich
Combat record: 24 personal victories.
Decorations: Gold Star of Hero of the Soviet Union on August 24, 1943 for 10 victories, 375 sorties, 55 of which were strafing ground targets as of August, 1943; the Orders of Lenin, the Red Banner (2), the Patriotic War 1st Class.

Fyodorov was born in the Podolsk area on March 8, 1918 and enrolled for service in 1939 being destined to become the highest scoring ace of the 32 GIAP. He completed his pilot training at Kacha military flying school a year later and was in the forefront of action from the beginning of the war. He engaged in heavy action at Stalingrad, Staraya Russa, Velikiye Luki, Demyansk and Kursk. His most memorable mission occurred on July 20, 1943 when he fought a furious battle with five enemy planes single-handedly and shot down one of them before he was badly shot up and wounded, causing him to bail out. He stayed in the service after the war and graduated from the Air Force Academy in 1945 prior to leaving active duty as a Major the following year. He rejoined the VVS later and wound up his military career in 1953.

FYODOROV, Arkadij Vasilyevich
Combat record: 24 personal victories, 18 fractional credits, 554 sorties, 183 encounters.
Decorations: Gold Star of Hero of the Soviet Union on April 13, 1944 for 16 kills, 4 fractional credits, 498 sorties as of September, 1943; the Orders of Lenin (2), the Red Banner (4), Aleksandr Nevskij, the Patriotic War 1st Class, the Red Star.

Fyodorov was born in Ivanovo on January 6, 1917 and began his distinguished military career in the VVS in 1938. He qualified as a pilot at Chkalov military flying school two years later and was in the forefront of action from the earliest days of the Patriotic War. He gained his initial combat experience as a flight leader in the 131 IAP completing as many as five sorties in I-16s on June 22, 1941, the first day of Operation Barbarossa – the German attack on Soviet Russia. Three days later Fyodorov was able to destroy his first enemy aircraft in the air when he forced down a Ju 88. It seems likely that his next score did not come until several months later when he was assigned to the 16 GIAP which was doing yeoman service in the Caucasus. From then on Fyodorov was in continuous action with the regiment developing into a thoroughly competent air fighter and veteran of numerous aerial encounters. He was to gain most of his victories flying the Airacobra and was happy with this mount as were most of his comrades in the regiment. They felt that for the first time they were at least on equal terms with anything the enemy had to offer as it was a solid craft, had great climbing at low to medium altitude where all the combat on the German Russian front took place and was an excellent gun platform. On top of that the Cobras were fitted with radio equipment. Over the Kuban victories in the spring of 1943 came thick and fast. On an unspecified date Fyodorov was shot down and wounded by Bf 109s. After a short stay in hospital he was back in the air again to destroy one of these in the vicinity of Abinskaya on April 16, 1943. For displaying exceptional skill, courage and devotion to duty he was promoted to Kapitan and deputy squadron leader. He became an ardent advocate of surprise attacks and a firm believer in teamwork. He later flew with great distinction in the big air battles above the Crimea and personally describes a scramble from a Crimean airfield in one of his distinctive, short to the point, reports: "We were flying at 150 meters with low ceiling. Soon after we detected them: 30 Lapotnikov (Soviet service slang for the Ju 87) and 18 Khudykh (Soviet service slang for the Bf 109). I ordered my flight to pull up and engage them head-on while I was hitting the deck to make surprise attack from underneath. In all, we destroyed 4 bombers and 2 fighters in a matter of minutes." Fyodorov remained in the ranks at the conclusion of the war and rose to Polkovnik before winding up his military career in 1955.

FYODOROV, Ivan Vasilyevich

Combat record: 36 personal victories, 9 fractional credits, 9 enemy aircraft on the ground, 416 sorties, 104 encounters.

Decorations: Gold Star of Hero of the Soviet Union on October 26, 1944 for 24 air victories and 9 enemy planes on the ground in 285 sorties as of August, 1944; the Orders of Lenin, the Red Banner (5), Aleksandr Nevskij, the Patriotic War 1st and 2nd Class, the Red Star (2).

Fyodorov was born in the Kalinin area on September 21, 1920 and entered military service in 1940. He received his pilot wings at Kacha military flying school a year later and in April, 1943 joined the 812 IAP to begin his rather spectacular combat career flying Yak-1s. He was to make a brilliant record through two years of bitter air fighting over the Kuban, the Crimea, Vitebsk, Poland and the Reich later successively flying the Yak-7B and Yak-9U fighters. When decorated with the Gold Star Fyodorov had become Starshij Lejtenant and leader of a fighter squadron. He was much of a close-in fighter using to pull in behind his victims until he was almost within ramming distance to assure the kill. He came out of World War II as the outfit's top-scoring ace and one of Russia's finest fighter pilots. He remained in the VVS after the war and graduated from the Air Force Academy in 1952. He concluded his active duty with the rank of General Major in 1978 with 38 years service and is living in Cherkassy.

GALCHENKO, Leonid Akimovich

Combat record: 24 personal victories, 12 fractional credits, 410 sorties, 90 air-to-air combats.

Decorations: Gold Star of Hero of the Soviet Union on June 6, 1942 for 7 kills in 77 sorties as of September, 1941; the Orders of Lenin, the Red Banner (4), the Patriotic War 1st Class (2), the Red Star.

The Lavochkin La-5 was gradually replaced by the powerful La-7 fighter. The removal of the supercharger and oil cooler intakes from the engine cowling resulted in essentially improved aerodynamics. Outstanding La-7 pilots were I.N. Kozhedub, who shot down 17 Luftwaffe planes while flying this type, and K.A. Yevstigneyev. (Author's collection)

Galchenko was born in Petrovsk-Port, Dagestan, on April 2, 1912 and enlisted in the Soviet Army in 1933. He received his pilot training at Stalingrad military flying school and during his first combat assignment won the Order of the Red Banner for his efforts against the Finns between 1939/40. The German attack on Soviet Russia in June, 1941 found him serving as a squadron leader in the 145 IAP. Although vastly outnumbered, the unit put up a spirited defense of the port of Murmansk flying I-16s. Under his leadership the squadron was credited with downing 16 enemy planes until late September 1941 in the course of 260 sorties and 76 air encounters. Most successful pilot was Galchenko himself, who accounted for seven of these kills. On September 13 he got a Ju 87 and two days later was leading a flight of I-16s to claim four victories in a tussle with 25-30 enemy aircraft. He was promoted Major in November, 1941 and later began a run of success after the regiment had converted to Airacobras. He was commanding officer of the 609 IAP between 1942/43 the unit running up a confirmed total of 60 kills in the air and 55 aircraft on the ground during 2,038 sorties and 95 encounters with Galchenko in the lead. He eventually was appointed deputy commander of the 261 AD. During his postwar career Galchenko graduated from the General Staff Academy and was put in command of an air division. In 1954 he concluded his active duty with the rank of Polkovnik. He died on September 26, 1986.

GAVRILIN, Pavel Fyodorovich

Combat record: 19 personal victories, 244 sorties, 54 encounters.

Decorations: Gold Star of Hero of the Soviet Union on May 15, 1946; the Orders of Lenin, the Red Banner (3), the Patriotic War 1st Class (2), the Patriotic War 2nd Class, the Red Star (2).

Gavrilin was born in the Gorkij area on February 12, 1920 and entered military service in 1940. He completed his training at Kacha military flying school a year later and joined combat with the Luftwaffe over the Kuban in April, 1943 when he was assigned to the 402 IAP. He did not have to wait long for action and on the 29th acquired his initial success by downing a Bf 109 when eight Yaks encountered 12 German fighters escorting four Ju 87s. After that he scored on a regular basis and by April, 1944 his score had risen to seven personal victories. He had his big day on April 12, 1944 with two Bf 109s and a Ju 52 during a fighter sweep over the Crimea. He was however bounced from out of the sun by two more fighters and was injured, force-landing near Kara-Kiyak. After a brief rest from operations he was back in the thick of the action at Sevastopol but was wounded again in a dogfight over Yassy. Following his recovery he gave a good account of himself in the skies above the Carpathians, Poland, the Reich and Czechoslovakia. He was credited with a single kill over East Pomerania on March 2, 1945 while participating in the air battles surrounding the

Two aces of the 145 IAP: Leonid Galchenko (left) came out of World War II as the regiment's top-scorer with 24 kills and 12 fractional credits while Kapitan V.P. Mironov was killed in a flying accident on February 16, 1943 after winning the Gold Star for his efforts on Karelian Front. The date is June, 1942. (Author's collection)

Soviet Oder bridgehead at Küstrin. On April 19 he was off with Lejtenant Nikiforov as his number two blasting a Fw 190 fighter-bomber out of the sky when they ran into four enemy aircraft. He remained in the ranks after the close of war and left active duty as a Podpolkovnik in 1955.

GERMAN, Grigorij Ivanovich

Combat record: 23+ personal victories.

Decorations: Gold Star of Hero of the Soviet Union on September 28, 1943 for 16 personal victories, 209 sorties, 37 encounters as of September, 1943; the Orders of Lenin, the Red Banner (2), Aleksandr Nevskij, the Patriotic War 1st Class (2).

German was born in Zhitomir on February 25, 1917 and commenced his military career in 1938. Two years later he qualified as a pilot at Odessa military flying school and was in action from the very start of the war in 1941. While flying the MiG-3 fighter German was able to achieve 42 IAP's first air victory near Orel in July. It was during the brutal fighting for Smolensk in 1943 that he built up a remarkable score with the Yak-9T, a modification of the standard Yakovlev fighter featuring a large-caliber 37-mm cannon for use against enemy bombers and tanks. A well-placed shot from this weapon would simply blow an enemy aircraft apart at once. On September 4 he knocked down a Do 217 in the vicinity of Dukhovshchina (NE Smolensk), the enemy plane exploding before it could take any evasive action. He blasted two bombers out of the sky later that month while Marshal A.A. Novikov was watching from the ground. He had his best day 24 hours later when he got a triple with two Ju 88s and one Fw 190. Further combats took his tally to 21 kills as of late 1943. He subsequently saw a great deal of action in the great aerial campaigns against the Luftwaffe over Nevel, Orsha, Borisov and East Prussia. On October 18, 1944 he claimed two Fw 190s while flying free hunt with Mladshij Lejtenant A.A. Solovyev in the Gumbinnen area. He served with the postwar VVS until 1955 when he wound up his military career with the rank of Polkovnik.

GERMAN, Ivan Moiseyevich
Combat record: 6 personal victories, 91 sorties, 27 encounters along with 30 planes, 2 tanks and 70 motor transports on the ground.
Decorations: Gold Star of Hero of the Soviet Union on August 24, 1943; the Orders of Lenin (2), the Red Banner (3), the Patriotic War 1st Class, the Red Star.

German was born in the Sumy area on September 23, 1915 and completed his flight training at Chuguyev military flying school. He was in the thick of the fighting from the earliest days of the war, entering combat in July, 1941. He made a brilliant war record serving with the 74 ShAP on Southwest, West, Northwest and 1st Byelorussian Fronts and was four times wounded in action. In February, 1943 he took over as leader of an Il-2 squadron and in September, 1944 was grounded and sent to the Air Force Academy not seeing any further action. His most memorable mission came on April 5, 1942 when he was leading four Shturmoviks to beat up ground targets but enroute they became involved in a series of encounters with some 30 enemy aircraft. Five Ju 87s were claimed destroyed, two of these being accounted for by German himself. After that they proceeded to strafe an enemy airfield where four more planes were left burning. On November 7, 1942 he was leading five Il-2s in a strafing attack on a German airfield in the vicinity of Demyansk, where they destroyed 10 aircraft on the ground whilst German also shot down one Ju 87 which was taking-off. He hit him from a range of 20 meters whereupon the dive-bomber blew up crashing on the perimeter. He remained in the VVS following World War II and concluded his active duty with the rank of Polkovnik in 1956. Reports conflict concerning his combat record: one source is suggesting 7 air victories along with 22 aircraft and 20+ tanks and armored vehicles destroyed on the ground as of June, 1943 which recommended him for the Gold Star award.

GES, Grigorij Ivanovich
Combat record: 5 personal victories, 21 sorties, 20 encounters during World War II; 9 personal victories in Korea 1950/53.
Decorations: Gold Star of Hero of the Soviet Union on October 10, 1951; the Orders of Lenin (2), the Red Star (3).

Ges was born in the Dnyepropetrovsk area on April 7, 1916 and enlisted in the VVS in September, 1937. He completed his training at Batajsk military flying school in 1941 and was a pilot instructor for some time prior to commencing his combat duty in October, 1944. He saw a great deal of action during the ferocious battles for Hungary and is credited with two kills in one sortie over Budapest. He served with the postwar VVS

A German column destroyed by a Soviet air attack in the Bobrujsk area on June 27, 1944. The tank on the extreme right is a PzKpfw. III. On June 22, 1944 – the third anniversary of Operation Barbarossa – a Soviet offensive ("Bagration") hit German Army Group Center with brutal force resulting in cataclysmic destruction of German forces. In late June the German 9.Armee was trapped at Bobrujsk and fell upon by forces of 1st Byelorussian Front. In a series of crushing air raids by 16 VA some 150 tanks and armored vehicles along with 6,000 motor transports were reduced to scrap. (Author's collection)

and next made a significant contribution to the fighting in Korea flying MiG-15s. On September 10, 1951 he bagged a Gloster Meteor as the 64 IAK was claiming 12 kills for no losses. Ges went on to emerge as one of the best fighter pilots of the conflict. He came off active duty with the rank of Major in 1957 and passed away on July 1, 1968.

GIRICH, Andrej Ivanovich
Combat record: 15 personal victories, 7 fractional credits, 479 sorties.
Decorations: Gold Star of Hero of the Soviet Union on February 23, 1945; the Orders of Lenin, the Red Banner, Suvorov 3rd Class, the Red Star (2).

Girich was born in the Kiev area on December 28, 1918 and joined the Soviet Army in 1939. He had his flight training at Odessa military flying school and was posted to the 486 IAP before the war. On June 25, 1941 he was in the public eye by blasting a Ju 88 in a head-on encounter near Stanislau. The German crew was taken prisoner the pilot turning out to be an Oberst and veteran of the aerial campaigns over Belgium and France. Unfortunately, his identity has not been established. Girich claimed another single over the Kerch Peninsula on March 16, 1942 and next added a Bf 109 in the same area on May 9. On this occasion he took six fellow pilots down to attack a large gaggle of some 40 enemy planes, five of these being shot down. On November 5, 1942 he forced down an He 111 over Ostashkov and then completed 103 missions on Central and Byelorussian Fronts during the period of July 15 to December 8, 1943 to run up a string of seven kills during 17 air-to-air combats. He eventually rose to Major and stayed in the service at the conclusion of the war. He graduated from the Air Force Academy in 1950 and from the General Staff Academy in 1958. He died on April 11, 1973.

GLAZOV, Nikolaj Yelizarovich
Combat record: 17 personal victories, 7 fractional credits, 537 sorties, 70 encounters.
Decorations: Gold Star of Hero of the Soviet Union on May 1, 1943 for 13 kills, 5 fractional credits, 475 sorties, 62 engagements as of March, 1943; the Orders of Lenin (2), the Patriotic War 1st Class.

Glazov was born in Shilka, Chita area, in 1919 and entered the VVS for flight training in 1938. Two years later he received his pilot wings at Batajsk military flying school and was in continuous action from the beginning of the Patriotic War. He proved his gunnery skills during the brutal battles for Moscow by running up a remarkable eight victories in the course of 40 air encounters although it seems likely that this figure comprises personal victories and fractional credits. He thus met the requirements for the award of the Order of the Patriotic War 1st Class and in September, 1942 was assigned to the 31 GIAP as a deputy squadron leader. He next fought in the hell of Stalingrad and on September 15 claimed a Ju 88 while leading nine Yak-1s to bounce 18 Ju 88s escorted by 12 Bf 109s, with six of these being shot down. On October 23 Glazov was decorated with his first Order of Lenin, and next destroyed a further Ju 88 near Mechetinskaya on January 27, 1943. He subsequently deployed with the unit to South Front where he was to see a great deal of action over the Donbas. On July 30, 1943 he perished while deliberately ramming a Fw 189 in the Voroshilovgrad area.

GLINKA, Boris Borisovich
Combat record: 30 personal victories, 200+ sorties.
Decorations: Gold Star of Hero of the Soviet Union on May 24, 1943 for 10 kills in 200 sorties as of April, 1943; the Orders of Lenin, the Red Banner (3), the Patriotic War 1st Class, the Red Star.

Glinka, the brother of the redoubtable Dmitrij Glinka, was born in Krivoj Rog on September 27, 1914 and entered military service in 1939. He completed his pilot training at Odessa military flying school a year later and was involved in pilot training prior to entering combat in June, 1941. He did not get an opportunity to score until the 45 IAP had converted to Airacobras in early 1943 but then made his mark against the Luftwaffe in the fury of the Kuban air engagements. He got his first, a Ju 88, at point-blank range Southeast of Abinskaya and then achieved six kills within two weeks. He claimed a double on April 15, 1943 when six enemy planes went down before the guns of seven Cobras in a running battle with 60 Ju 88s and He 111s. Later that same day Glinka added a single Bf 109 on a fighter sweep. The total of 39 kills claimed by the Glinka brothers over the Kuban earned them an almost legendary reputation for air combat skill and aggressiveness. Boris' share: 18 kills. He was rated as one of the best fighter pilots and had

Famous brothers, Boris (left) and Dmitrij Glinka during operations on North Caucasus Front in the spring of 1943. (Author's collection)

developed into a phenomenal shot. One day he attacked a Ju 87 near Mariupol but the rear gunner fought back spiritedly, scoring hits and wounding him in his left shoulder. He was rushed to hospital where he told Sasha Pokryshkin, the popular commander, that he already felt fairly well looking forward to resume combat "to get even with the Fritzen." Further combats along the Dnyepr River took his tally to 27 (almost certainly including fractional credits) and at Yassy assumed command of the legendary 16 GIAP. On July 15, 1944 his fighter was badly shot up in a dogfight with Bf 109s causing him to take to his parachute. Unfortunately he was struck by the tail of his aircraft breaking his legs and collarbone. Although he escaped with his life and recovered from his injuries, Glinka did not return to combat. He remained in the ranks after the war and graduated from the Air Force Academy in 1952. He subsequently was involved in the Soviet space program instructing cosmonauts at Borisoglebsk military flying school. He died on May 11, 1967.

GLINKA, Dmitrij Borisovich
Combat record: 50 personal victories, 300 sorties, 90 encounters.
Decorations: 1st Gold Star of Hero of the Soviet Union on April 24, 1943 for 15 victories, 146 sorties as of April, 1943, 2nd Gold Star on August 24, 1943 after 14 more kills; the Orders of Lenin, the Red Banner (5), Aleksandr Nevskij, the Patriotic War 1st Class, the Red Star (2).

Glinka, the seventh ranking Allied fighter ace, was born in the village of Aleksandrov Dar, Krivoj Rog area, on December 10, 1917. He began his rather spectacular career in the VVS in 1937 and won his wings at Kacha military flying school two years later. He was posted to the 45 IAP entering combat with the Luftwaffe in January, 1942. From then on Glinka was in continuous action until the close of war, participating in the great aerial campaigns on South, North Caucasus, 3rd and 1st Ukrainian Fronts. He was a thoroughly competent air fighter achieving a large number of his victories through surprise attacks while flying free hunt. He gained his first combat experience on Yak-1s scoring a triple with three Junkers Ju 87s on May 9, 1942. Transition to Airacobras was accomplished in early 1943 and it was over the Kuban that Glinka won fame for displaying exceptional combat skill. On March 31, 1943 he ran his tally to 16 and on April 15 he was credited with destroying three enemy planes leading a mission of five Cobras. Once over the front they immediately made contact with 30 Ju 87s and 12 Bf 109s, five of these being shot down without loss. Six days later he brought his score to 21 and was awarded his first Gold Star on this same day in recognition of 15 personal kills. In that theater he was shot down once in the Krymskaya area during a wild battle with Bf 109s being forced to bail out close to a mountain hamlet. Unfortunately he was too low for the canopy of his parachute to deploy and he was seriously injured in the resulting heavy fall. He was found by peasants and carried to the Soviet lines in his parachute. Following his recovery Glinka scored heavily during the summer of 1943 chalking up a string of 14 kills in but 37 sorties and 21 air encounters. With this outstanding effort he met the conditions for a second Gold Star award. His personal mount in 1943 was a P-39K, serial number 24403, and white tactical number "21" on its fuselage. He continued to enjoy considerable success in the subsequent battles over the Crimea, Yassy, Lemberg-Sandomierz, Poland and the crumbling Reich. He assumed command of a fighter squadron and by dynamic and decisive action this fought a very successful campaign at Yassy, where it was credited with downing 50 enemy planes to lead the regiment. During the final stages of the Yassy campaign he came within a hair of getting lost when the Li-2 transport he was a passenger of hit a mountain in adverse weather and crashed. He passed out as a result of wounds suffered and was rescued only a couple of days later. He had sustained such serious injuries that he required two months to recuperate. In late 1944 his tally stood at 46 personal kills and he rose to Major. He became greatly involved in the final battles over Germany and on April 18, 1945 was off on a free hunt leading six fighters when they sighted 12 Fw 190s and four Bf 109s near Cottbus. They attacked and shot down four of the unsuspecting Fw 190s between 1320 and 1435 hours. On the next day Glinka became embroiled in two separate tussles destroying two Fw 190s and one Bf 109 to run his score to 49. He closed out his scoring a short time later in the vicinity of Dresden. During his postwar career he graduated from the Air Force Academy in 1951 and was appointed deputy commander of a fighter aviation division. In 1960 he returned to civilian life with the rank of Polkovnik and passed away on March 1, 1979.

GLINKIN, Sergej Grigoryevich

Combat record: 30 personal victories, 200+ sorties.

Decorations: Gold Star of Hero of the Soviet Union on February 4, 1944 for 19 victories, 148 sorties, 45 encounters as of November, 1943; the Orders of Lenin, the Red Banner (4), Aleksandr Nevskij, the Patriotic War 1st Class, the Red Star (3).

Podpolkovnik D.B. Glinka, a fighter pilot of unsurpassed daring and skill. He was credited with 50 personal victories fighting through the great aerial campaigns of the Eastern Front ranking him seventh among Allied aces of World War II (Author's collection)

Glinkin was born in the Lipetsk area on October 2, 1921 and started his military career in December, 1939. Upon receiving his wings at Borisoglebsk military flying school he was sent to a unit in the Far East. He joined with the glorious 5 GIAP as a Mladshij Lejtenant on September 22, 1942 and subsequently proved his outstanding attributes in the contested air space above Byelgorod, Izyum, Dnyepropetrovsk and Zaporozhye eventually being rated as a fighter pilot of formidable skill and tenacity. On May 6, 1943 he claimed a Bf 109G near Kramatorsk and another of these on June 23. He next got an He 111 in the vicinity of Kamennaya Yaruga on July 5 and on the 23rd attacked a Ju 87 which blew apart after he had poured a stream of fire into it from almost within ramming distance. On July 15, 1944 he was badly hit during a dogfight between Lemberg (Lvov)-Lutsk and pulled his crippled fighter around sharply to resort to the extreme, ramming one of the Germans in a head-on pass. He parachuted and landed safely, suffering burns to his face, neck, arms and back. This action won him the Order of Aleksandr Nevskij. He later excelled in the ferocious battles over the Oder bridgeheads, destroying a Fw 190 between Sagan-Sorau on February 14, 1945. Five days later he was on free hunt leading four La-5s when they had a tussle with a superior number of Ju 88s and Bf 109s in the Guben area. Glinkin accounted for one of the bombers and shared a second with a fellow pilot. He closed out his scoring on April 18 forcing down another Fw 190 near Cottbus to emerge as the regiment's fourth ranking ace. He was with the postwar VVS and wound up his military career with the rank of Polkovnik in 1960.

GLOBIN, Nikolaj Ivanovich

Combat record: 10 personal victories, 180 sorties along with 50 tanks, 200 motor transports, 4 locomotives, 97 rail cars on the ground.

Decorations: Gold Star of Hero of the Soviet Union on June 29, 1945; the Orders of Lenin, the Red Banner (3), Aleksandr Nevskij, the Patriotic War 1st Class (2), the Red Star (3).

Globin was born in the Sumy area on July 21, 1920 and joined the VVS for flight training in 1940. He was graduated at Voroshilovgrad military flying school a year later following which he was assigned as a pilot instructor. He was posted to the 525 ShAP in November, 1943 entering combat on Il-2s. During his combat career Globin was to make a big name for himself both as an air fighter and in the ground attack role. He came out of World War II as one of the most accomplished Shturmovik pilots. He remained in the VVS at the conclusion of the war and retired with the rank of Polkovnik in 1961.

GNEZDILOV, Ivan Fyodorovich

Combat record: 24 personal victories, 376 sorties, 120 encounters.

Decorations: Gold Star of Hero of the Soviet Union on August 19, 1944 for 17 personal victories, 1 fractional credit, 245 sorties, 67 encounters as of February, 1944; the Orders of Lenin, the Red Banner (4), Aleksandr Nevskij, the Patriotic War 1st Class (2), the Red Star (2).

Gnezdilov was born in the Byelgorod area on June 17, 1922 and commenced military service in 1940. He qualified as a pilot at Chuguyev military flying school the following year entering combat in January, 1942. He destroyed his first enemy aircraft in the air, a Bf 109, while flying a Yak-1 during the struggle for Moscow. He later gave a good account of himself by downing four enemy planes during 70 sorties in the skies above Byelgorod. On July 11, 1943 he destroyed two Bf 109s in a fierce series of dogfights near Prokhorovka. He continued to fly with great distinction during the final stages of the war and closed out his scoring over Berlin, finishing as 153 GIAP's top-scoring ace. He wound up his military career with the rank of Polkovnik in 1961 and lives in Riga.

Legendary fighter pilot. S.G. Glinkin saw considerable fighting with the famous 5 GIAP and wound up as the regiment's fourth ranking ace with 30 air victories. (Author's collection)

GNIDO, Pyotr Andreyevich

Combat record: 34 personal victories, 300+ sorties.

Decorations: Gold Star of Hero of the Soviet Union on May 1, 1943 in recognition of 14 personal victories, 7 fractional credits, 206 sorties, 43 air-to-air combats as of April, 1943; the Orders of Lenin, the Red Banner (4), Aleksandr Nevskij, the Patriotic War 1st Class (2), the Red Star (3).

Gnido was born in the Odessa area on December 22, 1919 and enlisted in the VVS for flight training in 1940. He won his wings at Stalingrad military flying school later that same year and was posted to the 248 IAP before the outbreak of the war. He was in the forefront of action from the earliest days of Operation Barbarossa flying I-16s in the Taganrog area. In 1942 he was assigned to the 13 IAP and began his remarkable war record with the Lavochkin La-5 fighter. He performed brilliantly in the skies above the Kuban, his known victories in that theater including a single Ju 87 on April 20, 1943. On the next day he claimed a double to raise his confirmed tally to 15. He is said to have shot down a Luftwaffe ace and Oberst by the name of "Schmidt" in a furious dogfight over Poland one day, but unfortunately Soviet sources again are lacking in more details. No details of any such action can be found from the German side. If Gnido really shot down 173-victory ace Heinz Schmidt will remain a mystery; Schmidt failed to return after an encounter with Red fighters in the Markor area on September 5, 1943 and was promoted posthumously to Hauptmann. In a burst of energy and skill Gnido closed out his scoring over Czechoslovakia in 1945, chalking up a string of seven kills to head up the list of aces in that campaign. He served in various command positions following the close of hostilities graduating from the Air Force Academy in 1952 and from the General Staff Academy in 1960. He had become a General Major when he retired in 1975.

Kapitan P.A. Gnido of the 13 IAP, one of the most successful and enduring VVS pilots. He finished as the unit's top ace of the war. (Author's collection)

GOLOVACHYOV, Pavel Yakovlevich

Combat Record: 31 personal victories, 1 fractional credit, 457 sorties, 125 encounters.

Decorations: 1st Gold Star of Hero of the Soviet Union on November 1, 1943 for 17 kills, 225 sorties, 92 engagements as of November, 1943, 2nd Gold Star on June 29, 1945 in recognition of 26 kills, 385 sorties as of March, 1945; the Orders of Lenin (2), the Red Banner (6), the Patriotic War 1st Class, the Red Star (2).

Twice Hero of the Soviet Union Major P.Ya. Golovachyov was one of the most accomplished Soviet fighter pilots. Flying with the glorious 9 GIAP – the "regiment of aces" – he chalked up high scores on the 4th Ukrainian and 3rd Byelorussian Fronts. (Author's collection)

Golovachyov was born in the Gomel area on December 15, 1917 and when entering the Soviet Army in 1938 he was destined to become one of Russia's most capable and experienced fighter pilots. He completed his pilot training at Odessa military flying school two years later following which he was posted to the 69 IAP in the Odessa area. Golovachyov saw considerable fighting from the earliest days of the war and subsequently excelled over Odessa, Stalingrad, Rostov, the Kuban, the Crimea, Byelorussia, East Prussia and finally, Berlin through nearly four years of bitter air warfare. His most impressive display of combat skill took place during the epic battles for Stalingrad when he was credited with eight enemy planes in the air. He later flew Airacobras with above-average success in the wild air battles above the Kuban, at Taganrog, Dnyepropetrovsk and Sevastopol prior to converting to La-7s in mid-1944. He next saw a great deal of action over East Prussia and on December 30, 1944 successfully rammed a Ju 88 at 9,000 meters to raise his score to 20. He claimed two Fw 190s on January 18, 1945 and participated in the final aerial campaigns over the Reich. His last two victories occurred in his 125th aerial encounter over the German capital in April, 1945. He finished as the regiment's third highest scoring ace and in all, had been wounded in action four times. He vividly recalls an action that took place on August 21, 1943 when the regiment was deployed on 4th Ukrainian Front: "We took off at 1020 hours with Gv. Kapitan Amet-Khan Sultan and his wingman, Gv. Lejtenant Borisov, in the lead. Gv. Starshij

Lejtenant Safonov and his wingman, Gv. Kapitan Legkij comprised the other pair while Gv.Lejtenant Malkov was my number two. We were approaching the Kujbyshev area at an altitude of 4,500 meters. The sky was cloudless and we had the sun in our back. At 1040 hours we sighted three gaggles of enemy bombers headed for our ground forces and immediately bounced a formation of 20 enemy planes flying 500 meters beneath whilst one pair was remaining aloft as top cover. It was 1043 hours when Amet-Khan ordered the attack on the lead box of six bombers. On our first pass we dropped four of the bombers but the rear gunners were blazing away as we approached and one of our fighters was hit forcing him to set course for home with his wingman providing cover. The enemy broke formation and jettisoned their bombs. We dove down and used the speed we had built up to approach another group of Ju 88s. Ignoring the tracers flashing from the rear guns we destroyed two of them and damaged a third. Amet-Khan's wingman was shot up and began to develop engine trouble forcing him to break off and turn for home. I assigned Malkov to cover him and found myself left with Amet-Khan to carry on the fight. We reversed course and broke into a formation of He 111s pouring fire into two of them but I expended my ammunition in the process. The gunners fought back spiritedly scoring strikes on Amet-Khan's plane. I observed oil leaking out which fortunately did not catch fire. He switched off the ignition and feathered prop and tried to reach the airfield by gliding making a successful forced landing in a cornfield." Golovachyov and Amet-Khan were each credited with doubles in this affray while Safonov and Borisov had one apiece. Golovachyov remained in the VVS following World War II and graduated from the Air Force Academy in 1951 and from the General Staff Academy in 1959. He rose to General Major in 1957 and died on July 2, 1972.

Starshij Lejtenant G.G. Golubev, who spent his World War II career with the 16 GIAP. He joined the unit in September, 1942 and gave regular wingman support to the great Sasha Pokryshkin before qualifying for the flight leader position. Golubev summarizes his opinion on the P-39 in the following words, which reflect the findings of most of his fellow pilots: "I had flown wing to Pokryshkin on several occasions and entered combat four times. We now all felt that the new aircraft was a match for the vaunted Messerschmitts. I thought that for the first time we were now roughly equal." He received the title of Hero of the Soviet Union for displaying his skills on 1st Ukrainian Front on June 27, 1945 and had a final record of at least 12 personal kills during 252 sorties. (Author's collection)

GOLUBEV, Vasilij Fyodorovich

Combat record: 16 personal victories, 23 fractional credits, 546 sorties, 133 encounters.

Decorations: Gold Star of Hero of the Soviet Union on October 23, 1942 for 4 personal victories, 23 fractional credits, 339 sorties, 61 encounters as of June, 1942; the Orders of Lenin (2), the Red Banner (7), the Patriotic War 1st Class (2), the Red Star (2).

Golubev was born in the Leningrad area on November 16, 1912 and enlisted in the VMF in 1933. He qualified as a pilot at Yejsk military flying school in 1940 and first was assigned as a deputy squadron leader of a troop carrier unit prior to joining with the 13 OAK (Independent Aviation Squadron) of the Baltic Fleet's air service in July, 1940. When German forces knifed into Soviet Russia in June, 1941 Golubev became involved in the defense of the naval base of Hanko (SW Helsinki) flying an I-16 "White 33." He drew first blood on the 28th claiming a Ju 88. In early July he added a Bf 109E and next enjoyed considerable success in August gaining 12 victories, most of which were claimed jointly with Dmitrij Knyazov, including five Bf 109s. On November 2, 1941 he bagged two Hurricanes when running into five aircraft of HLeLv 32 and next claimed five aerial kills in the skies above Leningrad while operating from Kronshtadt. By June, 1942 his score stood at nine personal victories. He continued to fly the I-16 fighter well into 1943 and then switched to La-5s. He gave a good account of himself by downing five enemy planes within two months to raise his combined total to 20. On April 21, 1943 he was leading a flight on a fighter sweep when they found themselves in a dogfight with 12 Finnish Fiat G-50s, four of these reportedly going down in flames near Lavansaari. The most successful pilot in this mission was Golubev, who teamed with Kapitan Ye.T. Tsyganov in destroying three of the fighters. Finnish sources do not substantiate this claim, and the date may be in error. Golubev had risen to Podpolkovnik when he was put in command of the 4 GIAP-KBF in August, 1943. He subsequently participated in air operations over Tallin, Königsberg and Danzig, and although atrophied Luftwaffe units in that theater were capable of token resistance only Golubev continued to make his mark. While flying air patrol on February 8, 1944 he sighted a lone Bf 110 which he attacked and destroyed for his 38th victory including shares. He closed out his score with a Fw 190 on June 28, 1944. He came out of World War II as one of Russia's most accomplished naval fighter pilots. His tally record consists of a variety of more or less exotic ships such as Fiats or Fokkers while he also claimed two fighters that were identified as Spitfires. Soviet reports conflict concerning his total score, one source, Vestnik Vozdushnogo Flota (no.5-6, 1995, p.80), suggesting no fewer than 39 personal kills along with 12 fractional credits. In view of the confusion of the Soviet records this point must remain an imponderable one. Golubev stayed in the service after the war and graduated from the Naval Academy in 1951. He left active duty with the rank of General Lejtenant in 1975.

V.F. Golubev, one of Baltic Fleet's leading personalities. (Author's collection)

GOLUBIN, Ivan Filippovich
Combat record: 14 personal victories.
Decorations: Gold Star of Hero of the Soviet Union on March 4, 1942 for 7 personal victories, 2 fractional credits, 125 sorties and 10 encounters as of late 1941; the Orders of Lenin, the Red Banner.

Golubin was born in the Tula area in 1919 and enrolled for service in 1939. He completed his pilot training at Borisoglebsk military flying school later that year following which he was posted to the 16 IAP. He fought at Moscow claiming four victories until autumn 1941 while he was able to add four more in November with the MiG-3 fighter. He rose to deputy squadron leader but on November 1, 1942 was shot down and perished.

Beautiful shot of Yak-9s in flight in 1944. This version of the Yak fighter began to enter VVS service in late 1942, and when production was finally phased out in 1947, a total of 16,769 examples of this versatile and highly maneuverable plane had been built. One of the principal criticisms voiced by pilots was the tendency of the armorglass screen aft of the pilot's seat to come off during forced landings causing neck injuries. (Author's collection)

GOLUBOV, Anatolij Yemelyanovich
Combat record: 14 personal victories, 355 sorties, 43 encounters.
Decorations: Gold Star of Hero of the Soviet Union on June 29, 1945 for 10 kills as of April, 1945; the Orders of Lenin, the Red Banner (4), Suvorov 3rd Class, Aleksandr Nevskij, the Red Star.

Golubov was born in the Voronezh area on April 29, 1908 and entered military service at age 22. He was initially posted to the artillery and applied for a transfer to the VVS whereupon he was sent to Odessa military flying school. After training in 1933 he became a pilot instructor at Borisoglebsk and commenced his combat duty against the Luftwaffe in June, 1941. During his career Golubov saw a lot of action on Leningrad, Southwest, West and 3rd Byelorussian Fronts writing a distinguished war record as a fighter leader and being wounded in action once. In October, 1942 he took over as leader of the legendary 18 GIAP. Under his inspiring leadership the regiment was credited with destroying 220 enemy aircraft in the air during 279 air-to-air combats in 5,190 sorties. It had a big day on July 14, 1943 when 30 of its Yaks teamed with 15 fighters of the French Normandie-Neman regiment to send down 20 He 111s and several Fw 190s in running battles at Kursk. The unit was engaged in very heavy fighting over Smolensk and Byelorussia with Golubov continuing to set out on combat missions whenever possible. On October 15, 1943 he made a claim for a Ju 88 while leading 12 Yaks to attack 20+ bombers and their escort. In June, 1944 he claimed a double with one fighter and one bomber in one mission, the fighter pilot being captured. The Soviet reports read that the German was a Major and holder of "two Iron Crosses" serving with a Luftwaffe unit at Balbasovo but his identity unfortunately was not established. On June 28, 1944 he took off to reconnoiter the road between Borisov and Smolevichi and immediately became involved in a dogfight with two Bf 109s, in which he destroyed one and was in the process of finishing off the other when he was badly hit by a hail of groundfire. He was able to nurse his fighter back to the Soviet lines and was well below 100 meters altitude when his Yak-9D suddenly burst into flames forcing him to bail out. His parachute failed and he was severely injured in the resulting heavy fall suffering rib fractures and traumas of the hip-joints, collar-bone and skull. He was picked up immediately and taken to Moscow's central military hospital returning to his unit on October 6. Golubev finished World War II as a Podpolkovnik and deputy commander of the 303 IAD. After the war he graduated from the General Staff Academy in 1949 and left active duty with the rank of General Major in 1955. He died on January 29, 1978.

GONCHAR, Ivan Alekseyevich
Combat record: 16 personal victories, 87 sorties, 28 encounters.
Decorations: Gold Star of Hero of the Soviet Union posthumously on June 27, 1945; the Orders of Lenin, the Red Banner (2), Glory (SLAVA) 3rd Class.

Gonchar was born in the Dnyepropetrovsk area on September 21, 1921 and entered military service in 1941. He had his flight training at Chuguyev following which he was posted to a combat unit at Stalingrad. He is believed to have done well in this theater but unfortunately no details have emerged. He later enjoyed unequaled opportunities to increase his tally in the skies above Lithuania and on one occasion reported the destruction of four enemy planes – including fractional credits – when his flight bounced 16 bombers escorted by four fighters. Only a few days later he personally accounted for four kills while leading five of his regiment against 16 Junkers Ju 87s, no fewer than 11 of these being forced down. He later excelled with the 89 GIAP on 1st Ukrainian Front, taking part in the air operations of the Lemberg-Sandomierz campaign (July 13/August 29, 1944) and over Poland claiming the destruction of nine Fw 190s. In June, 1944 he was promoted flight leader and under his leadership his pilots would run up 21 victories in the air during 314 sorties. On April 20, 1945 Gonchar was assigned to a front-line patrol between Mittenwalde-Saarmund-Luckenwalde-Baruth where he ran through a rather heavy curtain of flak. Although he had been badly hit he was able to nurse his crippled aircraft back to his own airfield where he crashed. His fighter burst into flames and he was unable to get out. He was buried on the military cemetery of Lubsko, Poland, the former German village of Sommerfeld/ Niederlausitz.

GORBATYUK, Yevgenij Mikhajlovich
Combat record: 11 personal victories, 347 sorties.
Decorations: Gold Star of Hero of the Soviet Union on March 4, 1942 for 4 victories, 203 sorties, 26 encounters as of February, 1942; the Orders of Lenin (2), the Red Banner (3), Aleksandr Nevskij, the Patriotic War 1st Class, the Red Star.

Gorbatyuk was born in the Khmelnitskij area on October 23, 1914 and enrolled for service at age 22. He received his pilot wings at Kacha military flying school in 1938 and had become a squadron leader in the 28 IAP-PVO when German forces initiated Operation Barbarossa in June, 1941. The unit fought hard against great odds and although heavy losses were incurred, morale was high. By November, 1941 the squadron's score had risen to 13 victories in the air during 625 sorties with Gorbatyuk personally accounting for four of these himself. He seems to have been successful while flying the Airacobra later and eventually was promoted deputy commander of a fighter aviation division ending up in the battle for Berlin. He served in command positions after the war and graduated from the General Staff Academy in 1955. He advanced to General Polkovnik in 1967 and died on March 2, 1978.

GORBUNOV, Ivan Mikhajlovich
Combat record: 24 personal victories, 400+ sorties.
Decorations: Gold Star of Hero of the Soviet Union on September 2, 1943 in recognition of 14 kills, 3 fractional credits, 113 sorties consisting of 36 Il-2 escorts, 15 reconnaissance, 37 ground support, 23 strafing missions and 50 air encounters as of July, 1943; the Orders of Lenin, the Red Banner (3), Aleksandr Nevskij, the Red Star.

Gorbunov was born in the Kursk area on May 25, 1915 and enlisted in the Soviet Army in 1935. He completed his pilot training at Kacha military flying school two years later but it was not before August, 1942 that he had a chance to prove his skills. On the 13th he joined with the 8 IAP flying Yak-1s and four days later shot a Bf 109 off the tail of N.K. Naumchik when they were jumped by German fighters near Mozdok. Gorbunov then began a run of success, reporting the destruction of a Fw 200 and then claiming another Bf 109 in the vicinity of Anastasiyevka (NW Taganrog), but no further details have emerged. On April 2, 1943 he destroyed a Fw 189 in the Troitskoye area and then had his best day on May 14 when he made claims for one each Hs 123 and Bf 109 in a tussle near Novorossijsk. On June 3 he sighted a Ju 87 near Kievskaya which he attacked and claimed to have destroyed. He was promoted to Starshij Lejtenant and squadron leader soon after and was well qualified for the Gold Star award in September. Of his victories at this point in time, 10 were against the vaunted Bf 109s while he claimed a Fw 189, 24 motor vehicles, two antiaircraft guns and five horse-drawn vehicles in 23 ground attacks. He later successfully flew the Yak-3 and wound up as 42 GIAP's top-scoring ace. He remained in the VVS following World War II and graduated from the Air Force Academy in 1949. He then was involved in the Korean War but was killed on June 29, 1953 the circumstances not being known; if he further added to his scoring is uncertain.

Kapitan Ye.M. Gorbatyuk with his Aeracobra. (Author's collection)

GORBUNOV, Nikolaj Ivanovich
Combat record: 15 personal victories, 196 sorties, 40 encounters.
Decorations: Gold Star of Hero of the Soviet Union on August 2, 1944; the Orders of Lenin, the Red Banner, Aleksandr Nevskij (2).

Gorbunov was born in the Lipetsk area on January 15, 1918 and joined the Soviet Army in 1938. He was graduated as a pilot at Borisoglebsk military flying school a year later and was assigned to the 31 IAP on Southwest Front to commence his combat duty in April, 1943. He managed to put up a good performance with the La-5 fighter and is reputed to have shot down a German ace in an engagement near Krasnyj Liman (N Slavyansk) on July 17, 1943. Details are sparse, the Russians only recording that the enemy aircraft carried the rather unusual code number "17." Six days later Gorbunov and five fellow pilots were ordered off to escort an Il-2 mission and were bounced from the sun by six Bf 109s. They instantly broke up and turned into the enemy fighters. Gorbunov was able to get two of them before he was shot up and forced to break off and turn for home. He later rose to Kapitan and squadron leader and continued to do well after moving with the regiment to 3rd Ukrainian Front but was shot down and killed on May 19, 1944.

GOREGLYAD, Leonid Ivanovich
Combat record: 15 personal victories, 6 fractional credits, 146 sorties, 53 encounters.
Decorations: Gold Star of Hero of the Soviet Union on February 23, 1948; the Orders of Lenin, the Red Banner (5), Suvorov 2nd Class (2), the Patriotic War 1st Class, the Red Star (3).

Goreglyad was born in Ashkhabad on April 13, 1916 and enrolled for military service in 1934. He completed his pilot training at Orenburg military flying school and first fired his guns in anger against the Finns during the Winter War of 1939/40. He entered combat with the Luftwaffe as a squadron leader on South Front in October, 1941. He rapidly rose to Major and deputy commander of the 304 IAD participating in the violent action at Kirovograd in January, 1944. In April, 1944 he assumed command of the crack 22 GIAD and in this capacity was to distinguish himself during subsequent air operations on 1st and 2nd Ukrainian Fronts. In a fierce series of dogfights he was able to claim four kills in the course of the Lemberg-Sandomierz campaign (July 13/August 29, 1944). Goreglyad continued on active duty at the conclusion of the war and graduated from the General Staff Academy in 1950. He was appointed General-inspektor VVS in 1961 and had advanced to General Major when he returned to civilian life in 1976. He died on July 14, 1986.

GORELOV, Sergej Dmitriyevich

Combat record: 24 personal victories, 1 fractional credit, 214 sorties, 47 encounters.

Decorations: Gold Star of Hero of the Soviet Union on October 26, 1944; the Orders of Lenin (2), the Red Banner (7), Aleksandr Nevskij, the Patriotic War 1st Class (2), the Red Star.

Gorelov was born in the Tula area on June 23, 1920 and enrolled for service in 1938. He completed his pilot training at Borisoglebsk military flying school two years later and started flying combat in July, 1941. He was to enjoy considerable success while flying the La-5 and on October 14, 1943 Gorelov and eight of his squadron were assigned to a front-line patrol. While prowling around in the area of the Dnyepr River they spotted a very large formation of German bombers and immediately dove to attack. The La-5s stormed into the bomber force and claimed to have destroyed 10 in breaking up their attack. A few days later he was leading his squadron in another highly successful engagement when they reported the destruction of 15 enemy aircraft. Gorelov subsequently rose to Kapitan and gave a good account of himself in the ferocious battles above 1st Ukrainian Front. Following World War II he graduated from the Air Force Academy in 1952 and from the General Staff Academy seven years later. He later was assigned as deputy commander of the VVS academies serving in this capacity between 1977/81. He eventually advanced to General Polkovnik.

GORGOLYUK (also spelled GORGALYUK), Aleksandr Ivanovich

Combat record: 8 personal victories, 5 fractional credits, 376 sorties, 48 engagements.

Decorations: Gold Star of Hero of the Soviet Union on September 2, 1943; the Orders of Lenin, the Red Banner (2), the Patriotic War 1st Class.

Gorgolyuk was born in Odessa on August 27, 1919 and entered military service in 1937. He qualified as a pilot at Odessa military flying school in 1940 and entered combat with the Luftwaffe on the very first day of Operation Barbarossa, June

Major N.P. Gorodnichev scored 11 victories with the 5 GIAP in the wild battles on Kalinin Front in 1941. Here he is seen as a Kapitan posing with his LaGG-3 on December 8, 1941, one day after he had shot down a Ju 87. He met the requirements for the award of the title of Hero of the Soviet Union on May 5, 1942 but lost his life in an aircraft accident on March 1, 1943. (Author's collection)

22, 1941. He claimed his first victory, a Bf 109, shortly afterward and saw a lot of action on Kalinin Front. He really came into his own while becoming involved in the fury of the Kursk air engagements in 1943, by which time he had become a Starshij Lejtenant and flight leader in the 30 GIAP. On May 6 he forced down a Fw 190 when the regiment was fighting a pitched battle near Orel, three Bf 109s and a Fw 190 being shot down for the loss of one of their own. On June 6 he took off with four comrades from Fatezh (N Kursk) to intercept an enemy strike aimed at Kursk. They dove down on a large bomber formation and Gorgolyuk was able to send down a Ju 88 in flames in his first pass. He hurtled down on another and scored strikes on its starboard engine which caught fire. He was then bounced by six fighters and badly hit in his face forcing him to take to his parachute. Although he survived his serious injuries, his eyesight was destroyed. Reports conflict concerning his final tally, A.F. Semyonov suggesting a combined total of 15 kills ("Na vzlete", p. 69). Gorgolyuk was released from the service with the rank of Kapitan in 1946.

GOROKHOV, Yurij Ivanovich

Combat record: 23 personal victories, 10 fractional credits, 307 sorties, 57 air-to-air combats.

Decorations: Gold Star of Hero of the Soviet Union on February 4, 1944 in recognition of 16 kills, 10 fractional credits as of September, 1943; the Orders of Lenin, the Red Banner (3), Aleksandr Nevskij, the Patriotic War 1st Class.

Gorokhov was born in the Ivanovo area on August 1, 1921 an enlisted in the VVS in 1938. He won his wings at Chkalov military flying school a year later and was assigned to the 162 IAP on West Front in July, 1941 to enter combat. By June, 1943 his score had risen to five kills during 234 sorties. While flying a Yak-7B inscribed "Aleksandr Pushkin" he chalked up a string of nine victories in a series of dogfights in the areas of

Bryansk and Smolensk. August 12, 1943 proved to be a bright day for Gorokhov when he took off five times to hunt down the enemy in the Spas-Demensk area submitting claims for four planes destroyed in the air. He fell victim to German fighters on January 1, 1944 and was buried in a common grave in Krasnaya Gorka, a hamlet near Smolensk. At the time of his death he was his unit's highest scoring ace.

GOROVETS, Aleksandr Konstantinovich
Combat record: 11 personal victories, 6 fractional credits, 74 sorties, 11 encounters.
Decorations: Gold Star of Hero of the Soviet Union posthumously on September 28, 1943; the Orders of Lenin, the Red Banner.

Gorovets was born in the Vitebsk area on March 12, 1915 and entered military service in 1932. He received his pilot wings at Ulyanovsk military flying school three years later but then joined with the aeroklub of Shakhty in the Rostov area. He reenlisted in the Soviet Army in 1941 being posted to the 166 IAP on North Caucasus Front in June, 1942. His meteoric rise to fame was brief. His rate of scoring while flying the LaGG-3 fighter was far from spectacular and at the outset of the Battle of Kursk his record stood at two personal kills along with six being claimed jointly with fellow pilots. At that time he was flying a La-5 inscribed "Ot kolkhoznikov Gorkovskoj oblasti" ("From the kolkhoz workers of the Gorkij" area indicating that the aircraft was donated to the regiment). His real big day came on July 6, 1943 when he was able to set the all time record for victories in one sortie for Soviet aces. On this date he was returning from a mission to the Vladimirovka-Olkhovatka areas but found himself separated from his comrades after encountering intense flak. At 1940 hours he sighted a formation of some 20 enemy planes below and immediately hurtled down to attack. The Ju 87s were taken off guard as he stormed in closing on tail-end Charlie. He opened fire almost at ramming distance and the enemy plane exploded in midair. He got in behind another, firing until it went down to crash in flames and then worked his way forward. He succeeded in blasting nine Stukas out of the sky before he in turn was bounced by four Fw 190s. Soviet infantry elements later gave an account of the action reporting that he went in on fire giving him no chance of survival. He was buried in the village of Zorinskiye Dvory. Arsenij Vorozhejkin, 52-victory ace and one of Russia's most notable fighter pilots, commented: "This undoubtedly was one of the most astonishing exploits of the war. It is likely that he required but one short burst for each of his victories, which is tremendous. The whole action took only between 10 to 15 minutes and the enemy planes certainly had not been standing still in the air. He did contrary to the established theories of air fighting."

A.A. Grachyov, seen here as a Kapitan, became an ace fighting with the 272 IAP. He was in continuous action from October, 1941 receiving the title of Hero of the Soviet Union for his feats on West Front on February 4, 1944. By the close of hostilities his score was at least 16 personal victories. (Author's collection)

GRAZHDANINOV, Pavel Aleksandrovich
Combat record: 20 personal victories.
Decorations: Gold Star of Hero of the Soviet Union posthumously on May 1, 1943 for 6 personal victories in 16 sorties as of January, 1943; the Orders of Lenin, the Patriotic War 1st Class, the Red Star.

Grazhdaninov was born in the Tula area on December 19, 1920 and started his military career in 1938. He was graduated as a pilot at Borisoglebsk military flying school a year later and in November, 1942 was posted to the 169 IAP on Kalinin Front to commence combat duty flying La-5s. He immediately displayed exceptional skill, claiming one each Bf 109 and Fw 190 in his first scrap with the Luftwaffe in the vicinity of Velikiye Luki on December 8, 1942. He added another kill in the afternoon and then submitted claims for a Ju 88 and a Bf 109 destroyed on December 16. On the 29th he successfully rammed a Ju 87 but was wounded in the process. Although in great pain Grazhdaninov delivered a rear attack on a second and followed it down to the deck scoring many strikes before it crashed in a large cloud of dust and flying pieces. He continued to achieve victories at an astonishing pace after his recovery and on February 21, 1943, the last day of the Battle of Demyansk, was engaged in a mission led by Kapitan A.M. Chislov. The six La-5s were flying free hunt when they came under attack of several gaggles of fighters from JG 54 near Zaluchye, west of Demyansk. The vigilant Russians broke in all directions as the German fighters sped through them. It was Grazhdaninov and his wingman, Starshij Serzhant Davydov, who claimed the honors that day: they combined forces to destroy five fighters. As was later discovered, one of Grazhdaninov's victims was Major Hans Hahn, 108-victory ace and commander of II./JG 54, who was captured after making a forced landing in Soviet-held territory. One Russian report relates that Major Hahn during interrogation insisted that no Soviet pilot could shoot him down, and stated that he was hit by groundfire after he had shot down three Red fighters. In all, claims for six Bf 109s were submitted that day by pilots of the 169 IAP with Grazhdaninov accounting for two of them while one pilot was killed and another wounded. On March 5, 1943 he forced down a Ju 87 to run his tally to 20 but did not return and is presumed to have fallen victim to German fighters.

Hans "Assi" Hahn, who was forced down by P.A. Grazhdaninov on February 21, 1943 to spend seven arduous years in Soviet prison camps. He had 68 victories in the West and 40 more in the East. (Bundesarchiv)

Major A.D. Grebenyov, a brilliant officer and pilot of the 111 GIAP. Here he is seen wearing the Order of Lenin, three Orders of the Red Banner and the Guards badge in addition to the Gold Star which he was awarded in recognition of 18 personal victories, 4 shares, 340 sorties and 57 encounters on October 26, 1944. He ended the war with 24 confirmed kills. (Author's collection)

GRIB, Mikhail Ivanovich

Combat record: 15 personal victories, 500 sorties.
Decorations: Gold Star of Hero of the Soviet Union on October 23, 1942 for 10 kills, 250 missions and 56 encounters plus two tanks and five motor vehicles destroyed in 13 ground attacks as of August, 1942; the Orders of Lenin, the Red Banner (3), Aleksandr Nevskij, the Patriotic War 1st Class (2), the Red Star.

Grib was born in the Cherkassy area on October 2, 1919 and entered the VMF in 1937. He completed his pilot training at Yejsk military flying school in 1940 following which he was assigned to the Black Sea Fleet's air service. He fought from the very start of the war and made a big name for himself during the epic defense of Sevastopol by gaining four aerial victories. Subsequently he flew with great distinction with the 6 GIAP during the aerial campaigns over the Crimea, Rumania and Bulgaria. Grib served with the postwar VMF and graduated from the Naval Academy in 1955. He wound up his military career as a Polkovnik in 1968.

GRIGORYEV, Gerasim Afanasyevich

Combat record: 17 personal victories, 300 sorties, 18 encounters.
Decorations: Gold Star of Hero of the Soviet Union on February 14, 1943 for 13 personal victories together with 2 fractional credits as of November, 1942; the Orders of Lenin (2), the Red Banner (3).

Grigoryev was born in the Smolensk area on March 16, 1921 and joined the Soviet Army in 1939. He completed his flight training at Odessa military flying school in 1940 following which he was assigned to the 178 IAP. Grigoryev was in the forefront of action from the beginning of the war and while participating in the great battles for Moscow got his initial success, a Ju 88, on October 15, 1941 in an I-16. He converted to LaGG-3s a short time later and began to set a remarkable record by claiming a victory in each of his subsequent combats. On August 22, 1942 he was prowling around in the Yukhnov area

In this shot of 1942 M.I. Grib wears the basic flying equipment of Soviet fighter pilots of the period. Well worn paint job of his LaGG-3 denotes that both have seen heavy action. (Author's collection)

where he shot down a bomber to raise his tally to 13. He had by now become a Kapitan and deputy squadron leader and on February 5, 1943 engaged a lone Ju 88 while patrolling the Kaluga area with Lejtenant Dudnik. Grigoryev peeled off on him and closed to 100 meters opening fire. The bomber crashed without taking evasive action. He remained in the VVS following World War II and graduated from the Air Force Academy in 1955. He left active duty with the rank of Polkovnik and died on April 23, 1966.

M.I. Grib leading a mission of 6 GIAP-ChF Yak-9Ds over Sevastopol flying his personal mount "22." The date is May, 1944. (Author's collection)

The LaGG-3 "6" of Kapitan G.A. Grigoryev displays 13 victories dating this photo after August, 1942. Grigoryev's most impressive display of combat skill came in the great battles for the Russian capital. (Author's collection)

GRISHCHENKO, Pyotr Lukyanovich

Combat record: 27 personal victories, 380 sorties, 78 encounters.

Decorations: Gold Star of Hero of the Soviet Union on July 1, 1944 in recognition of 15 kills, 155 sorties, 31 engagements as of February, 1944; the Orders of Lenin, the Red Banner (3), the Patriotic War 1st Class, the Patriotic War 2nd Class, the Red Star.

Grishchenko was born in the Vitebsk area on August 1, 1921 and enlisted in the Soviet Army in 1940. He received his wings at Armavir military flying school two years later being posted to the 32 IAP in March, 1943 to start flying combat. He made his mark against the Luftwaffe during the Battle of Kursk when he submitted at least one victory. This occurred on July 15 when eight Yaks were sweeping the area of Prokhorovka where they had an encounter with 27 bombers escorted by eight Bf 109s. Five bombers were shot down in flames before the fighters could intervene with Grishchenko accounting for an He 111. He later was to make a brilliant war record in the skies above Kiev, Vinnitsa, Ternopol and Lemberg (Lvov). On January 25, 1945 he combined forces with his wingman to claim two kills when they ran into 30 bombers and eight escorting Fw 190s. He flew his last missions of the war in the dramatic battles over Berlin. Grishchenko served with the postwar VVS and graduated from the Air Force Academy in 1955. He was to become a Podpolkovnik before he concluded his active duty in 1961. He died on February 21, 1973.

GRISHIN, Aleksej Nikolayevich

Combat record: 13 personal victories, 378 sorties, 49 encounters.

Decorations: Gold Star of Hero of the Soviet Union on June 27, 1945; the Orders of Lenin, the Red Banner (3), Aleksandr Nevskij, the Patriotic War 1st Class, the Red Star.

Grishin was born in the Tula area in 1918 and entered military service in 1939. Upon completion of his training at Borisoglebsk military flying school Grishin commenced his combat duty in June, 1941. While serving with the 516 IAP he rose to Kapitan and took over as leader of a fighter squadron. He enjoyed considerable success during the hard fighting at Kharkov and on an unspecified date in September, 1943 was leading six Yak-1s on an Il-2 escort in the Borki area (SW Kharkov), where they became involved in a dogfight with 16 Bf 109s. The Messers tried to engage the Shturmoviks but Grishin successfully intervened claiming two of them shot down in flames. He subsequently put up a good performance during the great aerial campaigns on 1st Ukrainian Front. He remained in the ranks after the war winding up his military career in 1964 by which time he had advanced to Podpolkovnik. He died on August 22, 1974.

GRITSEVETS, Sergej Ivanovich
Combat record: 42 personal victories.
Decorations: 1st Gold Star of Hero of the Soviet Union on February 22, 1939, 2nd Gold Star on August 29, 1939; the Orders of Lenin (2), the Red Banner (2).

Gritsevets was born in the Brest area on July 19, 1909 and enrolled for service in 1931. He completed his pilot training at Orenburg military flying school a year later and rapidly rose from airman to regiment commander. He was a pilot instructor for a while before volunteering for action in Spain in 1938. He had by now become a Kapitan and in a burst of energy and skill he was to run up a string of 30 kills – a total unsurpassed by any other Soviet pilot during the conflict. It was not long before he started knocking down Japanese planes over the Khalkhin Gol after joining with the 22 IAP in May, 1939. He made good use of the virtues of his I-16 fighter and by September 7 had gained 12 more victories. He had developed into a brilliant officer and pilot, being admired and respected by his comrades, and fittingly was appointed regiment commander soon after. On September 16, 1939 however he perished when Major P.I. Khara's plane stalled whilst landing crashing into Gritsevets who was taxiing on the landing ground.

GROMAKOVSKIJ, Vladimir Aleksandrovich
Combat record: 16 personal victories, 186 sorties, 29 encounters.
Decorations: Gold Star of Hero of the Soviet Union on May 15, 1946; the Orders of Lenin, the Red Banner (3), the Patriotic War 1st Class, the Red Star.

Gromakovskij was born in Orenburg on March 15, 1922 and entered military service in 1940. He was graduated at Krasnodar military flying school two years later and was assigned to the 19 IAP in August. From then on Gromakovskij was in continuous action taking part in the great aerial battles at Kursk, Bobrujsk, over Poland and ultimately, over the Reich. He was to gain all of his score while flying the La-5 and La-7 fighters. On February 12, 1945 he claimed two Fw 190s shot down in flames near Küstrin while flying wing to Major I.N. Kozhedub, the Allied ace of aces. On March 22 he was flying a sweep out to the Seelow area with another great ace, Major A.S. Kumanichkin, to engage a large gaggle of some 30 German fighters. They went through the formation like lightning with Gromakovskij singling one Fw 190 out for attack, the enemy aircraft exploding before it could take any evasive action. He was a Starshij Lejtenant and flight leader at the end of the war and remained in the ranks until his retirement in 1954 by which time he had become a Polkovnik.

GROMOV, Georgij Vasilyevich
Combat record: 13 personal victories, 400 sorties, 64 encounters.
Decorations: Gold Star of Hero of the Soviet Union on May 15, 1946; the Orders of Lenin, the Red Banner (3), Aleksandr Nevskij, the Patriotic War 1st Class, the Red Star.

Gromov was born in the Smolensk area on April 1, 1917 and joined the Soviet Army at age 20. He completed his pilot training at Borisoglebsk military flying school later that year and

A.A. Gubanov of the 13 IAP made a big name for himself on North Caucasus Front. The title of Hero of the Soviet Union was bestowed upon him on August 24, 1943 in recognition of 14 kills in 358 sorties. He went on to finish as the regiment's third ranking ace with a bag of 25 victories. (Author's collection)

first fired his guns in anger during the Soviet-Finnish conflict in 1939/40. He next commenced his combat duty against the Luftwaffe in June, 1941 and in the dark months to follow would display remarkable skill and outstanding leadership. He eventually rose to command the 515 IAP which claimed 34 kills in a flurry of action between January 14 and February 3, 1945. His rank at the close of war was Podpolkovnik. During his postwar career Gromov graduated from the General Staff Academy in 1956 serving in various command positions until 1963 when he returned to civilian life as a General Major. He died on September 26, 1975.

GUCHYOK, Pyotr Iosifovich

Combat record: 20 personal victories, 3 fractional credits, 209 sorties, 56 air-to-air combats.

Decorations: Gold Star of Hero of the Soviet Union posthumously on June 27, 1945; the Orders of Lenin, the Patriotic War 1st Class.

Guchyok was born in the Minsk area on March 18, 1923 and entered the VVS for flight training in 1940. He won his wings at Batajsk military flying school two years later joining with the veteran 100 GIAP in August, 1943. He immediately began a run of success while flying Airacobras and subsequently made a remarkable combat career on 1st, 2nd and 4th Ukrainian Fronts. He excelled at Yassy in August, 1944 when he achieved a string of six air victories within a week. On April 18, 1945 he was hit by groundfire while strafing gun emplacements on the outskirts of Spremberg (S Cottbus) and crashed to his death. He was buried in Tschenstochau (now Czestochowa, Poland).

GUDKOV, Dmitrij Vasilyevich

Combat record: 19 personal victories, 314 sorties, 28 encounters.

Decorations: Gold Star of Hero of the Soviet Union on June 29, 1945; the Orders of Lenin, the Red Banner (3), Aleksandr Nevskij, the Patriotic War 1st Class (2), the Red Star (4).

Gudkov was born in the Ryazan area on January 11, 1921 and enrolled for service in 1940. He qualified as a pilot at Kacha military flying school a year later and commenced his combat duty in August, 1942 when he was posted to the 976 IAP. His most memorable mission occurred on September 11, 1942 when he was patrolling the Stalingrad area and spotted a lone Ju 88 below at 4,000 meters. He dove down and started to pour fire into it but the enemy plane refused to go down. Reluctant to let it go away he sliced off part of its tail with the propeller of his fighter whereupon it went out of control. Bleeding from a head wound, Gudkov lost consciousness momentarily and found he was losing altitude rapidly and unable to control his fighter. He took to his parachute at 2,000 meters and saw the Ju 88 crash near Kajsatskaya with two of its crew being captured by Soviet infantry hurrying to the scene. Gudkov later saw considerable fighting on 3rd Byelorussian Front and did well in the skies of East Prussia, especially at Insterburg. Following World War II he graduated from the Air Force Academy in 1951 and continued on command positions until his retirement with the rank of Polkovnik in 1977. He died on March 18, 1978.

GULAYEV, Nikolaj Dmitriyevich

Combat record: 57 personal victories, 3 fractional credits, 248 sorties, 69 encounters.

Decorations: 1st Gold Star of Hero of the Soviet Union on September 28, 1943 in recognition of 13 kills, 3 fractional credits, 95 sorties as of July, 1943, 2nd Gold Star on July 1, 1944 for 42 victories, 3 fractional credits, 125 sorties, 42 encounters; the Orders of Lenin (2), the Red Banner (4), the Patriotic War 1st Class (2), the Red Star (2).

Gulayev, the third ranking Allied fighter ace of World War II, was born in the Rostov area on February 26, 1918. He began his rather spectacular career in the VVS in 1938 completing his pilot training at Stalingrad military flying school two years later. He was assigned to Stalingrad Front in April, 1942 where he joined with the 27 IAP to start flying combat. During the fury of the air battles over the Volga River he was able to submit a claim for a bomber aircraft destroyed and then converted to P-39 Airacobras. He had his first big day on May 14, 1943 after the regiment had deployed to Voronezh Front when he blasted two Ju 87s and then successfully rammed a third after having expended his ammunition. Gulayev force-landed safely close to elements of the Soviet 52nd Rifle Division. It was at Kursk that Gulayev really began to display his outstanding talents as a fighter pilot. In a fierce series of dogfights he ran his score to 13 in a seven day period between July 5 and 11, 1943 and in turn was recommended for the coveted title of Hero of the Soviet Union, the highest Soviet military distinction. On July 9 he had the rare distinction of destroying a second enemy plane by ramming when he forced down a Ju 88. "You'd have acted exactly the same if you had been in my place", Gulayev later was telling his admiring comrades, his unassuming character expressing itself in these words. In the air though he was aggressive, uncanny and lethal. He was a Starshij Lejtenant and deputy squadron leader when he received his first Gold Star on September 28, by which time his tally had already risen to 27. Gulayev continued to score steadily and on October 24 got a double with one each Bf 109 and Ju 87 when Starshij Lejtenant F.F. Arkhipenko was leading six Cobras to bounce a superior Luftwaffe force between Likhovka-Lozovatka-Volnye Khutora. He then advanced to Kapitan and took over as leader of a fighter squadron but was shot down and wounded in early 1944 leaving the front for a short home leave. Upon his return to combat five Ju 87s fell to his guns within four minutes while leading six Cobras against a formation of 27 Stukas and seven fighters on March 5, 1944. In all, 11 claims were submitted by the P-39 pilots. Gulayev was greatly involved in the great Soviet summer offensive scoring victories whenever he entered combat. June 2, 1944 saw him claim his 50th kill. On this occasion he had taken off on a free hunt with five Cobras and while prowling in the Yassy area they had made contact with 30 bombers and their escorts. In an instant he had chased an Bf 109 down to the deck where the German fighter burst into flames. Gulayev saw the pilot bail out but due to the low altitude there was no time for his parachute to open. Gulayev then came in line astern slightly below another fighter and dispatched it with a short burst from point-blank range. A few days later he came within a hair of getting lost when he came embroiled in a dogfight with a novice flying wing to him. He was bounced by a German fighter and sustained serious injuries before his number two could intervene. Gulayev acted coolly, out turned his attackers and shot down two of them before breaking clear and setting course for home. He crashlanded on his own airfield where his strength gave out and he collapsed. He survived but did not return to combat operations. Without this misfortune, he might well have emerged as the top Allied ace of World War II. At this stage Gulayev was the leading fighter pilot of the VVS and had already met the requirements for a second Gold Star award which he received while in hospital. His nomination for the Gold Star reads: "Starshij Lejtenant Gulayev is an exceptional fighter pilot. Always eager for combat he delivers his attacks resolutely getting as close as possible before opening fire." Following World War II he continued on active duty with the PVO forces and graduated from the Air Force Academy in 1950 and from the General Staff Academy in 1960. He was appointed General Polkovnik in 1972 winding up his military career seven years later. He died on September 27, 1985.

Kapitan N.D. Gulayev, victor of 13 combats over Kursk, is rightfully proud of his tally of 32 kills displayed on his Aeracobra. He finished as the number three Allied ace with a confirmed score of 57, including two successful aerial rammings. (Author's collection)

This photo shows Major N.D. Gulayev after his recovery from serious injuries sustained in 1944 wearing his two Gold Stars of Hero of the Soviet Union. Few of his comrades doubt that had he not been wounded, he would have stayed on top as the leading ace! (Author's collection)

GUSAROV, Nikolaj Mikhajlovich

Combat record: 15 personal victories, 14 fractional credits, 432 sorties, 69 encounters.

Decorations: Gold Star of Hero of the Soviet Union on February 4, 1944; the Orders of Lenin, the Red Banner (2), Aleksandr Nevskij, the Patriotic War 1st Class (2), the Red Star (2).

Gusarov was born in the Orel area on December 4, 1917 and entered military service in 1936. He was graduated as a pilot at Kacha military flying school in 1939 and was in action from the beginning of the German-Soviet war. From then on he was greatly involved in the desperate fighting of 1941 and by October had logged no fewer than 230 sorties while serving as a flight leader with the 486 IAP on South Front. Of his sorties, 62 were escorts, 56 armed reconnaissance, 39 strafing and four dive-bombing missions. He entered combat on 35 occasions and was able to claim the destruction of seven aircraft while teaming with fellow pilots to bring down three more. He scored his first success on June 22, 1941, the first day of Operation Barbarossa, when he and four I-16s were ordered off to intercept a formation of 11 bombers and four fighters with Gusarov forcing down a Ju 88. He was in action seven days later when he added another of these and on August 10 shot down a fighter while engaged in an escort to Vinnitsa. He then saw a great deal of action at Dnyepropetrovsk and Novomoskovsk and by August his score had already risen to five. He claimed another victory on September 1 while leading four I-16s to attack 20 enemy aircraft, three of these being shot down. He was then appointed deputy commander of the 486 IAP and deployed with the unit to Crimean soil in January, 1942. During the course of the next five months Gusarov flew 104 sorties with 15 air encounters and two more kills. The regiment then was assigned to Central Front where it was tasked with providing ground support at the Desna and Dnyepr bridgeheads with Gusarov logging 60 sorties during the period of May to November, 1942. On July 5, 1943 he successfully rammed a Fw 190 after running out of ammunition near Maloarkhangelsk (Orel area) and parachuted safely while the German fighter crashed and blew up. He had his best day on August 5, 1943 when he got a triple while his squadron was submitting claims for 10 more enemy aircraft destroyed in a scrap over Kutafino. He stayed in the service after the war and retired with the rank of Polkovnik in 1955.

GUSKOV, Gavriil Gavriilovich
Combat record: 14 personal victories, 105+ sorties, 35+ encounters.
Decorations: Gold Star of Hero of the Soviet Union on May 24, 1943 for 10 personal victories as of April, 1943; the Orders of Lenin, the Red Banner, the Patriotic War 1st Class, the Red Star.

Guskov was born in the Orel area in 1923 and joined the VVS for flight training in April, 1941. He qualified as a pilot later that year and was posted as a Serzhant to the 653 IAP on Kalinin Front in November, 1942. He became heavily engaged in the air battles over Velikiye Luki scoring his initial success with the Yak-1 on January 3, 1943 when he shot down a Bf 109. He added a Fw 190 a week later and in February moved with the regiment to Northwest Front. Here Guskov piled up a good score while participating in the violent combats surrounding the Demyansk bridgehead and by the end of the month had run up a string of nine air victories. On March 7, 1943 he shot down another Bf 109 near Staraya Russa and in May 653 IAP was posted again, this time to Bryansk Front to take part in the Battle of Kursk. Guskov shot down a Ju 87 on July 12 and a few days later went off on two missions to destroy three Fw 190s although it is believed that some of his victories were actually claimed jointly with fellow pilots. On July 17, 1943 Guskov and his comrades S. Albinovich, A. Lebedev and V. Ponomarev were assigned on a ground-support mission in the Orel area but all of them failed to return. Twenty years later construction workers discovered the wreckage of a fighter plane and the remains of the pilot near the hamlet of Betovo Bolkhov. The registration numbers on the decorations found with the pilot's remains indicated that the awards had been bestowed upon Guskov.

GUTSALOV (also spelled GUTSALO), Aleksandr Semyonovich
Combat record: 18 personal victories, 3 fractional credits, 7 enemy planes on the ground, 494 sorties, 52 encounters.
Decorations: Gold Star of Hero of the Soviet Union on May 15, 1946; the Order of Lenin.

Gutsalov was born in the Kazakh SSR on March 20, 1917 and enlisted in the Soviet Army in 1937. Following his graduation at Groznyj military school for bomber gunners he was sent to Engels military flying school where he qualified as a pilot in 1941. He entered combat in November, 1941 when he was posted to the 691 SAP and later joined with the 845 IAP. His most impressive display of combat skill came with this unit when it was operating on 2nd Byelorussian and 3rd Baltic Fronts. On March 27, 1944 he was leading four Yak-9s on an Il-2 escort to Parkanovo airfield where they encountered 30 Fw 190s. Gutsalov peeled off to engage them head-on and shot down one on his first pass. He then dove to the rescue of his wingman, dispatching a Fw 190 with a long burst as it was working over his comrade. He went on to emerge as 845 IAP's top ace. He died on January 28, 1946, the circumstances of his untimely death not being known.

Luftwaffe graveyard. Remains of numerous shattered aircraft discovered by advancing Soviet forces at an airfield near Danzig, Germany, in 1945. (Author's collection)

IGNATYEV, Mikhail Trofimovich
Combat record: 28 personal victories.
Decorations: Gold Star of Hero of the Soviet Union on August 24, 1943 for 10 kills, 7 fractional credits, 171 sorties, 70 engagements as of May, 1943; the Orders of Lenin, the Red Banner (3), the Patriotic War 1st Class.

Ignatyev was born in the Chuguyev area on November 21, 1920 and enrolled for service in the VVS in 1938. He qualified as a pilot at Stalingrad military flying school two years later commencing his combat duty in June, 1942. He began a run of success while serving with the 13 IAP on North Caucasus Front and rapidly rose to deputy squadron leader. Ignatyev later was transferred to the glorious 5 GIAP seeing a great deal of action during the Lvov campaign in July, 1944 by which time he had become a Kapitan. He wound up his military career in 1946 and passed away on November 27, 1973.

INDYK, Semyon Leontyevich
Combat record: 8 personal victories, 93 sorties, 21 encounters.
Decorations: Gold Star of Hero of the Soviet Union on June 27, 1945; the Orders of Lenin, the Red Banner (4), the Red Star.

Indyk was born in the Sumy area on August 12, 1909 and entered military service in 1931. Upon qualifying as a pilot at Kacha military flying school in 1933 he was assigned as a bomber pilot instructor prior to joining with a fighter unit as a squadron leader. He first fired his guns in anger during the Russo-Finnish Winter War of 1939/40 and in April, 1941 was assigned as deputy commander of the 194 IAP. In this capacity he saw considerable fighting from the earliest days of the war with Germany and during the Battle of Stalingrad rose to command the 291 IAP. In June, 1943 he was posted again, this time taking over the 107 GIAP leading this with consummate skill during operations over the Dnyepr, the Oder and Neisse Rivers and at Dnyepropetrovsk, Sandomierz and ultimately, Berlin. Under his able leadership the unit was credited with destroying 120 enemy planes in the air along with 300 motor vehicles and three locomotives in ground attacks during the course of 4,266 sorties and 209 air-to-air combats between June, 1943 and May, 1945. He remained in the VVS after the war until 1954 when he came off active duty. He died on January 31, 1980.

ISKRIN, Nikolaj Mikhajlovich
Combat record: 16 personal victories, 297 sorties, 80 encounters.
Decorations: Gold Star of Hero of the Soviet Union on August 24, 1943 in recognition of 10 personal victories, 1 fractional credit, 218 sorties, 58 encounters as of May, 1943; the Orders of Lenin, the Red Banner (2), the Patriotic War 1st Class (2).

Major Pyotr Ivanovich Isayev of the 28 GIAP with his P-39 on June 20, 1944. Isayev's tally at that stage was four personal victories. (Author's collection)

Iskrin was born in the Kujbyshev area on April 14, 1918 and started his military career in 1939. He completed his pilot training at Batajsk military flying school a year later and flew with the 55 IAP from the beginning of the war. He excelled in the wild air battles above North Caucasus Front after the regiment had converted to Airacobras but was then seriously wounded in a scrap with German fighters. Although he survived, his left leg had to be amputated. He was determined to go on flying and returned to combat operations as soon as he had recovered, now fully mobile on an artificial leg. In a burst of energy and skill Iskrin was able to add six kills during 79 sorties and 22 encounters before the end of the war. He was released from active duty in 1945 and became an administrator with Kujbyshev airport. He died on August 28, 1985.

IVANOV, Nikolaj Pavlovich
Combat record: 15 personal victories, 50 sorties.
Decorations: Gold Star of Hero of the Soviet Union posthumously on September 2, 1943; the Orders of Lenin, the Red Banner, Aleksandr Nevskij.

Ivanov was born in the Yaroslavl area on November 26, 1908 and enrolled for military service in 1930. He won his pilot wings a year later at Borisoglebsk military flying school and in June,

1942 assumed command of the badly battered 169 IAP to get it into operational trim once more. The regiment resumed combat with Ivanov in the lead on November 29, 1942 and their aerial success came immediately. On this same day they became embroiled in a violent combat with a large gaggle of Luftwaffe planes near Velikiye Luki, where they claimed 21 kills. Ivanov personally accounted for a triple and then submitted a single victory the following day when the regiment was again having a field day with 11 kills. Victories continued at a high rate after the unit had deployed to the vicinity of Demyansk where it was to be credited with 25 victories in the air during 218 sorties in an eleven day period. In March, 1943 it was designated Guards and next moved to Bryansk Front to take part in the big air battles above Kursk. During a series of pitched battles the regiment claimed 37 victories in 189 sorties within five days and on July 12 Ivanov was flying a sweep with six La-5s out to the front where they made contact with 25 enemy planes, 10 of these being shot down. On August 7, 1943 he was shot down in an encounter between Orel-Bryansk and crashed to his death.

Lejtenant V.P. Ivanov first saw frontline action in June, 1941 and later rose to Kapitan and squadron leader in the 148 GIAP-PVO. His feats won him the title of Hero of the Soviet Union on August 22, 1944. He ran up a string of at least 14 personal victories during 556 sorties before the cessation of hostilities. (Author's collection)

IVANOV, Stepan Gavrilovich
Combat record: 22 personal victories, 463 sorties.
Decorations: Gold Star of Hero of the Soviet Union on August 2 1944 in recognition of 12 victories, 9 fractional credits, 325 sorties and 42 encounters as of April 1944; the Orders of Lenin (2), the Red Banner (5), the Red Star (2).

Ivanov was born in the Perm area on March 20, 1914 and entered military service in 1936. Following his graduation at Orenburg military flying school two years later Ivanov cut his teeth during the Russo-Finnish Winter War of 1939/40 but details are not available. He joined combat with the Luftwaffe in June, 1942 when he was assigned to the 910 IAP piling up a remarkable score during subsequent operations over Karelia, Stalingrad, Kursk, Korsun-Shevchenkovskij, Kiev, Rovno and finally, Berlin. He eventually rose to Major and deputy commander of the regiment, finishing as its top-scoring ace. On March 28, 1944 he led a strike against a German airfield in the Korsun area where five enemy planes were shot down as they were taking off while 10 Ju 52 and 60 motor vehicles were destroyed on the ground. Ivanov remained in the ranks after World War II and graduated from the Air Force Academy in 1951. He left active duty with the rank of Polkovnik eight years later and died on July 19, 1983.

KABEROV, Igor Aleksandrovich
Combat record: 8 personal victories, 18 fractional credits, 397 sorties, 92 encounters.
Decorations: Gold Star of Hero of the Soviet Union on July 24, 1943; the Orders of Lenin (2), the Red Banner (2), the Patriotic War 1st Class (2), the Red Star (2).

Kaberov was born in the Vologda area on April 25, 1917 and enrolled for service in the VMF in 1939. He received his wings at Yejsk military flying school a year later being assigned to the Baltic Fleet's air service. He entered combat with the 5 IAP-KBF in June, 1941 and during his time with the regiment was mostly occupied with close-support and ground targets during the epic defense of Leningrad. He flew LaGG-3s until well into 1943 and eventually advanced to Kapitan and deputy squadron leader. He served with the postwar VMF and graduated from the Air Force Academy in 1952. He came off active duty with the rank of Polkovnik in 1960.

KALABUSHKIN, Ivan Nikolayevich
Combat record: 15 personal victories.
Decorations: Gold Star of Hero of the Soviet Union on March 4, 1942 for 8 kills as of December, 1941; the Orders of Lenin, the Red Banner (2), Aleksandr Nevskij, the Patriotic War 1st Class, the Red Star (2).

Kalabushkin was born in the Vladimir area on January 23, 1915 and enrolled for service at age 21. He completed his pilot training at Voroshilovgrad military flying school in 1938 and was

Yakovlev Yak-3 "96" of an unknown regiment. This photograph shows to advantage the clean lines of the aircraft which ranks among the most formidable fighting machines of the war. The legendary A.I. Koldunov, the eighth ranking Allied ace of World War II, was the leading exponent of this fighter. (Author's collection)

La-5s rolling on takeoff for a free hunt in 1944. The Lavochkin fighter saw action across the skies of Eastern Europe and the Reich producing some of the most famous aces of the war. It was able to turn closer than the Bf 109 and the Fw 190 and faster than the enemy fighters in level flight on the deck leaving them only with the advantage of faster dives. (Author's collection)

posted to the 123 IAP before the Patriotic War. When the Germans knifed into Soviet Russia on June 22, 1941 Kalabushkin took off with his flight of I-153s and immediately made contact with swarms of enemy planes, four of these being shot down for no losses. In all, Kalabushkin set out three times that same day and entered combat on three separate occasions to submit claims for two each Bf 109s and Ju 88s together with an He 111 destroyed between Kobrin-Pinsk – a record that only was eclipsed late in the war. He was in the thick of the fighting next day claiming two more kills. He later was posted to the 562 IAP of the Moscow PVO and rapidly rose to Starshij Lejtenant and squadron leader. He remained in the VVS following World War II and graduated from the Air Force Academy in 1949 and from the General Staff Academy in 1958. He retired with the rank of General Major in 1964 and died on April 12, 1985.

KALARASH, Dmitrij Leontyevich
Combat record: 11 personal victories, 6 fractional credits, 242 sorties.
Decorations: Gold Star of Hero of the Soviet Union posthumously on December 13, 1942; the Orders of Lenin, the Red Banner, the "Badge of Honor."

Kalarash was born in Kiev on December 12, 1911 and entered the Soviet Army in 1929. He qualified as a pilot at Borisoglebsk military flying school three years later and was in action from the very start of the war. Because of his success during the dark months to follow Kalarash quickly rose to high positions and by the end of 1942 had become a Podpolkovnik and shturman in the 236 IAD on Transcaucasus Front. On July 19, 1942 Kalarash, then a Major, landed in a pasture close to General Major I.D. Klimov, commander of the 236 IAD who had been shot down and wounded in the Rostov area, effected a pick up and flew his crowded fighter back to safety. He was shot down in a fighter battle with Bf 109s in the vicinity of Lazarevskoye, between Tuapse and Sochi, on October 29, 1942 and although he managed to get out of his disabled fighter he died of his wounds in a Tuapse hospital a short time later. Soviet reports conflict concerning his last battle one suggesting he was killed while deliberately ramming a German fighter. Kalarash is remembered by his comrade, twice Hero of the Soviet Union Pavel Kamozin, as a dynamic, courageous personality, who originated substantial improvements to fighter tactics.

KAMENSHCHIKOV, Vladimir Grigoryevich
Combat record: 12 personal victories, 37 fractional credits.
Decorations: Gold Star of Hero of the Soviet Union on August 9, 1941 for 4 kills along with 4 fractional credits as of mid-July, 1941; the Orders of Lenin, the Red Banner.

Kamenshchikov was born in Stalingrad on March 18, 1915 and enrolled for service in 1934. He received his wings at Stalingrad military flying school in 1937 and by June, 1941 was serving as a Lejtenant in a regiment near Byelostok. On the 22nd he was attacked by three Bf 109s but turned into them and shot down one seeing its pilot bail out. He was then forced to bail out of his own blazing aircraft at 200 meters sustaining injuries in his face and arms. He was put back on combat duty only four days later and was successful in claiming four enemy planes jointly with fellow pilots. On July 7 he bagged another Bf 109 and three days later got a Ju 88. By mid-July he already had met the conditions for the award of the coveted title Hero of the Soviet Union and then made a big name for himself with the 126 IAP while taking part in the great battles for the Soviet capital and the fury of the Stalingrad air engagements. In a fierce series of dogfights he ran up 16 kills including fractional credits while flying the Tomahawk at Stalingrad and for his efforts was promoted to Major. Kamenshchikov eventually took command of a fighter aviation regiment but on May 22, 1943 he was shot down and killed being buried in a common grave in Volgograd (Stalingrad).

KAMOZIN, Pavel Mikhajlovich
Combat record: 35 personal victories, 13 fractional credits, 131 sorties, 56 encounters.
Decorations: 1st Gold Star of Hero of the Soviet Union on May 1, 1943 for 12 victories along with 7 fractional credits, 82 sorties, 23 encounters as of March, 1943; 2nd Gold Star on July 1, 1944 in recognition of 29 kills, 13 fractional credits; the Orders of Lenin, the Red Banner (2), Aleksandr Nevskij, the Patriotic War 1st Class.

Kamozin was born in the Bryansk area on July 16, 1917 and came to the VVS in 1937 qualifying as a pilot at Borisoglebsk military flying school a year later. He was a Mladshij Lejtenant and pilot instructor at the outbreak of the Patriotic War but did not commence his combat duty before October, 1942 when he was posted to the 269 IAP. He immediately proved his skills at blasting enemy aircraft astounding his comrades by scoring a triple in his first scrap with the Luftwaffe on an unspecified date soon after. On this occasion seven LaGG-3s were prowling around off the Black Sea coast when they were attacked by six Bf 109s and a running battle developed. Kamozin out turned one, opened fire, seeing strikes all over, following which a wing flew off and the fighter crashed. He claimed two others before 15 more Messerschmitts streaked in forcing them to disengage and turn for home. Kamozin then began to score victories at a formidable pace on North Caucasus Front and rapidly rose to deputy squadron leader. His highest scoring period came in the contested air space above the Crimea in 1944 when he claimed 19 kills including shares. He had by now become commanding officer of a fighter squadron in the 66 GIAP which was credited with the destruction of 63 enemy planes in the same time frame. His success was such that according to Soviet sources the Luftwaffe detailed one of its notables to bring him down as he was becoming a thorn in their side. When they met at last, Kamozin was able to get the better of his opponent in a head-on encounter, following which the 109 went down to explode on the ground. It is reasoned that his victim was a German pilot by the name of "Graf" but no evidence exists to confirm that this might have been the redoubtable Hermann Graf, who had become the first pilot in the history of warfare to achieve 200 aerial victories and survived as Kommodore of JG 52. The German's identity remains a mystery but is believed to have been a Graf, a German nobleman equivalent to an English earl. Kamozin came out of World War II as one of Russia's finest fighter pilots; he retired from the VVS in 1946 to join Soviet civil aviation and died on November 24, 1983.

Kapitan P.M. Kamozin, 269 IAP's highest-scoring ace, discussing a good day with fellow pilots. (Author's collection)

KANKOSHEV, Akhmet-Khan Tallovich

Combat record: 20 personal victories, 200 sorties, 100 encounters plus a Fw 190, 5 motor vehicles destroyed in ground attacks.

Decorations: Gold Star of Hero of the Soviet Union on September 2, 1943 for 8 personal victories, 3 fractional credits, 108 sorties, 45 air-to-air combats as of June, 1943; the Orders of Lenin, the Red Banner (2).

Kankoshev was born in the Kabardino-Balkar ASSR on August 28, 1914 and joined the Soviet Army in 1942. He was posted to the 42 GIAP on North Caucasus Front in March, 1943 and immediately began a run of success. He scored for the first time on the 14th when his squadron was off to intercept German transport aircraft but instead engaged a gaggle of fighters near Temryuk (N Novorossijsk) where Kankoshev claimed a Fw 190 destroyed and four more as damaged. He then chalked up 12 kills in two months combat, all but two of his victories being against single-engined fighters, the most difficult opponents. On May 14 he shot down a Bf 109F while patrolling the air space over Amakat and two days later made a claim for another of these when nine Yak-1s became embroiled in a dogfight with eight Bf 109s and two Fw 190s while heading for the Luftwaffe airfield of Krasnoarmejskaya. Kankoshev's quarry burst into flames whereupon the pilot bailed out to become a prisoner. On December 28, 1943 he failed to return from a mission in the Kerch area and is presumed to have fallen foul of fighters.

KARASYOV, Aleksandr Nikitovich

Combat record: 30 personal victories, 11 fractional credits, 380 sorties, 112 aerial engagements; plus 3+ victories in Korea.

Decorations: Gold Star of Hero of the Soviet Union on August 24, 1943 in recognition of 14 kills, 9 fractional credits, 301 sorties, 70 encounters as of May, 1943; the Orders of Lenin (3), the Red Banner (4), the Patriotic War 1st Class, the Red Star.

Karasyov was born in Vladikavkaz (Ordzhonikidze) on August 30, 1916 and enrolled for service in 1937. Upon qualifying as a pilot at Batajsk military flying school in 1941 he was in the forefront of action from the earliest days of the Patriotic War. Karasyov made a brilliant war record with the glorious 9 GIAP on South Front and was rapidly promoted to flight leader. He subsequently scored heavily while flying Airacobras and later La-7s in the ferocious battles over Sevastopol, Odessa and the Reich. He stayed in the service after the close of war and fought in Korea with the rank of Podpolkovnik. On September 19, 1950 flying the MiG-15, he destroyed three F-84s in one sortie. He graduated from the General Staff Academy in 1959 and retired as a General Major in 1968.

KARLOV, Valentin Andreyevich

Combat record: 19 personal victories, 7 fractional credits, 246 sorties, 71 encounters.

Decorations: Gold Star of Hero of the Soviet Union on June 27, 1945 for 18 victories along with 4 fractional credits during 172 sorties, 44 encounters; the Orders of Lenin, the Red Banner (2), the Patriotic War 1st Class (2), the Red Star (3).

Karlov was born in Simferopol on December 29, 1923 and entered military service in 1940. He was graduated at Kacha military flying school in 1942 and was assigned to the 129 GIAP commencing his combat duty in May, 1943. Under the tutelage of the experienced and very capable V.I. Bobrov, a tough veteran of the Spanish Civil War, Karlov was to develop into a skillful air fighter. He achieved his initial success with the Airacobra on May 14 when he rose to intercept a Luftwaffe strike against the regiment's own airfield at Grushka shooting down a Ju 87. Karlov later rose to Starshij Lejtenant and shturman of a fighter squadron and enjoyed considerable success while fighting on 1st Ukrainian Front. Bobrov provides the following revealing recollection of Karlov's eagerness for combat: "One day at Grushka the alert flight was scrambled. I noticed that Karlov was instructing his flight to warm up their engines as well and went over to ask him why. His answer was short to the point: 'Just in case I'm needed out there.'" He served with the postwar VVS and advanced to Polkovnik in 1956. He graduated from the Air Force Academy in 1970 and died on December 26, 1976.

KARNACH, Stepan Andreyevich
Combat record: 16 personal victories, 4 fractional credits, 346 sorties, 84 encounters.
Decorations: Gold Star of Hero of the Soviet Union on February 4, 1944 after 12 kills, 4 fractional credits, 270 sorties, 70 air combats as of September, 1943; the Orders of Lenin, the Red Banner (3), Suvorov 3rd Class, the Patriotic War 1st Class (2), the Red Star (2).

Karnach was born in the Minsk area on November 10, 1918 and enlisted in the VVS in 1938. He received his wings at Odessa military flying school two years later and went into action in June, 1941 while serving with the 247 IAP flying Yak-1s. He gave a good account of himself in the big air battles over the Crimea, the Caucasus, at Kursk and fighting the Luftwaffe above the Ukraine, Poland, the Reich and Czechoslovakia. When hostilities in Europe ceased he had become commanding officer of the regiment. During his postwar career Karnach graduated from the General Staff Academy in 1958 and concluded his active duty with the rank of General Major in 1973.

KARPOV, Aleksandr Terentyevich
Combat record: 27 personal victories, 10 fractional credits, 519 sorties, 130 encounters.
Decorations: 1st Gold Star on September 28, 1943 for 16 personal victories, 7 fractional credits, 370 sorties, 87 engagements as of August, 1943, 2nd Gold Star on August 22, 1944 in recognition of 26 kills, 7 fractional credits, 421 sorties, 94 air combats as of June, 1944; the Orders of Lenin, the Red Banner (3), Aleksandr Nevskij.

Karpov was born in the Kaluga area on October 17, 1917 and began his distinguished military career in 1939. He completed his pilot training at Kacha military flying school a year later and joined with the 123 IAP on Leningrad Front before the outbreak of war. During his combat career, Karpov achieved fame for his exploits over Kolpino, Ulyanovka, Sinyavino, Tosno, Krasnyj Bor and Vyborg (Viipuri). He scored for the first time on an unspecified date in August, 1941 when he made claims for two Bf 109s in an action on the outskirts of Leningrad following which he was able to build up a good score during the winter of 1941/42. He claimed another double on May 5, 1942 when Kapitan G.N. Zhidov's flight was flying a frontline patrol and they were engaged by lurking German fighters, three of these being shot down. He destroyed a Ju 88 over Mga (E Leningrad) on January 24, 1943 to bring his score to 13 and got another of these on September 3 which was victory number 22. He next reported the destruction of two Fw 190s near Sinyavino on the 15th by which time he had become a Kapitan and squadron leader. On June 30, 1944 Karpov had the distinction of destroying 2 GIAK's 1,000 enemy aircraft in the air which furthered his personal tally to 35 including fractional credits. He was shot down and killed on October 20, 1944. With his demise, Leningrad Front lost one of its most outstanding pilots.

KHARCHISTOV, Viktor Vladimirovich
Combat record: 10 personal victories, 367 sorties, 50 engagements.
Decorations: Gold Star of Hero of the Soviet Union on June 27, 1945; the Orders of Lenin, the Red Banner (2), Aleksandr Nevskij, the Patriotic War 1st Class.

Kharchistov was born in the Irkutsk area on December 11, 1918. He completed his pilot training at Ulyanovsk whereupon he was assigned as an instructor of Novosibirsk aeroklub. He entered military service in 1941 and from September engaged in heavy action during the brutal battles for Moscow while flying the Yak-1. He subsequently fought at Rzhev and in May, 1942 was decorated with the medal "For Valor" for 118 bombing missions in the U-2. He won his first Order of the Red Banner in recognition of 43 Il-2 escorts and one aerial victory in August, 1943 and a month later was awarded the Order of the Patriotic War 1st Class for 37 sorties and two more kills. He saw a great deal of action during the Byelgorod-Kharkov campaign claiming an Bf 109 near Gostishchevo (N Byelgorod) on July 7 and another of these on August 28 when 12 Yaks made contact with a gaggle of 20 Fw 190s and Bf 109s in the vicinity of Kovalenkovo. Two days later he added a further Bf 109 over Byelnkovka and subsequently took part in the operations against the enemy at Krasnograd, Poltava, Kremenchug, Dnyepropetrovsk, Kirovograd, Korsun-Shevchenkovskij, and Uman. In October, 1943 Kharchistov took over as leader of a fighter squadron with the rank of Kapitan. He then was assigned with 153 GIAP to the 2 VA flying sorties during the Yassy-Kishinyov campaign and over Sandomierz between May and September, 1944. On May 30 12 Yaks engaged 16 Fw 190s while escorting nine Il-2s and submitted claims for five enemy planes destroyed for no losses with Kharchistov getting a single. He achieved a further two kills during the Lemberg-Sandomierz fighting between July/August, 1944 and on September 14 bagged two Bf 109s in a scrap over Krosno. He was well qualified for a second Order of the Red Banner which was bestowed upon him in July and the Order of Aleksandr Nevskij in October. He completed 55 sorties over Krosno, Breslau (Wroclaw), Dresden and Berlin during the period of September 11, 1944 and May 9, 1945, 40 of which were to beat up ground targets, entering into four tussles with Luftwaffe aircraft and claiming three kills. Kharchistov returned to civilian life with the rank of Major in 1946 and passed away on January 14, 1982.

Yak-9T with the large caliber 37mm cannon which proved highly effective against tanks and bombers. One round could destroy a fighter or a light bomber, but the high G-forces experienced in combat often caused the weapon to jam. G.I. German of the 42 IAP is believed to be the leading exponent of the Yak-9T claiming a string of victories over Smolensk in 1943. (Author's collection)

KHARITONOV, Nikolaj Vasilyevich
Combat record: 16 personal victories, 300 sorties, 100 air-to-air combats.
Decorations: Gold Star of Hero of the Soviet Union on May 1, 1943 for 7 kills, 7 fractional credits, 197 sorties as of February, 1943; the Orders of Lenin, the Red Banner (2), Aleksandr Nevskij, the Patriotic War 1st Class (2), the Red Star.

Kharitonov was born in the Vladimir area on January 1, 1920 and enrolled for service in 1937. In 1940 he qualified as a pilot at Borisoglebsk military flying school and by June, 1941 had become a member of the 520 IAP in Byelorussia. During his combat career Kharitonov distinguished himself in the vicious fighting at Minsk, Vyazma, Stalingrad, Kursk, Orel, Byelgorod, Brest, Warsaw, Posen (Poznan) and Berlin. He excelled in the battles over Stalingrad where he scored a string of 12 kills to emerge as the regiment's highest scoring ace of the battle. Among his victories there was an He 111 which was destroyed on September 8, 1942. He was seriously wounded once, this occurring on April 14, 1945 when Kharitonov and his wingman, Boris Baranov, dove down to attack a superior enemy formation. They were able to send two bombers down on their first pass before they in turn were bounced by eight 109s who handled them roughly. While Baranov was able to nurse his crippled aircraft in safely at his own airfield, where he died of his wounds a short time later, Kharitonov bailed out but unfortunately was struck by the tailplane. Although in great pain he succeeded in opening his parachute before he collapsed. He woke up to find himself captured and tended by German soldiers but was liberated by armored elements of 2nd Byelorussian Front two weeks later. He remained in the ranks at the end of the war and graduated from the Air Force Academy in 1955. Five years later he was released from active duty with the rank of Polkovnik.

KHARLAMOV, Semyon Ilyich
Combat record: 17 personal victories, 6 fractional credits, 755 sorties, 147 encounters.
Decorations: Gold Star of Hero of the Soviet Union on February 23, 1945 for 4 personal victories, 2 fractional credits, 547 sorties, 85 encounters as of November, 1944; the Orders of Lenin, the Red Banner (5), Aleksandr Nevskij, the Patriotic War 1st Class, the Patriotic War 2nd Class, the Red Star (2).

Kharlamov was born in Saratov on April 30, 1921 and entered the Soviet Army in 1939. Upon qualifying as a pilot at Stalingrad military flying school in 1942, he was posted to the 249 IAP in the Kuban theater where he saw action for the first time in May. From then on Kharlamov was in continuous action over the Caucasus, the Kuban, at Taman, in the skies above the Crimea, Byelorussia, Poland and the Reich. He had trouble finding his shooting eye, and it was not until late in the war that he began to make his mark against the Luftwaffe. He eventually rose to squadron leader. During his postwar career he graduated from the Air Force Academy in 1955 and from the General Staff Academy six years later. He was promoted to General Polkovnik later and in 1985 he was serving as a deputy chairman of the DOSAAF Central Committee.

Starshij Lejtenant Ivan Ivanovich Khaustov, a successful pilot of the 21 IAP, with one of the regiment's La-5s on June 18, 1944. At this time Khaustov's score was 10 personal kills along with 12 fractional credits during about 400 sorties. It has not been possible to ascertain his final tally. (Author's collection)

KHIMICH, Fyodor Vasilyevich

Combat record: 13 personal victories, 4 fractional credits, 535 sorties, of which 100 were strafing ground targets.

Decorations: Gold Star of Hero of the Soviet Union on October 26, 1944; the Order of Lenin, the Red Banner (2), the Patriotic War 1st Class (2), the Patriotic War 2nd Class, the Red Star.

Khimich was born in the Kherson area on April 22, 1917 and enrolled for service in 1938. He was graduated as a pilot at Kacha military flying school a year later and entered combat with the Luftwaffe in July, 1941. He was able to put up a good performance as a flight leader in the 127 IAP, being credited with two kills during 122 sorties on West Front with the I-16 fighter during the fighting of 1941. He later converted to La-5s and gave a good account of himself in the great air battles at Stalingrad, Orel, Gomel, Bobrujsk, Lublin and Warsaw. He was promoted Major and appointed deputy commander of the 282 IAD being in the thick of the fighting during the latter stages of the war and over the Reich. Following the cessation of war Khimich graduated from the Air Force Academy in 1951 prior to his retirement as a Polkovnik in 1962.

A.S. Khlobystov, legendary Soviet fighter pilot. He performed three successful aerial rammings before being killed in action on December 13, 1943. (Author's collection)

KHLOBYSTOV, Aleksej Stepanovich

Combat record: 7 personal victories, 24 fractional credits, 335 sorties.

Decorations: Gold Star of Hero of the Soviet Union on June 6, 1942 after 4 kills, 6 fractional credits, 266 sorties and 16 air engagements as of April, 1942; the Orders of Lenin, the Red Banner (2).

Khlobystov was born in the Ryazan area on February 23, 1918 and entered military service at age 21. He won his wings at Kacha military flying school two years later and was assigned to the 20 IAP before the war. He was able to force down his first enemy plane on his very first sortie claiming a Ju 87 over the Karelian Isthmus on June 26, 1941, the fifth day of war. This was to be his only success for a while. He was to win fame for knocking down three enemy planes by deliberate ramming after being posted to the 147 IAP flying Kittyhawks. Soviet pilots were unanimous that the advent of the American fighter was no source of joy, as it did not have anything it could do better than the tried and tested Messerschmitt Bf 109. Morale in Kittyhawk units generally was below the zero point. In order to counteract the inferior performance of his aircraft, Khlobystov resorted to the extreme! On April 8, 1942 six of his squadron rose to intercept a formation of 15 Ju 87s and five Bf 110s. One of the 110s was badly shot up before eight Bf 109s streaked in. Khlobystov singled another 110 out for attack and chased it down to the deck but it simply refused to go down. He flew closer through the enemy's propwash and rammed the tailplane with one of his wings whereupon the 110 fell out of control and crashed. Khlobystov maintained effective control and rejoined formation with Kapitan A. Pozdnyakov and I. Fateyev to bounce the Stukas. One Ju 87 blew up and plunged earthward after their first attack while the others broke formation and dove away. Pozdnyakov was then seen to engage a Bf 109 head-on with both planes exploding in a mid-air collision as neither would waver. Khlobystov wound up with two more 109s on his tail but racked his ship around and struck the tailplane of one of these with his damaged wing. While breaking away Khlobystov observed his victim go down and explode, giving the pilot no chance of survival. In all, the Red fighters claimed the destruction of five planes including three by ramming. He performed a third successful TARAN on May 14, 1942 but on December 13, 1943 failed to return from a sortie. He was a Kapitan at the time of his death.

KHOLODOV, Ivan Mikhajlovich
Combat record: 26 personal victories, 400 sorties.
Decorations: Gold Star of Hero of the Soviet Union on March 4, 1942 for 6 kills, 225 sorties and 21 encounters as of February, 1942; the Orders of Lenin, the Red Banner (5), Suvorov 3rd Class, Aleksandr Nevskij, the Patriotic War 1st Class (2), the Red Star (2).

Kholodov was born in the Volgograd area on June 30, 1915 and entered military service in 1934. He completed his pilot training at Stalingrad military flying school three years later and gained his first combat experience during the Russo-Finnish Winter War of 1939/40. Before the Patriotic War he served in the 28 IAP and then saw a great deal of action during the great battles for the Soviet capital. On February 16, 1942 he was off on a front-line patrol with Lejtenant F.P. Glushko as his wingman and became embroiled in a dogfight with two Bf 109s near Zvenigorod, both of these being shot down in flames. Ten days later Kholodov and Mladshij Lejtenant N.Ye. Vorobyov combined forces to destroy a reconnaissance plane 23 SE Gzhatsk. He had been promoted Starshij Lejtenant and deputy squadron leader when he was recommended for the Gold Star award and was posted to the 32 GIAP with the rank of Kapitan shortly afterward. He flew with great distinction during subsequent aerial campaigns on Kalinin, Voronezh, Northwest, 1st and 4th Ukrainian Fronts. He claimed a Bf 109 on January 14, 1943 while leading eight Yak-1s in a scrap with 14 German fighters near Velikiye Luki. He added a Fw 190 over the Demyansk bridgehead on February 18 and then on March 6 successfully rammed a Bf 109 in an attempt to save his wingman Arkadij Makarov, safely bailing out of his own blazing aircraft. He performed well in the ferocious battles at Kursk, getting a Fw 190 on July 21 while leading 10 La-5s to engage 12 Luftwaffe fighters between Spasskoye-Somovo, five of these being claimed shot down. Eleven days later Kholodov made claims for two Ju 87s destroyed when eight La-5s under his leadership went after an unescorted formation of dive-bombers in the vicinity of Gorodok, four of these falling to their guns. He eventually assumed command of the 111 GIAP and finished the war as a Podpolkovnik in the skies of Berlin. Following World War II he continued on active duty with the VVS and wound up his military career with the rank of General Major in 1970 with 36 years service. He lives in Moscow.

KHOLZUNOV, Aleksej Ivanovich
Combat record: 12 personal victories, 265 sorties, 87 encounters.
Decorations: Gold Star of Hero of the Soviet Union posthumously on May 1, 1943; the Orders of Lenin, the Red Banner (2).

Kholzunov was born in the Saratov area on January 31, 1919 and entered the Soviet Army in 1938. He completed his pilot training at Engels military flying school a year later and was in action from the very first days of the war. He saw a great deal of action in the Volkhov area and then scored a string of seven air victories in the fury of the Stalingrad air engagements while serving with the 434 IAP. For his efforts he was promoted to deputy squadron leader and next took part in the operations over Kalinin but on March 7, 1943 he was shot down and killed while flying armed reconnaissance in the Yartsevo area (NE Smolensk).

KHRYAEV, Vasilij Ilyich
Combat record: 10 personal victories, 201 sorties, 56 engagements.
Decorations: Gold Star of Hero of the Soviet Union on October 23, 1942; the Orders of Lenin (2), the Patriotic War 1st Class.

Khryaev was born in the Moscow area in 1915 (or 1916 as suggested by another source) and enrolled for service in the VMF in 1936. He had his flight training at Yejsk military flying school and was posted to the 9 IAP of the Black Sea Fleet's air service before the war. He entered combat in June, 1941 and displayed his skills in the epic defense of Sevastopol. Khryaev was appointed squadron leader and in this capacity excelled, his squadron being credited with 71 enemy planes destroyed in the air. He eventually rose to Kapitan but on July 16, 1943 was killed in a melee with enemy fighters while engaged in escorting a formation of Il-2s.

KHUDOV, Pyotr Dmitriyevich
Combat record: 18 personal victories, 6 fractional credits, 235 sorties, 107 encounters.

Decorations: Gold Star of Hero of the Soviet Union on September 8, 1943 for 14 kills, 1 fractional credit, 71 sorties and 59 combats as of July, 1943; the Orders of Lenin, the Red Banner (3), the Patriotic War 1st Class, the Patriotic War 2nd Class, the Red Star.

Khudov was born in the Moscow area on December 23, 1918 and entered military service in 1940. He was graduated at Kacha military flying school a year later and was assigned to the 867 IAP in September, 1942 to start flying combat. From then on Khudov was in continuous action over the Volga, the Don, the Crimea, the Ukraine, the Vistula and ultimately, Berlin. He claimed a double with two Bf 109s on December 16, 1942 while leading a flight of Yak-1s in the Volkhov area, where combat occurred with 14 German fighters, six of these being shot down. He advanced to deputy squadron leader and converted to La-5s On July 9, 1943 Khudov and four of his squadron were assigned to fly a sweep out to the Donetsk area where they spotted two Ju 87s flying low on the deck towing gliders. Khudov flew in to point-blank range and started to pour fire into one enemy aircraft which blew apart to raise his score to 14. He then teamed with M.S. Konovalov, G.M. Muravitskij and A.G. Dolgov to destroy the second. On August 21, 1943 he was hit by groundfire and force-landed in enemy lines. He scrambled from the cockpit and ran for cover in nearby trees while enemy infantry was hurrying to the scene. He began walking towards the Soviet lines returning to his unit six days later. Khudov continued to score on a regular basis during subsequent combat assignments and finished in the battle for Berlin. He served with the postwar VVS until 1950 when he came off active duty with the rank of Major.

KISELYOV, Ivan Mikhajlovich

Combat record: 14 personal victories, 2 fractional credits, 156 sorties, 25 encounters.

Decorations: Gold Star of Hero of the Soviet Union on May 14, 1965; the Orders of Lenin, the Red Banner, the Patriotic War 1st Class (2).

Kiselyov was born in the Ryazan area on September 2, 1919 and started his military career in 1940. He completed his pilot training at Chernigov military flying school in Batajsk a year later and commenced his combat duty in November, 1943 when he joined the 274 IAP on 3rd Byelorussian Front. In mid-1944 the regiment was beginning to receive Yak-9Ks which were carrying a 45mm NS-P-45 hub mounted cannon for use against heavy tanks such as the Tiger and transport aircraft. He was flying one of these fighters on an unspecified date in August, 1944 when his squadron was having a tussle with enemy aircraft. Kiselyov destroyed a bomber but then sustained serious injuries when two shells from large caliber guns exploded in his cockpit. He evaded further attacks and managed to limb back to his own airfield near Kaunas where he made a successful landing before passing out as a result of his wounds. When he was picked up it was discovered that a shell had completely severed one of his legs which was lying on the cockpit's floor! Fitted with an artificial leg he rejoined his unit in May, 1945 before winding up his military career with the rank of Starshij Lejtenant in December that year. Soviet accounts conflict concerning his combat record one source suggesting 135 sorties and 26 combats. He died on April 6, 1987.

The Black Sea – stage for some of the toughest battles of World War II. This photo is dated April, 1942. (Author's collection)

KISLYAKOV, Anatolij Vasilyevich

Combat record: 17 personal victories, 539 sorties.

Decorations: Gold Star of Hero of the Soviet Union on August 18, 1945 in recognition of 15 victories, 532 sorties; the Orders of Lenin (2), the Red Banner (3), the Patriotic War 1st Class (2), the Patriotic War 2nd Class, the Red Star (2).

Kislyakov was born in the Moscow area on February 20, 1918 and entered military service at age 21. He was graduated as a pilot at Borisoglebsk military flying school a year later and was posted to the 153 IAP before the war. He scored for the first time on June 25, 1941 when he was on patrol over Ladoga Lake in an I-153 spotting a lone Finnish Fokker and shooting it down near Sortavala (N Ladoga Lake). He subsequently excelled in beating up enemy airfields around Tosno, Pushkino and Krasnoye Selo being credited with the destruction of 15 aircraft on the ground but in doing so was shot up by flak on four occasions and downed by fighters twice. He was appointed deputy commander of the regiment and deployed with it to the Stalingrad area. In a series of ferocious battles over the Volga he claimed six kills with Airacobras while the regiment was credited with downing 81 more. He next saw considerable fighting over the Demyansk bridgehead and on February 23, 1943 led a squadron to score seven air victories in a running battle with a superior enemy formation. Kislyakov flew his last sorties of the war over East Prussia in 1945. He remained in the ranks following World War II and graduated from the Air Force Academy in 1952. He concluded his active duty with the rank of Polkovnik in 1968.

Major A.V. Kislyakov was one of the stellar performers passing through the 28 GIAP. The date is March 6, 1945 by which time his score was 14 personal kills together with four fractional credits. (Author's collection)

Kapitan N.T. Kitayev, a noted 40 GIAP fighter ace. Kitayev fought against the Finns and later joined combat with the Luftwaffe in December, 1941. With eight kills, five fractional credits during 183 sorties on North Caucasus Front he met the requirements for the award of the title of Hero of the Soviet Union on May 1, 1943. He wound up with a total of 26 air victories coming off active duty as a Podpolkovnik in 1946. (Author's collection)

KIYANCHENKO, Nikolaj Stepanovich

Combat record: 17 personal victories, 4 fractional credits, 360 sorties, 46 encounters.

Decorations: Gold Star of Hero of the Soviet Union on June 27, 1945; the Orders of Lenin (3), the Red Banner (3), the Patriotic War 1st Class (2), the Red Star (2).

Kiyanchenko was born in the Kiev area on September 22, 1908 and enrolled for service in 1930. He first fired his guns in anger against the Japanese at Khasan Lake in the Far East between July/August, 1938 and later was sent to Kacha military flying school, graduating from flight training in 1940. He was able to gain his initial success on June 22, 1941, the very first day of the German-Soviet war, intercepting an He 111 which he had to chase for miles before it fell from the sky in flames. A few days later he forced down another of these in the vicinity of Minsk and had increased his tally to three when he was assigned to Leningrad Front at the end of the month. In November, 1942 he took over as leader of a fighter squadron in the 5 GIAP which was to run up 84 kills during 517 sorties and 201 clashes in eight months of combat with the La-5. In June, 1943 Kiyanchenko became deputy commander of the regiment and was to finish the war in command of the 106 GIAP as a Major. On April 2, 1945 he entered into his last combat with the Luftwaffe while leading a mission of 13 Yak-9s and mixed it up with 20 Fw 190s near Guben (NE Cottbus), where 10 enemy planes were claimed shot down. Kiyanchenko accounted for a single to bring his tally to 17. He served with the postwar VVS and retired with the rank of Polkovnik in 1958.

KLESHCHYOV, Ivan Ivanovich

Combat record: 16 personal victories, 32 fractional credits.

Decorations: Gold Star of Hero of the Soviet Union on May 5, 1942 for 6 personal victories, 13 fractional credits, 220 sorties, 30 combats as of March, 1942; the Orders of Lenin, the Red Banner (2), the Patriotic War 2nd Class.

Kleshchyov was born in the Voroshilovgrad area on January 26, 1918 and enlisted in the VVS for flight training in 1937. He had his baptism of fire fighting the Japanese along the Khalkhin Gol River in Mongolia in 1939 and flew with the 521 IAP as a squadron leader at the outbreak of the Patriotic War. He performed well in the dark months to follow on Kalinin Front and for his efforts was promoted Major. He assumed command of the 434 IAP shortly after being decorated with the Gold Star and developed into a masterful combat leader on many missions during the Battle of Stalingrad. On September

16, 1942 he was leading three flights to intercept a formation of 30 Ju 87s and their escorts and personally submitted claims for one each Ju 87 and Bf 109 destroyed. September 18 was a field day for the regiment with 19 enemy planes being blasted out of the sky, while 15 more were claimed the following day. On September 23 Kleshchyov was shot down and wounded by German fighters, being forced to take to his parachute but returned to his unit soon after. The regiment continued to exact a heavy toll from the attacking enemy formations but also began to experience heavy losses. During the period of September 14 to October 2 it was credited with 82 enemy planes in the air during 611 sorties but was down to one third of its original strength at the end of September. Kleshchyov met his untimely death on December 31, 1942 as a passenger of a transport plane that crashed enroute to Moscow. He was buried in Rasskazovo, SE Tambov.

KLIMANOV, Ivan Kirillovich
Combat record: 17 personal victories, 5 fractional credits, 284 sorties, 63 air engagements.
Decorations: Gold Star of Hero of the Soviet Union on February 23, 1945 for 16 kills, 5 fractional credits, 272 sorties, 60 encounters as of October, 1944; the Orders of Lenin, the Red Banner (3), Aleksandr Nevskij, the Patriotic War 1st Class, the Red Star.

Klimanov was born in the Ryazan area on August 18, 1923 and entered the Soviet Army in 1940. He won his pilot wings at Tbilisi military flying school the following year and in July, 1942 was posted to the 272 IAP in the Mozhajsk area flying LaGG-3s. He participated in the heavy air battles over Kozelsk a month later and by January, 1943 his score had risen to three kills which qualified him for the Order of the Red Star. In February he was promoted Mladshij Lejtenant and later was to enjoy considerable success in the air operations over Byelorussia, including Vitebsk and Polotsk. In early 1944 he was assigned to the La-5 equipped 49 IAP in the vicinity of Vitebsk and became engaged in the brutal fighting for Minsk and Grodno prior to taking part in the Soviet offensive in Poland. Klimanov remained in the ranks following the close of war and came off active duty as a Kapitan in 1953.

KLIMOV, Pavel Dmitriyevich
Combat record: 9 personal victories, 18 fractional credits, 306 sorties, 33 air-to-air combats.
Decorations: Gold Star of Hero of the Soviet Union on July, 24, 1943; the Order of Lenin, the Red Banner (3), the Patriotic War 1st Class (2), the Red Star (2).

Klimov was born in Baku on February 7, 1920 and enlisted in the VMF in 1939. He was graduated as a pilot at Yejsk military flying school two years later joining with the 2 GIAP-SF in January, 1942 to commence his combat duty. A little later he was in the public eye for achieving Northern Fleet's first nocturnal victory. Klimov gave a good account of himself while flying the Hawker Hurricane, claiming a triple with three Ju 87s in one interception sortie near Murmansk and added at least one further victory – a Bf 109 – before converting to Airacobras. Staying in the service after the war he graduated from the Air Force Academy in 1951 and from General Staff Academy in 1959. He was released from the service with the rank of Polkovnik in 1970.

KLUBOV, Aleksandr Fyodorovich
Combat record: 31 personal victories, 19 fractional credits, 467 sorties, 95 encounters.
Decorations: 1st Gold Star on April 13, 1944 in recognition of 14 victories, 19 fractional credits, 310 sorties, 84 engagements as of September, 1943, 2nd Gold Star posthumously on June 27, 1945 for 31 kills, 457 sorties, 95 combats as of October, 1944; the Orders of Lenin, the Red Banner (2), Aleksandr Nevskij, the Patriotic War 1st Class.

Klubov was born in the Vologda area on January 18, 1918 and began his brilliant career in the VVS in 1939. He completed his pilot training the following year at Chuguyev military flying school and entered combat on July 28, 1941 by which time he had become a member of the 10 IAP flying I-153s. He managed to make claims for a Ju 87 and an Bf 109 in one of his early encounters but was then badly wounded and out of action for several months. With his tally standing at four aerial victories plus 16 more destroyed in ground attacks during 150 sorties Klubov in May, 1943 was assigned to the glorious 16 GIAP. Under the tutelage of the great Aleksandr Pokryshkin he would run up a tremendous score in a series of vicious battles over Taman, Rostov and Novocherkassk requiring but 68 sorties and 28 combats to run his record to 14 in three months combat including four over the Kuban. One of his victims was a Bf 109 that he forced down near Slavyansk on July 13, 1943. On an unrecorded date he almost fell foul of a Messerschmitt whose pilot was his equal in every respect but finally managed to shake him off and turned for home to crashland his crippled P-39 on his own airfield. On one occasion he claimed a triple with three Ju 87s in the vicinity of Osipenko (W Yalta) and next excelled at Yassy where he chalked up nine kills with three more damaged within a week in June, 1944. He quickly rose to Kapitan and deputy squadron leader and eventually was appointed deputy regiment commander. He frequently flew an olive drab/neutral gray P-39N "White 45" with a red spinner. Klubov then participated in periods of intense activity during the Lemberg-Sandomierz campaign (July 13/August 29, 1944) and on July 16 bagged two Ju 87s while leading 12 Airacobras on a front-line patrol. On November 1, 1944 he crash-landed on return to base near Staleva-Volya in one of the new Lavochkin La-7s when his aircraft was carried away by a strong gust of wind. He was picked up immediately and taken to a hospital but died half an hour later. Klubov was admired and highly respected by his comrades; G. Golubev, a fellow 16 GIAP ace, provides the following recollection: "He was a cool and calculating leader, aggressive in the air, fast surprise attacks were his forte. He possessed a remarkable physique and stamina which combined with his great fighting spirit. He neither knew fear nor did he waver in the face of numerical enemy superiority. To take off on a mission with Klubov almost invariably meant success."

KNYAZEV, Vasilij Aleksandrovich
Combat record: 29 personal victories, 1,088 sorties, 139 encounters.
Decorations: Gold Star of Hero of the Soviet Union on August 24, 1943 for 11 victories, 9 fractional credits, 576 sorties as of June, 1943; the Orders of Lenin (2), the Red Banner (2), Aleksandr Nevskij, the Patriotic War 1st Class (2), the Red Star (2).

Knyazev was born in the Minsk area on January 9, 1920 and entered military service in 1938. He qualified as a pilot at Odessa military flying school two years later with his first assignment being to the 12 IAP in January, 1940. He then joined with the 88 IAP before the outbreak of the Patriotic War and was to see a great deal of action from the very first days of war. He was early in the public eye for forcing down a Ju 88 near Vinnitsa on June 23, 1941. He combined forces with Kubati Kardanov to destroy two Bf 109s on July 10 and nine days later teamed with Kardanov, Vasilij Kolesnik and an unidentified pilot to shoot down a Fw 189. On August 19 Knyazev was engaged in another patrol with Kardanov when they mixed it with two enemy planes identified as "He 113s" both of which went down in flames south of Dnyeprodzerzhinsk. On August 30 he was bounced by a German fighter in the Dnyepropetrovsk area and was obliged to carry out a force-landing. By the close of this year he had furthered his score to six kills, which possibly includes fractional credits. It is noteworthy that all of his victories were gained while flying the I-16 which was technically outclassed by all opposing Luftwaffe aircraft. He later converted to LaGG-3s and continued to prove his remarkable skills during the battles over the Northern Caucasus flying numerous missions. He was promoted Starshij Lejtenant and squadron leader and took part in the wild air battles along the Kuban in May, 1943 where he was credited with downing four enemy planes. Knyazev advanced to Kapitan in August, 1943 and during subsequent combat assignments gave a good account of himself over Novorossijsk, Taman, Kerch, Sevastopol and Byelorussia. He wound up as the regiment's highest scoring ace while his tremendous total number of sorties was to be surpassed by only one Soviet fighter pilot. He continued on active duty following the close of war winding up his military career with the rank of Polkovnik in 1962. He died on July 22, 1968.

Kapitan A.F. Klubov, pilot of surpassing willpower and courage. He drew first blood flying the I-153 biplane but really came into his own under the tutelage of Aleksandr Pokryshkin with Aeracobras. (Author's collection)

KOBYLETSKIJ, Ivan Ivanovich
Combat record: 15 personal victories, 9 fractional credits, 465 sorties, 95 encounters.
Decorations: Gold Star of Hero of the Soviet Union on May 15, 1946; the Orders of Lenin (2), the Red Banner (2), Aleksandr Nevskij, the Patriotic War 1st Class, the Red Star.

Kobyletskij was born in the Odessa area on August 10, 1916 and entered the Soviet Army in 1936. Two years later he was graduated as a pilot at Orenburg military flying school and saw action for the first time against the Japanese in China. He entered combat with the Luftwaffe in June, 1941 and during the dark months to follow was occupied primarily with reconnaissance missions completing 50 such sorties in the Kiev area alone. With two air victories he qualified for the award of the Order of Lenin and also won two Red Stars for his efforts during the dramatic battles of the 1941/42 air war. Kobyletskij had become a Starshij Lejtenant when he was posted to Stalingrad Front but no details have emerged. He eventually rose to Major and deputy commander of the 53 GIAP and flew with distinction on 1st Byelorussian Front. He served with the postwar VVS until September, 1948 when he retired with the rank of Podpolkovnik. He passed away on July 25, 1986.

KOCHETOV, Aleksandr Vasilyevich
Combat record: 34 personal victories, 8 fractional credits, 450 sorties.
Decorations: Gold Star of Hero of the Soviet Union on April 13, 1944 in recognition of 19 kills, 3 fractional credits, 262 sorties, 67 air-to-air combats as of October, 1943; the Orders of Lenin, the Red Banner (2), the Patriotic War 1st Class (3).

Kochetov was born in Alatyr (Chuvash ASSR) on March 8, 1919 and began his brilliant military career in 1938. He completed his pilot training at Engels military flying school two years later and gained his first combat experience with the 629 IAP on Southwest Front between June 22, 1941 and July 28, 1941 during which period he flew 83 sorties against great odds. He really came into his own after joining with the 43 IAP on Stalingrad Front on September 10, 1942. In a burst of energy and skill Kochetov was credited with downing five Ju 88s and two Bf 109s along with one fighter claimed jointly with fellow pilots during 105 sorties and 22 engagements until October 25. His best day was September 23 when he accounted for a double. He thus met the conditions for the award of the Order of the Patriotic War 1st Class and on April 18, 1943 was posted again this time moving with the regiment to North Caucasus Front. The skies above the Kuban saw a continuation of the fierce fighting. In this theater he was to claim the destruction of seven Bf 109s and one Ju 88 in the air during 45 sorties and 27 encounters qualifying him for the award of the Orders of the Red Banner and a second Patriotic War 1st Class. On June 3 he came within a hair of getting lost when he was bounced by four Messerschmitts having become separated from his squadron after encountering heavy flak. He reacted cooly and began to turn for his life. He throttled back as one 109 was closing in on him, forcing the German to overshoot, placing himself squarely in Kochetov's sight. It was all over in seconds, the 109 fell away in a spin and crashed. The demise of his comrade obviously disheartened the rest, who flew away! Kochetov left the front for a home leave and arrived on South Front on September 1, 1943 to add four more kills – two Ju 88s and two He 111s – along with shares in two enemy aircraft while flying 39 sorties and entering combat 18 times. He had by now become a Starshij Lejtenant and the regiment's highest-scoring ace. Under his decisive leadership his squadron had been credited with downing 15 Bf 109s, 12 Ju 87s, 11 Ju 88s and one each Bf 110, Hs 129, Fw 189, and Fw 190 during 672 sorties and 293 individual encounters; 10 locomotives, one tank and eight motor vehicles had been destroyed in ground attacks. Losses for the squadron were four pilots killed and six planes in air-to-air combat. Kochetov shortly afterward was promoted Kapitan and went on to score heavily in the subsequent air operations over Vitebsk, Poland and the Reich. He stayed in the service after the war rising to the rank of Major. In March, 1960 he returned to civilian life.

KOLDUNOV, Aleksandr Ivanovich
Combat record: 46 personal victories, 358 sorties – 194 of which were groundforce cover, 73 escorts, 50 reconnaissance, 10 scrambles, 30 ground attacks – for 373 combat hours, 96 encounters.
Decorations: 1st Gold Star of Hero of the Soviet Union on August 2, 1944 in recognition of 15 victories, 1 fractional credit, 223 sorties, 45 engagements as of May, 1944, 2nd Gold Star on February 23, 1948; the Orders of Lenin (3), the Red Banner (6), Aleksandr Nevskij, the Patriotic War 1st Class (2), the Red Star.

Koldunov, one of Russia's greatest fighter pilots and eighth ranking Allied ace of World War II, was born in the hamlet of Moshchinovo, Smolensk area, on September 20, 1923 and started his distinguished career in 1941. Two years later he completed his pilot training at Kacha military flying school cutting his combat teeth with the 866 IAP in June that same year. In his first combat sortie he was engaged in escorting Shturmoviks in a strafing attack on an airfield near Kramatorsk. On an unspecified date a short time later he was shot up by a Bf 109 in an action in the vicinity of Izyum, and was obliged to carry out a forced-landing in a cornfield. He was back in the air three days later beginning to chalk up victories at a formidable pace soon after. During the period of June 1, 1943 to February 11, 1945 Koldunov was credited with downing 31 enemy planes in the big air battles on Southwest and 3rd Ukrai-

Right: A.I. Koldunov, one of the most accomplished aces of the Eastern Front, seen here in a postwar photograph as a General Major. (Author's collection)

nian Fronts while conducting 296 combat sorties. With five kills to his credit he was appointed flight leader and on July 21, 1943 led an attack on 24 Ju 87s, three of these being shot down including a single by Koldunov. He perfected hit-and-run attacks from above and like most Russian or German high-scorers, closed right in before firing. His daring and aggressive style of flying and fighting quickly won him respect and admiration. By the spring of 1944 his score had risen to 20 air victories, and in time he was promoted Kapitan and squadron leader. He wrote a distinguished record on 3rd Ukrainian Front, and on May 4, 1944 was leading six Yaks that were tasked with covering a supply dropping mission to 23rd Armored Corps. Once over the front 16 Ju 87s were spotted forming up for an attack and in the ensuing melee Koldunov splashed two of them while his comrades got three more. He later was in the center of the fighting over Yugoslavia and Hungary, and on November 7, 1944 became inadvertently engaged with 15th USAAF Lightnings. On this particular day 60 fighters of the 82nd Fighter Group under the leadership of Colonel C.T. Edwinson were assigned to beating up ground targets along the roads from Sjenica to Novi Pazar, Raska and Mitrovica in Yugoslavia. Due to a navigational error they went down to attack General G.P. Kotov's Corps advancing towards Belgrade in the vicinity of Nisch (NW Sofia). A number of Russians including Kotov were killed before General V.A. Sudets, commander of the 17th Air Army, gave free reign to the alert flights of the 659 IAP which was based in the immediate vicinity. The Lightnings promptly turned into them shooting down one Yak. In the same time frame Koldunov's flight also rose trying to join formation with the Americans, but in an instant found themselves in a tough dogfight. The Russians lashed back and claimed to have shot down one P-38 that crashed onto the edge of the airfield while three more were reported to have fallen into the heart of the city. Koldunov, who reportedly accounted for three of these victories, then courageously closed into formation with the American leader and established mutual identification. The Americans admitted the loss of three fighters one of which was believed to have fallen to antiaircraft fire while five more sustained damage. Two Soviet pilots perished – Lejtenant Krivonogikh and Lejtenant Shipulin – while Lejtenant Zhestovskij was able to take to his parachute. Although more than 50 years since then have elapsed, Russian accounts on this incident have remained sketchy to this day. For a full American report see Appendix III. In late 1944 Koldunov was put in charge of forming a special duties squadron later known throughout the VVS as "gruppa po raschitske vozdukha" ("air cleanup group"). The unit was to focus on hunting down enemy aircraft in rear areas even in foul weather. Koldunov picked experienced and accomplished pilots such as Kapitan Shishov, Kapitan Sidorenko, Lejtenant Surnev, Lejtenant Shamanov and Lejtenant Guryev, and they were soon making their mark against the enemy, prowling over assigned areas as many as four times each day. In a very short time they submitted claims for 35 enemy planes in the air, 15 of these falling to Koldunov's guns. On November 22 four Yak-3s with Koldunov in the lead were tasked with covering the river crossing at Batino where they struggled with two gaggles of enemy fighters, Koldunov bagging two Fw 190s and one Bf 109 while his comrades got four more 190s and two 109s, all without loss. On December 9 he was ferrying to a new airfield in the vicinity of Tasar, where he spotted two Bf 109s attacking Il-2s on the ground. He immediately turned in behind them and bagged the first with a short burst. The other tried to race away just above the ground with the result that it crashed after taking two bursts. Koldunov then excelled in heavy action around Budapest and Vienna, running up a string of 22 kills between January 19 and April 13, 1945. It is possible that he encountered some of the leading Luftwaffe personalities there as JG 52 was mixing with the VVS during the same period over Hungary. On January 21, 1945 he claimed a double with two Bf 109s while leading six fighters to tackle with 18 Messerschmitts which were roaming about at high altitude in the area of Velencei Lake (SW Budapest), his squadron mates bringing the mission's tally to five, all without loss. On February 4 he was leading eight Yak-3s on a free hunt out to the Szekesfehervar area (SW Budapest) where they caught 12 Fw 190s approaching the frontline at tree-top level from behind. In a brief combat, three Fw 190s were destroyed, two by Koldunov, whose victims crashed in the vicinity of Bergend. He achieved another double on March 3 when eight of his squadron tore into a large gaggle consisting of 18 Fw 190 fighter-bombers escorted by 12 Bf 109s between Deg-Sarbogard (SW Budapest), six enemy planes going down before the Yaks' guns. Ten days later he reported the destruction of three Fw 190s while leading four Yaks to tie into three gaggles of 8-12 Fw 190s each escorted by 16 Messerschmitts. He claimed three Bf 109s for a change on the 17th when four Yaks tackled with an equal number of German fighters, all of these being knocked down. Koldunov closed out his scoring on an unspecified day in April, when he swept down on five unsuspecting Fw 190s while flying a free hunt in the St. Pölten area (E Vienna). When the fight was over, he had downed two of them. When hostilities ceased, Koldunov's squadron boasted a bag of 124 enemy planes in the air along with 107 motor vehicles and 71 horsedrawn vehicles destroyed in ground attacks during 2,139 sorties and 118 air combats. He stayed in the service to attain high rank with the VVS. In 1952 he graduated from the Air Force Academy and eight years later from General Staff Academy. In November, 1970 he took over as commander of Moscow air defense being promoted General Polkovnik a year later. Between 1978/87 he was commander in chief of the PVO defense forces with the rank of Marshal Aviatsii. He was in the public eye on September 1, 1983 when an Su-15 was tasked with intercepting a South Korean Airlines Boeing-747 over Sakhalin after this had strayed into Soviet air space, all 269 aboard perishing. When 19-year old German Mathias Rust on May 28, 1987 put his Cessna-172 down on Moscow's Red Square after dodging air defenses all the way from Helsinki, Koldunov took responsibility retiring two days later.

A.I. Koldunov's "nagradnoj list" can be found on the following four pages. This document recommended him for his second title of Hero of the Soviet Union, and as was common practice, there is a detailed outline of his exploits, his previous decorations, dates of birth, admission to the Communist party etc.; the list was forwarded by Podpolkovnik Chugunov, commander of the 866 IAP and successively approved by General Major Smirnov, commander of the 288 IAD, General Polkovnik Sudets, commander of the 17th Air Army and General Polkovnik Tsvetayev, deputy commander of Army Group South.

Вх № 019003

НАГРАДНОЙ ЛИСТ

1. Фамилия, имя и отчество – К О Л Д У Н О В Александр Иванович

2. Звание – Герой Советского Союза м а й о р.
3. Должность, часть – Командир эскадрилии 866 Истребительного Авиационного Измаильского ордена Суворова полка.

Представляется к званию Дважды ГЕРОЙ СОВЕТСКОГО СОЮЗА.

4. Год рождения – 1923г. 5. Национальность – Русский.
6. Партийность – Член ВКП/б/ с 1944 года.

7. Участие в гражданской войне, последующих боевых действиях по защите СССР и Отечественной войне / где, когда /– Участвовал в Отечественной войне с 1.6.1943 года по 8.5.1945 года на ЮЗФ и 3-м Украинском фронте.

8. Имеет ли ранения и контузии в Отечественной войне – Имеет одно легкое ранение в 1943 году.
9. С какого времени в Красной Армии – с 1941 года.
10. Каким РВК призван – Реутовским РВК Московской области.

11. Чем ранее награжден / за какие отличия /– орденом ЛЕНИНА и медалью "ЗОЛОТАЯ ЗВЕЗДА" – Указ Президиума Верховного Совета Союза ССР от 2.8.1944г., тремя орденами КРАСНОГО ЗНАМЕНИ – 9.1943г., 1.1944г., 4.1944г., орденом АЛЕКСАНДРА НЕВСКОГО – 9.44, орденом ОТЕЧЕСТВЕННАЯ ВОЙНА ПЕРВОЙ СТЕПЕНИ – 6.3.1945 года.

12. Постоянный домашний адрес представляемого к награждению и адрес его семьи. – гор. Москва, Соболевский проезд, дом №21, кв. 19.

I. Краткое, конкретное изложение личного боевого подвига или заслуг.

Участвовал в Отечественной войне в составе полка на ЮЗФ и 3-м Украинском фронте с 1.6.1943г. по 8.5.1945 года. За этот период проявил себя, как отличный организатор, смелый и отважный воздушный боец.

За период с 1.6.43 года по 8.5.45г. произвел лично триста пятьдесят восемь боевых вылетов с налетом триста семьдесят три часа. Из них: на прикрытие наземных войск сто девяносто четыре боевых вылета, на сопровождение штурмовиков и бомбардировщиков семьдесят три боевых вылета, на разведку войск противника пятьдесят боевых вылетов, на перехват самолетов противника десять боевых вылетов, на штурмовку войск противника тридцать один боевой вылет.

Участвовал в девяносто шести воздушных боях, в которых лично сбил сорок шесть самолетов противника. Штурмовыми действиями лично уничтожил: двадцать шесть автомашин, восемнадцать повозок и до ста семидесяти человек живой силы противника.

За этот период его эскадрилия произвела две тысячи сто тридцать девять боевых вылетов. В проведенных сто восемнадцати воздушных боях летным составом сбито сто двадцать четыре самолета противника. Штурмовыми действиями уничтожено: сто се[...] автомашин, семьдесят одна повозка с грузом, до восемьсот девяно[...] человек живой силы противника.

Майор КОЛДУНОВ за успешно проведенные двести девяносто шесть боевых вылетов и лично сбитые тридцать один самолет противника в период с I.6.43г. по II.2.45г. удостоин высшей правительственной награды звания Герой Советского Союза с вручением одновременно ордена ЛЕНИНА. Награжден тремя орденами КРАСНОГО ЗНАМЕНИ, орденом АЛЕКСАНДРА НЕВСКОГО, орденом ОТЕЧЕСТВЕННАЯ ВОЙНА ПЕРВОЙ СТЕПЕНИ.

При выполнении боевых заданий летал постоянно в качестве ведущего группы. Своим личным примером в воздушных боях показывал образцы храбрости, мужества и героизма. Благодаря отличного мастерства и выучки, обладая богатой техникой пилотирования на истребителе во всех воздушных боях постоянно выходил победителем. Летный состав, учась на личном примере своего командира, во всех воздушных боях постоянно захватывал инициативу в свои руки, заставляя противника часто превосходящего в количественном отношении пускаться в бегство с поля боя.

Участвуя в ожесточенных сражениях под Будапештом, в районе озера Балатон, в период уничтожения окруженной Будапештской группировки противника и в Венской наступательной операции провел ряд блестящих воздушных боев, с крупными группами истребителей и штурмовиков противника, сбивая в течении одного боя по 2-3 самолета противника. В этих боях сам лично не имел ни одного поражения.

Только за период с 19.1.45г. по 13.4.45г. провел двадцать девять воздушных боев, в которых лично сбил двадцать два самолета противника.

9 декабря 1944 года перелетая с аэродрома Лес на аэродром Тасар, в районе Капашвар, на самолете ЯК-3 с боевым распоряжением, при заходе на посадку, на аэродроме Тасар, заметил два МЕ-109, которые с бреющего полета стали штурмовать стоявшие на земле самолеты ИЛ-2. Произведя быстрый маневр, атаковал одного МЕ-109 и с первой же очереди сбил его. После этого сразу же обрушился на второго МЕ-109, который пытался удрать, перейдя на бреющий полет, двумя короткими очередями майор КОЛДУНОВ сбил и его. После боя, произвел посадку и своевременно доставил боевое распоряжение.

22 II.1944 года, прикрывая переправы в районе Батино в составе 4 ЯК-3, в двух воздушных боях сбил 2 ФВ-190 и одного МЕ-109, которые пытались штурмовать наземные войска в районе переправы. Ведомая им группа в этих двух воздушных боях сбила 4 ФВ-190 и 2 МЕ-109, не имея потерь своих самолетов.

21 января 1945 года, прикрывая наземные войска в районе озера Веленце, Ловашберень, в составе 6 ЯК-3, встретили в этом районе до 18 МЕ-109, патрулирующих на большой высоте. Зайдя со стороны солнца, майор КОЛДУНОВ со своей группой неожиданно атаковал противника. Группа МЕ-109, приняв организованно первую атаку, но в последствии чувствуя, что инициатива на стороне наших ЯК-3, по-одному и парами стали уходить из боя. Благодаря стремительным и дерзким действиям в этом бою майор КОЛДУНОВ взял инициативу в свои руки, несмотря на численное превосходство сил противника и вынудил его бежать с поля боя. В этом бою майор КОЛДУНОВ лично сбил два МЕ-109. Его группа, не имея потерь, сбила в общем итоге три МЕ-109.

4 Февраля 1945 года, прикрывая наземные войска, в районе Секешфехервар, встретили 12 ФВ-190, которые с бреющего полета пытались штурмовать наземные войска. Майор КОЛДУНОВ оставив 4 ЯК-3 для прикрытия, парой атаковал группу ФВ-190. Самолеты противника, сбросив бомбы в поле, в беспорядочном строю стали уходить на свою территорию. Майор КОЛДУНОВ ведя бои на бреющем со второй атаки сбил один ФВ-190. Преследуя отходящего противника сбил еще одного ФВ-190, которые упали в районе

гор. Секешфехервар и населенного пункта Бергенд.

13.3.1945 года майор КОЛДУНОВ вылетал в составе 4-х ЯК-3 на прикрытие наземных войск в районе Цеце, Шар-Егреш, в этом районе встретили 3 группы по 8-12 ФВ-190 в каждой, идущих под прикрытием до 16 МЕ-109 штурмовать наши наземные войска. Несмотря на численное превосходство противника, с группой вступили в бой. В результате боя противник беспорядочно сбросил бомбы не доходя до цели. В этом бою майор КОЛДУНОВ лично сбил 2 ФВ-190.

17.3.1945г. прикрывая наземные войска в районе Варполота Веспрем в составе 4-х ЯК-3, встретили 4 МЕ-109. Встретив их, навязал бой, майор КОЛДУНОВ дерзкими и молниеносными атаками связал боем группу МЕ-109, не дав им уйти с поля боя. В этом бою все 4 МЕ-109 были сбиты, майор КОЛДУНОВ лично сбил 3 МЕ-109.

За отличное выполнение боевых заданий командования и проявленные при этом храбрость, мужество и высокое мастерство, при ведении воздушных боев, за отличную организацию боевых действий эскадрилии, за произведенные триста пятьдесят восемь успешных боевых вылетов и лично сбитые сорок шесть самолетов противника, достоин высшей правительственной награды звания ДВАЖДЫ ГЕРОЙ СОВЕТСКОГО СОЮЗА.

КОМАНДИР 866 ИСТРЕБИТЕЛЬНОГО АВИАЦИОННОГО
ИЗМАИЛЬСКОГО ордена СУВОРОВА ПОЛКА
ПОДПОЛКОВНИК:- /ЧУГУНОВ/

12 Июня 1945 года.

---

2. Заключение вышестоящих начальников.

Достоин высшей правительственной награды присвоения зва[ния] ДВАЖДЫ ГЕРОЙ СОВЕТСКОГО СОЮЗА.

КОМАНДИР 288 ИСТРЕБИТЕЛЬНОЙ АВИАЦИОННОЙ
ПАВЛОГРАДСКО-ВЕНСКОЙ КРАСНОЗНАМЕННОЙ
ордена СУВОРОВА ДИВИЗИИ
ГЕНЕРАЛ-МАЙОР АВИАЦИИ
/СМИРНОВ/

"30" Июня 1945 года.

---

3. Заключение Военного Совета Армии

Достоин высшей правительственной награды присвоения звания ДВАЖДЫ ГЕРОЙ СОВЕТСКОГО СОЮЗА.

КОМАНДУЮЩИЙ 17 ВОЗДУШНОЙ АРМИИ
ГЕНЕРАЛ-ПОЛКОВНИК АВИАЦИИ
/СУДЕЦ/

"26" Сентября 1945 года.

1. Заключение Военного Совета Фронта.

Достоин высшей правительственной награды присвоения звания ДВАЖДЫ ГЕРОЙ СОВЕТСКОГО СОЮЗА

ЗАМЕСТИТЕЛЬ ГЛАВНОКОМАНДУЮЩЕГО ЮЖНОЙ ГРУППЫ ВОЙСК
ГЕНЕРАЛ-ПОЛКОВНИК
/ЦВЕТАЕВ/

ЧЛЕН ВОЕННОГО СОВЕТА ЮЖНОЙ ГРУППЫ ВОЙСК
ГЕНЕРАЛ-ЛЕЙТЕНАНТ
/ЛАЙОК/

"1" октября 1945 года.

Указом Президиума Верховного Совета СССР от 23.02.1948 г. награжден второй медалью "Золотая Звезда".

ОСНОВАНИЕ: ЦАМО РФ, ф.33, оп.I70415сс, д.I8, л.5I.

Копия верна: ЗАВ.АРХИВОХРАНИЛИЩЕМ (БРИЛЕВ)

KOLESNICHENKO, Stepan Kalinovich
Combat record: 16 personal victories, 4 fractional credits, 114 sorties, 24 encounters.
Decorations: Gold Star of Hero of the Soviet Union on September 2, 1943; the Orders of Lenin, the Red Banner, the Red Star.

Kolesnichenko was born in Grigoriopol on December 24, 1913 and entered the Soviet Army in 1935. He received his pilot wings at Odessa military flying school in 1942 being posted to the 519 IAP on West Front on April 23. He was not slow to get started and in only 12 aerial encounters claimed the destruction of four Bf 109s along with two Ju 88s, one each Bf 109 and Bf 110 claimed as damaged during 65 sorties up to October 30, 1942. Kolesnichenko next scored heavily after moving with the regiment to Central Front in April, 1943. In a burst of energy and skill he added eight Fw 190s, two Bf 110s and one each Ju 88 and Ju 87s together with two Ju 88s and an He 111 that were claimed jointly with fellow pilots during 49 sorties and but 12 air-to-air encounters. In the same time frame he claimed four more Fw 190s destroyed in ground attacks. He had a big day on May 16 when 15 Yak-7Bs rose from Shchigry (E Kursk) to engage 24 Bf 110s and six Fw 190s headed for the regiment's own airfield. In the ensuing melee Kolesnichenko accounted for two Bf 110s and a Fw 190. He got another triple with two Fw 190s and a Ju 88 on July 6 when four Yaks hurtled down on 20 Fw 190s and 15 Ju 88s near Yasnaya Polyana (SW Tula), five German planes being claimed shot down. Two days later he was flying a free hunt in the vicinity of Olkhovatka (NW Rossosh) where two Fw 190s were seen working with a Yak-1. He dove to the rescue but was too late to stop them from shooting down the Russian who reportedly was then strafed whilst helpless in his parachute. Kolesnichenko delivered an attack from underneath and closed in to point-blank range before firing. The enemy pilot failed to notice him and had no time to get out when Kolesnichenko's blast hit him. Kolesnichenko was killed in action on August 30 – or September 2 as suggested by another source – and was buried in the village of Beryoza, Sumy area. He was a Lejtenant at the time of his death.

KOLESNIK, Vasilij Artemyovich
Combat record: 8 personal victories, 13 fractional credits, 462 sorties, 106 encounters.
Decorations: Gold Star of Hero of the Soviet Union on August 24, 1943; the Orders of Lenin (2), the Red Banner (4), Aleksandr Nevskij, the Patriotic War 1st Class, the Red Star.

Kolesnik was born in the Kharkov area on July 5, 1914 and enrolled for service in 1936. He completed his pilot training in 1939 and entered combat right after the German invasion of Soviet Russia in June, 1941. He flew with the 88 IAP and was able to open his account on August 28, 1941 when he forced

Close-up of a derelict Bf 109 of an unidentified unit after being forced down in Soviet territory. Although the Fw 190 had superior level speed and firepower most Russian high-scorers felt that the Bf 109 was the more formidable opponent. (Author's collection)

down a Bf 109 near Dnyepropetrovsk. He became greatly involved in the battles over the North Caucasus and on August 19, 1942 sustained serious injuries in an encounter with Bf 109s NE Nalchik. He was off operations until late 1942 and next participated in the air operations along the Kuban in May, 1943. He had by now become a Kapitan flying the LaGG-3 fighter and on May 29 was leading six of these to engage 70 bombers and 20 fighters, five enemy planes being claimed destroyed for no losses. In August, 1943 he was promoted Major and in November, 1943 took command of the 805 IAP. Kolesnik served with the postwar VVS and graduated from the General Staff Academy in 1956. He wound up his military career with the rank of General Lejtenant in 1973 with 37 years service.

KOLOGRIVOV, Mikhail Mikhajlovich
Combat record: 10 personal victories, 2 fractional credits, 583 sorties, 130 encounters.
Decorations: Gold Star of Hero of the Soviet Union on November 5, 1944; the Orders of Lenin, the Red Banner (3), Aleksandr Nevskij, the Red Star.

Kologrivov was born in Kokshajsk, Zvenigovo area, on November 19, 1919 and enlisted in the VMF in 1937. Two years later he was graduated as a pilot at Yejsk military flying school and was assigned to the 8 IAP of the Black Sea Fleet's air service before the outbreak of the Patriotic War. During his time with the regiment he was to fight over Odessa, Sevastopol, the Caucasus and Rumania. He flew with distinction during the darkest hours of war completing 372 sorties for 478 combat hours up to June, 1942 entering into 67 air engagements with enemy aircraft. He achieved good results while being occupied with ground targets and during the month of December, 1941 alone he was credited with destroying three tanks, 12 motor vehicles and four antiaircraft guns in the vicinity of Perekop. On March 20, 1942 Kologrivov and four of his squadron fought a pitched battle with seven Bf 109s coming away with no less than six kills. He came under attack of four Bf 109s on April 9, 1943 after he had become detached from his squadron. By continually turning and firing he managed to shoot down two of his assailants before breaking clear. In May, 1943 he took over as leader of a fighter squadron, and under his leadership the outfit was to run up 22 kills during 923 sorties till June, 1944. He scored well after converting to Yak-9s getting a Bf 109 near Kerch on January 23, 1944 and another of these on February 10. He was promoted Kapitan and claimed a further Messerschmitt on April 4. Following World War II Kologrivov continued on active duty graduating from the Air Force Academy in 1955. Two years later he was released from the service by which time he had become a Podpolkovnik. He died on July 16, 1964.

Wrecked German aircraft at a base near Rostov-on-Don in February, 1943. Here a main Soviet thrust ("Operation Rostov") involving forces of South Front (General Polkovnik A.I. Yeremenko, as of February 2, 1943 General Lejtenant P.Ya. Malinovskij) cut deep wedges into the German front of Armeeabteilung Hollidt and Heeresgruppe Don (v.Manstein) between January 1 - February 18, 1943. (Author's collection)

KOLOMIN, Pyotr Ivanovich
Combat record: 16 personal victories, 7 fractional credits, 326 sorties, 75 encounters.
Decorations: Gold Star of Hero of the Soviet Union on August 18, 1945; the Orders of Lenin (2), the Red Banner (2), Suvorov 3rd Class, Aleksandr Nevskij, the Patriotic War 1st Class, the Red Star (2).

Kolomin was born in Dimitrovgrad, Ulyanovsk area, on December 28, 1910 and entered military service in 1931. He qualified as a pilot and an observer at Orenburg military flying school two years later and gained his first combat experience during the Soviet-Finnish Winter War of 1939/40. Kolomin entered combat with the Luftwaffe in June, 1941 when he was flying I-16s in the 162 IAP in the Bryansk area. During his combat career he successively flew MiG-3s, Yak-7Bs and Yak-3s seeing considerable fighting at Smolensk between August-September, 1943 and over Byelorussia in 1944. He eventually assumed command of the regiment and was a Podpolkovnik at the end of the war. He came off active duty in 1947 and is living in Kujbyshev.

KOLOMIYETS, Pyotr Leontyevich
Combat record: 18 personal victories, 400 sorties.
Decorations: Gold Star of Hero of the Soviet Union on November 5, 1944 for 13 kills, 118 sorties and 38 encounters as of October, 1944; the Orders of Lenin (2), the Red Banner (2), the Red Star.

Kolomiyets was born in the Chernigov area in 1917 and enlisted in the VMF for flight training in 1936. He had his flight training at Yejsk and started flying combat in January, 1942 when he joined with the 2 GIAP-SF. He was destined to become one of the greatest aces of the Northern Fleet's air service and eventually rose to command a squadron of Airacobras. Under his leadership the outfit was credited with 45 enemy planes in the air during 763 sorties from March, 1943 until October, 1944. He gave a good account of himself during the Petsamo(Pechenga)-Kirkenes campaign (October 7-29, 1944) and advanced to Kapitan. He remained in the VVS following World War II and graduated from the Air Force Academy in 1949. He retired with the rank of Podpolkovnik five years later and died on December 24, 1974.

KOLOMOYETS, Vasilij Nikolayevich
Combat record: 16 personal victories, 1 fractional credit, 365 sorties of which 106 were armed reconnaissance, 133 escorts, 116 air patrols, 10 ground attacks, and 67 air encounters.
Decorations: Gold Star of Hero of the Soviet Union on February 23, 1945; the Orders of Lenin, the Red Banner (2), Aleksandr Nevskij, the Patriotic War 1st Class, the Red Star (2).

Kolomoyets was born in the Dnyepropetrovsk area on November 30, 1918 and started his military career at age 21. He completed his pilot training at Kacha military flying school a year later and was posted to the 162 IAP on Kalinin Front as a flight leader on February 10, 1942. He scored a double with two Ju 88s on October 12, 1943 while leading six La-5s in an attack on 12 bombers escorted by six Bf 109s near Bayevo. Fifteen days later he added a single when four La-5s were headed out on a free hunt and got into three separate encounters with a total of 40-plus Ju 87s, three of these being shot down in flames. Kolomoyets saw a great deal of action during the aerial campaigns over Byelorussia in 1944 claiming five kills during 94 sorties in the areas of Mogilyov, Minsk and Grodno. He finished as a Kapitan and squadron leader in the 49 IAP in the final clashes over Berlin. He remained in the VVS at the conclusion of the war and graduated from the Air Force Academy in 1950. He left active duty with the rank of Polkovnik in 1957 and passed away on October 12, 1986.

KOLTSOV, Aleksej Ivanovich
Combat record: 14 personal victories, 6 fractional credits, 222 sorties, 60 encounters as of April, 1943.
Decorations: Gold Star of Hero of the Soviet Union on September 2, 1943; the Orders of Lenin, the Red Banner, the Patriotic War 1st Class, the Red Star.

Koltsov was born in Voronezh on September 14, 1917 and entered military service in 1936. He completed his pilot training at Borisoglebsk military flying school a year later and entered combat right after the German attack on Soviet Russia flying I-16s on West Front. He later converted to La-5s and took part in the ferocious fighting at Stalingrad. He claimed a double on an unspecified date taking off in the lead of nine Lavochkin fighters to intercept a formation of 38 bombers and four escorts, seven of the enemy planes being shot down. He was promoted Major and next was put in command of the 937 IAP deploying with the unit to Bryansk Front. The regiment made a significant contribution at Kursk while being tasked with conducting Il-2 escort, ground force cover and interdiction of enemy airfields. During the period of July 12 and August 10, 1943 it afforded 667 sorties which encountered 312 enemy bombers and 191 fighters the pilots making claims for 37 of the former and 32 of the latter. On November 7, 1943 the unit was ordered off to strafe a German airfield where nine parked planes were shot up before several Bf 109s streaked in to do battle. In the ensuing melee Koltsov shot down one of them but in turn was bounced by another crashing to his death southeast of Vitebsk.

KOLYADIN, Viktor Ivanovich
Combat record: 16 personal victories, 685 sorties including 500 ground attacks, 56 air patrols, 25 escorts, 4 armed reconnaissance.
Decorations: Gold Star of Hero of the Soviet Union on June 26, 1945; the Orders of Lenin (2), the Red Banner (6), the Patriotic War 1st Class (2), the Red Star.

Kolyadin was born in the Voroshilovgrad area on June 2, 1922 and entered the Soviet Army in 1938. He won his wings at Voroshilovgrad military flying school three years later and was assigned to the 68 GIAP on Northwest Front in March, 1942 to commence his combat duty. He was with the regiment through World War II seeing considerable action on 1st Baltic and 3rd Byelorussian Fronts. He eventually advanced to Starshij Lejtenant and took over as leader of a fighter squadron. He enjoyed considerable success in the air battles over Vitebsk and Polotsk claiming nine kills while flying Airacobras during 85 sorties and 17 air-to-air combats between June 22 and September 18, 1944. Kolyadin later added two aerial victories over the Samland (East Prussia). His highest scoring period was from June 22, 1944 until April 19, 1945 when he submitted claims for 15 enemy aircraft destroyed in 185 sorties and 30 encounters. He served with the postwar VVS and graduated from the General Staff Academy in 1966. He retired with the rank of General Major seven years later and is living in Sevastopol.

KOMARDINKIN, Konstantin Petrovich
Combat record: 19 personal victories, plus 3 more destroyed in ground attacks. *Decorations*: Gold Star of Hero of the Soviet Union on November 1, 1943; the Orders of Lenin, the Red Banner, the Patriotic War 1st Class and 2nd Class.

Major M.S. Komelkov, a brilliant officer and pilot of the 104 GIAP. He was honored with the title of Hero of the Soviet Union for his exploits on 1st Ukrainian Front on June 27, 1945. His final tally of 32 personal victories includes five over Yassy in a seven day period. (Author's collection)

Komardinkin was born in the Moscow area in 1918 and enlisted in the VVS for flight training in 1938. He qualified as a pilot at Engels military flying school a year later and became a member of the 274 IAP in April, 1943. He entered combat in the Kuban theater and while flying the Yak-9 destroyed his first enemy aircraft in the air on the 29th. Eight days later he claimed a double with one each Ju 87 and Bf 109 when six Yaks with Starshij Lejtenant V.V. Klimov routed an enemy formation near Krymskaya, 10 Luftwaffe planes being claimed destroyed. Komardinkin shot down two more Ju 87s while flying a sweep out to the same area on May 11 but he was then engaged by fighters and badly shot up forcing him to crash-land on return to base. He had furthered his tally to 6 in 36 sorties and 15 engagements when he was assigned to South Front flying Yak-1s. Victories came thick and fast and he required only 20 encounters to amass 12 more kills during 54 sorties for which he was promoted to Starshij Lejtenant and deputy squadron leader. In April, 1944 he advanced to Kapitan and participated in the air battles over the Crimea but failed to return from a sortie on the 17th. He was last seen tackling with several Fw 190s and is presumed to have fallen victim to one of the fighters.

KONDRASHYOV, Aleksandr Petrovich
Combat record: 15 personal victories, 100 sorties, 35 encounters.
Decorations: Gold Star of Hero of the Soviet Union on July 1, 1944; the Orders of Lenin, the Red Banner (3), Aleksandr Nevskij, the Patriotic War 2nd Class (2), the Red Star (2).

Kondrashyov was born in the Podolsk area on December 25, 1921 and started his military career in 1941. He completed his pilot training at Kacha military flying school a year later following which he joined with the 875 IAP as a Starshij Lejtenant in October. He made his mark two months later when he was participating in the ferocious fighting at Velikiye Luki. He subsequently developed into a capable fighter pilot taking part in the air operations on Northwest, Bryansk, 1st and 2nd Baltic, 1st and 3rd Byelorussian Fronts. He gained a large number of his kills flying the Yak-7B and was successful in achieving at least one victory during the Battle of Kursk, this occurring on July 12, 1943. He later rose to Kapitan and deputy squadron leader in the 66 GIAP, closing out his scoring in the skies of Berlin in April, 1945. Kondrashyov remained in the VVS following World War II advancing to Polkovnik. He returned to civilian life in 1960 and died on December 20, 1982.

KONOBAYEV, Vasilij Sergeyevich
Combat record: 18 personal victories, 2 fractional credits.
Decorations: Gold Star of Hero of the Soviet Union on April 13, 1944; the Orders of Lenin, the Red Banner, the Patriotic War 1st Class, the Red Star.

Konobayev was born in Dnyepropetrovsk on August 15, 1921 and entered the Soviet Army in 1940. Two years later he was graduated at Kacha military flying school prior to commencing his combat duty in March. He claimed a victory at Stalingrad but was himself shot down and badly wounded. Following his recovery he was assigned to the 291 IAP in the spring of 1943 and achieved a high level of success in the fury of the Kuban air engagements. He ran up a string of 17 victories along with two fractional credits during 56 sorties and 35 aerial engagements between April 20 and June 3, 1943. On May 5 six Yaks were engaged in providing ground force cover for elements of the 328th Rifle Division when they had a tussle with 20 Ju 87s escorted by 12 Bf 109s. Konobayev and his wingman successfully evaded the escorts and went through the bomber formation with two of these falling to the guns of Konobayev. He then rejoined the rest of his flight and combined forces with his comrades to send down two Bf 109s. On September 18, 1943 he was shot down crashing to his death near Malaya Tokmachka (SE Zaporozhye).

KONONENKO, Nikita Nikiforovich
Combat record: 15 personal victories, 9 fractional credits, 169 sorties, 52 encounters.
Decorations: Gold Star of Hero of the Soviet Union on May 15, 1946; the Orders of Lenin, the Red Banner (3), Aleksandr Nevskij, The Patriotic War 1st Class (2), the Red Star.

Kononenko was born in the Sumy area on April 16, 1922 and entered military service in 1940. He received his wings at Chuguyev military flying school later that year and in 1943 attended advanced training for navigators (shturmanov). He was assigned to a unit of the front reserves at Stalingrad prior to joining with the 297 IAP in February, 1943. He managed to put up a good performance during the Byelgorod-Kharkov campaign and at Sumy and Poltava, claiming a string of nine aerial victories with the La-5 fighter. Kononenko's big day was August 10, 1943 when the regiment was having a field day near Lozovaya. In all, 20 enemy planes were shot down with Kononenko accounting for a single and also sharing in eight more with fellow pilots. He was promoted Kapitan and on October 1 was leading nine La-5s to storm into a formation of 40 bombers escorted by 10 Bf 109s between Borodayevka and Domotkan (SE Kremenchug). In a running battle nine enemy aircraft were claimed destroyed. Kononenko's share – a single victory. He gained a double on an unspecified day during the Yassy-Kishinyov campaign (August 20-29, 1944) as his squadron destroyed 13 more. The regiment reequipped with La-7s a short time later and after the working up was completed Kononenko was successful in bagging one of the unit's first air victories with the new mounts on January 22, 1945. On that day he was leading a free hunt of six La-7s out to Budapest where they engaged four Bf 109s one of which he immediately shot down. He completed his last mission of the war – an escort to Prague – on May 9, 1945. His skill and courage have largely contributed to the high efficiency of his squadron which had been credited with downing 80 enemy planes. He remained in the ranks at the close of war and retired as a Polkovnik in 1965.

KONSTANTINOV, Anatolij Ustinovich
Combat record: 19 personal victories, 294 sorties, 90 encounters.
Decorations: Gold Star of Hero of the Soviet Union on May 15, 1946; the Orders of Lenin (2), the Red Banner (4), Aleksandr Nevskij, the Patriotic War 1st Class (2), the Patriotic War 2nd Class, the Red Star (2).

Konstantinov was born in Moscow on June 12, 1923 and started his military career at age 17. He completed his pilot training at Tbilisi military flying school in 1941 and started flying combat in August, 1942 while serving in the 85 GIAP. He eventually rose to Kapitan and squadron leader and wrote a distinguished record in the skies above 2nd Ukrainian Front. On

October 21, 1944 he led six Yak-1s against a gaggle of 30 enemy aircraft in the Bekescsaba area (SE Budapest) and personally accounted for a Fw 190. Konstantinov continued on active duty with the VVS following World War II rising to high positions. In 1964 he graduated from the General Staff Academy and commanded the Baku PVO between 1973-80 and Moscow PVO between 1980-87. He rose to Marshal Aviatsii in 1985.

Kapitan V.F. Korobov of the 34 IAP-PVO standing by his Yak. His score is quoted as 18 air victories over the approaches to Moscow though it seems likely that this in fact denotes the sum of his personal and shared victories. (Author's collection)

KORNIYENKO, Ivan Mikheyevich
Combat record: 24 personal victories.
Decorations: Gold Star of Hero of the Soviet Union on September 2, 1943 in recognition of 14 kills during 225 sorties as of August, 1943; the Orders of Lenin, the Red Banner (3), Aleksandr Nevskij, the Patriotic War 1st Class.

Korniyenko was born in the Rostov area on December 21, 1917 and enlisted in the VVS for flight training in 1938. He was graduated as a pilot at Borisoglebsk military flying school a year later and was in the forefront of action from December, 1941. He enjoyed considerable success in the heavy air battles on Steppe Front while flying in the crack 270 IAP. On August 4, 1943 Korniyenko was engaged in escorting a formation of Il-2s when they came under attack of 12 Bf 109s near Byelgorod. In the ensuing melee four enemy fighters were claimed destroyed with Korniyenko accounting for two of them. He went on to score a total of 11 aerial victories during the battles of Byelgorod-Kharkov (August 323, 1943). He remained in the ranks at the end of the war but was killed on March 17, 1948 the circumstances not being known.

Starshij Lejtenant K.I. Korshunov, a squadron leader in the 29 GIAP, with his Yak on Karelian Front in 1944. He excelled on Leningrad Front meeting the requirements for the award of the title of Hero of the Soviet Union on February 4, 1944. His final score was at least 15 personal kills. (Author's collection)

KOROLYOV, Vitalij Ivanovich
Combat record: 21 personal victories, 10 fractional credits, 435 sorties, 97 encounters.
Decorations: Gold Star of Hero of the Soviet Union on June 27, 1945; the Orders of Lenin, the Red Banner (3), the Red Star (2).

Korolyov was born in Bogolyubovo (N Kazakhstan) on May 5, 1916 and entered the Soviet Army in 1935. He completed his pilot training at Stalingrad military flying school three years later and fought from the very start of the Great Patriotic War. He made a brilliant war record on 1st Ukrainian Front and was to finish the war with the rank of Kapitan and deputy commander of the 482 IAP. He was a phenomenal shot and displayed his skills largely on free hunts later in the war. Usually two fighter elements – known as "okhotnikov" (hunters) – would prowl over assigned areas to destroy enemy aircraft or targets of opportunity such as command posts, bridges, locomotives or even lone motor vehicles on their initiative. On one such mission Korolyov and his wingman became embroiled in a dogfight with 20 Fw 190s, two of them being destroyed by Korolyov. Figures concerning his final record vary. One source, A.F. Semyonov "Na vzlete" p.180, suggests 558 sorties and 90 engagements. Korolyov served with the postwar VVS retiring with the rank of Polkovnik in 1957.

KOSOLAPOV, Filipp Markyevich (or Makarovich)
Combat record: 17+ personal victories.
Decorations: Gold Star of Hero of the Soviet Union on September 2, 1943 for 8 personal victories, 6 fractional credits, 107 sorties, 25 encounters as of August, 1943; the Orders of Lenin, the Red Banner, Kutuzov 3rd Class, Aleksandr Nevskij, the Patriotic War 1st Class, the Red Star (2).

Kosolapov was born in Volkovo (Bashkir ASSR) on January 9, 1919 and started his military career at age 19. He completed his pilot training at Chkalov military flying school in 1940 and was posted to the 2 GIAP in September, 1942 to start flying combat against the Luftwaffe. He quickly displayed outstanding leadership and tactical skill. On January 27, 1943 he led six La-5s to take on a formation of 21 German aircraft with three Ju 87s and two Messerschmitts being shot down. For his efforts he rapidly advanced to squadron leader and later took command of the 937 IAP. By February, 1945 Kosolapov had become a Podpolkovnik and on an unspecified date during that month scrambled to intercept two Fw 190s approaching the regiment's airfield near Sorau (SE Cottbus). He immediately made contact with the enemy fighters and shot one of them down which crashed at the edge of the airfield for his 17th kill. According to Soviet accounts the German was an Oberst and Knight's Cross holder but unfortunately no further details have emerged. Kosolapov remained in the VVS after the war and graduated from the Air Force Academy in 1955. He came off active duty two years later when he was a Polkovnik.

G.D. Kostylev poses with his steed of war carrying his impressive scoreboard. (Author's collection)

KOSTYLEV, Georgij Dmitriyevich

Combat record: 11 personal victories, 32 fractional credits, 418 sorties, 112 encounters.

Decorations: Gold Star of Hero of the Soviet Union on October 23, 1942 for 9 personal victories, 233 sorties, 59 engagements as of April, 1942; the Orders of Lenin (2), the Red Banner (2).

Kostylev was born in Oranienbaum (now Lomonosov), Leningrad area, on April 20, 1913 and entered the VMF in 1939. He fired his guns in anger for the first time during the Russo-Finnish Winter War of 1939/40, and then was in continuous action from the very start of the Great Patriotic War. He fought with the 5 IAP of the Baltic Fleet's air service flying LaGG-3 fighters. On July 15, 1941 he managed to destroy his first enemy aircraft in the air, a Bf 110 over Samro Lake (SW Leningrad). He chalked up a total of 10 kills including fractional credits with a LaGG-3 "White 64" with the inscription "Kolombinoj." On September 21, 1941 he caught a Ju 88 in the vicinity of Kronshtadt and sent it down in flames in spite of vicious return fire. He next combined forces with S.I. Lvov and M.A. Yefimov to destroy another of these on October 10 after the enemy aircraft had reconnoitered the regiment's airfield. On January 21, 1942 he was off with Lvov as his number two when they got into a scrap with an equal number of Bf 109s. Kostylev chased one into some clouds and opened fire, seeing strikes all over. He continued firing until he was almost within ramming distance and following which the 109 blew apart. By February his score had risen to 18 including frac-

Kostylev's well adorned sharkmouthed La-5 exhibited in Leningrad's Museum of Defense in 1945 bearing his victory markings, Guards badge below the cockpit and a faintly visible small Gold Star medal on the tail fin. (Author's collection)

tional credits but on the 5th he was shot down and wounded while flying armed reconnaissance in another aircraft. After a short stay in hospital, Kostylev teamed with Yefimov, Sukhov, and Kaberov to destroy 11 enemy aircraft in five days of fighting in March. In late 1942 he was flying a LaGG "Red 35" prior to converting to Hurricanes. The first Hurricane mission produced combat with six Finnish Fokker D-21s, two of these being shot down on an unrecorded date. In 1943 Kostylev was demoted to non-commissioned rank and deprived of his title Hero of the Soviet Union along with his range of decorations for disapproving with a rear services Polkovnik's living off the fat of the land whilst the people in Leningrad were starving to death. He subsequently flew wing to Vasilij Golubev and was fully rehabilitated in 1944. He later flew a La-5 "White 15" which was to be displayed in the Leningrad Museum of Defense in 1945. In 1944 he was appointed chief inspector of the Baltic Fleet's fighter arm serving in this capacity until the close of the war. Some sources suggest a final victory tally of some 40 personal kills as his victories as a fighter inspector conceivably were credited to his unit rather than to him individually. Kostylev stayed in the service after the war coming off active duty in 1953. He died on November 30, 1960.

KOVACHEVICH, Arkadij Fyodorovich
Combat record: 13 personal victories, 6 fractional credits, 356 sorties, 58 encounters as of February, 1943.
Decorations: Gold Star of Hero of the Soviet Union on May 1, 1943; the Orders of Lenin, the October Revolution, the Red Banner (3), the Patriotic War 1st Class, the Red Star (2).

Kovachevich was born in Kirovograd on May 3, 1919 and entered the Soviet Army in December, 1937. He was graduated as a pilot at Odessa military flying school in 1938 and was in action from the earliest days of the war. He spent his World War II career with the glorious 9 GIAP and successively flew MiGs, Yaks, Airacobras, La-5s and La-7s in combat and also flight tested the Bf 109. His choice was the Lavochkin fighter. "Stalingrad was our prime school," Kovachevich recalled. "I will never forget those cold autumn days of 1942. In the skies the aces of Geschwader "Mölders" and "Udet" were ruling supreme. They wouldn't forgive any mistake . . . Life again called for provisos: only thorough knowledge of the enemy's and our own facilities would enable us to exploit the advantages of our aircraft to the fullest extent." Kovachevich remained in the VVS at the conclusion of the war graduating from the Air Force Academy in 1948 and the General Staff Academy six years later. He eventually rose to General Lejtenant and deputy chief of the Air Force Academy and is living in Monino near Moscow.

KOVALENKO, Aleksandr Andreyevich
Combat record: 13 personal victories, 6 fractional credits, 207 sorties, 38 encounters.
Decorations: Gold Star of Hero of the Soviet Union on June 14, 1942 for 8 victories, 146 sorties, 22 air combats as of May, 1942; the Orders of Lenin, the Red Banner (2), the Patriotic War 1st Class, the British DFC.

Kovalenko was born in Kiev on February 7, 1909 and enrolled for service in the VMF in 1932. He completed his pilot training at Kacha military flying school a year later and gained his first combat experience during the Russo-Finnish Winter War of 1939/40. He was assigned to the Northern Fleet's air service before the war joining with the 72 IAP and was able to give a good account of himself during the dramatic battles of 1941. He quickly rose to Kapitan and took over as leader of 2nd fighter squadron and by mid-September had brought his score to 7 kills. In early 1942 Hurricanes were beginning to supplement the unit's I-16s and MiG-3s and on March 24, 1942 45 fighters were scrambled in an all-out effort to intercept a formation of 18 Ju 88s and their escorts and a terrific battle commenced. Kovalenko swept down on a Bf 110 and scored many strikes from the 3 o'clock position following which it glided downwards leaving a thick black smoke and crashed near Kuosli. On April 15 six Hurricanes and three MiG-3s engaged a formation of 18 Ju 87s escorted by eight Bf 110s and nine Bf 109s on the way to Murmansk. Despite effective intervention of German fighters which reportedly allowed only uncoordinated Soviet attacks, Kovalenko submitted claims for two of the Stukas destroyed. Kovalenko was released from the service with the rank of Podpolkovnik for health reasons in 1945 and died on June 21, 1984.

KOVALYOV, Konstantin Fyodotovich
Combat record: 21 personal victories, 13 fractional credits.
Decorations: Gold Star of Hero of the Soviet Union on January 22, 1944 for 12 personal victories, 12 fractional credits, 350 sorties, 35 encounters as of October, 1943; the Orders of Lenin, the Red Banner (3), the Patriotic War 1st Class.

Kovalyov was born in Abinskaya, area of Krasnodar, on May 20, 1913. He entered the Soviet Army and received his pilot training at Stalingrad military flying school in 1937 before he was released from the service the following year. He returned to active duty in 1941 when the war broke out and was posted to the Baltic Fleet's air service. He entered combat in January, 1942 while serving in the 13 IAP and was to gain a substantial proportion of his victories on a Yak-7B, an aircraft that now rests in a Leningrad war museum sporting 19 victory stars. His kills included an Bf 109 that fell to his guns on May 20, 1943 when he single-handedly tackled with eight German fighters near Krasnaya Gorka. He rose to deputy squadron leader and went on to become one of the most accomplished and successful Soviet naval pilots. He had advanced to Kapitan when he returned to civilian life in 1946.

KOVZAN, Boris Ivanovich
Combat record: 28 personal victories, 360 sorties, 127 encounters.
Decorations: Gold Star on August 24, 1943 in recognition of three successful aerial rammings and 142 sorties; the Orders of Lenin (2), the Order of the Red Banner, the Patriotic War 1st Class, the Red Star.

Kovzan was born in the Rostov area on April 7, 1922 and was destined to become one of Russia's most legendary war heroes. He enlisted in the VVS in 1939 receiving his pilot wings at Odessa military flying school a year later. He gained his initial combat experience while flying I-15s in the Gomel area at the outbreak of war and was a Mladshij Lejtenant when joining with the 42 IAP operating the MiG-3 in October, 1941. Kovzan later was posted to the 744 IAP and on October 29, 1941 performed his first successful Taran when he destroyed a Bf 110 near Zarajsk (SE Moscow) and parachuted to safety. His second such victory occurred on February 22, 1942 when he added a Ju 88 in the Torzhok area (Kalinin area) and then was credited with the destruction of a Bf 109 in this fashion in the vicinity of Lyubnitsa (NE Demyansk) on June 8, 1942. He was well qualified for the Gold Star which was bestowed upon him a month later, by which time he was a Starshij Lejtenant. On an unspecified date in August, 1943 Kovzan successfully rammed his fourth enemy aircraft when he became involved in a scrap with five Luftwaffe fighters near Staraya Russa. Unfortunately he was seriously injured and had to abandon his aircraft. Due to the low altitude at which the combat took place, his parachute did not deploy and he suffered various bone fractures. What was more, he had been badly hit in his face and his left eye was destroyed requiring nine months in hospital to recuperate. Following his recovery he flew operationally again and added further laurels to his already remarkable record. One source suggests that he claimed six more kills while others are crediting him with "some 10." Whatever the exact figures, Kovzan's performance was a spectacular one and he finished as the leading exponent of the Taran attack. He served with the postwar VVS and graduated from the Air Force Academy in 1954. Four years later he wound up his military career with the rank of Podpolkovnik. He passed away on August 31, 1985.

KOZHEDUB, Ivan Nikitovich
Combat record: 62 personal victories, 330 sorties, 120 encounters.
Decorations: 1st Gold Star on February 4, 1944 for 20 kills, 146 sorties, 27 air combats as of October, 1943, 2nd Gold Star on August 19, 1944 in recognition of 48 personal victories, 256 sorties as of mid-1944, 3rd Gold Star on August 18, 1945; the Orders of Lenin (2), the Red Banner (7), Aleksandr Nevskij, the Patriotic War 1st and 2nd Class, the Red Star (2).

Kapitan I.N. Kozhedub, the Allied ace of aces, climbs out of his La-5FN, "14", which was assigned to him in May, 1944. The inscription beneath the cockpit reads: "Ot kolkhoznika Konyeva" denoting the aircraft had been presented to the regiment by the father of Hero of the Soviet Union N. Konyev. Kozhedub's electrifying exploits earned him the title of Hero of the Soviet Union three times. (Author's collection)

Kozhedub, the Soviet ace of aces, was born in the Sumy area on June 8, 1920. He began his rather distinguished career in the VVS in 1940 and was graduated as a pilot at Chuguyev military flying school a year later. He spent some time as a pilot instructor prior to commencing his combat duty as a Starshij Serzhant in the 240 IAP on Voronezh Front on March 13, 1943 flying La-5s. He did not make his mark against the Luftwaffe until several months later when the regiment became greatly involved in the Battle of Kursk. Kozhedub, who had by now become a Mladshij Lejtenant, was off on July 6 with three fellow pilots providing ground force cover in the Pokrovka area where they stormed into a formation of 22 Ju 87s with Kozhedub destroying one of them. He claimed another of these the following day and on the 9th Kozhedub and his flight were assigned to a front-line patrol and became involved in a melee with nine Ju 87s, four Bf 109s and two Fw 190s. During this combat he bagged a Bf 109 on his first pass and with his fourth kill met the conditions for the award of his first Order of the Red Banner. A short time later he took over as leader of a fighter squadron which was to be credited with downing 12 Bf 109s, 11 Ju 87s and a Fw 190 during 165 combat sorties between

August 21 and October, 1943. Kozhedub became a devotee of the surprise attack closing right in before firing. He now began to pile up victories at a remarkable pace. On August 9 another Bf 109 fell to his guns while leading four fighters on a Pe-2 escort to Kharkov. Six Luftwaffe fighters rose to oppose them but broke away as the La-5s turned into their attack. Six days later he made a claim for two Bf 109s when enemy aircraft tried to bounce a Pe-2 reconnaissance plane and on August 22 was leading an escort for 14 Pe-2 bombers to Merefa (SW Kharkov). In the target area they came under attack of Fw 190s , one of them being shot down in flames by Kozhedub himself. He had by now become a Kapitan and on September 30 splashed a Ju 87 for a change while leading six of his squadron to bounce 18 Stukas in the Borodayevka area. He continued his streak into October, when the regiment became involved in the ferocious battles above the Dnyepr River. In 10 days of combat he ran up a string of 11 kills while runners-up were Vasilij Mukhin and Pavel Bryzgalov with five apiece. On October 1 he was leading six La-5s against two large gaggles of Ju 87s west of Pogrebnaya and blasted two of them as his squadron got two more. The following day he shot down another of these together with a Bf 109 when eight of his squadron took on 27 enemy planes destroying four dive-bombers along with three Messerschmitts for no losses. He was in action three days later claiming a Bf 109 shot down in flames when 14 La-5s tackled with 15 fighters near Borodayevka. Later that afternoon he added another 109 when combat occurred with 12 Ju 87s escorted by six fighters. The total claims for this affray were three Ju 87s and a Bf 109. He was wounded in a fighter battle on the

I.N. Kozhedub (left) receives congratulations on another victory. The aircraft in the background almost certainly is his own mount, Lavochkin La-7, "White 27," in which he ran up 17 kills. (Author's collection)

Below: Kozhedub's La-7 "White 27" on display in the Frunze Central House of Aviation in Moscow after the close of war. (Author's collection)

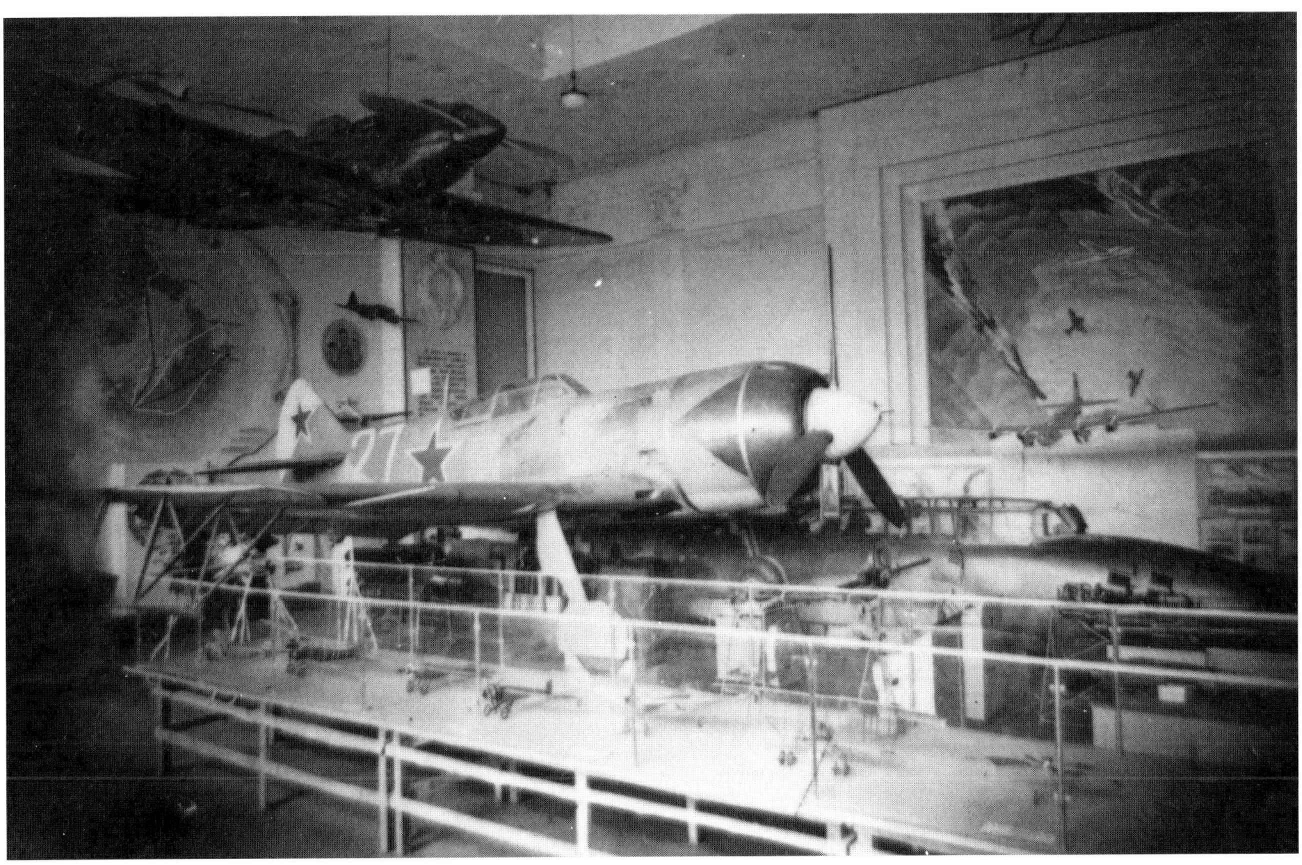

12th but was able to stagger back to his own airfield being back on duty a few days later. On October 29 Kozhedub and five of his comrades were off on a sweep and once over the front made contact with a formation of He 111s, Kozhedub claiming one of them destroyed. Shortly after this they met Luftwaffe dive-bombers engaged in bombing ground targets with Kozhedub blasting one out of the sky. With 20 personal kills he now was well qualified for his first award of the coveted title Hero of the Soviet Union and had already established a reputation for aggressiveness, skill and tenacity. His victims by type of enemy aircraft destroyed were:

Bf 109s 10
Ju 87s 8
Fw 190s 1
He 111s 1

It is particularly noteworthy that he required only 27 encounters to pile up his kills during the course of 146 sorties, 90 of which were escorts, 39 ground force cover, 9 armed reconnaissance and 8 scrambles. After a short rest from operations Kozhedub was again in the thick of fighting and on January 1, 1944 was providing ground force cover with five La-5s between Kapitanovka-Lebedin (NW Kirovograd), where they engaged nine Ju 87s, four of these being shot down. Kozhedub personally accounted for one as a Bf 109 fell to his guns a short time later. He participated in periods of intense activity that flared up along the Yuzhnyj Bug River and subsequently took part in the brutal battles over Rumania. In the same time frame he was in a highly competitive scoring race with another great fighter ace, Kirill Yevstigneyev. He claimed another Ju 87 shot down in flames on March 14, 1944 while leading five La-5s assigned to patrol the air space over the Yuzhoyj Bug and five days later forced down an He 111 when four fighters under his leadership took on 18 bombers escorted by six Messerschmitts in the vicinity of Vulturul. On the 29th six La-5s with Kozhedub in the lead were sweeping over the Yassy area where they engaged a formation of 10 Hs 129s and four Bf 109s. Kozhedub went after the assault aircraft, pulled in to point-blank range and after several bursts one of them blew up and crashed. In an outstanding effort Kozhedub's squadron had been credited with 65 enemy planes in the air since August, 1943 consisting of 23 Bf 109s, 30 Ju 87s, 5 He 111s, 2 Hs 129s, one Fw 190, three Fw 189s and one PZL-24 during 710 sorties (318 ground force cover, 357 escorts, 35 armed reconnaissance). Kozhedub's score now had risen to 34 and he was recommended for his second Gold Star award. His victories by type of enemy aircraft destroyed were as follows:

Bf 109s 13
Ju 87s 15
He 111s 2
Hs 129s 2
Fw 190s 1
PZL-24s 1

Kozhedub wearing his full range of World War II decorations. He believed that he had in fact destroyed more than 100 enemy planes forgoing many a victory credit in favor of younger pilots. (Author's collection)

Triumph followed triumph. At Yassy, victories continued to come thick and fast. He chalked up four more kills between June 1 and June 3 to run his tally to 43 but Yevstigneyev in the same time frame had increased his score to 44 by claiming five aerial victories. A short time later he was posted as deputy commanding officer of the 176 GIAP flying La-7s. On September 22 he took off with Lejtenant Sharapov on a patrol and engaged two gaggles of Fw 190 fighter-bombers comprising of 4-8 aircraft each and shot down two of them in quick succession opening fire at 150 meters. He added another of these on January 16, 1945 while victory number 50 came on February 10. On this day Kozhedub was carrying out a free hunt with Major Titarenko as his number two in the vicinity of the Oder River, two German fighters being seen, and Kozhedub shot down one of these. The enemy pilot made a forced landing in his crippled aircraft in a pasture and became a prisoner. It was discovered that he was an ace with eight victories but his identity has unfortunately not been established. Two days later he was off on another free hunt with Lejtenant Gromakovskij flying wing to him and while sweeping over the Konitz area they spotted 18 Fw 190s fighter-bombers flying at 400 meters. They immediately swept down and Kozhedub opened fire on "tail-end Charlie," seeing hits exploding all over him and pieces flying off in all directions whereupon he spun into the ground in a solid sheet of flame. He then destroyed two more in quick succession which crashed 10-12 km southwest of Konitz. Gromakovskij shot another off Kozhedub's tail for his second kill of the day. Kozhedub is believed to have shot down one of the first Me 262 jets to be encountered on Eastern Front during February but the date for this remains dubious. The date given by Kozhedub himself is the 19th while others are suggesting the 15th or 24th of February. It seems most likely that this claim has never been officially accepted as it cannot be traced in his "nagradnoj list" – the recommendation submitted by Polkovnik Chupikov, the commander of the 176 GIAP, for the award of his third title of Hero of the Soviet Union on March 31, 1945. On March 18 he claimed a Fw 190 that crashed 5-6 kilometers northwest of Küstrin and five days later four La-7s with Kozhedub and Major Kumanichkin in the lead tackled with some 30 Fw 190s in the Seelow area. Kozhedub and Major Titarenko attacked from the sun claiming single 190s each on their first pass before breaking away in a high speed climb. In continuing action Kozhedub bagged a second while in taking on another gaggle Kumanichkin and his wingman, Gromakovskij, both knocked down singles with the latter's victim taking to his parachute. By March 31, 1945 Kozhedub had reached 60 confirmed kills becoming the top Allied fighter pilot of the war. His victory credits by type as of this date were as follows:

Fw 190s 19
Bf 109s 18
Ju 87s 17
Hs 129s 3
He 111s 2
PZL-24s 1

He had by now logged 326 sorties, of which 116 were escorts, 109 ground force cover, 79 free hunts, 14 armed reconnaissance, 8 scrambles, during which he had entered into air combat 117 times. He closed out his scoring, fittingly perhaps, over Berlin on April 17 when he forced down two Fw 190s. Following the close of war he continued on active duty with the VVS and graduated from the Air Force Academy in 1949 and from the General Staff Academy seven years later. During the Korean War he commanded the 324 IAD at Antung comprising the 176 GIAP and 196 IAP but did not add to his score. Yet he displayed exceptional leadership, his unit claiming 207 U.N. aircraft destroyed for the loss of 27 MiG-15s in combat and 9 pilots. He later was assigned as an inspector of VVS flight training between 1956 and 1963 and in January, 1964 became deputy commander of the Moscow PVO forces. In 1967 Kozhedub was appointed president of the Aviation Sports Federation and vice president of the International Federation of Aviation (FAI). He later rose to Marshal Aviatsii and was assigned as an inspector of the Soviet Ministry of Defense.

Perhaps the last words should be left to Kozhedub himself, who provides the following revealing recollections: "I destroyed my first enemy aircraft in the air during the Battle of Kursk. Historians have been setting forth my total score as 62 victories. As a matter of fact this figure requires revision. There were many victories that either remained unconfirmed or were credited to fellow pilots. I reckon that my personal score actually is in excess of 100 victories while I never counted enemy aircraft destroyed jointly with my comrades." Kozhedub passed away in August, 1991.

KOZHEVNIKOV, Anatolij Leonidovich

Combat record: 27 personal victories, 300 sorties, 69 encounters.

Decorations: Gold Star of Hero of the Soviet Union on June 27, 1945 for 25 kills, 211 sorties, 62 engagements; the Orders

Right: Major A.L. Kozhevnikov, a top-notch ace of the Eastern Front. He served with the 212 GIAP and flew Hurricanes and Yak-7Bs with notable success. Soviet pilots generally had a low opinion of the British fighter. Recalls Kozhevnikov: "That same day we took off on two further missions to cover the return of Shturmoviks. The Messerschmitts always were above us once we approached the target area and would dive through us with their superior speed firing as they came. We only could form a defensive circle and try to repel them. Abaltusov's wingman, Zaborovskij, was shot down. Second Eskadrilya lost Khmylov while Olejnikov took to his parachute." (Author's collection)

of Lenin, the Red Banner (5), Aleksandr Nevskij, the Patriotic War 1st Class, the Red Star (3).

Kozhevnikov was born in Krasnoyarsk on March 12, 1917 and enlisted in the Soviet Army in 1938. He won his wings at Batajsk military flying school two years later and entered combat flying I-16s as a Mladshij Lejtenant between Batajsk-Rostov early in the war. He did not get an opportunity to score until he was posted to the 438 IAP when this was in the process of converting to Hawker Hurricanes. He deployed with the unit to Voronezh Front on July 20, 1942 scoring his first success on his 146th mission when he forced down a Bf 109 near Storozhevaya on September 13, 1942. He then began to claim victories on a regular basis. His highest scoring period came in June, 1943 when he chalked up seven kills in as many days on Yak-7Bs. Kozhevnikov subsequently proved his skills during the battles of the Korsun-Shevchenkovskij campaign (January 24/February 17, 1944) destroying a Fw 190 in the vicinity of Zhuravka on February 1. He later took part in the aerial operations above Moldavia, Yassy, and the Lemberg-Sandomierz campaign to run his tally to 20+ victories. He closed out his scoring in a scrap near Spremberg (SE Berlin) on April 18, 1945 when he shot down a Bf 109. Kozhevnikov remained in the VVS after the close of war and graduated from the Air Force Academy in 1950 and from the General Staff Academy eight years later. He eventually rose to General Lejtenant.

KOZICH, Ivan Semyonovich

Combat record: 16 personal victories, 4 fractional credits, 423 sorties, 31 encounters.

Decorations: Gold Star of Hero of the Soviet Union on April 21, 1943 in recognition of 9 victories, 4 fractional credits, 210 sorties as of February, 1943; the Orders of Lenin, the Red Banner (2), Aleksandr Nevskij, the Patriotic War 1st Class (3).

Kozich was born in the Minsk area on March 3, 1920 and entered military service at age 18. He completed his pilot training at Chuguyev military flying school three years later joining with the 721 IAP in October, 1941 to start flying combat. He was to see a great deal of action on Bryansk, Central and 1st Byelorussian Fronts gaining a large number of his victories with the La-5 and La-7 fighters. He wound up as the regiment's highest scoring ace. He served with the postwar VVS and returned to civilian life in 1950 when he had become a Major.

KOZLOV, Nikolaj Aleksandrovich

Combat record: 23 personal victories, 620 sorties, 130 encounters.

Decorations: Gold Star of Hero of the Soviet Union on February 14, 1943 for 12 kills, 5 fractional credits, 495 sorties, 101 air-to-air combats as of September, 1942; the Orders of Lenin, the Red Banner (2), Aleksandr Nevskij, the Patriotic War 1st Class (2), the Red Star (3).

Kozlov was born in Petrograd (Leningrad) on April 30, 1917 and enlisted in the Soviet Army in 1938. He was graduated at Chuguyev military flying school two years later and was in the thick of the fighting as a Starshij Lejtenant and deputy squadron leader in the 788 IAP from the earliest days of the war. He was able to open his account in an I-16 on June 23, 1941 when he shot down two Bf 110s near Baranovichi, a feat almost unheard of at the time. A short time later he converted to MiG-3s and on August 21 completed as many as nine sorties destroying a Ju 88. Kozlov's big day was September 24 when he shot down two Ju 88s in an encounter at Bryansk and in continuing action successfully rammed a third after running out of ammunition. He subsequently gave a good account of himself during the aerial campaigns on Bryansk, Stalingrad, Southwest, Central, 1st Ukrainian and 1st Byelorussian Fronts. He was credited with performing a second successful aerial ramming on May 27, 1942 destroying a Ju 88 reconnaissance plane near Morozovsk (SW Stalingrad) when his guns were jamming. On an unspecified day in August he claimed a double with two Ju 88s while leading 10 of his squadron against a force of 50 enemy aircraft. In September, 1943 Kozlov assumed command of the 907 IAP and served in this capacity until the end of war. The regiment made a major effort at Korsun, where six and a half German divisions were trapped in a pocket, and on February 8, 1944 six La-5s had a field day catching 12 Ju 52s, nine He 111s and a number of Fw 190s, with 11 enemy planes being claimed destroyed. The Luftwaffe continued to experience heavy losses in desperate attempts to sustain the besieged forces and 15 more German aircraft fell to the regiment's guns between February 10-11. Most successful pilot was Kozlov himself who personally accounted for three of the kills in two days combat. He went on to become a 23-victory ace, 20 of his kills being against bombers while under his leadership 907 IAP was credited with 119 enemy aircraft destroyed for the loss of 17 planes in combat. Kozlov remained in the VVS at the conclusion of the war and graduated from the General Staff Academy in 1954. He wound up his military career with the rank of General Major in 1976.

KOZLOVSKIJ, Vasilij Ivanovich

Combat record: 12 personal victories, 50 encounters.

Decorations: Gold Star of Hero of the Soviet Union on August 19, 1944 for 103 ground-attack sorties as of April, 1944; the Orders of Lenin, the Red Banner (3), Aleksandr Nevskij, the Patriotic War 1st Class, the Red Star.

Kozlovskij was born in the Kiev area on February 21, 1920 and was to become one of the greatest of all Soviet Shturmovik aces. He enlisted in the VVS for flight training in 1940 and was graduated at Tambov military flying school a year later. He began his remarkable combat career in July, 1942 and immediately was enjoying above-average success while serving in the 810 ShAP. He eventually rose to Kapitan and squadron leader. He made a big name for himself taking part in the dramatic battles along the Don River north of Voronezh in August, 1942. During this month the regiment was tasked with conducting strikes against advancing German forces and encountered heavy opposition. On one occasion Kozlovskij came within a hair of falling foul to enemy fighters when the regiment commander was leading a strafing attack of four Il-2s. In the target area they came under attack from 12 Bf 109s and two of the Shturmoviks went down and crashed on their first pass. Kozlovskij turned into their attack giving one a long burst and the aircraft went down vertically in a shower of sparks while ten Messerschmitts were knocking down the regiment commander. He was able to destroy a second fighter before he was forced to abandon his own burning ship his flight gear catching fire. Following his recovery he displayed his skills on 2nd Baltic Front and wound up with a total record of 12 aerial victories plus 68 tanks and self-propelled guns, 16 aircraft, 67 rail cars, 5 locomotives, 530 motor vehicles, 98 antiaircraft guns and 89 field guns destroyed in ground attacks. Following World War II he continued on active duty with the VVS until 1960 when he was retired with the rank of Polkovnik. He is living in Moscow.

Major N.F. Krasnov was one of the most distinguished VVS fighter pilots. He became an ace fighting with the 402, 31 and 116 IAPs finishing with at least 32 personal kills. (Author's collection)

KRASAVIN, Konstantin Alekseyevich
Combat record: 21 personal victories, 4 fractional credits, 376 sorties, 106 encounters.
Decorations: Gold Star of Hero of the Soviet Union on May 15, 1946; the Orders of Lenin, the Red Banner (3), the Patriotic War 1st Class (2).

Krasavin was born in the Moscow area on May 20, 1917 and entered military service in 1938. He was graduated as a pilot at Stalingrad military flying school two years later and joined combat with the Luftwaffe in December, 1941. He gained his first combat experience flying Hurricanes in the 485 IAP and on July 9, 1942 was flying wing to Starshij Lejtenant Yedkin when they engaged 20 Ju 88s and escorting fighters near Vasilyevshchina. They immediately swept down on the enemy formation and in the ensuing melee Krasavin claimed a Bf 109 which won him the award of his first Order of the Patriotic War. He later was assigned to the 150 GIAP and managed to put up a good performance on 2nd Ukrainian Front. He was a Major and deputy regiment commander when hostilities ceased. He remained in the VVS to advance to Podpolkovnik before winding up his military career in 1955.

KRASNOV, Nikolaj Fyodorovich
Combat record: 32 personal victories, 10 fractional credits, 300+ sorties.
Decorations: Gold Star of Hero of the Soviet Union on February 4, 1944 in recognition of 31 kills, 279 sorties, 85 engagements as of December, 1943; the Orders of Lenin, the Red Banner (2), Aleksandr Nevskij, the Patriotic War 1st Class (2).

Krasnov was born in the Vladimir area on December 9, 1914 and began his distinguished career in the VVS in 1930. He completed his pilot training at Tambov military flying school in 1934 and was a well-seasoned pilot when being posted to the 402 IAP in late June, 1941. He entered combat on Northwest Front a month later and it was not long before he proved his skills. On August 1 he achieved his initial success when he blasted a Ju 88 out of the sky near Novgorod. Nine days later the regiment got into its first scrap with enemy fighters when seven MiG-3s were engaged in escorting five SB bombers to an enemy airfield. In the vicinity of Shimsk, 50 kilometers southwest of Novgorod, 12 Bf 109s tried to bounce the bombers but were driven off. Two of them then closed on Krasnov from astern, who throttled back but the 109s accelerated away climbing back to altitude with their speed advantage. Krasnov then launched down on an 109 that was working with one of the bombers and sent it spinning down out of control. His next victory came on the 19th when he intercepted a German bomber approaching the regiment's airfield and shot it down close to base. He was seriously injured in a fighter battle on October 6 and required five months to recuperate. He was then assigned to the 31 IAP flying LaGG-3s but was wounded again on May

31, 1942 during in Il-2 escort to the Kursk area. On this occasion he had just downed a Bf 109F when he was in turn attacked by his victim's wingman and crashlanded with a leg wound 10 kilometers east of the target area. He began walking towards the Soviet lines eventually reaching his unit safely nine days later. He subsequently managed to put up a good performance flying La-5s in the Caucasus and later was posted to the 116 IAP. During his time with this he flew with great distinction in the air battles over Kursk, Byelgorod and along the Dnyepr River. He was promoted Major and took over as leader of a fighter squadron which he led with great fighting spirit to run up 71 air victories for the loss of three La-5s in air combat. During October, 1943 he was occupied with hunting down the elusive Luftwaffe Fw 189 reconnaissance planes known throughout the VVS as "rama" – frame – because of its distinctive structure. He was successful in destroying three of these planes, the first kill occurring near Barvenkovo, northwest of Kramatorsk, on the 13th. In a burst of energy and skill he submitted claims for 11 enemy aircraft destroyed in the skies above Zaporozhye before he took over as leader of the "eskadrilya okhotnikov" (hunter squadron) in January, 1944. The outfit was conceived as a special duty squadron and was composed of experienced and very capable volunteers to search out the enemy even in foul weather. On an unrecorded date he once ran into two Ju 52s and two Ju 87s while flying free hunt over the Crimea and shot down both transports in quick succession to bring his tally to 36 kills including fractional credits. In the skies above Budapest, Krasnov claimed a string of eight kills during 26 air encounters. On January 29, 1945 he perished while ramming a German fighter after running out of ammunition and was buried in Odessa. His place as leader of the "eskadrilya okhotnikov" was taken by another remarkable talent, Starshij Lejtenant Skomorokhov. Krasnov's final score is uncertain but is at least 32 personal victories.

KRASNOYURCHENKO, Ivan Ivanovich
Combat record: 8 personal victories, 16 fractional credits, 111 sorties, 55 encounters.
Decorations: Gold Star of Hero of the Soviet Union on November 17, 1939; the Orders of Lenin, the Red Banner (3), the Patriotic War 1st Class, the Red Star.

Krasnoyurchenko was born in the Volgograd area on September 3, 1910 and entered military service in August, 1934. He was graduated as a pilot at Kacha military flying school a year later and cut his teeth against the Japanese along the Khalkhin Gol in Mongolia between May 23 and September 16, 1939. During this period he was credited with downing five enemy planes in 31 air engagements. He next held the following assignments before the outbreak of the Great Patriotic War: squadron leader, commander of the 43 IAP and inspector of the Kiev military district. On June 22, 1941, the day of the German attack on Soviet Russia, Krasnoyurchenko was able to destroy an enemy bomber over Kiev. He subsequently was successively assigned as commander of the 92 IAP, 102 and 147 IAD-PVO and deputy commander of the 9 IAK-PVO displaying outstanding leadership in the ferocious battles over Kiev, Kharkov, Stalingrad, Yaroslavl and Rybinsk. At Stalingrad 102 IAD was to claim top honors for achieving 336 kills. Following World War II Krasnoyurchenko graduated from Voroshilov General Staff Academy and commanded various PVO units prior to becoming the head of Chkalov central aeroklub. He wound up his military career as a General Major in 1956. He died on April 1, 1970.

KRAVCHENKO, Grigorij Panteleyevich
Combat record: 20 personal victories.
Decorations: Gold Star of Hero of the Soviet Union on February 22, 1939; the Orders of Lenin (2), the Red Banner (2), the Patriotic War 2nd Class.

Kravchenko was born in the Dnyepropetrovsk area on October 12, 1912 and enlisted in the VVS in 1931. He completed his pilot training at A.F. Myasnikov military flying school at Kacha a year later and served as a pilot instructor until 1938. He next won the award of the Order of the Red Banner as a test pilot and then saw action for the first time against the Japanese at Khasan Lake (July 29/ August 11, 1938). He excelled in Mongolia while serving in the 22 IAP and rapidly rose to commander of the regiment for displaying exceptional leadership. In a fierce series of dogfights Kravchenko claimed 12 kills during the period of February to September, 1939 while his leadership resulted in an outstanding combat record for the regiment, setting it apart from similar units. On one occasion, 18 Japanese planes were blasted out of the sky in one day while between August 20-28, 1939 the regiment claimed 75 kills during 2,404 sorties. He then left the front but did not have to wait long for further action, taking part in the Russo-Finnish Winter War of 1939/40. In July, 1940 he was promoted General Lejtenant and was put in command of the Baltic military district's air service. A year later he took over the 64 SAD and saw a great deal of action right after the German attack on the Soviet Union in June, 1941. He next became commanding officer of the 11 SAD, a composite division consisting of five Yak-1, I-16 and Il-2 regiments and was greatly involved in the fighting on Bryansk Front. In July, 1942 he was posted to command the 215 IAD which would score 100 air victories under his leadership during the battles on Volkhov and Kalinin Fronts. On February 23, 1943 he was killed in air combat, and in him the VVS lost one of its legendary figures. He was interred in the Kremlin wall.

KRAVTSOV, Dmitrij Stepanovich
Combat record: 13 personal victories, 8 fractional credits, 430 sorties, 80 encounters.

Lavochkin La-7. Note Polikarpov I-16 in the background. (Author's collection)

Decorations: Gold Star of Hero of the Soviet Union on August 18, 1945; the Orders of Lenin, the Red Banner (2), Aleksandr Nevskij, the Patriotic War 1st Class (2), the Red Star.

Kravtsov was born in the Kursk area on October 12, 1916 and enrolled for service in November, 1937. He won his wings at Chuguyev military flying school three years later. Kravtsov was in continuous action from June, 1941 to January, 1945 and during his combat career saw considerable fighting at Stalingrad, over Kursk, Yassy-Kishinyov, Rumania, Bulgaria, Yugoslavia, Hungary and Austria. He would finish as a Major and squadron leader in the 31 IAP. He wrote a distinguished record on 3rd Ukrainian Front and on December 22, 1944 was leading six La-5s to take on 30 Fw 190s in the Balaton Lake area (Hungary) personally accounting for two of the four enemy aircraft destroyed in the ensuing melee. Three days later he claimed another of these when eight of his squadron tied into a formation of 12 Ju 87s, 12 Fw 190s and 10 Bf 109s, two of the German planes being shot down. On January 2, 1945 four Lavochkin fighters with Kravtsov in the lead engaged six Bf 109s and eight Fw 190s while escorting Il-2s near Budapest, where four enemy fighters were shot down. Most successful pilot in this affray was Kravtsov himself, with two 190s, who then unfortunately was badly wounded by shells exploding in his cockpit. Bleeding from several wounds in his arms and legs he succeeded in completing the mission and staggering back to his own airfield. He concluded his active duty in 1946.

KRAVTSOV, Ivan Savelyevich
Combat record: 15 personal victories, 4 fractional credits, 315 sorties, 85 encounters.
Decorations: Gold Star of Hero of the Soviet Union on July 22, 1944; the Orders of Lenin, the Red Banner (4), Nakhimov 2nd Class, the Patriotic War 1st Class (2).

Kravtsov was born in the Kirovograd area on February 19, 1914 and entered the VMF in 1936. He qualified as a pilot at Yejsk military flying school in 1939 and was assigned to the Baltic Fleet's air service before the outbreak of war. He commenced his combat duty in the 5 IAP-KBF in November, 1941 and for his efforts during the winter of 1941/42 was promoted to flight leader. He gave a good account of himself flying the Hawker Hurricane and on September 26, 1942 was leading four of these to bounce a formation of 12 Luftwaffe bombers and eight escorting fighters, three of the enemy planes being shot down without loss. Kravtsov served with the postwar VVS until 1950 when he was retired with the rank of Major.

KRIVOSHEYEV, Yefim Avtonomovich
Combat record: 5 personal victories, 15 fractional credits, 96 sorties, 29 encounters.
Decorations: Gold Star of Hero of the Soviet Union posthumously on February 22, 1943; the Orders of Lenin, the Red Banner.

Krivosheyev was born in Novomoskovsk, Dnyepropetrovsk area, on April 12, 1916 and enrolled for service in 1939. He graduated from flight training a year later and was posted as a Lejtenant to the 145 IAP on May 7, 1942 to start flying combat. The regiment was heavily committed to action in defense of Murmansk and on May 26 five Airacobras with Krivosheyev in the lead tackled with 20 enemy planes near Kitsa, four of these being claimed destroyed. A short time later he was shot down and wounded and after recovery claimed a Bf 109 on June 15, combined forces with a comrade to destroy another of these before successfully ramming a Ju 87 and nursing his crippled aircraft in safely at his own airfield. He reported the destruction of another German fighter the following day and also teamed to destroy a second with a fellow pilot. He had a big day on June 29 when he submitted claims for three enemy planes destroyed, almost certainly including shares, when he became embroiled in a dogfight low over Tuloma River. On September 9 he was killed deliberately ramming an 109 while attempting to rescue a comrade from trouble.

KRYUCHKOV, Vasilij Yegorovich
Combat record: 10 personal victories, 6 fractional credits, 572 sorties, 117 encounters.
Decorations: Gold Star of Hero of the Soviet Union on May 15, 1946; the Orders of Lenin, the Red Banner (3), Aleksandr Nevskij, the Patriotic War 1st Class (2), the Red Star (3).

Kryuchkov was born in the Ryazan area on October 22, 1921 and joined the Soviet Army in 1940. He completed his pilot training at Batajsk military flying school a year later and saw action for the first time in May, 1942 after being posted to the 249 IAP on South Front. During his time with the regiment he took part in numerous missions on Transcaucasus, North Caucasus, 4th Ukrainian and 2nd Byelorussian Fronts, 340 of his sorties being armed reconnaissance. When hostilities ceased he had become a Kapitan and squadron leader. He remained in the ranks and wound up his military career as a Polkovnik in 1971. He passed away on January 2, 1985.

KUBAREV, Vasilij Nikolayevich
Combat record: 46 personal victories.
Decorations: Gold Star of Hero of the Soviet Union on September 28, 1943 for 10 personal victories, 114 sorties, 53 air engagements as of August, 1943; the Orders of Lenin (2), the Red Banner (6), Aleksandr Nevskij (2), the Patriotic War 1st Class (2), the Red Star (2).

Kubarev was born in the Rzhev area on January 30, 1918 and started his military career in 1938. He completed his pilot training later that year at Odessa military flying school following which he was assigned as a flight leader at Konotop and subsequently Armavir military flying schools. He entered combat in November, 1941 and was to make a big name for himself in the aerial operations on Bryansk Front by which time he had become a Major and squadron leader in the veteran 65 GIAP. He excelled during the fighting above Kursk and Orel in July and early August, 1943. On one occasion he was leading six Yak-7Bs to patrol the air space over the Oka River where they had a tussle with two gaggles consisting of four Ju 88s and eight Fw 190s respectively 27 Ju 88s and 20 Fw 190s. In all, they destroyed four of the bombers and two escorts for no losses. Kubarev went on to finish as the eighth ranking Allied ace and is widely regarded as one of the greatest all-around Soviet fighter pilots. During his postwar career he graduated from the Air Force Academy in 1951 and from the General Staff Academy in 1960. He eventually rose to General Polkovnik and came off active duty in 1981.

KULAGIN, Andrej Mikhajlovich
Combat record: 32 personal victories, 7 fractional credits, 762 sorties, 142 encounters.
Decorations: Gold Star of Hero of the Soviet Union on July 1, 1944 in recognition of 22 kills, 4 fractional credits, 320 sor-

Lejtenant A.M. Kulagin, who enjoyed remarkable success in the Kuban theater while flying the LaGG-3. He emerged as the top ace of the 249 IAP with 32 confirmed victories. (Author's collection)

ties, 106 encounters as of February, 1944; the Orders of Lenin, the Red Banner (3), Aleksandr Nevskij, the Patriotic War 1st Class, the Red Star.

Kulagin was born in the Gomel area on September 4, 1921 and enlisted in the Soviet Army in 1940. He was graduated as a pilot at Armavir military flying school two years later and in July, 1942 started flying combat with the 249 IAP in the Kuban theater. Kulagin flew numerous missions in the ground support role and it was not before March 27, 1943 that he destroyed his first enemy aircraft in the air by downing a Bf 109 while beating up road traffic. He got another of these three days later when eight LaGG-3 became embroiled in a dogfight with 10 Bf 109s in the vicinity of Anastasiyevka, north of Taganrog. He continued to score on a regular basis and then enjoyed considerable success when the regiment was assigned to provide night cover in January, 1944 destroying a total of seven He 111s to rank him as one of the leading Soviet nightfighter aces. Kulagin came out of World War II as the regiment's top-scoring ace. After the war he graduated from the Air Force Academy in 1954 and retired with the rank of Polkovnik two years later. He died on August 9, 1980.

KULESHOV, Vladimir Kuzmich
Combat record: 16 personal victories, 6 fractional credits, 4 enemy planes destroyed in ground attacks, 351 sorties, 73 encounters.
Decorations: Gold Star of Hero of the Soviet Union on February 4, 1944; the Orders of Lenin, the Red Banner (2), the Red Star.

Kuleshov was born in the Uzbek SSR on January 5, 1918 and joined the Soviet Army for flight training in 1940. He was graduated as pilot at Odessa military flying school later that year following which he was assigned as a pilot instructor. He was posted as a Mladshij Lejtenant to the 88 IAP in August, 1942 and managed to put up a good performance flying I-16s in the air battles along the Terek River. On September 7 his squadron fought a pitched battle with enemy fighters. As several Messerschmitts were making things hot for A.K. Bazunov, Kuleshov dove to his rescue, shot down an 109 in flames and beat off the rest. Unfortunately he was wounded in the process and force-landed in the Voznesensk area (NW Nikolayev). He later rose to Kapitan and shturman and was deeply involved in the fighting on Voronezh Front. He was killed in action in the Kiev area on November 3, 1943.

KULIYEV, Adil Gusejnovich
Combat record: 18 personal victories, 265 sorties, 64 encounters.
Decorations: Gold Star of Hero of the Soviet Union on February 23, 1945 for 15 personal victories, 141 sorties, 38 air combats as of September 10, 1944; the Orders of Lenin, the Red Banner (3), Aleksandr Nevskij, the Patriotic War 1st Class, the Red Star.

Major A.S. Kumanichkin, a pilot of the 41 GIAP, who made a big name for himself on 1st Ukrainian Front. He was awarded the title of Hero of the Soviet Union on April 13, 1944 for 18 kills and 1 fractional credit during 196 sorties and 36 combats as of November, 1943. He later joined with the 176 GIAP excelling in the free hunt role during the final months of the war. On March 22, 1945 Kumanichkin and Major Kozhedub, the Allied ace of aces, tied into 30 Fw 190s near Seelow bagging singles each. When hostilities ceased his score was 31. (Author's collection)

Kuliyev was born in Baku on November 22, 1922 and entered military service at age 19. He completed his pilot training at Stalingrad military flying school a year later and was assigned to the 653 IAP. He joined combat with the Luftwaffe in October, 1942 and gave a good account of himself during subsequent assignments on Kalinin, Bryansk, 1st and 2nd Baltic and 3rd Byelorussian Fronts. He eventually advanced to Kapitan. His most memorable mission came on March 14, 1943 when his squadron was bounced by four Bf 109s while engaged in a front-line patrol near Staraya Russa. Kuliyev turned into their attack and destroyed one of them in a head-on encounter. He came in turn under attack by another being wounded in his arms and legs by shells exploding in his cockpit. He staggered back to the Soviet lines before he parachuted to safety. He got a double in the skies of Byelorussia on July 10, 1944 when his flight tackled with 17 enemy planes, four of these being shot down without loss. Kuliyev remained in the VVS following World War II and graduated from the Air Force Academy in 1956. He wound up his military career in 1966 by which time he was a Polkovnik.

KURZENKOV, Sergej Georgiyevich
Combat record: 12 personal victories, 225 sorties.
Decorations: Gold Star of Hero of the Soviet Union on July 24, 1943 for 9 victories, 209 sorties, 20 encounters as of March, 1943; the Orders of Lenin, the Red Banner (2), the Patriotic War 1st Class, the Red Star.

Kurzenkov was born in Omsk on July 7, 1911 and enlisted in the VMF in 1933. He won his pilot wings at Yejsk military flying school two years later and joined with the 78 IAP of the Northern Fleet's air service at Murmansk in October, 1941. By an unfortunate coincidence he attacked a Soviet Pe-2 shortly afterward which crash-landed after sustaining 138 strikes. Kurzenkov was taken into custody and almost court-martialed before being acquitted. On January 4, 1942 he got into his first aerial encounter with the Luftwaffe and was shot up by a Bf 109 his Hurricane bursting into flames while 20mm shell fragments pierced his upper thigh. Disregarding the pain he managed to shake his assailant off and blasted a yellow-nosed fighter out of the air before making a forced landing behind the Soviet lines. It was discovered that his victim was killed and although the German's identity has not been established Soviet accounts read that he was an Oberleutnant and recipient of "two Iron Crosses." Kurzenkov returned to his unit in March, 1942 and on the 24th forced down a Ju 88 west of Murmansk also scoring strikes on a second. He next added claims for a Ju 87 destroyed and a second damaged on April 15 and then bagged a Bf 109 two days later to bring his tally to nine kills plus five more destroyed in ground attacks during 209 sorties. He made a claim for a single on the 29th and shot down two Bf 110s in one sortie during May before he was hit, force-landing in enemy lines. Bleeding from a severe head injury he set out for the Soviet lines eventually reaching them safely 24 hours later. He resumed combat duty in July and in late 1942 was appointed deputy regiment commander. On February 28, 1943 he headed out on a nocturnal reconnaissance mission and shot up a Ju 88 on an enemy airfield but was badly hit by groundfire and was obliged to abandon his aircraft on his way home. Unfortunately his parachute failed to open fully and he was seriously injured in the resulting heavy fall. He never flew operationally again. He served with the postwar VMF until 1950 when he was released from active duty with the rank of Polkovnik.

P.S. Kutakhov, a man of outstanding leadership talent. He won his spurs during the Russo-Finnish Winter War of 1939/40 and later proved his attributes as commander of the 19 GIAP in Northern Russia. He remained in the ranks at the end of the war to become commander of the VVS (Author's collection)

KUTAKHOV, Pavel Stepanovich

Combat record: 14 personal victories, 28 fractional credits, 367 sorties, 79 encounters.

Decorations: Gold Star of Hero of the Soviet Union on May 1, 1943 for 7 kills, 24 fractional credits, 262 sorties, 40 engagements as of February, 1943; the Orders of Lenin (4), the Red Banner (5), Kutuzov 1st Class, Aleksandr Nevskij, the Patriotic War 2nd Class, the Red Star.

Kutakhov was born in the Rostov area on August 16, 1914 and started his remarkable military career in the VVS in 1935. He qualified as a pilot at Stalingrad military flying school three years later and first saw action during the Russo-Finnish Winter War of 1939/ 40, during the course of which he logged 131 sorties as a flight leader. He was posted to the 20 IAP before the outbreak of the Patriotic War and later was promoted to Major and squadron leader in the 19 GIAP for his efforts on Karelian Front. One of his most memorable missions came on May 26, 1942 when he was leading his fighters to intercept a Luftwaffe strike against a railroad station, five German planes being shot down without loss. In all, Kutakhov's squadron was credited with downing 40 enemy aircraft while flying Kittyhawks and Airacobras in the Murmansk area until late 1943. Kutakhov advanced to Polkovnik the following year and was put in command of the regiment displaying outstanding leadership through the close of war. He remained in the VVS following World War II and assumed many command assignments. He graduated from the General Staff Academy in 1957 and in March, 1969 succeeded Chief Air Marshal Vershinin as commander of the Soviet Air Force with the rank of Air Marshal. In November, 1972 he rose to Chief Air Marshal. On August 15, 1984 he was awarded a second title of Hero of the Soviet Union in recognition of his distinguished service career. He died on December 3, 1984.

KUZMIN, Georgij Pavlovich

Combat record: 21 personal victories, 7 fractional credits, 280 sorties.

Decorations: Gold Star of Hero of the Soviet Union on April 28, 1943 for 15 kills, 6 fractional credits, 270 sorties consisting of 30 escorts, 70 reconnaissance, 15 ground attacks and 90 air-to-air combats; the Orders of Lenin, the Red Banner.

Kuzmin was born in the Krasnoyarsk area on April 23, 1913 and entered the Soviet Army in 1930. He was graduated as an aircraft mechanic at Volsk and served in this capacity until 1939. He won the Order of the Red Banner for his efforts during the war with the Japanese at the Khalkhin Gol in Mongolia in 1939 and upon applying for pilot training was sent to Kacha military flying school. He was graduated as a pilot in 1940 being posted to the 161 IAP as a Starshij Lejtenant. He fired his guns in anger for the first time on June 26, 1941 when he combined forces with his wingman to knock down two Ju 88s near Lepel, south of Polotsk, flying the Polikarpov I-153 biplane. While returning home they spotted a lone Ju 88 which was attacked by Kuzmin. Just as he was on the point of firing he found his guns were jamming and resorted to ramming. The bomber went out of control and crashed while Kuzmin parachuted to safety. The regiment then withdrew to the Bryansk area where he single-handedly took on a formation of nine Ju 88s on November 19, 1941. Two of these fell from the sky in flames before a gunner made his mark and in an instant Kuzmin's fighter was engulfed in flames. He temporarily lost consciousness but was lucky enough to regain control and put his aircraft down in a snow-covered field. In the process he sustained such serious injuries that his left foot and part of his right foot had to be amputated. Following his recovery he joined with the 239 IAP as a squadron leader on Kalinin Front in March, 1942 and participated in a number of missions prior to moving with the unit to Stalingrad. He was to make a big name for himself in the hellish inferno over the Volga and on September 22 claimed a double while leading his La-5s to destroy five Ju 87s for no losses. Eleven days later Kuzmin achieved two more kills when his squadron stormed into a formation of 15 Ju 87s near Mamayev, six of these being shot down. Unfortunately, Kuzmin was hit by return fire and wounded in his abdomen but managed to make a successful forced landing. He returned to the regiment as a Kapitan in November, 1942 and claimed another double on January 29, 1943 while leading five La-5s to score six kills without loss. Further combats over Stalingrad ran his tally to 15 while his squadron was credited with downing 27 enemy planes throughout the battle. He was then posted to the glorious 9 GIAP forcing down a Bf 109 on his first sortie with the unit on May 30, 1943. On August 18, 1943 he was flying wing to Polkovnik Morozov, the regiment commander, when they had a tussle with Bf 109s near Pavlovsk. Kuzmin had to bail out but unfortunately his parachute did not open fully and he was killed.

KUZNETSOV, Anatolij Ivanovich

Combat record: 8 personal victories, 8 fractional credits, 1 enemy aircraft destroyed by strafing, 270 sorties, 60 encounters.
Decorations: Gold Star of Hero of the Soviet Union on February 22, 1943; the Orders of Lenin, the Red Banner (3).

Kuznetsov was born in the Tatarian ASSR in 1914 and enlisted in the VMF in 1936. He had flight training at Yejsk military flying school and saw action for the first time during the Russo-Finnish Winter War of 1939/40. He was decorated with two Orders of the Red Banner for his efforts during the conflict but no further details have emerged. By June, 1941 he had become a member of the 13 IAP-KBF and subsequently saw a lot of action over Hango (Hanko), southwest of Helsinki, and Tallin (Revel). He later fought with the regiment in the brutal battles of Leningrad and over the Volkhov front. He claimed a double with two Ju 87s over Ladoga Lake on May 29, 1942 and in doing so successfully broke up an attack on Soviet vessels. He finally rose to Kapitan and shturman but on January 19, 1943 was shot down by flak and crashed to his death. He was interred in Lebyazhye, Lomonosov area (W Leningrad).

KUZNETSOV, Mikhail Vasilyevich

Combat record: 22 personal victories, 6 fractional credits, 345 sorties, 72 encounters.
Decorations: Gold Star of Hero of the Soviet Union on September 8, 1943 in recognition of 17 victories, 6 fractional credits, 245 sorties, 53 encounters as of August, 1943, 2nd Gold Star on June 27, 1945; the Orders of Lenin, the Red Banner (4), Bogdan Khmelnitskij 2nd Class, the Patriotic War 1st Class, the Red Star (2).

Kuznetsov was born in Serpukhov near Moscow on November 7, 1913 and enrolled for service in 1933. He was graduated as a pilot at Yejsk naval flying school a year later and was to take part in the occupation of Polish soil in 1939 and in the Russo-Finnish Winter War of 1939/40. He was a squadron leader at the outbreak of the Patriotic War and saw considerable fighting in the great battles for Leningrad. In 1942 he was promoted Major assuming command of the 814 IAP. Under his dynamic leadership the unit fought a very successful campaign on Southwest Front and was designated Guards on August 24, 1943 becoming the 106 GIAP. Soon after Kuznetsov was awarded with his first title of Hero of the Soviet Union after writing a distinguished record over Leningrad, Kharkov, Dnyepropetrovsk, and Krivoj Rog. He had excelled over the Ukraine scoring 12 kills while flying MiG-3s and Yak-1s. The regiment was in the thick of the fighting during subsequent assignments on 3rd and 1st Ukrainian Fronts adding new laurels to its record during the Lemberg-Sandomierz campaign and in the air battles above Poland and the Reich. Kuznetsov advanced to Podpolkovnik but continued to go off on fighter sweeps whenever possible. On February 23, 1945 he was in the air leading six Yak-3s on a free hunt between Guben-Cottbus where they spotted some 40 Fw 190 fighter-bombers forming up for an attack on Soviet ground forces. Kuznetsov immediately ordered the attack and personally bounced a gaggle of fighters acting as top cover. Descending through a layer of clouds he closed in to 10-15 meters range before hitting tail-end Charlie with a stream of fire. The enemy plane exploded before it could take any evasive action. Kuznetsov added two more of the unsuspecting aircraft in quick succession while his flight got four more, all without loss. The regiment later took the fight to the Luftwaffe over Berlin winding up with a total of 299 confirmed victories with Kuznetsov in command. During his postwar career Kuznetsov graduated from the Air Force Academy in 1951 and was promoted General Major eight years later. He concluded his active duty in 1974 with 41 years service.

General Winter – a major factor on the Eastern Front. Shot of a typical Russian village, with inadequate mostly unsurfaced roads. (Author's collection)

KUZNETSOV, Nikolaj Aleksandrovich
Combat record: 14 personal victories, 12 fractional credits, 375 sorties, 35 encounters as of July, 1944.
Decorations: Gold Star of Hero of the Soviet Union on October 26, 1944; the Orders of Lenin (2), the Red Banner (3).

Kuznetsov was born in the Ivanovo area on October 10, 1918 and entered military service in 1938. He completed his pilot training at Chkalov military flying school two years later and became a member of the 191 IAP before the war. He started flying combat in I-16s on Karelian Front in June, 1941 and opened his account on August 27 downing a Ju 87. On September 11 Kuznetsov and four of his squadron bounced a formation of 20 Stukas near Krasnoye Selo, where eight of these were shot down. On another occasion in May, 1942 he led his flight against eight Ju 87s and two Bf 109s while conducting a front-line patrol, three of the dive-bombers being destroyed. On an unrecorded date Kuznetsov was successful in blasting a Bf 109 out of the sky close to the Luftwaffe airfield at Tungozera. He later was assigned to the 760 IAP and continued to see a great deal of action on Karelian Front rising to Major. He concluded his active duty in 1945 and died on October 24, 1982.

LANDIK, Ivan Ivanovich
Combat record: 16 personal victories, 160 sorties, 38 encounters.
Decorations: Gold Star posthumously on June 27, 1945; the Orders of Lenin, the Red Banner (2), the Patriotic War 2nd Class.

Landik was born in the Omsk area on February 18, 1919 and enlisted in the Soviet Army in 1940. He qualified as a pilot at Vyazniki military flying school two years later and saw action for the first time in June, 1942. Landik made a big name for himself while serving in the 482 IAP on 1st Ukrainian Front and eventually was promoted Kapitan and squadron leader. He is best remembered by fellow pilot and 19-victory ace A.F. Semyonov as "a courageous and ingenious fighter pilot and experienced squadron leader." On an unspecified date while flying armed reconnaissance he arrived over an enemy airfield and caught 10 Fw 190s as they were about to land. He dove down on one from above and immediately scored many strikes all along the fuselage whereupon it snapped and crashed in flames. On April 18, 1945 he became embroiled in a wild dogfight with a large gaggle of Fw 190s near Cottbus and destroyed two of them before he was shot down and killed.

LATYSHEV, Vladimir Aleksandrovich
Combat record: 17 personal victories, 232 sorties as of August, 1943.
Decorations: Gold Star of Hero of the Soviet Union on February 4, 1944; the Orders of Lenin, the Red Banner (3), the Patriotic War 1st and 2nd Class.

Latyshev was born in the Moscow area on July 21, 1921 and entered the VVS for flight training in 1941. He was graduated as a pilot at Vyazniki military flying school a year later commencing his combat duty in May that year. He served in the 67 GIAP through the close of war and rapidly rose to deputy squadron leader. During his time with the regiment Latyshev was greatly involved in the fighting at Demyansk, Stalingrad, Kursk, Minsk and Warsaw. His most memorable mission came on August 12, 1943 when he was leading eight Cobras on a fighter sweep and they engaged a large enemy formation, claiming the destruction of four Ju 88s and an equal number of Fw 190s. He was a Starshij Lejtenant at the end of the war and concluded his active duty in 1946.

LAVEJKIN, Ivan Pavlovich
Combat record: 24 personal victories, 15 fractional credits, 498 sorties, 106 encounters.
Decorations: Gold Star of Hero of the Soviet Union on August 24, 1943; the Orders of Lenin, the Red Banner (4), the Patriotic War 1st Class (2), the Red Star (2).

Lavejkin was born in Smolensk on August 2, 1921 and enrolled for service in the VVS in 1939. He received his pilot wings at Odessa military flying school a year later and saw

I.P. Lavejkin of the 5 GIAP, who ran up an impressive string of victories over Russia, Poland and the Reich. (Author's collection)

Kapitan Lavejkin photographed at Tarasovka, Dnyepr area, in 1943 wearing three Orders of the Red Banner, the Patriotic War 1st Class and the Guards badge. (V.I. Popkov)

action from the very start of the war. Lavejkin was with the crack 129 IAP through World War II and is remembered by his comrades as a phenomenal shot and a brilliant officer and pilot. On December 7, 1941 he shot down a Ju 87 and on March 21, 1942 claimed a Bf 110 between Gladovo-Tarutino when five LaGG-3s attacked a superior enemy formation destroying seven enemy planes without loss. He next gave a good account of himself at Rzhev during the period of June to July, 1942 and was well qualified for his first Order of the Red Banner for five kills soon after. In November, 1942 he was appointed Kapitan and squadron leader and saw a great deal of action over the Don River flying La-5s. On February 30, 1943 he was leading five La-5s on a front-line patrol when a running battle developed with 14 Ju 87s between Slavyansk-Kramatorsk, six of these being shot down. Lavejkin's share: one Stuka. He quickly advanced to Major and deputy squadron leader and continued his streak during subsequent assignments at Byelgorod, Izyum and Zaporozhye. Under his able leadership his squadron in eight months of combat was credited with 129 enemy aircraft in the air for 10 losses in air combat. Lavejkin enjoyed considerable success in the skies above Dnyepropetrovsk, Nikopol and Krivoj Rog when he was mainly occupied with free hunts and subsequently fought in the final air battles over Poland and the Reich. He remained in the VVS after the war and graduated from the Air Force Academy in 1950 and from General Staff Academy seven years later. He eventually rose to General Major and died on December 2, 1986.

LAVRENOV, Aleksandr Filippovich
Combat record: 22 personal victories, 150 sorties.
Decorations: Gold Star of Hero of the Soviet Union on November 1, 1943 in recognition of 17 kills, 3 fractional credits, 47 sorties, 26 engagements as of June, 1943; the Orders of Lenin, the Red Banner (2), the Patriotic War 1st Class, the Red Star.

Lavrenov was born in the Ryazan area on April 20, 1920 and started his military career in 1938. Two years later he was graduated as a pilot at Borisoglebsk military flying school and joined with the 291 IAP in April, 1943. In the Kuban theater Lavrenov was to write an indelible combat record racking up victories at a formidable pace. His number two at the time frequently was Mladshij Lejtenant Konobayev, who was to end the war as an ace with 17 kills, and both men became a dual scoring element combination. On April 29 Lavrenov blasted two Bf 109s out of the sky sweeping down on eight unsuspecting German fighters with his wingman in the vicinity of Krymskaya. Three days later he headed six of his squadron in an encounter with 14 Bf 109s escorting a Staffel of Ju 87s, and five Messerschmitts and a number of dive-bombers were destroyed. He next added a double with two Ju 87s to his personal tally on May 3 in a fierce battle with Luftwaffe aircraft near Kievskaya, seven of these going down in flames. On May 26 he got into two separate tussles while engaged in an escort mission reporting the destruction of two Bf 109s. Two days later he claimed two Ju 87s and a further Bf 109 in two sorties to bring his score to 17, all in just 26 air-to-air combats. He later proved his skills over the Crimea but on March 26, 1944 was shot down and killed.

V.D. Lavrinenkov, survivor of the Stalingrad ordeal, and destined to become one of the great aces of the German-Soviet front. He successfully evaded once and lived through a total of 46 months of combat racking up 35 personal victories (Author's collection)

LAVRINENKOV, Vladimir Dmitriyevich

Combat record: 35 personal victories, 11 fractional credits, 448 sorties for 415 combat hours, 134 encounters.

Decorations: 1st Gold Star on May 1, 1943 for 16 victories, 11 fractional credits, 322 sorties, 78 engagements as of February, 1943, 2nd Gold Star on July 1, 1944; the Orders of Lenin (2), the Red Banner (6), the Patriotic War 1st Class, the Red Star.

Lavrinenkov, brilliant officer and pilot, was born in the Smolensk area on May 17, 1919 and joined the VVS for flight training in 1940. He won his wings at Chuguyev military flying school a year later and first was assigned as an instructor to Chernigov flying school. He was in the forefront of action from the earliest days of the Patriotic War entering combat with the Luftwaffe as a Serzhant during the fighting for Rostov. He gained his first victory, a Bf 109, on a Yak-1 a short time later and this is reputed to have been an aircraft of Jagdgeschwader 2 *Richthofen*. It appears that this account was either a propaganda myth only or his opponent had been identified incorrectly as JG 2 at this stage was fairly active along the Channel coast. Lavrinenkov later took part in the air battles above Voronezh prior to moving with the 4 IAP to Stalingrad Front in August, 1942. He excelled in the fury of the air engagements over the Volga running up a string of nine kills along with 7 fractional credits while entering into 40 air-to-air combats, all with Yak-1s. In late 1942 Lavrinenkov and a select few of the regiment's fighter tigers were assigned to the crack 9 GIAP with Lavrinenkov taking over as leader of the 2nd Eskadrilya. He converted to Airacobras and enjoyed remarkable success at Batajsk and over the Kuban. In August, 1943 he destroyed one of the elusive Fw 189 reconnaissance planes over the Mius River by ramming, having expended the ammunition of his Cobra. He bailed out over enemy territory and became a prisoner but successfully evaded together with an Il-2 pilot. They decided to make a break when they were put on a train to Odessa, dropping off enroute. They went bolting into a field of man-high sunflowers beside the railroad and successfully pressed on toward the front line with the help of parti

Lavrinenkov with a Yak-7B on Stalingrad Front. (Author's collection)

Right: The indefatigable Lavrinenkov seen here as a Major. (Author's collection)

sans. He resumed combat duty soon after piling up a remarkable score in the skies of Melitopol, Dnyepropetrovsk, the Crimea and East Prussia. With the loss of Podpolkovnik A.A. Morozov he became his successor in command of the regiment in June, 1944 and served in this capacity through the close of war, by which time he had become a Major. His impressive total by type of enemy planes destroyed was as follows:

Bf 109s	15
Ju 88s	7
He 111s	5
Fw 190s	4
Bf 110s	2
Ju 52s	1
Fw 189s	1

Lavrinenkov's comrades praise his courage and vigor and remember him as a fine leader and tactician who could keep a clear tactical head even when things were going rough. He remained in the VVS following World War II and rose to command a fighter air division prior to his graduating from Frunze Military Academy in 1948. Six years later he graduated from General Staff Academy and later held various assignments in the PVO. In 1971 he rose to General Polkovnik.

LAVRONENKO, Ivan Vasilyevich
Combat record: 15 personal victories, 167 sorties, 32 encounters.
Decorations: Gold Star of Hero of the Soviet Union posthumously on October 26, 1944; the Orders of Lenin, the Red Banner, the Patriotic War 1st Class, the Red Star.

Lavronenko was born in Krivoj Rog on February 9, 1922 and entered military service in 1940. He received his flight training at Kacha military flying school a year later and in May, 1943 was posted to the 239 IAP commencing his combat duty over the Kuban. He was not slow to get started, racking up a string of six kills in a matter of a few weeks. For his efforts he was promoted to deputy squadron leader in August and on the 20th tore into an enemy formation near Kotelva (SW Akhtyrka) and quickly destroyed two Ju 87s and a Bf 109. The German fighter already had him squarely in his sights, blowing off his canopy, but then had the misfortune of overtaking Lavronenko, who had throttled back. The German found himself in front of Lavronenko's guns and after a few bursts he blew up and plunged earthward. On June 6, 1944 he became embroiled in a dogfight with two Bf 109s in the Stanislava area and blasted one of them out of the sky, the other escaping in a layer of cloud. On his way home he flew through a rather heavy curtain of flak and was killed. He was interred in Chortkov, Ternopol area, and was awarded a posthumous title of Hero Of the Soviet Union in recognition of his remarkable record.

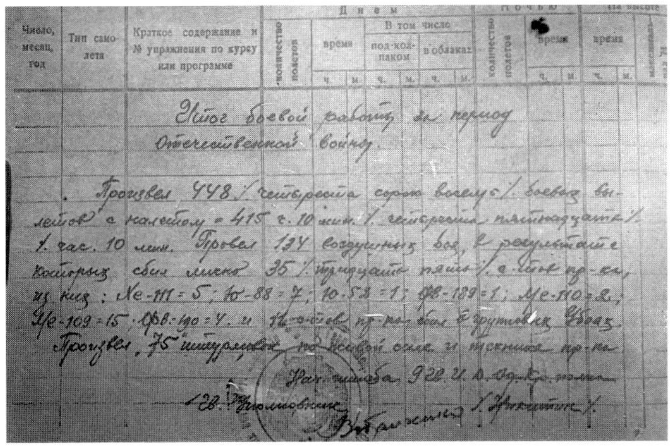

Last spread of Lavrinenkov's logbook giving an outline of his combat record: number of sorties, combat hours, aerial encounters and victories by type of enemy aircraft destroyed. (Author's collection)

LAZAREV, Sergej Ivanovich
Combat record: 15 personal victories, 3 fractional credits, 131 sorties, 48 encounters as of March, 1944.
Decorations: Gold Star of Hero of the Soviet Union on October 26, 1944; the Orders of Lenin, the Red Banner (2), Aleksandr Nevskij, the Patriotic War 1st Class.

Lazarev was born in the Vladimir area on June 23, 1923 and joined the Soviet Army in 1941. He completed his pilot training at Krasnodar military flying school later that year and started flying combat with the 728 IAP in July, 1942. He gained his initial combat experience on I-16s in the heavy fighting for Rzhev and by September 8 had chalked up a kill over a Ju 88 along with three fractional credits. He converted to Yak-7Bs in the spring of 1943 and during subsequent combat assignments managed to put up a good performance at Kursk, Byelgorod, Poltava, over the Dnyepr River, Krakau (Krakov) and the Reich. He rose to squadron leader and Starshij Lejtenant but on March 1, 1945 he was killed in action near Bunzlau (Boleslawiec), northwest of Breslau.

LEBEDEV, Fyodor Mikhajlovich
Combat record: 17 personal victories, 2 fractional credits, 351 sorties, 36 encounters.
Decorations: Gold Star of Hero of the Soviet Union on June 27, 1945; the Orders of Lenin, the Red Banner (2), Aleksandr Nevskij, the Patriotic War 1st and 2nd Class, the Red Star.

Lebedev was born in the Mozhajsk area on January 26, 1923 and enlisted in the VVS in 1939. He qualified as a pilot at Kacha military flying school a year later and started flying combat in June, 1941. He made a brilliant combat record serving with the 482 IAP on 1st Ukrainian Front and eventually rose to Major and took over as leader of a fighter squadron. On April 24, 1945 four La-5s with Lebedev in the lead caught a formation of 10 Bf 109s and four Fw 190s from behind in the vicinity of Berlin as these were harassing a Soviet tank column. Two Messerschmitts and a Fw 190 were claimed destroyed for no losses in breaking up the enemy attack. Lebedev remained in the VVS following World War II and in 1953 graduated from Frunze Military Academy. He came off active duty with the rank of Polkovnik in 1960.

LEBEDEV, Semyon Andrianovich

Combat record: 22 personal victories, 2 fractional credits, 220 sorties, 55 encounters.

Decorations: Gold Star of Hero of the Soviet Union on February 23, 1945 for 19 victories, 2 fractional credits, 169 sorties and 37 engagements as of August, 1944; the Orders of Lenin, the Red Banner (3), Aleksandr Nevskij, the Patriotic War 1st Class (2), the Red Star.

Lebedev was born in the Karaganda area on December 5, 1919 and started his military career in 1937. Two years later he qualified as a fighter pilot at Kacha military flying school being posted to the 43 IAP on North Caucasus Front in April, 1943, flying Yaks. He was not slow to get started and was given credit for six kills over the Kuban in 10 weeks combat. He continued to score on a regular basis during subsequent assignments on South, 4th Ukrainian, 1st and 3rd Byelorussian Fronts. He eventually advanced to Major and took over as leader of a fighter squadron, which was being credited with 17 enemy planes in the air during 276 sorties and 13 air encounters on 3rd Byelorussian Front. On July 7, 1944 Lebedev was leading six of his squadron to engage 10 German bombers and 18 fighters and they were successful in breaking up their formation scoring six kills. After the close of war he graduated from the Air Force Academy and became a lecturer there. He wound up his military career with the rank of Polkovnik in 1975 and is living in Monino near Moscow.

LEONOV, Nikolaj Ivanovich

Combat record: 20 personal victories.

Decorations: Gold Star of Hero of the Soviet Union on April 13, 1944 in recognition of 15 kills, 173 sorties, 31 encounters as of November, 1943; the Orders of Lenin, the Red Banner (3), the Patriotic War 1st Class, the Red Star (2).

Leonov was born in the Kursk area on April 20, 1919 and entered the Soviet Army in 1937. Two years later he graduated from flight training and was posted to the 183 IAP joining combat with the Luftwaffe in May, 1942. He made a big name for himself in the contested air space above Kharkov, Borodayevka and Domotkan. On July 10, 1943 he claimed a double with two Fw 190s while leading 12 Yak-1s and Yak-7Bs in an attack on 15 Focke-Wulfs escorting four Bf 109 fighter-bombers near Prokhorovka. He required just 31 aerial encounters to chalk up 15 kills during 173 sorties of which 116 were escorts, 22 ground force cover, seven scrambles and two air patrols qualifying him for the award of the title of Hero of the Soviet Union. His victories by type of enemy planes destroyed were as follows:

Ju 88s	4
Ju 87s	4
He 111s	1
Fw 190s	3
Bf 109s	3

He later participated in periods of intense activity over Hungary and was able to add at least one Fw 190 during November, 1944 when he got into a tussle with enemy fighters near Jaszbereny (E Budapest). He had by now become a Kapitan in the 150 GIAP. He stayed in the service after the war and retired with the rank of Polkovnik in 1957.

LEONOVICH, Ivan Semyonovich

Combat record: 28 personal victories, 340 sorties, 51 encounters.

Decorations: Gold Star of Hero of the Soviet Union on November 2, 1944 in recognition of 26 kills, 330 sorties, 50 air combats as of November, 1944; the Orders of Lenin, the Red Banner (2), the Patriotic War 1st Class.

A laughing I.S. Leonovich poses for the photographers. He is wearing the typical winter attire including the shapka/ushanka (synthetic pile winter cap), which was introduced by NKO (Narodnyj Komissariat Oborony – People's Commissariat of Defense) order no.187 dated July 5, 1940 for more protection against the cold. On his big day Leonovich got six confirmed kills. (Author's collection)

Leonovich was born in Borisov on November 14, 1920 and entered military service in 1940. He won his wings at Krasnodar military flying school later that year following which he was assigned as an instructor at Stalingrad Aviation Club between 1939/40 and Krasnodar flying school between 1941/42. He then was posted to the 29 GIAP on Leningrad Front and fired his guns in anger for the first time in December, 1942. He opened his account with a Ju 87 on May 26, 1943 when he was flying Yak-7Bs and then began to achieve aerial victories at a formidable pace. By May 30, 1944 his score had risen to 25 personal kills and three days later accounted for another victory hitting the enemy plane from a range of 50 meters. He had excelled in the fury of Volkhov and Karelian air battles and on his big day in January, 1944 racked up six kills during four sorties while engaged in providing assault area cover at Leningrad. He was promoted Starshij Lejtenant and deputy squadron leader and went on to come out of World War II as the regiment's second highest scoring ace. He was killed in an automobile accident on November 2 or 13, 1946.

LESHCHENKO, Vyacheslav Sergeyevich

Combat record: 13 personal victories, 10 fractional credits, 285 sorties, 45 encounters as of May 20, 1943.

Decorations: Gold Star of Hero of the Soviet Union on August 24, 1943; the Orders of Lenin, the Red Banner, Aleksandr Nevskij, the Patriotic War 2nd Class, the Red Star (3).

Leshchenko was born in Chernigov on May 6, 1916 and enrolled for service in the VVS in 1940. He was graduated as a pilot at Ulyanovsk military flying school a year later and was assigned to the 4 IAP. He saw considerable fighting at Kishinyov, Tiraspol, Nikolayev, Odessa and Kherson from the very start of the war initially flying the Polikarpov I-16 fighter. He later converted to Yak-7Bs and participated in the ferocious battles over Stalingrad. On October 16, 1942 he got a single when seven Yaks tore into a formation of 18 Ju 87s and eight Bf 109s, three of the dive-bombers being shot down. He claimed two Bf 109s on April 29, 1943 when Leshchenko and six of his squadron mates were bounced by four German fighters. Without hesitating they reportedly engaged the Messerschmitts head-on and in a fierce series of dogfights claimed to have destroyed all four of them. He reported another single on May 8 and next made a claim for a Bf 109 the following day. He advanced to Lejtenant and deputy squadron leader and almost certainly added to his score during the later stages of the war but no details are available. He served with the postwar VVS and graduated from the Air Force Academy in 1945 and from the General Staff Academy in 1959. He had become a General Major when he left the ranks in 1971. He died on March 30, 1978.

Two great aces share a quiet moment: S.G. Yankovskij (left) flew Shturmoviks with great distinction on 1st Baltic Front, I.D. Likhobabin was the top ace of the 72 GIAP with 30 kills. The date is March, 1945. (Author's collection)

LIKHOBABIN, Ivan Dmitriyevich

Combat record: 30 personal victories, 9 fractional credits, 321 sorties.

Decorations: Gold Star of Hero of the Soviet Union on October 26, 1944 for 17 kills, 9 fractional credits, 276 sorties and 45 engagements as of August, 1944; the Orders of Lenin, the Red Banner (5), Aleksandr Nevskij, the Patriotic War 1st Class, the Red Star.

Likhobabin was born in the Voronezh area on January 27, 1916 and started his distinguished military career in 1939. He completed his pilot training a year later and entered combat with the 402 IAP in November, 1941. He achieved fame for displaying great courage and fighting spirit with complete disregard for his personal safety. He single-handedly engaged two enemy aircraft on one occasion in late 1941, took on four planes on July 18, 1942 and tore into five hostile planes on an unspecified day in August, 1942. He had become a Kapitan when he was assigned to the 485 IAP in late 1942 to become greatly involved in the fighting over the Demyansk bridgehead. He enjoyed above-average success during subsequent assignments on Northwest, 2nd Baltic, 2nd and 3rd Byelorussian Fronts and was wounded twice before the cessation of hostilities. He got one of the elusive Fw 189s near Staraya Russa on March 13, 1943 and had his best day on July 27, 1943 when he bagged three Fw 190s in quick succession. He rapidly rose to Major and deputy commander of the 72 GIAP eventually being put in command of the unit. With Likhobabin in the lead, the regiment had a field day on an unrecorded date in September, 1944, when 14 kills were submitted by the pilots. Likhobabin's share: two victories. He went on to become the regiment's ranking ace and in his own fraternity was known as "khozyain neba" – master of the skies. He stayed in the service after the war and graduated from the Air Force Academy in 1951 leaving active duty as a Polkovnik in 1962.

LIKHOVID, Mikhail Stepanovich
Combat record: 16 personal victories, 11 fractional credits plus 6 enemy aircraft destroyed in ground attacks, 208 sorties, 44 encounters.
Decorations: Gold Star of Hero of the Soviet Union posthumously on June 27, 1945; the Orders of Lenin, the Red Banner (3).

Likhovid was born in the Sumy area on February 28, 1922 and entered the Soviet Army in 1940. He graduated from flight training a year later and entered combat in July, 1941 fighting with the 298 IAP on South Front. During its first actions the regiment was operating I-16s but it was not before transition to Airacobras had been accomplished that Likhovid really began to pile up his score. He got a single on March 21, 1943 with his squadron mates bringing the day's tally to four in a series of tussles in the Taman area. On April 21 six Cobras ran into eight Bf 109s while flying a front-line patrol in the vicinity of Krymskaya with Likhovid quickly destroying one of them and on a further mission later that day adding another of these. By August, 1944 he had brought his combat record to 16 kills along with 11 fractional credits and six planes, seven locomotives and 20 motor vehicles destroyed in strafing attacks and was recommended for the award of the title of Hero of the Soviet Union. On August 12, 1944 he force landed due to engine failure in a pasture in the Rava-Rusakaya area near Lvov and sent a radio request for two mechanics to take care of the damage. The aircraft quickly was repaired but as it was discovered that the boggy ground wouldn't allow him to takeoff, they were ambushed by a bunch of Ukrainian nationalists (OUN). They were wounded, overwhelmed and subjected to horrible mistreatment. Finally Likhovid and the mechanic Krasnyanskij were doused with gasoline and lit on fire to die an excruciating death while the other mechanic, Fonkevich, was left to his fate. Likhovid was interred in Rava-Rusaka.

Ace of Leningrad Front. P.Ya. Likholetov is credited with 25 kills in the epic roll-back of German forces at Leningrad. (Author's collection)

LIKHOLETOV, Pyotr Yakovlevich
Combat record: 25 personal victories, 5 fractional credits, 382 sorties, 78 air-to-air combats.
Decorations: Gold Star of Hero of the Soviet Union on February 4, 1944 for 19 personal victories, 5 fractional credits, 366 sorties, 72 encounters as of October, 1943; the Orders of Lenin, the Red Banner, the Patriotic War 1st Class, the Red Star.

Likholetov was born in the Donetsk area on July 18, 1917 and entered military service in 1937. He completed his pilot training at Kharkov military flying school a year later and saw action for the first time during the Russo-Finnish Winter War of 1939/40. In 1940 he attended Chuguyev military flying school and then was in continuous action from the very first days of the Patriotic War. He displayed his remarkable skills while serv-

Right: Happy warrior Likholetov. Like many other high scorers who survived air combat he lost his life in an accident. (Author's collection)

ing with the 159 IAP on Leningrad Front. On one occasion he claimed a Bf 109 in a head-on encounter but had to abandon his own burning aircraft parachuting to safety near the railroad station of Novyj Byt. He later advanced to Kapitan and squadron leader and gave a good account of himself in June, 1944 achieving six kills within three days. He was seriously injured in an automobile accident later dying of his wounds on July 13, 1945. He was buried in Leningrad.

LIPILIN, Aleksandr Alekseyevich

Combat record: 9 personal victories, 112 sorties as of October, 1941.

Decorations: Gold Star of Hero of the Soviet Union on February 24, 1942; the Orders of Lenin (2), the Red Banner (2), the Patriotic War 1st Class (2), the Red Star (2).

Lipilin was born in the Tambov area on January 18, 1913 and joined the Soviet Army in 1934. He received his wings at Orenburg military flying school three years later and was posted to the 41 IAP before the outbreak of war. He was early in the public eye for destroying a Ju 88 near Mogilyov on June 26, 1941. He completed as many as 10 sorties daily between August 19-22 in a desperate attempt to support the hard-pressed Soviet ground forces. During the period of August to September he was wounded twice and shot down by flak once having to take to his parachute. Lipilin's final score is uncertain but it is possible that he added to his tally during subsequent combat assignments. He served with the postwar VVS and returned to civilian life with the rank of Polkovnik in 1961.

LITAVRIN, Sergej Gavrilovich

Combat record: 19 personal victories, 5 fractional credits, 462 sorties, 90 encounters.

Decorations: Gold Star of Hero of the Soviet Union on January 28, 1943 in recognition of 10 kills, 311 sorties and 55 encounters as of December, 1942; the Orders of Lenin, the Red Banner (2), Aleksandr Nevskij, the Red Star.

Litavrin was born in the Lipetsk area and enrolled for service in the VVS at age 18. He was graduated as a pilot at Borisoglebsk military flying school in 1940 and joined with the 158 IAP flying I-16s before the war. He combined forces with Lejtenant Yelkin to shoot down a Ju 88 on June 26, 1941 and the following day made a claim for another of these in the vicinity of Pskov single-handedly. In September, 1941 he was promoted squadron leader and saw a lot of action during the rest of the year running his score to six. In early 1942 he converted to Airacobras and on May 29, 1942 was leading six of these on a front-line patrol in the Volkhov area where they stormed into a formation of 18 bombers escorted by 12 fighters. They destroyed three Ju 88s in a frontal attack and then rejoined formation to force down two Bf 110s with two Bf 109s being damaged. Most successful pilot in this affray was Litavrin himself with two kills. He was promoted Kapitan and by December, 1942 his score had risen to 10. On January 13, 1943 he was successful in making his mark against the new Fw 190 fighters which were beginning to reach JG 54 early in 1943 sending down one in flames. A second was obliged to make a force-landing on frozen Ladoga Lake from where it was removed by the Russians to be test-flown. Litavrin racked up his 14th air victory near Kolpino on June 24, 1943 and continued to fly Airacobras throughout 1943. In February, 1944 the regiment reequipped with Yak-9s with Litavrin flying an aircraft with the inscription "Lipetskij komsomolets" – komsomol of Lipetsk. He achieved his last victory of the war on June 18, 1944 when he claimed a Finnish Brewster B-239. No such casualty can be found in Finnish records, and it is possible that this combat actually occurred on June 12, when 2/HLeLv. 26 reported one Brewster missing in action. In 1945 he advanced to deputy regiment commander and finished as the unit's second ranking ace. Following World War II he continued on active duty with the VVS and graduated from the Air Force Academy in 1952. He was killed in an aircraft accident on February 4, 1957, and was a Polkovnik at the time of his death.

LITVINCHUK, Boris Mikhajlovich

Combat record: 18 personal victories, 9 fractional credits, 459 sorties, 44 encounters.

Decorations: Gold Star of Hero of the Soviet Union on May 16, 1944 for 17 kills as of April, 1944; the Orders of Lenin, the Red Banner (3), the Patriotic War 1st Class (2), the Red Star.

Litvinchuk was born in the Azerbaijan SSR on June 1, 1917 and entered the VMF in 1937. He was graduated as a pilot at Yejsk military flying school a year later and by the outbreak of the Patriotic War had become a member of the 32 IAP of the Black Sea Fleet's air service. He participated in the great battles over Novorossijsk, Taman, Nikolayev and Odessa and allegedly shot down a Luftwaffe fighter ace at Novorossijsk in September, 1943 but the German's identity has unfortunately not been established. On November 1 he teamed with Lejtenants G.P. Kolontayenko and P.A. Krasnov to destroy two Ju 87s and a Bf 109 in the vicinity of Kerch and five days later he combined forces with the regiment commander, K.D. Denisov, to force down two Bf 109s. His number of victories steadily increased during subsequent air battles over Konstanza (Rumania), the Dnyepr and Perekop with four missions daily being commonplace. On March 10, 1944 18 Airacobras were assigned to providing cover for some 23 ShAP Il-2s to the Luftwaffe airfield at Kulbakino, Nikolayev area. Some 40 Fw 190s and Bf 109s rose to engage them but it was to prove a black day for the Luftwaffe as claims for 11 enemy aircraft destroyed were submitted by the 11 GIAP with Litvinchuk accounting for a double. He had by now made Kapitan and taken over as leader of a fighter squadron which was to be credited with 102 enemy aircraft in the air until the close of war. Litvinchuk remained in the VMF following World War II and concluded his active duty with the rank of Polkovnik in 1961.

LITVINENKO, Trofim Afanasyevich

Combat Record: 23 personal victories, 519 sorties.

Decorations: Gold Star of Hero of the Soviet Union on November 2, 1944 in recognition of 20 kills, 167 sorties, 41 encounters; the Orders of Lenin (2), the Red Banner, Aleksandr Nevskij.

Litvinenko was born in the Cherkassy area on October 18, 1910 and enrolled for service in the Soviet Army in 1932. A year later he was graduated at Odessa tank training school and upon applying for flight training was sent to Odessa military flying school. He received his pilot wings in 1934 and later attended Voroshilovgrad military flying school prior to cutting his teeth against the Finns during the Winter War of 1939/40. His efforts won him the Order of Lenin and next managed to put up a good performance during the darkest hours of the Patriotic War while serving with the 191 IAP. By September, 1941 he had brought his tally to five during 38 sorties and by now had become a Major and shturman. On September 28 he was shot down and wounded in a scrap with Bf 109s and although he managed to get out of his crippled fighter his parachute snagged in a tree, trapping him in the air without food and water before he was rescued three days later. He was sent to hospital but enroute the medical echelon was caught in an air attack and he sustained major injuries. It was only through luck that he escaped with his life requiring 16 months to recuperate. He was put back on duty in 1944 and was to enjoy considerable success during the later stages of the war, finishing as regiment commander. He wound up his military career with the rank of Podpolkovnik in 1946 and passed away on September 14, 1963.

LITVYAK, Lidiya Vladimirovna

Combat record: 12 personal victories including 1 reconnaissance balloon, 4 fractional credits, 168 sorties.

Decorations: Gold Star of Hero of the Soviet Union posthumously on May 5, 1990; the Orders of the Red Banner, the Red Star.

Litvyak was born in Moscow on August 18, 1921 and was destined to become the most successful of Soviet women fighter pilots. Aged 15 she went on her first solo flight and later graduated from Kherson military flying school. She was an instructor at Kalinin Aeroklub following which she served with the famous 586 IAP, the women's fighter regiment which had been

Major T.A. Litvinenko of the 191 IAP (Author's collection)

Litvinenko strapped in for another mission (Author's collection)

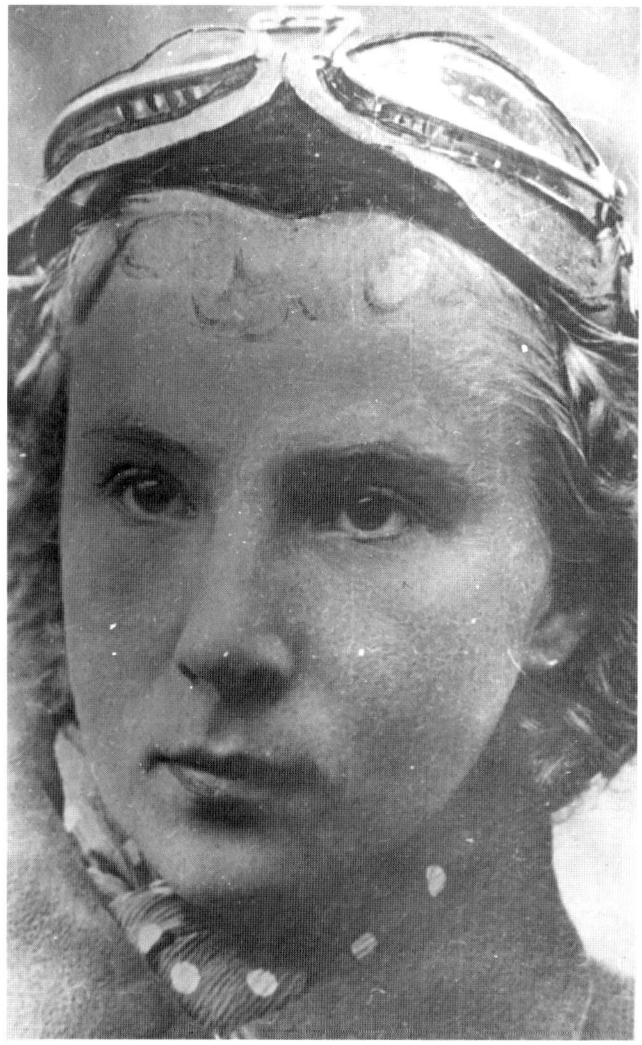

Lidiya Litvyak. This pretty aviatrix scored 12 air victories to emerge as the World's leading female fighter ace. She was killed in air combat on August 1, 1943 while flying her fourth mission of the day. (Author's collection)

Left: Litvyak on the wing of her fighter. She is rugged up against the brutal winter wearing cold weather flying gear typical of the early stages of the war – fleece lined canvas suit and heavy fur boots. No badges were applied to this kind of clothing. (Author's collection)

Lidiya Litvyak (left) and Kuznetsova gathering around Yekaterina Budanova (center) to receive some last minute advice. Budanova had 11 victories before she was killed in action on May 6, 1943. (Author's collection)

activated at Engels in October, 1941, between January and August, 1942 flying Yak-1s. In September Litvyak and her squadron mates Belyaeva, Budanova and Kuznetsova were assigned to the 437 IAP which was seeing a great deal of action over Stalingrad and along the Volga River. Litvyak destroyed her first enemy plane in the air during her second combat sortie which occurred on September 13 when four Yaks with Major S. Danilov in the lead became involved in a melee with a superior enemy force. Litvyak quickly wracked her fighter around in a tight turn to close on a Ju 88 which fell from the sky in flames after several bursts. She next shot a Bf 109 off Raya Belyaeva's tail, the German pilot being captured. The following day she combined forces with Yekaterina Budanova to down another Bf 109 and next claimed a Ju 88 on September 27, the gunner having shot up the regiment commander, Major M.S. Khvostnikov. In further action that day

Litvyak teamed with Starshij Lejtenant Belyaeva to force down a Bf 109. On October 10 she went off on five sorties through the day most of which were escorts and by the close of the year her tally stood at four personal kills in 20 air-to-air combats. A short time later she was posted to the 296 IAP and on February 19, 1943 was promoted Mladshij Lejtenant. She got another Ju 88 on February 11 also sharing a Fw 190 as four Yaks led by Major N. Baranov were achieving five victories without loss. On March 1 she got another Fw 190 while flying wing to Baranov and on the 22nd was scrambled with six of her squadron to intercept Ju 88s approaching Rostov. After destroying one of the bombers she was bounced by six Bf 109s and force-landed. She was picked up by a Shturmovik landing in a nearby field and taken to the hospital. She was out of action until May making a claim for a Bf 109 on the 5th while engaged in escorting a formation of Pe-2s. Her strength though gave out and she was grounded but resumed combat duty two days later claiming a further Bf 109. She was escort for Il-2s on July 16 with six squadron mates when they engaged a formation of 30 bombers and six Messerschmitts on the way to the front. In the ensuing melee she downed one of the bombers and shared in the destruction of a fighter before she was caught in a burst of fire and wounded again. Determined to return to combat she was unwilling to follow the physicians' advise and bagged a Bf 109 soon after as the German fighter was working with I. Golyshev. She was in turn attacked by another and had to force-land again. On August 1, 1943 she went off on three sorties claiming a Bf 109 jointly with fellow pilots. On a fourth mission in the afternoon six Yaks had a tussle with 30 Ju 88s and 12 escorts near Marinovka, Donetsk area, and she was shot down and crashed to her death.

LOBANOV, Aleksandr Vasilyevich

Combat record: 26 personal victories, 14 fractional credits, 811 sorties, 83 encounters.

Decorations: Gold Star of Hero of the Soviet Union on September 28, 1943 for 11 kills, 12 fractional credits, 376 sorties and 52 air engagements as of July, 1943; the Orders of Lenin, the Red Banner (3), Aleksandr Nevskij, the Patriotic War 1st Class.

Lobanov was born in the Pskov area on April 28, 1917 and enlisted in the VVS for flight training in 1937. He qualified as a pilot at Borisoglebsk military flying school a year later and was in the thick of the fighting from August, 1941. He wrote a distinguished combat record while serving with the 41 GIAP in the great aerial campaigns above the Donbas, the North Caucasus, Kursk-Orel, the Ukraine, Poland and finally the Reich. He rapidly rose to Starshij Lejtenant and deputy squadron leader and enjoyed considerable success in the ferocious fighting at Kursk and Kharkov. On July 7, 1943 he claimed two kills while leading four La-5s to tie into a superior enemy formation. He went on to finish as the regiment's ranking ace; his total of combat sorties is a matter of dispute, one source suggesting 850. Following the close of war Lobanov continued on active duty until his retirement in 1953 when he had made Podpolkovnik and regiment commander. He died on October 4, 1986.

LOBAS, Pyotr Kalinikovich

Combat record: 19 personal victories, 3 fractional credits, 160 sorties.

Starshij Lejtenant A.V. Lobanov (left) and Major A.G. Pavlov of the 41 GIAP in front of parked La-5FNs photographed on 1st Ukrainian Front in 1944. Pavlov was among the unit's more successful aces gaining at least 10 personal victories and 16 more shares. Note the regiment's insignia on the engine cowling of the fighters, which possibly was "borrowed" from JG 54 "Grünherz." (Author's collection)

Decorations: Gold Star of Hero of the Soviet Union on April 19, 1945 in recognition of 15 kills, 106 sorties as of January, 1945; the Orders of Lenin, the Red Banner (2), Aleksandr Nevskij, the Patriotic War 1st Class, the Red Star (2).

Lobas was born in the Primorsk area on June 23, 1916 and entered the Soviet Army in 1940. He was graduated as a pilot at Armavir military flying school a year later and was assigned to the 744 IAP in September, 1942 to enter combat. On June 1, 1943 six Yak-7Bs with Kapitan A.V. Zazayev in the lead were scrambled to intercept Luftwaffe bombers but instead were attacked by eight Fw 190s and a running battle developed. In all, four enemy fighters were claimed destroyed with Lobas accounting for one of them. He then began to score on a regular basis and by the end of the month his score had risen to six. Lobas subsequently flew with great distinction over Smolensk, Nevel, Orsha, Borisov and East Prussia. He rose to Kapitan and on October 16, 1944 blasted a Bf 109 out of the sky south of Schirwindt (East Prussia) while flying escort for Il-2s in a Yak-3. He added a Fw 190 on the 23rd and destroyed his 14th enemy aircraft with another Bf 109 on November 4. During January, 1945 he reported the destruction of three Luftwaffe planes including a Fw 190 that he shot down in the vicinity of Königsberg on the 28th. On March 18 he was hit by groundfire twice while flying an escort for Il-2s in the Bladiau area (SW Königsberg) and parachuted to safety behind the Soviet lines. Lobas served with the postwar VVS and graduated from the Air Force Academy in 1951. He left active duty with the rank of Polkovnik nine years later and passed away on April 1, 1985.

General Major G.A. Lobov, donning a fur-lined flying jacket manufactured by the Allies, by his Yak on which 20 victory stars are visible. He ended World War II with 19 personal victories along with eight fractional credits and was destined to add four more in Korea. (Author's collection)

Lobov (left) seen here as a Podpolkovnik conferring with V.N. Buyanov, chief political officer of the 322 IAD, alongside Lobov's aircraft. The score speaks for itself. This photo is dated May 8, 1945. (Author's collection)

LOBOV, Georgij Ageyevich

Combat record: 19 personal victories, 8 fractional credits, 346 sorties in World War II plus 4 personal victories during 15 sorties in Korea 1950/53.

Decorations: Gold Star of Hero of the Soviet Union on October 10, 1951; the Orders of Lenin, the Red Banner (4), Kutuzov 2nd Class, the Patriotic War 1st Class (2), the Red Star (3).

Lobov was born Yekaterinodar (Krasnodar) on April 23, 1915 and entered the Soviet Army in 1935. He completed his pilot training at Stalingrad military flying school in 1939 following which he gained his first combat experience against the Finns during the Winter War of 1939/40. He saw a great deal of action from the very first days of the Patriotic War and rapidly rose from deputy squadron leader to commander of a Guards fighter regiment. By late 1944 he had advanced to Podpolkovnik and deputy commander of the 322 IAD. He was promoted General Major assuming command of the crack 7 GIAD in February, 1945 and served in this capacity with great distinction through the close of war. He attained high rank with the postwar VVS and in March, 1951 deployed with the 303 IAD to Korea to see action against the United Nations air forces. Under his leadership the MiG-15 equipped units achieved impressive scores particularly against fighter-bombers. In time he rose to commander of the 64 IAK which parented three fighter aviation divisions which were to produce a total of 51 aces in Korea. In 1955 Lobov graduated from the General Staff Academy winding up his military career with the rank of General Lejtenant in 1976.

LOGVINENKO, Nikolaj Pavlovich

Combat record: 20 personal victories, 6 fractional credits.

Decorations: Gold Star of Hero of the Soviet Union on August 24, 1943 for 16 victories, 2 fractional credits, 245 sorties, 76 encounters plus 5 tanks, 40 motor vehicles destroyed in ground attacks as of May, 1943; the Orders of Lenin, the Red Banner (3), Aleksandr Nevskij, the Patriotic War 1st and 2nd Class.

Logvinenko was born in the Sumy area on January 15, 1920 and entered military service in 1939. He graduated from flight training a year later and entered combat as a flight leader in the 92 IAP in June, 1941. During his combat career he saw considerable fighting on Northwest, Stalingrad, North Caucasus and other Fronts proving his skills after joining with the 293 IAP. He was promoted Kapitan and squadron leader and was able to write a distinguished record in the skies above the Caucasus. On April 1943 he scored a single victory while leading 10 of his squadron mates on an escort for Il-2s. They became involved in a dogfight with 20 Bf 109s near Krymskaya where four of these were shot down in flames. He next claimed a double on May 5 when 10 Yak-1 tore into a formation of 40 bombers and their escorts and chalked up three kills. Logvinenko again forced down two enemy planes two days later when eight Yaks under his leadership mixed it with a superior Luftwaffe force coming away with five victories. He wound up his military career with the rank of Major in July, 1946 and died on January 7, 1974.

LUGANSKIJ, Sergej Danilovich

Combat record: 37 personal victories, 6 fractional credits, 417 sorties, 200 encounters.

Decorations: 1st Gold Star on September 2, 1943 in recognition of 18 kills, 1 fractional credit, 221 sorties as of August, 1943, 2nd Gold Star for 33 kills, 5 fractional credits, 355 sorties as of December, 1943; the Orders of Lenin (2), the Red Banner (2), Aleksandr Nevskij, the Red Star (2).

Luganskij, one of the great characters of Soviet fighter aviation, was born in Alma Ata on October 1, 1918 and enrolled for service in 1938. He completed his pilot training at Orenburg military flying school two years later and fought during the Russo-Finnish Winter War of 1939/40 flying 59 combat sorties. He was posted as a squadron leader to the 162 IAP in October, 1941 to begin his brilliant combat career against the Luftwaffe. At Stalingrad he was credited with the destruction of a Bf 109 by ramming on September 14, 1942 while flying a Yak-1. During further action over the Volga he allegedly shot down an Italian fighter ace quoted by some Soviet sources as "Gibelli with some 50 victories"; no evidence exists to confirm this claim. Top-scoring ace of the Regia Aeronautica actually was Teresio Martinoli with 22 kills, and as no further information has been forthcoming this event probably will remain a mystery. Luganskij performed a second successful ramming in the Kirovograd area in 1943 this time bringing down a German bomber. He was given credit for a total of four kills on South Front and had made Kapitan and squadron leader in the 270 IAP when he took part in very heavy fighting at Kursk. In a burst of energy and skill he ran up a string of 14 air victories between July 5 and August 6, 1943 to lead the regiment while his squadron was credited with downing 25 enemy planes during 372 sorties and 89 air-to-air combats. He claimed a double

Invincible Sergej Luganskij, who survived 200 encounters to achieve 37 air victories together with six fractional credits. Here he is seen as a Kapitan. (Author's collection)

Major Luganskij. He stayed in the VVS following the close of war and eventually made General Major. (Author's collection)

on August 4 while leading and escort for Il-2s and got another double the following day when he entered into two separate scraps. In May, 1944 he took over as commander of the regiment and was to lead it with consummate skill over Bucharest and Ploesti. In early 1945 he was sent to the Air Force Academy his place being taken by Major Shevchuk. In Luganskij's judgment, Soviet fighter pilot morale was exceptional and superior to the enemy's. Recalls Luganskij: "Without hesitating, we always were ready to utilize aerial ramming or to deliver a head-on attack whereas the fascists never were inspired by this kind of morale." As a matter of fact, many Luftwaffe pilots were far from enthusiastic about these forms of attack as the Bf 109 proved to be particularly vulnerable in frontal attacks. Luganskij was a brilliant leader and phenomenal shot; he emerged unscathed from some 200 aerial battles which he personally attributed to his strict attention to elementary tactics. The lesson he taught his young bucks was: "Do not separate from your leader. Maintain the PARA (i.e. two-plane formation)." This basic lesson had kept him alive on those occasions when enemy fighters had already cornered him – he was saved by his wingmen, 18-victory ace Major Ivan Kuzmichev, no fewer than four times. He remained in the VVS after the war and had become a General Major when he left active duty in 1964. He died on January 16, 1977.

LUKIN, Afanasij Petrovich
Combat record: 14 personal victories, 4 fractional credits, 325 sorties, 120 encounters.
Decorations: Gold Star of Hero of the Soviet Union on October 26, 1944; the Orders of Lenin, the Red Banner (2), Aleksandr Nevskij, the Patriotic War 1st and 2nd Class, the Red Star.

Lukin was born in the Vladimir area on August 22, 1919 and entered the VVS for flight training in 1938. He was graduated as a pilot at Perm military flying school a year later and was posted to the 88 IAP, starting flying combat in August, 1942. He saw a great deal of action over the Terek River and then excelled in the fury of the Kuban air engagements, racking up six kills on LaGG-3s. Among his victories there was a Ju 87 that was destroyed on June 3, 1943 while on November 21 he got two more of these when eight LaGGs tied into a formation of 20 Luftwaffe planes, shooting down four dive-bombers and a Bf 109. During his postwar career Lukin graduated from the Air Force Academy in 1949. He concluded his active duty with the rank of Polkovnik in 1979.

LUKIN, Vasilij Petrovich
Combat record: 16 personal victories, 2 fractional credits, 349 sorties, 48 encounters.
Decorations: Gold Star of Hero of the Soviet Union on October 26, 1944; the Orders of Lenin, the Red Banner (3), the Patriotic War 1st and 2nd Class, the Red Star (2).

Lukin was born in the Lipetsk area on February 12, 1918 and joined the Soviet Army in 1938. He qualified as a pilot two years later and fought from the very start of the Patriotic War while serving with the 287 IAP. He subsequently was in continuous action on Southwest, Bryansk, Voronezh, Volkhov, Leningrad and 3rd Baltic Fronts eventually advancing to squadron leader. On March 19, 1944 he was leading a flight on a front-line patrol when combat occurred with 26 enemy aircraft, four of these being shot down. Lukin excelled in the ferocious fighting for Tartu (August 10/September 9, 1944) scoring seven kills within five days to emerge as the top-scoring pilot of the campaign. He went on to come out of World War II as the regiment's second ranking ace. He served with the postwar VVS until 1966 when he wound up his military career with the rank of Polkovnik. He passed away on December 7, 1985.

LUKYANOV, Sergej Ivanovich
Combat record: 15 personal victories, 19 fractional credits plus 2 more enemy planes destroyed in ground attacks, 361 sorties, 70 encounters.
Decorations: Gold Star of Hero of the Soviet Union on April 13, 1944 in recognition of 14 kills, 15 fractional credits, 356 sorties as of September, 1943; the Orders of Lenin, the Red Banner (3), Aleksandr Nevskij, the Patriotic War 1st and 2nd Class.

Lukyanov was born in the Voronezh area on October 16, 1910 and entered the Soviet Army in 1931. He won his pilot wings at Orenburg military flying school four years later and commenced his combat duty as a squadron leader in the Donbas in August, 1941, flying I-16s. He racked up his first kill on the 20th destroying a reconnaissance plane over the immediate battle area. His squadron claimed the honors during the bitter defensive battles of 1941/42, running up 48 kills during the course of 1,810 sorties and 287 encounters in 10 months combat. This performance was particularly noteworthy in that all victories were gained while flying the Polikarpov fighter. On May 22, 1942 he was badly shot up by a Bf 109 in a dogfight between Izyum-Barvenkovo but was able to nurse his crippled aircraft back to his own airfield. As he was about to touch down, his engine cut and he crashed, being hurled out of his ship on impact together with his pilot's seat and armor plate and seriously injured. The medical staff fought to safe his life for some time, and he survived to be put back on duty in the spring of 1943, joining with the crack 16 GIAP in the Kuban theater. Now flying Airacobras he had his best day on August 29, 1943 when he submitted claims for three Ju 88s in the Kalinovka area. A month later he assumed command of the 100 GIAP and served in this capacity with great distinction through the close of war. He left active duty with the rank of Podpolkovnik in 1946 and is now living peacefully in Voronezh.

LUSTO, Mikhail Vasilyevich
Combat record: 19 personal victories, 1 fractional credit, 251 sorties, 49 engagements.
Decorations: Gold Star of Hero of the Soviet Union on June 27, 1945; the Order of Lenin, the Red Banner (2), the Red Star (2), the Order of Glory 3rd Class.

Lusto was born in Mogilyov on September 21, 1921 and started his military career in 1940. He completed his pilot training at Armavir military flying school two years later and was assigned to the Airacobra-equipped 129 GIAP in March, 1943. He immediately began to pile up an impressive score in the heavy air battles over Kursk and later fought over Rumania, Poland and the Reich. He eventually rose to Starshij Lejtenant and squadron leader and gave a good account of himself on 1st Ukrainian Front. Following World War II Lusto graduated from the Air Force Academy in 1954 and the General Staff Academy seven years later. He left active duty with the rank of Polkovnik in 1974 and died on March 16, 1979. Some sources quote his final record as 18 personal victories, 1 fractional credit, 169 sorties including 26 armed reconnaissance, and 36 encounters.

LYSENKO, Nikolaj Kalistratovich
Combat record: 8 personal victories plus 22 aircraft, 35 tanks, 400 motor vehicles, 108 guns and one armored train destroyed in ground attacks, 250 sorties, 60 encounters.
Decorations: Gold Star of Hero of the Soviet Union on October 26, 1944 after 115 sorties as of March, 1943; the Orders of Lenin (2), the Red Banner (3), Suvorov 3rd Class, the Patriotic War 1st Class, the Red Star.

Lysenko was born in the Dnyepropetrovsk area on December 9, 1916 and entered military service in 1935. He completed his pilot training at Perm military flying school a year later and joined combat in August, 1941 when he was serving with the 218 ShAP on Bryansk Front flying the Il-2 Shturmovik. From then on he was in the thick of the fighting quickly establishing a reputation for skill and aggressiveness. He was promoted Major and was put in command of the regiment leading this with above-average success at Kursk. His most memorable mission came on July 9, 1943 when he was leading 14 Il-2s assigned to beat up German tanks in the Ponyri area (N Kursk). Over the front they were viciously attacked by two gaggles of 14 Fw 190s each but handled them roughly claiming three kills for no losses. Lysenko eventually advanced to Podpolkovnik. In all, he was shot down 14 times but survived the war. He remained in the VVS following the cessation of hostilities and came off active duty with the rank of Polkovnik in 1954. He died on March 26, 1984.

LYUBIMOV, Ivan Stepanovich
Combat record: 10 personal victories.
Decorations: Gold Star of Hero of the Soviet Union on January 22, 1944 for 8 kills, 109 sorties, 21 encounters as of September, 1943; the Orders of Lenin (2), the Red Banner (3), Ushakov 2nd Class, the Patriotic War 1st Class, the Red Star.

Lyubimov was born in Kiev on March 25, 1909 and enrolled for service in the VMF at age 23. He graduated from flight training a year later and was posted to the 32 IAP of the Black Sea Fleet's air service before the war. He saw considerable

MiG-3s warming up on a snow-covered airfield. Moscow area, winter 1941/42. (Author's collection)

fighting as a squadron leader in the epic defense of Odessa (August 5/October 16, 1941). He was seriously wounded in a hard-fought, protracted duel with Bf 109s on October 9, his left leg being shattered by a heavy caliber bullet and the right one maimed. His left leg was subsequently amputated but he was determined to fly again and upon his recovery returned to combat duty on October 2, 1942 fully mobile on an artificial leg. He was put in command of his original regiment and displayed outstanding leadership in the wild air battles over Tuapse. By March, 1943 the unit had run up a tally of 152 enemy aircraft in the air and 10 on the ground during 12,000 sorties and 750 aerial encounters. Subsequent combat assignments saw the regiment engage the Luftwaffe along the Kuban and at Novorossijsk while flying Airacobras. Lyubimov next was assigned as commander of the 4 IAD-ChF which was to make a significant contribution to the fighting in Rumania. He used to head out on combat sorties whenever possible to add a total of three kills to his previous score before he had been wounded. He remained in the ranks at the conclusion of the war and graduated from the General Staff Academy in 1950 winding up his military career as a General Major in 1973.

MAJOROV, Aleksandr Ivanovich
Combat record: 27 personal victories, 460 sorties, 68 encounters.
Decorations: Gold Star of Hero of the Soviet Union on September 2, 1943 for 7 victories, 8 fractional credits, 220 sorties, 44 encounters as of March, 1943; the Orders of Lenin, the Red Banner (2), Aleksandr Nevskij, the Patriotic War 1st and 2nd Class, the Red Star and the British Empire.

Majorov was born in the Kalinin area on April 1, 1921 and joined the VVS for flight training in 1940. A year later he was graduated as a pilot at Borisoglebsk military flying school and in April, 1942 was posted to the 2 GIAP on Volkhov Front to enter combat. He deployed with the regiment to the Leningrad area in January, 1943 and shortly afterward took over as leader of the Mongolian fighter squadron "Mongolskij arat." On January 22, 1943 he claimed a Bf 109 while flying free hunt and then shot a Fw 190 off an Il-2's tail at point-blank range. He managed to put up a good performance in the contested air space above Orel-Bryansk and by August, 1943 had brought his score to 15 personal victories along with 10 fractional credits. One of his victims was an He 111 that he caught and shot down on July 13, 1943 at 1230 hours with three of its crew being captured. He was promoted Kapitan in early 1944 and in August began to range deep into East Prussia. On August 2 he swept down on four Fw 190s from the sun with Ivan Zakharov flying wing to him and quickly dispatched two of the unsuspecting fighters near Schirwindt. He advanced to Major in 1945 and on April 26 was caught by a flak burst and force-landed, hurting his spine in the process. Carefully concealing the pain from the medical officer he resumed combat duty soon after and ended the war as 2 GIAP's ranking ace. He stayed in the service after the war and graduated from KUOS (kursy usovershenstvovaniya ofitserskogo sostava – commissioned staff refresher courses) in 1949 concluding his active duty with the rank of Polkovnik in 1973.

MAKAROV, Valentin Nikolayevich
Combat record: 30 personal victories, 9 fractional credits, 638 sorties, 150 encounters.
Decorations: Gold Star of Hero of the Soviet Union on January 28, 1943 in recognition of 15 kills, 7 fractional credits, 462 sorties of which 23 were strafing ground targets and 118 air combats as of January, 1943; the Orders of Lenin (2), the Red Banner (3), Aleksandr Nevskij, the Patriotic War 1st Class, the Red Star (2).

Makarov was born in Sevastopol on August 30, 1919 and entered the Soviet Army in 1937. He won his pilot wings at Kacha military flying school a year later and was assigned to the 512 IAP before the war. He was in the forefront of action at Kiev

Kapitan V.N. Makarov who developed into an exceptionally capable fighter pilot during the struggle for Stalingrad and went on to wind up as one of the most eminent aces of the Eastern Front. (Author's collection)

from the very start of the war but would not score his initial success until October 10, 1941 when he was conducting a front-line patrol with Ivan Motornyj flying wing to him. Once over the target area they joined formation with a number of Il-2s tasked with striking a Luftwaffe base in the vicinity of Poltava. Over the airfield they saw several enemy planes that apparently had just taken off, and the two LaGG-3s broke onto them forcing down two Bf 109s and a Ju 87 while the Shturmoviks wrought successful havoc in the destruction of parked planes and flak emplacements. For his efforts in 1941 Makarov was decorated with two Orders of the Red Banner and then scored steadily in the air battles over Kharkov in May, 1942. He converted to Yak-1s and on August 30, 1942 was shot down by four Bf 109s and reportedly strafed whilst helpless in his parachute. He was promoted squadron leader and then made a big name for himself in the brutal fighting for Stalingrad. As many as six sorties daily were commonplace for the period September to October, 1942. He reported the destruction of an enemy plane on October 16 while leading six of his squadron against a formation of 26 Bf 109s and 30 Ju 88s with his comrades bringing the day's tally to five. He added a Bf 109 in the vicinity of Razgulyaevka four days later and continued to make his mark as the regiment was keeping up a steady battle for supremacy in the air. In the fiercest fighting ever fought Makarov's squadron was credited with 48 kills over Stalingrad while his personal tally had risen to 15 by the end of January, 1943 when the Germans were forced to surrender. Makarov's personal steed of war was now carrying the inscription "Za Sevastopol" – for Sevastopol – and he was again in the thick of the fighting at Kursk where he combined forces with his number two, Lejtenant Komolikov, to destroy four enemy planes. On July 9 fifteen Yak-1s with Makarov in the lead tore into a large enemy force near Khmelevoye and claimed to have shot down five Ju 87s, two Ju 88s and a Fw 190. He chalked up three more kills in subsequent air operations over Bobruijak, Minsk, Baranovichi, Warsaw and Radom. He was promoted Podpolkovnik and took over the 176 IAP and in this capacity displayed exceptional leadership through the end of war. He achieved a single victory near Küstrin on February 1, 1945 and a further one on April 17. The following day he was leading a sweep of six Yak-3s out to the Seelow area where they caught eight Fw 190s from behind with Makarov and Major Yefimov each blasting one of them out of the sky. He closed out his scoring with another of these on May 1, 1945. In two weeks of brutal fighting the regiment had claimed 110 kills over Berlin while it had been mainly responsible for driving the Luftwaffe from the skies. He stayed in the VVS after the war and assumed command of the 351 IAP which was to see some action during the Chinese Civil War in 1951 flying La-11s. In April P. Dushin and V. Sidorov were successful in opening the account with one each B-26 while N. Gushev claimed two Mustangs in one sortie near Shanghai later that month. Makarov was promoted General Major in 1954 and graduated from the General Staff Academy two years later. He wound up his military career in 1975 and passed away on May 20, 1978.

MAKOVSKIJ, Spartak Iosifovich

Combat record: 23 personal victories, 2 fractional credits, 218 sorties, 79 encounters.

Decorations: Gold Star of Hero of the Soviet Union on April 13, 1944 for 18 kills, 1 fractional credit, 92 sorties, 49 air engagements as of January, 1944; the Orders of Lenin, the Red Banner (3), Aleksandr Nevskij, the Patriotic War 1st Class (2), the Red Star.

Makovskij was born in Pavlodar on November 27, 1920 and entered military service in 1937. He qualified as a pilot at Kacha military flying school two years later following which he was posted to a unit in the Far East. In late 1942 he joined with the 43 IAP at Novosibirsk as a squadron leader and deployed with the unit to the Byelgorod area on April 19, 1943. A short time later he moved again, this time to the Kuban where he destroyed his first enemy aircraft in the air on May 3. On this day eight Yak-1s stormed into 20 Ju 87s intent on beating up targets in the vicinity of Novosibirsk with Makovskij destroying one in an attack from astern. Five days later he was leading six Yaks on ground support duty near Krymskaya where they became engaged in a dogfight with a number of Bf 109s. He was working with a Messerschmitt when he came under attack from another and broke away. He wracked around in a tight turn to engage the enemy fighter head-on and deliberately rammed it with his right wing seeing the enemy ship go down and crash. Makovskij made a successful force-landing returning to combat duty a little later. On January 3, 1944 he landed in a pasture near Apostolovo (SW Dnyepropetrovsk) to pick up his wingman, Mladshij Lejtenant Kuznetsov, and tookoff smoothly in spite of vicious enemy fire. He advanced to Starshij Lejtenant and squadron leader and enjoyed considerable success in the big air battles over Poland, Pomerania and finally, Berlin. He got a double over the German capital on April 19, 1945 and closed out his scoring with two Fw 190s ten days later. Makovskij continued on active duty with the VVS following World War II and returned to civilian life with the rank of Podpolkovnik in 1958. His total score is a matter of dispute, some sources quoting it as 30 personal kills plus 7 more fractional credits.

MAKSIMENKO, Vasilij Ivanovich

Combat record: 17 personal victories, 8 fractional credits, 516 sorties.

Decorations: Gold Star of Hero of the Soviet Union on November 23, 1942 for 7 kills, 250 sorties, 15 encounters as of October, 1942; the Orders of Lenin (2), the Red Banner (3), Suvorov 3rd Class, Aleksandr Nevskij, the Patriotic War 1st Class (2), the Red Star.

Maksimenko was born in the Donetsk area on February 12, 1913 and enrolled for service in 1935. Three years later he was graduated as a pilot at Orenburg military flying school and was serving in the 88 IAP at the outbreak of the war. He participated in periods of intense activity at Slavyansk, Izyum and Mozdok flying the Polikarpov I-16 fighter. He rapidly rose to Starshij Lejtenant and squadron leader but was seriously wounded over the North Caucasus in late 1942. He resumed combat duty in January, 1943 and was put in command of the regiment in August, 1943. Maksimenko remained in the ranks after the war retiring with the rank of Polkovnik in 1961.

MAKSIMOV, Aleksandr Yefimovich
Combat record: 22 personal victories, 444 sorties, 68 encounters.
Decorations: Gold Star of Hero of the Soviet Union on April 4, 1945 in recognition of 19 victories, 396 sorties and 53 air combats as of January, 1945; the Orders of Lenin, the Red Banner (3), Aleksandr Nevskij, the Patriotic War 1st Class, the Red Star (2).

Maksimov was born in the Vladimir area on August 15, 1914 and entered the Soviet Army in 1940. He won his wings at Ostafyev military flying school and saw action for the first time in December, 1941. He made an impressive combat record during the great battle for the Russian capital, at Korsun, Yassy-Kishinyov and in the aerial campaigns over Poland, the Reich and Czechoslovakia. He spent his World War II career with the 156 GIAP and eventually advanced to Major and squadron leader. In all, he was shot down three times and wounded twice. He saw considerable fighting in the epic defense of Moscow in the winter of 1941/42 flying Yak-1s. He opened his account on February 19, 1942 when he was off on a frontline patrol and spotted five Ju 88s near Uvarovka (W Mozhajsk) headed for the local rail station. With complete disregard for his own safety he single-handedly attacked and loosing off his RS-82 missiles he gained hits on a bomber which was blown apart. On his second pass he shot down another and scored strikes on a third whereupon the bombers peeled away and turned for home. He was promoted Kapitan and squadron leader and on July 5, 1943 was leading six of his squadron on an escort for Il-2s. Near Tomarovka (NW Byelgorod) they engaged 30 bombers and 12 escorting fighters with Maksimov scoring two kills before in turn, he was hit and badly wounded in his face, arms and legs. He nevertheless maintained effective control of his crippled aircraft and struggled back to his own base. He reportedly refused to be taken to hospital his impression being that he was needed at the front, where his squadron was. He chalked up another double on December 11 leading four fighters against 45 Ju 87s and their escorts, six German planes being shot down. He later advanced to Major and continued to do well in the air operations on 1st Ukrainian Front. He stayed in the service after the war and retired with the rank of General Major in 1961. He died on March 23, 1984.

MALTSEV, Konstantin Savelyevich
Combat record: 15 personal victories, 1 fractional credit plus 3 planes destroyed in ground attacks, 180 sorties, 32 encounters.
Decorations: Gold Star of Hero of the Soviet Union on May 15, 1946; the Orders of Lenin, the Red Banner (3), Aleksandr Nevskij.

Maltsev was born in the Borisov area in May, 1915 and enlisted in the VVS for flight training in 1936. He won his wings at Borisoglebsk military flying school a year later but would not commence his combat duty until May, 1944 when he was posted to the 177 GIAP. He excelled during the Yassy-Kishinyov campaign (August 20-29, 1944) while flying the Lavochkin La-5 fighter. On August 20, 1944 he made claims for two Fw 190s one of which he shot off Kapitan N.S. Artamonov's tail. He claimed a Ju 87 on October 6 when six fighters with Kapitan Artamonov in the lead tied into a formation of Luftwaffe dive-bombers near Sokodor (Hungary), seven of these being shot down. Maltsev rose to Kapitan and squadron leader but was killed in a plane crash on August 27, 1948.

MANKEVICH, Viktor Mikhajlovich
Combat record: 17 personal victories, 5 fractional credits, 240 sorties, 58 encounters.
Decorations: Gold Star of Hero of the Soviet Union on August 18, 1945 for 17 kills, 182 sorties, 45 engagements as of February, 1945; the Orders of Lenin, the Red Banner (4), Aleksandr Nevskij, the Patriotic War 1st Class, the Red Star.

Mankevich was born in Smolensk on April 10, 1918 and entered the Soviet Army at age 20. He completed his pilot training at Borisoglebsk military flying school in 1939 and at Konotop two years later becoming a pilot instructor. He was posted to the 163 IAP in May, 1943 to start flying combat and was to give a good account of himself during subsequent assignments on Central, 1st Ukrainian, 1st, 2nd and 3rd Byelorussian, 1st Baltic and Leningrad Fronts. Between 1943 and 1944 he was primarily occupied with fighter escorts, frontline patrols and armed reconnaissance in the skies of Gomel, Mozyr, Pinsk and Brest. He was promoted to Major and shturman before the end of the war. He served with the postwar VVS leaving active duty with the rank of Polkovnik in 1959. He is living in Kharkov.

MANOJLOV, Ivan Antonovich
Combat record: 9 personal victories, 190 sorties.
Decorations: Gold Star of Hero of the Soviet Union posthumously on March 31, 1943; the Orders of Lenin, the Red Banner.

Manojlov was born in the Zaporozhye area on December 4, 1910 and served with the Soviet Army between 1930/32 and from 1941. He was graduated at Moscow aviation technical school and at civil aviation school following which he joined with Zaporozhye Aeroklub in 1936. He was a member of the 774 IAP at the outbreak of the war and was to gain a large number of his victories flying Yak-1s in the big air battles over Stalingrad. On November 7, 1942 he destroyed a Ju 88 northwest of the city and next claimed a double in the vicinity of Surovikino on the 30th. The following day he reported the destruction of two Bf 109s but on December 17 he was shot down and killed. He was a Starshij Lejtenant and deputy squadron leader at the time of his death.

MARESYEV, Aleksej Petrovich
Combat record: 11 personal victories, 86 sorties.
Decorations: Gold Star of Hero of the Soviet Union on August 24, 1943; the Orders of Lenin (2), the Red Banner, the Patriotic War 1st Class, the Red Star.

Maresyev was born in the Volgograd area on May 20, 1916 and was destined to become a national hero and legendary figure in the VVS like his counterpart in the RAF, Douglas Bader, or the famous Luftwaffe pilot Hans-Ulrich Rudel. He completed his pilot training at Batajsk military flying school in 1940 and was posted to the 580 IAP joining combat with the Luftwaffe in August, 1941. By March, 1942 his score had risen to four personal victories but on April 4 he was hit in a fierce, protracted dogfight over the Demyansk bridgehead and crashed into a forest being seriously injured. Although in great pain, he set out for the Soviet lines where he arrived with the help of partisans 18 days later. Unfortunately his legs had both developed gangrene and were amputated. Maresyev was determined to fly again and after his recovery joined with the 63 GIAP as a Starshij Lejtenant in June, 1943 fully mobile on artificial legs. He next saw a great deal of action at Kursk while flying La-5s. He was credited with the destruction of a Fw 190 on his first combat sortie on July 6 and added a double the following day. He eventually rose to Major and was released from the service in 1946.

The indomitable A.P. Maresyev. Shot down in enemy territory in 1942 he set out for the Soviet lines where he arrived 18 days later. His legs were amputated but he fought an epic battle back to health making a distinguished record at Kursk in 1943. (Author's collection)

MARKIN, Nikolaj Vasilyevich
Combat record: 17 personal victories, 220 sorties, 42 encounters.
Decorations: Gold Star of Hero of the Soviet Union posthumously on November 1, 1943; the Orders of Lenin, the Patriotic War 1st Class, the Red Star.

Markin was born in the Ryazan area on September 30, 1920 and entered military service in 1938. He completed his pilot training at Engels military flying school two years later and was assigned as a Lejtenant to the 247 IAP on North Caucasus Front in April, 1943. In three months combat he ran up a string of 12 kills in the Krymskaya and Kerch areas while flying Yak-9 fighters. On September 15, 1943 he bagged two Ju 87s when three Yaks led by Kapitan M.N. Tomarev tied into German dive-bombers harassing Soviet emplacements. Thirteen days later eight of his squadron were flying a sweep out to the Najdorf-Barvinkovo areas. At 1750 hours they caught 12 Ju 87s escorted by four Bf 109s at 1,500 meters altitude near Najdorf and in an instant found themselves in a tough battle. Markin blasted one of the Stukas out of the sky at point-blank range but was then bounced by two Messerschmitts and shot down before Kapitan Tomarev could intervene. Although he was seen to abandon his ship he was only found dead.

MARKOV, Aleksej Ivanovich
Combat record: 16 personal victories, 255 sorties.
Decorations: Gold Star of Hero of the Soviet Union on February 23, 1945; the Orders of Lenin, the Red Banner (2), Aleksandr Nevskij, the Patriotic War 1st Class.

Markov was born in the Moscow area on February 2, 1921 and started his military career in 1940. He qualified as a pilot at Kacha military flying school a year later and joined the 434

IAP on Stalingrad Front in July, 1942 to see a great deal of action during the ferocious battle over the Volga. He later flew La-5s with marked success in the aerial operations on Kalinin, Northwest, Bryansk, 1st and 2nd Baltic and 3rd Byelorussian Fronts managing to put up good performance at Orsha, Borisov and Minsk. After the close of war Markov served with the VVS Air Transport Command. He left active duty with the rank of Podpolkovnik in 1955 and passed away on April 1, 1966.

MASTERKOV, Aleksandr Borisovich
Combat record: 18 personal victories, 195 sorties, 40 encounters.
Decorations: Gold Star of Hero of the Soviet Union posthumously on June 27, 1945; the Orders of Lenin, the Red Banner (2), the Patriotic War 1st and 2nd Class.

Masterkov was born in Moscow on September 12, 1921 and entered the Soviet Army in 1940. He qualified as a pilot at Borisoglebsk military flying school a year later and first was assigned as an instructor. He was posted to the crack 5 GIAP in November, 1942 when it was in the process of reequipping with Lavochkin La-5 fighters and entered combat over the Don a month later. He subsequently saw a great deal of action during the heavy air battles over Slavyansk, Kharkov, Byelgorod and Izyum. He shot up a Ju 52 on the Luftwaffe airfield at Gartmashevka on January 16, 1943 and shot down a Ju 87 on July 23 the enemy aircraft crashing near Rogan. He later fought above the Dnyepr and at Zaporozhye, Nikopol and Krivoj Rog. In the same time frame he was flying a personal mount with the inscription "Vesyolye rebyata" – merry children – a La-5 donated to the regiment by the famous Russian Utesov jazz orchestra. He chalked up two kills in this fighter and then took part in the great aerial campaigns at Kovel, over the Vistula River and the crumbling Reich. He combined forces with I.S. Glazkov to destroy a Fw 190 near Glogau, between Breslau and Berlin, on February 16, 1945 and shortly afterward forced down three Ju 87s in one sortie in the vicinity of Guben. On March 20 Kapitan V.I. Popkov's squadron was tasked with beating up a marshaling yard in the Bautzen area where they dive-bombed tanks on flatcars. Vitalij Popkov told the author that Masterkov took a direct hit from one of the tanks into his fuselage the round passing completely through. Masterkov bailed out but was struck by the tail of his aircraft and killed. Popkov's wingman, Pchyolkin, landed close to his body and affected a successful pick-up. Masterkov was interred at Moscow Kalitnikov cemetery.

MERENKOV, Viktor Alekseyevich
Combat record: 22 personal victories, 166 sorties, 39 encounters plus 36 motor vehicles and 2 locomotives in ground attacks.

Starshij Lejtenant F.M. Mazurin of the 28 GIAP, who displayed his skills in the contested air space over 3rd Byelorussian Front. He was honored with the title of Hero of the Soviet Union on August 18, 1945 and had a score of 18 kills together with two fractional credits. This photo shows him with his P-39 on June 20, 1944 when his tally stood at eight with two shares. (Author's collection)

Decorations: Gold Star of Hero of the Soviet Union on February 23, 1945; the Orders of Lenin, the Red Banner (3), Aleksandr Nevskij, the Patriotic War 1st Class, the Red Star.

Merenkov was born in Orel on September 1, 1923 and joined the Soviet Army in 1941. Two years later he completed pilot training at Stalingrad military flying school and was posted to the 897 IAP in August. He achieved an impressive scoring during combat assignments on Southwest and 3rd Ukrainian Fronts emerging as the regiment's top-scoring ace. He claimed a double on September 21, 1943 when eight of his squadron became embroiled in a dogfight with 18 Bf 109s and six Fw 190s while engaged in an Il-2 escort. He got another double with two Ju 87s while flying escort for Il-2s to Grigoriopol (NE Kishinyov) on May 22, 1944 and then had his best day on December 21, 1944 with a triple. He remained in the ranks after the close of hostilities and retired from the VVS with the rank of Podpolkovnik in 1953. He passed away on December 14, 1975.

MERKULOV, Vladimir Ivanovich
Combat record: 21 personal victories.
Decorations: Gold Star of Hero of the Soviet Union on October 26, 1944 in recognition of 19 kills, 4 fractional credits, 195 sorties and 82 aerial engagements as of April, 1944; the Orders of Lenin, the Red Banner (4), the Patriotic War 1st Class (3), the Red Star (3).

Merkulov was born in the Orel area on December 28, 1922 and entered military service in 1940. He was graduated at Armavir military flying school a year later and in April, 1943 joined the 43 IAP in the Caucasus to enter combat. Over the Kuban he logged 56 sorties during the period of April 13 to June 22, 1943 with six kills in 23 air encounters. In September, 1943 he moved with the regiment to South Front and later to

4th Ukrainian Front, where he really began to score. In six months combat he was given credit for 13 more victories along with four shares, nine of which had occurred on free hunt missions. On February 13, 1944 he reported the destruction of two Ju 87s when his flight took on 10 bombers and four Fw 190s. Merkulov served with the postwar VVS and graduated from the Air Force Academy in 1957. He wound up his military career with the rank of General Lejtenant in 1979 with 39 years service.

MERKUSHEV, Vasilij Afanasyevich
Combat record: 29 personal victories, 418 sorties.
Decorations: Gold Star of Hero of the Soviet Union on September 2, 1943 for 12 victories, 264 sorties as of August, 1943; the Orders of Lenin (2), the Red Banner, the Red Star.

Merkushev was born in the Udmurtian ASSR on April 25, 1910 and started his remarkable military career in 1931. He qualified as a pilot at Odessa military flying school two years later and was a member of the 270 IAP before the outbreak of war. He was early in the public eye, claiming two Bf 109s shot down in flames on June 24, 1941 and two more of these during the following month. He scored steadily during the fierce fighting at Sevastopol and in the Caucasus and by the close of 1942 his tally had risen to 8 enemy planes in the air plus 12 tanks, 28 motor vehicles and 6 AAA emplacements destroyed in ground attacks during 220 sorties for 218 combat hours. He was promoted Major and took over command of the 270 IAP displaying outstanding leadership during its assignments on Steppe Front. Merkushev made an impressive combat record at Kursk and in the air battles over Poltava, Cherkassy and Kirovograd. On July 4, 1944 he was hit and obliged to carry out a forced landing in enemy lines and became one of the very few Soviet aces to be captured by the Germans. He remained in the VVS after his repatriation and had become a Podpolkovnik when he retired in 1954. He died on August 20, 1974.

MIKHAJLIK, Yakov Danilovich
Combat record: 17 personal victories, 6 fractional credits, 316 sorties, 73 encounters.
Decorations: Gold Star of Hero of the Soviet Union on May 15, 1946; the Orders of Lenin, the Red Banner (3), Aleksandr Nevskij, the Patriotic War 1st Class, the Red Star (3).

Mikhajlik was born in Kremenchug on May 7, 1922 and entered military service in 1940. He was graduated as a pilot at Chuguyev military flying school a year later and became a member of the 237 IAP. He entered combat in February, 1942 initially flying Yak-1s, later successively converting to Yak-7Bs and Airacobras. He began to make his mark in the ferocious fighting at Stalingrad claiming seven kills along with two shares and then gave a good account of himself in the skies above Kursk. During the battle he was at least credited with two Fw 190s in the air on July 2, 1943 but no further details are known. Mikhajlik subsequently saw a great deal of action in the aerial campaign over Byelorussia, and over the Vistula and Oder bridgeheads eventually rising to Starshij Lejtenant and deputy squadron leader. He served with the postwar VVS and graduated from the Air Force Academy in 1955. He came off active duty with the rank of Polkovnik in 1976.

MIKRYUKOV, Vitalij Vasilyevich
Combat record: 16 personal victories, 226 sorties of which 20 were reconnaissance, 99 escorts, 21 free hunts, 86 air patrols and 34 aerial encounters.
Decorations: Gold Star of Hero of the Soviet Union posthumously on June 29, 1945; the Orders of Lenin, the Red Banner (3), Aleksandr Nevskij, the Patriotic War 1st Class, the Red Star.

Mikryukov was born in the Udmurtian ASSR on October 25, 1923 and enlisted in the VVS for flight training in 1941. He qualified as a pilot at Krasnodar military flying school later

Tomahawks on alert. Winter 1941/42. (Author's collection)

that year and was posted to the 897 IAP commencing his combat duty in June, 1943. He fought in the great aerial campaigns at Kursk, along the Dnyepr and over Krivoj Rog, Odessa, Moldavia, Rumania, Yugoslavia and Hungary. He gained all or most of his victories on the Yakovlev Yak-9 fighter. On April 4, 1945 he was bounced by 15 German fighters and turned for his life, giving them a good fight. By continually turning and firing he managed to work his way back to Soviet territory, bleeding from several wounds and dying shortly afterward. He was a Kapitan and deputy squadron leader at the time of his death.

MILOVANOV, Aleksej Mikhajlovich
Combat record: 17 personal victories, 5 fractional credits, 215 sorties, 30 encounters.
Decorations: Gold Star of Hero of the Soviet Union posthumously on July 1, 1944; the Orders of Lenin, the Red Banner (3), the Patriotic War 1st Class.

Milovanov was born in Ivanovo in 1913 and entered the Soviet Army at age 18. He was graduated as a pilot at Engels military flying school in 1935 and saw action for the first time during the Russo-Finnish Winter War of 1939/40. He was in the forefront of action from the earliest days of the Patriotic War in June, 1941 and was to make a distinguished record while serving with the 193 IAP on 2nd Ukrainian Front. He was promoted Kapitan and took over as leader of a La-5 squadron that was to be credited with downing 82 enemy planes while under his leadership. On an unspecified date he was leading a flight to tackle with a superior enemy force in the vicinity of Krivoj Rog where they claimed to have shot down nine Luftwaffe planes. He made a claim for a Ju 87 on October 23, 1943 leading five of his squadron mates to intercept six dive-bombers while providing ground force cover. He claimed another single in the afternoon when his flight forced down five Luftwaffe planes that were trying to beat up Soviet positions at tree top level. On March 6, 1944 he was hit by groundfire while reconnoitering the Cherkassy area, staggered back to his airfield but then his engine cut and he crashed to his death onto the perimeter of the airfield. He was buried in Rotmistrova.

MIROSHNICHENKO, Dmitrij Grigoryevich
Combat record: 15 personal victories, 108 sorties, 26 encounters.
Decorations: Gold Star of Hero of the Soviet Union on October 26, 1944; the Orders of Lenin, the Red Banner (2), the Patriotic War 1st and 2nd Class.

Miroshnichenko was born in the Krasnodar area on September 29, 1921 and entered military service in 1941. He won his pilot wings at Krasnodar military flying school a year later and was assigned to the 248 IAP on August 20, 1942. Miroshnichenko during his combat career participated in the heavy fighting on West, Central, Bryansk and Byelorussian Fronts. He was promoted flight leader and in a series of encounters at Mozyr-Kalinikovichi (SW Gomel) his fighters would claim nine kills during 61 encounters. He rose to Starshij Lejtenant and squadron leader in time and took part in the final air battles over Berlin. He remained in the VVS after the war and assumed command of a fighter air regiment. He concluded his active duty with the rank of Polkovnik in 1955. His total score is a matter of dispute, some sources suggesting 18 kills.

MISHUSTIN, Vasilij Ivanovich
Combat record: 17 personal victories, 8 fractional credits, 388 sorties, 68 encounters.
Decorations: Gold Star of Hero of the Soviet Union on June 27, 1945; the Orders of Lenin (2), the Red Banner (3), Aleksandr Nevskij, the Patriotic War 1st Class, the Red Star.

Mishustin was born in the Byelgorod area on December 20, 1916 and joined the VVS for flight training in 1937. He was graduated as a pilot at Odessa military flying school and was posted to the 166 IAP before the war. On August 1, 1942 he shot down a Bf 110 near Majkop and was on his way home when he was bounced by two Bf 109s who showered him with a veritable hail of bullets. He broke into them and pressed the triggers but no gun would fire. Without hesitating he now deliberately rammed the canopy of an 109 with the wing of his LaGG-3 and parachuted to safety, seeing his victim go down and crash. He later flew La-5s in the Battle of Kursk scoring another double on July 3, 1943 when his flight was attacked by some 20 Bf 109s, five of these being shot down without loss. Mishustin went on to end the war as the regiment's top-scoring ace. A break down of his aerial victories by type of enemy planes destroyed shows that most of his victims were single-engined fighters:

Ju 88s	2
Ju 87s	3
Bf 109s	9
Fw 190s	1
He 111s	1
Bf 110s	1

Of his fractional credits, five were He 111s, and one each Ju 88, Fw 190 and Hs 126. In ground attacks he had accounted for 13 motor vehicles, two locomotives and 17 rail cars. What was more, his squadron was credited with destroying 81 planes in the air during 1,838 sorties and 163 engagements together with eight locomotives, 48 rail cars, 54 motor vehicles shot up in ground attacks. He had become a Major by the cessation of hostilities and served with the postwar VVS until 1960 when he retired as a Polkovnik.

MITROFANOV, Fyodor Vasilyevich
Combat record: 10 personal victories, 3 fractional credits, 250 sorties, 18 encounters as of November, 1942.
Decorations: Gold Star of Hero of the Soviet Union on February 14, 1943; the Orders of Lenin, the Red Banner (2), Aleksandr Nevskij.

Mitrofanov was born in the Sumy area on August 6, 1916 and entered the Soviet Army in 1936. He qualified as a pilot at Chuguyev military flying school in 1939 and had become a member of the 445 IAP when the Germans initiated Operation Barbarossa, the attack on the Soviet Union, in June, 1941. He flew with great distinction against the all-conquering Luftwaffe during the darkest hours of the 1941/42 air war and then was posted to the 562 IAP. He made a specialty of tracking Luftwaffe bombers on their withdrawal and picking off unsuspecting aircraft deep in enemy territory. On January 17, 1943 he was successful in forcing down a Ju 88 25 kilometers south of Gzhatsk. A short time later he was promoted Kapitan and in late 1944 was assigned to the 813 IAP with the rank of Major. On February 4, 1945 he was shot down crashing to his death near Elbing (SW Königsberg) in East Prussia. His final score is uncertain but is probably higher than his tally of 1942 that won him the title Hero of the Soviet Union.

MITROKHIN, Vasilij Borisovich
Combat record: 17 personal victories, 174 sorties, 36 encounters.
Decorations: Gold Star of Hero of the Soviet Union on November 2, 1944; the Order of Lenin, the Red Banner, Aleksandr Nevskij, the Patriotic War 1st Class (2), the Red Star.

Mitrokhin was born in the Tula area on April 5, 1918 and enlisted in the Soviet Army in 1938. He completed his training at Borisoglebsk military flying school a year later and spent some time as a pilot instructor. He saw action for the first time in November, 1942 but was wounded in an encounter over Velikiye Luki soon after. Upon his recovery he was posted to the 191 IAP and took over as leader of an Airacobra squadron which would run up 56 confirmed kills in 12 months combat on Leningrad Front. Mitrokhin went on to finish as the regiment's second ranking ace his number two on many missions being his younger brother Sergej. He was a Kapitan at the end of war. During his postwar career with the VVS Mitrokhin advanced to Polkovnik before leaving active duty in 1961.

MORGUNOV, Sergej Nikolayevich
Combat record: 27 personal victories, 16 fractional credits.
Decorations: Gold Star of Hero of the Soviet Union on May 15, 1946 in recognition of 22 kills, 234 sorties, 68 air-to-air combats as of September, 1944; the Orders of Lenin, the Red Banner (4), the Patriotic War 1st and 2nd Class.

Morgunov was born in the Moscow area on November 30, 1918 and started his military career in 1937. He won his wings at Kacha military flying school in 1941 but he would not start flying combat until April, 1943, when he joined with the 15 IAP. He gained his first success a month later and from then on was in continuous action through the close of war. He rapidly rose to squadron leader and in this capacity distinguished himself on 1st Byelorussian Front flying the Lavochkin La-5 fighter. He took part in the big air battles over Poland, Pomerania, East Prussia and finally, Berlin. He really came into his own during the closing stages of war, running up a string of victories over the Reich including a double in the Küstrin area on February 12, 1945 and four over Berlin on April 18, 1945 which was his highest scoring day. He was killed in a plane crash on July 19, 1946 and interred in Kashira (SE Moscow).

MOROZOV, Anatolij Afanasyevich
Combat record: 24 personal victories, 8 fractional credits, 400 sorties.
Decorations: Gold Star of Hero of the Soviet Union on March 27, 1942 for 7 personal victories, 2 fractional credits and 8 aircraft on the ground as of July, 1941; the Orders of Lenin, the Red Banner (3), Aleksandr Nevskij.

Morozov was born in Bryansk on July 4, 1916 and enrolled for service in the Soviet Army in 1934. Three years later he was graduated as a pilot and gained his first combat experience during the Russo-Finnish Winter War of 1939/40. At the outbreak of the Patriotic War he was a Starshij Lejtenant and flight leader in the 4 IAP and received much publicity during the dark months to follow. On July 7, 1941 he was able to destroy a German bomber near Kalfa (Moldavia) and successfully rammed a second after experiencing problems with his guns. He parachuted to safety and to cap an already good day, he captured a pilot of one of the planes he had forced down. He continued to score on a regular basis in the skies above Tiraspol, Nikolayev, Odessa and Kherson, and because of his success was put in command of the regiment in good time. He flew Hawker Hurricanes for a while and recalled: "We were penalized with the Hurricane. The British for obvious reasons withdrew them from the frontline in Africa to leave them to us. The aircraft certainly lacked performance and an effective armament." The regiment reequipped with Yak-1s in the Voronezh area in July, 1942 and came under command of the 287 IAD on Stalingrad Front. Here it operated with notable success but suffering heavy losses so that by October only 1-2 aircraft were available for combat duties. Morozov was promoted Podpolkovnik and in the autumn of 1943 took the place of the legendary L.L. Shestakov as commander of the 9 GIAP. He subsequently fought with the unit across the skies of Russia in the great aerial campaigns of late 1943 and early 1944 but on June 18, 1944 was shot down and killed. With his death, the VVS lost one of its outstanding fighter leaders, his place as leader of the 9 GIAP being taken by Major V.D. Lavrinenkov.

MOSHIN, Aleksandr Fyodorovich
Combat record: 11 personal victories, 299 sorties.
Decorations: Gold Star of Hero of the Soviet Union August 29, 1939; the Orders of Lenin, the Red Banner, the Red Star.

Moshin was born in the Vladimir area on August 28, 1917 and entered the Soviet Army in 1935. He qualified as a pilot at Voroshilovgrad military flying school three years later and on June 16, 1939 arrived with the 56 IAP in Mongolia and became engaged in fierce border battles with the Japanese along the Khalkhin Gol. On August 4 he shot down an I-97 fighter and successfully rammed a second after running out of ammunition near Khamar-Daban and was able to nurse his I-16 in safely at his own airfield. He racked up his fifth victory on September 1 but in turn was badly shot up and wounded. Upon his recovery he was posted to the 25 IAP and took an active part in the Russo-Finnish Winter War of 1939/40 winning the Order of the Red Banner for his efforts during the conflict. He next joined with the 402 IAP and saw some action between June and August, 1941. He returned to combat duty in November, 1942 when he was assigned to the 32 GIAP near Velikiye Luki as a squadron leader and participated in the steady battle for aerial supremacy. He deployed with the regiment to Northwest Front in February, 1943 and to Bryansk Front two months later where it became heavily involved in the Battle of Kursk. Here the unit added 42 kills to its record in a fierce series of battles, 22 of these being claimed by Moshin's squadron during 272 sorties and 86 encounters between June and July, 1943. Moshin personally shot down one each Ju 87 and Fw 190 on July 12 and the following day was leading seven La-5s to engage four Fw 190s. He quickly destroyed one of the fighters but in the heat of combat got too low his wings brushing the ground under full power. He lost control and crashed being killed instantly.

Battle of Moscow, autumn 1941. Red Army riflemen examine the burnt-out wreckage of a Junkers Ju 87 shot down by fighters (Author's collection)

Downed He 111. This one was forced down in the Kalinin area on December 17, 1941. (Author's collection)

MOSKOVENKO, Vasilij Ivanovich
Combat record: 14 personal victories, 3 fractional credits, 175 sorties, 37 encounters.
Decorations: Gold Star of Hero of the Soviet Union on June 27, 1945; the Orders of Lenin, the Red Banner (2), the Patriotic War 1st and 2nd Class, the Red Star.

Moskovenko was born in the Kazakh SSR on August 8, 1915 and entered military service in 1936. Upon receiving his wings at Stalingrad military flying school two years later he was posted to the 2nd Army's air service in the Far East. He next was assigned to the 29 IAP before the war and was to achieve his initial success during the Battle of Moscow probably while flying a Hawker Hurricane. In March, 1942 he was shot down by Bf 110s in a tussle near Chertolino on Kalinin Front but survived and returned to his unit later that month. During the war three of his brothers – Andrej, Roman and Mikhail – were killed, and from then on Moskovenko was waging his own private war against the Luftwaffe. He subsequently fought over Leningrad, Rzhev, Zubtsov, Orel, Vitebsk, Orsha, Berlin and Prague. He eventually rose to Starshij Lejtenant and took over as leader of a fighter squadron which was to put up a good performance on 1st Ukrainian Front scoring 22 kills while engaging enemy planes on 39 occasions without loss. Moskovenko remained in the VVS after the war and had become a Major when he retired in 1954.

MOTORNIJ, Ivan Porfiryevich
Combat record: 15 personal victories, 435 sorties, 117 encounters as of December, 1942.
Decorations: Gold Star of Hero of the Soviet Union on January 28, 1943; the Orders of Lenin (2), the Red Banner (2), Aleksandr Nevskij, the Patriotic War 1st Class.

Motornij was born in the Nikolayev area on August 29, 1918 and enlisted in the VVS for flight training in 1937. He was graduated as a pilot at Odessa military flying school a year later and was a Lejtenant and flight leader in the 512 IAP at the outbreak of the Patriotic War. He flew with great distinction during the darkest hours of 1941 and in recognition of his efforts was put in command of the regiment. With Motornij in the lead the unit performed brilliantly at Stalingrad although experiencing heavy losses. During the period of October 9, 1942 to February 1, 1943 the regiment was credited with 53 enemy aircraft in the air. Motornij personally accounted for a double on August 23, 1942 leading six Yak-1s against 60 German aircraft near Vertyachij and then began to pile up a remarkable score although no details have emerged. He submitted claims for a single on October 16 and was decorated with the Order of Lenin and two Orders of the Red Banner. He later assumed command of the 58 GIAP and wound up his military career with the rank of Major in 1946 and died on July 11, 1973. It seems possible that Motornij added to his tally during the later stages of war but no such information has been forthcoming from Soviet sources so far.

A young 28 GIAP pilot just beginning to make a name for himself during mid-1944 was flight leader Boris Aleksandrovich Mukhin, seen here on June 20, 1944 with his Aeracobra. At that time he had five confirmed kills with three more fractional credits. (Author's collection)

MUKHIN, Vasilij Filippovich
Combat record: 19 personal victories, 340 sorties.
Decorations: Gold Star of Hero of the Soviet Union on February 23, 1945 for 15 kills, 227 sorties, 64 encounters as of July, 1944; the Orders of Lenin, the Red Banner (4). the Patriotic War 1st Class, the Red Star.

Mukhin was born in the Gomel area on December 31, 1917 and entered military service in 1938. He was graduated as a pilot at Chuguyev military flying school three years later and was posted to the 240 IAP in July, 1942. From then on he was in continuous action at Kursk and over the Ukraine, Moldavia, Rumania, Hungary, and Austria. He got a Bf 109 near Liptsy on August 10, 1943 and excelled during the fighting over the Dnyepr River, submitting claims for two Bf 109s, two Fw 189s and a Ju 87 in October, 1943 while flying as wingman for the great Ivan Kozhedub. He took part in the Yassy-Kishinyov campaign and on August 20, 1944 racked up his 11th victory with another Bf 109, all gained while flying La-5s. Mukhin remained in the VVS after the war and had made Podpolkovnik when he concluded his active duty in 1950. He died on July 17, 1984.

MURASHOV, Aleksej Andrianovich (also spelled MURASHEV)
Combat record: 22 personal victories, 9 fractional credits, 450 sorties, 125 encounters.
Decorations: Gold Star of Hero of the Soviet Union on September 28, 1943 in recognition of 17 victories, 9 fractional credits, 328 sorties, 69 air combats as of August, 1943; the Orders of Lenin (2), the Red Banner (3), Aleksandr Nevskij, the Patriotic War 1st Class (2), the Red Star.

Murashov was born in the Irkutsk area on July 30, 1919 and started his military career in September, 1938. Two years later he won his pilot wings at Batajsk military flying school and

Right: Major A.A. Murashov, high-scoring ace of the 3 GIAP, who built up a good score in a fierce series of dogfights over the Kuban. (Author's collection)

became a member of the 155 IAP before the war. He was in action from the very start of the war and successively fought on Karelian, Volkhov, Leningrad, Stalingrad, North Caucasus, Voronezh and 1st Ukrainian Fronts. He destroyed his first enemy aircraft in the air at Leningrad and then gave a good account of himself in the skies of Stalingrad, the Kuban and Kursk. He claimed a Ju 87 with a La-5 near Karpovka on November 24, 1942 and a Bf 109 over Tsybenkovo the following day. He was credited with a double in the vicinity of Buzinovka on December 10 and then saw considerable fighting over the hamlets of Russkaya, Krymskaya and Moldavanskaya reporting the destruction of four enemy aircraft, including three Bf 109s, in a three day period between June 1-3, 1943. On August 4 he forced down a Ju 88 near Tamarovka and the following day added two He 111s engaging an enemy formation in the same area. Four days later he bagged an Hs 123 in the Bogodukhova area and on August 18 was leading four La-5s on a sweep out to Akhtyrka, where they mixed it with 25 dive-bombers covered by fighters. Murashov destroyed two Ju 87s while his squadron mates brought the day's tally to four. He eventually rose to regiment commander and participated in the final aerial operations over Prague. He remained in the VVS at the conclusion of the war and returned to civilian life with the rank of Polkovnik in 1972.

Starshij Lejtenant P.I. Muravyov. He was in continuous action from October, 1941 earning the title of Hero of the Soviet Union on May 1, 1943 for nine kills, five fractional credits, 185 sorties as of February, 1943. On the left breast he is wearing the Gold Star of Hero of the Soviet Union, the Order of Lenin and two Orders of the Red Banner. On the right there is the Guards badge and the Order of the Patriotic War (1st version). He ended the war as 271 IAP's top-scoring ace with a total of 28 victories. (Author's collection)

NAGORNIJ, Viktor Sergeyevich

Combat record: 24 personal victories.

Decorations: Gold Star of Hero of the Soviet Union on July 1, 1944 for 19 kills, 6 fractional credits, 169 sorties, 59 aerial engagements as of February, 1944; the Orders of Lenin, the Red Banner (2), Aleksandr Nevskij, the Patriotic War 1st Class, the Red Star (4).

Nagornij was born in the Sumy area on October 26, 1922 and enlisted in the VVS for flight training in 1940. He was graduated as a pilot at Chuguyev military flying school a year later and entered combat with the 293 IAP in August, 1942. He soon proved his skills at blasting enemy aircraft and made a remarkable combat record during his assignments on Stalingrad, South, North Caucasus, Bryansk and 2nd Baltic Fronts. At Stalingrad he reportedly shot down a 13-victory Luftwaffe ace who perished, but his identity has unfortunately not been established. Nagornij went on to become the regiment's highest scoring ace and was a squadron leader at the cessation of hostilities. During his postwar career he advanced to Podpolkovnik and retired from the VVS in 1960. He passed away on July 12, 1964.

NAJDENKO, Vasilij Mikhajlovich

Combat record: 22 personal victories, 57 fractional credits, 550 sorties, 350 encounters.

Decorations: Gold Star of Hero of the Soviet Union on April 21, 1943 for 5 victories along with 13 fractional credits as of March, 1943; the Orders of Lenin, the Red Banner (3), the Red Star.

Najdenko was born in Krivoj Rog on December 7, 1915 and started his rather spectacular career in the VVS in 1934. He completed his pilot training at Odessa military flying school two years later and was to become famous for taking part in as many as four conflicts and enter into more aerial encounters than any other Allied fighter pilot. He saw action for the first time in the Spanish Civil War and was given credit for three kills and six more shares in 27 air combats. Najdenko next enjoyed considerable success against the Japanese along the Khalkhin Gol River in Mongolia in 1939 chalking up five more kills and 19 fractional credits prior to being assigned as a squadron leader to a fighter air regiment close to the Finnish border. He came out of the Russo-Finnish Winter War as one of the high-scorers of the conflict with four confirmed victories and had already developed into an exceptionally capable fighter pilot when he was assigned as a squadron leader to the 126 IAP before Operation Barbarossa commenced in June, 1941. The regiment was thrown into the fray against the all-conquering Luftwaffe on West and Central Fronts and performed brilliantly but experienced heavy losses in doing so. During this period Najdenko's squadron bore the brunt of action and was able to claim 56 victories in the air plus 40 enemy aircraft destroyed in ground attacks. On August 15, 1941 he was leading a sweep of six MiG-3s out to the front where they intercepted 12 Ju 88s and nine Bf 109s, claiming four destroyed without loss. August 24 proved to be a bright day for the regiment when 34 fighters with Najdenko in the lead were sent out to engage 80 Luftwaffe planes and in a pitched battle gained 17 kills. During October Tomahawks were beginning to replace the MiG-3s and the unit was assigned to the Moscow PVO. Although the new fighter was to cause endless technical and logistical problems effecting a decline in morale, the regiment put up 685 sorties in support of ground forces on West and Kalinin Fronts, claiming 17 air victories during the period of October 12 to November 30, 1941. In all, 126 IAP chalked up 29 kills in 47 air encounters during the great battle for the Soviet capital before it was posted to Stalingrad Front with Najdenko becoming its commanding officer. At Stalingrad he added four more victories to his tally with the regiment bringing the campaign's total to 36. On September 5, 1942 he shot down two Bf 109s before he was badly hit in his legs and forced to bail out. He then reportedly was strafed by two Fw 190s whilst helpless in his parachute but fortunately escaped further harm. Although one of his legs was subsequently amputated, Najdenko was determined to return to combat duty and upon his recovery was to lead the regiment with consummate skill through the close of war. He wound up with a total of 10 personal victories and 29 fractional credits during the Patriotic War period to add to his previous record of 12 kills and 28 shares. He served with the postwar VVS and came off active duty with the rank of Polkovnik in 1953. He died on January 13, 1969.

NAJDYONOV, Nikolaj Alekseyevich
Combat record: 29 personal victories.
Decorations: Gold Star of Hero of the Soviet Union on August 24, 1943 for 9 kills, 3 fractional credits, 281 sorties and 32 encounters as of July, 1943; the Orders of Lenin, the Red Banner (2), Aleksandr Nevskij, the Patriotic War 1st Class (2), the Red Star.

Najdyonov was born in the Altajsk area on November 9, 1918 and entered the Soviet Army in 1938. Two years later he qualified as a pilot at Stalingrad military flying school and was posted to the 563 IAP before the war. He was in action from the beginning of the war and in 1942 was promoted Starshij Lejtenant and squadron leader. He next gained a number of victories in the skies of Stalingrad flying Kittyhawks and next became involved in the air battles at Kursk. On May 22, 1943 he submitted claims for two Fw 190s and a Bf 110 and on June 2 got into eight separate encounters claiming two kills and damage to two more. His aircraft was then badly hit forcing him to peel away and turn for home where he effected a successful wheels-up landing. He was flying Yak-1s when he became involved in heavy fighting over Korsun (January/February, 1944), Uman (March/April), and Batajsk (June) and rose to Kapitan. He later converted to Yak-3s and closed out his scoring in the contested air space over Berlin. He achieved a triple on April 16, 1945 and three days later knocked down a Fw 190 when six of his squadron led by Major V.I. Byvshev tackled with 16 German fighters. He remained in the service following World War II and retired from the VVS with the rank of Polkovnik in 1957.

NARZHIMSKIJ, Vladimir Aleksandrovich
Combat record: 18 personal victories, 404 sorties.
Decorations: Gold Star of Hero of the Soviet Union on March 6, 1945 in recognition of 13 victories, 5 fractional credits, 339 sorties, 35 air engagements as of August, 1944; the Orders of Lenin, the Red Banner (3), the Patriotic War 1st Class (2), the Red Star (3).

Narzhimskij was born in the Minsk area on February 14, 1915 and enrolled for service in the VMF in 1936. Upon graduating from flight training at Yejsk in 1941 he was assigned to the Black Sea Fleet's air service. He made his mark against the Luftwaffe early in the war and subsequently saw a lot of action over Tuapse, Novorossijsk, Kerch and Sevastopol. He excelled at Tuapse where he chalked up six kills within two days late in 1942. He was promoted Kapitan and assigned to the crack 11 GIAP-ChF which at that stage was operating a collection of Airacobras and Yaks fighting a very successful campaign over Anapa and Feodosiya. After the war Narzhimskij graduated from the Air Force Academy in 1951 and made Polkovnik before leaving active duty in 1970.

NAUMCHIK, Nikolaj Kuzmich
Combat record: 13 personal victories, 9 fractional credits, 319 sorties, 54 encounters as of December, 1943.
Decorations: Gold Star of Hero of the Soviet Union on May 1, 1943 for 8 victories, 8 fractional credits plus 1 enemy aircraft destroyed in ground attacks, 270 sorties, 39 air combats as of February, 1943; the Orders of Lenin (2), the Red Banner (3), the Patriotic War 1st Class (2), the Red Star.

Naumchik was born in Minsk on July 15, 1916 and enlisted in the VVS at age 21. He completed his pilot training at Borisoglebsk military flying school in 1938 and was posted to the 8 IAP on South Front in September, 1941. He gained his initial combat experience in Yak-1s and later reequipped with Yak-3s. He gave a good account of himself in the Caucasus and over the Kuban, and by April, 1943 his score had risen to 10 personal victories. He was promoted Kapitan and squadron leader but his subsequent combat career then is somewhat obscure. It is possible that he added to score of 13 kills as of December, 1943 but is not certain. He served with the postwar VVS and graduated from the Air Force Academy in 1946 winding up his military career with the rank of Polkovnik in 1957.

NAZARENKO, Dmitrij Pavlovich
Combat record: 24 personal victories, 8 fractional credits, 500 sorties, 120 encounters.
Decorations: Gold Star of Hero of the Soviet Union on December 13, 1942 for 11 kills, 7 fractional credits, 323 sorties as of November, 1942; the Orders of Lenin (2), the Red Banner (2), the Patriotic War 1st and 2nd Class, the Red Star.

Nazarenko was born in the Dnyepropetrovsk area on November 26, 1917 and entered military service in 1936. He received full flight training at Kacha military flying school in 1938 following which he saw action for the first time during the Russo-Finnish Winter War of 1939/40. By June, 1941 he had become a member of the 131 IAP and in the dark months to follow would display exceptional skill and tenacity. The regiment was occupied with ground support in the Donbas its I-16s claiming 21 kills within two days between October 22-23, 1941. With four air victories Nazarenko was most successful pilot and next he moved with the unit to the Kuban where he was to add new laurels to his record. In 1942 he was promoted Kapitan and squadron leader and subsequently saw a lot of action during the great aerial battles at Kursk, Voronezh, Smolensk and over Poland and the Reich flying his last mission in the Berlin area on May 5, 1945. He remained in the VVS following World War II and graduated from the Air Force Academy in 1951 and from General Staff Academy six years later. He had made General Major when he concluded his active duty in 1967.

Major N.K. Naumchik was among the successful aces of the 8 IAP running up a good score in the Caucasus. (Author's collection)

NAZIMOV, Konstantin Savelyevich
Combat record: 24 personal victories.
Decorations: Gold Star of Hero of the Soviet Union on October 26, 1944 in recognition of 15 kills, 2 fractional credits, 240 sorties, 27 engagements as of August, 1944; the Orders of Lenin, the Red Banner (2), Aleksandr Nevskij, the Patriotic War 1st Class.

Nazimov was born in Leningrad on March 3, 1915 and entered the VVS for flight training in 1939. He was graduated as a pilot at Chuguyev military flying school a year later and was a pilot instructor for a while. He was posted to the 254 IAP as a Starshij Lejtenant and started flying combat on Volkhov Front in March, 1943. Over the next 12 months he ran up a string of 12 air victories with the Lavochkin La-5 fighter and next distinguished himself on 3rd Baltic Front. He rose to Kapitan and squadron leader and on an unspecified day led four of his squadron mates against a formation of 40 enemy aircraft, 10 of these being shot down. Although his aircraft was badly shot up, Nazimov stayed in the fight to turn in three kills. On December 23, 1944 he was shot down and killed, and in him the regiment lost one of its most outstanding characters and second ranking ace.

NEPRYAKHIN, Pavel Markovich
Combat record: 17 personal victories, 149 sorties, 28 encounters.
Decorations: Gold Star of Hero of the Soviet Union on June 27, 1945; the Orders of Lenin, the Red Banner (2), the Patriotic War 2nd Class.

Nepryakhin was born in the Perm area on January 21, 1923 and joined the Soviet Army in 1941. He completed his pilot training at Rustav military flying school a year later and was posted to the 2 GIAP in May, 1942. He entered combat with the Luftwaffe the following month and quickly established a reputation for aggressiveness and air combat skill on free hunt missions. During his time with the regiment Nepryakhin saw action on Volkhov, Kalinin, Bryansk, 1st Baltic and 3rd Byelorussian Fronts building up a good score over Leningrad, Velikiye Luki, Orel, Bryansk, Vitebsk, Minsk, East Prussia and Berlin. He scored a single with an He 111 on August 1, 1943 when 10 La-5s engaged 40 bombers and 12 escorting Fw 190s in the Bryansk area getting nine kills. Nepryakhin had his best day five days later when eight of his squadron tore into 25 Ju 88s and 12 Fw 190s approaching the front-line area and personally accounted for four Fw 190s and a Ju 88 with his com-

Viktor Korabin of the 254 IAP reports to the regiment commander after a sortie in Estonia, autumn 1944. From left, the pilots are: Viktor Korabin, Aleksandr Gorchakov, Ivan Vasilyev, Konstantin Nazimov, who was at the time leading the 2nd Eskadrilya, the regiment commander Stepan Mikhajlin, Anissi, Izmodenov, Vadim Ivanov, Viktor Lesin, and Sergej Sarkasyan. (Author's collection)

Members of the 254 IAP. From left they are: K.S. Nazimov, Mikhajlin, I.V. Vasilyev, Izmodenov and Sarkasyan. Note victory stars marked beneath the La-5's cockpit. (Author's collection)

rades bringing the day's tally to nine kills without loss. Further combats on Bryansk Front saw him claim two more Fw 190s while he combined forces with fellow pilots to destroy a Ju 87, an He 111 and two Fw 190s which qualified him for the award of the Order of the Patriotic War 2nd Class. In 1945 the regiment began to range deep into East Prussia, and he was credited with the destruction of one each Ju 52 and Fw 190 in the Inkstein area on an unspecified date while on March 18 he sent down a Bf 109 over an enemy airfield near Cottbus. He stayed in the service after the war and retired from the VVS with the rank of Major in 1955. Nepryakhin died on May 23, 1958.

NEUSTROYEV, Ivan Pavlovich (also spelled NEUSTRUYEV)
Combat record: 23 personal victories, 6 fractional credits, 400 sorties, 85 encounters.
Decorations: Gold Star of Hero of the Soviet Union on September 28, 1943 for 11 personal victories, 6 fractional credits, 128 sorties, 55 encounters as of August, 1943; the Orders of Lenin, the Red Banner (3), Kutuzov 3rd Class, the Patriotic War 1st Class, the Red Star (3).

Neustroyev was born in Kamensk on August 15, 1915 and entered military service in 1934. He graduated from flight training at Kharkov three years later and cut his teeth against the Finns during the Winter War of 1939/40. Neustroyev was in continuous action from the very first days of the Patriotic War while serving in the 195 IAP. He destroyed his first enemy aircraft in the air in the vicinity of Kingisepp (SW Leningrad) a short time later when he forced down a Ju 88. In three months combat he chalked up nine kills in a series of pitched battles with the Luftwaffe over Leningrad while a fighter squadron under his leadership was given credit for 46 air victories. On one occasion Neustroyev claimed a double with one each Bf 109 and Ju 87 in one sortie and this was to be his best day. Because of his success he rapidly was promoted Major and put in command of the 11 GIAP which he was to lead with consummate skill during subsequent combat assignments. He was released from the service with the rank of Polkovnik in 1949 and passed away on February 19, 1965.

NIKOLAYENKOV, Aleksandr Ignatyevich
Combat record: 8 personal victories, 23 fractional credits, 229 sorties, 28 encounters.
Decorations: Gold Star of Hero of the Soviet Union posthumously on August 24, 1943; the Orders of Lenin, the Red Banner.

Nikolayenkov was born in Smolensk on April 2, 1920 and enlisted in the Soviet Army in 1938. He was trained at Odessa military flying school receiving his wings two years later and saw action as a member of the 126 IAP from the earliest days of the Patriotic War. He later was posted to the 760 IAP on Karelian Front advancing to deputy squadron leader. On February 21, 1942 he destroyed a Ju 88 near Kovda regardless of vicious return fire, and upon his return to base 130 hits were counted in his aircraft. He reported the destruction of two more of these in the vicinity of Kemi (Karelia) on June 15 while leading four Kittyhawks to attack a formation of 23 enemy planes, seven bombers and one fighter being claimed shot down. He was killed in action on July 7, 1943 and was a deputy squadron leader at the time of his death.

NIKONOROV, Pyotr Mikhajlovich
Combat record: 17 personal victories, 5 fractional credits, 167 sorties, 44 encounters.
Decorations: Gold Star of Hero of the Soviet Union on July 1, 1944; the Order of Lenin, the Red Banner (3), the Patriotic War 1st Class, the Red Star.

Nikonorov was born in Chistopol, Tatarian SSR, on January 13, 1923 and entered the Soviet Army in 1941. He completed his pilot training at Tsnoris-Tskhalinsk military flying school a year later and joined with the 166 IAP in December, 1942. He achieved his initial success in the big air battles above the Kuban and subsequently fought in the skies above Kursk, the Dnyepr River and Zhitomir eventually making flight leader. He built up a good score on 1st Ukrainian Front and on August 14, 1944 Nikonorov and his wingman, Mladshij Lejtenant Novichkov, were successful in breaking up a formation of Ju 88s approaching Soviet forces at the Vistula bridgehead, one of the bombers falling before their guns. He remained with the VVS until 1957 retiring as a Major. He died on July 5, 1983.

NOGA, Mitrofan Petrovich
Combat record: 22 personal victories.
Decorations: Gold Star of Hero of the Soviet Union on November 17, 1939; the Orders of Lenin, the Red Banner (4), Suvorov 2nd Class, Kutuzov 2nd Class, the Patriotic War 1st Class (2), the Red Star (2).

Noga was born in the Kharkov area on August 19, 1914 and enlisted in the VVS in 1932. He was graduated from flight training at 9th military flying school and rapidly rose from pilot to squadron leader while serving with units of Kiev and Transbaikal military districts. In May, 1939 he was assigned as a Starshij Lejtenant and squadron leader to the 70 IAP becoming involved in the air operations against the Japanese at the Khalkhin Gol in Mongolia. He emerged as one of the high-scorers of the conflict with a confirmed tally of nine fighters along with two fractional credits during 109 sorties and 22 aerial engagements. His squadron also put up a good performance, claiming the destruction of 16 Japanese aircraft in ground attacks during the period of August 20-30, 1939 only. He then assumed command of the 41 IAP and attended the Air Force Academy between January and June, 1941. When the Germans initiated their attack on the Soviet Union Noga commenced his combat duty as commander of the 182 IAP and was to serve in various command positions through the close of war successive assignments seeing him lead the 144, 322 and 256 IADs. During the war he took part in the aerial campaigns on South, North Caucasus, West, Bryansk, 3rd Byelorussian and 1st Ukrainian Fronts being wounded in action twice. Following World War II Noga graduated from Voroshilov General Staff Academy in 1949 and eventually advanced to General Lejtenant. He wound up his military career in 1963 and died on December 22, 1986. Noga's final score is a matter of dispute, some sources quoting his tally as 27 personal kills along with 6 fractional credits.

NOVIKOV, Yegor Pavlovich

Combat record: 11 personal victories, 6 fractional credits, 60 sorties.

Decorations: Gold Star of Hero of the Soviet Union posthumously on January 16, 1942; the Orders of Lenin, the Red Banner.

Novikov was born in the Bryansk area on October 1, 1915 and enrolled for service in the VVS in 1938. He received his pilot wings at Borisoglebsk military flying school a year later and then won the Orders of Lenin and the Red Banner for his efforts against the Finns during the Winter War of 1939/40 being shot down and wounded once. He was posted to the 191 IAP before the war and by June, 1941 had become a Mladshij Lejtenant and flight leader. He was in the thick of the fighting on Leningrad Front from the earliest days of the war flying I-16s. In a few weeks he became one of the outstanding pilots of the theater scoring victories on a regular basis. He drew first blood on August 25 claiming a Bf 109 near Gatchina, and two days later led three fellow pilots in achieving three victories, where he personally accounted for a Ju 87. His big day came on the 29th when he bagged two more Ju 87s along with a Bf 109 near Mga but was wounded and had to force-land on his own airfield. He returned to his unit on September 6 and three days later scared away two German fighters that were reportedly attacking Lejtenant Savchenko in his parachute. On the 11th he forced down another Stuka near Krasnoye Selo (SW Leningrad) by ramming , having expended his ammunition, and returned safely to his base. On September 17 he was engaged by six Bf 109s and Bf 110s and never had a chance. His tally at the time of his death consists of nine Ju 87s and two Bf 109s; Soviet sources do not agree on the circumstances of his last combat, one suggesting he was killed ramming an enemy plane, though this would appear to be in error and possibly confusion with his September 11th feat.

NOVOSYOLOV, Kuzma Vasilyevich

Combat record: 19 personal victories, 5 fractional credits plus 18 tanks, 4 locomotives, 36 motor vehicles destroyed in ground attacks, 235 sorties.

Decorations: Gold Star of Hero of the Soviet Union on June 27, 1945; the Orders of Lenin, the Red Banner (2), the Patriotic War 1st Class.

Novosyolov was born in Sernur on February 8, 1919 and started his military career in 1939. He initially was serving with the infantry but in 1942 came to the 16 Zapasnyj Aviapolk (reserve air regiment) where he was trained on Po-2s. Upon completion of training he was assigned as a Starshij Lejtenant to the 115 GIAP and claimed his first enemy plane in the air over Orel with the Yak-9 fighter. He subsequently enjoyed above-average success in the contested skies above Bryansk, Minsk, Vilnyus, Kaunas, Tilsit, Memel and finally, Berlin. His most memorable mission occurred on the night of July 28, 1944 when Novosyolov and five of his squadron mates were scrambled to intercept enemy aircraft over the Neman River. They broke up the attack claiming 14 night kills with Novosyolov personally accounting for two Ju 87s. He closed out his scoring near Dresden on May 8, 1945 to finish as the regiment's ranking ace. He stayed in the ranks after the cessation of hostilities retiring as a Podpolkovnik in 1953. He died on March 20, 1985.

OBORIN, Aleksandr Vasilyevich

Combat record: 13 personal victories, 13 fractional credits, 283 sorties, 119 encounters.

Decorations: Gold Star of Hero of the Soviet Union posthumously on April 10, 1945; the Orders of Lenin (2), the Red Banner (3), the Red Star.

Oborin was born in the Perm area in 1908 and entered military service in 1929. He received his basic training at Leningrad in 1932 prior to qualifying as a pilot at Engels military flying school. He was posted to the 563 IAP on July 12, 1941 to start flying combat and in June, 1942 took over as leader of a fighter squadron. He saw considerable fighting at Stalingrad and on September 9, 1942 downed a Bf 109 in the Ersovka area and successfully rammed a second having expended the ammunition of his fighter. He was able to nurse his aircraft in safely at his own airfield. Oborin later took over as commander of the 438 IAP and made Podpolkovnik taking part in the aerial operations on 1st Ukrainian Front. On August 7, 1944 while leading a fighter sweep out to the Sandomierz bridgehead he claimed two kills when they became involved in melees with Luftwaffe planes and then deliberately rammed a German fighter in the Lagov area, 31 kilometers southeast of Kielce, Poland, but was unable to bail out being killed. With Oborin's loss, the VVS was deprived of one of its fine tacticians.

Polikarpov I-16s passing low over central Russia. This nimble fighter first saw action against nationalist forces in Spain and later did yeoman service in many roles until more advanced aircraft were introduced into combat, some frontline regiments continuing to operate them until well into 1943. The great S.I. Gritsevets was the outstanding exponent of the I-16, gaining all or most of his victories on this type. (Author's collection)

ODINTSOV, Mikhail Petrovich
Combat record: 12 personal victories plus numerous targets on the ground, 215 sorties.
Decorations: 1st Gold Star of Hero of the Soviet Union on February 4, 1944 for 2 air victories and 4 enemy planes on the ground, 96 sorties as of September, 1943, 2nd Gold Star on June 27, 1945; the Orders of Lenin (2), the October Revolution, the Red Banner (5), Aleksandr Nevskij, the Patriotic War 1st Class (2), the Patriotic War 2nd Class, the Red Star.

Odintsov was born in the Perm area on November 18, 1921 and started his remarkable career in the VVS in 1938. He graduated from Perm and Engels military flying schools in 1939 resp. 1940 and went to war as a Mladshij Lejtenant in a bomber unit on June 26, 1941. He was wounded in action shortly afterward and upon his recovery was assigned to the 820 ShAP flying Il-2s. From then on Odintsov was in continuous action enjoying considerable success at Demyansk, Velikiye Luki, Byelgorod-Kharkov, Korsun-Shevchenkovskij, Lemberg-Sandomierz, Berlin, Potsdam and Dresden. On May 30, 1942 he was leading a strafing attack on a Luftwaffe airfield in the Kursk area where he personally accounted for the destruction of two Ju 88s, six antiaircraft guns, one locomotive and six rail cars on the ground. He claimed two Bf 109s in the air on July 6, 1942 when his squadron was bounced by four fighters. He saw a great deal of action during the Soviet counteroffensive at Byelgorod-Kharkov and over a five weeks period between August 3 and September 6, 1943 was credited with four tanks, 10 motor vehicles and two antiaircraft guns destroyed during 20 ground-attack missions. He eventually was promoted Major and deputy regiment commander serving in this capacity through the end of war. He became greatly involved in the dramatic fighting of the Korsun-Shevchenkovskij campaign – known to the Germans as the Cherkassy pocket where 56,000 men were caught and trapped by half a dozen Soviet armies. On February 11, 1944 Odintsov led a massive strafe of Shturmoviks out to an assigned area northwest of Korsun where eight Ju 52 transport were reduced to scrap. Odintsov went on to emerge as one of the outstanding ground attack pilots of World War II and was to attain high rank with the postwar VVS. He graduated from the General Staff Academy in 1959 and was promoted to General Polkovnik in 1976. In the 1970s he was commander of the Moscow military district air service and in 1981 was appointed assistant chief of Warsaw Pact air forces in Poland.

Shturmovik ace. M.P. Odintsov made a brilliant war record serving with the 820 ShAP. (Author's collection)

OGANESOV, Vozgen Mikhajlovich
Combat record: 23 personal victories, 324 sorties.
Decorations: Gold Star of Hero of the Soviet Union on May 15, 1946 in recognition of 16 kills, 290 sorties, 67 encounters as of March, 1945; the Orders of Lenin, the Red Banner (3), the Patriotic War 1st Class (2), the Red Star.

Oganesov was born in the Artik area, Armenian SSR, on February 10, 1920 and enlisted in the VVS for flight training in 1940. He won his pilot wings at Tbilisi military flying school a year later and commenced his combat duty in December, 1941. His most impressive display of combat skill came on 1st Byelorussian Front during the latter stages of war when he was flying Yak-9s with the 347 IAP. On September 20, 1943 he combined forces with his wingman to destroy two Ju 88s near Koselets (NE Kiev) and on August 9, 1944 claimed a Fw 190 when 12 of his squadron tackled with 30 Fw 190s over the Vistula River, three of these being shot down. He later saw a lot of action during the big air battles over Berlin, scoring a double on April 16, 1945. Oganesov came out of World War II as the regiment's highest scoring ace. He remained in the VVS at the conclusion of the war and had become a Polkovnik when leaving active duty in 1956.

OKHAJ, Grigorij Ulyanovich
Combat record: 11 personal victories, 122 sorties (all Korean War).
Decorations: Gold Star of Hero of the Soviet Union on November 13, 1951; the Orders of Lenin, the Red Banner, the Patriotic War 1st and 2nd Class, the Red Star (2).

Okhaj was born in the Zaporozhye area on January 5, 1917 and destined to become one of the notable pilots of the Korean conflict. He enrolled for service in the VVS in 1935 and had flight training at Voroshilovgrad military flying school. He participated in the Russo-Finnish Winter War of 1939/40 and then fought on the German-Russian Front but no details have emerged. His meteoric rise to fame began after World War II when he was posted as deputy commanding officer of the 523 IAP to North Korea, flying MiG-15s. He quickly proved his skills at blasting U.N. aircraft and on September 5, 1951 claimed a double with two Meteors while leading 24 fighters to storm into a formation of Australian fighters. He got another of these on November 3, 1951 when the regiment again pitilessly ambushed enemy fighter-bombers forcing down five F-84s and two Meteors. Okhaj stayed in the service after the war and wound up his military career with the rank of Polkovnik in 1960.

OLKHOVSKIJ, Nikolaj Ivanovich

Combat record: 19 personal victories, 128 sorties.

Decorations: Gold Star of Hero of the Soviet Union on February 4, 1944 for 12 victories, 84 sorties, 17 air-to-air combats as of September, 1943; the Orders of Lenin, the Red Banner (4), Aleksandr Nevskij, the Red Star.

Olkhovskij was born in the Vitebsk area on October 10, 1909 and entered the Soviet Army in 1927. He qualified as a pilot at Orenburg military flying school three years later and in 1936 graduated from the Air Force Academy. Olkhovskij was posted to the 193 IAP in January, 1943 and subsequently served with great distinction on Bryansk, Voronezh, Steppe and 2nd Ukrainian Fronts, finishing as a Podpolkovnik and commander of the 178 GIAP. He developed into a crack shot, achieving victories at a formidable pace. He excelled during the Byelgorod-Kharkov campaign, claiming three Bf 109s in quick succession near Liptsy on August 10, 1943. On September 9 he was leading his squadron to destroy four more of these when German fighters tried to bounce Pe-2s in the Kovyagi area (W Kharkov). When he was recommended for the award of the coveted title of Hero of the Soviet Union soon after he had acquired a total of 12 kills in just 17 encounters. He remained in the ranks following World War II retiring from the VVS in 1953. He died on August 26, 1978.

ONUFRIYENKO, Grigorij Denisovich

Combat record: 29 personal victories, 405 sorties.

Decorations: Gold Star of Hero of the Soviet Union on April 12, 1942 in recognition of 7 kills, 110 sorties, 31 encounters as of August, 1941; the Orders of Lenin, the Red Banner (4), Aleksandr Nevskij, the Patriotic War 1st Class (2), the Red Star (2).

G.D. Onufriyenko casting a pensive look, Kalinin Front, 1941. He became an ace fighting with the glorious 5 GIAP and later assumed command of the 31 IAP on 3rd Ukrainian Front as a Podpolkovnik with 29 confirmed victories. (Author's collection)

Onufriyenko was born in Voroshilovgrad (Lugansk) on June 22, 1916 and joined the Soviet Army in 1936. He had flight training at Voroshilovgrad military flying school and participated in the occupation of Poland in 1939 prior to entering into combat against the Finns during the Winter War of 1939/40. When Operation Barbarossa commenced in June, 1941 Onufriyenko was a well-seasoned pilot serving as a Starshij Lejtenant and leader of the 1st Eskadrilya in the 129 IAP. He flew with great distinction during the dark months to follow, fighting against great odds at Dukhovshchina, Yelnya, and Yartsevo. By September he had brought his score to nine, all or most of which were gained on the MiG-3 fighter. On September 24 he was leading a highly successful strafing attack of eight squadron mates on a Luftwaffe airfield where they claimed to have destroyed seven bombers and damaged three more. Nine LaGG-3s with Kapitan Zajtsev in the lead then swept in to finish off the rest. He was shot down and wounded by Bf 109s in the vicinity of Yartsevo on October 2 and on December 5 was sent out with several comrades to intercept a formation of Ju 88s approaching elements of 243rd Rifle Division near Kalinin. In the ensuing melee five bombers were destroyed, one of which fell before the guns of Onufriyenko himself. Two days later he reported the destruction of a Ju 87 and on August 4, 1942 was leading a front-line patrol of six LaGG-3s when they became embroiled in a dogfight with an equal number of Bf 109s in the Chertolino area, Onufriyenko forcing one of them down in flames. He rose to Major and in late 1942 was tasked with picking up the new Lavochkin La-5 fighters near Gorkij. In 1943 he was promoted Polkovnik assuming command of the 31 IAP on 3rd Ukrainian Front. He was to lead the unit with consummate skill during the ferocious air battles of the Yassy-Kishinyov campaign (August 20-29, 1944), over Yugoslavia and Hungary, being heavily involved in the Budapest fighting. The regiment's final score was 350 confirmed victories during 17,000 sorties. Following World War II Onufriyenko continued on active duty until 1971 when he retired from the VVS with the rank of Polkovnik.

ORLOV, Aleksandr Ivanovich
Combat record: 14 personal victories, 8 fractional credits, 629 sorties, 56 encounters.
Decorations: Gold Star of Hero of the Soviet Union on June 27, 1945; the Orders of Lenin, the Red Banner (2), the Patriotic War 1st Class, the Red Star (2).

Orlov was born in Serpukhov on August 15, 1913 and entered military service at age 23. He won his pilot wings at Kacha military flying school in 1940 but would not start flying combat until December, 1942, having joined with the glorious 5 GIAP the previous month. He began to make his mark against the Luftwaffe in the big air battles over the Don River flying La-5s. He claimed a double over Izyum on August 17, 1943 but in turn was shot down bailing out wounded in his face and arms. He later rose to Starshij Lejtenant and squadron leader and gave a good account of himself during combat operations on 1st Ukrainian Front. Orlov returned to civilian life with the rank of Kapitan in 1946 and is living in Serpukhov.

ORLOV, Pavel Ivanovich
Combat record: 11 personal victories, 276 sorties, 24 encounters.
Decorations: Gold Star of Hero of the Soviet Union posthumously on July 24, 1943; the Orders of Lenin, the Red Banner (2).

Orlov was born in the Moscow area in 1914 and enlisted in the VMF in 1933. He received his pilot training at Yejsk and in October, 1941 was posted to the 2nd Eskadrilya of 2 GIAP-SF. He opened his account with a Hs 126 in January, 1942 and on April 15 bagged a Ju 87. He got a Bf 109 on May 8 when four Hurricanes with Podpolkovnik Safonov in the lead tangled with seven German fighters over Vichany Bay claiming three kills. Two days later he forced down another of these and on May 30, the day the famous and able tactician Boris Safonov was lost, destroyed a Ju 88. On an unspecified date he reportedly attacked a Bf 109 head-on and shot it down in flames as it broke away. Orlov fell foul of eight Bf 109s and Fw 190s in an action near Murmansk on May 15, 1943.

A.I. Orlov, who won acedom with the 5 GIAP flying 629 combat sorties with 14 personal victories. (V.I. Popkov)

OSADCHIYEV, Aleksandr Dmitriyevich
Combat record: 26 personal victories, 250 sorties, 100 encounters.
Decorations: Gold Star of Hero of the Soviet Union on May 15, 1946 in recognition of 18 kills, 6 fractional credits, 230 sorties as of September, 1944; the Orders of Lenin, the Red Banner (2), Aleksandr Nevskij, the Patriotic War 1st Class (3), the Red Star (2).

Osadchiyev was born in Borisoglebsk on April 25, 1919 and entered the Soviet Army in 1936. He was sent to Kacha military flying school where he won his wings in 1939. He was involved in training pilots for some time before he was assigned to the 43 IAP in April, 1943 flying Yak-7Bs. He was not slow to get started and in a burst of energy and skill ran up four kills – two Ju 87s and one each Bf 109 and Ju 88 – over the Kuban. He next saw a good deal of action in the skies above the Donbas and subsequently would score steadily during combat assignments on 3rd and 1st Byelorussian Fronts. He wound up as the regiment's second ranking ace and had been wounded in action four times. When hostilities in Europe ceased he had become a Starshij Lejtenant and squadron leader. He remained in the VVS after the war and graduated from the Air Force Academy in 1950 and from General Staff Academy nine years later. He wound up his military career with the rank of General Major in 1981.

OSIPENKO, Aleksandr Stepanovich

Combat record: 17 personal victories, 34 fractional credits, 360 sorties.

Decorations: Gold Star of Hero of the Soviet Union on February 22, 1939; the Orders of Lenin, the Red Banner (3), Kutuzov 1st and 2nd Class, Suvorov 2nd Class, the Patriotic War 1st Class, the Red Star.

Osipenko was born in Tursevo-Kula (Finland) on June 1, 1910 and enlisted in the Soviet Army in 1929. He qualified as a pilot at Borisoglebsk military flying school three years later and then was to make a big name for himself in the Spanish Civil War of 1936-39. In eight months combat he chalked up 17 kills along with 34 more fractional credits to emerge as one of the outstanding pilots of the conflict. In 1940 he became deputy commander of the Moscow air defense and by June, 1941 had assumed command of the 20 SAD with the rank of General Major. The unit escaped the initial Luftwaffe strikes virtually unscathed with only four of its total of 360 aircraft being destroyed and managed to put up a good performance in the subsequent clashes at Kishinyov. In 1942 Osipenko was appointed commander of PVO fighter forces and on June 16, 1944 was assigned as commander of the 8 IAK, serving in this capacity through the end of war. He served with the postwar PVO concluding his active duty as a General Lejtenant in 1959.

OSKALENKO, Dmitrij Yefimovich

Combat record: 14 personal victories.

Decorations: Gold Star of Hero of the Soviet Union on February 14, 1943 for 11 personal victories, 1 fractional credit, 197 sorties, 23 engagements as of June, 1942; the Orders of Lenin, the Red Banner, the Red Star.

Oskalenko was born in the Mogilyov area on November 7, 1920 and entered military service in 1937. He was graduated as an aircraft mechanic at Leningrad two years later and during his first combat assignment saw action against the Finns in the Winter War of 1939/40. He was then sent to Kacha military flying school where he received his pilot wings in 1941 and next went to war with the 26 IAP flying I-16s. He was able to build up a good score during the darkest hours of 1941, claiming three kills on August 18 while entering into three different tussles. Seven days later a German fighter fell before his guns also shooting up three aircraft on the ground while taking part in a massive airfield strafe in the Leningrad area. On August 28 Oskalenko and his wingman took on a large enemy force reportedly consisting of some 40 bombers and fighters with Oskalenko knocking down a Bf 109 and scoring strikes on two bombers before breaking off and turning for home. He was promoted Kapitan and got another victory with a Ju 88 a short time later. On September 26 though, while leading six I-16s on a sweep out to Dubrovka (E Leningrad), combat occurred with eight Bf 109s at 1230 hours. In a vicious, protracted duel Oskalenko's aircraft was badly hit forcing him to bail out but he did not survive. He was interred in Dubrovka. It is particular noteworthy that Oskalenko achieved his scoring on the Polikarpov I-16 fighter which was obsolete and outclassed by all German aircraft under normal circumstances.

OVODOV, Yakov Leontyevich

Combat record: 19 personal victories.

Decorations: Gold Star of Hero of the Soviet Union on May 15, 1946 for 18 victories, 224 sorties, 69 encounters as of April, 1945; the Orders of Lenin, the Red Banner (3), the Patriotic War 1st Class (2), the Red Star.

Ovodov was born in the Saratov area on October 20, 1917 and enlisted in the Soviet Army in 1938. He had his flight training at Borisoglebsk military flying school and joined combat with the Luftwaffe in February, 1942 after having been posted to the 133 IAP. He quickly rose to Starshij Lejtenant and saw considerable fighting at Kursk. On July 11, 1943 he got a double with two Fw 190s and eight days later was leading a fighter sweep of Yak-7Bs when they engaged a force of 27 Ju 87s between Oleshnya-Bortnoye, eight of these being shot down. He later made Major and flew with great distinction during the final stages of the war. He took part in the Vistula-Oder campaign (January 12/February 3, 1945) and participated in the flurry of action surrounding the Küstrin bridgeheads. He claimed two kills between March 5-8, 1945 including a single on the 6th while leading six Yak-3s on an escort for four 173 GShAP Il-2s when they became embroiled in a dogfight with 12 Fw 190s. In all, five German fighters were destroyed for no losses. Ovodov closed out his scoring in the final clashes over Berlin. Following World War II he continued on active duty retiring from the VVS as a Podpolkovnik in 1954.

PANIN, Pavel Alekseyevich

Combat record: 13 personal victories, 114 sorties, 18 encounters.

Decorations: Gold Star of Hero of the Soviet Union posthumously on January 22, 1944; the Orders of Lenin, the Red Banner (2), the Patriotic War 1st Class, the Red Star.

Panin was born in Volgograd in 1909 and joined the Soviet Army in 1932. After qualifying as a pilot Panin cut his teeth during the Spanish Civil War of 1936/39 and next fought against the Finns in the Winter War of 1939/40, but unfortunately no

A beautifully restored Yak-3 displayed at a national air show in Moscow. (Author's collection)

details are available. He saw considerable action right after the German attack on Soviet Russia in June, 1941 and in May, 1942 took over the 255 IAP of Northern Fleet's air service as a Major. Under his leadership the unit was given credit for 87 enemy planes in the air until August, 1943, all while flying Airacobras. On the 26th, however, Panin was shot down and killed.

PANOV, Aleksej Borisovich

Combat record: 14 personal victories, 241 sorties, 41 encounters.

Decorations: Gold Star of Hero of the Soviet Union posthumously on February 23, 1945; the Orders of Lenin, the Red Banner (4), Aleksandr Nevskij, the Patriotic War 1st Class, the Red Star.

Panov was born in the Sumy area on October 15, 1914 and enlisted in the VVS for flight training in 1934. Two years later he was graduated as a pilot and in 1937 entered combat in Spain but was seriously wounded. He was posted to the 185 IAP before the outbreak of the Patriotic War and by June, 1941 had become a Kapitan and deputy commander of the regiment. He enjoyed considerable success during the bitter fighting of 1941 and for his efforts was promoted Major in 1942. In May he was put in command of the 436 IAP by which time his score stood at six kills during 70 sorties and 15 aerial encounters. He molded and vitalized it into one of the hottest fighter units of the Eastern Front and in time it was honored with the Guards banner. Although the Hurricane under normal conditions was no match for Luftwaffe fighters, the regiment was able to build up a good score on this machine by destroying 20 enemy aircraft within five days in July, 1942. After converting to Airacobras they were able to achieve a remarkable victory on August 2, 1943 when Panov led 17 fighters in an aggressive attack against 70 bombers covered by 40 fighters between Lomovets-Gostomlya-Chuvardino-Krasnikovo, 25 enemy planes being claimed destroyed. Panov personally accounted for a Ju 87 on his first pass and then successfully rammed a second, carrying out a forced landing in the Soviet lines. He advanced to Podpolkovnik in 1944. On September 12, 1944 he was leading four Yak-3s on an escort mission to the Warsaw area when they came under attack of enemy fighters. Turning into them Panov claimed two kills in quick succession before his aircraft was badly shot up, causing him to attempt a force-landing. Unfortunately his fighter crashed and burst into flames, giving him no chance of survival. Russian cavalry hurrying to the scene was unable to pull him from the flaming wreckage. He was a Polkovnik at the time of his death, and under his decisive leadership the 67 GIAP had been given credit for 268 air victories during 4,250 sorties producing 10 Heroes of the Soviet Union.

PARSHIN, Georgij Mikhajlovich

Combat record: 10 personal victories plus 34 tanks, 200 motor vehicles, 8 locomotives, 51 field guns destroyed in ground attacks, 253 sorties.

Decorations: 1st Gold Star of Hero of the Soviet Union on August 19, 1944 after 138 sorties as of March, 1944, 2nd Gold Star on April 19, 1945 in recognition of 10 air victories and 96 more sorties as of February, 1945; the Orders of Lenin, the

Red Banner (4), Suvorov 3rd Class, Aleksandr Nevskij, the Patriotic War 1st Class.

Parshin was born in the Orel area on May 23, 1916 and destined to become one of the finest ground-attack pilots of World War II. In 1936 he graduated from flight training at Kherson Osoaviakhim flying school following which he was involved in training pilots at Dnyepropetrovsk, Cheboksary and Groznyj Aeroklubs. He entered the Soviet Army in 1941 and in January, 1942 was assigned to the 943 ShAP flying the Ilyushin Il-2 Shturmovik. During his combat career Parshin enjoyed above-average success on Central, Kalinin, West, North Caucasus, Leningrad and 3rd Byelorussian Fronts. He excelled during the period of January 26, 1942 and February 29, 1944 when he was credited with the destruction of 19 enemy aircraft, 34 tanks, eight locomotives, 124 rail cars, 47 antiaircraft guns, 50 field guns and some 200 motor vehicles either personally or jointly with squadron mates. On February 26, 1944 six Il-2s with Parshin in the lead were sent out to beat up the Luftwaffe airfield at Tartu (Estonia), where they destroyed seven bombers and one fighter. He rose to Kapitan and on July 2 led a massive airfield strafe to Immalan with claims for 17 aircraft and one hangar destroyed being submitted for no losses in spite of vicious fighter attacks. Parshin then was promoted Major assuming command of the regiment and flying with great distinction during the East Prussian campaign. Between January 13 and February 1, 1945 he personally logged 44 sorties while displaying first-class leadership. In the same time frame the regiment was credited with 46 tanks, 271 motor vehicles, 28 field guns, and 20 mortars destroyed during 589 sorties for one aircraft lost to enemy action. Parshin wound up his military career with the rank of Major in 1946 to join with Soviet civil aviation. He later became a test pilot but on March 13, 1956 was killed in a plane crash. He was interred in Moscow.

PASHKEVICH, Aleksej Vasilyevich
Combat record: 16 personal victories, 115 sorties.
Decorations: Gold Star of Hero of the Soviet Union on February 23, 1945; the Orders of Lenin (2), the Red Banner (4), the Patriotic War 1st Class, the Red Star (2).

Pashkevich was born in the Leningrad area on December 24, 1916 and joined the VVS for flight training in 1939. He completed his pilot training a year later and in 1942 was posted to the 169 IAP to start flying combat. He claimed at least a single victory during the Battle of Kursk, forcing down a Bf 109 on July 8, 1943. He assumed command of a fighter squadron and quickly proved his outstanding attributes, the squadron running up 48 kills during 686 sorties between July, 1943 and September, 1944. On September 15, 1944 he was leading eight La-7s on a front-line patrol when they became embroiled in a dogfight with 24 Fw 190s. In a vicious duel four Luftwaffe fighters were shot down in flames with Pashkevich personally

The Dnyepr at Berislav. September, 1941. Here, in bloody fighting against strong Russian resistance, the mighty river was crossed by 11.Armee between August 24 and September 1 during its drive to the Crimea. Covering these operations JG 51, under the legendary Werner Mölders, claimed the destruction of 77 unescorted Russian bombers in a two day period. (Author's collection)

accounting for one of them. His big day came four days later when he made claims for four more of these. When hostilities in Europe ceased he was a Major. He stayed in the service after the war and took over as commander of the 29 GIAP which saw some action during the Chinese Civil War in 1950. The unit was equipped with 45 MiG-15s scoring its initial success during the night of May 11 when I. Shinkarenko downed a Liberator which possibly was the first kill for the MiG-15. Pashkevich graduated from the Air Force Academy in 1955 concluding his active duty with the rank of General Major four years later. He died on August 28, 1967.

PASKO, Nikolaj Fyodorovich
Combat record: 15 personal victories, 265 sorties, 32 encounters.
Decorations: Gold Star of Hero of the Soviet Union on August 18, 1945; the Orders of Lenin, the Red Banner (3), the Patriotic War 1st Class, the Red Star.

Pasko was born in the Kharkov area on December 12, 1918 and entered military service at age 21. He graduated as a pilot at Kacha military flying school a year later and in December, 1942 went to war with the 28 GIAP. He participated in the great aerial campaigns on Northwest, 1st and 2nd Baltic Fronts and was to gain a large number of his victories while flying the Airacobra. He managed to put up a good performance on 3rd Byelorussian Front and on an unspecified date reported the destruction of two bombers in one sortie near Zimmerbude (W Königsberg). He finished the war as a Starshij Lejtenant and squadron leader. He remained in the ranks to make Polkovnik before his retirement in 1956. He passed away on July 16, 1982.

PAVLOV, Grigorij Rodionovich
Combat record: 11 personal victories, 5 fractional credits plus 4 enemy aircraft in ground attacks, 378 sorties, 60 encounters as of June, 1943.

Decorations: Gold Star of Hero of the Soviet Union on September 2, 1943; the Orders of Lenin, the Red Banner (4), the Patriotic War 1st Class (2), the Red Star (2).

Pavlov was born in the Tatarian ASSR on February 10, 1920 and enlisted in the Soviet Army in 1938. Two years later he won his pilot wings at Chkalov military flying school and first saw action in August, 1941. He really came into his own in the contested air space over the Kuban in 1943 when he was a Starshij Lejtenant and deputy squadron leader in the 42 GIAP. On April 20 he claimed a Bf 109 while flying escort for Il-2s northwest of Glebovka (NE Krasnodar) and added another of these the following day when he was engaged in escorting bombers to Novorossijsk. He was well qualified for the Gold Star with 11 personal victories along with 5 shares – 14 of which were against Bf 109s, the most difficult opponents. It would appear that he subsequently added to his tally but unfortunately no further details have emerged. During his postwar career Pavlov graduated from the Air Force Academy in 1949 and from General Staff Academy in 1960. He eventually advanced to General Lejtenant and came off active duty in 1980.

PAVLOV, Pavel Ilyich

Combat record: 10 personal victories, 3 fractional credits, 557 sorties, 40 encounters as of July, 1944.
Decorations: Gold Star of Hero of the Soviet Union on July 22, 1944; the Orders of Lenin, the Red Banner (4), the Red Star.

Pavlov was born in the Novgorod area on November 16, 1919 and entered the VMF in 1939. Upon completion of training at Yejsk military flying school in 1940 he was assigned to the Baltic Fleet's air service. He commenced his combat duty with the 21 IAP early in the war and saw a great deal of action over Tallin, Leningrad and Kotka. He seems to have been successful flying the Yakovlev Yak-9 and eventually rose to Kapitan and squadron leader. Following World War II Pavlov continued on active duty with the VMF graduating from the Naval Academy in 1956. He died on September 15, 1963.

PAVLOV, Pavel Ivanovich

Combat record: 10 personal victories, 5 fractional credits, 454 sorties, 44 encounters as of October, 1944.
Decorations: Gold Star of Hero of the Soviet Union on November 5, 1944; the Orders of Lenin (3), the Red Banner (4), Ushakov 2nd Class, the Red Star.

Pavlov was born in Moscow on September 11, 1908 and entered the VMF in 1929. He completed his pilot training three years later cutting his teeth against the Finns during the Winter War of 1939/40. By June, 1941 when Operation Barbarossa commenced, Pavlov had become a squadron leader and from then on was in continuous action through the end of war. He finished as a Podpolkovnik and commander of the 21 IAP-KBF. After the war he graduated from the General Staff Academy in 1948 and left active duty with the rank of General Major in 1956. He died on February 2, 1967.

PAVLUSHKIN, Nikolaj Sazonovich

Combat record: 35 personal victories.
Decorations: Gold Star of Hero of the Soviet Union on July 1, 1944 in recognition of 13 kills, 134 sorties, 37 air combats as of January, 1944; the Orders of Lenin, the Red Banner, the Patriotic War 1st and 2nd Class, the Red Star.

Pavlushkin was born in Penza on November 8, 1917 and enlisted in the Soviet Army in 1938. He received military training at Tambov cavalry school two years later prior to applying for transfer to pilot training. He passed his pilot's examination at Stalingrad military flying school in 1942 and in April, 1943 went to war with the 402 IAP. He soon began to pile up a tremendous score with the Yak-1 fighter over the Kuban and subsequently enjoyed above-average success in the skies above Sevastopol, Yassy, Byelorussia and the Reich. He came out of

Starshij Lejtenant A.I. Pchyolkin, 5 GIAP ace. Pchyolkin joined combat with the Luftwaffe in October, 1941 and was able to perform brilliantly in the great aerial campaigns on 1st Ukrainian Front, eventually making flight leader. He ended the war with 14 confirmed air victories during 387 sorties being awarded the title of Hero of the Soviet Union on June 27, 1945. (V.I. Popkov)

World War II as a squadron leader and the regiment's ranking ace but details of his combat career are only sketchy. Pavlushkin achieved numerous fractional victories, one source ("Geroi i podvigi," p.145) quoting his tally as of an unspecified date as 17 personal kills along with 48 fractional credits. When honored with the title of Hero of the Soviet Union for his efforts in July, 1944 his record had risen to 25 personal victories during 495 sorties. He remained in the ranks following World War II making Podpolkovnik but was killed on June 19, 1958 the circumstances not being known.

PECHYONYJ, Nikolaj Nikolayevich

Combat record: 20 personal victories, 3 fractional credits, 219 sorties, 88 encounters.

Decorations: Gold Star of Hero of the Soviet Union on May 15, 1946; the Orders of Lenin, the Red Banner (2), the Patriotic War 1st Class (2), the Red Star.

Pechyonyj was born in the Kiev area on February 15, 1919 and joined the Soviet Army in 1937. He was graduated at Odessa military flying school a year later and commenced his combat duty with the 8 IAP. During his time with the regiment he was to write a distinguished record in the great air battles over the Caucasus, Voronezh, Kursk, and on 2nd Byelorussian Front. He was wounded in action twice and when hostilities in Europe ceased was a Major and squadron leader. On one particular day in June, 1943 Pechyonyj led six Yak-3s to engage a mixed formation of German bombers escorted by 12 Bf 109s, three Ju 87s, two He 111s and one Bf 109 being shot down. Others sources credit him with only 153 sorties and 64 encounters but it seems possible that these figures qualified him for the award of the title of Hero of the Soviet Union rather than representing his final record. He served with the postwar VVS concluding his active duty with the rank of Polkovnik in 1957.

PEPELYAEV, Yevgenij Georgiyevich

Combat record: 19 personal victories, 108 sorties, 38 encounters all in Korea (1950-1953) plus 42 sorties in WW II.

Decorations: Gold Star of Hero of the Soviet Union on April 22, 1952; the Orders of Lenin (2), the Red Banner (3), the Patriotic War 1st and 2nd Class, the Red Star (2).

Pepelyaev was born in the Irkutsk area on March 18, 1918 and started his military career in 1936. Two years later he won his wings at Odessa military flying school following which he was posted to the 300 IAP in the Far East. He had become a squadron leader when the Germans initiated the attack on Soviet Russia in June, 1941 but it was not until November, 1943 that he started flying combat with the 162 IAP. He logged 12 sorties with the Yak-7B on Byelorussian Front getting into three scraps with German aircraft without scoring. He once came within a hair of falling foul of German fighters and then rejoined the 300 IAP to take part in the operations against the Japanese on 2nd Far East Front. Being occupied with ground support duties he afforded 30 missions on Yak-9Ts with one locomotive destroyed and was promoted commander of the regiment at Mukden. In late 1947 Pepelyaev was assigned as deputy commander of the 196 IAP and advanced to Podpolkovnik. In January, 1951 he deployed with the unit to China now as its commander where the essential working up on MiG-15s was completed. On April 1 they moved to Antung close to the South Korean border coming under command of Ivan Kozhedub's 324 IAD. The regiment went to war that same day, assigned to protecting the railroad bridge and the hydroelectric power plant, claiming the destruction of two Sabres for the loss of two MiGs. Following this modest start, Pepelyaev made his mark against the USAF the following month when he hurtled down on an unsuspecting F-86 pouring a stream of fire into it whereupon it spun in before taking any evasive action. He then began to enjoy considerable success by downing Sabre after Sabre. Day after day he was off to search them out and when he found them usually managed to chalk up one or two kills. In August, 1951 he was promoted Polkovnik and then on one particular day in September led the regiment to bounce 12 F-94s, seven of these being shot down. He personally accounted for one and continued his streak into 1952. On January 15 he closed out his scoring with another F-86 to bring his tally to 19. When he was rotated back to the Soviet Union in February, 1952 Pepelyaev had become the second ranking jet-ace of all time while the 196 IAP had claimed 104 kills at the cost of five pilots killed and 24 aircraft destroyed. By type of enemy aircraft he had shot down:

F-86s 14
F-84s 2
F-94s 2
F-80s 1

His final score is a matter of dispute; some sources are suggesting 20 resp. 23 kills, while recent research indicates that the latter figure would appear to be a sum up of personal victories and shares. Pepelyaev graduated from the General Staff Academy in 1958 and wound up his military career in 1973. During his time with the VVS he had logged 2,020 hours in numerous types of aircraft including Po-2s, I-15s, I-16s, LaGG-3s, La-5s, La-15s, Yak-3s, Yak-7s, Yak-9s, MiG-15s, MiG-19s and Su-9s.

PERESUMKIN, Pyotr Petrovich

Combat record: 18 personal victories, 2 fractional credits, plus 2 aircraft destroyed in ground attacks, 113 sorties, 38 encounters.

Decorations: Gold Star of Hero of the Soviet Union on August 18, 1945; the Orders of Lenin, the Red Banner (2), the Patriotic War 2nd Class, the Red Star.

Peresumkin was born in the Volgograd area on July 14, 1918 and entered military service in 1937. He completed his pilot training at Borisoglebsk military flying school a year later but did not start flying combat until October, 1943 when he was posted to the 149 IAP. From then on he was in continuous action through the close of war, displaying his skills in the skies above Smolensk, Bobrujsk, Warsaw, Breslau, and Berlin. He flew 15 close support missions in Byelorussia claiming a double near Baranovichi on July 8, 1944. He next added 47 sorties over East Prussia and finished as a Kapitan and squadron leader. Peresumkin remained in the ranks after the war and retired from the VVS with the rank of Podpolkovnik in 1956. He died on October 6, 1981.

PESKOV, Pavel Ilyich
Combat record: 26 personal victories, 326 sorties.
Decorations: Gold Star of Hero of the Soviet Union on May 5, 1942 for 7 personal victories, 164 sorties, 32 of which were ground attacks, and 13 air engagements as of January, 1942; the Orders of Lenin, the Red Banner (4), Aleksandr Nevskij, the Patriotic War 1st Class (2), the Red Star.

Peskov was born in Orekhovo-Zuyevo near Moscow on January 26, 1918 and enlisted in the Soviet Army in 1936. Three years later he won his wings at Kacha military flying school and fought with the 129 IAP from the very start of the war. He was not slow to get started and on August 19, 1941 Peskov and six of his squadron mates were flying escort for nine 215 ShAP Il-2s in an attack on the Luftwaffe airfield at Shatolovo. Several Bf 109s were scrambled with Peskov destroying one which crashed on the perimeter of the airfield. He next saw a good deal of action on Kalinin Front and in May, 1942 moved with the regiment to the Kholm area to be occupied with Il-2 and Pe-2 escorts to Rzhev and Velikiye Luki. During the course of these missions his aircraft was once badly shot up but he managed to struggle back to base. He rose to Kapitan and continued to score regularly in the big air battles over Stalingrad, Byelgorod-Kharkov, Poland and the Reich. Following World War II he continued on active duty graduating from the Air Force Academy in 1950. He returned to civilian life with the rank of General Major in January, 1979 and is living in Moscow.

P.I. Peskov, a very capable 5 GIAP pilot, photographed with a LaGG which is believed to be his personal mount. The date is December 8, 1941. (Author's collection)

PETRENKO, Yevgenij Vasilyevich
Combat record: 11 personal victories, 1 fractional credit, 261 sorties, 69 encounters as of July, 1944.
Decorations: Gold Star of Hero of the Soviet Union on August 19, 1944; the Orders of Lenin, the Red Banner (2), Ushakov 2nd Class, the Red Star.

Petrenko was born in the Sumy area on December 22, 1918 and enrolled for service in the VMF in 1936. He completed his pilot training at Yejsk military flying school three years later and was posted to the 20 IAP of the Northern Fleet's air service before the war. He saw considerable fighting in the defensive battles at Murmansk and on July 19, 1942 was leading a formation of Kittyhawks to intercept an incoming raid of 20 Ju 88s escorted by 16 fighters. Ignoring the escorts, they dove on the bombers with Petrenko destroying the lead aircraft in a head-on attack. In all, six Ju 88s and four fighters were shot down and the rest driven off. He later converted to Airacobras and took part in the Petsamo-Kirkenes campaign between October 7-29, 1944. He finished as a Kapitan and squadron leader. After the close of war he graduated from the Air Force Academy in 1949 coming off active duty with the rank of Polkovnik in 1974. He passed away on July 22, 1976.

PETROV, Nikolaj Stepanovich
Combat record: 5 personal victories, 6 fractional credits, 170 sorties.
Decorations: Gold Star of Hero of the Soviet Union on June 27, 1945 in recognition of 93 ground-attack sorties, 2 kills, 2 fractional credits and 2 planes destroyed on the ground; the Orders of Lenin, the Red Banner (2), the Patriotic War 2nd Class, Glory 3rd Class.

Petrov was born in the Vologda area on December 25, 1922 and joined the Soviet Army in 1941. Upon qualifying as a pilot at Tambov military flying school two years later Petrov in September, 1943 went to war with the 141 GShAP flying Il-2 Shturmoviks. He was able to build up a good score in the ferocious fighting at Kirovograd, Yassy-Kishinyov, Lemberg, Tschenstochau (Czestochowa) and Krakau (Krakov). On March 6, 1945 Petrov and five of his squadron caught German tanks and armored vehicles as they were deploying in the Timmendorf and Seifersdorf areas and wrought successful havoc. On his first pass Petrov, rockets sizzling from his wing runners, knocked out a tank with a direct hit and disregarding vicious and accurate antiaircraft fire returned for another attack with his cannon claiming a second kill. During his combat career, Petrov was shot down twice, force-landing his stricken aircraft and returning to his unit later. He finished the war as a Lejtenant and flight leader and retired as a Starshij Lejtenant in 1946. Six years later he reenlisted in the VVS and graduated from Ryazan Air Force Officers School in 1953. He eventually made Podpolkovnik winding up his military career in 1962. He died on June 29, 1981.

Major Pyotr Mikhajlovich Petrov won fame while flying with the 68 IAP in the Russo-Finnish Winter War. On February 2, 1940 he landed on frozen Muojarvi Lake to successfully pick up a downed comrade and was decorated with the title of Hero of the Soviet Union on April 7, 1940. Petrov again was in the center of action from the earliest days of Operation Barbarossa commanding a fighter regiment but was killed in action near Alekseyevka, Kursk area, on November 23, 1941. It has not been possible to ascertain his final score. (Author's collection)

PIDTYKAN, Ivan Dmitriyevich

Combat record: 11 personal victories, 5 fractional credits, 217 sorties, 58 encounters.

Decorations: Gold Star of Hero of the Soviet Union on June 6, 1942; the Orders of Lenin, the Red Banner.

Pidtykan was born in Kujbyshev on April 13, 1918 and entered the Soviet Army in 1937. He was graduated as a pilot at Chuguyev military flying school in 1940 and started flying combat with the 123 IAP in June, 1941. Flying the nimble Polikarpov I-16 fighter Pidtykan was to enjoy above-average success in the dark months to follow. He opened his account with a Bf 109 over the Gulf of Finland on the 24th and then ran up a string of 10 kills including fractional credits during his next 10 missions. On September 10 he forced down a Ju 88 and on December 1 was leading three fellow pilots to engage 14 Ju 88s and 10 Bf 109s over Ladoga Lake and personally destroyed an enemy plane at 50 meters range. He was killed in action on August 2, 1942, and in him the VVS lost one of its outstanding I-16 pilots. He was interred in Krasnyj Bor (Tosno area).

PILIPENKO, Ivan Markovich

Combat record: 13 personal victories, 29 fractional credits plus three aircraft, 180 motor vehicles and 30 field guns in ground attacks, 520 sorties, 83 encounters.

Decorations: Gold Star of Hero of the Soviet Union posthumously on December 13, 1942; the Orders of Lenin (2), the Red Banner (2).

Pilipenko was born in the Donetsk area on August 15, 1912 and started his military career in 1933. Four years later he qualified as a pilot at Borisoglebsk military flying school and then gained his first combat experience against the Finns during the Winter War of 1939/40. His meteoric rise to fame began in August, 1941 when he joined combat with the Luftwaffe serving as a Starshij Lejtenant in the 40 IAP. He flew with great distinction on Transcaucasus Front, his number two on many occasions being A.V. Lobanov, who was to emerge as a 20-victory ace himself. On May 26, 1942 Pilipenko was leading six I-16s on a front-line patrol and fought a pitched battle with 40 bombers near Izyum, two of these being shot down and four more damaged, all without loss. Eight fighters with Pilipenko in the lead had a big day on July 22 when they became embroiled with 14 Messerschmitts in the vicinity of Rostov and in a hard-fought, protracted melee claimed six kills. He rose to Kapitan and by September his record had risen to 10 kills, 28 fractional credits, 470 sorties and 76 air combats. On October 2 15 I-16s and six I-153s were sent out to beat up Soldatskaya airfield where Pilipenko and his wingman, P. Dodonov, watched two Bf 109s takeoff. In a shallow dive they overhauled the enemy fighters whose pilots did not appear to be aware of their presence and opened fire. Both planes hit the ground at the far end of the field, and then Pilipenko went down to shoot up two more Bf 109s on the ground. All of a sudden they were jumped by six German fighters and without hesitating, immediately engaged them head-on. Their shells reportedly struck home with two Bf 109s going down in flames before hits sent Pilipenko crashing down to his death. At that time the famous Luftwaffe unit III./JG 52 was based at Soldatskaya but no details of any such action can be found from the German side, and it is possible that this combat actually occurred on another date.

PILYUTOV, Pyotr Andreyevich

Combat record: 23 personal victories, 1,945 sorties, 76 encounters.

Decorations: Gold Star of Hero of the Soviet Union on February 10, 1943 for 6 kills, 4 fractional credits, 170 sorties as of December, 1941; the Orders of Lenin (4), the Red Banner (4), the Patriotic War 1st Class, the Red Star (2).

Pilyutov was born in the Rogachyov area on December 23, 1906 and began his remarkable career in the VVS in 1928. He became an aircraft mechanic in 1932 and two years later his engineering feats as crewchief of the famous Soviet airman Vasilij Molokov won him his first Order of Lenin (registration number 40). He later was sent to Kacha military flying school being graduated as a pilot in 1935. He saw action for the first time against the Japanese at Khazan Lake in 1938 and during the Russo-Finnish Winter War of 1939/40 brought his score to 6. He was in the thick of the fighting from the earliest days of the Patriotic War managing to put up a good performance with the 154 IAP in the hell of Leningrad. He rapidly advanced to deputy regiment commander and in December, 1941 converted to Tomahawks. Flying one of these he reported the destruction of two Bf 109s over Ladoga Lake on the 17th but in turn was hit and wounded, 21 fragments being removed from his body by surgeons later. He returned to his unit a month later and on March 13, 1942 combined forces with Major Matveyev, and Kapitans Pokryshev and Chirkov to destroy three enemy planes when they tackled with a force of 18. Two days later he was decorated with the Order of the Red Banner and was promoted Kapitan. On March 24, 1943 he destroyed a bomber at night and finished the war as commander of the 154 IAP with the rank of Podpolkovnik. His impressive total of 1,945 combat sorties was not to be outdone by any Allied fighter pilot in the war. After the war he joined the select few who were assigned to fly the new Russian jet fighters and retired from the VVS as a Polkovnik with a lifetime total of 8,788 sorties in military aircraft in 1955. He died from heart attack on March 24, 1960.

Somewhat grainy picture of P.A. Pilyutov, who was one of the most experienced Soviet fighter pilots amassing 1,945 sorties through the war. Here he is seen featuring in a photographic session by which time he had made Podpolkovnik and commander of the 154 IAP. (Author's collection)

PINCHUK, Nikolaj Grigoryevich

Combat record: 22 personal victories, 2 fractional credits, 307 sorties, 68 encounters.

Decorations: Gold Star of Hero of the Soviet Union on April 19, 1945 in recognition of 18 kills, 226 sorties; the Orders of Lenin, the Red Banner (4), the Red Star (2).

Pinchuk was born in the Mogilyov area on February 4, 1921 and entered military service at age 19. He completed his pilot training at Armavir military flying school in 1942 and started flying combat in August. Two months later he joined with the crack 18 GIAP on West Front quickly establishing a reputation for aggressiveness and air combat skill. He was greatly involved in the fighting at Kursk, claiming a Fw 190 on July 17, 1943 while engaged in escorting Il-2s. He added another of these near Spas-Demensk in early August and on the 28th reported the destruction of an He 111. Two days later he successfully rammed a Ju 87 in the vicinity of Yelnya (SE Smolensk), bailing out wounded. He was back in the air soon after running up a string of five kills in the contested air space above Smolensk. In December, 1943 his tally stood at 13 kills and on June 26, 1944 a Fw 190 fell before his guns in the Borisov area. He converted to the Yakovlev Yak-3 fighter claiming another 190 shot down in flames over East Prussia on October 10. Six days later he got two more in an action in the vicinity of Insterburg and on the 17th forced down a further one while conducting ground force cover. On January 19, 1945 he shot down a Fw 190 that blew up and crashed into a forest and destroyed another of these near Heiligenbeil on February 11. He finished the war as a Kapitan and deputy squadron leader. He served with the postwar VVS and graduated from the Air Force Academy in 1954. He came off active duty as a Polkovnik in 1975 and died on January 12, 1978.

PIVOVAROV, Mikhail Yevdokimovich

Combat record: 21 personal victories, 269 sorties, 69 encounters.

Decorations: Gold Star of Hero of the Soviet Union on May 15, 1946; the Orders of Lenin, the Red Banner (3), Aleksandr Nevskij, the Red Star.

Pivovarov was born in the Rostov area on January 22, 1919 and entered the Soviet Army in 1937. He won his pilot wings at Krasnodar military flying school four years later and in September, 1943 was assigned to the 402 IAP on 4th Ukrainian Front to enter combat. He excelled in Byelorussia in 1944, scoring a string of 11 victories while engaging the enemy on 21 occasions over Vitebsk, Orsha, Borisov and Minsk to head up the list of fighter aces in that campaign. He subsequently was able to perform brilliantly in the air battles over Poland and during the Vistula-Oder campaign (January 12 - February 3, 1945) and gained two kills between March 5-8. He closed out his scoring with a double in the Küstrin area on April 18. Pivovarov remained with the VVS until 1947, retiring as a Kapitan. He died on May 15, 1949.

PLEKHANOV, Andrej Filippovich
Combat record: 17 personal victories, 621 sorties.
Decorations: Gold Star of Hero of the Soviet Union on May 15, 1946 in recognition of 16 victories plus 8 damaged, 596 sorties; the Orders of Lenin, the Red Banner (3), Aleksandr Nevskij, the Patriotic War 1st Class (3).

Plekhanov was born in the Saratov area on August 15, 1918 and entered military service in 1939. He graduated from flight training two years later and was in the forefront of action from December, 1941 flying Po-2 nightbombers. In 12 months combat he logged 215 sorties, including 10 in one night beating up targets between the areas of Sobolevka and Glubokaya. In late 1942 Plekhanov was posted to the 73 GIAP flying Yak-1s and later wrote a distinguished record on 2nd Ukrainian Front. He eventually rose to Kapitan and deputy squadron leader and gave a good account of himself in the final clashes over Czechoslovakia, claiming a Fw 190 on April 24, 1945 and two more of these near Brno the following day. He wound up his military career in 1948 and passed away on June 21, 1986.

PLEKHANOV, Ivan Yefimovich
Combat record: 11 personal victories, 2 fractional credits, 244 sorties, 34 encounters as of August, 1942.
Decorations: Gold Star of Hero of the Soviet Union on January 28, 1943; the Orders of Lenin, the Red Banner, the Patriotic War 1st Class, the Red Star (2).

Plekhanov was born in the Kursk area on September 27, 1917 and joined the Soviet Army in 1936. He completed his pilot training at Kacha military flying school two years later and was posted to the 158 IAP before the war. He began flying I-16s in defense of Leningrad and later converted to Kittyhawks. On May 29, 1942 he racked up his second confirmed victory with a Bf 109 when 11 of his squadron were storming into a formation of 30 bombers escorted by 33 fighters in the Volkhov area, where nine enemy planes were shot down. Plekhanov had a big day on August 2 when he got a triple with two Ju 87s and a Bf 109 in the vicinity of Uritskij, but on his fifth mission that day his aircraft was badly shot up by German fighters, his right arm being shattered by shells exploding in the cockpit and severed below the elbow. He required six months to recuperate and never flew operationally again. He stayed in the VVS after the war rising to the rank of Polkovnik and was released from the service in 1956.

POKROVSKIJ, Vladimir Pavlovich
Combat record: 12 personal victories, 6 fractional credits, 350 sorties, 60 encounters as of May, 1943.
Decorations: Gold Star of Hero of the Soviet Union on July 24, 1943; the Orders of Lenin, the Red Banner (2), the Patriotic War 1st Class, the Red Star.

V.P. Pokrovskij, fighter ace of Northern Fleet's 72 IAP, in flying gear with his I-16 in 1942. (Author's collection)

Pokrovskij was born in the Kaluga area on July 22, 1918 and enrolled for service in the VMF in 1937. Upon completion of training at Yejsk military flying school three years later he was assigned to the Northern Fleet's air service. When the Germans initiated Operation Barbarossa on June 22, 1941 Pokrovskij was a flight leader in the 72 IAP-SF. From then on he was in continuous action over Murmansk and on September 15, 1941 got a double. He brought his tally to four until late September and later was to fly Hawker Hurricanes with some success. On April 15, 1942 he shot down a Ju 87 when six Hurricanes and three MiG-3s with Kapitan Kovalenko in the lead engaged a force of 26 Ju 87s and their escorts enroute to Murmansk. He was once wounded in a fighter battle but managed to stagger back to his own airfield. He rose to Kapitan, and there is a possibility that he added to his score but details are not available. Following World War II he graduated from the Air Force Academy in 1954 and retired from the VMF as a Podpolkovnik two years later.

POKRYSHEV, Pyotr Afanasyevich
Combat record: 23 personal victories, 7 fractional credits, 300 sorties, 72 encounters.

This photo shows Pokryshev posing in front of P-40E "White 65" in which Podpolkovnik A.A. Matveyev became an ace. The cyrillic nomenclature on his parachute straps translates "Pokryshev." Plekhanovo airfield, Leningrad Front, in 1942. (Author's collection)

Decorations: 1st Gold Star of Hero of the Soviet Union on February 10, 1943 for 11 kills, 7 fractional credits, 211 sorties, 38 engagements as of July, 1942, 2nd Gold Star on August 24, 1943 in recognition of 22 kills, 7 fractional credits, 282 sorties and 50 air combats; the Orders of Lenin, the Red Banner (3), Aleksandr Nevskij, the Patriotic War 1st Class, the Red Star (2).

Legendary fighter pilot: Podpolkovnik P.A. Pokryshev, who drew first blood against the Finns in 1939 and later rose to command the 159 IAP. This photograph was taken in the autumn of 1944 when he was flying La-7s. (Author's collection)

Major P.A. Pokryshev passes the time with "Boyevaya Trevoga" (Battle Alert), a frontline newspaper. (Author's collection)

Pokryshev was born in the Kherson area on August 24, 1914 and was destined to become one of the most outstanding VVS pilots and fighter leaders. He enlisted in the VVS for flight training in 1934 and was graduated as a pilot at Odessa military flying school a year later. He saw action for the first time flying I-153s during the Russo-Finnish Winter War of 1939/40 and is credited with scoring two victories but was shot down himself on two occasions (November 30 resp. December 18, 1939), serving with the 7 IAP. By June, 1941 he had become a Starshij Lejtenant in the 154 IAP and on the 25th had the distinction of achieving the second kill of Leningrad Front when he claimed a Ju 88 with the I-16 fighter. He next added doubles on June 29 and July 3 possibly consisting of fractional credits. He later proved his gunnery skills in the Tomahawk, and on December 17, 1941 the first Bf 109F to be destroyed on Leningrad Front fell before his guns while flying escort for Li-2s. The enemy fighter reportedly crashed in the Soviet lines killing its pilot and displaying 15 victory bars on its rudder. Unfortunately his victim's identity has not been established. In 1942 Pokryshev's personal mount was a Kittyhawk "White 50", while the P-40E "White 65", considered by some sources to have been his steed of war, actually was flown by 15-victory ace Podpolkovnik A.A. Matveyev. He was promoted Kapitan and squadron leader and in January, 1943 the regiment re-equipped with the Yakovlev Yak-7B, turning over its war-weary Tomahawks and Kittyhawks to the 196 IAP. Pokryshev in July, 1943 assumed command of the 159 IAP with the rank of Major and was to serve in this capacity until the close of war earning a reputation for cool, decisive leadership. On August 24, 1943, the day he was honored with his second title of Hero of the Soviet Union, he was hit hard by enemy fighters and returned in a blazing La-5. He was unlucky enough to hit a ditch while landing and cartwheeled. He survived returning to combat duty two months later and subsequently flew La-5FNs and La-7s in sweeps, escorts and patrols. His final score is a matter of dispute, one source suggesting 38 kills along with 8 fractional credits ("Dvazhdy Geroi Sovyetskogo Soyuza," p.162). Pokryshev stayed in the service at the conclusion of the war graduating from the General Staff Academy in 1954. He came off active duty with the rank of General Major in 1961 and passed away on August 22, 1967.

Sasha Pokryshkin just back from a combat sortie wearing the three-quarter length leather coat of World War I inspiration which was still common to the VVS early in the war. His MiG-3 has seen some weather as well. (Author's collection)

The illustrious Pokryshkin seen here as a Polkovnik and commander of the famous 9 GIAD which ranked highly amongst the top- scoring VVS fighter divisions with 1,147 kills between May, 1942 and May, 1945. Pokryshkin's principles of air fighting significantly influenced the Soviet fighter arm. (Author's collection)

POKRYSHKIN, Aleksandr Ivanovich

Combat record: 59 personal victories, 560 sorties, 156 encounters. (Some sources suggest a tally of 53 individual kills plus 6 shared)

Decorations: 1st Gold Star of Hero of the Soviet Union on May 24, 1943 for 13 kills, 6 fractional credits, 354 sorties, 54 encounters as of April, 1943, 2nd Gold Star on August 24, 1943 in recognition of 30 kills, 455 sorties as of July, 1943, 3rd Gold Star on August 19, 1944 in recognition of 53 kills, 550 sorties, 137 air combats; the Orders of Lenin (6), the October Revolution, the Red Banner (4), Suvorov 2nd Class (2), the Patriotic War 1st Class, the Red Star (2).

Pokryshkin, one of the leading VVS personalities and second ranking Allied fighter ace, was born in Novosibirsk on March 6, 1913 and began his rather spectacular military career in 1932. He attended Perm aircraft mechanics school in 1933 and three years later was posted to the 55 IAP. He applied for transfer to pilot training and eventually was sent to Kacha military flying school where he was to pass his pilot's examination in 1939. He went to war as a Starshij Lejtenant and deputy squadron leader with the 55 IAP, being based at Beltsy (NW Kishinyov) in Moldavia. Flying a MiG-3 fighter, Pokryshkin inadvertently forced down a Soviet Su-2 bomber on June 22, 1941, the day German forces started their onslaught on Soviet Russia. He made his mark against the Luftwaffe the following day when he reported the destruction of a Bf 109 "with a yellow spinner" and shortly afterward two Hs 126s fell before his guns in one sortie. April saw him claim a total of 10 Bf 109s ranking him second only to St.Lej. V.I. Fadeyev who had knocked down 12 of the German fighters. He then became involved in very heavy fighting under appalling conditions largely being occupied with ground targets and patrols. The regiment was gradually whittled down and plagued by the lack of replacements. What was more, one day all 12.7mm UB machine guns were removed from the MiGs in response to an order demanding the return of all available heavy machine guns to the aircraft factories – while the production tempo of fighters was building up rapidly, the output of machine guns was dramatically lagging behind. As a result armament was restricted to a pair of 7,62mm ShKAS machine guns; apart from these serious restrictions, the aircraft were neither provided with radios nor did they have armorglass windscreens. By the close of 1941 Pokryshkin's score had risen to four kills during 316 sorties and 26 air combats. He had been forced down to a wheels-up landing into enemy territory by flak once, evading capture and returning to his unit four days later. Not at all satisfied with this modest start, Pokryshkin diligently devoted himself to devise new fighter tactics under combat conditions. From the early weeks of the war it became painfully obvious to him that with tactics inherited from prewar doctrines the VVS was decidedly at a disadvantage against the tried and tested Luftwaffe. Recalls Pokryshkin: "Our young pilots were taught to fly and fight according to old-fashioned fighter doctrine on aircraft such as the Chajka or the I-16. The front to them was a new reality. The tactical abilities they had acquired during flight training did not comply with the demands of hot war." Pokryshkin never ceased studying tactical maneuvers and his enemies. He carefully conveyed his findings to the young bucks, and remarkable talents such as Aleksandr Klubov, Andrej Trud or Konstantin Sukhov learnt the ropes from him. Pokryshkin is largely responsible for originating fundamental improvements to Soviet tactical development. During his combat career he had ample opportunity to perfect and verify his famous four-step mode of attack: "vysota – skorost – manevr – ogon" (altitude – speed – maneuver – fire). He was a brilliant leader and pilot of uncanny gifts; his forte became high speed surprise attacks from above, make a run and then climb back to altitude with his speed advantage built up in a dive, closing right in before firing. Pokryshkin conquered his opponents in the air and battled with the rigid structures within the VVS. "We were called to give an account of our combat experience and to compare our planes with the enemies," Pokryshkin said later, "In comparing the MiG-3 with the Bf 109 I frankly said that in spite of having many advantages our machine was appreciably heavier and less maneuverable at low altitudes than the Messerschmitt while its armament had proved inadequate. I wound up by saying that our aircraft designers certainly would soon have rendered new, more perfect planes. My words however did not meet with approval but rather were interpreted as unpatriotic. Henceforth I decided to better hold my tongue during any such consultations to come." During 1942 the regiment was flying a collection of Yak-1s and MiG-3s primarily in the low-level close support role meeting stiff resistance with operations being fairly expensive. Pokryshkin continued to achieve victories on a regular basis while flying the Yak fighter and by the close of the year had brought his tally to 12, eight of which had been gained against Bf 109s. The regiment then was rested, reformed and kept busy on training schedules while being reequipped with Bell P-39 Airacobras. These were introduced into combat over the Kuban in the spring of 1943 immediately enjoying considerable success. Pokryshkin was very happy with this equipment feeling that it was an outstanding aircraft at low to medium altitude even in the fighter versus fighter role particularly when used in hit-and-run passes. On the very first mission he splashed a Bf 109 near Krymskaya and then began piling up a tremendous score. In the hands of pilots of the standing of Pokryshkin, Bobrov, Gulayev and

Pokryshkin smiling for the camera. He emerged as the most famous of the Stalin's eagles gaining a staggering 59 kills before he was pulled out of combat and grounded. (Author's collection)

Rechkalov the Airacobra undoubtedly helped to establish aerial supremacy over the Eastern Front while units such as the 16, 100 and 129 GIAPs will be permanently identified with this mount. On April 12 he was leading eight Cobras on a sweep out to the Krasnodar area where they got into two separate scraps with Bf 109s, six of these being shot down by Pokryshkin (2), Starshij Lejtenant Rechkalov, Mladshij Lejtenant Naumenko, Serzhants Savin and Sutyrin. Pokryshkin then claimed singles on the 15th, 16th and 20th, and on April 29 had a big day with four Bf 109s in one sortie. He logged nine more missions in the contested skies above the Kuban with one further kill in six aerial encounters and was well qualified for the award of his first title of Hero of the Soviet Union in May. On June 8 he advanced to Major and in time took over as commander of the regiment. Under his cool and decisive leadership the unit was to knock the opposing enemy for six in the big air battles over the Crimea and at Yassy. On an unspecified date Pokryshkin bagged three Ju 87s in one sortie while flying his first Airacobra, "White 13." With this particular ship he was to run up some 20 kills before receiving a new personal mount, his famous "White 100." In no time two more Ju 87s, two Ju 88s, three Ju 52s and several Bf 109s fell before his guns including one each Bf 109 and Ju 88 in the vicinity of Slavyansk on July 13. With 30 kills and 6 shares to his credit as of July, 1943 he was recommended for the award of his second title of Hero of the Soviet Union but further combats had taken his score past 40 when this was bestowed upon him on August 24. He rose to Podpolkovnik and in February, 1944 received orders to the VVS high command headquarters in Moscow being offered promotion to commander of fighter operations, the highest appointment in the Soviet Fighter Arm. Pokryshkin though had a front line soldier's aversion to staff duty and refused requesting a combat assignment. In May, 1944 high command complied with his request putting him in command of the crack 9 GIAD to be back in combat with some of his most accomplished comrades. He next saw a great deal of action during the Lemberg-Sandomierz campaign (July 13/ August 29, 1944) and on July 14 led 12 Cobras against 40 bombers, four Ju 88s being destroyed without loss. On August 19 he had the distinction of becoming the first recipient of three titles of Hero of the Soviet Union but was then grounded for fear that he might be exposed to further prospect of injury or death. His score stood at 59 kills, although there are some

Two aces talk things over. Pokryshkin (left) and K.V. Sukhov, who had gained his first combat experience with the 84 IAP in the Caucasus before being assigned to the 16 GIAP. Sukhov gained all or most of his 22 victories with the Aeracobra. (Author's collection)

This propaganda photograph is purporting to show Pokryshkin celebrating another victory with admiring comrades. The aircraft in the background evidently is G.A. Rechkalov's personal mount. Pokryshkin highly valued the sleek Bell fighter gaining most of his success on this type. (Author's collection)

sources suggesting 6 group kills in his final tally. What was more, 13 further victories were never officially confirmed as they had been obtained over enemy territory. Pokryshkin subsequently was responsible for planning and coordinating combat operations against the Luftwaffe in Poland, Silesia and at Cottbus and Prague and was also able to devote himself to the essential task of converting the regiments to the Lavochkin La-7. The division finished the war as one of the VVS' topscorers with 1,147 victories. With his brilliant combat record and outstanding gifts for command and organization, Pokryshkin was destined for a significant high command career following World War II. In 1948 he graduated from Frunze Academy and from the General Staff Academy nine years later becoming Inspector of the Fighter Arm. In 1968 he was assigned as commander of the PVO forces and served in this capacity until 1971. A year later he was promoted Marshal Aviatsii and then was Chairman of the Central Committee of DOSAAF between 1972-1981 before becoming a General Inspector in the Soviet Ministry of Defense. He died on November 13, 1985. He was interred in Moscow's Novodyevichi cemetery.

POLOGOV, Pavel Andreyevich
Combat record: 18 personal victories, 12 fractional credits, 365 sorties, 90 encounters.
Decorations: Gold Star of Hero of the Soviet Union on September 2, 1943; the Orders of Lenin, the Red Banner (3), the Patriotic War 1st Class, the Patriotic War 2nd Class (2), the Red Star.

Pologov was born in the Sverdlovsk area on September 23, 1913 and entered military service in 1934. He graduated as a pilot at Borisoglebsk military flying school three years later and fired his guns in anger for the first time against the Japanese at the Khalkhin Gol in 1939. He next saw some action during the Russo-Finnish Winter War of 1939/40 and then joined with the 737 IAP before the outbreak of the Patriotic War. He was able to give a good account of himself on Southwest Front and advanced to Shturman. He was promoted to Podpolkovnik in time and assumed command of the 163 IAP. In this capacity he was greatly involved in the fighting at Kursk. On one occasion in July, 1943 he was leading a flight on a fighter sweep out to the front where they engaged eight Fw 190s and six Ju 88s. In the ensuing melee Pologov reported the destruction of one fighter and one bomber with his comrades bringing the day's tally to five with two more damaged. His final total of sorties is a matter of dispute, one source suggesting 750. He remained in the VVS following World War II retiring with the rank of Podpolkovnik in 1949.

POPKOV, Vitalij Ivanovich
Combat record: 41 personal victories, 1 fractional credit, 300+ sorties, 117 encounters plus 7 more kills disallowed by order of General Zhukov; 3 aerial victories in Korea 1950-53.
Decorations: 1st Gold Star of Hero of the Soviet Union on September 8, 1943 in recognition of 17 kills, 168 sorties, 45

V.I. Popkov with his steed of war, Lavochkin La-5 "Yellow 01" bearing 33 of his total bag of 41 victories. This aircraft is also shown in the profile section. Popkov was destined to add three more kills in Korea against the UN air forces. The photo is dated early 1945. (Author's collection)

encounters as of August, 1943, 2nd Gold Star on June 27, 1945 for 36 victories, 1 fractional credit, 325 sorties – 124 of which were groundforce cover, 75 escorts, 17 ground attacks, 37 free hunts, 52 reconnaissance – 83 air combats as of February, 1945; the Orders of Lenin (3), the Red Banner (2), Aleksandr Nevskij, the Patriotic War 1st Class (2), the Patriotic War 2nd Class, the Red Star.

Popkov, one of the greatest aces of them all, was born in Moscow on May 1, 1922 and began his distinguished military career on September 15, 1940. He won his pilot wings at Chuguyev military flying school a year later and in 1942 attended Batajsk military flying school. Intent on aviation from boyhood, Popkov was eager to become a fighter pilot. In April, 1942 he was posted as a Serzhant to the 5 GIAP flying LaGG-3s. He saw action for the first time in May, getting a Ju 88 near Kholm soon after to draw first blood. He then flew Il-2 and Pe-2 escorts in the Rzhev and Velikiye Luki areas and was wingman for Ivan Lavejkin on many occasions. By August he had logged 45 sorties qualifying him for the award of the Order of Lenin on the 26th. On August 5 he had been successful in racking up his fifth victory with a Bf 109 near Rzhev and was promoted flight leader. Once the regiment had converted to the nimble and speedy Lavochkin La-5, it deployed to Stalingrad. Popkov added a number of victories during the course of this dramatic battle, including a Bf 109F in the vicinity of Gartmashevka on January 16, 1943, but STAVKA representative General Zhukov on an unrecorded date nullified the combat records attained by the fighter arm in this front sector in enforcing disciplinary action. In consequence, Popkov's tally of seven kills chalked up at Stalingrad was never officially allowed. On April 10, 1943 he caught a Bf 109 in its landing approach near Kramatorsk, fired a quick burst whereupon the enemy fighter crashed. On May 23 he was awarded the Order of the Patriotic War 1st Class for four victories and next was greatly involved in the fighting at Millerovo and Kantemirovka. On July 23 he reported the destruction of two Bf 109G-2s while participating in the battles of Byelgorod-Kharkov and seven days later was decorated with the Order of the Red Banner in recognition of five victories. On August 3 he became embroiled in a dogfight with two Bf 109s and shot down one but was in turn hit hard by the other, forcing him to bail out at 3,000 meters sustaining serious burns. Upon his recovery he took over as leader of 1st Eskadrilya. Popkov by now had become one of Russia's hottest aerial fighters and was to make a big name for himself in the months to follow. He had developed a distinctive style of his own, tearing into the enemy at high speed and getting as close as possible before firing. Popkov told the author that he once nailed Wilhelm Batz, high scoring ace of JG 52 in a wild melee near Izyum. He is almost certain that this particular en-

Popkov posing for the photographers on the wing of La-5 "75" which was not his personal aircraft. (Author's collection)

Popkov and Kapitan Nikolaj Grigoryevich Ilin, one of his squadron mates. (V.I. Popkov)

Wilhelm Batz, whose 237 victories make him the sixth ranking ace of all time, seen here as a Hauptmann and Gruppenkommandeur of II./JG 52. He was once forced down by Vitalij Popkov becoming a prisoner but managed to escape. (Bundesarchiv)

counter had taken place in August, 1943, when Batz was still having problems in finding his range. Batz fell into Russian hands and during his interrogation had a meeting with Popkov before he managed to escape to eventually run up a most amazing combat record. On August 28 Popkov had the distinction of scoring the regiment's 499th aerial victory claiming another single later that same day. Further combats over Zaporozhye, Dnyepropetrovsk and Krivoj Rog took his bag to 30 confirmed in early 1944. He next put up a good performance during the Lemberg-Sandomierz and Oder-Vistula campaigns being slightly wounded by flak on June 16, 1944. On August 17 he received the Order of Aleksandr Nevskij for 14 kills. He destroyed a Fw 190 near Sprottau on February 11, 1945 while leading five La-5s to take on 10 Luftwaffe fighters, his squadron mates bringing the day's tally to four. Five days later two Ju 87s and another 190 fell to his guns in an action over Glogau. By February 27, when he was recommended for his second title of Hero of the Soviet Union by Podpolkovnik Rulin, the regiment commander, his squadron had run up 27 kills during 562 sorties. On April 16, while flying a sweep out to the Cottbus area, he caught a Fw 190 taking-off, attacked and saw it crash onto the perimeter of the airfield. The following day he successfully rammed a Ju 88 right over Berlin-Tempelhof airport and although being wounded in the process he managed to nurse his plane in safely at his own airfield. He was in action again on the 18th leading six of his squadron on an escort for Il-2s when they engaged 16 Fw 190s. In the ensuing scrap, Popkov, Glinkin and Belyakov all claimed singles. He closed out his scoring with another 190 in the vicinity of Berlin on May 1 and flew his last wartime mission out to Prague on the 12th, coming out of World War II as the regiment's ranking ace. He is best remembered by his comrades for his lightning reactions and his brilliant leadership. His regard for the safety of his squadron mates evoked confidence and devotion among those who fought with him. He next was put in command of the 739 IAP and served with the postwar VVS attaining high rank. He again proved his skills at blasting enemy aircraft in the skies above Korea while serving as deputy commander of the 324 IAD, adding one each B-29, RB-26 and F-86 to his impressive record. He attended the Air Force Academy and in 1964 graduated from General Staff Academy. Four years later he was promoted General Lejtenant and in 1980 became a lecturer at the Soviet Air Force Academy. When he eventually returned to civilian life, he had flown 53 types of aircraft. Now in his seventies, Popkov is a friendly man with undiminished vigor, and whenever he speaks of his glory days in the VVS and of his comrades, his unique photographic memory provides thoughtful and revealing recollections.

Popkov's "nagradnoj list" recommending him for his second title of Hero of the Soviet Union can be found on the following pages 177-179. In this document, forwarded by the regiment commander, Podpolkovnik Rulin, his combat record is outlined in detail along with his rank, date of birth, previous awards. This recommendation was successively approved by Polkovnik Osadchij, commander of the 11 GIAD, General Major Slyusarev, commander of the 2 GShAK, General Polkovnik Krasovskij, commander of the 2 VA.

PROKOPENKO, Georgij Nikolayevich
Combat record: 12 personal victories, 15 fractional credits, 217 sorties.
Decorations: Gold Star of Hero of the Soviet Union on September 8, 1943 for 11 kills, 15 fractional credits, 189 sorties, 47 air combats as of July, 1943; the Orders of Lenin, the Red Banner (2), Aleksandr Nevskij.

Prokopenko was born in the Sumy area on April 25, 1914 and entered the Soviet Army in 1933. He graduated from flight training three years later and saw action for the first time during the Spanish Civil War in 1938 being once wounded in action prior to taking part in the Soviet occupation of East Poland a year later. He was posted to the 155 IAP before the outbreak of the Patriotic War and then fought from the very start of the war. He subsequently flew sorties on Karelian, Volkhov, Leningrad and Stalingrad Fronts and in May, 1943 was transferred with the unit to Northwest Front where he would add six more missions seeing only little air combat. In late 1943 he assumed command of the 3 GIAP but on June 14, 1944 (or July 14 as suggested by another source) fell victim to enemy fighters northwest of Ternopol.

PULOV, Grigorij Ivanovich
Combat record: 10 personal victories, 120 sorties all Korea.
Decorations: Gold Star of Hero of the Soviet Union on April 22, 1952; the Orders of Lenin, the Red Banner (3), the Patriotic War 1st Class (2), the Red Star.

Pulov was born in the Vladimir area on January 18, 1918 and enlisted in the Soviet Army in 1942. He entered combat in July, 1942 but his World War II combat career has remained somewhat obscure. He graduated from the Air Force Academy in 1949 and then was to make a big name for himself as a Major and commanding officer of the 17 IAP in Korea, flying MiG-15s. On August 25, 1951 he opened his account with a Gloster Meteor and went on to emerge as one of the accomplished pilots of the conflict. During his postwar career Pulov eventually made General Major.

PUSHKIN, Nikolaj Petrovich
Combat record: 19 personal victories, 8 fractional credits, 380 sorties, 52 encounters.
Decorations: Gold Star of Hero of the Soviet Union on September 2, 1943 in recognition of 7 victories, 8 fractional credits as of May, 1943; the Orders of Lenin, the Red Banner (2), the Patriotic War 1st Class (2), the Red Star.

225
7025

НАГРАДНОЙ ЛИСТ

Фамилия, имя и отчество – ПОПКОВ Виталий Иванович.
Военное звание – Герой Советского Союза гвардии капитан.
Должность, часть – Командир эскадрильи 5 Гвардейского Истребительного Авиаполка 11 Гвардейской Истребительной Авиационной Днепропетровской Краснознаменной Дивизии.

ПРЕДСТАВЛЯЕТСЯ К ВЫСШЕЙ НАГРАДЕ –
ЗВАНИЮ ДВАЖДЫ ГЕРОЯ СОВЕТСКОГО СОЮЗА.

1. Год рождения – 1.5.1922г. 2. Национальность – Русский.
3. С какого времени в КА – С 15.9.1940 года.
4. Партийность – Член ВКП/б/ с 1943 года.
5. Участие в боях – В Отечественной войне с 15.5.1942г. – Калининский, Юго-Западный, 3 и 1 Украинские фронта.
6. Имеет ли ранения и контузии – 3.8.43г. тяжело ранен в воздушном бою, 16.6.44г. легко ранен осколками от ЗА.
7. Чем ранее награжден – Герой Советского Союза – Указ Президиума Верховного Совета ССР от 8.9.43г. за 17 сбитых самолетов противника; орденом Ленина – приказ ВКФ № 033 от 26.8.42г. за 1 сбитый самолет противника; орденом Красного Знамени – приказ 17 ВА № 026 от 30.7.43. за 5 сбитых самолетов противника; орденом Отечественной войны 1 степени – приказ 3 САК № 06 от 23.5.43. за 4 сбитых самолета противника; орденом Александра Невского – приказ 2 ВА № 029/Н от 17.8.44. за 14 сбитых самолетов противника.
8. Каким РВК призван – Краснопресненским РВК г. Москва.
9. Постоянный домашний адрес: Грузинская ССР, п/о Гантиази, п/я 1. Отец – Попков Иван Максимович.

Краткое, конкретное изложение личного
боевого подвига или заслуг.

Свою боевую работу начал с мая 1942 года на Калининском фронте, когда наши войска вели ожесточенные бои за овладение Ржевским плацдармом. Он является прославленным летчиком части, замечательным мастером воздушного боя, не знающим страха перед врагом.

Он участвовал в боях под Ржевом, в прорыве обороны и уничтожении итальянской армии в среднем течении р. Дона, при взятии г. Миллерово, Кантемировки и последующем развитии наступления наших войск. Участвовал в ликвидации наступления немцев в 1943г., на Белгородском направлении, в Изюм-Барвенковской, Запорожской и Днепропетровской операциях, на Владимир Волынском и Львовском направлениях, при форсировании р. Висла и р. Одер с последующим развитием наступления наших войск на территории немцев.

За отличное выполнение боевых заданий на фронте борьбы с немецкими захватчиками тов. Попков имеет четыре правительственных награды и удостоен звания Героя Советского Союза.

Первую правительственную награду – орден Ленина получил 26.8.42. за 1 сбитый самолет противника.

319

Вторую награду – орден Отечественной войны 1 степе-
ни – получил 23.5.43. за 4 сбитых самолета противника.
Третью награду – орден Красного Знамени – получил
30.7.43. за 5 сбитых самолетов противника.
Четвертую награду – орден Александра Невского – по-
лучил 17.8.44. за 14 сбитых самолетов противника.
8.9.43. за 168 успешных произведенных боевых выле-
и 17 сбитых самолетов противника присвоено звание Геро
Советского Союза.
В ответ на высокие правительственные награды тов.
ков с новой силой, энергией и жгучей ненавистью к вра
стал громить немецких захватчиков в воздухе и на зем
с честью оправдал высокие награды правительства.
После последней правительственной награды тов.Попк
произвел 75 успешных боевых вылетов, из них: 2 на шту
вые действия, 13 на разведку, 27 на охоту, остальные
прикрытие и сопровождение. Произвел 26 вылетов с бомб
танием, провел 12 воздушных боев, в которых лично сби
самолетов противника. Штурмовыми и бомбардировочными
виями уничтожил и вывел из строя: 10 автомашин с боепр
сами, 6 самолетов, 4 паровоза, подавил до 12 зенитных
За все время боевой работы в Отечественной войне
произвел 325 успешных боевых вылетов на самолетах ЛАГГ
ЛА-5, из них: на прикрытие 124, на сопровождение 75, на
штурмовку войск и аэродромов противника 17, на свобод
охоту 37, на разведку 52. Произвел 58 вылетов с бомбом
нием. Провел 83 воздушных боя, в результате которых ли
сбил 36 и 1 в группе самолетов противника.
Тов.Попков все задания выполняет в качестве веду
грамотно и умело командует группой по радио в воздушн
и при штурмовках. Своими действиями наносит большой ур
противнику.
Особенно отличился гвардии капитан Попков в после
дних операциях 1 Украинского фронта при прорыве оборон
тивника на Сандомирском плацдарме и в дальнейших насту
тельных действиях наших войск за Одером.
11.2.45., вылетев ведущим группы 5 ЛА-5 на свобо
охоту, Попков при подходе к Шпротау заметил группу 10
ФВ-190. Сразу же, подав команду по радио, Попков повел
группу на Фокеров, находившихся ниже на 200 м. Стреми
вая атака ошеломила противника и летчики ФВ-190, несм
на двухкратное превосходство, заметались в панике. С
вой же атаки Попков сбил 1 ФВ-190, который горящим вр
ся в землю. После этого Попков прикрыл атаку своего в
го, который так же сбил 1 ФВ-190. Атаки были настольк
кими и смелыми, что противник даже не пытался оказать
тивление. Еще двух Фокеров сбили ведомые Попкова.
Потеряв 4 самолета, оставшаяся группа противника
пешно удрала на запад, а наши истребители без единой
вернулись на свой аэродром.
За время командования эскадрильей, летным состав
произведено 562 боевых вылета, произведено 175 вылето
бомбометанием, сбито 27 самолетов противника.

ВЫВОД: За 36 лично сбитых самолетов противника
неоднократно проявленные мужество, отвагу и
при выполнении боевых заданий, достоин пр
ния звания – ДВАЖДЫ ГЕРОЯ СОВЕТСКОГО СОЮ

КОМАНДИР 5 ГВАРДЕЙСКОГО ИАП
ГВАРДИИ ПОДПОЛКОВНИК /ГРУЛИН/

"27" февраля 1945 года

20 221

II. ЗАКЛЮЧЕНИЕ ВЫШЕСТОЯЩИХ НАЧАЛЬНИКОВ. 7025

...тоин Высшей Правительственной награды - присвоения звания

"ДВАЖДЫ ГЕРОЙ СОВЕТСКОГО СОЮЗА".

...ДИР 11 ГВ. ИСТРЕБИТЕЛЬНОЙ АВИАЦИОННОЙ

...ПЕТРОВСКОЙ КРАСНОЗНАМЕННОЙ ДИВИЗИИ

...ИЙ ПОЛКОВНИК /ОСАДЧИЙ/

" марта 1945 года.

Достоин высшей Правительственной награды - звания

ДВАЖДЫ ГЕРОЙ СОВЕТСКОГО СОЮЗА.

КОМАНДИР 2 ГВ. ШТУРМОВОГО АВИАЦИОННОГО

...ИМИР ВОЛЫНСКОГО КРАСНОЗНАМЕННОГО КОРПУСА

ГЕНЕРАЛ-МАЙОР АВИАЦИИ /СЛЮСАРЕВ/

16 " марта 1945г.

III. ЗАКЛЮЧЕНИЕ ВОЕННОГО СОВЕТА АРМИИ.

Достоин высшей Правительственной награды - звания

Дважды Герой Советского Союза

Командующий 2й Воздушной Армии

Генерал-Полковник авиации

/Красовский/

марта 1945.

IV. ЗАКЛЮЧЕНИЕ ВОЕННОГО СОВЕТА ФРОНТА.

Присвоено звание
Героя Советского Союза
с вручением ...
2 медали „Золотая Звезда".
Указ Президиума Верховного Совета Союза ССР
от „27. 06 1945г.

ОСНОВАНИЕ: ЦАМО РФ, ф.33, оп.793756, д.60, л.225.

Копия верна: ЗАВ. АРХИВОХРАНИЛИЩЕМ (БРИЛЕВ)

Pushkin was born in the Ryazan area on December 4, 1918 and joined the Soviet Army in 1937. Three years later he passed his pilot's examination at Kacha military flying school and was in the thick of the fighting with a fighter unit from the earliest days of the war. On an unspecified date in July he was leading six I-16s to take on 40 bombers escorted by 18 fighters and personally accounted for a double with his comrades bringing the day's tally to nine. In May, 1942 he was posted to the 2 GIAP on Kalinin Front and on one particular day during that month managed to claim two Bf 109s when four LaGG-3s mixed it with 10 Luftwaffe fighters, six of these being shot down. In early 1943 he took over as leader of 2nd Eskadrilya "Mongolskij Arat" and on January 14 again reported the destruction of two Bf 109s. He then saw a great deal of action in the ferocious fighting at Orel and on July 14 eight La-5s with Pushkin in the lead hurtled down on 27 bombers and eight Fw 190s forcing down four He 111s without loss. By August his score had risen to 10 along with 8 fractional credits and in July, 1944 Pushkin was appointed deputy commander of the regiment serving in this capacity through the close of war. He remained in the VVS following World War II and graduated from the Air Force Academy in 1955. He left active duty as a Polkovnik in 1966 with 29 years service.

PYLAYEV, Yevgenij Alekseyevich

Combat record: 16 personal victories, 4 fractional credits, 285 sorties, 94 sorties.

Decorations: Gold Star of Hero of the Soviet Union on October 26, 1944; the Orders of Lenin, the Red Banner (3), the Patriotic War 1st and 2nd Class, the Red Star.

Pylayev was born in the Yaroslavl area on November 5, 1919 and enrolled for military service in 1938. He won his pilot wings at Chuguyev military flying school two years later and started flying combat with the 88 IAP in August, 1942 and saw a lot of action over the Terek River. During his time with the regiment Pylayev participated in the aerial campaigns on Caucasus, 4th Ukrainian and 2nd Byelorussian Fronts finishing as a Kapitan and deputy regiment commander. He had a big day on October 2, 1942 when three regiments, the 40, 84 and 88 IAPs, were assigned to fly a massive airfield strafe to Soldatskaya where 24 Luftwaffe planes were reportedly shot up. Pylayev's share: one on the ground and two fighters shot down while they were scrambling for takeoff. He built up a good score over the Kuban with five kills on the LaGG-3 fighter. On June 3, 1943 he gained another double when six LaGGs became embroiled in three separate tussles while flying a frontline patrol submitting claims for nine enemy aircraft destroyed. He was decorated with the Order of the Red Banner for his contribution to this combat and later would continue to do well in the air battles over Novorossijsk, Taman, Kerch, Sevastopol and Byelorussia. He served with the postwar VVS but died on September 5, 1951.

RATNIKOV, Pyotr Petrovich

Combat record: 11 personal victories, 4 fractional credits, 220 sorties, 85 encounters.

Decorations: Gold Star of Hero of the Soviet Union posthumously on August 24, 1943; the Orders of Lenin, the Red Banner (2), the Patriotic War 2nd Class.

Ratnikov was born in the Kamensk area in 1918 and entered military service at age 22. He had flight training at Ulyanovsk military flying school commencing his combat duty in January, 1942. He fought with great distinction in the Battle of Stalingrad by which time he had become a Starshij Lejtenant and squadron leader in the 512 IAP. He scored a single victory on October 16, 1942 and four days later was leading a number of Yaks on a sweep out to the Razgulyaevka area where they claimed six kills in an encounter with 12 Messerschmitts, all without loss. He next saw considerable fighting at Kursk and on July 5, 1943 combined forces with Starshij Serzhant Zhigalov to destroy three enemy aircraft. He was shot down and killed on July 24.

RECHKALOV, Grigorij Andreyevich

Combat record: 56 personal victories, 5 fractional credits, 450 sorties, 122 encounters.

Decorations: 1st Gold Star of Hero of the Soviet Union on May 24, 1943 for 12 victories, 2 fractional credits, 194 sorties, 54 encounters as of May, 1943, 2nd Gold Star on July 1, 1944 in recognition of 48 kills, 6 fractional credits, 415 sorties, 112 air combats as of June, 1944; the Orders of Lenin, the Red Banner (4), Aleksandr Nevskij, the Patriotic War 1st Class, the Red Star (2).

Rechkalov was born in the Sverdlovsk area on February 9, 1920 and when entering the VVS in 1938 was destined to enter aerial history as the fourth-ranked Allied fighter ace of World War II. Determined to fly fighters, Rechkalov completed his training at Perm military flying school a year later but was grounded after a medical commission had diagnosed Daltonism. He nevertheless made it into a fighter unit, and when German forces knifed into Soviet Russia on June 22, 1941 was flying I-153s on South Front. On the very first day of the war he flew six sorties in this relic of the past and added seven more next day beating up ground targets. Shortly after this he converted to I-16s and quickly proved his outstanding attributes. He destroyed his first enemy aircraft in the air a short time later when he had a tussle with 12 Ju 88s near Kishinyov while flying escort for Il-2s sending one of the bombers down in flames. A little later he was bounced by German fighters while engaged in escorting I-153s sustaining serious injuries to his head and right leg. He was out of action for several months and upon his recovery brought his score to four kills together with two shares in 20 air-to-air combats with the Yak-1 during the rest of 1942. Rechkalov's rise to fame began in early April, 1943 when he

G.A. Rechkalov who ranks fourth among Allied aces of World War II. He became famous as the enfant terrible of the VVS, a rule breaker who constantly disregarded regulations. He began to pile up a tremendous score once the 16 GIAP had reequipped with the Bell P- 39 Aeracobra. Here he is seen with his victory-flourishing P-39Q-15. (Author's collection)

An exuberant Grigorij Rechkalov in front of his personal aircraft which bore a three letter code group "RGA" denoting his initials. The pilot standing on the COBRA's wing is D.B. Glinka, famous fighter tiger of the 100 GIAP. (Author's collection)

deployed with the 16 GIAP to the Kuban theater after transition to the Bell P-39 had been accomplished. He came to value the Cobra for its outstanding performance at low to medium altitudes and began to write an indelible combat record. During the regiment's very first P-39 mission Rechkalov and Sasha Pokryshkin both claimed single 109s in a dogfight at Krymskaya. Rechkalov was promoted Starshij Lejtenant and flight leader in Pokryshkin's squadron and on April 15 a Ju 88 fell before his guns as his flight was breaking up a formation of bombers. The following day he knocked down another Bf 109 in the vicinity of Kholmskaya and blasted two more of these out of the sky on the 21st. Eight days later six Cobras with Kapitan Pokryshkin in the lead became engaged with four Stukas escorted by an equal number of fighters while prowling around in the frontline area. Pokryshkin immediately ordered the attack personally tearing into the bomber formation while assigning Rechkalov to cover his attack. In the ensuing melee Pokryshkin and Rechkalov both made claims for two enemy planes each. Triumph followed triumph. April proved to be a big month for Rechkalov with seven Bf 109s and one Ju 88 downed, while Pokryshkin downed 10 Luftwaffe fighters and St.Lej. Fadeyev 12. In chalking up a total of 19 kills over the Kuban Rechkalov verified his own fighting techniques. "See the enemy first – hit them hard and shoot them from the sky with a blast of fire at point-blank range," Rechkalov said, emphasizing the importance of surprise and the devastating effect of point-blank firing. He took over as leader of 1st Eskadrilya and a short time later claimed three Ju 87s in one sortie. Although Rechkalov was raised amid rigid Soviet military traditions which tended to favor team work and collective operations he had a propensity to break away to chase the enemy – routine, discipline and staying strictly in formation were alien to his spirit. He was constantly rebuked for violating flying discipline and his character study draws many interesting parallels with the brilliant Luftwaffe ace, Hans-Joachim Marseille. Rechkalov was one of the quickest and deadliest aces, possessed of an aggressive fighting spirit to go with outstanding marksmanship. Sasha Pokryshkin once provided the following revealing recollection of his days as commander of the 9 GIAD: "Individual efforts to further personal scores of enemy aircraft destroyed obviously resulted in our formation breaking up and even Rechkalov demonstrated this lack of discipline. There followed a sharp discussion with Rechkalov. In his capacity as regiment commander he did not ensure combat discipline but rather violated the principles of leadership him-

Rechkalov when he was a Kapitan wearing two Gold Stars of Hero of the Soviet Union. (Author's collection)

self as he was carried away by his strife for aerial victories." Rechkalov continued to pitilessly ambush enemy aircraft wherever they could be found scoring heavily in the skies above the Donbas and the Crimea and during the Lemberg-Sandomierz campaign. When the regiment commander, Boris Glinka, was seriously wounded in a fighter battle in July, 1944 his place was taken by Rechkalov. He got a Ju 87 on July 16 and continued to go off whenever possible. In February, 1945 he was appointed inspector of 9 GIAD with little opportunity to add to his scoring. He got into his last scrap with the Luftwaffe over Berlin in April, 1945 and was at this stage flying the Lavochkin La-7, one of the most advanced Soviet fighter aircraft, but like many fighter aces preferred the old workhorse P-39. He stayed in the service after the war and graduated from the Air Force Academy in 1951. He retired from the VVS as a General Major eight years later.

RENTS, Mikhail Petrovich

Combat record: 20 personal victories, 5 fractional credits, plus 96 motor vehicles and four locomotives destroyed in ground attacks, 294 sorties, 56 encounters.

Decorations: Gold Star of Hero of the Soviet Union on May 15, 1946 for 18 kills as of April, 1945; the Orders of Lenin, the Red Banner (4), the Patriotic War 1st Class, the Red Star.

Rents was born in Kursk on November 22, 1916 and entered military service in 1938. Upon qualifying as a pilot at Odessa military flying school in 1939 he was sent to a unit in the Far East. In March, 1943 he joined with the 30 GIAP on Central Front and from then on was in continuous action until the close of war. He took part in the great aerial campaigns over Kursk, Rogachyov, Minsk, Bobrujsk, Brest, Warsaw and Berlin, advancing to Major. He took over as leader of a fighter squadron which would be given credit for 58 air victories along with 11 locomotives, 48 rail cars and 136 motor vehicles destroyed on the ground during 1,183 sorties and 92 engagements to lead the division. On August 12, 1944 Rents scored a double with two Ju 87s while leading a flight of Yak-3s to attack 10 dive-bombers escorted by Fw 190s in the Warka area, seven enemy planes being shot down for no losses. He later saw a great deal of action during the Vistula-Oder Campaign in early 1945 and took part in the big air battles over the Küstrin bridgeheads. On March 11, 1945 he got a single as 273 IAD was claiming 16 kills. In a flurry of action over Berlin his squadron then chalked up 15 kills during 112 sorties between April 16-19, all without loss. During the fighting Rents excelled, bagging doubles each on the 18th and 20th respectively. He served with the postwar VVS and wound up his military career with the rank of Polkovnik in 1958.

The P-39 became a must on the Eastern Front. M.P. Rents, fighter ace of the 30 GIAP, was amongst those who flew this fighter with notable success. Here he is seen seated third from left posing for a photograph with his squadron mates. Note the elaborate squadron emblem. Rents emerged as the regiment's ranking ace with 20 confirmed victories. (Author's collection)

RESHETOV, Aleksej Mikhajlovich
Combat record: 35 personal victories, 8 fractional credits, 821 sorties, 200 encounters.
Decorations: Gold Star of Hero of the Soviet Union on May 1, 1943 in recognition of 11 kills, 8 fractional credits, 432 sorties, 100 air combats as of February, 1943; the Orders of Lenin, the Red Banner (2), Suvorov 3rd Class, Aleksandr Nevskij, the Patriotic War 1st Class (2), the Red Star (3).

Reshetov was born in the Moscow area on March 23, 1921 and started his remarkable career in the VVS in 1938. He graduated from flight training at Borisoglebsk military flying school two years later and became a member of the 239 IAP before the war. He drew first blood on June 22, 1941 when a Ju 88 fell before his guns at 0430 hours. He rapidly was promoted Starshij Lejtenant and then made a big name for himself during the hell of Stalingrad. On August 17, 1942 he conducted three armed reconnaissance missions claiming a Bf 109 destroyed and a second damaged. The following day he was off on four missions bagging another Bf 109 and on the 19th entered into three scraps with enemy planes. In all, he was credited with five kills and one damaged during that month while logging 52 sorties. On January 27, 1943 he led four Yak-1s to engage seven Ju 88s and four Bf 109s and personally accounted for one of the bombers while Lejtenant N.Ye. Glazov destroyed a second. Reshetov went on to become one of the high scorers of the battle with 11 kills – it is possible that this is actually a summation of personal victories and shares – during 150 sorties and 50 air encounters. He subsequently wrote a distinguished record in the skies above the Ukraine, the Crimea, Poland, Rumania, Hungary and Czechoslovakia, gaining a large number of his victories flying the Lavochkin La-5. He came out of World War II as the regiment's ranking ace. He remained in the ranks after the war and graduated from the Air Force Academy in 1954 concluding his active duty as a Polkovnik in 1964.

RIDNYJ, Stepan Grigoryevich
Combat record: 21 personal victories, 100 sorties, 60 encounters.
Decorations: Gold Star of Hero of the Soviet Union on August 9, 1941; the Order of Lenin.

Ridnyj was born in the Sumy area on March 26, 1917 and entered military service in 1937. He received his pilot wings at Odessa military flying school a year later and was posted to the 126 IAP before the war. He was early in the public eye running up an impressive string of victories and flying as many as 6-8 sorties a day during the darkest hours of 1941. On an unrecorded date in June, 1941 he caught a Ju 88 near Gomel and chased it deep into enemy territory but the bomber simply refused to go down. With complete disregard to vicious return fire he continued firing until he was almost within ramming distance, whereupon the enemy plane blew up and plunged earthward. Ridnyj staggered back to his own airfield where some 200 hits were counted in his I-16. He kept up a fierce battle with the Luftwaffe in July his aircraft being badly shot up on three occasions between the 1st and 12th of that month. On July 10 he forced down another Ju 88 and claimed an He 111 the following day while on the 12th he combined forces with his wingman, Mladshij Lejtenant Ivan Levshoj, to destroy two more Ju 88s. He was among the first recipients of the coveted title of Hero of the Soviet Union and in October was promoted flight leader. Later that month he converted to Tomahawks and continued to achieve victories at a formidable pace during the great battle for the Soviet capital. On December 14, 1941 he intercepted two He 111s one of which he was able to destroy jointly with his wingman while on February 3, 1942 he became involved in two separate melees coming away with claims for a fighter and a reconnaissance plane. The following day he was in action again splashing a Ju 52 and combining forces with Lejtenant Matyushkin to force down a second. On February 8 another He 111 fell to his guns but on the 17th he was bounced by four Bf 109s while returning from a mission. Without hesitating Ridnyj turned into them hitting one with a long burst whereupon it crashed but at that moment was hit hard from behind by another and crashed to his death. With his

Polkovnik I.G. Romanenko, who won the title of Hero of the Soviet Union for his decisive leadership of the Baltic Fleet's 13 IAP during the Russo-Finnish Winter War of 1939/40. He wound up his military career with 40 years service as a General Lejtenant in 1970. (Author's collection)

loss, the VVS was deprived of one of its finest pilots of the time. He was interred in the village of Chkalovskaya, Shchelkovo area (NE Moscow).

ROMANENKO, Ivan Ivanovich
Combat record: 16 personal victories, 1 fractional credit, 85 sorties, 23 encounters as of July, 1943.
Decorations: Gold Star of Hero of the Soviet Union on February 4, 1944; the Orders of Lenin, the Red Banner (5), Aleksandr Nevskij, the Patriotic War 1st Class, the Red Star.

Romanenko was born in the Poltava area on November 5, 1918 and joined the Soviet Army in 1935. He was graduated as a pilot at Chuguyev military flying school three years later and went to war with the 774 IAP in October, 1942 flying Yak-1s. He built up a good score on Central Front and had a big day on July 7, 1943 when he was engaged in escorting some 221 BAD aircraft to Kursk and using mutual support tactics with his wingman, Serzhant P.I. Pshenov, reported the destruction of three Fw 190s with Pshenov getting a fourth. He rose to Kapitan and Shturman and possibly added to his tally but details are not available. Romanenko stayed in the service after the war and graduated from the Air Force Academy in 1951. He retired from the VVS as a General Major in 1974 and died on June 8, 1978.

RUBAKHIN, Anatolij Yermolayevich
Combat record: 20 personal victories.
Decorations: Gold Star of Hero of the Soviet Union on February 23, 1945 for 16 kills, 123 sorties, 51 encounters as of September, 1944; the Orders of Lenin, the Red Banner (3), Aleksandr Nevskij, the Patriotic War 1st Class (2), the Red Star.

Rubakhin was born in the Voronezh area on July 7, 1918 and entered military service in 1936. He graduated from flight training at Kacha three years later and started flying combat with the 402 IAP in April, 1943. He subsequently did remarkably well during his assignments over the Caucasus, the Kuban, the Donbas, the Crimea, Byelorussia, Poland and the Reich. He eventually rose to command the regiment with the rank of Major and was to build up a high score on the Yak-3 fighter. He was in the thick of the fighting during the Vistula-Oder campaign in January, 1945 and over the Oder bridgehead at Küstrin, scoring a double on February 10. During his World War II career Rubakhin was once wounded in action. He remained in the VVS at the conclusion of the war and graduated from the Air Force Academy in 1955. He left active duty with the rank of General Major eight years later and passed away on October 4, 1986.

RUDENKO, Nikolaj Sergeyevich
Combat record: 21 personal victories, 2 fractional credits, 186 sorties, 38 encounters.
Decorations: Gold Star of Hero of the Soviet Union on June 29, 1945; the Orders of Lenin, the Red Banner (3), the Patriotic War 1st Class.

Rudenko was born in the Voronezh area on December 12, 1920 and entered the Soviet Army for flight training in 1940. Two years later he won his pilot wings at Batajsk military flying school and in October, 1942 became a member of the 19 IAP. He was with the unit through World War II seeing a lot of action on Stalingrad, South, 1st Ukrainian, 1st and 3rd Byelorussian Fronts. He began to come into prominence under the tutelage of the great Ivan Kozhedub during the latter stages of the war, gaining all or most of his victories on La-5s and La-7s. On March 17, 1944 he blasted two Bf 109s out of the sky while flying free hunt in the Proskurov area and on September 26 caught and destroyed a Fw 189 reconnaissance plane right over a Luftwaffe airfield in the vicinity of Warsaw and then spotted a fighter taking-off and attacked from abeam with a long burst, scoring many strikes following which the aircraft exploded giving the pilot no chance of survival. He claimed another double with two Fw 190s near Küstrin on February 15, 1945 and then added a single on March 11. He forced down another Fw 190 in the Seelow area on the 23rd and next saw considerable fighting over Berlin, reporting the destruction of two Fw 190s near Bernau on April 16 and another of these two days later. He served with the postwar VVS and in 1953 was assigned to the Soviet Naval Air Service. He wound up his military career with the rank of Major a year later.

RYAZANOV, Aleksej Konstantinovich
Combat record: 32 personal victories, 16 fractional credits, 551 sorties, 97 encounters.
Decorations: 1st Gold Star of Hero of the Soviet Union on August 24, 1943 for 16 kills, 16 fractional credits, 300 sorties, 67 air combats, 2nd Gold Star on August 18, 1945 in recognition of 31 kills, 16 fractional credits, 509 sorties as of February, 1945; the Orders of Lenin (3), the Red Banner (4), Aleksandr Nevskij, the Patriotic War 1st Class (2), the Red Star (2).

Ryazanov was born in the Tambov area on February 27, 1920 and enlisted in the VVS in 1939. He was graduated as a pilot at Borisoglebsk military flying school later that year and when the Germans initiated Operation Barbarossa on June 22, 1941 was flying I-16s with the 736 IAP. On the very first day of the war the Luftwaffe hit the regiment's airfield near Lutsk. Only a few surviving aircraft got airborne to make a number of uncoordinated attacks with Ryazanov bringing down an He 111 for his first kill. By the end of 1941 his score had risen to 4, all while flying I-16s, and was appointed Kapitan and squadron

A Yak-7B gets airborne. A total of 6,399 examples of this excellent derivative of the Yak-1 were built. After a trickle of but 166 deliveries in 1941, 2,431 fighters already went off the assembly lines the following year. (Author's collection)

leader. He later joined with the 4 IAP and during his time with this was to develop into one of Russia's deadliest fighter tigers. On July 12, 1942 he was leading eight Yak-1s against a formation of 24 Ju 87s and eight Bf 109s near Zemlyansk (NW Voronezh) and personally accounted for one of the dive-bombers while his squadron mates brought the day's tally to seven. He then made a big name for himself in the contested air space over Stalingrad running up a string of seven kills which qualified him for the award of the Order of Lenin. He destroyed a Bf 109 on August 21 while leading six Yaks flying escort for Il-2s when combat occurred with eight German fighters, two of these being shot down. In early 1943 the regiment deployed to the Kuban where it became involved in some very heavy fighting. Six to seven sorties a day were commonplace, and in a series of fierce dogfights Ryazanov's squadron was credited with downing some 30 enemy planes over Taman, Krasnodar and Anapa while losing only three of its own. The dramatic battles over the Kuban took his tally to 19 kills along with 16 fractional credits and he had a big day on April 29, 1943 with a triple. He next fought over Gomel and Bryansk in September, 1943 and subsequently flew Yak-9s on 2nd Baltic Front. In time he was ranging deep into East Prussia with Valerij Shman frequently flying wing to him. On January 26, 1945 13 Yak-9s with Ryazanov in the lead tangled with a bevy of 20 Fw 190s claiming 10 kills. Ryazanov personally accounted for one of them but was then wounded and force-landed behind the Soviet lines. In all, he was wounded in action three times. He remained in the VVS after the war graduating from Frunze Military Academy in 1950 and from General Staff Academy eight years later. He eventually made General Major and returned to civilian life in 1975.

RYKACHYOV, Yurij Borisovich

Combat record: 19 personal victories, 280 sorties.

Decorations: Gold Star of Hero of the Soviet Union on February 10, 1942 for 3 kills, 11 fractional credits, 104 sorties as of September, 1941; the Orders of Lenin (3), the Red Banner (3), Kutuzov 2nd Class, the Patriotic War 1st Class, the Red Star.

Rykachyov was born in Tiflis (Tbilisi) on December 16, 1909 and started his military career in 1928. Two years later he graduated as a pilot at Volsk military school for pilots and aircraft mechanics, attended advanced training for flight leaders in 1936 and graduated from the Air Force Academy five years later. He was a well-seasoned pilot when commencing combat duty at the very start of the war flying with great distinction as a Kapitan and deputy commander of the 69 IAP which was keeping up a fierce battle with the Luftwaffe over Kishinyov and Odessa in 1941. During his postwar career Rykachyov graduated from General Staff Academy in 1949 assuming various command assignments. He left active duty as a General Lejtenant in 1969 with 41 years service.

RYZHIJ, Leonid Kirillovich

Combat record: 17 personal victories, 250 sorties, 89 encounters.

Decorations: Gold Star of Hero of the Soviet Union on May 15, 1946; the Orders of Lenin, the Red Banner (4), Aleksandr Nevskij, the Patriotic War 1st Class (2), the Red Star (2).

Ryzhij was born in Kiev on September 23, 1941 and enrolled for service in the VVS at age 18. A year later he won his wings at Kacha military flying school and started flying combat in October, 1941. He enjoyed considerable success while serving as a Kapitan and squadron leader in the 347 IAP during the latter stages of the war. On September 20, 1943 he was leading four Yak-9s to tear into a large bomber formation near Koselets (NE Kiev) and in spite of vicious return fire destroyed a Ju 88 while his comrades got two more. His fighter had been badly hit but he maintained effective control completing the mission. His big day came on August 9, 1943 when he claimed a triple with three Fw 190s when 12 Yaks under his leadership tackled with 22 German fighters in the vicinity of Magnuszew (SE Warsaw). He next saw a great deal of action during the Vistula-Oder campaign (January 12/February 3, 1945) and above the Oder bridgehead at Küstrin. While flying free hunt with his number two, Mladshij Lejtenant N.P. Bugayev, in the Beeskow area on March 7 combat occurred with six Fw 190s, with both pilots claiming single victories. Ryzhij stayed in the service after the cessation of hostilities graduating from the Air Force Academy in 1951. He concluded his active duty as a Polkovnik in 1973.

RYZHOV, Yefgraf Mikhajlovich
Combat record: 13 personal victories, 6 fractional credits, 250 sorties, 54 encounters.
Decorations: Gold Star of Hero of the Soviet Union on October 23, 1942; the Orders of Lenin, the Red Banner (2).

Ryzhov was born in Moscow on December 16, 1916 and enrolled for service in the VMF in August, 1936. He completed his pilot training at Yejsk military flying school in late 1938 and was assigned to the 32 IAP of the Baltic Fleet's air service before the war. He was early in the public eye, destroying an He 111 in a ramming attack off Sevastopol on July 25, 1941. This feat won him the award of the Order of the Red Banner on August 13. He then excelled in November, submitting claims for five enemy planes destroyed with the LaGG-3 fighter. Shortly afterward he was promoted Kapitan and flight leader and by June, 1942 had brought his tally to 10. He was well qualified for his second Order of the Red Banner on August 9, 1942 and next was posted to the 7 IAP-ChF to become commanding officer of a squadron. In July, 1943 he rose to Major and deputy regiment commander but was seriously wounded later that month never flying operationally again. He was released from the service with the rank of Major in 1946.

SAFONOV, Boris Feoktistovich
Combat record: 30 personal victories, 3 fractional credits, 234 sorties, 34 encounters.
Decorations: 1st Gold Star of Hero of the Soviet Union on September 16, 1941 for 11 victories, 130 sorties as of September, 1941, 2nd Gold Star posthumously on June 14, 1942; the Orders of Lenin, the Red Banner (3), the British DFC.

The redoubtable B.F. Safonov seen here as a Podpolkovnik in 1942. (Author's collection)

Safonov was born in the Tula area on August 26, 1915 and when entering military service in 1933 was destined to become a national hero and legendary figure in the VVS. He won his wings at Kacha military flying school a year later and in 1938 joined with the 15 IAP. In December 1939 his squadron was assigned to the Northern Fleet's 72 SAP where he took an active part in the Russo-Finnish Winter War flying I-16s. By June, 1941 the regiment was operating a motley collection of I-16s, I-15bis', I-153s and a few MiG-3s. Safonov was leader of the 4th Eskadrilya and on June 24, 1941 had the distinction of destroying Northern Fleet's first enemy plane in the air claiming an He 111 over the Kola Peninsula at 1645 hours. It seems more likely that his victim was actually a Ju 88 of 6./KG 30 reported missing that day. He next scored three days later when he combined forces with the regiment commander, Major G.P. Gubanov, to destroy an Hs 126 in the Petsamo area. He added another of these single-handedly on July 16 and forced down a Ju 87 the following day. On the 18th a Ju 88 fell to his guns in the vicinity of Vaenga and a further one seven days later. On August 5 he was able to down a Bf 109 for a change and then made claims for single Ju 88s on the 9th and 23rd. Four days later he was credited with destroying a Hs 126 and on September 9 bagged a Ju 87. On the 15th he was engaged in providing ground force cover in the Zapadnaya Litsa area where he dispatched one each Ju 88, Hs 126 and Ju 87 in two sorties. By mid-September Safonov had become the top-scoring naval fighter pilot with 14 kills, and what makes his record particular noteworthy is that he gained all of his score on the Polikarpov I-16. At this stage followers-up in the regiment were A.A. Kovalenko and Z.A. Sorokin with 7 and 5 kills apiece. In October he assumed command of the newly formed 78 IAP-SF and on December 17 destroyed a Bf 109 while flying a Hurricane. He claimed an He 111 on New Year's Eve and reportedly shot down a German 36-victory ace identified as a Willi Frenger by Soviet sources on an unrecorded date during the year (possibly May 17). The enemy pilot fell into Russian hands but his eventual fate remains a mystery. On March 20, 1942 Safonov was put in command of his old regiment and on April 15 led 13

Hurricanes, Tomahawks and MiG-3s against a formation consisting of 18 Ju 87s and 17 Bf 110s enroute to Murmansk, seven Stukas and a Bf 110 being shot down for the loss of one MiG. On May 17 he caught a Ju 88 near Vaenga and quickly sent it down in flames with his Tomahawk. On May 30 he took off with Major Kukharenko, Kapitan Orlov and Starshij Lejtenant Pokrovskij to provide combat air patrol for PQ 16 enroute to Murmansk. They ran into six Ju 88s of I./KG 30 on the way to the convoy three of which reportedly were destroyed by Safonov before hits sent him crashing down to his death. In Safonov the VVS lost its then top-scoring ace and one of its remarkable characters. His final score yet is a matter of dispute, some sources quoting his tally as 25 kills together with 14 shares (V.S. Bojko: "Krylya Severnogo Flota") or even 41 personal victories ("Krylya Rodiny). His personal log book which could serve to settle this query remains entrenched in 2 GIAP's archives.

SAFRONOV, Sergej Ivanovich

Combat record: 27 personal victories, 4 fractional credits, 147 sorties.

Decorations: Gold Star of Hero of the Soviet Union on August 24, 1943 in recognition of 11 kills, 2 fractional credits, 65 sorties as of May, 1943; the Orders of Lenin, the Red Banner (2), the Patriotic War 1st Class (2).

Safronov was born in the Gorkij area on August 25, 1918 and entered the VVS for flight training in 1938. He qualified as a pilot at Engels military flying school a year later and went to war with the 293 IAP in October, 1942 flying Yak-1s. He made a big name for himself in the skies above the Kuban by scoring five kills while his squadron was credited with downing 24 enemy planes during the period of April 23 to May 20, 1943. His victories included a Bf 109 that he forced down in an action near Krymskaya on April 28, 1943. Safronov continued to achieve victories at a remarkable pace during subsequent assignments and came out of World War II as the regiment's ranking ace. He left active duty with the rank of Major in 1945 and later was instructor of the famous cosmonaut Yuri A. Gagarin, the first man in space, at Saratov Aeroklub. He died on September 29, 1983.

SAVITSKIJ, Yevgenij Yakovlevich

Combat record: 22 personal victories, 2 fractional credits, 216 sorties, 81 encounters.

Decorations: 1st Gold Star of Hero of the Soviet Union on May 11, 1944 for 15 kills, 107 sorties as of March, 1944, 2nd Gold Star on June 2, 1945; the Orders of Lenin (3), the October Revolution, the Red Banner (5), Suvorov 2nd Class, Kutozov 2nd Class, the Patriotic War 1st Class, the Red Star (2).

Lejtenant N.T. Samonov spent his savings on a fighter plane and reportedly scored 13 victories while flying this machine in the contested skies above Stalingrad. It seems likely that he served with the 126 IAP. (Author's collection)

Savitskij, brilliant Soviet fighter leader and top tactician, was born in Novorossijsk on December 24, 1910 and started his distinguished military career in 1929. He graduated from flight training in 1932 and by 1937 had become a Starshij Lejtenant and flight leader. A short time later he was promoted to squadron leader and subsequent assignments include deputy commanding officer of the I-153 equipped 29 IAP in the Far East and commanding officer of the 3 IAP on West Front. At age 28 he took over the 31 IAD as a Major seeing some action during the Battle of Moscow. He was a staff officer with 25th Army's air service between March-April, 1942 and the following month he gave up the position to assume command of the 205 IAD which at the time was flying Yak-1s and Airacobras becoming involved in the fierce battles over Stalingrad. He served in this capacity until November when he was posted to command the 3 IAK on December 10. In this capacity he was to display outstanding leadership while participating in the great aerial campaigns over the Kuban, the Crimea, Byelorussia, the Reich and finally, Berlin. He finished as one of the most accomplished Soviet fighter leaders, whose skill and devotion have largely contributed to the remarkable record attained by his unit. In late 1943 he was promoted General Major and on May 11, 1944 advanced to General Lejtenant. In November, 1944 the corps was deployed to 1st Byelorussian Front adding new laurels to its record. Over a three months period the pilots claimed 171 victories during 4,552 sorties until March 4, 1945. Savitskij continued to go off on combat missions whenever possible chalking up four kills in 43 sorties in the same time frame. On January 19, 1945 he got a Fw 190 in the Kutno area (W Warsaw) when he was in the air searching for adequate airfields to deploy his units on. He claimed another single on March 11 and closed out his scoring in the contested air space of Berlin in April, 1945. At the end of the war, 3 IAK had the second highest score of any VVS air corps with 1,653 victories during 28,860 sorties. Savitskij continued on active duty with the VVS following World War II attaining high rank. In 1948 he was appointed commander of the PVO air service and seven years later graduated from General Staff Academy. He was promoted Marshal Aviatsii in 1961 and became deputy commander of the national air defense forces. During his distinguished career Savitskij logged a total of 12,943 hours in the air of which 1,201 came at night during 5,586 sorties. He flew numerous types of aircraft including I-16s, La-5s, La-7s, MiG-3s, LaGG-3s, Il-2s, Yak-1s, Yak-3s, Yak-6s, Yak-7s, Yak-9s, Yak-11s, Yak-12s, Yak-15s, Yak-17s, Yak-25s, Yak-28s, Yak-50s, MiG-19s, MiG-21s, captured Bf 109s and Me 262s along with lend-lease Hurricanes, Spitfires and Airacobras.

General Lejtenant Ye.Ya. Savitskij, the esteemed commander of the glorious 3 IAK, which finished the war with a total of 1,653 confirmed. Savitskij was known throughout the VVS as "drakon" (dragon). (Author's collection)

SEMENISHIN, Vladimir Grigoryevich

Combat record: 23 personal victories, 13 fractional credits.
Decorations: Gold Star of Hero of the Soviet Union on May 24, 1943 for 8 kills, 7 fractional credits, 136 sorties, 29 encounters as of May, 1943; the Orders of Lenin (2), the Red Banner, the Patriotic War 1st Class.

Semenishin was born in St. Petersburg (Leningrad) on June 15, 1910 and entered military service in 1932. He was graduated as a pilot at Kacha military flying school four years later and first saw action during the Russo-Finnish Winter War of 1939/40. By June, 1941 he had become a member of the 131 IAP and then was in the thick of the fighting from the earliest days of the war flying I-16s. On an unspecified date he led several squadron mates in a strafing attack on a Luftwaffe airfield near Belaya Tserkov (S Kiev), where nine parked planes and two antiaircraft guns were left destroyed. A short time later he came within a hair of getting lost on a mission to Novomirgorod (NW Kirovograd) but survived with serious injuries to his legs and arms. He was wounded again in 1942 by which time his record stood at eight kills together with seven fractional credits during 136 sorties, 56 of which were ground attacks. It is particularly noteworthy that Semenishin had acquired this record with the I-16 fighter which proved to be outclassed by most of the enemy aircraft it met. Upon his recovery he was posted to the 298 IAP to command a fighter squadron. Now flying the sleek Airacobra, he was to make a big name for himself in the ferocious fighting over the Kuban. Under his able leadership the squadron was credited with down-

One of the best: 298 IAP ace V.G. Semenishin by the nose of his P-39 carrying 12 victory stars. Kuban, 1943. (Author's collection)

ing 41 enemy planes between February and May, 1943 while personally accounting for eight kills and six fractional credits. On May 3 he reported the destruction of two Bf 109s when three Cobras tackled with six German fighters in the vicinity of Krymskaya. He had a big day on May 27 chalking up four kills in two sorties with his squadron bringing the day's tally to 11. On September 29, 1943 he was off on a sweep out to Bolshoj Tokmak with eight fellow pilots but six of them became separated after encountering foul weather. All of a sudden nine Bf 109s swept down on them and one Cobra immediately exploded before it could take any evasive action. Semenishin acted coolly and wracked his fighter around in a tight turn to engage his attackers head-on. He managed to blast three 109s out of the sky before hits sent him crashing down. He was a Major and Shturman at the time of his death.

SEMENTSOV, Mikhail Ivanovich

Combat record: 19 personal victories, 12 fractional credits plus 48 motor vehicles, 15 field guns, two armored vehicles, five antiaircraft guns destroyed in ground attacks, 363 sorties, 83 encounters.

Decorations: Gold Star of Hero of the Soviet Union on September 29, 1943 for 12 victories, 9 fractional credits, 270 sorties, 69 air engagements as of July, 1943; the Orders of Lenin, the Red Banner (2), the Red Star.

Sementsov was born in the Kiev area on September 26, 1917 and joined the Soviet Army in 1938. Upon qualifying as a pilot at Odessa military flying school two years later he was sent to the 40 IAP in the Far East. He commenced his combat duty flying I-16s in August, 1941 and on March 3, 1942 was shot down and wounded by antiaircraft fire near Izyum. He was put back on duty two weeks later and then saw a great deal of action at Rostov, the "Gateway to the Caucasus." He was wounded again by groundfire while conducting a mission in the Achikulak area (NE Nalchik) on October 20 being out of action for two months. He next ran up a string of six kills with the Lavochkin La-5 during the Kursk-Byelgorod fighting. On an unspecified date in August Sementsov and his wingman became involved in a fierce dogfight with eight Luftwaffe fighters, Sementsov personally blasting two Bf 109s out of the sky. He was credited with a Taran victory near Kiev in October when he destroyed a Fw 190 after having expended his ammunition but during the process was injured again. During his combat career Sementsov altogether was wounded in action eight times and this may well be the highest record of any Allied pilot. Fittingly, he once described his eagerness for combat in his own words: "I won't stop fighting as long as there are any Fritzen for my bullets left." In early February, 1945 he deployed with the regiment to an airfield at Brieg being occupied with escorts to Breslau, the capital of Silesia. On the 12th he was leading several La-5s on an escort for Pe-2s when they engaged a superior force of enemy fighters in the Breslau-Oppeln area. Sementsov immediately destroyed a Fw 190 turning into their attack but was then hit hard by another diving straight into a Bf 109 with both planes blowing up and plunging earthward.

SEMENYUK, Ivan Ivanovich

Combat record: 19 personal victories, 8 fractional credits, 430 sorties, 125 encounters.

Decorations: Gold Star of Hero of the Soviet Union on July 1, 1944 in recognition of 16 kills, 8 fractional credits, 278 sorties as of February, 1944; the Orders of Lenin (2), the Red Banner (2), the Patriotic War 1st Class, the Red Star (2).

Semenyuk was born in Minsk on February 15, 1917 and entered military service in 1938. Two years later he qualified as a pilot at Batajsk military flying school commencing his combat duty in June, 1941. He fought across the skies of Russia in the wild air battles at Tiraspol, Dnyepropetrovsk, Taganrog and Kursk-Orel successively flying I-16s, LaGG-3s, and La-5s. He later rose to Kapitan and squadron leader in the 40 GIAP and gave a good account of himself on 1st Ukrainian Front. He stayed in the service after the war retiring from the VVS as a Polkovnik in 1961. He died on April 26, 1973.

SEMYONOV, Aleksandr Fyodorovich

Combat record: 19 personal victories, 12 fractional credits, 315 sorties, 70 encounters.

Decorations: Gold Star of Hero of the Soviet Union on March 21, 1940 for 4 victories, 75 sorties and 5 air combats; the Orders of Lenin (2), the Red Banner (4), Kutuzov 2nd Class, Bogdan Khmelnitskij 2nd Class, the Patriotic War 1st Class, the Red Star.

Semyonov was born in the Kalinin area on April 7, 1912 and entered the Soviet Army in 1933 for flight training. He won his wings at Kharkov military flying school and in late 1937 volunteered for combat duty in Spain. He next excelled during the Russo-Finnish Winter War of 1939/40 being honored with the highest Soviet distinction, the title Hero of the Soviet Union in turn. He was then a Kapitan and deputy squadron leader serving in the 7 IAP. Semyonov was posted to the 122 IAP shortly afterward and joined combat with the Luftwaffe flying MiG-3s in July, 1941. In September he was decorated with his third Order of the Red Banner (previous awards had been in 1938 resp. 1940) and won the Order of Lenin a month later. He was posted to the 180 IAP later that month and saw considerable fighting at Rzhev, Kholm-Zharkovskij, and Zubtsov being occupied with furnishing ground force cover and beating up enemy columns. In late December he was sent to officers advanced training courses and in May, 1942 was posted as a Major and fighter inspector to Stalingrad. In February, 1943 he was assigned to the badly battered 286 IAD to get this into operational trim once more. He found this in a demoralized state but soon got it into shape. In February, 1944 he applied for transfer to combat duty and was given command of the 32 GIAP. In May he was appointed deputy commander of the 3 GIAD following which he participated in the huge Soviet offensive against Army Group Center in Byelorussia in June, 1944 and subsequently fought in Courland. In October, 1944 he rose to command the 322 IAD and displayed outstanding leadership in the final aerial campaigns over the Reich with the pilots claiming 152 kills over Silesia, Berlin and Prague during 4,369 sorties. During his postwar career Semyonov graduated from the General Staff Academy and eventually made General Lejtenant retiring from the VVS in 1970. He died on February 13, 1979.

SEREDA, Pyotr Seliverstovich

Combat record: 18 personal victories, 500 sorties.

Decorations: Gold Star of Hero of the Soviet Union on November 23, 1942 for 7 kills, 270 sorties, 30 engagements as of July, 1942; the Orders of Lenin (4), the Red Banner (4), the Red Star.

Sereda was born in Melitopol on December 3, 1917 and enlisted in the Soviet Army in 1938. Later that year he passed his pilot's examination at Kacha military flying school and was posted to the 88 IAP flying I-16s before the war. He drew first blood on June 22, 1941 reporting the destruction of a Bf 109 while engaged in an escort mission and next scored on November 5 when he combined forces with three squadron mates to shoot down an He 111 in the Shakhty area (NE Rostov). Later in the month he spotted a Ju 88 that apparently had made a forced landing and made several passes until it blew up. He subsequently saw a lot of action at Rostov and was promoted Kapitan and squadron leader. On February 20, 1942 he was leading a flight out to the Novo-Orlovka area where they found two Luftwaffe planes undergoing repair on an airfield leaving them destroyed. In all, his pilots were credited with 42 enemy aircraft in the air plus 10 more destroyed in ground attacks along with 300 motor vehicles, four locomotives, eight armored vehicles during 2,300 sorties. He later was in the thick of the fighting over Slavyansk and Izyum. He remained in the ranks after the war retiring from the VVS as a General Major in 1963. He died on December 7, 1984.

SEREDIN, Vladimir Alekseyevich

Combat record: 15 personal victories, 195 sorties, 76 encounters.

Decorations: Gold Star of Hero of the Soviet Union on August 19, 1944; the Orders of Lenin, the Red Banner (2), Aleksandr Nevskij.

Seredin was born in Borisoglebsk on February 9, 1917 and joined the Soviet Army at age 21. He was graduated as a pilot at Borisoglebsk military flying school in 1940 and fought from the very start of the war seeing first action at Lvov (Lemberg). He subsequently put up a good performance on Bryansk, Southwest, Stalingrad, Voronezh and 3rd Ukrainian Fronts while serving in the 866 IAP. On one occasion in July, 1943 six Yaks with Seredin in the lead took on a formation of some 50 enemy planes in the vicinity of Izyum, five of these being shot down. A single claimed by Seredin himself brought his tally to 10. He rose to Kapitan and Shturman but on April 6, 1945 he deliberately rammed a Bf 109 in an action over Hungary and was killed.

SEREGIN, Vasilij Georgiyevich

Combat record: 16 personal victories, 8 fractional credits, 332 sorties, 35 encounters.

Decorations: Gold Star of Hero of the Soviet Union on February 23, 1948; the Orders of Lenin (2), the Red Banner (6), Aleksandr Nevskij, the Patriotic War 1st Class (2), the Red Star (2).

Seregin was born in the Tula area on March 12, 1915 and enrolled for service in 1939. A year later he was graduated at Perm military flying school following which he attended Chkalov flying school. He fought from the very start of the war and on March 7, 1942 led six LaGG-3s of the 168 IAP to take on 12 Ju 87s near Yukhnov (SE Vyazma). The day's total claims were seven dive-bombers of which a single fell to the guns of Seregin himself. He later claimed an He 111 jointly with Mladshij Lejtenant V.M. Shalev in July but most of his victories came in the big air battles over Byelorussia in late 1943. On October 13 he forced down another Ju 87 near Vitebsk and added two more of these next day. He bagged a Fw 190 on May 26, 1944 while carrying out a free hunt between Vitebsk-Bogushevsk-Orsha. He converted to Yak-3s and put up a good performance in the skies of East Prussia, downing a Fw 190 on October 10. Six days later he claimed another of these whilst taking-off at Budupenen airfield and in the afternoon reported the destruction of a second closing in to 50 meters. On the 18th he received credit for two Bf 109s and eventually rose to Major and Shturman of the 303 IAD. He remained in the VVS at the conclusion of the war retiring as a Polkovnik in 1958.

SERZHANTOV, Ivan Yakovlevich

Combat record: 14 personal victories, 8 fractional credits, 258 sorties, 85 encounters.

Decorations: Gold Star of Hero of the Soviet Union posthumously on August 24, 1943; the Orders of Lenin, the Red Banner, the Red Star.

Serzhantov was born in the Vitebsk area on February 17, 1919 and entered the Soviet Army in 1938. He qualified as a pilot at Chuguyev military flying school three years later and went to war with the 9 GIAP in January, 1942. He became involved in the heavy air battles above Kharkov, Izyum, Stalingrad and Rostov opening his account with an Hs 126 on April 3. He then built up a respectable score and in a few months became one of the unit's top-scorers. On the 9th he destroyed a Bf 109 and on May 1 shot down a Bf 110. He shot down a Ju 87 on the 11th and another of these eleven days later. June 13 saw him add a Bf 109 to his bag and on July 11 he got a Macchi C-200 Saetta and an He 111. Six days later he forced down a Bf 109 and a further one together with a Saetta on August 6. On October 27 he racked up his 12th kill with a Ju 52. He took a short home leave and on February 26, 1943 a Ju 87 fell to his guns and on March 27 destroyed a Ju 88. On April 28 he was shot down in a fierce fighter battle and sustained serious injuries, dying of his wounds the following day. He was buried in Rostov.

Vladimir Georgiyevich Serov, top-scoring ace of Leningrad Front. Serov tallied 20 kills during 203 sorties in La-5s between April, 1942 and April, 1944 and had a total of 36 before his final flight on June 26, 1944. On that particular day he single-handedly took on seven enemy fighters in the Vyborg area, knocked down two but was then killed successfully ramming a third. He received a posthumous title of Hero of the Soviet Union on August 2, 1944. (Author's collection)

SGIBNEV, Pyotr Georgiyevich

Combat record: 19 personal victories, 318 sorties, 38 encounters.

Decorations: Gold Star of Hero of the Soviet Union on October 23, 1942 in recognition of 10 kills, 290 sorties as of September, 1942; the Orders of Lenin, the Red Banner (3).

Sgibnev was born in the Kalinin area in 1920 and enrolled for service in the VMF in 1937. Three years later he qualified as a pilot at Yejsk military flying school and was assigned to the Baltic Fleet's air service. He entered combat early in the war chalking up four air victories during 186 sorties and 14 air combats before joining with the 78 IAP-KBF in 1942 flying Hurricanes. In a very short time he amassed six more kills while flying 74 sorties and for his efforts was decorated with the highest Soviet degree of merit, the title Hero of the Soviet Union. He shot down a Bf 109 on May 8 when four Hurricanes tackled with six German fighters over Vichany Bay and claimed another of these two days later. On the 12th he received credit for a double and a short time later was promoted Kapitan taking over as leader of a fighter squadron. In early 1943 he re-equipped with Bell P-39 Airacobras and on April 19 was lead-

Above: Starshij Lejtenant P.G. Sgibnev, a high-scoring ace of the Northern Fleet with his Hawker Hurricane IIB in 1942. (Author's collection)

Right: Lejtenant Nikolaj Dmitriyevich Serykh of the 21 IAP on October 15, 1944 by which time his tally was three personal victories along with four fractional credits. It has not been possible to ascertain his final tally. (Author's collection)

ing four of his squadron to engage six Bf 109s in a hard-fought duel over Vaenga and personally submitted claims for two enemy fighters. There are some Soviet reports suggesting that one of his victims was Luftwaffe ace Rudolf Müller of JG 5, but an objective investigation of the records leaves no doubt that Müller was shot down by N.A. Bokij. On May 3 he was hit hard by fighters and crashed dying of wounds shortly afterward.

Two shots of an He 111 successfully rammed by Mladshij Lejtenant A.T. Sevastyanov of the 26 IAP over Leningrad in the night of November 4, 1941. Sevastyanov lost his last battle on April 23, 1942 receiving a posthumous title of Hero of the Soviet Union on June 6, 1942. (Author's collection)

SHADRIN, Gennadij Alekseyevich
Combat record: 14 personal victories, 503 sorties of which 73 were reconnaissance and 75 ground attacks, 76 encounters.
Decorations: Gold Star of Hero of the Soviet Union on June 29, 1945; the Orders of Lenin (2), the Red Banner (5) , Aleksandr Nevskij, the Patriotic War 1st Class (2), the Red Star (2).

Shadrin was born in the Perm area on March 15, 1922 and entered military service in 1941. He went to war with the 117 GIAP in August, 1942 and subsequently fought on Caucasus, North Caucasus, South, 1st, 3rd and 4th Ukrainian Fronts. In time he advanced to Major and squadron leader. On March 16, 1943 he sustained serious injuries in an encounter with Bf 109s in the Myskhako area (SW Novorossijsk) but was able to complete the mission and nurse his crippled aircraft back to his own airfield. Upon his recovery he was greatly involved in the fighting at Rostov and over the Donbas. He racked up his 13th kill by downing a reconnaissance plane over Yugoslavia on October 14, 1944. Shadrin remained in the VVS after the war leaving active duty as a General Major in 1979.

SHAMANSKIJ, Anatolij Fyodorovich
Combat record: 16 personal victories, 1 fractional credit, 253 sorties, 61 encounters.
Decorations: Gold Star of Hero of the Soviet Union on April 10, 1945; the Orders of Lenin, the Red Banner (3), the Patriotic War 2nd Class, the Red Star.

Shamanskij was born in the Irkutsk area on November 9, 1918 and enrolled for service in 1940. He won his pilot wings at Stalingrad military flying school two years later and started flying combat on South Front on May 25, 1942. He spent his World War II career with the 156 GIAP on Crimean, Transcaucasus, Steppe, Voronezh, 1st and 2nd Ukrainian Fronts. With one air victory and 36 sorties he met the conditions for his first award, the medal "For Valor" on June 16, 1943. He took part in the big air battles of Kursk-Orel, and on July 8, 1943 claimed a Fw 190 in the vicinity of Teterevino when six Yak-1s became involved in a dogfight with four enemy fighters while engaged in an escort. Eight days later he forced down a Bf 109 on his second mission that day when he was off on another Il-2 escort. On August 4 he destroyed his fifth enemy aircraft of the Battle of Kursk with another Fw 190 near Tamarovka. For his efforts at Kursk he won the Orders of the Red Star on July 11 for one kill and 12 sorties and the Patriotic War 2nd Class on July 24 in recognition of two kills and 20 more sorties. During further assignments on Steppe Front Shamanskij managed to run up a string of five further victories. On September 6, 1943 he took on three Bf 109s over the hamlet of Borki blasting two of them out of the sky. He added another 109 in the Borodayevka area a month later, destroyed one over Pyatikhatki (W Dnyepropetrovsk) two weeks later and forced down a fifth near Verkhovtsevo (W Dnyepropetrovsk) the following day. He continued his streak during the subsequent campaigns of Korsun-Shevchenkovskij (January 24/February 17, 1944) and Yassy-Kishinyov (August 20-29, 1944) claiming three Bf 109s and one each Ju 87 and Hs 126. On September 16 he brought his score to 16 in a tussle over the Vistula River. He conducted his last mission over Berlin in April, 1945. Shamanskij served with the postwar VVS in Hungary and left active duty as a Kapitan in 1954. He died on July 16, 1965.

SHAMENKOV, Ivan Frolovich
Combat record: 18 personal victories, 200 sorties.
Decorations: Gold Star of Hero of the Soviet Union on May 15, 1946 for 15 kills, 127 sorties, 28 air combats; the Orders of Lenin, the Red Banner (3), the Patriotic War 1st Class, the Red Star (2).

Shamenkov was born in the Saratov area on October 1, 1918 and entered the Soviet Army in 1937. He had his flight training at Bataijsk military flying school and went to war right after the German attack on Soviet Russia in June, 1941. He excelled as a Starshij Lejtenant and flight leader in the 150 GIAP participating in the great aerial campaigns against the Luftwaffe on 2nd Ukrainian Front. He scored heavily in the skies above Hungary, gaining at least a single victory in November, 1944 by forcing down a Fw 190 near Jaszbereny (E Budapest). In a flurry of action over the Danube River three more of these fell to his guns between December 20-21, 1944. He stayed in the service after the war and made Polkovnik before retiring in 1958. He passed away on February 15, 1980.

SHARDAKOV, Igor Aleksandrovich
Combat record: 21 personal victories, 483 sorties.
Decorations: Gold Star of Hero of the Soviet Union on September 8, 1943 for 16 victories, 156 sorties, 18 engagements as of July, 1943; the Orders of Lenin, the Red Banner (3), the Red Star (2).

Shardakov was born in the Perm area on April 19, 1922 and started his distinguished career in 1939. He passed his pilot's examination at Kacha military flying school and destroyed his first enemy aircraft in the air on June 22, 1941. He then fought at Smolensk, Demyansk, Yelnya, Velikiye Luki and Staraya Russa and when being posted to the glorious 5 GIAP his score already had risen to four. He put up a good performance in the Rzhev area with five Ju 87s and Bf 109s in August, 1942. In December, 1942 he deployed with the regiment to Southwest Front and on the 16th was credited with its first kill in the new Lavochkin La-5 fighter when he bagged a Bf 109 near Novaya Kalitva. With a tally of 9 personal kills he met the requirements for the award of his third Order of the Red Banner and then ran up a string of seven air victories in the heavy air battles above Slavyansk and Kramatorsk in February, 1943. On the 27th he led four La-5s against a formation of 16 Ju 87s and four Bf 109s, with two Stukas being destroyed and one Messerschmitt making a forced landing. Shardakov later took over as leader of 3rd Eskadrilya and saw considerable fighting over Kharkov, Izyum, Zaporozhye, Dnyepropetrovsk, Nikopol, Krivoj Rog. He rose to Kapitan and on August 31, 1944 bagged a Bf 109 over the Sandomierz bridgehead while engaged in escorting a formation of Il-2s. He racked up his 21st kill during a fighter escort to Breslau on March 14, 1945 but later that day was pulled out of combat and sent to Air Force Academy. Shardakov remained in the VVS following World War II leaving active duty with the rank of Podpolkovnik in 1956. He passed away on August 2, 1982.

SHARENKO, Vasilij Denisovich
Combat record: 12 personal victories, 4 fractional credits, 223 sorties, 51 encounters as of November, 1943.
Decorations: Gold Star of Hero of the Soviet Union on April 13, 1944; the Orders of Lenin, the Red Banner, the Red Star (2).

Sharenko was born in the Sumy area in 1916 and enlisted in the VVS for flight training in 1938. He was graduated as a pilot at Kacha military flying school a year later and in January, 1942 was posted to the 45 IAP. During his time with the regiment he fought on North Caucasus, Southwest, South, and 4th Ukrainian Fronts and was wounded in action twice. On January 29, 1942 he reported the destruction of a Ju 87 in the Kerch area and on June 12, 1942 became embroiled in three separate encounters at Sevastopol claiming a Ju 88 before he was forced to abandon his stricken Yak-1. In 1943 he advanced to squadron leader and converted to Airacobras, sending down a Ju 87 over the Kuban on May 23, 1943. He was killed in a Po-2 on July 30, 1944 by which time he had become a Major and shturman. He was interred in Lemberg (Lvov).

SHCHERBAKOV, Viktor Ivanovich
Combat record: 11 personal victories, 7 fractional credits, 359 sorties, 35 encounters.
Decorations: Gold Star of Hero of the Soviet Union on March

6, 1945; the Orders of Lenin, the Red Banner (2), the Patriotic War 1st Class (2), the Red Star.

Shcherbakov was born in the Rostov area on January 1, 1922 and joined the VMF in 1939. He won his wings at Yejsk military flying school two years later and became a member of the 32 IAP-ChF before the war. He took part in the air battles over Kerch and Novorossijsk and was given credit for five enemy planes in the air at Tuapse while flying Airacobras. On November 6, 1943 he dispatched a Bf 109 and a Ju 87 in the Eltigen area and then combined forces with three squadron mates to destroy two Ju 52s, an He 111 and a "Bücker 133" over Kherson on the 22nd. He was promoted Starshij Lejtenant and flight leader and on January 31, 1944 he claimed two Ju 52s jointly with Mladshij Lejtenant Karpunin. Shcherbakov was killed on May 21, 1947 but the circumstances are not known.

SHEMENDYUK, Pyotr Semyonovich
Combat record: 16 personal victories, 8 fractional credits.
Decorations: Gold Star of Hero of the Soviet Union on August 24, 1943 for 13 victories, 6 fractional credits, 261 sorties, 40 encounters as of June, 1943; the Orders of Lenin (2), the Red Banner, the Patriotic War 1st Class (2).

Shemendyuk was born in the Kirovograd area on June 29, 1916 and entered the Soviet Army in 1938. Two years later he qualified as a pilot at Batajsk military flying school and started flying combat with the 158 IAP on Leningrad Front in June, 1941. He later was posted to the 157 IAP seeing a lot of combat on Kalinin and Central Fronts. On January 3, 1942 he claimed two kills while engaged in an Il-2 escort and a little later shot down a Bf 109 near Rzhev but was also hit and force-landed. On August 1, 1943 he became involved in a wild melee with enemy fighters in the vicinity of Orel and splashed two Fw 190s before hits forced him to bail out, severely wounded in his left hand. Unfortunately he developed gangrene and his hand had to be amputated. He was determined to go on flying and fitted with a prosthesis he would add three personal victories together with two shares to his score after his recovery. He later was assigned as an instructor to a fighter unit that was to claim 81 enemy planes in the air and 41 on the ground during the East Prussian campaign between October 18, 1944 and May 1, 1945. He wound up his military career as a Major in 1946 and is living in Kherson.

SHESTAKOV, Lev Lvovich
Combat record: 23 personal victories, 44 fractional credits, 400 sorties
Decorations: Gold Star of Hero of the Soviet Union on February 10, 1942 for three kills, 8 fractional credits as of September, 1941; the Orders of Lenin (2), the Red Banner (2), the Patriotic War 1st Class.

Shestakov was born in the Donetsk area on December 28, 1915 and entered military service in 1934. After completion of training at Voroshilovgrad military flying school he volunteered for combat duty in Spain. He was to emerge as one of the most accomplished pilots of the conflict with eight personal victories and 31 fractional credits which qualified him for the award of the Orders of Lenin and the Red Banner. He rose to Kapitan and was to get the newly formed 69 IAP off and running before the outbreak of the Patriotic War. By June, 1941 the unit had moved to Kishinyov from where it was putting up a spirited defense against great odds. He drew first blood on the 22nd when he managed to destroy two Ju 88s and displayed outstanding leadership and tactical skill in the dark months to follow. In August he became commanding officer of the regiment and was to develop into one of the finest combat leaders in the VVS during the early days of World War II. Under his leadership the unit enjoyed above-average success in the ferocious battles over Odessa, Kharkov, Stalingrad, and Rostov. The pilots ran up a string of 54 kills during 784 sorties in the skies above Stalingrad and an equal number of victories was claimed during its combat assignment on South Front while affording 1,393 sorties. When Shestakov was posted as deputy division commander in late 1943 9 GIAP already boasted a tally of 200 air victories. He later assumed command of the 19 IAP but on March 13, 1944 was killed attacking a large gaggle of enemy planes in the Proskurov area. He reportedly destroyed two Ju 87s at point-blank range but damaged his aircraft as he flew through the wreckage of his second victim. He was forced to bail out but due to the low altitude at which the combat took place his parachute failed to open fully and he died hitting the ground. He was buried in a common grave near Khmelnitskij. During the Patriotic War period Shestakov had added a further 15 personal victories, 11 fractional credits, 200 sorties and 82 air combats to his record and his personal overall tally by the time of his death thus had risen to 23 along with 44 shares; his final score though is quoted by some sources as 29 kills, 45 fractional credits, 600 sorties and 130 encounters. Whatever the exact figures, there can be no doubt that his war record was impressive and his great skill and decisive leadership had largely contributed to the high efficiency attained by his units.

SHEVCHUK, Vasilij Mikhajlovich
Combat record: 14 personal victories, 1 fractional credit plus 1 enemy aircraft destroyed in ground attacks, 194 sorties, 40 of which were strafings, 42 encounters.
Decorations: Gold Star of Hero of the Soviet Union on June 27, 1945; the Orders of Lenin, the Red Banner (5), the Patriotic War 1st Class (2), the Patriotic War 2nd Class, the Red Star.

Shevchuk was born in the Kiev area on August 14, 1919 and enrolled for service in 1936. He won his wings at Kacha military flying school three years later and was assigned as a

Komissar to the 247 IAP, entering combat in January, 1942. He destroyed his first enemy aircraft in the air while flying wing to 16-victory ace Kapitan S.A. Karnach soon after and chalked up a total of three kills with the Yak-1 fighter in four months combat. He was seriously wounded in May, 1942 and required 12 months to recuperate. On May 5, 1943 he was appointed deputy regiment commander and moved with the unit into the Ukraine being occupied with escorts and beating up ground targets in the assault areas. The greatest number of kills claimed in one day was 22 on an unspecified date in May, 1943 when 40 Yaks ran into 60 Ju 87s and 40 Bf 109s near Prokhorovka while flying escort for 16 Il-2s. Shevchuk's share: one victory. In January, 1945 he was put in command of the 152 GIAP and closed out his scoring as a Major over Berlin with a Fw 190 and an Hs 126 in April, 1945. He continued to serve in command positions with the postwar VVS retiring with the rank of General Lejtenant in 1979.

SHEVTSOV, Aleksandr Grigoryevich
Combat record: 15 personal victories, 270 sorties, 52 encounters.
Decorations: Gold Star of Hero of the Soviet Union on September 8, 1943 in recognition of 10 kills, 6 fractional credits, 220 sorties, 47 engagements as of August, 1943; the Orders of Lenin (3), the Red Banner (4), Aleksandr Nevskij, the Patriotic War 1st Class (2), the Red Star (2).

Shevtsov was born in the Byelgorod area on October 17, 1918 and enlisted in the Soviet Army in 1937. He was graduated as a pilot at Chuguyev military flying school three years later and fought from the very start of the war on Leningrad Front. From then on he was in continuous action putting up a good performance at Kursk, Gomel, Riga and Königsberg. By mid-1942 his score had risen to five and on July 13, 1942 he scored a triple with one each Bf 109, Bf 110 and Ju 88. He later rose to Kapitan and Shturman in the 171 IAP. Following World War II Shevtsov graduated from Frunze Military Academy in 1949 and from General Staff Academy seven years later and in time became deputy commander of the Soviet Strategic Missile Command. He retired from the VVS with the rank of General Polkovnik in 1976 and died on April 28, 1988.

SHISHKAN, Ilya Minovich
Combat record: 16 personal victories.
Decorations: Gold Star of Hero of the Soviet Union on January 28, 1943 for 12 victories, 2 fractional credits, 373 sorties and 56 encounters as of December, 1942; the Orders of Lenin, the Red Banner, the Red Star.

Shishkan was born in the Dnyepropetrovsk area on August 1, 1918 and entered military service at age 19. He passed his pilot's examination at Chuguyev military flying school in 1940 and when the Germans initiated Operation Barbarossa in June, 1941 he was serving as a flight leader in the 158 IAP on Leningrad Front flying I-16s. He successively flew Tomahawks and Kittyhawks and on March 30, 1943 shot down a Bf 109 near Leningrad, but these are the only details of his score that could be found. He fell foul of German fighters on June 21, 1943 and was interred in the Vsevolozhsk area (E Leningrad).

Major P.F. Shevelyov became an ace with the 67 GIAP. He was to make a big name for himself as a squadron leader on Central Front by downing 13 enemy planes during 189 sorties as of August, 1943 qualifying him for the award of the title of Hero of the Soviet Union on February 4, 1944. His final score is uncertain. (Author's collection)

SHISHKIN, Yakov Vasilyevich
Combat record: 18 personal victories, 244 sorties, 36 encounters.
Decorations: Gold Star of Hero of the Soviet Union on June 27, 1945 in recognition of 17 victories, 205 sorties, 27 encounters as of April, 1945; the Orders of Lenin, the Red Banner (2), the Patriotic War 1st Class, the Red Star (2).

Shishkin was born in the Saratov area on December 23, 1920 and started his military career in 1938. Two years later he completed his pilot training at Engels military flying school and commenced his combat duty with the crack 32 GIAP in December, 1943. Shishkin scored heavily in the big air battles over Poland and the Reich eventually advancing to Kapitan and squadron leader. On February 4, 1945 he shot a Fw 190 off a P-39's tail in the vicinity of Breslau and added another of these in a scrap near Steinau on March 22, 1945. He remained in the VVS until 1968 retiring as a Polkovnik. He passed away on December 27, 1979.

SHMELYOV, Ilya Vasilyevich
Combat record: 23 personal victories.
Decorations: Gold Star of Hero of the Soviet Union on August 24, 1943 for 14 personal victories, 10 fractional credits, 198 sorties, 35 air combats as of May, 1943; the Orders of Lenin, the Red Banner (5), Aleksandr Nevskij, the Patriotic War 1st Class, the Red Star (2).

Shmelyov was born in Moscow on August 2, 1917 and joined the Soviet Army in 1938. He won his pilot wings at Borisoglebsk military flying school two years later and was posted to the 4 IAP before the war. He made a big name for himself flying the Yakovlev Yak-1 in the contested air space above the Kuban in 1943. On April 23 he claimed a double leading six squadron mates to tear into an unescorted force of 35 Ju 87s near Krymskaya, four of these being shot down. A little later they reported another successful encounter with 25 Stukas escorted by four fighters and quickly achieved five more kills, with Shmelyov personally accounting for another double. In a burst of energy and skill he then chalked up eight air victories in a two day period between April 30 and May 1 to emerge as one of the highest scoring pilots of this campaign. He had by now become a Major and squadron leader and was able to give a good account of himself during subsequent combat assignments over the Baltic and Courland while flying Yak-7Bs and Yak-9s. He wound up his military career with the rank of Polkovnik in 1957 and died on December 25, 1979.

SHMELKOV, Nikolaj Ivanovich
Combat record: 18 personal victories.
Decorations: Gold Star of Hero of the Soviet Union on December 31, 1936; the Orders of Lenin, the Red Banner.

Shmelkov was born in the Vladimir area on May 5, 1912 and entered military service in 1930. Two years later he qualified as a pilot at Lugansk military flying school and in October, 1936 was one of the first Soviet pilots to arrive in Spain to fight with the Republican forces. He was able to put the good qualities of the Polikarpov I-16 fighter to best advantage, claiming 13 kills on the Madrid front over a three months period while his Escuadrilla de Moscas was credited with 53 more. In January, 1937 he returned to the Soviet Union and attended advanced command courses prior to taking over as commander of the 54 IAB of Leningrad Military District. He took part in the Russo-Finnish Winter War of 1939/40 winning the Order of the Red Banner on March 21, 1940 but no details of his efforts are available. When the invasion of Soviet Russia commenced the morning of June 22, 1941 Shmelkov was a Polkovnik and deputy commander of the 1 SAD in the Murmansk area. He later was assigned as deputy commander of the 5th Reserves Air Brigade of the Siberian Military District and commander of an air force unit of the Transbaikal Military District. He returned to combat duty in 1944 joining with the 234 IAD as deputy commander to participate in the aerial operations over Byelorussia, Poland and the Reich. On his last mission of the war his aircraft was shot up by groundfire in the Berlin area. Shmelkov came off active duty in 1945 and passed away on March 24, 1967.

This photo shows Lejtenant V.A. Shishov of the 233 IAP wearing the Order of the Red Star in September, 1942. With 13 air victories during 215 sorties and 40 encounters he met the conditions for the award of the title of Hero of the Soviet Union on November 23, 1942. (Author's collection)

SHUTT, Nikolaj Konstantinovich
Combat record: 22 personal victories, 444 sorties, 120 encounters.
Decorations: Gold Star of Hero of the Soviet Union on February 4, 1944 for 14 kills, 1 fractional credit, 315 sorties, 86 air combats as of September, 1943; the Orders of Lenin, the Red Banner (2), Aleksandr Nevskij.

Shutt was born in the Minsk area on December 30, 1916 and enlisted in the VVS for flight training in 1938. He was graduated as a pilot at Borisoglebsk military flying school later that year and gained his first combat experience against the Japanese over the Khalkhin Gol River in Mongolia in 1939. He joined combat with the Luftwaffe in December, 1941 when he was posted to the 270 IAP and from then on was in continuous action on Crimean, North Caucasus, Voronezh, Steppe, 1st and 2nd Ukrainian Fronts through the close of war. When hostilities in Europe ceased he had made Major and in August, 1945 resumed combat duty to take part in the Soviet offensive that hit and smashed Japanese Kwantung Army. He remained in the VVS until 1949 and died on March 30, 1977.

S.A. Sibirin of the 18 GIAP, an ace officially credited with 14 kills while flying Yak fighters. The aircraft's paintwork is badly weathered. (Author's collection)

SIBIRIN, Semyon Alekseyevich
Combat record: 14 personal victories, 1 fractional credit, 246 sorties, 36 encounters.
Decorations: Gold Star of Hero of the Soviet Union on July 1, 1944; the Orders of Lenin, the Red Banner (2), Suvorov 3rd Class, Aleksandr Nevskij, the Patriotic War 2nd Class.

Sibirin was born in the Orenburg area on February 12, 1914 and entered the Soviet Army in 1937. Three years later he completed his pilot training at Batajsk military flying school and was in action from the beginning of the Patriotic War. He enjoyed considerable success while serving with the 18 GIAP at Kursk in July, 1943 by which time he was a Kapitan and squadron leader and then fought at Spas-Demensk. He destroyed an He 111 near Yelnya on August 28, 1943 and got a Ju 87 two days later. He excelled in the wild air battles over Smolensk where he chalked up a string of six victories and then reported the destruction of a Ju 87 in the Vitebsk area on October 13. He converted to the sleek Yak-3 fighter and participated in the aerial campaign over East Prussia. On October 16, 1944 a Fw 190 fell to his guns in the vicinity of Insterburg and on April 13, 1945 claimed another of these near Gross-Hubniken airfield when 12 Yaks under his leadership roughly handled a gaggle of German fighters bringing the day's tally to seven Fw 190s at the cost of one of their number. He finished as deputy regiment commander. Sibirin's final score is uncertain. F.S. Gnezdilov in "Na vysotakh muzhestva" (p. 185) quotes his score as 18 as of June, 1944 when Podpolkovnik A.Ye. Golubov, the regiment commander, was badly wounded his place temporarily being taken by Sibirin. He remained in the ranks at the close of war but was killed on May 6, 1949 the circumstances not being known.

SIDORENKOV, Vasilij Kuzmich
Combat record: 25 personal victories, 350 sorties.
Decorations: Gold Star of Hero of the Soviet Union on August 19, 1944 in recognition of 17 kills, 2 fractional credits, 219 sorties, 36 air engagements as of May, 1944; the Orders of Lenin, the Red Banner (3), the Patriotic War 1st Class, the Red Star (2).

Sidorenkov was born in Orel on February 18, 1918 and started his military career in 1937. He won his wings at Chuguyev military flying school three years later and went to war on Volkhov Front with the 254 IAP in March, 1943. He was a phenomenal shot and skillful pilot and immediately began to achieve a remarkable string of victories. On August 2, 1943 he got a double with one each Fw 190 and Bf 109 near Mga and then blasted two Ju 87s and a Fw 190 out of the sky in a running battle in the Bateskij area (W Novgorod) on March 6, 1944. His La-5 in turn was badly shot up but he was able to stagger back to his own airfield. He gained further triples on April 4 and August 15, 1944 the latter occurring in the vicinity of Riga. He later rose to deputy squadron leader and went on to finish as the regiment's ranking ace of the war. During his postwar career with the VVS Sidorenkov graduated from the Air Force Academy in 1950 and from General Staff Academy in 1960. He had made General Lejtenant when he left active duty in June, 1974.

SIDOROV, Ivan Dmitriyevich
Combat record: 16 personal victories, 7 fractional credits, 400 sorties, 130 encounters.
Decorations: Gold Star of Hero of the Soviet Union posthumously on September 2, 1943; the Orders of Lenin, the Red Banner (2), the Patriotic War 1st Class.

Sidorov was born in the Volgograd area on September 24, 1916 and enlisted in the Soviet Army in 1934. He completed his pilot training at Stalingrad military flying school three years later commencing his combat duty on Volkhov Front in June, 1942 flying I-16s. His first success was a Ju 88 that skillfully had evaded his attacks before Sidorov's shells struck home at point-blank range. He really began to score while serving with the 92 IAP on Central Front. On an unspecified date during the Battle of Kursk he claimed a triple with three Fw 190s with his

254 IAP at Ivanovo in March, 1944. Starshij Lejtenant V.K. Sidorenkov, who finished as the unit's top-scoring ace, is fifth from left. (Author's collection)

squadron mates bringing the day's total to 12. On July 6, 1943 he had set course for home when he came under attack of four Fw 190s and turned for his life, his valiant fight taking place over elements of Kapitan Ponomaryov's 74th Independent Motorized Battalion. They later recalled that Sidorov managed to pull in behind one of the fighters which blew up and crashed but the others were steadily scoring strikes on him. Without hesitating he then wracked his fighter around in a tight turn to ram one of his attackers with both planes exploding in mid-air. His remains were buried in a common grave in Brusovoye, Ponyri area.

SINCHUK, Vasilij Prokofyevich
Combat record: 18 personal victories, 305 sorties.
Decorations: Gold Star of Hero of the Soviet Union posthumously on April 13, 1944; the Orders of Lenin, the Red Banner (2).

Sinchuk was born in Kazakhstan on February 15, 1921 and joined the Soviet Army in 1938. A year later he completed his pilot training at Chkalov military flying school and was posted to the 22 IAP in November. He would not start flying combat until September, 1942 when he was posted to the 662 SAP on Volkhov Front flying Yak-1s. He had a big day on October 25, 1942 when he was engaged in flying escort for Il-2s and first shot down a Bf 109 near Spasskaya Polist. While returning home he ran into three transport aircraft dispatching all of them in quick succession. He next added to his score on November 10, 1942 forcing down two "Heinkels" which were operating as artillery observers in the Podberezye area (N Velikiye Luki). In May, 1943 he was posted as a flight leader to the 254 IAP and began flying Lavochkin La-5s. In a very short time he brought his score to 11 personal kills during 240 sorties and 35 aerial encounters. On July 29, 1943 he reported the destruction of two Bf 109s in a tussle near Mga and on August 1 two more of these fell to his guns while leading three fighters on a free hunt out to the Karbusel-Sologubovka-Turyshkino areas. In the target area two Luftwaffe fighters dove to the attack but were out turned by Sinchuk. On February 1, 1944 five La-5s with Sinchuk in the lead took on 25 Ju 87s and 12 Fw 190s in the vicinity of Peredelskaya, where he destroyed two of the Stukas and a fighter before his aircraft was badly shot up, causing him to make a wheels-up landing. He was helped back to his regiment by partisans but was then killed ramming a bomber near Novgorod. Most sources suggest that Sinchuk's last combat took place on February 1, 1944, and the date for the successful encounter over Peredelskaya thus may be in error.

SIVTSOV, Nikolaj Stepanovich
Combat record: 22 personal victories, 78 sorties, 34 encounters.
Decorations: Gold Star of Hero of the Soviet Union on Sep-

tember 8, 1943; the Orders of Lenin, the Red Banner (2), the Red Star.

Sivtsov was born in the Kursk area on June 26, 1917 and enlisted in the VVS in 1939. He was graduated as a pilot at Kacha military flying school a year later and started flying combat with the 867 IAP in September, 1942. His success was immediate. He was able to make a brilliant record on Southwest Front before he fell victim to enemy fighters on September 23, 1943 by which time he had become a Starshij Lejtenant and deputy squadron leader. Confirmed victories by N.S. Sivtsov:

Bf 109s 4
Ju 87s 5
Ju 88s 2
Do 215s 2
He 111s 4
Fw 189s 1
Bf 110s 1
Hs 126s 1
Unrecorded 2

SKOBARIKHIN, Vitt Fyodorovich
Combat record: 12 personal victories, 169 sorties, 23 encounters.
Decorations: Gold Star of Hero of the Soviet Union on August 29, 1939 for 2 kills including one aerial ramming in 10 encounters; the Orders of Lenin, the Red Banner (2), the Patriotic War 1st Class (3), the Red Star.

Skobarikhin was born in Moscow on June 25, 1910 and entered the Soviet Army at age 21. He passed his pilot's examination at Engels military flying school in 1933 and was assigned to the Transbaikal Military District successively serving as a pilot, flight leader and deputy squadron leader flying R-5s and I-16s. He was then posted to the 22 IAP and saw action for the first time in May, 1939. He gained his initial success on June 22 and on July 20 successfully rammed an I-97 over Buir Nur Lake. He returned to Russia in September and next would see considerable fighting during the Patriotic War. He eventually advanced to deputy commander of the crack 10 GIAD and took part in the aerial campaigns on Stalingrad, South, North Caucasus, Voronezh, 1st and 4th Ukrainian Fronts. Skobarikhin remained in the VVS at the conclusion of the war and came off active duty as a Polkovnik in July, 1954.

SKOMOROKHOV, Nikolaj Mikhajlovich
Combat record: 46 personal victories, 8 fractional credits, plus 3 enemy planes destroyed in ground attacks, 605 sorties, 143 encounters.
Decorations: 1st Gold Star of Hero of the Soviet Union on February 22, 1945 for 25 kills, 8 fractional credits, 483 sorties, 104 air combats as of December, 1944, 2nd Gold Star on August 18, 1945 in recognition of 35 kills, 520 sorties, 119 encounters as of March, 1945; the Orders of Lenin, the Red Banner (5), Aleksandr Nevskij, the Patriotic War 1st Class (2), the Red Star.

Excellent close-up of Major V.F. Sirotin and markings on his P-39. Sirotin won the title of Hero of the Soviet Union on February 23, 1945 for 15 kills during 233 sorties flying with the 17 IAP. The 21 victories shown in this picture possibly constitute his final bag. (Author's collection)

Skomorokhov, one of Russia's finest fighter pilots and tenth ranking Allied ace, was born in the Saratov area on May 19, 1920 starting his spectacular military career in December, 1940. He won his pilot wings at Batajsk military flying school in 1942 and went to war with the 31 IAP on November 29 that same year flying LaGG-3s. From then on he was on the forefront of action on Caucasus, North Caucasus, Southwest and 3rd Ukrainian Fronts. He destroyed his first enemy aircraft in the air with a Fw 189 over Tuapse, and really came into his own once he had reequipped with the Lavochkin La-5 fighter. He was decorated with his first Order of the Red Banner on July 30, 1943 and then was promoted Kapitan. On December 4, 1943 he shot down two Bf 109s while engaged in escorting some 951 ShAP Il-2s. He received his second Order of the Red Banner on January 25, 1944 and the following month took over as leader of the "eskadrilya okhotnikov" (hunter squadron)

Legendary fighter ace N.M. Skomorokhov meets his father at his home, village of Lapot, Saratov area, in 1946. Skomorokhov's prowess became legend even before the course of the war was run. (Author's collection)

Major Skomorokhov (center) at Frunze Academy in 1946 with Podpolkovnik A.S. Simochkin and Polkovnik V.D. Morozov, who gained the title of Hero of the Soviet Union commanding the 207 Artillery Regiment. (Author's collection)

which was tasked with hunting down enemy planes and targets of opportunity behind the enemy lines even in foul weather. Within 20 days between February 1-20 the pilots bagged 10 air victories along with shooting up 46 motor vehicles in ground attacks. For two further air victories Skomorokhov was awarded the Order of the Patriotic War 1st Class on April 29 and later was able to perform brilliantly in the skies of Hungary while flying the La-5FN fighter. On December 17 he was decorated with the Order of Aleksandr Nevskij for scoring four victories and four days later combined forces with Mladshij Lejtenant Filippov to destroy three Fw 190s in a running battle with 24 German fighters in the vicinity of Velencei Lake (SW Budapest) before peeling away and turning for home. He scored a triple on January 16, 1945 when he was off with his number two flying free hunt in the Tata area (NW Budapest). While prowling around in the assigned area they spotted a large gaggle consisting of 16 Ju 52s and 38 Messerschmitts. Skomorokhov dove to attack and before the escorts could intervene had destroyed two transports. He then latched onto the tail of a fighter pouring a stream of fire into him whereupon he plunged down and crashed. Six days later a Bf 109 fell to his guns while leading six of his squadron on an Il-2 escort to Szekesfehervar (SW Budapest). While returning home, four Bf 109s were spotted, one of these being attacked by Skomorokhov whereupon it crashed two kilometers west of Szukarr. On February 17 six La-5s under his leadership tackled with six Bf 109s and four Fw 190s in the Libad area, where two Luftwaffe fighters were destroyed, one 190 by Skomorokhov. When recommended for his second title of Hero of the Soviet Union on March 16, 1945 by Podpolkovnik G.A. Onufriyenko, Skomorokhov's tally stood at 35 kills plus three aircraft, 11 motor vehicles, seven rail cars destroyed in ground attacks during 520 sorties for 509 combat hours 09 minutes. His air victories by type of enemy planes destroyed then were as follows:

Bf 109s 15
Fw 190s 10
Fw 189s 3
Ju 52s 2
Ju 87s 3
Ju 88s 2

He continued to score heavily against atrophied Luftwaffe formations in the skies of the crumbling Reich. On April 10 he was returning from a mission with his number two, Lejtenant B.S. Gorkov, but joined formation with three La-7s near

Postwar photograph of Skomorokhov when he had made General Polkovnik. He was one of the most distinguished Soviet military figures. (Author's collection)

Gerasdorf (NE Vienna) to escort a large force of Shturmoviks out to the front. Once in the target area they found themselves in a furious battle with Fw 190 fighter bombers and escorting Bf 109s. In Skomorokhov's first high speed pass one 190 blew up at 150 meters range. He next pulled in behind a second, throttled back to increase his firing time and saw numerous strikes and pieces flying off in all directions before the enemy plane burst into flames. He turned his ship around in a tight turn to make an overhead attack on several 190s that were beginning to harass Soviet ground forces and quickly achieved another kill. He glanced back to see two Germans closing in on him but Gorkov dove to his rescue, splashing one and forcing the other to break away. In all, the Red fighters reported eight kills for no losses that day. On April 26 he forced down two more 190s when six La-7s under his leadership caught 10 of these from behind north of Vienna and blasted seven out of the sky in quick succession. During his combat career Skomorokhov was never touched by an enemy bullet though he entered combat over 140 times. Podpolkovnik Onufriyenko wrote in his recommendation document ("nagradnoj list") for his second title of Hero of the Soviet Union: "Kapitan Skomorokhov is one of the best aerial fighters of the 17th Air Army. He displays courage and tenacity in aerial combat, and is a fine and capable pilot, skillfully employing his radio equipment." Until these days Skomorokhov has remained one of the most admired and respected fighter pilots in the eyes of his contemporaries. Following World War II he continued on active duty with the VVS and graduated from Frunze Academy in 1949 and from General Staff Academy in 1958. He rose to General Polkovnik in 1972 and to Marshal Aviatsii nine years later but was killed in an automobile accident in the Monino area near Moscow some time later.

SLIZEN, Leonid (Leontij) Nikolayevich

Combat record: 19 personal victories, 2 fractional credits, 222 sorties, 95 encounters.

Decorations: Gold Star of Hero of the Soviet Union on May 15, 1946; the Orders of Lenin, the Red Banner (3), Aleksandr Nevskij, the Patriotic War 2nd Class.

Slizen was born in the Kingisepp area near Leningrad on April 24, 1918 and enlisted in the VVS for flight training in 1937. He won his wings at Borisoglebsk military flying school a year later and started flying combat with the 15 IAP in April, 1943. He rapidly rose to Kapitan and squadron leader for his efforts on 4th Ukrainian Front and on January 23, 1944 was in the public eye for performing a successful aerial ramming having expended his ammunition and parachuted safely. He later fought with above-average success on 1st Byelorussian Front taking part in the Vistula-Oder campaign (January 12/February 3, 1945) and in the final air battles over the Reich. On January 29, 1945 he claimed a single in the Posen (Poznan) area and another single over the Küstrin bridgehead on February 12. He eventually made Major. He remained in the ranks after the close of war but on January 13, 1953 was killed in a car accident.

SMIRNOV, Aleksej Semyonovich

Combat record: 34 personal victories, 15 fractional credits, 457 sorties of which 100 were ground attacks, 72 encounters.

Decorations: 1st Gold Star of Hero of the Soviet Union on September 28, 1943 for 13 kills, 312 sorties, 39 air combats as of August, 1943, 2nd Gold Star on February 23, 1944 in recognition of 31 kills, 396 sorties as of September, 1944; the Orders of Lenin (2), the Red Banner (5), Aleksandr Nevskij, the Patriotic War 1st Class (2), the Red Star.

Smirnov was born in the Kalinin area on February 7, 1917 and when starting his military career in 1938 he was destined to become one of the most talented VVS fighter pilots. He completed his pilot training at Odessa military flying school later that year and cut his teeth against the Finns during the Winter War of 1939/40. He was serving in the 153 IAP at the outbreak of the Patriotic War engaging in the threefold mission of carrying out armed reconnaissance, bomber escort and ground attack at Leningrad. He opened his account with a Bf 109 while

Major A.S. Smirnov who excelled on Northwest and 1st Baltic Fronts while fighting with the 28 GIAP becoming one of Russia's deadliest aces. This photo is dated March 6, 1945. (Author's collection)

flying the Polikarpov I-153 biplane before the regiment converted to I-16s but on September 14, 1941 he was badly hit and wounded in a fighter battle managing to nurse his blazing aircraft back to friendly territory before bailing out. By December, 1941 he had brought his score to three personal kills and reequipped with Airacobras in mid-1942. He flew this fighter with notable success during subsequent assignments on Voronezh, Northwest, Kalinin, 1st and 2nd Baltic and 3rd Byelorussian Fronts to come out of World War II as the regiment's top ace. On July 23, 1942 he was leading six Cobras to tear into a formation of six Ju 87s and an equal number of fighters near Zemlyansk. Before the escorts could intervene Smirnov had destroyed one of the Stukas and then pulled in behind a Bf 109 and started to pour fire into him. The German pilot knew how to protect his skin and gave him a good fight. By continually turning, side-slipping and fish-tailing he managed to work his way back into German territory forcing Smirnov to break off and turn for home when fuel was getting low. In March, 1943 Smirnov got into a hard, protracted duel with a Fw 190 flown by a pilot of equal ability. The combat came to a rapid end when he allowed the German to get close, then throttled back allowing him to overshoot. Smirnov latched onto his tail getting strikes all over him following which the 190 hit the ground in a splash of flame. He was promoted Kapitan and in October, 1943 took over as leader of a fighter squadron. His highest scoring day was October 9, 1943 when he shot down four German planes and for this feat was decorated with the Order of Aleksandr Nevskij three days later. He then flew with great distinction over Byelorussia and East Prussia adding a string of 15 victories to his score. In January, 1945 he advanced to deputy commander of the regiment and participated in the final clashes over Berlin. His number two on many occasions was 14-victory ace Pyotr Uglyanskij. Following World War II Smirnov assumed command of a fighter air regiment and later became a fighter inspector of a military district. He retired from the VVS as a Polkovnik in 1954 and died on August 7, 1987.

Smirnov (second from left) with noted members of the 28 GIAP. They are I.I. Logvinov (11+ kills), Kozlovskij and Yu.M. Chapliyev (9+). Photo was made on June 20, 1944. (Author's collection)

Major Smirnov festooned with two Gold Stars and a range of high awards for his remarkable combat career. (Author's collection)

SMIRNOV, Oleg Nikolayevich

Combat record: 20 personal victories, 7 fractional credits, 404 sorties, 120 encounters.

Decorations: Gold Star of Hero of the Soviet Union on August 18, 1945 for 18 kills, 6 fractional credits, 314 sorties, 93 air engagements as of February, 1945; the Orders of Lenin, the Red Banner (2), the Patriotic War 1st Class (2), the Red Star, Glory 3rd Class.

Smirnov was born in the Kostroma area on July 11, 1919 and joined the VVS in November, 1941. After completion of training at Chuguyev military flying school a year later he started flying combat with the 31 IAP in March, 1943. He was not slow to get started and in no time had run up a string of victories with the Lavochkin La-5 in the Millerovo area. He next was in the thick of the fighting at Kursk where he made a claim for at least one Bf 109 this occurring between Solomino-Bezlyudovka on July 11. Smirnov then built up a good score in September, 1943 when he chalked up six kills within three days. He got a double with two Fw 190s on the 12th and destroyed another a few days later. He saw a good deal of action at Krivoj Rog and on November 28 was shot down by a Bf 109 while providing ground force cover parachuting to safety. A short time later he claimed another double with two Ju 87s while leading four La-5 fighters against a force of 27 dive-bombers near Dubossary (NE Kishinyov). A few days later Smirnov and six of his squadron were prowling around in the front-line area where he again reported the destruction of two Stukas also forcing a third to make a wheels-up landing in Soviet territory. He later rose to Starshij Lejtenant and deputy to squadron leader Nikolaj Skomorokhov. In this capacity he saw a great deal of action in September, 1944 when forces of 3rd Ukrainian Front knifed into Yugoslavia. In the course of these operations he was credited with destroying four enemy planes in the air and then was promoted Kapitan. He took part in the final aerial campaigns over Hungary and Austria and finished as the regiment's fourth ranking ace. He wound up his military career as a Kapitan in 1947 and is living in Moscow.

SNESARYOV, Vladimir Semyonovich

Combat record: 12 personal victories, 4 fractional credits, 302 sorties, 32 encounters.

Decorations: Gold Star of Hero of the Soviet Union on May 16, 1944; the Orders of Lenin, the Red Banner (2), Suvorov 3rd Class, the Patriotic War 1st Class, the Red Star (2).

Snesaryov was born in the Voroshilovgrad area on July 15, 1914 and served with the VMF between 1936-38 returning to active duty in 1939. Two years later he was graduated as a pilot at Yejsk military flying school and started flying combat in August, 1941 with the Black Sea Fleet's air service. His brothers Viktor and Vasilij were both killed in action in the dramatic battles for the Crimea with Vladimir from then on vengefully seeking out the Germans wherever they could be found. He put up a good performance while serving with the 11 GIAP-ChF at Sevastopol, Novorossijsk and Taman, and in the skies of Tuapse was given credit for six enemy aircraft destroyed. By November, 1943 he had become a Kapitan and squadron leader his score standing at about 10 kills. He next fought over Kerch and Eltigen flying Airacobras. Snesaryov served with the postwar VMF and graduated from the Naval Academy in 1954. He concluded his active duty as a Polkovnik in 1960. His final score is a matter of dispute, one source suggesting 14 kills and 313 sorties.

SOBIN, Vasilij Vasilyevich

Combat record: 15 personal victories, 379 sorties, 122 encounters.

Decorations: Gold Star of Hero of the Soviet Union posthumously on August 19, 1944; the Orders of Lenin, the Red Banner, the Patriotic War 2nd Class, the Red Star.

Sobin was born in the Byelgorod area on August 7, 1923 and entered the Soviet Army in November, 1941. After completion of training in May, 1942 he was posted to the 88 IAP a month later and entered combat flying the I-16. He drew first blood on August 18, 1942 claiming the destruction of two Bf 109s near Elkhotovo. Six days later he got a single victory thus meeting the conditions for the award of the Red Banner. He converted to LaGG-3s and ran up a string of four victories over the Kuban. On June 3, 1943 Sobin claimed a double when he and five fellow pilots tied into a formation of 30 Ju 88s escorted by Bf 109s in the vicinity of Kievskaya, where six German bombers were shot down. By August, 1943 his score had risen to eight kills during 256 sorties. He took over as leader of a fighter squadron and excelled in the contested air space over the Crimea where he added six air victories to his tally while flying some 100 sorties. On February 7, 1944 he became embroiled in a dogfight over the Kerch bridgehead and shot down a fighter but in turn was badly wounded and died of his injuries the following day.

SOBOLEV, Afanasij Petrovich

Combat record: 15 personal victories, 9 fractional credits.

Decorations: Gold Star of Hero of the Soviet Union on August 24, 1943 for 11 kills, 7 fractional credits, 322 sorties, 46 encounters as of June, 1943; the Order of Lenin, the Red Banner (2), Kutuzov 3rd Class, the Patriotic War 1st Class, the Red Star (2).

Sobolev was born in the Shilka area on May 1, 1919 and enlisted in the Soviet Army in 1938. Two years later he won his wings at Batajsk military flying school and was in action from the very first days of the war. He began a run of success once he had been posted to the 2 GIAP on Volkhov Front in April, 1942. He quickly rose to Kapitan and squadron leader and on January 14, 1943 shot down a Bf 109 at 100 meters range in the Leningrad area. On the 23rd he engaged a Ju 87 and flew in to 25 meters before firing, and after a few bursts, the enemy plane blew up. He assumed command of the regiment in June, 1943 and became involved in very heavy fighting at Kursk, Orel, and Bryansk. On July 17, 1943 16 La-5s with Sobolev in the lead engaged a mixed gaggle of 20 Ju 88s and Ju 87s escorted by 30 Fw 190s, six bombers and two fighters being shot down for the loss of one Lavochkin. In late 1944 he was promoted to Podpolkovnik. Sobolev remained in the VVS after the war and made Polkovnik but was killed on February 10, 1958 the circumstances not being known.

SOKOLOV, Anatolij Mikhajlovich

Combat record: 8 personal victories, 148 sorties, 37 encounters (Patriotic War period only).

Decorations: Gold Star of Hero of the Soviet Union posthumously on April 12, 1942, the Orders of Lenin, the Red Star.

Sokolov was born in Kishinyov on December 2, 1911 and entered military service in 1933. He qualified as a pilot at Kacha military flying school a year later and saw action for the first time during the Russo-Finnish Winter War of 1939/40. He appears to have gained a number of victories but details have not been established. Shortly afterward he became one of the original members of the 129 IAP when this was formed in Byelorussia, and was a Komissar flying MiG-3s when the Wehrmacht launched Operation Barbarossa on June 22, 1941. On the very first day of the war Sokolov had the distinction of scoring the unit's first success by destroying a Bf 109 in the Tarnovo area. In the dark months to follow he was mostly occupied with ground-support duties and reconnaissance and was credited with seven further victories consisting of three Ju 88s and one each Bf 109, Hs 113, Fw 156 and Fw 190. The squadron to which he was attached reported the destruction of 67 planes in the air plus 12 aircraft, 12 tanks, 14 field guns and 205 motor vehicles in ground attacks during 2,427 sorties and 387 individual combats at the cost of seven aircraft and four pilots. It seems likely that losses given are in fact only those known definitely to be to enemy aircraft according to the VVS practice of differentiating between losses to all causes, non-operational losses and losses to enemy action. On January 25, 1942 he fell victim to enemy fighters and was buried in the village of Lukovnikovo, Kalinin area.

Hugged up against the brutal winter, 5 GIAP aces G.D. Onufriyenko (left) and A.M. Sokolov pose for a portrait on Kalinin Front in December, 1941. Both pilots wrote distinguished records during the darkest hours of the 1941/42 air war. The date is December 8, 1941. (Author's collection)

Somov was born in the Gorkij area on September 20, 1921 and enlisted in the VVS for flight training in 1940. He completed his pilot training at Engels military flying school a year later and was assigned to the 744 IAP. He commenced his combat duty in February, 1942 and was a Mladshij Lejtenant when he destroyed an He 111 with a Yak-7B near Zhikharevo (Volkhov area) on May 27, 1943. By late June, 1943 he had brought his score to five and later was promoted Kapitan. In November, 1944 he was greatly involved in the fighting around Gumbinnen, East Prussia. He remained in the VVS after the close of war and graduated from the Air Force Academy in 1950. He came off active duty with the rank of Polkovnik in 1976.

SOKOLOV, Leonid Mikhajlovich

Combat record: 17 personal victories, 6 fractional credits, 230 sorties, 62 encounters.

Decorations: Gold Star of Hero of the Soviet Union on June 27, 1945; the Orders of Lenin, the Red Banner (3), the Red Star (2).

Sokolov was born in the Tatarian ASSR on April 28, 1908 and was with the Soviet Army between 1932-33 and from May, 1942. He went to war with the 867 IAP at Stalingrad in December, 1942 and later proved his gunnery skills over Kursk. He was appointed squadron leader and in this capacity took part in the great aerial campaigns on 1st Ukrainian Front his pilots running up a total of 45 air victories. Sokolov finished as a Major in the final battles over Berlin. Following World War II he continued on active duty with the VVS until his retirement as a Polkovnik in 1958. He died on May 12, 1981.

SOMOV, Ivan Konstantinovich

Combat record: 16 personal victories, 3 fractional credits, 276 sorties, 35 encounters.

Decorations: Gold Star of Hero of the Soviet Union on February 4, 1944; the Orders of Lenin, the Red Banner (2), Bogdan Khmelnitskij 3rd Class, Aleksandr Nevskij, the Patriotic War 1st Class, the Red Star (3).

SOMOV, Pyotr Arsentyevich

Combat record: 17 personal victories, 1 fractional credit, 102 sorties, 24 encounters.

Decorations: Gold Star of Hero of the Soviet Union on April 10, 1945; the Orders of Lenin, the Red Banner (3), the Red Star.

Somov was born in the Orel area on January 28, 1921 and entered military service in 1940. He passed his pilot's examination at Borisoglebsk military flying school two years later and was posted to the 482 IAP in October, 1943 to start flying combat. He subsequently flew with great distinction on 1st Baltic, 3rd Byelorussian and 1st Ukrainian Fronts, winning the Orders of the Red Banner and the Red Star for eight kills on 1st Baltic Front. On an unspecified date he reportedly shot down a Fw 190 the pilot of which fell into Soviet hands the records relating that he was a Major with some 20 years service and "dozens of victories" to his credit. Unfortunately Soviet sources are lacking in more detail. He rose to deputy squadron leader and during subsequent assignments on 3rd Byelorussian and 1st Ukrainian Fronts the pilots gained 46 air victories during

406 sorties. On February 7, 1944 he led four La-5s to tear into a formation of 27 Ju 87s escorted by eight fighters near Vitebsk, where four enemy planes were shot down. He scored a triple with two Ju 87s and a fighter during two sorties on February 10, 1945. After the war Somov graduated from the Air Force Academy in 1951 and from General Staff Academy nine years later. He retired from the VVS as a General Major with 33 years service in 1973. He passed away on May 8, 1979.

SOROKIN, Zakhar Artyomovich
Combat record: 18 personal victories.
Decorations: Gold Star of Hero of the Soviet Union on August 19, 1944 in recognition of 11 kills, 103 sorties and 19 air-to-air combats as of July, 1944; the Orders of Lenin, the Red Banner (3).

Sorokin was born in the Sverdlovsk area in 1917 and started his spectacular career with the VMF in 1937. Two years later he received his wings at Yejsk military flying school and entered combat with Northern Fleet's 72 IAP in July, 1941. By September he had racked up five kills in the MiG-3 fighter and on October 25 had an experience that earned him a niche in the history of aerial warfare. On that day he was off on a mission with Dmitrij Sokolov flying wing to him when they became involved in a melee with four Bf 110s. Sorokin managed to destroy two of the fighters before he in turn was badly hit and wounded in his legs. He nevertheless pulled up a high, tight turn and ended up on the tail of another 110 that was giving Sokolov a hard time. He sliced off part of the enemy plane's tail section with the propeller of his fighter and made a forced landing on a frozen lake within 30 kilometers from his airfield while the 110 plunged earthward out of control. One of his victims crashed close by and in an instant Sorokin found himself attacked by the two German airmen. He shot one of his assailants right away with his Tokarev but the other German pounced on him, trying to strangle him to death with his hands. He managed to shake him off by thrusting his sound knee into his abdomen and killed him with his remaining ammunition. Sorokin then set out for the nearest Soviet outpost where he arrived six days later. His legs unfortunately had developed gangrene and were subsequently amputated. He was determined to fly again and, fully mobile on artificial legs, he returned to his unit in November, 1942 to be put back on combat duty. On March 23, 1943 he claimed a single victory and then ran up a string of success. On April 19 he reported the destruction of a Bf 109 and next added another of these on May 13. On the 23rd he forced down a further Messerschmitt while providing top cover for naval vessels off Ejna-Guba (NW Murmansk) and destroyed another the following day. He then converted to Airacobras and after the essential working up was completed the unit resumed operations against the enemy in October, 1943. He later rose to Kapitan and Shturman. Sorokin served with the postwar VVS retiring as a Kapitan in 1955. He died on March 19, 1978.

Z.A. Sorokin who won fame for making an indelible combat record with Northern Fleet's 2 GIAP while flying with artificial legs. (Author's collection)

SPIRIDENKO, Nikolaj Kuzmich
Combat record: 15 personal victories, 6 fractional credits, 337 sorties, 85 encounters.
Decorations: Gold Star of Hero of the Soviet Union on February 23, 1945; the Orders of Lenin, the Red Banner (2), Suvorov 3rd Class, the Patriotic War 1st Class, the Red Star (3).

Spiridenko was born in the Vitebsk area on January 12, 1917 and entered the Soviet Army in 1937. He completed his pilot training at Borisoglebsk military flying school a year later and received his baptism of fire during the Russo-Finnish Winter War of 1939/40. He was serving in the 172 IAP at the outbreak of the Patriotic War in June, 1941 and subsequently gave a good account of himself on Northwest, Southwest, West and 2nd Byelorussian Fronts. He finished as a Major and squadron leader and the regiment's ranking ace. He remained in the VVS after the war graduating from the Air Force Academy in 1950 and from General Staff Academy in 1957. Four years later he was promoted General Major and left active duty in 1970. He died on December 27, 1980.

STARIKOV, Dmitrij Aleksandrovich
Combat record: 21 personal victories, 6 fractional credits, 479 sorties of which 30 were ground attacks and 11 reconnaissance, 51 encounters.

Decorations: Gold Star of Hero of the Soviet Union on January 21, 1944 for 11 victories, 399 sorties, 26 engagements as of January, 1944; the Orders of Lenin, the Red Banner (3), the Patriotic War 1st Class.

Starikov was born in the Krasnodar area on May 1, 1921 and enrolled for service in the VMF in 1939. On June 15, 1941 he won his wings at Yejsk military flying school and was posted as a Serzhant to the 32 IAP of the Black Sea Fleet's air service on July 21. Eight days later he commenced his combat duty becoming involved in the epic defense of Sevastopol. In the course of the battle he flew 113 sorties and entered combat with enemy aircraft eight times. He rose to Mladshij Lejtenant and on November 11, 1941 deployed with the regiment to the Caucasus. He would not achieve his first success until July 17, 1942 when he blasted a Ju 88 out of the sky near Tuapse. In a burst of energy and skill Starikov then racked up eight kills consisting of six He 111s, a Ju 88 and a Fw 189 between August 6 and September 5. He was promoted Lejtenant and took over as leader of a flight of Airacobras, his pilots being credited with 18 planes in the air during 471 sorties and 43 encounters over Novorossijsk and Sevastopol from January 1 until November 15, 1943. Starikov had a big day on November 6, 1943 claiming four kills in a scrap between Eltigen and Kerch with his flight bringing the day's tally to eight. In January, 1944 he became the unit's first recipient of the title of Hero of the Soviet Union for 11 kills, by which time he actually had already brought his record to 17 victories along with six shares during 450 sorties and 40 combats. He favored point-blank attacks, closing in to 30-40 meters before firing. At this range his fire was devastating. He next made a claim for two Bf 109s on March 10, 1944 while engaged in escorting Il-2s to Kulbakino airfield. Eleven days later he racked up his 21st and last victory, a Bf 110, becoming Black Fleet's top-scoring ace. He was pulled out of combat and became a pilot instructor serving in this capacity until the close of war. On October 2, 1945 Starikov was killed in a car accident.

Kapitan I.N. Stepanenko of the 4 IAP in 1944. He began to come into prominence in the big air battles over Stalingrad. (Author's collection)

STEPANENKO, Ivan Nikiforovich

Combat record: 33 personal victories, 8 fractional credits, 414 sorties, 118 encounters.

Decorations: 1st Gold Star of Hero of the Soviet Union on April 13, 1944 in recognition of 14 kills, 8 fractional credits, 232 sorties, 75 air combats as of August, 1943, 2nd Gold Star on August 18, 1945 for 32 kills, 395 sorties as of February, 1945; the Orders of Lenin, the Red Banner (3), Aleksandr Nevskij, the Patriotic War 1st Class (2), the Red Star (5).

Stepanenko was born in the Cherkassy area on April 13, 1920 and entered military service in 1940. On June 25, 1941 he passed his pilot's examination at Kacha military flying school and

Right: Stepanenko in the cockpit of his Yak-7B "17" when the unit was engaged in heavy fighting in the Kuban theater. (Author's collection)

joined with 4 IAP as a Serzhant in July. He started flying combat in the Crimea logging 60 sorties within four months prior to withdrawing with the regiment to Bryansk Front. Here he got into his first dogfight with German fighters on June 12, 1942. Recalls Stepanenko: "I tried to attract as little attention as possible. Aircraft were everywhere, spinning, rolling, diving, turning, and I could virtually smell the German gunpowder as they came flashing down. Swinging wide I was unable to get accustomed to German tactics." Three days later he drew first blood with a Ju 88 near Zemlyansk. With one kill, two fractional credits during 77 sorties on Bryansk Front Stepanenko met the conditions for the award of the Order of the Red Star. In July the regiment was withdrawn from combat and scheduled to be reequipped with Yak-7Bs at Tula. He next moved with the unit to Stalingrad where he was to make a big name for himself for piling up a remarkable score. He destroyed a Fw 189 on September 7, 1942, added a Ju 88 seven days later and then reported the destruction of two Bf 109s on the 29th. He knocked down two more of these on October 6 when Stepanenko and his wingman were bounced by four Luftwaffe fighters southwest of the Volga. When things were getting rough Stepanenko often used the head-on attack into which he had noticed the Germans were loath to enter (the Bf 109 from the experience of many Luftwaffe pilots in fact proved to be very vulnerable in frontal attacks). Following the disastrous defeat of German forces at Stalingrad he saw a great deal of action over the Kuban between May and July, 1943 and on Bryansk Front where he was to score eight more victories in 60 sorties during the rest of the year. He then took over as leader of a fighter squadron his pilots racking up 40 kills during 893 sorties after deploying to 2nd Baltic Front in 1944. Stepanenko continued to score on a regular basis in Estonia and Lithuania and destroyed his last enemy plane in an encounter over the Baltic on May 8, 1945. He stayed in the service after the close of war retiring as a General Major in 1976.

SUTYAGIN, Nikolaj Vasilyevich

Combat record: 22 personal victories, 149 sorties, 66 encounters, all Korean War.

Decorations: Gold Star of Hero of the Soviet Union on October 10, 1951; the Orders of Lenin, the Patriotic War 1st Class, the Red Star (3).

Sutyagin was born in the Gorkij area on May 5, 1923 and entered military service in 1941. He qualified as a pilot at Chernigov military flying school the following year getting his combat initiation against the Japanese in 1945 but did not see any aerial combat. He made up for that in Korea. Flying MiG-15s as a Starshij Lejtenant with the 17 IAP Sutyagin drew first blood over North Korea on June 19, 1951 and then claimed three kills in the next three days. On August 25 he blasted a Gloster Meteor out of the sky and added another of these on September 26 to bring his tally to nine. He excelled in December when he reported the destruction of five jets over the Yalu while in January, 1952 he added three more. He finished as a Kapitan and deputy squadron leader and the top ace of that conflict, and the world's number one jet ace of all time. Yevgenij Pepelyaev, the brilliant fighter pilot and commander of the 196 IAP, is credited by some sources with 23 victories but this figure would appear to be the sum of personal victories and shares. Sutyagin's record by type of enemy aircraft destroyed ran as follows:

F-86s 15
F-80s 2
F-84s 3
Meteors 2

He was rotated out of combat in February, 1952 and remained in the VVS to graduate from the Air Force Academy in 1956 and from General Staff Academy in 1964. He wound up his military career as a General Major in 1978 and died on November 12, 1986.

Starshij Lejtenant Anatolij Vasilyevich Sudarenkov of the 21 IAP with his La-5FN. The date is June 18, 1944 by which time his score stood at nine personal kills together with five fractional credits. It is possible that he added to his tally later but no details are available. (Author's collection)

K.V. Sukhov, an ace of the 16 GIAP, is being congratulated on his victory over a Fw 189 by Sasha Pokryshkin. He was awarded the title of Hero of the Soviet Union for 20 kills during 250 sorties as of March, 1945 on June 27, 1945 and wound up with a total of 22 confirmed. (Author's collection)

SUVIROV, Viktor Ivanovich
Combat record: 25 personal victories, 7 fractional credits, plus 10 planes destroyed in ground attacks, 200 sorties, 50 encounters.
Decorations: Gold Star as Hero of the Soviet Union on April 13, 1944 for 14 kills, 122 sorties and 32 air combats as of February, 1944; the Orders of Lenin, the Red Banner (3), Aleksandr Nevskij, the Patriotic War 1st Class (2), the Red Star.

Suvirov was born in the Ryazan area on April 29, 1919 and enrolled for service in the VVS in 1937. He completed his pilot training at Borisoglebsk military flying school a year later and saw action for the first time against the Japanese at the Khalkhin Gol River in Mongolia in 1939. He opened his account with an I-97 fighter early in August and ran up a total of three kills in just 10 sorties before being pulled out of combat and sent back to Russia. His next combat assignment would not come until April, 1943 when he was posted as a Starshij Lejtenant and squadron leader to the 15 IAP on North Caucasus Front. When the unit moved to Melitopol on South Front in August, 1943, he had already made Kapitan. On September 28, 1943 Suvirov and his number two, Mladshij Lejtenant Kanashenkin, were off on a front-line patrol in the Nikopol area, where they spotted eight Bf 109s prowling around. Without hesitating, they delivered a rear attack and destroyed two of the fighters on their first pass before diving away. Two days later six Yak-1s with Suvirov in the lead tackled with an equal number of Bf 109s, one of these falling to the guns of Suvirov at 50 meters range. In the afternoon he racked up his 15th kill with another of these. On November 28, 1943 he claimed a Ju 87 when Kapitan L.N. Slizen took 10 Yaks down on 15 German bombers, four of these being shot down. Suvirov later converted to Yak-9s and then achieved an impressive score against Luftwaffe transports between Ochakov-Odessa-Nikolayev-Snegirevka. Within 15 days he sent down four Ju 52s over the Black Sea and five more over Crimean soil, although the author is convinced that these figures actually consist of personal victories and fractional credits. Suvirov displayed outstanding leadership as a squadron leader, his pilots running up 61 kills during 962 sorties and 222 individual combats up to April, 1944. He was promoted Major and deputy regiment commander in early 1945 and next participated in the aerial campaign against the Luftwaffe over Poland. On January 25, 1945 he destroyed a Fw 190 in a dogfight west of Posen (Poznan) with his comrades bringing the day's tally to four. He reported another single over the Küstrin bridgehead on February 12 and on April 14 claimed a Ju 88 in the vicinity of Schwedt, the German crew being captured. Two days later he combined forces with Mikhail Baranov to destroy two Fw 190s in a pitched battle with as many as 20 German fighters. He served with the postwar VVS and graduated from the Air Force Academy in 1955. Three years later he left active duty as a Polkovnik.

SYROMYATNIKOV, Sergej Vasilyevich
Combat record: 15 personal victories, 5 fractional credits, 122 sorties for 500 combat hours, 65 encounters.
Decorations: Gold Star of Hero of the Soviet Union posthumously on May 1, 1943; the Orders of Lenin, the Red Banner, the Patriotic War 1st Class, the Red Star.

Syromyatnikov was born in Kursk in 1921 and entered the Soviet Army. in 1939. After completion of pilot training at Kacha military flying school he served with a unit in the Far East for a while before being posted to the 875 IAP on May 18, 1942 to start flying combat. He logged 59 sorties on Southwest Front between May 18 and July 31, 1942 reporting the destruction of three Bf 109s while flying the Yak-1 fighter. On July 19 he was hit by groundfire while strafing motorized infantry between Mitrofanovka-Rossosh (Voronezh area) and was obliged to carry out a force-landing. With German soldiers hurrying to the scene, Mladshij Lejtenant Makarov landed in a nearby field to attempt a rescue. Syromyatnikov shoehorned into the cockpit and Makarov managed to takeoff smoothly and fly his crowded fighter back to safety. Syromyatnikov next deployed with the regiment to Kalinin Front where he was to claim seven more kills consisting of two Fw 190s, three Bf 109s and two Ju 87s while completing 49 sorties during the period of October 26, 1942 and February 10, 1943 winning him the Order of the Red Star. He then added 16 sorties on Northwest Front from February 10 until March 16, 1943 and claimed a double with one each Fw 190 and Bf 109 near Zavaly on February 27. On March 4 he forced down another Fw 190 in the vicinity of Sheldukovo and knocked down a Bf 109 in the Rukatk area the following day. Two days later a further Fw 190 fell to his guns between Bor-Teremovo. On the 19th he fell victim to German fighters. He was a Lejtenant and deputy squadron leader at the time of his death.

SYRTSOV, Dmitrij Dmitriyevich
Combat record: 16 personal victories, 343 sorties, 120 encounters.
Decorations: Gold Star of Hero of the Soviet Union on August 18, 1945; the Orders of Lenin (2), the Red Banner (2), Aleksandr Nevskij, the Patriotic War 1st Class (2), the Red Star.

Syrtsov was born in the Chelyabinsk area on November 8, 1913 and started his military career in 1934. He completed his pilot training at Orenburg military flying school three years later and took part in the occupation of Eastern Poland in 1939. He next saw action against the Finns during the Winter War of 1939/40 and was in the forefront of action from the earliest days of the Patriotic War as a Lejtenant. He enjoyed considerable success while serving with the 866 IAP at Stalingrad, Kursk, Yassy, and over Bulgaria and Hungary, finishing as a Major. He was only once wounded in action though he entered combat over 100 times. Syrtsov remained with the VVS until 1969 retiring as a Polkovnik. He died on November 29, 1985.

SYTOV, Ivan Nikitovich
Combat record: 34 personal victories.
Decorations: Gold Star of Hero of the Soviet Union on September 8, 1943 for 19 kills, 4 fractional credits, 150 sorties, 81 encounters as of August, 1943; the Orders of Lenin, the Red Banner, the Patriotic War 1st Class.

Sytov was born in the Saratov area on June 13, 1916 and enrolled for service in 1938. He passed his pilot's examination at Stalingrad military flying school two years later but would not see action for the first time until November, 1942 when he was posted to the crack 5 GIAP to fly La-5s in the great battles over the Don River. He was not slow to get started and was decorated with the Order of the Red Banner in recognition of two personal victories along with two fractional credits after three months combat. He really came into his own during the spring of 1943 when the regiment was fighting a very successful campaign over the Donbas with Sytov gaining his fifth victory on March 29. He next scored heavily at Kramatorsk knocking down three Bf 109s and a Bf 110 in a four day period between April 3-6. He later excelled over Byelgorod, Kharkov and Izyum blasting seven more Luftwaffe planes out of the sky between July 16-18. On the 17th he had a double with two Ju 87s when Sytov, Lejtenants Nikitin and Lavrenko tied into a gaggle of 18 Stukas escorted by six Fw 190s, four of the dive-bombers being claimed shot down. In August he took the place of Kapitan Dmitriyev as leader of 3rd Eskadrilya after he had been wounded in action leading it with exceptional skill. On the 28th Sytov racked up his 28th and 29th victories with two He 111s to run the regiment's tally to 497. On October 1943 he mixed it single-handedly with four Bf 109s while conducting ground force cover near Zaporozhye and was seen to destroy one of the fighters by ramming but was unable to abandon his machine. At the time of his death Sytov was the regiment's ranking ace and remained so until late in the war when his score was outdone by Vitalij Popkov.

Lejtenant I.N. Sytov who was rated as one of Russia's best fighter pilots. He was able to build up a remarkable score before being killed in a "Taran" (ramming) attack. At the time of his death he was 5 GIAP's ranking ace with 34 air victories. (Author's collection)

TARANENKO, Ivan Andreyevich
Combat record: 11 personal victories, 265 sorties, 50 encounters.
Decorations: Gold Star of Hero of the Soviet Union on September 2, 1943 after 4 kills, 4 fractional credits, 205 sorties, and 18 combats as of June, 1943; the Orders of Lenin (2), the Red Banner (5), Bogdan Khmelnitskij 2nd Class, the Patriotic War 1st Class (2), the Red Star.

Taranenko was born in the Dnyepropetrovsk area on April 28, 1912 and entered the Soviet Army in 1933. He received his pilot wings at Kharkov military flying school a year later and gained his first combat experience against the Finns during the Winter War of 1939/40. He joined combat with the Luftwaffe at the outbreak of the Patriotic War and rapidly rose to command the 298 IAP, which later was acknowledged as one of the top fighting outfits of the Eastern Front. With Taranenko in the lead it came into prominence in the big air battles over the Kuban where its pilots racked up 112 kills while further combats would take the record to 189 air victories in 277 encounters along with 373 motor vehicles, 44 locomotives, and 385 antiaircraft and machine gun emplacements destroyed in ground attacks before he took over the 294 IAD on July 27, 1943. He next displayed outstanding leadership during the Byelgorod-Kharkov campaign with the unit reporting the destruction of 84 German fighters in August, 1943 alone. He remained in the VVS after the war leaving active duty with the rank of General Lejtenant in 1972.

TARASOV, Pavel Timofeyevich
Combat record: 24 personal victories, 235 sorties, 81 encounters as of December, 1943.
Decorations: Gold Star of Hero of the Soviet Union on April 13, 1944; the Orders of Lenin, the Red Banner (2), the Patriotic War 1st Class.

Tarasov was born in the Dnyepropetrovsk area in 1914 and entered military service in 1934. Two years later he passed his pilot's examination at Voroshilovgrad military flying school and was in the forefront of action from the very first days of the war. He made a big name for himself in the Kuban theater while flying the Yak-1 fighter. On August 28, 1943 (or August 20 according to some sources) Tarasov and his number two, Lejtenant S.P. Kalugin, were able to force a Bf 109 of 7./JG 52 to land at their own airfield after a melee near Taman. The German officer, Uffz. Herbert Meissler, was captured. It is interesting to not that this Bf 109G-4/R6 (Werknummer 14997) "White 2" was actually the aircraft of Lt. Erich Hartmann, who had left the front for a brief home leave with 17 kills at this stage of the war. Hartmann was to finish as the greatest fighter pilot of all time with 352 aerial victories. Tarasov posed for a famous set of photographs in front of his unique trophy. He later assumed command of the regiment and was promoted Major, flying with great distinction on 4th Ukrainian Front. He was shot down and killed during a dogfight over Lithuania on July 29, 1944 his score at the time of his death being at least 24. He was buried in Ukmerge.

Kapitan P.T. Tarasov (right) and fellow pilots of the 812 IAP examine the nose art of Tarasov's August 28, 1943 kill. The aircraft sports the I./JG 52 gruppe emblem denoting its former owner. (Author's collection)

TATARENKO, Dmitrij Mitrofanovich
Combat record: 16 personal victories, 598 sorties.
Decorations: Gold Star of Hero of the Soviet Union on July 24, 1943 in recognition of 14 victories, 8 fractional credits, 550 sorties, 102 air combats as of March, 1943; the Orders of Lenin, the Red Banner (3), Nakhimov 2nd Class, the Patriotic War 1st Class, the Red Star (2).

Tatarenko was born in the Novosibirsk area on May 23, 1921 and enlisted in the VMF in 1939. He was graduated as a pilot at Yejsk military flying school a year later and fought from the very start of the war. He saw a lot of action while serving with the Baltic Fleet's 3 IAP over Leningrad, Hanko and Ladoga Lake-and was called "rubaka" – broadsword – by his comrades because of his ability to knock down his opponents in one lightning strike from behind. He was promoted Kapitan and squadron leader and on January 27, 1943 claimed a double with two Ju 87s and also damaged a third while leading four LaGG-3s to attack eight dive-bombers. Tatarenko excelled during the roll-back of German forces at Leningrad in early 1943 gaining seven victories and two shares in a short time.

Tarasov explaining his victory to General Major Ye.Ya. Savitskij, commander of the 3 IAK. Note 15 victories marked on the l09's rudder. The aircraft was Lt. Erich Hartmann's personal mount, then a rising star of 7./JG 52 with seventeen kills. Hartmann finished the war as the world's highest scoring fighter ace with 352 kills. (Author's collection)

Kapitan D.M. "Rubaka" (broadsword) Tatarenko, who was considered to be one of Baltic Fleet's best fighter pilots. His nickname derives from his ability to knock his victims down on his first pass.

Starshij Lejtenant N.V. Tikhonov in flying gear beside his LaGG-3 in August, 1942. (Author's collection)

He served with the postwar VMF graduating from the Naval Academy in 1953 and from General Staff Academy nine years later. He was released from active duty with the rank of General Major in 1967.

TIKHONOV, Nikolaj Viktorovich
Combat record: 16 personal victories, 1 fractional credit, 229 sorties, 53 encounters.
Decorations: Gold Star of Hero of the Soviet Union posthumously on February 4, 1944; the Orders of Lenin, the Red Banner (3), the Patriotic War 1st Class.

Tikhonov was born in the Leningrad area on December 4, 1914 and entered the Soviet Army in 1935. He completed his pilot training at Kacha in 1939 and was serving in the 42 IAP at the outbreak of the war. He subsequently was in continuous action on Bryansk, West, Northwest and Kalinin Fronts, making Kapitan and squadron leader. At Stalingrad he was credited with destroying at least one Bf 109, the combat occurring on January 21, 1943. On September 10, 1943 Tikhonov fell foul of four Fw 190s in the Dukhovshchina area north of Smolensk.

TIKHONOV, Viktor Pavlovich
Combat record: 11 personal victories, 4 fractional credits, 140 sorties, 48 encounters.
Decorations: Gold Star of Hero of the Soviet Union posthumously on August 24, 1943; the Orders of Lenin, the Patriotic War 2nd Class, the Red Star.

Tikhonov was born in the Penza area on January 10, 1923 and enlisted in the VVS for flight training in 1941. He won his wings at Chernigov military flying school a year later and in June, 1942 was posted to the 236 IAP on Voronezh Front to start flying combat. He opened his account with a Ju 88 on August 1 and the following month deployed with the regiment to Stalingrad. He later saw a good deal of action on North Caucasus and Bryansk Fronts, but on August 15, 1943 was killed in a scrap with 10 Fw 190s and Bf 109s near Kharkov. He was a Mladshij Lejtenant and deputy squadron leader at the time of his death.

TIMOFEYENKO, Ivan Vasilyevich
Combat record: 21 personal victories, 6 fractional credits, 436 sorties, 107 encounters.

Decorations: Gold Star of Hero of the Soviet Union on July 1, 1944 for 15 kills, 6 fractional credits, 336 sorties and 76 engagements as of February, 1944; the Orders of Lenin, the Red Banner (4), the Patriotic War 1st Class (2), the Red Star.

Timofeyenko was born in the Kharkov area on December 15, 1918 and entered the Soviet Army in 1937. After completion of training at Stalingrad military flying school in 1940 he was assigned to the 168 Air Reserves Regiment in the Far East and drew first blood on June 5, 1941 forcing down a Japanese reconnaissance aircraft over the Manchurian border the enemy pilot being captured. A short time later he was greatly involved in the fighting in the Ukraine flying the Polikarpov I-16 fighter. On one occasion he was hit and wounded by groundfire while reconnoitering the Balakleya area (SE Kharkov) but was able to stagger back to his own airfield. On another unspecified date he found himself left behind with five mechanics when German tanks were closing on the airfield. Everyone scrambled for the last airplane available – a U-2 – and Timofeyenko shoehorned into the cockpit with two of the mechanics while two others held on to the wings with the fifth squatting down on the axle of the landing gear. Takeoff went smoothly and all of them escaped with a fright! He next flew a number of sorties in the I-153 but was wounded again. He gained his first success before joining with the 9 GIAP in 1942 and then was flying Yak-1s. In a fierce series of battles over the Volga River he claimed six kills and then racked up his eighth victory by downing a Messerschmitt during an escort in the Matveyev Kurgan area (NE Rostov). He next forced down two He 111s near Melitopol in October, 1943 and shot down two Fw 190s while engaged in escorting a bomber formation to Sapun-Gora in early May, 1944. He was pulled out of combat as a Major and squadron leader in March, 1945. Timofeyenko remained in the VVS following World War II and graduated from the Air Force Academy in 1955. He returned to civilian life with the rank of Polkovnik in 1972.

TIMOSHENKO, Afanasij Ivanovich
Combat record: 13 personal victories, 250 sorties, 67 encounters.
Decorations: Gold Star of Hero of the Soviet Union posthumously on June 27, 1945; the Orders of Lenin, the Red Banner (2), the Patriotic War 1st Class, the Red Star.

Timoshenko was born in the Kursk area on May 1, 1913 and enlisted in the Soviet Army in 1933. Three years later he qualified as a pilot at Rogan military flying school and was posted to the 814 IAP in December, 1942. He rose to Kapitan and took over as leader of a fighter squadron, his pilots gaining a remarkable 80 kills during 1,800 sorties and 225 encounters. On December 1, 1944 he was promoted Major and appointed deputy regiment commander and subsequently saw a great deal of action on 1st Ukrainian Front. He was shot down and killed on March 3, 1945 being interred in Lemberg (Lvov).

TISHCHENKO, Aleksandr Trofimovich
Combat record: 21 personal victories, 3 fractional credits, 397 sorties, 83 encounters.
Decorations: Gold Star of Hero of the Soviet Union on May 15, 1946 for 16 kills, 1 fractional credit, 351 sorties as of February, 1945; the Orders of Lenin, the Red Banner (3), Aleksandr Nevskij, the Red Star (2).

Tishchenko was born in the Cherkassy area on November 20, 1916 and entered military service in 1938. He was graduated as a pilot at Odessa military flying school a year later but he would not commence his combat duty until April, 1943 when he joined with the 812 IAP flying Yak-1s. Tishchenko enjoyed considerable success in the air battles over Byelorussia in 1944 claiming a string of eight victories at Vitebsk, Orsha, Borisov and Minsk. He finished as a Kapitan and Shturman. He served with the postwar VVS and graduated from the Air Force Academy in 1952. He was released from active duty as a Polkovnik eight years later and passed away on April 8, 1976.

TOKAREV, Moisej Stepanovich
Combat record: 22 personal victories.
Decorations: Gold Star of Hero of the Soviet Union on December 13, 1942 in recognition of 10 kills, 2 fractional credits, 160 sorties, 32 combats as of September, 1942; the Orders of Lenin (2), the Red Banner, the Patriotic War 1st Class.

Tokarev was born in the Donetsk area on November 9, 1913 and started his military career at age 20. He completed his pilot training at Kharkov military flying school in 1936 and saw action for the first time during the Russo-Finnish Winter War of 1939/40. He started flying combat against the Luftwaffe while serving as a Starshij Politruk in the 131 IAP at the outbreak of the Patriotic War. He was early in the public eye, drawing first blood with a Ju 88 near Tiraspol on June 22, 1941 when nine I-16s under his leadership encountered a force of 20 bombers escorted by 12 Bf 109s. He later fought at Stalingrad and enjoyed considerable success over the Kuban , scoring 14 kills in a burst of energy and skill. For his performance he was promoted Major taking over as commanding officer of the 862 IAP. The unit then made a move to the Kursk area where it fought a hard battle against large Luftwaffe forces inflicting heavy losses. On July 12, 1943 Tokarev achieved four kills in a hard-fought battle near Staryj Oskol (NE Byelgorod) but was then shot down crashing to his death.

TRUD, Andrej Ivanovich
Combat record: 24 personal victories, 1 fractional credit, 420 sorties, 120 encounters.
Decorations: Gold Star of Hero of the Soviet Union on April 13, 1944 for 18 victories, 1 fractional credit, 314 sorties, 71 engagements as of September, 1943; the Orders of Lenin, the

Red Banner (3), the Patriotic War 1st Class (2), the Red Star (2).

Trud was born in the Kirovograd area on August 20, 1921 and joined the VVS for flight training in 1940. He was graduated as a pilot at Kacha military flying school a year later and went to war with the 55 IAP flying MiG-3s in July, 1941. The unit was largely occupied with ground-support duties and by spring 1942 Trud had totaled 79 sorties and entered air combat eight times without scoring though. He really began to display his skills once the regiment had accomplished transition to P-39 Airacobras in early 1943. These were thrown into the fray at the Kuban where they fought an extremely successful battle against the Luftwaffe. Learning the ropes from the great Sasha Pokryshkin, Trud claimed single Bf 109s on April 13, 16 and 20. Further combats during the month took his tally to seven while he went on to emerge as one of the high scorers of the battle with 14 kills. He rose to flight leader and was able to perform brilliantly in the campaigns of Yassy-Kishinyov and Lemberg-Sandomierz. On an unspecified date in July, 1944 Trud and Starshij Lejtenant Zherdev tangled with an unescorted formation of Ju 87s while flying armed reconnaissance and in a furious few minutes shot down four between them. He subsequently became engaged in the heavy fighting over Poland, the Reich and Czechoslovakia, finishing as the regiment's fourth ranking ace. During his postwar career Trud graduated from the Air Force Academy in 1955 retiring from the VVS as a Polkovnik in 1972.

TSAPOV, Ivan Ivanovich
Combat record: 15 personal victories, 530 sorties, 58 encounters.
Decorations: Gold Star of Hero of the Soviet Union on July 22, 1944; the Orders of Lenin, the Red Banner (4), Aleksandr Nevskij, the Patriotic War 1st Class (2), the Red Star.

Tsapov was born in the Smolensk area on November 13, 1922 and entered military service in 1940. He had flight training at Serpukhov military flying school and was posted to the Baltic Fleet's air service. He saw a great deal of action at Leningrad and over Kronshtadt and Lavansaari from the very start of the war and later rose to Kapitan and squadron leader in the 3 GIAP-KBF. His most memorable mission occurred on February 14, 1944 when four La-5s with Tsapov in the lead attacked a formation of 18 Ju 87s and four fighters over Chudskoye Lake (N Pskov). In the ensuing melee, Tsapov accounted for a Ju 87 and a Fw 190 with his squadron mates bringing the day's tally to four. Tsapov stayed in the service after the war and graduated from the Air Force Academy in 1955 and from General Staff Academy five years later. He had made General Lejtenant when he wound up his military career in 1985.

9 GIAD luminaries. From left they are: A.F. Klubov (31 kills plus 19 fractional credits), G.A. Rechkalov (56+5), A.I. Trud (24+1) and B.B. Glinka (30) pose in front of Rechkalov's P-39Q in 1944. (Author's collection)

TSYGANOV, Yevgenij Terentyevich
Combat record: 14 personal victories, 492 sorties, 65 encounters as of December, 1943.
Decorations: Gold Star of Hero of the Soviet Union on January 22, 1944; the Orders of Lenin, the Red Banner (4), the Red Star.

Tsyganov was born in Baku on August 22, 1921 and enlisted in the VMF in 1939. He won his wings at Yejsk military flying school a year later and was in continuous action with the 13 IAP-KBF from the earliest days of the war. He quickly earned a reputation for aggressiveness and air combat skill in the wild air battles over Kronshtadt, Hanko and Leningrad, and for his efforts was promoted Kapitan and squadron leader. In January, 1943 he racked up his 18th victory with a Bf 109 although this figure conceivably contains an unspecified number of shares. On April 21, 1943 he combined forces with Kapitan V.F. Golubev to destroy three Fiat G.50 fighters near Lavansaari but no such casualties can be found in Finnish records, and the date may be in error. When hostilities ceased Tsyganov continued on active duty with the VMF assuming many assignments. In 1953 he graduated from the Air Force Academy and from General Staff Academy seven years later. He returned to civilian life as a General Major in 1968 and died on May 23, 1971.

TYULKIN, Mikhail Nikolayevich
Combat record: 15 personal victories, 254 sorties, 64 encounters.
Decorations: Gold Star of Hero of the Soviet Union on May 15, 1946; the Orders of Lenin, the Red Banner (2), Aleksandr Nevskij, the Patriotic War 1st Class (3), the Red Star.

Tyulkin was born in Izhevsk on November 22, 1918 and entered the Soviet Army in 1940. He completed his pilot training at Ulyanovsk military flying school a year later but would not commence his combat duty until joining with the 515 IAP in

May, 1942. During his time with the regiment he fought on Bryansk, Southwest, Steppe and other Fronts claiming two kills along with two shares during the great battle for Stalingrad. He took over as leader of a fighter squadron on July 10, 1943 and finished as a Major and Shturman. Tyulkin remained with the VVS until 1960 retiring as a Polkovnik.

ULITIN, Ivan Semyonovich
Combat record: 17 personal victories, 202 sorties, 64 encounters.
Decorations: Gold Star of Hero of the Soviet Union on February 4, 1944; the Orders of Lenin, the Patriotic War 1st Class (2), the Red Star.

Ulitin was born in the Rostov area in 1923 and entered the VVS for flight training in 1940. He completed his pilot training at Chernigov military flying school a year later but would not start flying combat until January, 1943 when he was assigned to the 116 IAP on North Caucasus Front. Between January 1 and February 25 he flew 51 sorties claiming a Bf 109 during the course of 13 air-to-air combats. After this modest start he deployed with the regiment to Southwest Front on May 10, 1943 where he was able to make a brilliant war record. On July 21 four La-5s were assigned to escorting a formation of Il-2s to beat up ground targets in the Mayak area (SW Kujbyshev) where they got into a fierce series of encounters with several German gaggles consisting of 18 Ju 87s, 12 Hs 123s, six Bf 109s and four Fw 190s. Leading the way into the action, Ulitin knocked down two Fw 190s and a Hs 123. On August 17 he was off on a fighter sweep to the Dolgonkaya area where he spotted four Bf 109s in a turning battle with two Yak-1s. He bore in on the enemy fighters closing to 50 meters before firing and watched his victim go down in flames while pulling away. Eight days later a Fw 189 went down before his guns but on May 20, 1944 he was shot down and killed. He was buried in Odessa.

Kapitan I.T. Tushev, a fighter ace in the 191 IAP, prepares to board his P-40, August, 1944. Tushev went through pilot training at Odessa military flying school in 1940 and was in the forefront of combat from June, 1942. Because of his success in the fighting on Karelian Front he was awarded the title of Hero of the Soviet Union on November 2, 1944. His final score was at least 15 kills during 359 sorties. (Author's collection)

Soviet servicemen examine the remains of a Ju 87 that fell victim to flak near Sevastopol in April, 1942. (Author's collection)

VASILYEVSKIJ, Yegor Vasilyevich
Combat record: 21 personal victories, 296 sorties.
Decorations: Gold Star of Hero of the Soviet Union on May 15, 1946 for 17 kills, 2 fractional credits, 217 sorties, 54 encounters as of November, 1944; the Orders of Lenin, the Red Banner (4), Aleksandr Nevskij, the Patriotic War 1st Class (2), the Red Star.

Vasilyevskij was born in the Vitebsk area on January 1, 1922 and entered the Soviet Army in 1939. He qualified as a pilot at Odessa military flying school a year later but it was not until May, 1943 that he commenced his combat duty when being posted to the 151 GIAP. He subsequently served with distinction over Byelgorod, Poltava, Kremenchug, Rumania, Hungary, Austria and Czechoslovakia. He claimed at least a single in the skies of Hungary with a Fw 190 on October 6, 1944, by which time he was a Starshij Lejtenant. Vasilyevskij finished as a Kapitan and squadron leader. He served with the postwar VVS and graduated from the Air Force Academy in 1955 retiring as a Polkovnik three years later.

VASKO, Aleksandr Fyodorovich
Combat record: 15 personal victories, 303 sorties, 49 encounters all in World War II.

Starshij Lejtenant M.Ya. Vasilyev of the 4 GIAP-KBF made a big name for himself in the air over Khanko by claiming two kills along with 16 shares during 325 sorties as of April, 1942. His feats won him the title of Hero of the Soviet Union on June 14, 1942 but on May 4, 1943 he failed to return from a mission. His final total is uncertain. (Author's collection)

Starshij Lejtenant V.I. Vedeneyev, skillful fighter tiger of the 159 IAP. He saw action for the first time in April, 1942 and was to survive the Leningrad ordeal. Six of his kills came in a two day period between April 21-22, 1944. He received the title of Hero of the Soviet Union on February 23, 1945 and finished with a final tally of at least 24 air victories. (Author's collection)

Decorations: Gold Star of Hero of the Soviet Union on May 15, 1946; the Orders of Lenin, the Red Banner (3), the Patriotic War 1st Class (2), the Patriotic War 2nd Class, the Red Star.

Vasko was born in the Poltava area on August 29, 1920 and joined the Soviet Army in 1940. The following year he passed his pilot's examination at Chuguyev military flying school and fought from the very start of the war. Vasko won fame while serving with the glorious 176 GIAP on 1st Byelorussian Front during the later stages of the war. He closed out his scoring with a double over Berlin on April 18, 1945. He remained in the VVS at the conclusion of the war and later proved his gunnery skills with 176 GIAP in Korea flying MiG-15s. On December 1, 1951 he blasted a Gloster Meteor out of the sky but no further details are available. In 1956 he graduated from the Air Force Academy and came off active duty in 1960 with the rank of Polkovnik.

VERNIKOV, Yakov Ilyich
Combat record: 14 personal victories, 1 fractional credit, 302 sorties, 64 encounters.
Decorations: Gold Star of Hero of the Soviet Union on November 18, 1944; the Orders of Lenin (2), the Red Banner (4), the Patriotic War 1st Class, the Red Star (3).

Vedeneyev with his Lavochkin La-5 fighter. (Author's collection)

Vernikov was born in Spas-Demensk on October 31, 1920 and entered military service in 1938. Two years later he was graduated as a pilot at Odessa military flying school and became a member of the 234 IAP before the war. He was in continuous action from the very first days of the war and had his greatest day in the air on March 25, 1943 when he combined forces with Kapitan N.K. Durakov to destroy four enemy fighters in a scrap near Batajsk. He reported the destruction of two Bf 109s on August 2, 1943 and later was posted to the 147 GIAP eventually making Kapitan. Vernikov remained in the ranks until 1975 retiring as a Major with 37 years service.

VILYAMSON, Aleksandr Aleksandrovich

Combat record: 18 personal victories, 6 fractional credits, 382 sorties, 66 encounters.

Decorations: Gold Star of Hero of the Soviet Union on June 27, 1945; the Orders of Lenin, the Red Banner (2), Aleksandr Nevskij, the Patriotic War 1st Class (2), the Patriotic War 2nd Class, the Red Star (2).

Vilyamson was born in the Kalinin area on August 13, 1918 and enrolled for service in the VVS in 1940. He won his wings at Kacha military flvina school on June 22, 1941 – the day the Germans initiated Operation Barbarossa – and was posted to the 298 IAP. He opened his account with an "He 113" over the Donbas in December, 1941 but was to achieve a large number of his victories on Airacobras in the big air battles over the Kuban, the Crimea, Poland and the Reich. He finished as a Kapitan and squadron leader. He served with the postwar VVS until 1955 coming off active duty as a Polkovnik.

VISHNYAKOV, Ivan Alekseyevich

Combat record: 20 personal victories, 3 fractional credits, 296 sorties, 125 of them being escorts, 48 reconnaissance, 91 patrols, 11 free hunts, and 100 encounters.

Decorations: Gold Star of Hero of the Soviet Union on February 23, 1948; the Orders of Lenin, the Red Banner (4), Aleksandr Nevskij, the Patriotic War 1st Class (2), the Red Star.

Vishnyakov was born in the Lipetsk area on June 15, 1917 and entered military service in 1937. He graduated as a pilot at Borisoglebsk military flying school a year later following which he was assigned as a pilot instructor to a flying school in Siberia. In July, 1941 he was posted to the 296 IAP to enter combat in the Kirovograd area flying the Polikarpov I-16 fighter. The regiment converted to MiG-3s three months later but Vishnyakov was then posted to the 171 IAP to go into action at Tula. He was promoted squadron leader in December, 1941 and on June 27, 1942 forced down a Ju 87 in the vicinity of Voronezh where four Yaks took on 16 Stukas escorted by four Bf 109s. During the heavy air battles over Orel he frequently flew as wingman for Viktor Aleksandryuk while on August 27, 1942 he was leading four of his squadron on an escort for six Il-2s to an enemy airfield in the Orel area. 21 Bf 109s reportedly rose to engage them but lost five of their number while the Shturmoviks were credited with shooting up 10 Ju 88s on the ground. The regiment later reequipped with La-5s and on July 12, 1943 he combined forces with Starshij Serzhant Borisov to destroy two Fw 190s while flying escort for Il-2s. The following day he personally claimed a double when 12 La-5s tied into a force of 60 enemy planes forming for an attack on Soviet ground forces in the vicinity of Orel, 11 of these being shot down. On July 17, 1944 he scored another double by destroying two Fw 190s near Rezekne (Latvia), where eight La-5s under his leadership became embroiled in a scrap with 12 German fighters. He converted to La-7s later that month and a short time later acquired his 13th victory while flying aircraft "76." He took over as commander of 1st Eskadrilya which would be credited with 86 enemy aircraft in the air and 19 on the ground during 2,140 sorties. He later rose to Major and deputy regiment commander closing out his scoring with a single Fw 190 on February 23, 1945. In late June, 1945 he was posted to the Far East joining the 147 IAP which was at the time operating Yak-9s. He flew his first combat sortie against the Japanese on August 9 and logged 17 more in a very short time. Vishnyakov remained in the VVS after the war and graduated from the Air Force Academy in 1953. He came off active duty as a General Major in 1975.

VOLKOV, Viktor Fyodorovich

Combat record: 15 personal victories, 8 fractional credits, 236 sorties, 59 encounters.

Decorations: Gold Star of Hero of the Soviet Union on July 1, 1944; the Orders of Lenin (2), the Red Banner, Aleksandr Nevskij, the Patriotic War 1st Class, the Red Star.

Volkov was born in the Yaroslavl area on February 7, 1917 and started his military career in 1936. Two years later he completed his pilot training at Odessa military flying school being posted to the 157 IAP before the war. On an unspecified date in August, 1941 Volkov and his wingman were successful in breaking up a formation of 10 bombers approaching Kholm with one of them falling to his guns. A little later he was leading six of his comrades in a strafing attack on an airfield near Borovsk, where they made claims for 30 planes destroyed or damaged. Volkov was hit hard by antiaircraft fire but managed to bring his damaged aircraft back. On August 9, 1942 he forced down a Ju 87 near Rzhev but was in turn shot down by the rear gunner of another returning to his unit soon after. He was promoted Major and assumed command of the regiment displaying high-caliber leadership in the skies above Kursk and Byelorussia. He had his greatest day in the air on February 23, 1944 taking 12 Yaks against 42 Luftwaffe planes in the Rogachyov area (NW Gomel), and in a furious few minutes his pilots shot down 12 German aircraft, a double by Volkov. When hostilities ceased he was a Podpolkovnik and had been wounded twice in the course of his combat duty. Following World War II he remained in the ranks and graduated from the Air Force Academy in 1951 retiring as a Polkovnik in 1972.

VOLOSHIN, Aleksandr Iovich
Combat record: 16 personal victories, 4 fractional credits, 293 sorties, 65 encounters.
Decorations: Gold Star of Hero of the Soviet Union on June 27, 1945; the Orders of Lenin, the Red Banner (3), the Patriotic War 1st Class, the Red Star (3).

Voloshin was born in Dnyepropetrovsk on January 1, 1922 and joined the VVS in April, 1940. He won his wings at Kacha military flying school a year later and started flying combat right after the German attack on Soviet Russia. He served with distinction with the 107 GIAP on 1st Ukrainian Front his biggest day coming on August 22, 1944 when he and his number two, Mladshij Lejtenant A.I. Penyaz, tangled with four Fw 190s while prowling around in the San River area (SE Poland). One enemy fighter came all to pieces after his first burst but he then wound up with a second on his tail, this proving to be flown by a really skillful pilot. His cockpit soon began to fill with fumes as his aircraft was trailing heavy smoke. He broke hard and wracked his fighter around in a tight turn to engage the 190 head-on, slicing off part of its wing in a deliberate ramming attack. The German fell out of control whilst Voloshin dove away from the fight attempting to bring his blazing ship back to friendly territory. He was struck by two more 190s but by skillful maneuvering he escaped their attacks and sent one of them crashing down before crash-landing behind the Soviet lines, sustaining serious burns. By the time hostilities closed he had made Starshij Lejtenant and deputy squadron leader. He remained with the VVS until 1972 retiring as a Polkovnik.

VOROBYOV, Ivan Alekseyevich
Combat record: 6 personal victories, 6 fractional credits plus numerous ground targets, 217 sorties in Il-2s and 171 Po-2 nightbomber sorties.
Decorations: 1st Gold Star of Hero of the Soviet Union on August 19, 1944, 2nd Gold Star on June, 29, 1945; the Orders of Lenin, the Red Banner (2), Aleksandr Khmelnitskij 3rd Class, Aleksandr Nevskij, the Patriotic War 1st Class (2), the Patriotic War 2nd Class, the Red Star (2).

Vorobyov was born in the Tula area on August 26, 1921 and started his distinguished career in the VVS in 1940. The following year he completed his pilot training at Tambov military flying school and in August, 1942 commenced his combat duty flying Po-2 nightbombers. He was seriously wounded at Stalingrad in January, 1943 and upon his recovery was assigned

S.Ye. Vojtenko gave a good account of himself fighting with Black Sea Fleet's 6 GIAP from the very start of the war. He made Major and deputy regiment commander winning the title of Hero of the Soviet Union on November 5, 1944 in recognition of 12 kills during 241 sorties and 45 air combats. His total score was 13. His Yak in this picture displays the Guards emblem and the Order of the Red Banner. (Author's collection)

to the crack 76 GShAP flying Shturmoviks. Vorobyov excelled in the hellish inferno along the Molochnaya River south of Zaporozhye and next logged 23 sorties during the fighting for Sevastopol in May, 1944. With three air victories, plus 12 enemy planes and nine motor vehicles destroyed in ground attacks during 117 sorties he met the conditions for the award of his first title of Hero of the Soviet Union. He later flew with great distinction in Byelorussia and Lithuania and wrought havoc in the destruction of German ground forces at Königsberg and Pillau and in Courland. He submitted claims for three more kills, six shares, eight tanks, eight self-propelled guns and 33 motor vehicles until the end of the war, by which time he had become a Major and squadron leader. During his postwar career Vorobyov served as squadron leader and regiment commander. In 1952 he graduated from the Air Force Academy concluding his active duty with the rank of Polkovnik in 1973.

VOROZHEJKIN, Arsenij Vasilyevich
Combat record: 52 personal victories, 13 fractional credits, 300 sorties, 90 encounters.
Decorations: 1st Gold Star of Hero of the Soviet Union on February 4, 1944 in recognition of 19 kills, 78 sorties and 32 encounters, 2nd Gold Star on August 19, 1944 for 11 more kills during 28 sorties and 14 air combats; the Orders of Lenin, the Red Banner (4), Suvorov 3rd Class, Aleksandr Nevskij, the Patriotic War 1st Class, the Red Star (2).

Vorozhejkin was born in the Gorkij area on October 28, 1912 and when entering the Soviet Army in 1931 he was destined to become one of Russia's finest fighter pilots and the sixth ranking Allied ace of World War II. Following three years with cavalry units he had flight training at Kharkov military flying school winning his wings in 1937. He gained his first combat experience with the 22 IAP against the Japanese in Mongolia in 1939, flying his first combat sortie on June 27. He emerged as one of the high-scorers of the conflict with six kills during 160 sorties for some 140 combat hours and 30 air combats within 10 weeks. Vorozhejkin next participated in the Russo-Finnish Winter War of 1939/40 but did not seem to have added to his score. He attended the Air Force Academy in 1942 and when assigned to the battered 728 IAP on Kalinin Front in September, he already was a tough veteran with 600 hours in fighter aircraft under his belt. The unit had achieved 100 air victories with the Polikarpov I-16 but suffered fairly heavy casualties at this stage having only six planes and 10 pilots on strength. Recalls Vorozhejkin: "To successfully attack enemy aircraft that were some 100 kilometers faster was quite an impossible task. We just managed to cover the Shturmoviks or to drive the enemy off. They seemed to have all the advantages on their side: speed, altitude and even initiative. With our I-16s we were in no position to overhaul or to accelerate away from them. We only had superior maneuverability which permitted us to effectively use the defensive circle. But if the Fascists managed to break up this circle, the outcome was a foregone conclusion!" The regiment converted to Yak-7Bs in mid-March, 1943 and Vorozhejkin was promoted Kapitan and squadron leader in July to become heavily involved in the fighting at Kursk. He drew first blood against the Luftwaffe on the 14th while leading a fighter sweep of six Yaks. Between Bogorodetskoye-Velenikhino-Shakovo they got into a tussle with some 40 Ju 87s and six Bf 109s. Vorozhejkin ordered the attack and immediately bounced a Stuka and closed to 50 meters before firing. He continued firing until he was within 25 meters and pieces barely missed him as the bomber exploded. He then got in behind another, pulled in to pointblank range and poured a stream of fire into it until it went down to explode on the ground and combined forces with one of his squadron mates to destroy a third. In all, they claimed nine kills for no losses. He now began to pile up a tremendous score. He had a big day on August 4 while leading six of his squadron against 12 Ju 87s escorted by 10 Bf 109s between Rakovo-Pushkarnoye-Tomarovka, where eight German planes were blasted out of the sky three Stukas and a Messerschmitt by Vorozhejkin. He next added a double with two Ju 87s ten days later. In two months combat his pilots had accounted for 36 kills with two more damaged although it seems likely that most of the victories had been gained by Vorozhejkin himself. By September 20 his score had risen to 19 making him the regiment's ranking ace. He had adopted hit-and-run tactics, positioning himself in the sun and hurtling down on the enemy to hit him from pointblank range and climb back to altitude using his greater speed. Seven Yaks under his leadership again had a field day on November 6 while assigned to providing assault area cover for

Major A.V. Vorozhejkin, whose name stands out in the annals of the VVS. A veteran of the undeclared war with the Japanese in Mongolia in 1939 with six kills and of the Winter War against Finland, Vorozhejkin later rose to deputy commander of the 728 IAP piling up a tremendous score against the Luftwaffe. He had chalked up some 50 kills when he was grounded to become an instructor. He claimed one of the few Arado Ar 234 jet bombers that fell foul of the VVS over Berlin in April, 1945. (Author's collection)

elements of 3rd Guards Tank Army. In the vicinity of Byelaya Tserkov (SW Kiev) they stormed into two formations of dive-bombers, 11 of these being shot down for no losses. In February, 1944 he was well qualified for the award of his first title of Hero of the Soviet Union for 19 kills by which time his tally already stood at 27. He scored another triple with three Ju 87s on April 19, 1944 while leading six Yaks to engage a large Luftwaffe formations over the Carpathians and in a furious combat, five Stukas and a Fw 190 were shot down. On May 1 he reported the destruction of a Bf 109 while engaged in a Pe-2 escort to bring his score to 45 confirmed victories. He rose to Major and deputy regiment commander but in October, 1944 was pulled out of combat to spend the rest of the war as a front-line instructor after repeated conflicts with the unit's commander, V.S. Vasilyaka, over "senseless orders." Henceforth he saw very little combat but in April, 1945 downed one of the elusive Arado Ar 234 jets. He served with the postwar VVS to attain high rank serving as regiment and division commander prior to his being appointed deputy commander of the Black Sea Fleet's air defense forces. In 1952 he graduated from the General Staff Academy and retired from the VVS with the rank of General Major in 1957.

VOSTRUKHIN, Pyotr Mikhajlovich

Combat record: 28 personal victories.

Decorations: Gold Star of Hero of the Soviet Union on May 1, 1943 for 12 kills, 3 fractional credits, 83 sorties; the Orders of Lenin, the Red Banner (2), the Patriotic War 1st Class, the Red Star.

Vostrukhin was born in the Moscow area on July 15, 1921 and started his military career in 1940. Upon completion of pilot training at Borisoglebsk military flying school later that year he served as an instructor for a while prior to receiving orders to the 271 IAP in October, 1942. He started flying combat with the Yakovlev Yak-7 fighter and immediately proved his gunnery skills seeing a great deal of action over Demyansk. On March 16, 1943 he knocked down a Fw 190 between Ramushovo-Kobylkino and had a big day on May 1 when he scored four kills during two sorties. On that day he took off with five squadron mates meeting seven Fw 190s, six of these being claimed shot down. Later in the afternoon seven Yaks reported attacking a formation of 18 Ju 87s escorted by 10 Fw 190s and four Bf 109s claiming four kills. Vostrukhin next performed brilliantly in the heavy air battles over Kursk and on July 12 claimed a double when six of his squadron tackled with eight Bf 110s and six Bf 109s sending five German fighters down. Eleven days later he was shot down in an encounter with enemy fighters and crashed, being killed instantly. He was interred in Mokhovoye (E Orel), and in him the regiment lost its highest scoring ace.

VYBORNOV, Aleksandr Ivanovich

Combat record: 20 personal victories, 190 sorties, 42 encounters.

Decorations: Gold Star of Hero of the Soviet Union on June 27, 1945; the Orders of Lenin, the Red Banner (4), Aleksandr Nevskij, the Patriotic War 1st Class (3), the Red Star (2).

Vybornov was born in the Moscow area on September 17, 1921 and enlisted in the VVS for flight training in 1939. He graduated as a pilot at Chuguyev military flying school a year later and in October, 1942 was posted to the 728 IAP on Kalinin Front to start flying combat in I-16s. He was decorated with the medal "For Military Merit" for 30 combat sorties and one confirmed air victory and learnt the ropes from the great Arsenij Vorozhejkin flying as his number two on many occasions. Realizing that they could depend on each other they would team up to form a deadly fighting duo until well into 1944 when both had already made squadron leader. In March, 1943 the regiment had accomplished transition to Yak-7Bs deploying to Buturkinovka near Kursk to become heavily engaged in the major clashes for the Kursk salient. Vybornov claimed a Ju 87 on July 13 and next day added two more kills. He was promoted flight leader and on one particular day in August he landed in enemy lines to pick up A. Chetveryakov, who had force-landed after being wounded by the gunner of an He 111, and successfully flew his crowded Yak back to safety. He racked up his 10th victory on September 11 combining forces with Mikhail Sachkov to destroy a Ju 87 which qualified him for the Order of the Red Banner. He converted to Yak-9s and took part in the aerial campaign along the Dnyepr. He was once shot down abandoning his aircraft and returned to his unit a short time later. He took over as leader of a fighter squadron in late 1943 by which time his unofficial tally was 21 kills. During the great air battles of 1944 he gained six more victories and flew his last combat sortie in the vicinity of Prague in 1945. In all, Vybornov personally claimed 28 victories although eight of these were never officially confirmed:

Bf 109s	10
Fw 190s	5
Ju 87s	10
Ju 88s	2
unidentified	1

He remained with the regiment at the close of hostilities and had become a Major and deputy regiment commander when moving with it to Kacha airfield on the Crimea. In 1947 he attended the Air Force Academy in Monino and in 1953 was posted as commander of a fighter regiment to Poland. Later he took command of a reconnaissance air regiment and by 1958 had been assigned as commander of a fighter division. In 1965 he was put in charge of PVO fighter pilot training. In 1967 the Soviet command considered plans for massive Arab support one calling for the deployment of substantial forces to the

Middle East including seven VVS and five PVO regiments. A military delegation headed by General Polkovnik P.N. Lashchenko went to Egypt to investigate into the feasibility of these plans with Vybornov being earmarked for command of the Soviet air forces. In Egypt he flew some 12 sorties within three months every single one of them having to be authorized by the Ministry of Defense. He was twice tasked with reconnoitering Israeli territory in a MiG-25 but was not opposed by fighters. He was decorated with the Order of the Red Banner for his efforts in the Middle East.

In the night of July 22, 1941 the Luftwaffe dispatched the first bombing raid against the Soviet capital. Eight days later this Ju 88 "F6+AK" of Aufkl.Gr.(F) 122 reposes on its belly in Moscow's Sverdlov Square. Local people are taking a great interest in this war booty. (Author's collection)

YAKHNOV, Gennadij Mikhajlovich

Combat record: 12 personal victories, 5 fractional credits, 572 sorties, 112 encounters.

Decorations: Gold Star of Hero of the Soviet Union on August 22, 1944 for 8 victories, 5 fractional credits, 518 sorties, 52 air engagements as of April, 1944; the Orders of Lenin, the Red Banner (3), the Patriotic War 1st Class, the Red Star.

Yakhnov was born in the Ivanov area on August 30, 1918 and joined the Soviet Army in 1937. He was graduated as a pilot at Perm military flying school two years later and entered combat as a Mladshij Lejtenant in the 33 IAP early in the war. He took part in the epic defense of Brest but a month later the fortress had to capitulate and Soviet forces were driven back. The regiment performed brilliantly against great odds but was gradually whittled down. By August, when the unit with all remaining aircraft was withdrawn to the Smolensk area, Yakhnov's score had risen to 5 kills including shares. From then on he was in continuous action fighting in the great battle for Moscow and at Staraya Russa. In 1942 he became a deputy squadron leader and in May, 1943 took over as leader of a fighter squadron when the regiment was seeing a great deal of action on Volkhov Front. He finished as commanding officer of the 33 IAP. Yakhnov remained with the VVS until 1958 retiring as a Polkovnik.

YAKIMENKO, Anton Dmitriyevich

Combat record: 13 personal victories, 35 fractional credits, 241 sorties, 29 encounters.

Decorations: Gold Star of Hero of the Soviet Union on August 29, 1939 for 3 kills; the Orders of Lenin, the Red Banner (4), Suvorov 3rd Class, the Patriotic War 1st Class (2), the Red Star (3).

Yakimenko was born in the Donetsk area on December 5, 1913 and enlisted in the VVS at age 21. He completed his pilot training at Voroshilovgrad military flying school in 1935 and during his first combat assignment managed to put up a good performance against the Japanese in Mongolia in 1939. He entered combat in May serving in the 22 IAP and was given credit for three victories before his being wounded in action on July 12. Successive assignments included fighter inspector and deputy commander of the 67 IAP before the outbreak of the Patriotic War. He joined combat with the Luftwaffe in June, 1941 and during his World War II career flew on Southwest, Northwest, Kalinin, Voronezh and 2nd Ukrainian Fronts being twice wounded in action. He rose to deputy commander of the 427 IAP and finished as commander of the 150 GIAP displaying outstanding leadership in the skies of Leningrad, Stalingrad and Kursk and over Rumania, Hungary, Austria and Czechoslovakia. He claimed a Bf 109 near Jaszbereny (E Budapest) in November, 1944 while his pilots excelled in a burst of activity along the Danube River by claiming 11 kills between December 20-21, 1944. Yakimenko remained in the VVS after the war assuming command of a fighter air division. In 1955 he graduated from Voroshilov General Staff Academy and was appointed deputy chairman of DOSAAF Central Committee. He left active duty as a General Lejtenant in 1972.

YASHIN, Viktor Nikolayevich

Combat record: 16 personal victories, 184 sorties, 42 encounters.

Decorations: Gold Star of Hero of the Soviet Union on October 26, 1944; the Orders of Lenin, the Red Banner (2), the Patriotic War 1st Class (2).

Yashin was born in Khabarovsk on January 29, 1922 and entered military service in 1938. Two years later he won his pilot wings at Kacha military flying school and went to war with the 133 IAP in July, 1942. During his time with the regiment Yashin flew with great distinction on 1st Byelorussian Front and rapidly rose to Kapitan and squadron leader. He scored most of his victories during the last months of the war engaging in heavy action during the Vistula-Oder campaign and over the Oder bridgehead at Küstrin. He claimed two kills between March 5-8, 1945 and closed out his scoring with a double on May 1. He retired from the VVS in 1949 and died on October 28, 1952.

YEDKIN, Viktor Dmitriyevich
Combat record: 15 personal victories, 3 fractional credits, 294 sorties, 53 encounters.
Decorations: Gold Star of Hero of the Soviet Union on August 18, 1945; the Orders of Lenin, the Red Banner (3), Aleksandr Nevskij, the Patriotic War 1st Class (3), the Red Star (2).

Yedkin was born in the Kirovograd area on June 21, 1917 and entered the Soviet Army in 1937. He completed his pilot training at Chuguyev military flying school three years later and fought from the very start of the war. He was with the 485 IAP through World War II fighting in the great aerial campaigns on Leningrad, Northwest, 1st and 2nd Baltic Fronts. Flying Hurricanes on Northwest Front he was shot down and wounded by Bf 109s near Kirilovshchina in May, 1942 after he had knocked down a fighter. On June 19 he brought his score to five with another Bf 109 when seven Hurricanes with Major Zimin in the lead reported 10 kills in a running battle with 27 German aircraft. He bagged another Bf 109 while attacking a formation of 20 Ju 88s with his wingman near Vasilyevshchina on July 9 which won him the Order of the Patriotic War 1st Class. On March 13, 1943 he destroyed a Fw 190 in a head-on encounter in the vicinity of Staraya Russa. He later rose to Major and in 1944 was greatly involved in the fighting in Byelorussia. He got another single on June 26 leading his squadron mates against a bomber formation between Ulla-Beshenkovichi (W Vitebsk), three of these being shot down. He served with the postwar VVS making Polkovnik. Yedkin wound up his military career in 1955.

Flight leader Aleksandr Fyodorovich Yakovenko of the 21 IAP with his Lavochkin La-5. He gained at least five victories in some 120 sorties. The date is June 18, 1944. (Author's collection)

I.F. Yakubov was a deputy squadron leader during his World War II combat days with the 653 IAP. He earned the title of Hero of the Soviet Union for his exploits on February 22, 1943 and achieved a total of at least 10 confirmed victories in just 23 combats. The photo is dated May, 1945. (Author's collection)

YEFIMOV, Matvej Andreyevich
Combat record: 9 personal victories, 29 fractional credits, 350 sorties, 106 encounters.
Decorations: Gold Star of Hero of the Soviet Union on June 14, 1942 in recognition of 3 kills, 19 fractional credits, 280 sorties as of April, 1942; the Orders of Lenin (2), the Red Banner.

Starshij Lejtenant Ivan Nikiforovich Yemelyanenko of the 21 IAP, photographed on October 15, 1944 with a Yak fighter. His total score was at least nine personal kills together with nine more fractional credits. (Author's collection)

Yefimov was born in the Smolensk area in 1909 and enrolled for service in the VMF in 1931. He graduated from flight training at Yejsk military flying school following which he was involved in training pilots. He was posted to the Black Sea Fleet's 5 IAP before the war and on June 22, 1941 flew four sorties claiming one enemy aircraft destroyed. He rapidly advanced to flight leader and on September 11, 1942 became embroiled in two separate encounters coming away with two kills. He was shot down and killed on January 7, 1943 being buried in Kronshtadt.

YEFREMOV, Vasilij Vasilyevich
Combat record: 12 personal victories.
Decorations: Gold Star of Hero of the Soviet Union on May 5, 1942 for five kills, 172 sorties as of December, 1941; the Orders of Lenin (3), the Red Banner (5), the Patriotic War 1st Class (2), the Red Star.

Yefremov was born in Orenburg on March 1, 1914 and started his military career in 1936. Upon completion of training at Orenburg military flying school two years later he cut his teeth against the Finns during the Winter War of 1939/40. During the fighting he excelled, heading up the list of fighter aces with five kills which qualified him for the award of the Order of Lenin and the medal "For Valor." He was posted to the 129 IAP before the war and would see a great deal of action on West Front right after the German attack on Soviet Russia. He participated in periods of intense activity at Smolensk and Kalinin and for his efforts was promoted Kapitan. On March 21, 1942 he claimed a Bf 109 while leading five LaGG-3s to engage a superior Luftwaffe formation between Gladovo-Tarutino, seven enemy planes being claimed shot down for no losses. Yefremov remained in the ranks following the close of hostilities graduating from the General Staff Academy in 1953. He came off active duty as a Polkovnik in 1971 with 35 years service.

V.V. Yefremov, an accomplished 5 GIAP fighter pilot, by the nose of his LaGG-3. Note he is still wearing the three-quarter length leather coat which had already been rendered obsolete by the cramped confines of modern fighters. The date is October 10, 1942. (Author's collection)

YELDYSHEV, Anatolij Petrovich
Combat record: 7 personal victories plus numerous ground targets, 160 sorties.
Decorations: Gold Star of Hero of the Soviet Union on August 18, 1945 in recognition of 139 sorties, 18 tanks destroyed in ground attacks as of February, 1945; the Orders of Lenin, the Red Banner (2), Aleksandr Nevskij, the Patriotic War 1st Class (2), the Red Star (2).

Yeldyshev was born in the Irkutsk area on November 4, 1922 and joined the VVS in December, 1940. He won his pilot wings at Perm military flying school a year later serving as an instructor for a while. In March, 1943 Yeldyshev commenced his combat duty with the 995 ShAP flying Il-2 Shturmoviks and while with the unit was involved in air operations on Southwest and 3rd Ukrainian Fronts, emerging as one of the outstanding ground-attack pilots of the war. On August 19, 1943 he was leading eight Il-2s in a strafing attack on Kajdaki airfield where they came under attack of German fighters, two Bf 109s being shot down in the ensuing melee following which they worked over the airfield for claims of eight transport aircraft and three bombers. On December 3, 1943 Yeldyshev's flight went down to break up a German tank counterattack and reported the destruction of a heavy Tiger tank and two Ferdinand heavy self-propelled tank destroyers. Further combats in Bulgaria and Hungary took his record to 18 tanks, three locomotives, 41 rail cars, 47 motor vehicles and four bombers destroyed in ground attacks plus two Bf 109s and a Fw 190 shot down in air combat as of February, 1945. He had by now become a Kapitan and squadron leader and during the subsequent fighting in Austria flew 21 sorties with four more kills in the air. He stayed in the service after the war and graduated from the Air Force Academy in 1953. He later was appointed deputy director of this institution with the rank of General Major.

YEREMIN, Aleksej Ustinovich
Combat record: 18 personal victories, 93 sorties.
Decorations: Gold Star of Hero of the Soviet Union on June 27, 1945; the Orders of Lenin, the Red Banner (4), Aleksandr Nevskij, the Patriotic War 2nd Class, the Red Star.

Yeremin was born in the Volgograd area on February 11, 1911 and entered military service in 1932. Two years later he completed his pilot training at Stalingrad military flying school and joined combat with the Luftwaffe at age 32 in April, 1943. He was not slow to get started, scoring his first success a short time later while leading six of his squadron to tangle with 12 Bf 109s over the Kuban. He knocked down the lead aircraft on his first pass with his comrades bringing the day's tally to four. He rose to Major while serving in the 402 IAP and on September 6 was off on a sweep with Kapitan A.Ye. Rubakbin and Mladshij Lejtenant V.A. Yegorovich when they ran into enemy planes near Marinka each getting a Ju 52. He next saw action in the Ukraine and the Criméa and was promoted Podpolkovnik and regiment commander. On an unspecified date he led six Yaks to engage seven German aircraft over the Sivash River, six of these being shot down. He later took command of the 355 IAP and though not among the highest scorers, he was one of the outstanding leadership talents to emerge from the war. Under his command the two regiments had been credited with a combined total of 408 air victories during 5,544 sorties. Yeremin remained in the VVS following World War II returning to civilian life as a Polkovnik in 1955. He died on March 30, 1977.

YEREMIN, Boris Nikolayevich
Combat record: 23 personal victories, 342 sorties, 60 encounters.
Decorations: Gold Star of Hero of the Soviet Union on May 5, 1990; the Order of Lenin.

Yeremin was born in Saratov on March 18, 1913 and in 1932 joined Volsk aircraft mechanics school. Between 1938 and early 1939 he took part in the conflict against the Japanese and during the same time frame learnt to fly the R-5. After receiving full flight training at Kacha military flying school in late 1939 he was posted to the 160 Reserve Air Regiment at Kirovograd. In January, 1941 he was appointed squadron leader and joined combat with the Luftwaffe on June 22, 1941. He destroyed his first enemy aircraft in the air with a Do 17 later that month but was shot down and wounded by antiaircraft fire shortly afterward. Upon his recovery he was assigned to the 296 IAP and in November, 1941 was put in command of a fighter squadron. He had his biggest day on March 9, 1942 while leading seven Yak-1s against a mixed gaggle of Ju 88s, Ju 87s and Bf 109s between Shebelinka-Cherkasskij Bishkin. Before the escorts could intervene they had loosed off their RS-82 82mm rockets knocking down four bombers on their first pass and breaking up the enemy formation. In continuing action three Bf 109s were destroyed in running battles to the deck. Yeremin's share that day: two Bf 109s. In November, 1942 he assumed command of the 273 IAP as a Major and eventually rose to command the crack 6 GIAD. He closed out his scoring with a single Fw 190 over Czechoslovakia on May 10, 1945 – one day after the surrender had taken place, as fighting with isolated German units in Czechoslovakia continued until the 11th. During his postwar career Yeremin headed Kacha military flying school and joined the select few to fly the MiG-15 jet fighter. He graduated from the General Staff Academy in 1959 and during successive assignments commanded North Caucasus Military District's air service and an Air Army of Northern Army Group. He had become a General Lejtenant when decorated with the title Hero of the Soviet Union in 1990.

Lejtenant D.V. Yermakov, a crack shot of the 159 IAP, who scored the majority of his victories in the ferocious fighting on Leningrad Front. (Author's collection)

YERMAKOV, Dmitrij Vasilyevich
Combat record: 25 personal victories, 247 sorties, 64 encounters.
Decorations: Gold Star of Hero of the Soviet Union on February 23, 1945; the Orders of Lenin, the Red Banner (3), the Patriotic War 1st Class, the Red Star (3).

Yermakov was born in the Kalinin area on November 2, 1920 and entered military service in 1940. He passed his pilot's examination at Batajsk military flying school two years later commencing his combat duty with the 123 IAP in May, 1942. Yermakov developed into a brilliant pilot and top marksman once he had joined with the crack 159 IAP on Leningrad Front. He rose to Starshij Lejtenant and flight leader and in a burst of energy and skill ran up a string of eight kills over the Karelian Isthmus in June, 1944. His exact score is a matter of dispute, one source quoting 25 kills, 322 sorties and 54 air-to-air combats as of November, 1944 which recommended him for the award of the title of Hero of the Soviet Union. Yermakov remained with the VVS until 1958 retiring as a Polkovnik.

YEVSTIGNEYEV, Kirill Alekseyevich
Combat record: 53 personal victories, 3 fractional credits, 283 sorties, 109 encounters.
Decorations: 1st Gold Star of Hero of the Soviet Union on August 2, 1944 in recognition of 23 kills, 3 fractional credits, 144 sorties, 53 combats as of November, 1943, 2nd Gold Star on February 23, 1945 for 20 more kills, 83 sorties as of October, 1944; the Orders of Lenin, the Red Banner (4), Suvorov 3rd Class, the Patriotic War 1st and 2nd Class, the Red Star, the British Empire.

Yevstigneyev, fifth-ranking Allied fighter ace, was born in the Kurgan area on February 17, 1917 and enlisted in the Soviet Army on September 21, 1938. Upon receiving his wings at Bijnsk military flying school three years later he was sent to the Far East where he was involved in training pilots. Anxious to get into action he persisted in filing request for transfer to the front. His opportunity finally came on March 17, 1943 when he arrived with the 240 IAP in the Kharkov area flying the Lavochkin La-5 fighter. Yevstigneyev immediately got hot and once having flown his first combat sortie two days later he ran up a string of three kills during his next 17 sorties. He drew first blood later that month when he engaged a Ju 88 knocking it down at 70 meters range. He continued to score on a regular basis in a fierce series of dogfights around Kharkov and had brought his tally to nine when he was shot down, wounded in both legs. He returned to his unit a little later to see considerable action at Kursk. On June 7 he claimed a Ju 87 while leading six squadron mates to tear into a formation of 10 dive-bombers and next day added two more of these. All hell broke loose in this area in July as the Germans initiated Operation Zitadelle – the attempted reduction of a huge salient around Kursk. The battle started with the most intensive air fighting of the war and saw Yevstigneyev gain six kills in July, including a triple on the 5th, a mission which he recalls as follows: "I was assigned on a frontline patrol encountering a heavy layer of cloud at 5,000 meters. Kapitan Podorozhnij's attack group consisting of six fighters was flying below so as to intercept enemy bomber formations while three comrades were assigned as top cover to engage any fighters that might appear. Once over the front the first bombers were spotted going in to hammer our ground forces. Podorozhnij immediately ordered the attack and bounced one Junkers from astern teaming with his number two to destroy it on his first pass. Flying slightly behind him I hit the left-hand aircraft with a burst from starboard at 50 meters range and saw it blew up and hit the ground. While this was going on, a second enemy bomber force was spotted. I swept down and went through their formation, and banked around for a second pass, downed one of them as they were breaking formation and trying to race away just above the ground. I pulled in behind another and started to pour fire into him at 50-60 meters range and saw him crash for my third victory of the day." On July 7 he flew six sorties in the Byelgorod area and then reported the destruction of single Bf

Kapitan K.A. Yevstigneyev, the extremely talented young fighter ace of the 240 IAP. He cut a wide swath through enemy formations flying the La-5 and La-7 fighters, and in the great aerial campaigns of 1943/44 was in a highly competitive scoring race with the redoubtable Ivan Kozhedub. His big day was October 7, 1943 when he racked up five kills. (Author's collection)

109s on July 9, 13 and 16. In August he was promoted squadron leader and then ran up victories along the Dnyepr River at a formidable pace. As the regiment was exacting a heavy toll from opposing Luftwaffe formations in early October with 50 kills for the loss of three fighters through enemy action, Yevstigneyev entered combat nine times coming away with 12 kills. Runners-up during this period were Ivan Kozhedub with six and A. Kolesnikov with five. His victories ran as follows: On October 2 a Bf 109 and a Ju 87 fell to his guns while three days later he claimed another Ju 87 together with a Fw 190. He had his biggest day on the 7th while leading six La-5s to take on 27 Stukas escorted by six Bf 109s. Storming into the bomber formation, they forced them to jettison their loads and then Yevstigneyev and two fellow pilots returned for a second attack while four fighters were assigned to tackle with the German escorts. Yevstigneyev blasted three Ju 87s out of the sky in quick succession before being diverted by six more Bf 109s streaking in. He wracked his fighter around in a tight turn to close on the lead fighter pouring a stream of fire into him whereupon he blew up the pilot bailing out. In all, he got five kills that day. During the rest of the month he submitted claims for two Bf 109s, two Ju 87s, and one each He 111 and Fw 190. At that time he had entered into a keen scoring race with one of his fellow pilots, whose career was equally meteoric, Ivan Kozhedub. They scored heavily in the contested air space above Rumania in the spring of 1944. In early March Yevstigneyev racked up his 29th and 30th victories when 22 La-5s became embroiled in a hard-fought battle with 100+ Luftwaffe aircraft. Leading the way into action, Yevstigneyev's squadron accounted for six of the day's total of nine victories with Kozhedub running his score to 35. On March 29 he polished off a Bf 109 and next claimed a Fw 190 and a Ju 88 in an action over Yassy on April 17. Six days later he got into a scrap with four Fw 190s and put a burst into a fighter that rolled over and went down to crash. On the 28th he forced down a Fw 190 and a Ju 87 while engaged in a fighter sweep north of Yassy and next day shot down another Fw 190 in the vicinity of Vulturul. On May 5 he claimed a Hs 126 near Podul for a change while two days later two Bf 109s fell to his guns when eight La-5s tore into a formation of 36 Ju 87s and 10 Bf 109s between Frumos-Dumbrovina. He next bagged another Fw 190 in the Skulyany area on May 30 and on June 1 submitted claims for a Bf 109 and a Ju 87 returning to the same area. 14 La-5s were prowling around in the Vulturul-Skulyany areas on the 2nd where they engaged a large gaggle consisting of some 60 aircraft. Yevstigneyev exploded a Stuka on his first pass while his squadron mates got two Hs 129s and a Bf 109 without loss. The following day he was off on several frontline patrols sending down a Hs 129 antitank aircraft, a Fw 190 and a Bf 109. He got another triple with two Fw 190s and a Bf 109 two days later during two combat sorties in the Larga area. By August, 1944 Yevstigneyev's squadron had chalked up 71 kills during 1,370 sorties and 97 air encounters in 13 months combat over Byelgorod, Poltava, Kishinyov, Yassy and the Carpathians. Yevstigneyev was promoted Kapitan and continued his streak during the subsequent air battles over Rumania while flying a La-5FN "Black 96." In October, 1944 he was recommended for his second title of Hero of the Soviet Union for 46 air victories and three fractional credits consisting of the following:

Bf 109s	17
Ju 87s	13
Bf 110s	2
Ju 88s	2
Fw 190s	9
Fw 189s	1
Hs 129s	1
Hs 126s	1

With fellow pilots he jointly claimed a Ju 88, a Ju 87 and an He 111. Yevstigneyev's prowess in combat by now had become legend. Like most Soviet high-scorers he favored the point-blank and high speed attack. He later rose to Major and deputy commander of the 178 GIAP and closed out his scoring over Budapest on March 26, 1945 while leading eight La-7s to bounce 18 Fw 190s. Yevstigneyev peeled off on one of them and shot him down at point-blank range. When hostilities ceased his squadron had been credited with an impressive total of 140 kills. He remained in the VVS following World War II graduating from the Air Force Academy in 1955 and the General Staff Academy in 1960. Six years later he was promoted General Major and concluded his active duty in 1972.

Postwar photograph of Kirill Yevstigneyev by which time he had become a Polkovnik. He retired in 1972 after a 29-year career as a military aviator. He is considered by many to have been one of the finest pilots of World War II. (Author's collection)

ZAJTSEV, Aleksandr Petrovich

Combat record: 14 personal victories, 21 fractional credits, 200 sorties.

Decorations: The Orders of Lenin, the Red Banner, the Red Star.

Zajtsev was born in Nizhnyj Novgorod in 1912 and graduated from flight training at Kharkov military flying school in 1936. He was decorated with the Order of the Red Star for his efforts against the Japanese during the fighting along the Khalkhin Gol River in 1939 and next won the Order of the Red Banner during the Russo-Finnish Winter War of 1939/40. He had become a member of the 145 IAP by June, 1941 and then was to see a great deal of action at Murmansk in the dark months to follow. His great fighting spirit earned him the award of the Order of Lenin on July 22 and soon after he was promoted Major. On August 4 he was off on an early morning mission leading seven squadron mates to engage 13 Bf 110s. In the ensuing melee Zajtsev reported the destruction of one German fighter while his comrades got two more. Soviet accounts identify his victim as an "Hauptmann Schaschke", who was killed while attempting to force-land in Soviet lines, the fin and rudder of his 110 carrying his victory markings being put on display in Murmansk. He was killed in a flying accident on May 30, 1942.

ZAJTSEV, Aleksandr Andreyevich

Combat record: 15 personal victories.

Decorations: Gold Star of Hero of the Soviet Union on November 17, 1939; the Orders of Lenin, the Red Banner (2), Suvorov 3rd Class, Aleksandr Nevskij, the Red Star (2)

Zajtsev was born in Moscow on December 12, 1911 and commenced flight training at Yejsk in April, 1933. He entered combat duty in Spain in December, 1936 and is reported to have achieved a total of eight victories to emerge as one of the high-scorers of the conflict. There followed assignments as squadron leader and deputy commander of the 19 IAP prior to his taking over as commanding officer of the 70 IAP in Mongolia on May 11, 1939. He had by now become a Kapitan and immediately began to make his mark against the Japanese chalking up a total of six air victories during 118 sorties and 29 combats in that theater. Zajtsev later participated in the Russo-Finnish Winter War of 1939/40 while commanding the air units of 8th Combined-Arms Army following which he was assigned as an inspector to Transcaucasus Military District. He attended the Air Force Academy between July, 1941 and January, 1942 and next became a test pilot. In August, 1942 he joined combat with the Luftwaffe assuming command of the 431 IAP as a Podpolkovnik in February, 1944. He was engaged in heavy action over Stalingrad, Leningrad and the Baltic being given credit for one further victory during 76 sorties. He commanded an air regiment while serving with the postwar VVS retiring as a Podpolkovnik in 1952. He died on December 25, 1965.

ZAJTSEV, Vasilij Aleksandrovich

Combat record: 34 personal victories, 19 fractional credits, 427 sorties, 163 encounters.

Decorations: 1st Gold Star of Hero of the Soviet Union on May 5, 1942 for 12 kills, 115 sorties, 16 air combats as of January, 1942, 2nd Gold Star on August 24, 1943 in recognition of 22 kills, 299 sorties as of August, 1943; the Orders of Lenin, the Red Banner (3), Bogdan Khmelnitskij 2nd Class, the Patriotic War 1st Class.

V.A. Zajtsev, great fighter leader. Here he is seen as a Major in mid-1942 when he was deputy commander of the 129 IAP. He is wearing the Gold Star of Hero of the Soviet Union, the Orders of Lenin and the Red Banner. (Author's collection)

Zajtsev was born in the Moscow area on January 10, 1911 and enlisted in the VVS in 1932. He completed his pilot training at Lugansk military flying school a year later and attended advanced training for flight leaders at Borisoglebsk in 1936. He was involved in training pilots before commencing his combat duty right after the German attack on the Soviet Union. He drew first blood on July 5, 1941 and was a Kapitan when posted to the 129 IAP shortly afterward. By August his score had risen to six including two victories that were obtained with RS-82 air-to-air rockets while flying the LaGG-3 fighter. Zajtsev dedicated himself to the study of enemy tactics and technology acquiring a thorough knowledge of what he believed to be their weaknesses. His forte were surprise attacks, holding his fire until within point-blank range and knocking his adversary down in the last instant before breaking away. He saw a lot of action at Smolensk, Yelnya, Yartsevo and Kalinin. On December 7 he reported the destruction of a Ju 87 and on the 29th was credited with a double while leading an interception sortie on the outskirts of Moscow that resulted in claims for 11 enemy aircraft destroyed. He had by now become a Major and deputy commander of the regiment and in mid-1942 was to display his outstanding leadership talent in the wild air battles over Kholm and Byelyj. He later fought along the Vazuza and Osuga Rivers assuming command of the unit in September. With Zajtsev in the lead the regiment fought with distinction in the epic Battle of Stalingrad being engaged in intercepting

Luftwaffe transports and interdicting enemy airfields. In four weeks combat the pilots chalked up 45 kills mostly while flying free hunt searching out unescorted Ju 52s, Ju 88s and He 111s. Zajtsev's contribution: six kills. The regiment later did yeoman service in the skies above Slavyansk, Kramatorsk, Kharkov, Byelgorod and Izyum with Mladshij Lejtenant Nikolaj Marisayev earning the distinction of gaining the 500th kill on August 29, 1943. Zajtsev claimed another double with two Ju 87s on March 10, 1943 while leading six La-5s on a fighter sweep out to Yarovaya-Bannovskij-Priship, where they knocked down a total of five Stukas and three Fw 189s. 5 GIAP fought with above-average success in the great aerial campaigns above the Dnyepr, the Vistula, the Oder and finally, Berlin, finishing as the highest scoring Soviet fighter regiment of the war with a confirmed total of 739 victories. On April 5, 1944 Zajtsev was appointed deputy commander of the 11 GIAD also temporarily leading the 105 GIAP. During his World War II career he scored a total of three triples and is widely regarded as one of the greatest of all Soviet fighter leaders. He remained with the VVS until 1946 retiring as a Polkovnik. He died on May 19, 1961 and is buried in Kolomna near Moscow.

ZAJTSEV, Vasilij Vladimirovich
Combat record: 16 personal victories, 448 sorties including 69 ground attacks, 42 encounters.
Decorations: Gold Star of Hero of the Soviet Union on June 27, 1945; the Orders of Lenin, the Red Banner (3), the Patriotic War 1st Class, the Red Star (2).

Zajtsev was born in the Kursk area on April 18, 1920 and joined the VVS at age 18. He won his wings at Voroshilovgrad military flying school in 1938 and saw action for the first time in December, 1941. During his World War II career he fought on Bryansk, 1st Baltic, 3rd Byelorussian and 1st Ukrainian Fronts. On March 10, 1942 he was off on a front-line patrol in his I-153 biplane when he spotted a formation of 18 He 111s approaching the Novotitarovskaya area (N Krasnodar) at 6,000 meters altitude. Without hesitating he delivered a head-on attack scoring strikes on the lead bomber at 1,200 meters range, seeing its starboard-engine blow up and burst into flames whereupon it crashed. On August 6 Zajtsev and Lejtenant Kulishev were ordered off to strafe ground targets in the vicinity of Kurganskaya (35 kilometers southwest of Armavir)but ran into five Bf 110s, two Ju 88s and two Fw 189s harassing Soviet motor vehicles. They dove down to attack and both claimed singles but Zajtsev was then badly hit by two Bf 110s being obliged to carry out a force-landing near Majkop. He later became a Major and squadron leader flying with the 482 IAP and had a big day on March 2, 1944. On this day four La-5s with Zajtsev leading were prowling around in the Vitebsk-Gorodok-Nevel areas where they engaged five Ju 87s, four of them falling in the area of Gusino Lake, three by Zajtsev. On an unspecified date he took off on a sortie with Lejtenant Grinko as his wingman and once over the front near Sagan immediately made contact with 16 Ju 87s and six Fw 190s. In a furious few minutes, one Ju 87 and one Fw 190 were knocked down by Zajtsev. In August, 1944 he took over as leader of a fighter squadron which would be given credit for 46 kills during 1,031 sorties, 189 of which were ground attacks, during subsequent assignments on 3rd Byelorussian and 1st Ukrainian Fronts. Zajtsev contribution in the same time frame: seven air victories, 44 sorties, 12 engagements. His final victory claims were as follows:

Fw 190s	8
Ju 87s	5
Fw 189s	1
Bf 109s	1
He 111s	1

In ground attacks he destroyed one Ju 88, 107 motor vehicles, five railcars, three antiaircraft guns. He remained in the VVS after the war and graduated from the Air Force Academy in 1957. He wound up his military career as a Polkovnik in 1964.

ZAKHAROV, Georgij Nefyodovich
Combat record: 10 personal victories, 153 sorties, 48 encounters (Patriotic War period only).
Decorations: Gold Star of Hero of the Soviet Union on April 19, 1945; the Orders of Lenin (2), the Red Banner (4), Kutuzov 2nd Class, Aleksandr Nevskij, the Patriotic War 1st Class, the Red Star (2).

Zakharov was born in the Kujbyshev area on April 24, 1908 and entered the Soviet Army in 1930. He passed his pilot's examination at Stalingrad military flying school and attended General Staff Academy prior to cutting his teeth in Spain fighting with the Republicans. He scored a total of six victories there and next was assigned to the Far East, putting up a good performance against the Japanese at Khasan Lake in 1938. He had by now become a squadron leader his pilots reportedly "downing numerous Japanese aircraft" but details are not available. In 1940 he was promoted General Major and was in the forefront of action right after the German attack as commander of the 43 IAD. The unit was based in the Minsk area initially consisting of the 160, 161, 162 and 163 IAPs and was to see a great deal of action over Minsk, Bobrujsk, Mogilyov, Smolensk and Vyazma. During the period of June 22 to August 2, 1941 it was credited with downing 167 enemy planes for the loss of 63 aircraft on the ground and 26 in the air. In early 1943 he took over the newly formed 303 IAD containing the 18 GIAP, 20, 523 and 168 IAPs while later the all-French Normandie-Nyeman regiment was assigned. The first sorties were undertaken on February 22 and subsequently the unit would make an auspicious contribution to the fighting at Kaluga, Orel, Spas-Demensk, Smolensk, Orsha, Vitebsk, Borisov, Vilnyus, Kaunas and over East Prussia. Zakharov scored two personal kills above the Byelorussian capital and continued to go off whenever the opportunity arose. He continued on active duty with the post-war VVS serving in command positions until 1960. In addition to his Soviet decorations he holds the French Legion d'Honneur.

ZAKHAROV, Konstantin Fyodorovich
Combat record: 15 personal victories, 1 fractional credit, 190 sorties, 41 encounters.
Decorations: Gold Star of Hero of the Soviet Union posthumously on August 2, 1944; the Orders of the Red Banner (2), the Patriotic War 1st Class.

Zakharov was born in Ivanovo in January, 1919 and enrolled for service in the Soviet Army in 1937. Two years later he was graduated as a pilot at Perm military flying school and began his combat career at the outbreak of the war. He spent his World War II career with the 233 IAP taking part in the aerial campaigns on West, Central and Byelorussian Fronts. He eventually rose to Kapitan and squadron leader but while flying a mission in the Mozyr area on January 13, 1944 was hit hard by flak and reportedly directed his burning Yak to crash into an enemy column being killed on impact.

ZELENOV, Nikolaj Andrianovich
Combat record: 24 personal victories, 9 fractional credits.
Decorations: Gold Star of Hero of the Soviet Union on February 10, 1943 in recognition of 9 kills, 8 fractional credits, 382 sorties, 47 air combats as of July, 1942; the Orders of Lenin, the Red Banner (2), the Patriotic War 1st Class (2).

Zelenov was born in the Kostroma area in 1917 and entered the VVS for flight training in 1936. Upon completion of training at Lugansk military flying school Zelenov won his spurs during the Russo-Finnish Winter War of 1939/40. He was in action again right after the German attack on Soviet Russia in June, 1941 and fought with great distinction with the 154 IAP on Leningrad Front. He rapidly advanced to Kapitan and on March 30, 1942 reported the destruction of two Ju 87s in one sortie. He claimed another double on April 30 and on March 23, 1943 combined forces with his wingman to destroy two more Stukas. On April 3 he was successful in shooting a German fighter off a comrade's tail also damaging a second. Zelenov fell foul of Luftwaffe fighters in an action near Vyborg on June 29, 1944 and was interred in Leningrad (St. Petersburg). In Zelenov the regiment lost one of its most deadly fighter pilots.

ZHERDEV, Nikolaj Prokofyevich
Combat record: 14 personal victories, 105+ sorties, 46+ encounters.

N.A. Zelenov, another of the great aces of the hell of Leningrad. He achieved a remarkable score while fighting with the 154 IAP before he was lost on June 29, 1944. He is wearing the Gold Star of Hero of the Soviet Union, the Orders of Lenin, the Red Banner, the medal "For Gallantry" (1st version) on the left breast and the Order of the Patriotic War (1st version) and the Guards badge on the right. Between the latter two decorations there are two wound stripes. (Author's collection)

Decorations: Gold Star of Hero of the Soviet Union on November 17, 1939; the Orders of Lenin (2), the Red Banner.

Zherdev was born in the Donetsk area on May 5, 1911 and entered military service in 1934. In December, 1936 he joined with the 56 IAE at Bobrujsk and from March, 1938 was involved in fierce fighting over Spain. His most memorable mission came on June 27, 1938 when he shot down a Fiat and then deliberately rammed a second having expended the ammunition of his fighter. For this feat he was decorated with his first Order of Lenin on February 22, 1939. He next excelled fighting the Japanese along the Khalkhin Gol River in Mongolia. He arrived in this theater on May 29, 1939 to join with the 70 IAP and quickly proved his skills at blasting enemy aircraft. He took over as leader of a fighter squadron which was to run up a total of 42 kills with Zherdev in the lead. With 14 air victories during 105 sorties and 46 combats he emerged as one of the high-scorers of the conflict meeting the conditions for the award of the title of Hero of the Soviet Union. Zherdev was again in the thick of the fighting at the start of Operation

Barbarossa, the German attack on Soviet Russia, fighting with the 821 IAP during the darkest hours of 1941/42 on Southwest, South, Transcaucasus, and North Caucasus Fronts. He was shot down and killed in the Caucasus on November 15, 1942, by which time he had become a Major and Shturman.

he joined in late 1942 taking part in the heavy air battles over the Demyansk pocket while flying Hurricanes. Ziborov rose to deputy squadron leader and later gave a good account of himself in the air operations on 1st Baltic Front. He remained with the VVS until 1960 retiring as a Polkovnik.

ZHIGULENKOV, Boris Vasilyevich

Combat record: 20 personal victories, 200 sorties, 50 encounters.

Decorations: Gold Star of Hero of the Soviet Union on October 26, 1944 for 16 victories, 184 sorties, 46 engagements as of July, 1944; the Orders of Lenin, the Red Banner, the Patriotic War 1st Class.

Zhigulenkov was born in the Moscow area on May 2, 1922 and started his military career in July, 1940. Two years later he qualified as a pilot at Zernograd military flying school being assigned to the 240 IAP in March, 1943. He destroyed his first enemy aircraft in the air during the brutal battles of the Kursk-Kharkov campaign in August, 1943 claiming a Bf 109. He rapidly developed into a brilliant pilot and top marksman running up a string of 10 victories during his next 60 sorties and 20 combats in three months frontline duty. He achieved a remarkable score over the Ukraine scoring six kills during 28 sorties in October alone. On the 4th he bagged a Bf 109 while leading 14 La-5s to tie into a formation of 60 Ju 87s and 12 Bf 109s near Borodayevka. He added a Fw 190 in the vicinity of Mishurin Rog next day when 11 of his squadron tangled with six Luftwaffe fighters. On the 12th he made a claim for a Ju 87 when seven La-5s stormed into a formation of 18 Stukas escorted by five Bf 109s to shoot five down in an action near Kutsevalovka. For his efforts that month Zhigulenkov was decorated with the Order of the Patriotic War 1st Class. He claimed another Ju 87 on January 30, 1944 and continued to score on a regular basis in the skies of Rumania and Hungary. On February 7, 1945 (or November 10, 1944 as suggested by another source) he was badly wounded in a fighter battle and was able to limp home where he died before he was pulled from the aircraft.

ZIBOROV, Vasilij Mikhajlovich

Combat record: 22 personal victories.

Decorations: Gold Star of Hero of the Soviet Union on August 18, 1945 in recognition of 15 victories, 134 sorties, 24 combats as of January, 1945; the Orders of Lenin, the Red Banner (2), Aleksandr Nevskij, the Patriotic War 1st Class, the Red Star (2).

Ziborov was born in the Stavropol area on April 19, 1923 and entered the Soviet Army in 1941. After completion of training a year later he was posted to the 402 IAP in September to start flying combat. He became an ace flying with the 485 IAP which

ZIMIN, Georgij Vasilyevich

Combat record: 19 personal victories, 20 fractional credits, 249 sorties, 69 encounters.

Decorations: Gold Star of Hero of the Soviet Union on September 28, 1943 for 13 kills, 4 fractional credits, 163 sorties, 39 engagements as of September, 1943; the Orders of Lenin (3), the Red Banner (4), Suvorov 2nd Class, Kutuzov 2nd Class, the Patriotic War 1st Class, the Red Star (2).

Zimin was born in St. Petersburg (Leningrad) on May 6, 1912 and commenced his military service in 1931. Four years later he graduated from flight training at Engels military flying school and gained his first combat experience against the Japanese at Lake Khasan in 1938. The following year he was promoted Kapitan and assigned to the 53 IAP. In June, 1941 he became a member of the 42 IAP flying MiG-3s and the following month saw some action at Orel. He moved with the unit to the Tula area in October where he managed to run his tally to seven until November 15, 1941. In March, 1942 Zimin rose to Major being posted to Northwest Front where he took over the Hurricane equipped 485 IAP. One criticism the pilots had was the armament of their mount which was inferior to that carried by the Luftwaffe fighters initial sorties proving to be a very costly business. On April 18 the regiment claimed four Bf 109s but one pilot was killed and a second seriously wounded. Two days later six Hurricanes reported the destruction of three German fighters while engaged in escorting a formation of Il-2s but again two pilots were bested and killed by 109s. Success was not long in coming for on June 19 Zimin was leading six pilots to tear into a force of 12 Ju 87s and 15 Bf 109s, 10 enemy planes being shot down for the loss of one fighter, two Ju 87s and one Bf 109 by Zimin. He claimed a Fw 190 near Staraya Russa on March 13, 1943 by which time his tally stood at nine kills, four fractional credits during 93 sorties and 26 air combats. On April 13, 1944 he became commanding officer of the 240 IAD and deployed with the unit to Leningrad Front coming under command of the 13 VA. Under his leadership the division did yeoman service over Smolensk, Nevel, Orsha and Königsberg. Zimin brought down a Fw 190 over the Frische Nehrung promontory (SW Königsberg) on March 26, 1945 and on April 25 knocked down another of these while flying free hunt over Berlin seeing his victim fall into the heart of the city not far from the Olympic Stadium. Following World War II Zimin continued on active duty with the VVS graduating from the General Staff Academy in 1948. In 1960 he was appointed deputy commander-in-chief of the PVO forces and in 1973 rose to Marshal Aviatsii.

ZOTOV, Viktor Alekseyevich
Combat record: 28 personal victories, 10 fractional credits, 416 sorties.
Decorations: Gold Star of Hero of the Soviet Union on February 4, 1944 for 17 kills, 10 fractional credits, 336 sorties, 87 encounters as of October, 1943; the Orders of Lenin, the Red Banner, Aleksandr Nevskij, the Patriotic War 1st Class (2), the Red Star.

Zotov was born in Moscow on November 23, 1919 and enlisted in the VVS in 1939. He completed his pilot training at Borisoglebsk military flying school a year later and fought from the very first days of the Patriotic War. He enjoyed considerable success flying La-5s with the 159 IAP on Leningrad Front and rapidly rose to Starshij Lejtenant and deputy squadron leader. His highest scoring day was June 19, 1943 when he was leading a number of young bucks out to a frontline patrol. In an instant they found themselves in a dogfight with German fighters with Zotov claiming a Bf 109 on his first pass and then shooting a second off his wingman's tail at point-blank range. With fuel getting low they peeled away and turned for home coming across a reconnaissance plane which Zotov promptly sent down in flames for his third victory of the day. Zotov gave a good account of himself during subsequent combat assignments over Novgorod, Volkhov and Narva coming out of World War II as the regiment's second highest scoring ace. His final total of combat sorties is a matter of dispute, one source quoting 750. He stayed in the service after the war graduating from the Air Force Academy in 1950. Zotov wound up his military career with the rank of Polkovnik in 1968.

ZUYEV, Mikhail Aleksandrovich
Combat record: 12 personal victories, 4 fractional credits, 335 sorties, 63 encounters.
Decorations: Gold Star of Hero of the Soviet Union on February 4, 1944; the Orders of Lenin, the Red Banner (2), Aleksandr Nevskij, the Patriotic War 1st Class, the Red Star.

Zuyev was born in the Saratov area on June 18, 1918 and entered military service in 1937. Three years later he received his wings at Engels military flying school commencing combat duty right after the German attack on Soviet Russia. Zuyev made a big name for himself in the skies above Stalingrad acquiring eight kills during 46 sorties and 25 air engagements in 103 days of combat. On October 26, 1942 he bagged a Bf 109 while flying Pe-2 escort and on December 8 he destroyed a Ju 52 but in turn was badly hit and wounded. He was out of action for four months and returned to 73 GIAP to fight with distinc-

V.A. Zotov (left), a skillful air fighter, who made a distinguished combat record on Leningrad Front. He emerged as the second ranking ace of the crack 159 IAP with 28 kills. (Author's collection)

Fighter ace of Leningrad Front. P.D. Zyuzin, who had a significant share in the success achieved by the 29 GIAP in the tough air battles fought over Northern Russia. His final bag was 19 confirmed victories. (Author's collection)

Zyuzin (second from right) and an informal gathering of fellow pilots. Karelian Front, July, 1944. (Author's collection)

tion at Batajsk, Mariupol and Kharkov. He eventually made Kapitan and squadron leader. Zuyev served with the postwar VVS until 1957 concluding his active duty as a Polkovnik.

ZYUZIN, Dmitrij Vasilyevich
Combat record: 14 personal victories, 535 sorties, 51 encounters.
Decorations: Gold Star of Hero of the Soviet Union on May 16, 1944; the Orders of Lenin, the Red Banner (2), the Patriotic War 1st Class (2), the Red Star.

Zyuzin was born in Majkop on November 1, 1921 and enlisted in the VMF at age 17. Two years later he graduated from flight training at Yejsk military flying school and in September, 1942 went to war with the Black Sea Fleet's 11 GIAP. Zyuzin managed to put up a good performance during the heavy fighting for Nikolayev scoring seven kills including shares while flying Airacobras during the period of November 25, 1943 to March 19, 1944. His 500th combat sortie saw him claim a Ju 88 at night on November 30, 1943 when he intercepted eight Luftwaffe aircraft enroute to Skadovsk (SE Kherson). Zyazin later became a squadron leader in the Pacific Fleet's air service and took part in the great campaign that would smash the Japanese Kwantung Army in August, 1945. He served with the postwar VMF leaving active duty as a Polkovnik in 1957. He died on July 12, 1976.

ZYUZIN, Pyotr Dmitriyevich
Combat record: 19 personal victories, 211 sorties, 41 encounters.
Decorations: Gold Star of Hero of the Soviet Union on November 2, 1944 in recognition of 16 victories, 208 sorties and 35 encounters as of November, 1944; the Orders of Lenin, the Red Banner (3), the Patriotic War 1st Class (2), the Red Star (3).

Zyuzin was born in the Moscow area on July 24, 1922 and joined the Soviet Army in 1941. He graduated from flight training a year later and in March, 1943 was posted to the crack 29 GIAP on Volkhov Front to enter combat. During his time with the regiment Zyuzin took part in the air operations on Leningrad and Karelian Fronts excelling in a series of aerial encounters at Auvere, Narva, Ust-Zherdyanka and Vajvara by claiming 12 kills between March-June, 1944. He had his biggest day on March 26, 1944 when he was credited with a triple over Auvere. He remained with the VVS until 1958 retiring with the rank of Podpolkovnik. He is living in Moscow.

3

THE TANKBUSTERS (Shturmovik Aces)

The aircraft that does not really need any type of introduction is the Il-2 Shturmovik, the single-engined close-support aircraft that came from the drawing boards of the design team around the brilliant S.V. Ilyushin.

When going into action with the 4 ShAP in late June, 1941, the Il-2 was destined to become one of the most formidable fighting machines of the war, enjoying a long and remarkable service career. Early Il-2 armament consisted of two wing-mounted 20mm ShVAK (ShVAK Shpitalnyj-Vladimirov, aviatsionnaya krupnokalibernaya or heavy aircraft cannon)) cannon and two 7.62mm ShKAS (ShKAS Shpitalnyj-Komaritskij, aviatsionnyj, skorostrelnykh or rapid-firing aircraft gun) guns in the upper portion of the fuselage nose with 500 resp. 750 rpg. In addition, there were provisions for eight unguided 82mm RS-82 (RS=raketnykh snaryadov or rocket missiles) air-to-ground rocket missiles or bombs under the wings. The missiles had a range of 5,200 meters. Heavy armor plates were fitted to guard the pilot and the aircraft's vitals. The plane quickly proved to be the most deadly weapon system available to battle enemy armor or any other ground target; pilots were equally impressed with their mount's ability to absorb punishment.

The rapid German advance caused a dramatic decline of production as the plants had to be evacuated and re-erected beyond the Urals, with the result that only 1,542 had been completed by the end of 1941. Stalin himself urged the acceleration of production, and in an outstanding effort 8,225 rolled off the assembly lines throughout the following year. The Russians soon were beginning to deploy Il-2s in great numbers everywhere at points of main effort. They were committed as "flying artillery" in support of infantry and armored forces, focusing on enemy tanks, artillery positions, the softening up of enemy defenses and disorganizing of supplies and the retreat of enemy forces.

By 1944 no less than 150 assault air regiments had been equipped with the steel clads, and when hostilities ceased, 36,163 examples of the Il-2 family had been built, 33,700 of these going into service with the VVS.

The Shturmovik was not born "fully fledged," but the impetus placed behind the production program was allowing only piecemeal refinements. Firepower was improved considerably with the installation of two 23mm VYa-23 (VYa Volkov-Yartsev) cannon to replace the unreliable ShVAKs. The new weapon was developed in 1941 to penetrate 25 millimeters of armor at a range of 400 meters; gunsights were rudimentary only while radio equipment was confined to formation leaders. The most serious shortcoming, though, was the aircraft's lack of defensive armament and its extreme vulnerability to fighter attack from astern. Strangely enough, Ilyushin had originally planned to make provisions for a rear gunner, but this had not proceeded further for fear of an overall performance loss due to added weight and impaired aerodynamics. The Shturmovik regiments were suffering crippling losses in combat and frontline engineering teams began to field-modify their equipment.

General F.P. Polynin, who commanded the 6th Air Army between January 8, 1943, and September 27, 1944, vividly recalls the early setbacks: "As a matter of fact, the results achieved by Shturmoviks in defending themselves often were insignificant. Their fire went wide as the gunners were poor shots." After combat practicing with fighters, the Il-2s were sent out to engage sluggish Ju 52 transports, reputedly with much success. Between September 7-8, 1942, the Air Army's 243 ShAD (Podpolkovnik I.V. Delnov) began to convert its aircraft to adopt a gunner with a flexibly mounted 7.62mm ShKAS gun. In Polynin's judgment, German fighters after that were no longer quite so eager, the rear gunners' wide field of fire now keeping them at bay while they previously had aggressively closed to

Going hunting. Shturmoviks of an unknown regiment taxi for takeoff. Soviet ground-attack pilots duly earned the Germans' respect for their courage and tenacity in carrying out their assigned duties. The Il-2s proved to be the top Allied tank killers of World War II. (Author's collection)

100 meters or less. General Polynin is neglecting to say that the element of surprise actually allowed only brief moments of glory, as the Luftwaffe fighters before long got the measure by striking from below and behind.

The cockpit was extended further aft with armor plates being installed for the protection of the gunner, and the aircraft was cleared for production. The first two-seaters became operational on October 30, 1942, as Il-2Ms, but the change in the center of gravity made it unforgiving, and any but a highly-experienced pilot found it a difficult machine to fly. The ultimate phase in the process of refinement was reached with the introduction of the Il-2M-3, which featured a more powerful engine and a newly designed wing to compensate for its poor stability. It was delivered with two large 37mm 11-P-37 cannon with 32 rpg in the wings replacing the VYa-23s, as their weight of fire was proving insufficient against the heavy armor of the new Tiger and Panther tanks. The new type demonstrated its armor-defeating potentials for the first time at Kursk in July, 1943, and on the first day of Operation Zitadelle claims for 70 tanks and armored vehicles destroyed were submitted within a furious 20 minutes! Another Soviet answer to the heavy German tanks that was used for the first time during the battle were the PTAB-2.5-1.5 (PTAB – protivotankovaya aviabomb, or antitank air bomb) hollow charge antitank bombs, which proved to be highly effective, being capable of penetrating up to 70 millimeters of armor.

The Il-2 air assault regiments caused mayhem to German forces across Russia, Poland, Hungary, Rumania, and the crumbling Reich. The veteran outfits made brilliant war records in accomplishing their missions, and even managed to make their mark against enemy aircraft in air-to-air combat.

Sturmgeschütz knocked out by Il-2s somewhere in Russia. (Author's collection)

Battle damage. Friend and foe equally marveled at the Il-2's ability to take punishment. More than 150 hits were counted in this aircraft but the pilot was able to get it back safely! (Author's collection)

A.N. Yefimov, the greatest tank-hunter of them all. He went to war as a Serzhant with the 198 ShAP in the Rzhev area in August, 1942 and piled up a tremendous score on 2nd Byelorussian Front. On July 13, 1943 he took over as leader of 2nd Eskadrilya and in February, 1945 joined the 62 ShAP as a Shturman. His 222nd and last mission was a strike against the port of Swinemünde on May 5, 1945. His impressive tally consists of 126 tanks, 85 enemy planes (including fractional credits) on the ground, two aerial victories (one each Bf 109 and Bf 110) and five fractional credits. Photo is dated November, 1951. (V.I. Popkov)

Master Shturmovik pilot. Twice Hero of the Soviet Union V.I. Andrianov commenced his combat duty at Kursk in 1943 and subsequently fought with great distinction during the great clashes at Korsun-Shevchenkovskij, Uman, Kishinyov-Yassy. He is credited with destroying 50 tanks along with numerous other ground targets during 177 sorties. (Author's collection)

A case in point is the glorious 1 GShAD, which was credited with 150 air victories, along with the destruction of 400 planes, 2,500 tanks and armored vehicles, 12,000 motor transports, 50 locomotives, and 450 railcars in ground attacks during some 30,000 sorties. The division had written a distinguished record at Stalingrad, but it was while taking part in the ferocious fighting over the Donbas in September, 1943 that its pilots acquired 89 of these air victories alone!

On December 6, 1941 the 215 ShAP (Major L.D. Rejno) was awarded the title of Guards, becoming the 6 GShAP for distinguishing itself in violent combat on the outskirts of Moscow – during the period of August 28 to October 10 the pilots had accounted for 205 tanks, 800 motor vehicles, 82 aircraft, 205 railcars and 102 anti-aircraft batteries.

The pilots of the 74 GShAP also built up a good score, claiming to have destroyed 480 tanks and 2,635 motor transports while affording 9,121 sorties throughout the war. The 672 ShAP was in the forefront of the action, finishing the war with a confirmed record of 108 enemy aircraft in the air and on the ground, 203 tanks together with 1,890 motor vehicles during 6,556 sorties. The first air victory in an Il-2 reportedly was achieved in July 1941 by Major A.N. Vitruk when he blasted an He 111, and adding a Bf 109 several days later. Vitruk was to make a big name for himself as commander of the 291 Voronezhskaya ShAD which was credited with the staggering total of 422 tanks destroyed during Zitadelle!

It is not without reason that the Soviet ground-attack arm produced the top Allied strafing aces of the war. Kapitan I.I. Zinovyev, a pilot of formidable skill and tenacity, who served with the 108 GShAP, chalked up the tremendous bag of 87 aircraft on the ground, plus nine more in the air, a record that was never equalled by an Allied pilot.

But the price was heavy. During the course of the war, the Shturmoviks continued to suffer fearful losses at the hands of Luftwaffe fighters. In fact, their ratio of losses was the highest in the VVS. In 1943 the ratio was one Il-2 for 26 sorties compared with 40 La-5 sorties, 45 Yak-1 sorties, and 54 Pe-2 sorties.

The Luftwaffe kept a special note of Il-2 credits. Joachim Brendel lead the way with 88 kills, while runners-up were Günther Josten and Johannes Wiese with 70 each, Erich Hartmann with 62, Kurt Dombacher 43, Helmut Lipfert 39, and others.

Walter Krupinski gave the author this account of his experiences: "The Il-2 was a very effective ground-attack aircraft. Their pilots were of a remarkable courage. My favorite tactic

Major M.G. Gareyev made a brilliant war record flying with the 76 GShAP in the Battle of Stalingrad, over the Donbas, the Crimea, Byelorussia, Poland and the Reich. He totaled 250 sorties bagging numerous ground targets. (Author's collection)

Major Yu.M. Balabin, a notable pilot of the glorious 144 GShAP, photographed in 1950. He won the coveted title of Hero of the Soviet Union with 232 Il-2 sorties under his belt on June 27, 1945. (V.I. Popkov)

was to concentrate my fire on their wings, where they tended to burn relatively easily." Generalleutnant (ret.) Krupinski was one of the most accomplished aerial fighters of the Eastern Front, winding up with a total of 197 victories; unfortunately, he does not recall how many Shturmoviks fell to his guns as his personal logbook was snatched from him by his American captors at Heilbronn POW camp.

Alfred Grislawski, another of JG 52's luminaries with 133 kills, 20 of them against Il-2s, recalls to me that he favored strikes from below and astern.

The Il-2 pilots earned the Germans' admiration and respect for their bold courage, executing their assigned duties even in the face of staggering losses. There are numerous eerie tales about Russian rear gunners who were still fighting back furiously while their aircraft was already ablaze and plunging earthward!

According to Soviet records, 23,600 Shturmoviks were lost during the war, representing 70% of the total number of 33,700 at hand! Of this figure, 12,400 were known definitely to be to enemy action. The following losses were recorded by year:

YEAR	TOTAL LOSSES	LOSSES TO ENEMY ACTION ONLY	% OF STRENGTH at HAND
1941	1,100	600	73.3
1942	2,600	1,800	34.2
1943	7,200	3,900	45
1944	8,900	4,100	46.6
1945 (1-1/5-10)	3,800	2,000	27.3
TOTAL	**23,600**	**12,400**	**70.03**

For reasons of historical value I have compiled a list of the top Shturmovik aces. Many of these notables were also able to build up good scores in air combat apart from wreaking havoc on enemy ground forces. As of this date, it is the most detailed list available. The entries are listed in order of number of tanks destroyed. Additional data include the pilot's surname, given name, father's name, combat unit, rank, and a listing of ground targets shot up.

YEFIMOV, Aleksandr Nikolayevich, Kap., 198 ShAP, 62 ShAP
126 tanks, 2 e/a air (Bf 109, Bf 110) and 5 fractional credits, 30 locos, 85 e/a ground, 193 artillery guns, 43 AA guns
BONDAR, Aleksandr Afanasyevich, Kap., 59 GShAP; KIA 10-28-1943
70 tanks, 250 motor vehicles, 2 e/a air plus 4 fractional credits, 6 e/a ground, 7 gun emplacements
KOPAYEV, Grigorij Ivanovich, Maj., 59 GShAP
70 tanks, 3 e/a air, 14 e/a ground
GOLUBEV, Viktor Maksimovich, Maj., 285 ShAP, 58 GShAP; KIA 5-17-1945
69 tanks, 875 motor vehicles, 80 e/a air/ground
KITALISHVILI, Zakhar Solomonovich, Kap., 232 ShAP
69 tanks, 31 armored cars, 29 e/a ground
KOZLOVSKIJ, Vasilij Ivanovich, Kap., 810 ShAP
68 tanks, 530 motor vehicles, 12 e/a air, 16 e/a ground, 5 locos, 67 rail cars
KADOMTSEV, Anatolij Ivanovich, Kap., 688 ShAP, 59 GShAP; KIA 2-21-1944
65 tanks, 340 motor vehicles, 4 e/a air, 16 e/a ground

Several of the most experienced pilots of Karelian Front gather for a council of war. They are, left to right: Lejtenant Korotkov, twice Hero of the Soviet Union V.I. Mykhlik, Hero of the Soviet Union Starshij Lejtenant A.A. Artemyev, Hero of the Soviet Union L.V. Obelov and three unknown officers. The date is June, 1944. (Author's collection)

The Il-2 proved to be notoriously difficult to bring down. The Luftwaffe Experten, who had learnt how to deal with the steel clads, though were taking a heavy toll. This IL-2M-3 was forced down in the Kiev area during the ferocious fighting in late 1943 and is being examined by curious soldiers. (Bundesarchiv)

Below: The war is over. Historic shot of Shturmoviks cruising over the ruins of Berlin. (Author's collection)

MARKOVTSEV, Stepan Kharitonovich, Podpolk., 208 ShAP
63 tanks, 201 motor vehicles, 4 e/a air, 5 locos
PISKUNOV, Vasilij Grigoryevich, St.Lej., 232 ShAP
58 tanks, 12 e/a air/ground, 17 gun emplacements
KOLENNIKOV, Vasilij Fyodorovich, Kap., 78 GShAP
56 tanks, 180 motor vehicles, 5 e/a air ground, 66 heavy guns
MALEN, Arsentij Antonovich, Kap., 74 GShAP
53 tanks, 3 e/a air/ground, 117 motor vehicles, 32 heavy guns, 23 rail cars
BYKOV, Mikhail Semyonovich, Kap., 571 ShAP
52 tanks, 12 e/a ground, 40 guns
STOLYAROV, Nikolaj Georgiyevich, Kap., 667 ShAP, 141 GShAP
52 tanks, 201 motor vehicles, 8 e/a air, 24 AA guns
ANDRIANOV, Vasilij Ivanovich, Kap., 667 ShAP, 141 GShAP
50 tanks, 200 motor vehicles, 2 e/a air plus 7 fractional credits, 25 gun emplacements
GLOBIN, Nikolaj Ivanovich, St.Lej., 525 ShAP
50 tanks, 200 motor vehicles, 10 e/a air, 4 locos, 97 rail cars
KARABULIN, Nikolaj Mikhajlovich, Kap., 215 ShAP; KIA 7-5-1943
50 tanks, 15 e/a air/ground, 70 motor vehicles
MYKHLIK, Vasilij Ilyich, Kap., 566 ShAP
50 tanks, 200 motor vehicles, 13 e/a air ground, 7 locos, 150 rail cars, 100 heavy guns
KARASEV, Anton Andreyevich, Kap., 57 ShAP-KBF
43 tanks, 113 motor vehicles, 51 AA guns
LOZENKO, Ivan Arkadyevich, Kap., 431 ShAP; KIA 12-15-1943
43 tanks, 125 motor vehicles, 2 e/a air, 7 e/a ground, 2 SPG, 1 loco, 13 heavy guns, 12 AA guns
MOSPANOV, Ilya Petrovich, St.Lej., 7 GShAP; KIA 7-25-1942
42 tanks, 160 motor vehicles, 37 e/a air/ground
AMELIN, Georgij Ivanovich, Lej., 208 ShAP
41 tanks, 11 armored cars, 104 motor vehicles, 3 e/a air, 4 e/a ground, 42 heavy guns

Two aces of the 218 ShAP: Starshij Lejtenant N.F. Pisarevskij (left) and Starshij Lejtenant V.S. Gavrilov, both of whom excelled in the fighting on 1st Byelorussian Front. (Author's collection)

V.I. Belousov of the 9 ShAP is decorated on Northwest Front in 1942. He won the title of Hero of the Soviet Union for proving his skills during the Russo-Finnish Winter War of 1939/40 and next saw frontline service from the earliest days of Operation Barbarossa. (Author's collection)

Three aces pose in front of Moscow's Kremlin. From left, they are: Kapitan A.N. Yefimov (62 ShAP), who knocked out 126 tanks – a total unsurpassed by any other Allied pilot – Major I.N. Stepanenko (4 IAP) and Major S.Ye. Artyomenko (447 SP), the able commander of a rifle battalion. (Author's collection)

BRYUKHANOV, Stepan Stepanovich, St.Lej., 966 ShAP; KIA 5-3-1945
40 tanks, 150 motor vehicles, 3 SPG, 30 heavy guns
RUDENKO, Pyotr Ivanovich, Lej., 7 GShAP; KIA 12-10-1942
40 tanks, 110 motor vehicles, 30 e/a air/ground, 20 heavy guns
VIKTOROV, Grigorij Petrovich, St.Lej., 74 GShAP, KIA 12-8-1944
40 tanks, 200 motor vehicles, 2 e/a air
ZAVARYKIN, Ivan Aleksandrovich, Kap., 806 ShAP; KIA 2-21-1945
40 tanks, 130 motor transports, 7 e/a ground, 20 heavy guns
YERMAKOV, Ivan Ivanovich, St.Lej., 91 GShAP
39 tanks, 2 e/a ground, 137 motor vehicles
FATKIN, Sergej Stepanovich, St.Lej., 165 GShAP
38 tanks, 3 e/a air, 18 locos
YELISEYEV, Nikolaj Trofimovich, Maj., 142 GShAP
38 tanks, 2 e/a air, 5 e/a ground
SMIRNOV, Dmitrij Ivanovich, St.Lej., 431 ShAP
37 tanks, 76 motor vehicles, 6 e/a air/ground, 20 heavy guns
ZHULOV, Fyodor Yegorovich, Ml.Lej., 235 ShAP; KIA 4-23-1944
36 tanks, 7 e/a air, 8 e/a ground, 90 motor vehicles
FOMIN, Sergej Semyonovich, St.Lej., 525 ShAP
35 tanks, 93 motor vehicles, 5 e/a ground, 40 rail cars, 27 AA guns
GRIDINSKIJ, Aleksandr Ivanovich, St.Lej., 144 GShAP; KIA 6-7-1944
35 tanks, 20 e/a air/ground, 90 motor vehicles, 3 gun emplacements
KLIMENKO, Mikhail Gavrilovich, St.Lej., 57 ShAP-KBF
34 tanks, 104 motor vehicles, 30 AA guns, 12 armored cars
MIKHALENKOV, Yefim Andreyevich, Kap., 78 GShAP
34 tanks, 27 e/a air/ground, 118 heavy guns
PARSHIN, Georgij Mikhajlovich, Maj., 943 ShAP
34 Tanks, 200 motor vehicles, 8 locos, 10 e/a air, 51 heavy guns
YUSHIN, Sergej Vasilyevich, Kap., 637 ShAP
34 tanks, 78 motor vehicles, 2 locos, 18 rail cars, 12 heavy guns
ALEKSENKO, Vladimir Avramovich, Maj., 15 GShAP
33 tanks, 118 motor vehicles, 15 armored cars, 2 e/a ground, 53 rail cars, 81 heavy guns
KARPOV, Aleksandr Alekseyevich, St.Lej., 806 ShAP
32 tanks, 90 motor vehicles, 5 e/a air/ground
KOLESNIKOV, Aleksandr Nikiforovich, Kap., 232 ShAP
32 tanks, 12 e/a air/ground, 150 motor transports, 23 armored vehicles
POPOV, Nikolaj Isaakovich, Kap., 724 ShAP
32 tanks, 1 e/a air plus 35 fractional credits, 55 motor vehicles

Kapitan A.N. Manokhin of the 15 GShAP, who received a Gold Star for his performance on August 19, 1944. Apart from wreaking havoc on enemy ground forces, Manokhin had three air victories and eight more fractional credits. (Author's collection)

A.K. Novikov, seen here as a Podpolkovnik in 1959, received the title of Hero of the Soviet Union for his exploits with the 108 GShAP on 1st Ukrainian Front on June 27, 1945. He passed away on July 8, 1984. (V.I. Popkov)

CHERNETSOV, Grigorij Ustinovich, Podpolk., 155 GShAP
31 tanks, 58 motor vehicles, 2 e/a air, 5 e/a ground
KAPUSTNIKOV, Nikolaj Ilyich, St.Lej., 637 ShAP; KIA 4-2-1945
31 tanks, 3 e/a air, 2 e/a ground, 74 motor vehicles, 25 heavy guns
ROSHCHIN, Lev Mikhajlovich, St.Lej., 190 ShAP
31 tanks, 137 motor vehicles, 1 e/a air, 12 e/a ground, 3 locos, 31 rail cars, 59 heavy guns
ROZHNOV, Nikolaj Andreyevich, Kap., 217 ShAP
31 tanks, 3 e/a air, 146 motor vehicles, 49 heavy guns
ZAJTSEV, Nikolaj Ilyich, St.Lej., 208 ShAP
31 tanks, 87 motor vehicles, 2 e/a ground, 4 gun emplacements
BALDIN, Anatolij Mikhajlovich, Lej., 92 GShAP
30 tanks, 75 motor vehicles, 5 e/a air/ground, 10 locos, 100 rail cars, 40 heavy guns
BRANDYS, Anatolij Yakovlevich, Kap., 75 GShAP
30 tanks, 9 SPG, 2 e/a air, 24 e/a ground, 64 motor vehicles, 4 locos, 70 rail cars, 35 gun emplacements
INASARIDZE, Georgij Moiseyevich, St.Lej., 683 ShAP
30 tanks, 10 armored cars, 108 motor vehicles, 15 locos, 105 rail cars, 13 gun emplacements
BUZIKOV, Fyodor Petrovich, St.Lej., 74 GShAP; KIA 1-24-1944
29 tanks, 3 e/a air/ground, 15 heavy guns
MININ, Yakov Kireyevich, Lej., 667 ShAP
29 tanks, 3 e/a air plus 7 fractional credits, 58 motor vehicles, 8 gun emplacements, 12 AA guns
TAVADZE, David Yelizbarovich, Kap., 190 ShAP
29 tanks, 150 motor vehicles, 7 e/a air, 9 e/a ground
BURAK, Aleksandr Kondratyevich, St.Lej., 208 ShAP
28 tanks, 3 gun emplacements, 3 e/a ground
DZHINCHARADZE, Israfil Kemalovich, Ml.Lej., 673 ShAP; KIA 10-15-1943
27 tanks, 82 motor vehicles, 6 e/a ground
KALASHNIKOV, Anatolij Stepanovich, St.Lej., 637 ShAP
27 tanks, 1 e/a air, 125 motor vehicles, 8 heavy guns
KARACHUN, Vladimir Grigoryevich, Kap., 947 ShAP
27 tanks, 112 motor vehicles, 3 e/a ground, 2 fractional credits air, 2 locos, 19 rail cars, 73 heavy guns
MACHNEV, Afanasij Gavrilovich, St.Lej., 566 ShAP
27 tanks, 3 e/a air, 21 e/a ground, 1 loco, 16 rail cars, 33 heavy guns
NOSOV, Aleksandr Andreyevich, Lej., 288 ShAP
27 tanks, 11 e/a ground, 15 heavy guns
BERNIKOV, Mikhail Mikhajlovich, Maj., 809 ShAP
26 tanks, 87 motor vehicles, 13 e/a air/ground, 18 heavy guns
GULKIN, Ivan Tikhonovich, St.Lej., 667 ShAP; KIA 3-4-1945
26 tanks, 112 motor vehicles, 3 fractional credits air, 17 heavy guns
MARKELOV, Nikolaj Danilovich, Lej., 806 ShAP
25 tanks, 4 e/a ground, 20 heavy guns
OLEJNIKOV, Vasilij Semyonovich, Lej., 143 GShAP
25 tanks, 90 motor vehicles

A Pz.Kpfw.III, or rather what is left of it, after it had been struck by rockets and/or bombs before an internal explosion blew off the turret. (Author's collection)

BLINOV, Pavel Fyodorovich, St.Lej., 141 GShAP
24 tanks, 207 motor vehicles, 3 e/a ground, 5 fractional credits air, 12 AA guns
LATSKOV, Nikolaj Sergeyevich, St.Lej., 431 ShAP
24 tanks, 76 motor vehicles, 20 guns, 3 e/a air, 2 locos
LOBANOV, Yevgenij Ivanovich, St.Lej., 18 ShAP-ChF; KIA 3-11-1942
24 tanks, 19 motor vehicles

Major L.I. Beda of the 75 GShAP was one of the legendary Shturmovik pilots emerging as a leading tank killer of World War II. He lost his life on December 26, 1976 the circumstances of his death not known. (Author's collection)

VVS stalwart – the ubiquitous Il-2 ground-attack aircraft played a major role on the German-Soviet Front proving its superior performance against tanks, gun emplacements, troop concentrations, airfields and anything that moved. The Shturmovik units produced 860 Heroes of the Soviet Union – more than any other air arm. Note RS-82 rockets on underwing rails. (Author's collection)

Ilyushin Il-10 with four 23mm NR-23 cannon (150 rpg). The Il-10 was the ultimate refinement of the Il-2 incorporating aerodynamic improvements and a more powerful engine for a considerable performance gain boosting the maximum level speed of the Il-2-AM-42 (1943) by 115 km/h to 550 km/h at sea level. It began to appear in small numbers in October, 1944 and was to soldier on for years after the cessation of hostilities. The 108 GShAP was the first regiment to put the Il-10 into operation, and on February 2, 1945 Hero of the Soviet Union F.A. Zhigarin led the first successful strike against enemy emplacements in the Sprottau area. When production was finally phased out, more than 41,000 examples of the Il-2 and Il-10 families had been delivered. Note the windscreen wiper. (Author's collection)

SEMEJKO, Nikolaj Illarionovich, Kap., 15 GShAP; KIA 4-20-1945
24 tanks, 4 SPG, 17 e/a ground, 64 motor vehicles, 3 locos, 40 rail cars, 34 heavy guns
UTKIN, Yevgenij Ivanovich, St.Lej., 996 ShAP
24 tanks, 3 SPG, 80 motor vehicles, 2 locos, 35 rail cars
ZVYAGIN, Aleksandr Yevstafyevich, Lej., 208 ShAP
24 tanks, 3 e/a air plus 2 fractional credits, 54 motor vehicles
BARANENKO, Vladimir Yakovlevich, St.Lej., 947 ShAP
23 tanks, 8 SPG, 85 motor vehicles
BEDA, Leonid Ignatyevich, Maj., 75 GShAP
23 tanks, 9 armored cars, 1 e/a air plus 3 fractional credits, 4 e/a ground, 1 loco, 32 rail cars, 37 heavy guns
PADALKO, Boris Mikhajlovich, Kap., 683 ShAP
23 tanks, 10 fractional credits air, 97 motor vehicles, 1 loco, 125 rail cars
BALAMUTKIN, Grigorij Vasilyevich, St.Lej., 431 ShAP
22 tanks, 95 motor vehicles, 17 artillery guns, 12 AA guns, 1 loco, 10 rail cars, 1 Ju 87 air
CHEKIN, Boris Sergeyevich, Lej., 566 ShAP
22 tanks, 61 motor vehicles, 37 heavy guns
ISHMUKHAMEDOV, Tamerlan Karimovich, St.Lej., 43 GShAP
22 tanks, 60 guns, 49 motor vehicles, 1 e/a air, 14 e/a ground
KIRILLOV, Aleksandr Semyonovich, Kap., 41 ShAP
22 tanks, 77 motor vehicles, 1 e/a air, 37 guns
KORCHAGIN, Lev Pavlovich, Kap., 566 ShAP
22 tanks, 84 motor vehicles, 7 e/a ground, 3 locos, 35 rail cars
KRASILOV, Aleksej Pavlovich, Kap., 235 ShAP
22 tanks, 2 e/a air, 5 armored cars, 90 motor vehicles, 75 locos, 16 rail cars
MOSHKOV, Boris Nikolayevich, St.Lej., 431 ShAP
22 tanks, 5 e/a air, 11 motor vehicles, 20 heavy guns
SELYANIN, Yevgenij Nikolayevich, St.Lej., 174 GShAP
22 tanks, 6 e/a air/ground, 75 motor vehicles, 20 heavy guns
ARTEMYEV, Aleksandr Alekseyevich, St.Lej., 566 ShAP
21 tanks, 1 e/a air, 39 motor vehicles
BEGELDINOV, Talgat Yakubekovich, Kap., 144 GShAP
21 tanks, 5 SPG, 7 e/a air, 5 e/a ground, 37 motor vehicles, 2 locos, 7 rail cars
MILASHENKOV, Sergej Vasilyevich, St.Lej., 109 GShAP
21 tanks, 65 motor vehicles, 22 heavy guns
VASILYEV, Nikolaj Konstantinovich, Kap., 594 ShAP
21 tanks, 170 motor vehicles, 1 e/a air
BIBISHEV, Ivan Frolovich, Lej., 285 ShAP
20 tanks, 50 motor vehicles
BOJKOV, Ivan Timofeyevich, St.Lej., 155 GShAP
20 tanks, 1 Ju 87 air, 10 e/a ground, 50 motor vehicles
BREKHOV, Konstantin Vladimirovich, Kap., 62 ShAP
20 tanks, 8 e/a ground
BUSLOV, Fyodor Vasilyevich, St.Lej., 136 GShAP
20 tanks, 5 e/a air, 7 e/a ground
GERMAN, Ivan Moiseyevich, Kap., 70 GShAP
20 tanks, 7 e/a air, 22 e/a ground, 70 motor vehicles
IVLIYEV, Yurij Dmitriyevich, Kap., 312 ShAP; KIA 1-29-1945
20 tanks, 1 e/a air, 11 e/a ground, 100 motor vehicles
YERMILOV, Pavel Aleksandrovich, St.Lej., 766 ShAP
20 tanks, 1 e/a air, 115 motor vehicles, 2 locos, 30 rail cars, 60 heavy guns
YERMOLAYEV, Vladimir Ivanovich, Lej., 143 ShAP
20 tanks, 98 motor vehicles
ZAJTSEV, Nikolaj Yakovlevich, St.Lej., 996 ShAP
20 tanks, 80 motor vehicles

4

SOVIET FIGHTER ACES IN KOREA

On Sunday, June 25, 1950, the North Korean Peoples Army suddenly launched its invasion of South Korea by crossing the 38th Parallel. Spearheaded by T-34/85 tanks and supported by swarms of Il-10 Shturmovik ground-attack aircraft, the offensive rapidly pushed South Korean and UN troops back.

USAF F-80s, F-51s, F-82s, and B-26s were quickly in the fray, wreaking successful havoc on Communist supply lines, and some big scores were built up against obsolescent Russian-built piston-engined aircraft; as the tide of war was beginning to turn and the North Korean advance slowed down to a halt, the advent of the Mikoyan-Guryevich MiG-15 mid-wing monoplane jets came to the Allies as one of the nastiest surprises of the war.

On November 1, 1950, UN pilots submitted first sighting reports of MiG-15s in Korean colors and, although 12 days later the first victory was reported, it soon became very obvious that the F-80s, F-84s, and Meteors had at a stroke become obsolete. The MiGs could even outclimb the F-86s that entered combat in December, 1950, and enjoying an untouchable ceiling of 15,200 meters, they could dive down on their prey and climb back up to a safe position after striking with relative impunity. From their experience Russian pilots determined that the MiG's main strength though lay in its enormous firepower, offered by one N-37 37mm cannon and two NS-23KM 23 mm cannon. A two-second burst would pour a devastating 14 kilograms of lead into the enemy plane, tearing it to pieces, while the MiG could take a lot of punishment from the Sabres' .50 caliber guns thanks to its heavier armor protection.

United States military authorities have always felt certain that skilled Soviet airmen fought in Korea. The actual Soviet involvement has long been due to continuous Soviet attempts to hide their participation at all. Glasnost and Perestrojka as late as 1993 have laid open fragments of Russian files, allowing to make a fairer comparison of the history of aerial warfare. Although there are many Russian participants who are still reluctant to talk freely about their experiences, there is no more denying that the combatants in Korea in terms of technical and psychological quality were actually more evenly matched, and that UN estimates of their air-to-air losses were grossly underestimated.

The VVS posted its 64 IAK on secret mission to Korea primarily tasked with blunting the Allied air offensive against the north. It was comprised of some elite fighter divisions which were rotated in and out after six to twelve months of combat. Commanding officer at its peak was General Major G.A. Lobov, late of the crack 7 GIAD of World War II fame with 19 air victories to his credit, who was destined to add four more kills to his already distinguished record in the ferocious air battles fought over Korea. In 1952 the 64 IAK commanded three fighter air divisions along with two antiaircraft divisions (85mm and 57mm guns), having a total of 26,000 men in strength. Recent information from Russia reveals that a total of 10 fighter divisions were committed to action in Korea at one time or another. The following units have been traced so far:

32 IAD	913 IAP
151 IAD	29 GIAP
216 IAD	518 IAP
303 IAD	18 GIAP, 523 IAP, 17 IAP
304 IAD	
324 IAD	176 GIAP, 196 IAP

As the Soviet Air Force was undergoing a complete transformation in modern equipment, units were deployed not uniformly prepared, some containing a relative proportion of pilots with an all too brief training period on jets; the tough vet-

Top-scoring ace of the Korean War. This postwar portrait shows Nikolaj Sutyagin as a General Major. He was awarded the title of Hero of the Soviet Union for his feats performed against the UN air forces in Korea. 15 of his kills were against F-86 Sabres. (Author's collection)

Polkovnik Ye.G. Pepelyaev ranks as the world's number two jet ace. He commanded the 196 IAP in Korea and personally claimed 19 kills including 14 F-86s before being rotated out of combat while his regiment was credited with blasting 100 enemy planes out of the sky for the loss of 24 MiG-15s. (Author's collection)

erans of the Patriotic War, however, formed the bulk and guts of the Soviet fighter force in Korea. They devised tactics under combat conditions that put the good qualities of the MiG to best advantage. In fact, the aircraft itself was confidence-inspiring, as it proved a clear ascendancy in many respects over the best enemy fighter, the F-86.

For fear of Soviet airmen falling into enemy hands, orders were given that prohibited pilots from penetrating a restricted area 100 kilometers wide north of the 38th Parallel, and from flying over coastal areas with the risk of imminent enemy naval vessels. Some Russians said that American pilots were quick to make good use of these restrictions when things were beginning to become too rough, running for the safety of these areas.

One of the first divisions to become operational was the 324 IAD under the high caliber leadership of the legendary Ivan Kozhedub, the Allied ace of aces of World War II with 62 kills. The unit had distinguished itself against the Luftwaffe during the so-called Svir-Petrozavodsk campaign (June-August, 1944) and was now tasked with neutralizing the Allied bombing campaign against North Korea, producing six more Heroes of the Soviet Union, the highest Soviet military distinction; whereas Kozhedub did not see any combat in Korea, his deputy, Vitalij Ivanovich Popkov, did. Popkov, a brilliant pilot and able tactician with 41 air victories against the Luftwaffe, went off whenever the opportunity arose, reporting the destruction of three more enemy planes in the skies above Korea.

On September 19, 1950, well before the first MiG-sightings were reported by the Allies, Podpolkovnik Aleksandr Karasyov, another notable fighter ace of World War II with 30 kills, again proved his attributes by flaming three F-84 Thunderjets in quick succession. On December 24 Kapitan Stepan Naumenko of the crack 29 GIAP had the distinction of becoming the first Soviet fighter ace in Korea by scoring his 5th air victory.

Aggressive, flying a formidable fighting machine and almost always enjoying the advantage of height, the Russians in time enjoyed moments of glory in their principal function of stopping the B-29s from systematically bombing North Korean industries, airfields, and bridges. On April 12, 1951, 48 B-29s were ordered off to strike the railroad bridges at Andong and Sinuiju, but 36 MiGs rose to engage them and claimed to have knocked down nine heavies, while the Americans admitted the loss of three of their number with seven more sustaining damage. On May 20 Starshij Lejtenant Fyodor Shabanov became the first fighter pilot in history to destroy five jets in

Ivan Kozhedub, the Allied ace of aces of World War II, proved his leadership talent as commander of the 324 IAD in this first virtually all-jet war. Although a serious fighter tiger, he did have a humorous side on occasion. This photo was made following the award of his third title of Hero of the Soviet Union in 1945. (Author's collection)

Vitalij Popkov, a battle-hardened World War II veteran, who had achieved 41 kills battling the Luftwaffe on the Eastern Front, was destined to add three more in Korea as deputy to Ivan Kozhedub. (V.I. Popkov)

air combat when he forced down an F-86 to bring his tally to six – five against jets – tying him with the American Jim Jabara of the 335th FIS, who, by coincidence, racked up his fifth and sixth victories that same day.

The MiGs appeared in increasing numbers as the war wore on, with poorly trained Chinese and North Korean units entering the fray, only to be whittled down by the battle-hardened Sabre pilots. The Allied fighters, though, again fared badly engaging Soviet MiGs on September 10, when the 64 IAK submitted claims for five F-86s, five F-84s, and one each F-80 and Gloster Meteor, all without loss; Kapitan G.I. Ges, an ace with five kills in World War II, accounted for the Meteor. Two weeks later, on September 26, Starshij Lejtenant N.V. Sutyagin claimed another of these to raise his bag to nine as the 303 and 324 IADs were claiming a total of four F-86s, three F-84s, and two Meteors, again without loss. In fact, the Soviet fighter elite in Korea considered the Americans less aggressive and flexible when met on equal terms, and lagging behind in fighting morale considering them unmotivated, fighting without cause.

The B-29s took another terrible battering on October 23. This time the MiGs were really ready. 56 fighters were put into the air during the raid, 12 of which were kept in reserve to intercept any bombers that might break through. 44 relentlessly attacked the bombers, 12 of these being claimed destroyed despite an escort of 55 F-84s, four of the Thunderjets also being knocked down. One MiG fell victim to the screening force of 34 F-86s over North Korean territory. As is so often the case, accounts from the opposing sides vary, and the exact figures are a matter of dispute. Whatever the truth, the B-29s were relegated to night raids following their heavy losses.

The hopelessly inferior Meteors were again meat on the table on December 1, 1951, when the glorious 176 GIAP got into its last scrap with the Australians, coming away with nine kills. Kapitan S.M. Kramarenko was high-scorer that day with a double, while singles were turned in by Podpolkovnik S.F. Vishnyakov, Major S.P. Subbotin, Kapitan A.F. Vasko, who was a 15-victory in World War II, Starshij Lejtenant F.A. Zubakin, P.S. Milaushkin, A.F. Golovachyov, and I.N.Gulyj.

The number one jet ace of all time is squadron leader Kapitan Nikolaj Sutyagin. He went to war as a deputy squadron leader with the 17 IAP and claimed his first success on June 19, 1951. Three days later he was able to bring his tally to three with two F-86s. He continued to chalk up victories on a regular basis and excelled in December, 1951, reporting the destruction of five enemy planes in the air. He finished with a confirmed total of 22 kills during 149 sorties, his score running as follows: 15 F-86s, three F-84s, two F- 80s, and two Meteors.

The runner-up was the highly talented commander of the 196 IAP, Polkovnik Yevgenij Pepelyaev, whose score is quoted by some sources as 23, although this is considered a combined total of his personal victories and shares. Pepelyaev required only 108 sorties to amass his impressive score of 19 kills, all of which were achieved against jets: 14 Sabres, two F-84s, one F-94, and one F-80. He also made a distinguished record as leader of the regiment, which finished the conflict as one of the top-scorers with 100 air victories against 24 aircraft and five pilots lost to enemy action during the period of April, 1951 to February, 1952. Among stellar performers in Korea was Major Dmitrij Oskin, who scored a string of eight victories in 23 days of combat between October-December, 1951 and wound up as an ace with 15 confirmed kills. Major S.A. Bakhayev is credited with 11 victories in Korea and one RB-29 intruder during the cold war period on December 29, 1950, while serving with the 523 IAP.

The Korean War produced 51 Russian fighter aces scoring five or more confirmed air victories; numerous other pilots made acedom by combining their World War II bag with credits in Korea. The 303 IAD boasted a total of 12 Heroes of the Soviet Union in MiG-15s.

The war ended on July 27, 1953. Total losses are a matter of dispute. Material disclosed by the VVS General Staff in 1993 indicates that the 64 IAK was credited with downing 1,106 enemy aircraft, 650 of which were F-86s, in 1,872 aerial encounters. Overall losses (conceivably not including missing in action or non-operational causes) were 335 planes and 120 pilots. Some Soviet sources quote a final score (not including Chinese and Korean victories) of some 1,300 for the loss of 345 MiGs. The Chinese and Korean air forces claimed a combined total of 231 victories at the cost of 271 of their number; the Americans reported the destruction of 954 aircraft, 827 of which were MiGs (or 893 resp. 841 as suggested by other sources), admitting the loss of 78 Sabres, 14 F-80s, and 18 F-84s in air-to-air combat and 971 losses overall, mostly to groundfire and non-operational causes.

I have compiled this partial list of Russian fighter aces in Korea. Certain pilots may have been left out due to the lack of available material. The list features:

Name, given name and father's name – rank (latest wartime ratings) – combat unit – number of air victories – number of missions

SUTYAGIN, Nikolaj Vasilyevich Kap., 17 IAP, 523 IAP	22	149
PEPELYAEV, Yevgenij Georgiyevich Polk., 196 IAP	19	108
OSKIN, Dmitrij Pavlovich Maj., 523 IAP	15	150
SHCHUKIN, Lev Kirillovich Kap., 18 GIAP; shot down three times	15	212
SMORCHKOV, Aleksandr Pavlovich Podpolk.	15	191
PONOMAREV, Mikhail Sergeyevich Maj.; 4 V 9-11-1951	14	140
KRAMARENKO, Sergej Makarovich Kap., 176 GIAP	13	149
SHEBERSTOV, Konstantin Maj.	12	
BAKHAYEV, Stepan Antonovich Maj.	11	166
DOKASHENKO, Nikolaj Grigoryevich Kap.	11	148
MILAUSHKIN, M.S. Kap., 176 GIAP	11	
OKHAJ, Grigorij Ulyanovich Kap., 523 IAP, 18 GIAP	11	122
BOJTSOV, Arkadij Sergeyevich Maj.	10+	
PULOV, Grigorij Ivanovich Podpolk., 17 IAP	10	120
SAMOJLOV, Dmitrij Aleksandrovich St.Lej.	10	161
GES, Grigorij Ivanovich Kap., 176 GIAP	9	120
SUBBOTIN, Serafim P. Kap., 176 GIAP	9	
FEDORETS, Semyon Alekseyevich Kap., 913 IAP	7	98
KARELIN, Anatolij Mikhajlovich Maj., 351 IAP; all night kills	6	50
SHABANOV, Fyodor Akimovich St.Lej.	6	150

5

THE UNITS

Order of battle of the VVS FIGHTER AIR CORPS (Istrebitelnye Aviatsionnye Korpusa)

1 IAK
Designated the 1 GIAK on 3-18-1943
Key commanders : Gen.Maj., as of 3-17-1943 Gen.Lej.Ye.M. Beletskij (9-10-1942/end of war)
Combat record: The unit ended World War II with a confirmed total of 1,789 air victories during 32,438 sorties

2 IAK
Key commanders: Gen.Maj., as of 4-30-1943 Gen.Lej.A.S. Blagoveshchenskij (10-10-1942/2-10-1945), Gen.Maj.V.M. Zabaluyev (2-11-1945/end of war)

3 IAK
Key commanders: Gen.Maj., as of 5-11-1943 Gen.Lej.Ye.Ya. Savitskij (12-10-1942/end of war)
Combat record: By May, 1945, when hostilities in Europe ceased, the score was 1,653 air victories during 28,860 sorties

4 IAK
Designated the 3 GIAK on 7-2-1944
Key commanders: Gen.Maj., as of 9-13-1944 Gen.Lej.I.D. Podgornyj (12-6-1942/end of war)
Combat record: The corps enjoyed considerable success in October, 1943 when claims for 276 enemy planes destroyed in air-to-air combat were submitted in 2,049 sorties. Final total not available.

5 IAK
Key commanders: Gen.Maj. I.D. Klimov (2-15-1943/6-26-1943), Gen.Maj. D.P. Galunov (6-27-1943/8-27-1944), Polk., as of 4-20-1945 Gen.Maj. M.G. Machin (8-28-1944/end of war)

6 IAK
Key commanders: Gen.Maj. A.B. Yumashev (2-19-1943/6-29-1943), Gen.Maj.Ye.Ye. Yerlukin (7-10-1943/5-28-1944), Gen.Maj. I.M. Dzusov (5-20-1944/end of war)
Combat record: By the end of the war the unit's score was 832 air victories during 18,654 sorties and 1,243 encounters; of the victories, 219 were claimed in the final battles over Berlin.

7 IAK
Designated the 6 GIAK on 10-27-1944
Full title: 6 Istrebitelnyj aviatsionnyj Lvovskij Krasnoznamennyj ordena Suvorova korpus
Key commanders: Gen.Maj., later Gen.Lej. A.V. Utin (6-23-1943/end of war)
Combat record: Casualties to the unit during October, 1943 ran high as dramatic battles flared up along the Dnyepr with 47 Airacobras and 25 pilots being lost during this month. Final record not available.

8 IAK
Key commanders: Gen.Maj. F.F. Zherebchenko (6-24-1943/6-13-1944), Gen.Lej. A.S. Osipenko (6-16-1944/end of war)
Combat record: At the close of hostilities the 8 IAK boasted a record of 21,586 sorties, 676 encounters, 735 aerial victories along with 151 enemy planes destroyed on the ground.

10 IAK
Key commanders: Polk., as of 8-7-1943 Gen.Maj. M.M. Golovnya (7-13-1943/end of war)

11 IAK
Key commanders: Gen.Maj. G.A. Ivanov (2-1-1944/end of war)

13 IAK
Key commanders: Gen.Maj. B.A. Sidnev (12-29-1943/end of war)
Combat record: At the end of the war the unit's confirmed victories totaled 405 enemy aircraft destroyed in the air during 11,828 sorties

14 IAK
Key commanders: Gen.Maj. S.P. Danilov (9-28-1944/end of war)

Order of Battle of the VVS FIGHTER AIR DIVISIONS (Istrebitelnye Aviatsionnye Divizii)

1 GIAD – see 220 IAD

1 GIAD-KBF
The unit was formed in 1938 as the 61 Aviatsionnaya Brigada being composed of the 5, 13 and 71 IAPs. In June, 1943 it was reformed as the 3 IAD-KBF and later was designated Guards for distinguishing itself in the epic fighting for Leningrad.
Key commanders: Polk. A. Morozov (until 8-26-1941), Polk. I. Romanenko (8- 30-1941/2-14-1942), Gen.Maj. N. Petrukhin (2-16-1942/6-24-1942), Polk. P. Kondratyev (6-29-1942/6-1-1943), Polk.V. Koreshkov (6-1-1943/8-26-1943), Podpolk.V. Katkov (9-28-1943/12-24-1943), Polk.V. Koreshkov (4-24-1944/end of war).
Combat record: The unit performed brilliantly in the defense of Leningrad, Tallin and the island of Kronshtadt east of Leningrad, claiming 200 kills during 9,200 sorties in 10 weeks of combat after the outbreak of the war. It added new laurels to its record taking part in the Soviet counteroffensive at Leningrad with 67 kills being chalked up in 700 sorties and 80 encounters from January to March, 1943. The division finished as the Baltic Fleet's highest scoring fighter outfit with a confirmed total of 1,021 air victories during 52,000 sorties.

2 GIAD-PVO – see 102 IAD-PVO

3 IAD – no trace

3 GIAD – see 210 IAD

3 IAD-KBF – see 1 GIAD-KBF

4 GIAD – see 274 IAD

5 GIAD – see 239 IAD

6 IAD
Key commanders: Polk. N.T. Petrushkin

A military correspondent is taking shots as fighter pilots are discussing their mission before take-off. (Author's collection)

An He 111 of KG 53 after crash-landing at Proskurov in 1944. (Author's collection)

6 GIAD – see 268 IAD

7 IAD – no trace

7 GIAD – see 209 IAD

8 IAD
Key commanders: Polk. N.S. Toropchin
Assignments: 1 VA

8 GIAD – no trace to original unit
Full title: 8 Gvardejskaya istrebitelnaya aviatsionnaya Krasnoznamennaya ordenov Suvorova i Bogdana Khmelnitskogo Kievskaya diviziya
Key commanders: Polk. V.I. Davidkov
Assignments: 2 VA

9 GIAD – see 216 IAD

10 GIAD – no trace to original unit
Full title: 10 Gvardejskaya istrebitelnaya aviatsionnaya Krasnoznamennaya ordena Suvorova Stalingradskaya diviziya
Key commanders: Gen.Maj. A.P. Zhukov
Assignments: 2 VA
Combat record: The unit finished as one of the VVS' top scorers with 1,098 air victories in 1,062 encounters

11 GIAD – see 207 IAD

14 GIAD – see 302 IAD

15 GIAD – see 235 IAD

22 GIAD – see 205 IAD

23 GIAD – no trace to original unit
Full title: 23 Gvardejskaya istrebitelnaya aviatsionnaya Krasnoznamennaya ordena Bogdana Khmelnitskogo Cherkasskaya diviziya
Key commanders: Polk. P.P. Kryukov
Assignments: 2 VA

24 IAD
Key commanders: Polk. I.D. Klimov
Assignments: 3 VA

29 IAD
Assignments: 10 VA

32 IAD
Assignments: 9 VA

36 IAD-PVO
Key commanders: Polk. V.V. Zelentsov
Combat record: 6,000 sorties, 92 air victories during the period of June 22 to September 1, 1941. Final total not available.

38 IAD
Key commanders: Gen.Maj. I.I. Yevseyev
Combat record: In heavy action on West Front the unit claimed the destruction of 235 enemy planes in the air and on the ground along with 35 tanks and 50 motor vehicles during 2,230 sorties in July, 1941.

39 IAD
Key commanders: Polk. Ye.Ya. Kholzakov
Combat record: 100 kills on Leningrad Front in August, 1941. Division score at the close of hostilities not available.

41 IAD – no trace

43 IAD
Key commanders: Polk. G.N. Zakharov

44 IAD
Key commanders: Polk. V.M. Zabaluyev
Assignments: 6 VA

47 IAD – no trace

54 IAD – no trace

Master Soviet fighter pilots pose for a group portrait. They are, left to right: P.D. Zyuzin (19 kills), A.D. Bilyukin (22), I.S. Leonovich (28), I.T. Tushev (15) and T.A. Litvinenko (23). (Author's collection)

Meeting of a fighter unit's party bureau discussing a pilot's admission to the Communist Party. The Aeracobra has been flown by one of the more accomplished pilots, as can be seen by the 20 victory stars painted on the forward fuselage. (Author's collection)

56 IAD
Assignments: 16 VA

57 IAD – no trace

73 IAD – no trace

78 IAD – no trace

96 IAD
Assignments: 11 VA

101 IAD-PVO
Key commanders: Polk. N.I. Shvedov, Polk. A.T. Kostenko
Combat record: 101 IAD operated with particular success during the period of June 28 to July 3, 1941, claiming 40 kills. It fought with great distinction at Voronezh and Borisoglebsk, where it afforded 13,089 sorties from October 16, 1942, until March 15, 1943, with 320 air encounters resulting in 256 kills.

102 IAD-PVO
Designated the 2 GIAD-PVO on 3-31-1943
Full title: 2 Gvardejskaya istrebitelnaya aviatsionnaya Krasnoznamennaya ordena Suvorova Stalingradskaya diviziya

Key commanders: Gen.Maj. I.I. Yevseyev, Polk. I.I. Krasnoyurchenko, Polk. I.G. Puntus (as of October, 1942)
Combat record: After activation in November, 1941 the division entered combat flying a miscellaneous collection of I-15bis, I-153s and I-16s. In July, 1942 the pilots reported the destruction of 17 enemy planes while entering combat 47 times. During the Battle of Stalingrad the unit finally realized its full potential, claiming 34 kills during 4,895 sorties and 47 combats between July 1 and August 7, 1942, for the loss of 33 aircraft to enemy action. At the end of the Battle 336 enemy planes had been shot down, 216 of which were bombers, though suffering very heavy losses. Serviceability as of November 29, 1942, was 30 aircraft. The unit's final tally at the close of war stood at 400 air victories during 16,919 sorties.

104 IAD-PVO – no trace

105 IAD-PVO
Key commanders: Polk. L.G. Rybkin
Combat record: The unit was particularly successful during the period of January 1, 1942, to June 1, 1943, when it was greatly involved in the fighting at Rostov and over the Kuban, submitting claims for 248 enemy planes in the air and 16 in ground attacks. May 9, 1943, was a field day for the unit when it put up 93 sorties in the Batajsk area claiming 40 victories. In all, 134 enemy aircraft were destroyed throughout 1943. The division was disbanded on June 1, 1943.

106 IAD-PVO
Key commanders: Gen.Maj. A.I. Gusev, Gen.Maj. P.K. Demidov
Combat record: The division was activated in December, 1941 and drew first blood on March 2, 1942. It was fairly active during the fighting at Demyansk, claiming 16 Luftwaffe planes in the air plus 53 more destroyed in ground attacks between February 26 and March 21, 1942. During the later stages of the war victories for the PVO forces were much harder to come by, but 106 IAD was able to add nine kills in March, 1943, one of which was a night intruder.

122 IAD-PVO
Honorifics: Pechengskaya
Key commanders: Polk. F.A. Pogreshayev
Combat record: The unit saw a lot of action in the defense of Murmansk, experiencing prohibitive losses. By November, 1942 strength at hand was down from 69 to three serviceable Hurricanes.

125 IAD-PVO – no trace

126 IAD-PVO – no trace

127 IAD-PVO – no trace

129 IAD-PVO – no trace

130 IAD-PVO
Key commanders: Polk. F.I. Shinkarenko
Assignments: 1 VA

133 IAD
Key commanders: Polk. A.M. Ryazanov

141 IAD-PVO – no trace

142 IAD-PVO
Key commanders: Podpolk. V.P. Ivanov

144 IAD-PVO
Key commanders: Maj. I.P. Suvorov, Polk. M.P. Noga

147 IAD-PVO
Key commanders: Polk. I.I. Krasnoyurchenko (as of November, 1942)

148 IAD-PVO
Key commanders: Polk. A.A. Tereshkin
Combat record: The unit saw only limited action scoring two air victories during 619 sorties in March, 1942. In 1944, however, as activity against Luftwaffe intruders increased, it was credited with 142 more victories at the cost of 13 aircraft and

Two photographs showing the mangled wreckage of an He 111 that was knocked down by Russian fighters near Mozhajsk, winter 1941. (Author's collection).

nine pilots killed through enemy action. The unit's final bag is uncertain.

178 IAD
Assignments: 5 VA

181 IAD
Key commanders: Gen.Maj. A.A. Demidov
Assignments: 2 VA

190 IAD
Key commanders: Polk. V.V. Fokin
Assignments: 3 VA, 12 VA

193 IAD
Honorifics: Demblinskaya
Key commanders: Polk. S.I. Mironov
Assignments: 16 VA

194 IAD
Key commanders: Polk. F.N. Dementyev
Assignments: 16 VA

197 IAD – no trace

201 IAD
Key commanders: Polk. A.P. Zhukov
Assignments: 8 VA, 1 VA, 5 VA
Combat record: It is possible that 201 IAD was designated Guards becoming the 10 GIAD for fighting a very successful campaign against the Luftwaffe. It is credited by one source with a total of 1,118 air victories, which does not match with the total quoted for the 10 GIAD, i.e. 1,098 kills, but this figure may be in error.

202 IAD
Key commanders: Polk. B. Yansen
Assignments: 1 VA

203 IAD
Designated the 12 GIAD on 2-5-1944
Full title: 12 Gvardejskaya istrebitelnaya aviatsionnaya Krasnoznamennaya ordena Bogdana Khmelnitskogo Znamenskaya diviziya
Key commanders: Gen.Maj. K.G. Baranchuk
Assignments: 1 VA, 5 VA (as of August, 1943), 2 VA

204 IAD – no trace

205 IAD
Designated the 22 GIAD on 10-27-1944
Full title: 22 Gvardejskaya istrebitelnaya aviatsionnaya ordena Lenina Krasnoznamennaya ordena Kutuzova Kirovogradskaya diviziya
Key commanders: Polk. Ye.Ya. Savitskij (May-November, 1942), Polk. Yu.A. Nemtsevich (November, 1942-April, 1944), Podpolk. L.I. Goreglyad (April-June, 1944), Polk. M.G. Machin (June-August, 1944), Podpolk. L.I. Goreglyad (August, 1944-end of war)
Assignments: 2 VA (Until July, 1943), 5 VA (until July, 1944), 2 VA
Combat record: The unit saw a great deal of activity at Orel in 1942 prior to deploying to Voronezh, destroying many enemy aircraft. It later fought with great success during the Korsun-Shevchenkovskij operation (January 24-February 17, 1944) and over Berlin. 58 German aircraft were destroyed during 1,500 sorties between July and October, 1942, while at Korsun 170 more fell before the pilots' guns. Final total not available.

206 IAD
Key commanders: Polk. V.A. Sryvkin
Assignments: 2 VA, 8 VA

207 IAD
Designated the 11 GIAD on 8-24-1943
Full title: 11 Gvardejskaya istrebitelnaya aviatsionnaya Krasnoznamennaya ordena Bogdana Khmelnitskogo Dnyepropetrovskaya diviziya
Key commanders: Polk. A.P. Osadchij
Assignments: 2 VA, 17 VA

208 IAD – no trace

209 IAD
Designated the 7 GIAD on 5-1-1943
Full title: 7 Gvardejskaya istrebitelnaya aviatsionnaya Krasnoznamennaya ordenov Suvorova i Kutuzova Rzhevskaya diviziya
Key commanders: Gen.Maj. V.M. Zabaluyev (May, 1942-February, 1945), Podpolk. G.A.Lobov (February, 1945-end of war)
Assignments: 3 VA (until December, 1942), 14 VA (until March, 1943), 5 VA (until June, 1943), 1 VA (July-August, 1943), 15 VA (Until October, 1943), 3 VA (until March, 1944), 1 VA (until end of war).
Combat record: The unit was activated in May, 1942 comprising of the 5 GIAP and 521 IAP and was assigned to the 3 VA on the Kalinin Front. It became involved in the defensive operations at Byelyj in July and took part in the Soviet offensive at Rzhev between July-August, 1942. Its regiments (1 GIAP, 12 and 900 IAPs) later enjoyed above-average success during the period of November-December, 1942 when they engaged in heavy action over Velikiye Luki. By May, 1943 the tally had risen to 200 kills during 10,000 sorties. It performed brilliantly during subsequent aerial operations over Vyazma, Orel, Bryansk, Nevel, Gorodok, Vitebsk, Sandomierz, Silesia and Berlin, finishing with a final record of 800 air victories and 21,000 sorties.

210 IAD
Designated the 3 GIAD on 3-21-1943
Full title: 3 Gvardejskaya istrebitelnaya aviatsionnaya Krasnoznamennaya ordena Suvorova Bryanskaya diviziya
Key commanders: Maj. L.Ya. Pinskij, Gen.Maj. V.P. Ukhov, Polk. V.I. Stalin
Assignments: 3 VA
Combat record: The division excelled in September, 1944, claiming 113 kills for 16 fighters lost through enemy action during 2,240 sorties and 65 air engagements. Final total not available.

215 IAD
Key commanders: Gen.Lej. G.P. Kravchenko (as of July, 1942, KIA 2-23-1943), Polk. M.N. Yakushin
Assignments: 1 VA, 16 VA

216 IAD
Designated the 9 GIAD on 6-17-1943
Full title: 9 Gvardejskaya istrebitelnaya aviatsionnaya ordena Lenina, Krasnoznamennaya, ordena Bogdana Khmelnitskogo, Mariupolsko-Berlinskaya diviziya
Key commanders: Gen.Maj. V.I. Shevchenko (May-October, 1942), Gen.Maj. A.V. Borman (October, 1942-May, 1943), Polk. I.M. Dzusov (May, 1943-May, 1944), Polk.A.I. Pokryshkin (May, 1944-end of war)
Assignments: 4 VA (until May, 1943), 8 VA (until January, 1944), 5 VA (as of May, 1944), 2 VA (as of July, 1944)
Battle honors: Donbas, Kuban, Taganrog, Mariupol, Yassy, Lemberg-Sandomierz, Silesia including Breslau, Berlin, Prague
Combat record: The division was activated in May, 1942 and became heavily engaged in the fighting over the Donbas, scoring 95 air victories between May-July, 1942 during 2,000 sorties. It began to pile up a tremendous score once the transition to Airacobras – the steed of war with which it would be permanently identified – had been completed. May 26, 1943 proved to be a bright day for the unit when 30 Luftwaffe planes were shot down and 27 more damaged in hard-fought, protracted duels over the Kuban. The pilots claimed 58 kills in a seven day period between July 13-19 for the loss of seven P-39s through enemy action. The Cobras had their biggest day on July 24, claiming 37 kills at the cost of three of their number. At Yassy the division again caused mayhem to enemy formations when 139 victories were claimed within seven days for the loss of some 10 pilots and 20 aircraft. Klubov was top-scoring ace of the campaign with nine kills, while runners-up were Dmitrij Glinka and Pyotr Guchyok with six each and Grigorij Dolnikov and Mikhail Komelkov getting five each. The unit closed out its scoring with 66 kills over Berlin, including 42 that were achieved on April 16, 1945, the first day of the Soviet assault on the German capital. The number of enemy aircraft destroyed by the 9 GIAD totaled 1,147 in the air during 33,654 sorties and 1,333 encounters. By the close of hostilities it had produced 61 Heroes of the Soviet Union, including four who had won this highest distinction twice and one (Aleksandr Pokryshkin) three times.

Sevastopol was knocked apart by super heavy artillery and bombs holding out for 250 days. When it fell on July 4, 1942 it was a smoking brickyard. (Author's collection)

217 IAD
The unit is believed to have been designated 8 GIAD, but this has not yet been substantiated.
Key commanders: Polk. D.P. Galunov
Assignments: 4 VA

220 IAD
Designated the 1 GIAD on 2-4-1943
Full title: 1 Gvardejskaya istrebitelnaya aviatsionnaya Krasnoznamennaya Stalingradsko-Berlinskaya diviziya
Key commanders: Polk. A.V. Utin (until June, 1943), Podpolk. I.V. Krupyenin (as of 6-19-1943), Polk. V.V. Sukhoryabov (August, 1943-end of war)
Assignments: 8 VA, 16 VA (as of September, 1943)
Battle honors: Stalingrad, Kursk, Byelorussia, Poland, Berlin
Combat record: The unit came into prominence during the Battle of Stalingrad, receiving the Guards Banner for amassing the formidable total of 334 aerial victories during the course of the fighting. The battle reached its climax in September, 1942 when the pilots claimed 93 kills, but 91 planes were lost while 48 pilots were killed and 16 wounded! The division again harshly treated enemy formations at Kursk, 33 kills being claimed on July 5, 1943, plus 28 more two days later. In all, 245 enemy planes were shot down before the end of the battle. It counted a total of 1,000 air victories at the end of the war.

223 IAD
Key commanders: Polk. P.P. Ryabakov

229 IAD
Honorifics: Tamanskaya
Key commanders: Polk. M.N. Volkov, Polk. P.G. Stepanovich
Assignments: 8 VA, 4 VA (as of May, 1944)
Combat record: The unit won fame for its operations over the Kuban where it ran up 100 kills in 120 air combats. Final total not available.

230 IAD
Honorifics: Kubanskaya
Assignments: 8 VA, 4 VA (as of May, 1944)

234 IAD
Honorifics: Mozyrskaya
Key commanders: Polk. Ye.Z. Tatanashvili
Assignments: 1 VA, 15 VA, 16 VA (as of July, 1943)

235 IAD
Designated the 15 GIAD, date not available
Full title: 15 Gvardejskaya istrebitelnaya aviatsionnaya Krasnoznamennaya, ordena Bogdana Khmelnitskogo Stalingradskaya diviziya
Key commanders: Polk. I.D. Podgornyj, Gen.Maj. I.A. Lakeyev
Assignments: 1 VA, 8 VA (as of 6-12-1942), 2 VA
Combat record: At Stalingrad the unit's four regiments – the 191, 436, 46 and 180 IAPs – fought hard while flying Hurricanes and were able to give as good as they received. 29 enemy planes were shot out of the skies between July 1-5, 1942 while losses that month amounted to 17 aircraft. By the end of hostilities in May, 1945 the division had destroyed 910 enemy planes in the air.

236 IAD
Key commanders: Gen.Maj. I.D. Klimov, Polk. V.Ya. Kudryashov
Assignments: 5 VA (as of June, 1942), 4 VA (as of April, 1943), 8 VA, 5 VA (as of May, 1944)

237 IAD
Key commanders: Gen.Maj. Ye.M. Beletskij
Assignments: 5 VA (as of June, 1942)

239 IAD
Designated the 5 GIAD in March, 1943
Key commanders: Polk. G.A. Ivanov

240 IAD
Honorifics: Nevelskaya
Key commanders: Polk. S.Ya. Simonenko (until April, 1943), Gen.Maj. G.V. Zimin (until October, 1945)
Assignments: 13 VA (as of April, 1943), 3 VA (as of August, 1943), 4 VA (as of 5-12-1944), 16 VA (as of 4-14-1945)
Combat record: The unit engaged in very heavy action on Leningrad Front. After two months combat available strength was down to 26 aircraft (86 GIAP – 15 Yak-7Bs, 156 GIAP – 6 LaGG-3s) and on July 11, 1943, it was withdrawn to Moscow, handing over its remaining planes to the 275 IAD. At this stage the score was 83 air victories plus four planes destroyed in ground attacks. It next saw considerable fighting at Smolensk, 1,784 sorties being flown within three weeks up to September 19, 1943, and 155 Luftwaffe planes (58 bombers, 97 fighters) were claimed destroyed. The price was heavy: 49 fighters were lost and 32 pilots KIA, including Podpolkovnik S.N. Najdenov, the commander of the 86 GIAP. As of October 3, 1943, 87 fighter aircraft stood ready to take part in the aerial operation of Nevel and claims for the period of October 6-11 amounted to 94 during 1,450 sorties. This raised the total record for the period August to mid-October, 1943 to 222 kills in 111 air combats involving 564 Soviet fighters and 1,125 enemy aircraft. The victories by type of aircraft destroyed were as follows:

He 111s	32
Ju 88s	29
Ju 87s	11
Do 215s	3
Do 217s	4
Hs 126s	1
Fw 190s	125
Bf 109s	17

In the same time frame losses were 62 aircraft and 58 pilots, 14 of which were KIA and 44 MIA. The division then took an active part in the fighting for Orsha and Borisov being tasked with escorting Il-2 and Pe-2 formations between June 23-30, 1944. Air opposition had decreased considerably and only 17 victories were claimed for the loss of 16 planes and nine pilots. Between June 23 and August 1, 1944, the division conducted 2,637 sorties in support of the Lida and Grodno fighting gaining 22 more kills. Casualties continued at a relatively high rate with 17 aircraft being lost in air combat and two Yak-9s being shot down by flak while 12 pilots were killed.

During August the unit carried out 789 escort sorties for 878 Il-2s and 81 Pe-2s in the Kaunas area. The Luftwaffe lost 22 planes while eight Yaks and five pilots fell to German guns. On October 10 the division moved to an advanced airfield close to the East Prussian border. From there it was engaged in escorting 1 GShAD and 311 ShAD Il-2s on ground-support missions, paving the way for General K.N. Galitskij's 11th Guards Army in the Gumbinnen area. Between late September and late October the unit afforded 3,169 sorties escorting a total of 2,659 Il-2s while it reported the destruction of 21 German aircraft in 72 encounters for the loss of 12 fighters, seven of these falling victim to groundfire, and four pilots.

The number of fighters on establishment as of December 1, 1944, was 139 (95 Yak-9s, 44 Yak-3s), of which five were undergoing repair, and 160 pilots. During January, 1945 1,690 fighters were sent out to escort 2,616 Il-2s and dive-bombers with all bombers returning safely. Only few enemy fighters rose to engage these missions and were successfully driven off, losing 20 of their number in the air and 12 more on the ground. Only one pilot, Mladshij Lejtenant N.Z. Golovchenko, failed to return. February witnessed a further decline of enemy air activity which resulted in only eight kills in the Konigsberg area for the loss of three pilots. The following month 240 IAD afforded 2,671 sorties with 16 enemy planes being shot down in 21 encounters involving 81 Yak-3s and Yak-9s resp. 151 Fw

190s and Bf 109s. Of six losses, only one was known definitely to be to enemy fighters. On April 14 it came under command of the 16 VA to participate in the final drive on Berlin four days later. In a final burst of activity, some 400 sorties resulted in 22 air engagements with 15 kills, Kapitan P.Ya. Golovachyov, Kapitan D.P. Motsakov and Starshij Lejtenant A.I. Kalugin all claiming doubles. These actions brought the unit's final record to 757 air victories, 20,206 sorties (18,743 combat hours) and 664 encounters.

245 IAD
Key commanders: Polk. G.P. Pleshchenko
Assignments: 12 VA

246 IAD
Assignments: 12 VA

250 IAD
Assignments: 9 VA

254 IAD
Key commanders: Polk. N.A. Silayev

256 IAD
Honorifics: Kievskaya
Key commanders: Polk. N.S. Gerasimov, Polk. M.P. Noga (11-17-1944-end of war)
Assignments: 3 VA, 2 VA

258 IAD
Full title: 258 Istrebitelnaya aviatsionnaya Krasnoznamennaya Svirskaya diviziya
Key commanders: Polk. M.M. Golovnya, Podpolk. G.A. Rejfshnejder (Kalugin) (as of 12-11-1942)
Assignments: 7 VA

259 IAD
Key commanders: Polk. Ya.A. Kurbatov, Podpolk. as of 3-18-1943 Polk. S.S. Yakhmenev
Assignments: 3 VA, 7 VA

260 IAD – no trace

265 IAD
Honorifics: Melitopolskaya
Key commanders: Podpolk. P.T. Korobkov, Polk. A.A. Koryagin
Assignments: 5 VA (as of June, 1942), 1 VA, 8 VA, 16 VA

268 IAD
Designated the 6 GIAD on 3-18-1943
Full title: 6 Gvardejskaya istrebitelnaya aviatsionnaya Krasnoznamennaya Donsko-Segedskaya diviziya
Key commanders: Podpolk. A.M. Ryazanov (June-July, 1942), Polk. B.A. Sidnev (July, 1942-October, 1944), Polk. I.I. Gejbo (October, 1944-end of war)

Fighter leaders discuss the next mission. Polkovnik A.A. Matveyev (right), commander of the 275 IAD, and Major Grinko, commander of the 191 IAP. Leningrad area, 1944.

Assignments: 8 VA, 5 VA (as of 9-13-1944)

269 IAD
Honorifics: Novgorodskaya
Key commanders: Polk. N.P. Laryshkin, Polk. A.P. Nikolayev, Polk. V.Ya. Dodonov
Assignments: 2 VA, 14 VA (as of July, 1943), 13 VA (as of February, 1944), 4 VA (as of October, 1944)
Combat record: The division was activated in the Voronezh area in late 1942 and was to achieve a high level of success during the period of January 11 to March 23, 1943, with 62 kills consisting of 41 bombers and 21 fighters being chalked up during 1,500 sorties and 86 air combats. It again scored heavily between July 7 and December 31, 1943, when it was credited with 76 enemy planes destroyed in the air during 3,800 sorties and 87 encounters. Final tally not available.

273 IAD
Honorifics: Gomelskaya
Key commanders: Polk. I.Ye. Fyodorov, Polk. N.V. Isayev
Assignments: 16 VA

274 IAD
Designated the 4 GIAD on 3-21-1943
Full title: 4 Gvardejskaya istrebitelnaya aviatsionnaya Krasnoznamennaya, ordena Suvorova Orshanskaya diviziya
Key commanders: Podpolk. P.K. Moskovets, Gen.Maj. V.A. Kitayev (as of 12-26-1942)
Assignments: 3 VA, 1 VA

275 IAD
Honorifics: Pushkinskaya
Key commanders: Podpolk. F.M. Mishchenko, Polk. A.A. Matveyev
Assignments: 13 VA

278 IAD
Full title: 278 Istrebitelnaya aviatsionnaya Krasnoznamennaya Svirskaya diviziya

Key commanders: Polk. V.T. Lisin, Polk. K.D. Orlov
Assignments: 1 VA, 14 VA, 8 VA
Combat record: Lejtenant Borovskij, Mladshij Lejtenant Bannikov and an unknown pilot had the distinction of scoring the unit's first successes on April 19, 1943 when they knocked down two Ju 87s and one Bf 109 in a melee over the Kuban. In this theater the division was to make a brilliant war record, and by June 16, 1943, the tally stood at 233 air victories including 79 bombers during 1,993 sorties, 133 group encounters and 519 individual scraps. It then fought a very successful campaign along the Dnyepr where it reported the destruction of 309 enemy planes in the air plus 95 motor transports, 28 rail cars, 25 locomotives and seven guns in ground attacks during 4,620 sorties and 278 group encounters along with 1,164 individual combats from September 7 until December 31, 1943. It saw a lot of action over the Crimea where 240 more kills were added while conducting 4,838 sorties between January 1 and May 12, 1944. The division furthered its high reputation during subsequent aerial operations over Orsha, Borisov, Vilnyus, Kaunas, the Berezina and Neman Rivers and East Prussia, exacting a heavy toll from opposing enemy aircraft. Between June 23 and September 9, 1944, it ran up a string of 125 air victories during 3,563 sorties and next took an active part in the Soviet Vistula-Oder offensive, the main thrust towards Berlin. The final assault on Berlin in April, 1945 saw the division claim 308 kills, 16 of which fell to their guns on April 16 and a record 43 two days later.

279 IAD
Key commanders: Polk. F.N. Dementyev, Polk. V.G. Blagoveshchenskij
Assignments: 14 VA, 16 VA (as of May, 1943)

281 IAD – no trace

282 IAD
Full title: 282 Istrebitelnaya aviatsionnaya Krasnoznamennaya, ordena Suvorova II stepeni Gomelskaya diviziya
Key commanders: Podpolk. A.M. Ryazanov, Polk. S.P. Danilov, Polk. Yu.M. Byerkal
Assignments: 16 VA (as of May, 1943)

283 IAD
Honorifics: Kamyshinskaya
Key commanders: Polk. V.A. Kitayev, Gen.Lej. S.P. Denisov, Polk. S.N. Chirva (December, 1943-end of war)
Assignments: 16 VA
Combat record: The division was in the thick of the fighting at Stalingrad scoring many victories but suffering inordinate losses. During September, 1942 it reported the destruction of 105 enemy planes for a loss of 66 aircraft (43% of the strength on hand). Losses of pilots were also high, amounting to 35 KIA in the same time frame (30%). The unit had a big day on April 16, 1945, when it was engaged in the final assault on Berlin, scoring 42 victories.

Interesting close-up of an unknown Lejtenant of a Guards unit posing with his Aeracobra. Four stars beneath the cockpit denote victories. (Author's collection)

286 IAD
Full title: 286 Istrebitelnaya aviatsionnaya Krasnoznamennaya, ordena Suvorova II stepeni Nezhinskaya diviziya
Key commanders: Polk. I.I. Ivanov, Podpolk. I.G. Trilyevich, Polk. V.I. Stalin
Assignments: 15 VA, 16 VA (as of March, 1943)

287 IAD
Key commanders: Polk. S.P. Danilov
Assignments: 8 VA, 5 VA (as of 4-20-1943), 4 VA (as of April, 1943)
Combat record: The 287 IAD was the first fighter division to fly the Lavochkin La-5, introducing it to combat on the Stalingrad Front on August 20, 1942. Its success was immediate, and within 27 days of combat the pilots had been credited with 97 kills while being engaged in frontline patrols and airfield defense. A total of 205 enemy planes were shot down through the battle during 3,142 sorties. Final score not available. It is believed that the unit later was designated the 10 GIAD.

288 IAD
Full title: 288 Istrebitelnaya aviatsionnaya Krasnoznamennaya, ordena Suvorova II stepeni Pavlogradsko-Venskaya diviziya
Key commanders: Polk. S.F. Konovalov, Gen.Maj. B.A. Smirnov (1943-45)
Assignments: 8 VA, 17 VA

289 IAD – no trace

294 IAD
Honorifics: Poltavsko-Aleksandrijskaya
Key commanders: Polk. V.V. Sukhoryabov, Polk. I.A. Taranenko (as of 7-27-1943)
Assignments: 5 VA (as of August, 1943), 2 VA
Combat record: The unit was in the forefront of action at Kursk, scoring 47 air victories during the period of July 5-8, 1943. It

scored heavily again in August, 1943 when it submitted claims for 84 Fw 190s and Bf 109s destroyed. The division ended World War II as one of the high scoring outfits with 1,105 air victories.

295 IAD
Key commanders: Polk. N.F. Balanov, Polk. A.A. Silvestrov, Polk. F. S. Shatilin
Assignments: 17 VA, 5 VA

296 IAD
Assignments: 10 VA

298 IAD-PVO
Key commanders: Polk. V.A. Lushchin

302 IAD
Designated the 14 GIAD on 7-2-1944
Full title: 14 Gvardejskaya istrebitelnaya aviatsionnaya Krasnoznamennaya, ordena Suvorova Kirovogradsko-Budapeshtskaya diviziya
Key commanders: Polk. B.I. Litvinov (December, 1942-February, 1944), Podpolk. V.I. Zinovyev (February, 1944-June, 1944), Polk. A.P. Yudakov (June, 1944-end of war)
Assignments: 2 VA (March, 1943-July, 1944), 5 VA (July, 1944-end of war)
Combat record: The division was activated in December, 1942 and was to make a brilliant war record during its subsequent assignments at Voronezh, Kursk, Byelgorod-Kharkov, Korsun-Shevchenkovskij, Uman, Yassy-Kishinyov, Budapest and Vienna. It chalked up 100 kills in the skies above Kursk, and the greatest number of air victories claimed in one month was 180 in 88 encounters in October, 1943. One of its regiments, the 240 IAP, was largely responsible for this success accounting for more than half of the kills. It reached 500 victories in July, 1944 and continued to see considerable fighting during the later stages of the war.

303 IAD
Honorifics: Smolenskaya
Key commanders: Gen.Maj. G.N. Zakharov
Assignments: 1 VA
Battle honors: Spas-Demensk, Smolensk, Vitebsk, Borisov, Kaunas, East Prussia
Combat record: The division fought with great distinction at Smolensk between August-September, 1943 getting 188 kills. Two of its fighter regiments, the 18 GIAP and the French Normandie-Neman regiment, were among the most illustrious outfits of the Eastern Front, the former claiming 427 kills and the latter 273. It later added more luster to an already bright record against UN air forces in Korea under the fabled Georgij Lobov, producing 12 Heroes of the Soviet Union and claiming some 200 kills for the loss of 30 MiG-15s.

309 IAD
Key commanders: Polk. V.N. Vuss
Assignments: 1 VA, 4 VA

310 IAD-PVO
Key commanders: Polk. A.T. Kostenko
Combat record: In a flurry of action around Breslau the unit reported the destruction of eight Luftwaffe planes during 386 sorties on May 6, 1945, as the remains of the garrison tried to fly to the west.

315 IAD
Honorifics: Rizhskaya
Key commanders: Polk. V.Ya. Litvinov
Assignments: 15 VA
Combat record: The division was activated in April, 1943. It entered combat at Kursk, seeing a great deal of action and inflicting heavy losses on the enemy. By August 5, 1943, the score had risen to 108 during 1,027 sorties and 71 air encounters. At Karachev and Bryansk few enemy planes were encountered and only 13 kills were added between August 5-September 17. The amount of air combat also fell off in March, 1944 and kept claims for the month down to 32, while two months later nine Fw 190s, one Bf 109, and 10 Ju 87s were shot down, plus 13 planes destroyed in ground attacks. The bag for the period January-July, 1944 was 59 air victories during 3,230 sorties and 52 combats. Air opposition continued to be weak during subsequent operations over Daugavpils and Rezekne (Latvia), 1,793 sorties until August, 1944 drawing up the Luftwaffe only on nine occasions with the division knocking down 14 Fw 190s and two Bf 109s. Of these sorties, 682 were escorts, 450 free hunts, 211 frontline patrols, and 450 reconnaissance. German fighters appeared during the fighting for Riga between August-October, 1944 putting up a fierce resistance. During the same period, the 315 IAD received credit for 63 victories in 3,152 sorties and 61 encounters. From October, 1944 until January, 1945 the unit conducted 1,471 sorties over Courland, but no combat was seen at this late stage. The final score was 387 air victories, consisting of 216 fighters, 83 bombers, 33 reconnaissance planes plus 66 aircraft, 37 locomotives, and 86 rail cars destroyed in ground attacks, 16,913 sorties, 286 group encounters and 93 individual combats.

320 IAD-PVO
Key commanders: Polk. A.G. Panov

322 IAD
Full title: 322 Istrebitelnaya aviatsionnaya Krasnoznamennaya, ordena Suvorova Minskaya diviziya
Key commanders: Polk. M.P. Noga, Polk. A.F. Semyonov (October, 1944-end of war)
Assignments: 1 VA, 2 VA
Combat record: In a last burst of heavy activity the unit ran up 152 air victories during 4,369 sorties between January-May, 1945. Final record not available.

The awesome results of Shturmovik attacks southeast of Minsk, where the bulk of German 4.Armee and elements of 9.Armee were caught in an enormous pocket. (Author's collection)

323 IAD
Honorifics: Baranovichskaya
Key commanders: Polk. P.P. Rybakov
Assignments: 1 VA, 16 VA

324 IAD
Honorifics: Svirskaya
Key commanders: Polk. F.I. Fomin, Polk. I.P. Laryshkin (as of 4-17-1944)
Assignments: 7 VA, 16 VA
Combat record: In Korea, the division later operated with equal success under the high-caliber leadership of the great Ivan Kozhedub, producing six Heroes of the Soviet Union while flying MiG-15s.

328 IAD-PVO
Key commanders: Gen.Maj. A.I. Gusev

329 IAD
Key commanders: Polk. A.A. Osipov
Assignments: 4 VA

331 IAD
Key commanders: Polk. I.A. Semyonenko
Assignments: 5 VA, 8 VA

336 IAD
Key commanders: Polk. S.M. Petrov, Polk. S.P. Grashchenko (as of June, 1944)
Assignments: 6 VA, 16 VA, 3 VA

Order of Battle of the VVS FIGHTER AIR REGIMENTS (Istrebitelnye Aviatsionnye Polki)

1 GIAP – see 29 IAP

2 IAP
Key commanders: Polk. Grisenko
Assignments: 36 IAD, 220 IAD
Aircraft: I-153s, LaGG-3s, Yak-1s, MiG-3s
Battle honors: Kiev 1941, Kharkov 1942

2 GIAP – see 526 IAP

2 GIAP-SF – see 72 IAP-SF

3 GIAP-KBF – see 5 IAP-KBF

4 IAP
Key commanders: Podpolk. V.I. Melikov, Podpolk. K.P. Malinov

3 GIAP – see 155 IAP

3 GIAP-KBF – see 5 IAP-KBF

4 IAP
Key commanders: Podpolk. N.I. Mironov, Podpolk. A.A. Morozov (until late 1943)
Assignments: 20 SAD, 147 IAD, 185 IAD, 287 IAD (as of August, 1942)
Aircraft: I-153s, I-16s, Hurricanes (as of January, 1942), Yak-1s, Yak-7Bs, Yak-9s
Battle honors: Kishinyov, Tiraspol, Nikolayev, Odessa (all 1941), Yaroslavl, Voronezh, Stalingrad, Kuban, the Baltic, Courland
Combat record: Over 150 enemy planes were destroyed by September, 1942. It claimed 18 kills over the Kuban on April 23, 1943. The unit's Yak-9s were fitted with 37mm cannon in September, 1943, and these were flown with notable success against transports and in the ground support role.

Aces: I.N. Stepanenko 33, A.K. Ryazanov 32, M.S. Pogorelov 29, A.A. Morozov 24, I.V. Shmelev 23

4 GIAP-KBF – see 13 IAP-KBF

5 IAP-KBF

Activated in August, 1938
Designated 3 GIAP-KBF on 1-18-1942
Full title: 3 Gvardejskij istrebitelnyj aviatsionnyj Krasnoznamennyj ordena Ushakova II stepeni polk
Key commanders: Podpolk. P.V. Kondratyev, Podpolk. N. Nikitin (as of 6-29-1942), Maj. N. Shmelev (as of 1-1-1944), Podpolk. V. Katkov (as of 5-18-1944), Maj. G.A. Romanov (as of 7-15-1944)
Aircraft: LaGG-3s, Hurricanes, La-5s
Battle honors: Leningrad, Kronshtadt, Lavansaari
Combat record: The regiment was in the forefront of action from the earliest days of the war, achieving a high level of success between June-August, 1941 by claiming 57 air victories. Further combats took the score to 105 during 5,899 sorties by January, 1942 winning it the Guards Banner. During the period of August 14 to October 22, 1942, it ran up a string of 79 air victories, 11 of these being claimed on September 5 for two fighters lost. It finished as the top-scoring Soviet naval fighter regiment with a confirmed bag of 500 kills, plus 17 planes, 71 tanks and armored vehicles, and 750 motor transports destroyed in ground attacks.
Aces: D.M. Tatarenko 16, I.I. Tsapov 15

5 GIAP – see 129 IAP

6 IAP

Activated at Khabarovsk in June, 1938
Designated the 18 GIAP on 3-7-1942
Full title: 18 Gvardejskij istrebitelnyj aviatsionnyj dvazhdy Krasnoznamennyj ordena Suvorova Vitebskij polk
Key commanders: Maj. B.R. Aristov (KIA), Maj. S.I. Chertov, Podpolk. A.Ye. Golubov (as of October, 1942)
Assignments: 234 IAD (as of June, 1942), 303 IAD
Aircraft: I-16s, Yak-1s (as of March, 1942), Yak-7Bs, Yak-9s, Yak-3s (as of July, 1944)
Battle honors: Novgorod, Staraya Russa, Kozelsk, Rzhev, Bryansk, Kursk, Spas-Demensk, Smolensk, Vitebsk, Orsha, Mogilyov, Bobrujsk, East Prussia
Combat record: The regiment started flying combat on Northwest Front on July 24, 1941, reporting the destruction of 61 enemy planes in the air and six on the ground over Novgorod and Staraya Russa during 4,420 sorties and 217 combats within seven months. Outstanding pilots during this time were G.A. Tsvetkov, V.S. Karpov, I.I. Molchanov, N.I. Gurin, V.I. Zapaskin, A.P. Gruzdev and A.V. Nikolayev with 5-6 victories each. Between March-June, 1942 Yak-1s began to arrive to replace the I-16 fighters following which the unit came under command of the 234 IAD to enter into a fierce battle at Kozelsk and later Rzhev. In two months' combat the pilots added 63 victories with 14 more damaged to the record during 1,735 sorties and 251 air engagements. The regiment next enjoyed above-average success in the contested air space above Kursk, racking up 30 more victories for a loss of four pilots in air-to-air combat between June 12-27, 1943. During the same period, the regiment afforded 503 sorties, 425 of which were Il-2 and bomber escorts. Operations continued on an ever-increasing scale with 32 more enemy planes falling to the regiment's guns from August 29 until September 6 at the cost of four pilots. On September 4, 1943, eight Yak-9s with Lejtenant B.I. Lyapunov in the lead were roughly handled by 24 Fw 190s while engaged in a frontline patrol. In a protracted dogfight, the regiment lost four promising air fighters, who boasted tallies of some 10 kills each – Boris Lyapunov, Dmitrij Lobashev, Ivan Sobolev, Vasilij Loginov – against three victories. In all, the regiment gained 62 kills at Smolensk before fighting a series of combats over Vitebsk where 22 more German planes were destroyed between October 12-15. The bag for the period February-December, 1943 was 150 kills during some 3,000 sorties and 295 encounters, and when comparing the unit's aerial victory record with its four fellow regiments operating with the 303 IAD the magnitude of its accomplishments comes into true perspective: 40% of the division's victory total was accounted for by the 18 GIAP. The regiment took a heavy toll of enemy aircraft after moving into East Prussia, and on October 16, 1944, had a field day with 20 Fw 190s in the air plus four planes by strafing in the Insterburg area without loss. Major Zapaskin, Major Terentyev, and Kapitan Barakhtayev all scored singles in the last air battle fought by the regiment near Pillau on April 25, 1945. It ended the war with a total of 12,638 sorties, 940 air combats, 427 kills and 30 planes destroyed in ground attacks. A total of 49 pilots were killed in action, along with five more who lost their lives in enemy air attacks. The unit later fought in Korea while flying MiG-15s and was one of the outstanding regiments, scoring many victories. High-scorer in this conflict was Kapitan L.K. Shchukin with 15 kills.
Aces: V.N. Barsukov 22, N.G. Pinchuk 22, N.N. Danilenko 16

6 GIAP-ChF – see 8 IAP-ChF

7 IAP

Designated the 14 GIAP on 3-7-1942
Full title: 14 Gvardejskij istrebitelnyj aviatsionnyj Krasnoznamennyj Leningradskij polk
Key commanders: Podpolk. G.M. Galytsin
Aircraft: I-153s, I-16s, MiG-3s
Battle honors: Russo Finnish Winter War 1939/40, Leningrad Front
Combat record: During the Winter War the regiment claimed eight Fokker D-21s without loss on January 31, 1940, and later had a big day on September 16, 1941, with 16 kills while fighting during the darkest hours of the 1941/42 air war on Leningrad Front.

Polikarpov I-153 biplane of the 7 IAP attached to truck mounted Hucks-type starter. Leningrad Front, autumn 1941. (Author's collection)

7 IAP-ChF
Key commanders: Podpolk. A.Z. Dushin, Podpolk. K.D. Denisov (as of July, 1942), Podpolk. V.M. Yankovskij (as of October, 1943)
Aircraft: I-15ls, MiG-3s, Yak-1s, LaGG-3s, Yak-7s (as of October, 1942), Kittyhawks
Battle honors: Crimea, Kerch, Novorossijsk, Anapa, Taman, Gelendzhik, Sevastopol (1944)

8 IAP
Designated the 42 GIAP on 2-8-1943
Key commanders: Podpolk. Ya.A. Kurbatov
Assignments: 216 SAD, 269 IAD, 9 GIAD
Aircraft: Yak-1s, Yak-3s
Battle honors: Caucasus 1942/43, Voronezh, Orel, Byelgorod
Aces: I.M. Gorbunov 24, N.N. Pechyonyj 20, A.Kh. Kankoshev 20, V.V. Isayev 17, M.I. Kossa 15

8 IAP-ChF
Activated in 1939.
Designated the 6 GIAP-ChF on 4-3-1942
Key commanders: Polk. K.I. Yumashev, Podpolk. M.V. Avdeyev (as of 4-26-1943), Maj. I. Lokinskij (as of 12-30-1944)
Aircraft: I-15bis, I-16s, Yak-1s, Yak-7s, Yak-9s (as of 1944)
Battle honors: Odessa, Sevastopol 1941/42, Crimea, Novorossijsk, Sevastopol 1944, Rumania
Combat record: The regiment ended World War II with a total of 300 air victories, 54 enemy planes destroyed on the ground along with 19 tanks and 669 motor vehicles, 21,600 sorties, 2,219 encounters

9 IAP-ChF
Key commanders: Podpolk. K.P. Malinov (1942), Maj. A.D. Dzhaparidze
Aircraft: Yak-1s, MiG-3s
Battle honors: Nikolayev 1941, Sevastopol 1942, Kerch, Perekop

9 IAP-KBF
Full title: 9 Istrebitelnyj aviatsionnyj Krasnoznamennyj Klajpedskij ordena Ushakova II stepeni polk
Key commanders: Podpolk. A.D.Dzhaparidze

9 GIAP – see 69 IAP

10 IAP
Key commanders: Maj. N.V. Terekhin (as of August, 1941/KIA 12-30-1942)
Aircraft: I-16s, MiG-3s, Yak-1s, Kittyhawks
Battle honors: Lithuania June, 1941, Kalinin, Volkhov and Northwest Fronts

10 GIAP-KBF – see 71 IAP-KBF

11 IAP
Key commanders: Podpolk. G.A. Kogrushev (1941), Maj. N.G. Kukharenko
Assignments: 268 IAD
Aircraft: Yak-1s
Battle honors: Moscow, Stalingrad, Leningrad, Karelia
Aces: Although no details are available, one source ("Vozmaya Vozdushnaya", p.102) suggests that as of October, 1942 the regiment had two aces with 10 or more kills

11 IAP-KBF – no trace

11 GIAP – see 44 IAP

11 GIAP-ChF – see 32 IAP-ChF

12 IAP
Key commanders: Maj. P.T. Korobkov
Assignments: 64 SAD, 209 IAD, 265 IAD, 7 GIAD
Aircraft: I-153s, I-16s, Yak-1s, MiG-3s
Battle honors: Stanislau, Kiev, Moscow, Rzhev, Bryansk, Sandomierz, Silesia
Combat record: The regiment suffered inordinate losses on the very first day of the Patriotic War when Luftwaffe strikes claimed 36 of its 66 I-153s on the ground. In their desperate attempt to give what cover they could to their airfield the pilots claimed the destruction of eight Ju 88s around Stanislau at the cost of three of their number. Mladshij Lejtenant L.G. Butelin knocked down two of the attackers, getting his second victory by ramming near Galich at 5:42 a.m.

12 IAP-KBF
Full title: 12 Istrebitelnyj aviatsionnyj Krasnoznamennyj, ordena Ushakova II stepeni polk
Key commanders: Podpolk. V.V. Volochnev

12 GIAP – see 120 IAP

13 IAP
Designated the 111 GIAP, on 8-25-1943
Full title: 111 Gvardejskij istrebitelnyj aviatsionnyj Stalingradskij polk
Key commanders: Podpolk. I.M. Kholodov
Assignments: 201 IAD, 10 GIAD
Aircraft: I-16s, La-5s, La-7s
Battle honors: Stalingrad, Kuban, Lemberg-Sandomierz, the Reich, Czechoslovakia
Aces: P.A. Gnido 34, M.T. Ignatyev 28, A.A. Gubanov 25, S.D. Gorelov 24, A.D. Grebenyov 24

13 IAP-KBF
Activated in April, 1938
Designated the 4 GIAP-KBF on 1-18-1942
Full title: 4 Gvardejskij istrebitelnyj aviatsionnyj ordena Ushakova II stepeni polk
Key commanders: Podpolk. I. Romanenko, Maj. M. Okhten (as of October, 1941), Polk. B.I. Mikhajlov (as of 1-9-1942), Polk. V. Koreshkov (as of 10-10-1942), Podpolk. L. Borisov (as of 11-13-1942), Podpolk. V. Golubev (as of August, 1943)
Aircraft: I-16s, La-5s

Familiar shot of Yak-9s of the 6 GIAP-ChF prowling over the Sevastopol area in May, 1944. Aircraft "22" is flown by Mikhail Grib, leader of the 3rd Eskadrilya. (Author's collection)

Battle honors: Hanko, Tallin, Kronshtadt, Leningrad, Volkhov, Königsberg
Combat record: The regiment was in the thick of the fighting from the earliest days of the war and by January, 1942, when it was awarded the title of Guards, the score had risen to 117 during 5,945 sorties. It had a big day on March 28, 1942, when 11 enemy planes were destroyed. By the close of hostilities the record was 431 air victories plus ground claims of 20 tanks and armored vehicles, 358 motor transports, 22,000 sorties.
Aces: K.F. Kovalyov 21, V.F. Golubev 16, A.M. Selyutin 16, P.A. Brinko 15

14 GIAP – see 7 IAP

14 GIAP-KBF – no trace to original unit
Designated Guards on 7-29-1944
Full title: 14 Gvardejskij istrebitelnyj aviatsionnyj dvazhdy Krasnoznamennyj, ordena Ushakova II stepeni Klajpedskij polk
Key commanders: Podpolk. A.A. Mironenko

15 IAP
Full title: 15 Istrebitelnyj aviatsionnyj Krasnoznamennyj, ordena Suvorova Orshanskij polk
Key commanders: Maj. V.N. Kalachev (KIA 6-28-1942), Podpolk. G.V. Gromov
Assignments: 278 IAD
Aircraft: Yak-1s (until late 1943), La-5s
Battle honors: Stalingrad, Kuban, Crimea, Vistula-Oder campaign, the Reich, Berlin
Combat record: The regiment was involved in a fierce series of dogfights on June 22, 1941, claiming nine kills. High scorer of the day was deputy commander Kapitan A. Dovzhenko, who

Podpolkovnik Romanenko, commander of the 13 IAP-KBF, relaxing in front of an I-16 fighter. The date is July, 1941. Romanenko was awarded the title of Hero of the Soviet Union for displaying his leadership talent during the Russo-Finnish Winter War, the unit claiming 13 kills as of February, 1940. (Author's collection)

knocked down three Luftwaffe planes in eight sorties. It destroyed 19 enemy planes on April 19, 1945, and on May 1 A. Odnoblyudov racked up the 581st and last air victory, the regiment finishing as one of the top-scoring VVS fighter units.
Aces: S.N. Morgunov 27, V.V. Klimov 27, V.I. Suvirov 22 of 25, L.N. Slizen 19

16 IAP
Key commanders: Podpolk. F.M. Prutskov (1941)
Assignments: 6 IAK-PVO
Aircraft: Yak-1s, MiG-3s
Battle honors: Moscow
Combat record: The regiment reportedly put the good qualities of the RS-82 air-launched rocket to best advantage, I.F.

An I-16 of the 4 GIAP-KBF taxis out for a mission on Kronshtadt Island, off Leningrad, in August, 1942. (Author's collection)

Golubin, M.G. Trunov, N.P. Buryan, I.P. Shumilov and A.M. Filimonov claiming the destruction of six Luftwaffe planes with salvoes of this 82mm rocket in October, 1941.
Aces: I.P. Shumilov 16, I.F. Golubin 14, I.N. Zabolotnyj 12

16 GIAP – see 55 IAP

17 IAP
Assignments: 14 SAD, 205 IAD, 190 IAD
Aircraft: I-16s, LaGG-3s, Yak-1s, La-5s, Airacobras, Kingcobras (as of June, 1945)
Battle honors: Kiev 1941, Voronezh, Kursk, Korsun-Shevchenkovskij, Uman-Botosani, Manchuria 1945
Combat record: The regiment was in the forefront of action from the earliest days of the war, scoring many victories and finishing as one of the most accomplished fighter outfits. It concurrently operated LaGG-3s and Yak-1s until the close of the war alongside a number of P-39s and La-5s. In June, 1945 it was based in the Transbaikal, becoming one of the first units to convert to P-63 Kingcobras. In August, 1945 it went to war with the Japanese in Manchuria, and on the 15th Mladshij Lejtenant I.F. Miroshnichenko gained the Kingcobra's only victory of the war by destroying a fighter identified as either a Ki.27 or Ki.43. The regiment later fought with distinction in Korea while flying MiG-15 jets, producing the top ace of the war, Kapitan N.V. Sutyagin.
Aces: V.F. Sirotin 15

Major V.F. Sirotin, 17 IAP's ranking ace with his Aeracobra. He was killed in a flying accident on August 7, 1948. The photo is dated March 6, 1945. (Author's collection)

18 GIAP – see 6 IAP

19 IAP
Activated in March, 1938
Designated the 176 GIAP on 8-19-1944
Full title: 176 Gvardejskij istrebitelnyj aviatsionnyj Krasnoznamennyj ordena Aleksandr Nevskogo Proskurovskij polk
Key commanders: Kap. A.G. Tkachenko (June, 1941-October, 1942), Maj. L.A. Orlov (October, 1942-March, 1943), Maj. G.A. Pustovojt (March-August, 1943), Podpolk. L.L. Shestakov (September, 1943-March, 1944), Polk. P.F. Chupikov (March, 1944 – end of war)
Assignments: 7 IAK-PVO (as of 8-8-1941), 269 IAD (as of March, 1943), 324 IAD
Aircraft: I-16s, La-5s, La-7s
Battle honors: Russo-Finnish Winter War 1939/40, Leningrad, Volkhov, Stalingrad, Voronezh, Kursk, Proskurov, Bobrujsk, Poland, Pomerania, Berlin, Manchuria 1945
Combat record: When German forces initiated Operation Barbarossa in June, 1941 the regiment was operating on North Front prior to being assigned to the 7 IAP-PVO on August 8, 1941. It was to write a distinguished record during the epic defense of Leningrad, claiming 76 kills in the I-16 fighter during 2,826 sorties and 415 combats until December, 1941. It next saw action during the brutal battles for the Soviet capital and in February, 1942 deployed to Volkhov Front. After heavy fighting it was reformed at Moscow between August-December, 1942 before returning to combat on Voronezh Front as part of the 269 IAD. The regiment gained a high reputation for its fighting prowess in the skies above Stalingrad, Ostrogozhsk-Rossosh, Voronezh, and Kharkov. In January, 1944 it was posted to 1st Ukrainian Front, exacting a heavy toll of opposing enemy aircraft over Proskurov and Byelorussia excelling in "free hunt" fighter sorties. On August 11, 1944, it came under command of the 16 VA to fight a very successful campaign over Poland and the Reich. By May, 1945, when hostilities ceased, the score was 398 enemy planes in the air and 56 on the ground during 9,450 sorties, 4,016 of which were free hunts and 750 air encounters. The regiment later enjoyed considerable success against UN air forces in Korea, claiming 103 kills for the loss of 17 MiG-15s and five pilots.
Aces: N.S. Rudenko 21, A.A. Karayev 18, I.N. Kozhedub 17 of 62, A.S. Kumanichkin most of his 31 kills, V.A. Gromakovskij 16

19 GIAP – see 145 IAP

20 IAP
Designated the 139 GIAP, date not established
Key commanders: Maj. S.N. Najdenov 1941, Maj. I.I. Gejbo, Maj. P.S. Kutakhov

Lavochkin La-5 "20" of the 21 IAP on the way in. 1st Baltic Front, June 18, 1944. Note stars beneath the cockpit indicating aerial victories. (Author's collection)

Yak-9s of the 21 IAP-KBF taxi out for take-off on September 21, 1944. (Author's collection)

Assignments: 63 SAD, 203 IAD, 303 IAD
Aircraft: I-153s, Yak-1s, Yak-9Us
Battle honors: Karachev, Moscow, Kaluga, Orel, Smolensk, Orsha, Borisov, Vilnyus, Kaunas, East Prussia
Combat record: The regiment was taken completely by surprise on June 22, 1941, when it was caught by heavy Luftwaffe strikes, smashing most of its 60 I-153s and 61 Yak-1s on the ground in the vicinity of Karachev.

20 GIAP – see 147 IAP

21 IAP
Key commanders: Maj. Miroshnichenko, Maj. P.I. Pavlov
Assignments: 259 IAD
Aircraft: LaGG-3s, La-5s
Battle honors: Riga, Moscow, Kalinin Front, Vitebsk, East Prussia
Combat record: The regiment joined combat with the Luftwaffe on June 22, 1941, intercepting enemy bombers in the Riga area. Throughout the day it claimed nine air victories, doubles each by Lejtenant Garkusha and Lejtenant Komissarov. In the dark months to follow losses were very heavy, but a good score was built up with 87 kills being claimed, along with 42 tanks and armored vehicles and 46 motor transports being destroyed in ground attacks during 2,366 sorties between July-August, 1941.
Aces: V.V. Yegorov 11

21 IAP-KBF
Full title: 21 Istrebitelnyj aviatsionnyj Krasnoznamennyj, ordena Suvorova III stepeni Kenigsbergskij polk
Key commanders: Podpolk. P.I. Pavlov
Aircraft: Yak-9s

21 GIAP – see 38 IAP

22 IAP
Key commanders: Maj. T.F. Kutsevalov (1938-April, 1939), Maj. N.G. Glazykin (April, 1939/KIA 6-22-1939), Podpolk. G.P. Kravchenko
Aircraft: I-153s, I-16s
Battle honors: Khalkhin Gol 1939
Combat record: The regiment made a big name for itself fighting the Japanese along the Khalkhin Gol River in Mongolia, emerging as the top-scoring fighter units of the conflict. The first combat saw the regiment lose two pilots – Starshij Lejtenant N.S. Cherenkov and Mladshij Lejtenant V.G. Paksyutov – on May 27, 1939. It suffered a further setback the following day when Japanese fighters were able to bounce them, losses for the two days amounting to 12. The situation was about to change radically for the better, however, once I-16 fighters arrived. These quickly restored the balance in the air, and on June 22 the unit had a big day with 13 enemy planes being destroyed while 42 fighters and 33 bombers were knocked down during 2,404 sorties in a nine day period between August 20-28.
Aces: V.F. Skobarikhin 12, G.P. Kravchenko 8 of 20, V.G. Rakhov 8

23 IAP
Activated at Kiev in 1938
Key commanders: Polk. A.I. Sidorenko
Aircraft: I-15s, I-153s, MiG-3s
Battle honors: Russo-Finnish Winter War 1939/40, Lemberg 1941
Combat record: The regiment operated during the Winter War against the Finns, reporting the destruction of four enemy planes while losing one of its own to groundfire. On the eve of Operation Barbarossa it had 40 I-15s, I-153s and 45 MiG-3s on strength, but at least five fighters were destroyed and five pilots wounded in the heavy Luftwaffe air attacks of June 22, 1941. Throughout the day the regiment flew 130 interception sorties. By July 15, 1941, when it was disbanded and the regiment's personnel and remaining aircraft being absorbed by the 28 IAP-PVO, it had been credited with downing 28 enemy aircraft during 790 sorties.

24 IAP
Key commanders: Maj. A.M. Stepanov (1941)
Aircraft: Yak-1s
Battle honors: Moscow

25 IAP
Key commanders: Polk. N.S. Toropchin
Battle honors: Russo-Finnish Winter War 1939/40, Crimea 1944

26 IAP-PVO
Designated the 26 GIAP on 11-22-1942
Key commanders: Podpolk. B.N. Romanov
Assignments: 7 IAK-PVO, 2 GIAK-PVO
Aircraft: I-16s, I-153s, Yak-1s, MiG-3s, LaGG-3s, Hurricanes, Tomahawks, Kittyhawks, Spitfires, Airacobras, Yak-9s, La-5s
Battle honors: Leningrad Front
Combat record: With the German attack on Soviet Russia the regiment saw a great deal of action, but experienced heavy losses. 13 pilots were lost in September and 14 more the following month.
Aces: D.Ye. Oskalenko 14

26 GIAP -see 26 IAP

27 IAP
Designated the 129 GIAP, on 10-9-1943
Full title: 129 Gvardejskij istrebitelnyj aviatsionnyj ordenov Bogdana Khmelnitskogo i Aleksandra Nevskogo Sandomirskij polk
Key commanders: Podpolk. P.K. Demidov (1941), Polk. V.I. Bobrov, Podpolk. V.A. Figichev
Assignments: 205 IAD, 22 GIAD

Aircraft: Airacobras
Battle honors: Moscow, Kalinin Front, Stalingrad, Kursk-Byelgorod, Poltava, Kovel, Rovno, Novograd, Lemberg-Sandomierz, Moldavia, Rumania, Berlin, Prague
Combat record: The regiment wrote a distinguished record during the early months of the war, claiming 61 victories during 3,950 sorties from June until December, 1941. It really came into its own once it had re-equipped with P-39 Airacobras, and between May 10 and July 5, 1943, reported the destruction of 23 enemy planes while engaged in intercepting German reconnaissance aircraft. On May 14 it broke up an attack on its own airfield at Grushka, knocking down nine Ju 87s for the loss of two Cobras. It next excelled during the Battle of Kursk, claiming 88 kills between July 5-August 5, 1943, including 19 on the first day of the fighting. By the time hostilities in Europe ceased, the regiment had established itself as a top-scoring outfit, destroying a total of 549 enemy planes in the air.
Aces: N.D. Gulayev – a large number of his 57 kills, F.F. Arkhipenko 30, V.I. Bobrov 30 of 43, P.P. Nikiforov 20, V.A. Karlov 19, A.L. Karmin 19, M.V. Lusto 19, Ye.P. Mariinskij 19, M.V. Bekashonok 18

27 GIAP – see 123 IAP

28 IAP
Key commanders: Podpolk. N.F. Demidov
Assignments: 15 SAD, 6 IAK-PVO
Aircraft: I-16s, MiG-3s
Battle honors: Lemberg, Moscow, Rzhev
Combat record: The regiment entered combat on June 22, 1941, when it was based near Lemberg (Lvov), fighting hard against great odds. It afforded 157 sorties throughout the day, coming away with six air victories. It had a big day on September 29, 1942, with victory claims of 10 destroyed, including a triple by A.Ya. Fyodorov.
Aces: A.V. Rudenko 14, Ye.M. Gorbatyuk 11

28 GIAP – see 153 IAP

29 IAP
Activated in 1938
Designated the 1 GIAP on 12-6-1941
Full title: 1 Gvardejskij istrebitelnyj aviatsionnyj ordena Lenina, Krasnoznamennyj i Kutuzova Krasnogvardejskij polk
Key commanders: Polk. A.P. Yudakov (June, 1941-September, 1942), Komissar A.I. Zotov (September-December, 1942), Maj. P.T. Logvinov (December, 1942-February, 1943), Maj. I.M. Dzyuba (February-March, 1943), Maj. I.I. Kajnov (March, 1943-October, 1944), Maj. V.I. Zinov (October, 1944-February, 1945), Maj. I.A. Malinovskij (February, 1945-end of war)
Assignments: 31 SAD (1938), 210 IAD, 209 IAD
Aircraft: I-153s, I-16s, Hurricanes (as of December, 1941), Yak-1s (as of May, 1942), Yak-7Bs (as of October, 1942), Yak-3s (as of October, 1944)

N.D. Gulayev of the 129 GIAP. With 57 personal victories he ranks as number three Allied ace of World War II. (Author's collection)

Battle honors: Kursk 1941, Rzhev, Vitebsk, Lemberg-Sandomierz, Poland, Silesia, Berlin
Combat record: The regiment drew first blood on July 18, 1941, when Mladshij Lejtenant I.L. Yukhimovich, in an I-153 biplane, destroyed a Ju 88. On August 8 it reported the destruction of seven enemy planes, and by October, 1941 the score had risen to 67. The unit's biggest day came on July 31, 1943, when 16 German planes were blasted out of the sky in five separate tussles. May 8, 1945, was the last time the 1 GIAP was to fire its guns in anger, and saw Starshij Lejtenant I.D. Sviridov bring down an He 111 over Czechoslovakia. The regiment's final record was 347 aerial victories, 11,508 sorties, 900 combats.
Aces: A.K. Laukhin 20, I.I. Zabegajlo 16, V.K. Ishchenko 14

29 GIAP – see 154 IAP

30 GIAP – see 180 IAP

31 IAP
Full title: 31 Istrebitelnyj aviatsionnyj ordena Bogdana Khmelnitskogo Nizhnednyeprovskij polk
Key commanders: Podpolk. G.D. Onufriyenko
Assignments: 206 IAD, 295 IAD

Aircraft: LaGG-3s, La-5s, La-7s
Battle honors: Byelgorod-Kharkov, Dnyepropetrovsk, Krivoj Rog, Yassy-Kishinyov, Yugoslavia, Hungary, Austria
Combat record: The regiment came out of World War II as one of the outstanding fighter units with a record of 350 confirmed kills, 17,301 sorties, 608 engagements.
Aces: N.M. Skomorokhov 46, P.G. Yakubovskij 23, V.V. Kirilyuk 22, O.N. Smirnov 20, N.I. Gorbunov 15, M.D. Tsykin 15

31 GIAP – see 273 IAP

32 IAP
Key commanders: Maj. A.P. Zhukov (1941)
Assignments: 43 IAD (July, 1941), 256 IAD
Aircraft: MiG-3s
Battle honors: Smolensk, Yartsevo, Yelnya, Vyazma 1941, Kalinin Front, Moscow, Caucasus, Kursk-Byelgorod, Poland, Berlin, Czechoslovakia
Aces: V.G. Denisenko 30, P.L. Grishchenko 27, N.V. Khudyakov 19, Ya.V. Shishkin 17, A.N. Konyaev 15

32 IAP-ChF
Activated in March, 1938
Designated the 11 GIAP on 5-31-1943
Honorifics: Nikolayevskij
Key commanders: Podpolk. N. Pavlov (until 9-23-1942), Podpolk. I.S. Lyubimov (10-2-1942/10-3-1943), Podpolk. K. Denisov (10-3-1943/10-11-1944), Maj. N. Vasilyev (as of 12-11-1944)
Aircraft: Yak-1s, Airacobras(as of September, 1943)
Battle honors: Odessa, Sevastopol, Kuban, Novorossijsk, Taman, Kerch, Perekop
Combat record: During its first year of combat the regiment achieved 86 air victories in 401 encounters. In a series of ferocious battles for Tuapse (September-December, 1942) it received credit for 50 more kills, and in March, 1943 the record stood at 152 air victories, eight more damaged and 10 planes destroyed on the ground during 12,000 sorties and 750 encounters. The regiment saw considerable fighting covering the Eltigen landings on the Crimea (November 1-9, 1943), getting four kills on November 1 and five more the following day, all without loss. On the 3rd two Bf 109s and one Ju 87 fell to its Cobras in four separate scraps. Starshij Lejtenant D.A. Starikov was the big gun on the 6th with four kills, his squadron mates bringing the day's tally to nine. The regiment had a field day on March 10, 1944, when it bagged 11 Luftwaffe planes while attacking the enemy Kulbakino airfield near Nikolayev for the loss of three P-39s. The unit's total bag was 304 kills, 25 damaged and 12 planes destroyed in ground attacks, 16,000 sorties.
Aces: D.A. Starikov 21, B.M. Litvinchuk 18, D.V. Zyuzin 14

32 GIAP – see 434 IAP

33 IAP
Key commanders: Maj. P.O. Petrov, Maj. G.M. Yakhnov
Assignments: 10 SAD, 106 IAD-PVO
Aircraft: I-16s
Battle honors: Brest 1941, Demyansk, Volkhov, Velikiye Luki
Combat record: The regiment was based at Pruzhan, 70 kilometers northeast of Brest, and saw action for the first time on June 22, 1941, at 3:30 a.m. when Lejtenant Mochalov's flight ran into an enemy aircraft, which they shot down near Brest. Shortly afterward the regiment's own airfield was attacked by 20 He 111s escorted by several Bf 109s, but these were intercepted by three fighter squadrons returning from air patrol. In the action that followed the regiment submitted claims for five He 111s destroyed, two by Lejtenant Gudimov, who claimed his second victim by ramming, having expended the ammunition of his I-16.
Aces: G.M. Yakhnov 12

34 IAP
Key commanders: Maj. L.G. Rybkin (1941)
Aircraft: MiG-3s
Battle honors: Moscow
Combat record: The regiment performed brilliantly in the defense of Moscow, claiming 12 kills on October 23 and eight on November 14, 1941. The total for the period June 22, 1941, until December 22, 1941, was 68 air victories during 3,427 sorties, 299 of which were nocturnal interceptions. In March, 1943 Starshij Lejtenant V.F. Korobov racked up the unit's 100th confirmed victory.
Aces: Yu.S. Seldyakov 11

35 IAP
Aircraft: Yak-1s
Battle honors: Moscow

36 IAP
Designated the 57 GIAP on 2-8-1943
Key commanders: Maj. A.A. Osipov (1942)
Aircraft: I-16s, Spitfires, Airacobras
Combat record: The regiment engaged in heavy action over the Kuban salient and along the northeastern coast of the Black Sea, totaling 1,976 sorties and 13 air victories in 56 air-to-air combats between June-July, 1942.

38 IAP
Designated the 21 GIAP on 5-3-1942
Full title: 21 Gvardejskij istrebitelnyj aviatsionnyj Krasnoznamennyj ordena Kutuzova Cherkasskij polk
Key commanders: Maj. A.I. Sergov
Assignments: 57 SAD
Aircraft: I-153s, LaGG-3s
Battle honors: Northwest and Leningrad Fronts
Aces: L.S. Chapchakhov 11, I.F. Balyuk 5 of 22

38 GIAP – see 629 IAP

39 GIAP – see 731 IAP

40 IAP
Designated the 41 GIAP on 2-8-1943
Full title: 41 Gvardejskij istrebitelnyj aviatsionnyj ordena Kutuzova Chernovitskij polk
Key commanders: Maj. P.F. Chupikov
Assignments: 217 IAD, 229 IAD, 8 GIAD
Aircraft: I-153s, I-16s, La-5s
Battle honors: Caucasus, Kursk-Byelgorod, the Dnyepr, Silesia
Combat record: The regiment's biggest day came on April 23, 1943 when it downed 18 enemy planes without loss. By May, 1945, when hostilities in Europe ceased, the regiment's tally was 425 air victories.
Aces: A.V. Lobanov 26, M.I. Sementsov 19, I.M. Pilipenko 10

40 GIAP – see 131 IAP

41 GIAP – see 40 IAP

41 IAP
Key commanders: Maj. M.P. Noga (1940), Maj. Yershov (1941)
Assignments: 9 SAD, 43 IAD
Aircraft: MiG-3s
Battle honors: Mogilyov, Smolensk, Vyazma, Moscow
Aces: I.D. Chulkov 9, A.A. Lipilin 9+

42 IAP
Designated the 133 GIAP on 10-9-1943
Honorifics: Orshanskij
Key commanders: Podpolk. F.I. Shinkarenko, Maj. A.V. Osipov (as of 5-28-1944)
Assignments: 240 IAD (as of 7-19-1943), 211 ShAD (as of October, 1943)
Aircraft: MiG-3s, LaGG-3s (as of November, 1941), Yak-7Bs, Yak-9Ts
Battle honors: Orel 1941, Tula 1941, Staraya Russa 1942, Demyansk, Smolensk September, 1943, Dukhovshchina September, 1943, Nevel October, 1943, Orsha June, 1944, Borisov June, 1944, Minsk July, 1944, Kaunas August, 1944, Gumbinnen October, 1944, East Prussia, Berlin
Combat record: The first enemy planes in the air were destroyed by G.I. German, D.I. Romanenko, and V.G. Mironov in the Orel area in July, 1941. At Tula the regiment ran up 30 kills in six weeks' combat between October-November, 1941 and was then pulled out of combat for a rest and transition to LaGG-3s on November 15. There was heavy air fighting at Smolensk and Nevel in 1943, and several pilots were able to give a good account of themselves, Kapitan S.M. Brazhnets getting six kills between late August and mid-October, as did Major A.V. Osipov, while Kapitan A.M. Legchakov received credit for four. In September, 1944 the regiment was engaged in intercepting enemy intruders in the Kaunas area at night, but no details of any successes are available.
Aces: G.I. German 23+, N.V. Tikhonov 16, V.N. Orlov 14

42 GIAP – see 8 IAP

43 IAP
Honorifics: Sevastopolskij
Key commanders: Maj. Ye.P. Melnikov, Podpolk. N.T. Syusyukalov (KIA), Maj. A.A. Doroshenkov
Assignments: 36 IAD, 220 IAD (1942), 278 IAD
Aircraft: I-16s, Yak-1s, Yak-7Bs
Battle honors: Kiev 1941, Stalingrad, Kuban, Kharkov, Sevastopol, Vitebsk, Vistula-Oder campaign, Berlin
Combat record: The regiment operated with particular distinction during the epic fighting for Kiev (July 7-September 26, 1941) claiming 67 victories but suffering heavy losses. It later fought a very successful campaign in the skies above Stalingrad, Starshij Lejtenant Kochetov being top-scoring ace with seven kills. It then deployed to the Kuban theater in the spring of 1943 where it was to add new laurels to its record, gaining 82 air victories during 650 sorties in three months' combat. Starshij Lejtenant Kochetov again was high-scorer of the battle, chalking up eight more kills. After being assigned to South Front the regiment shot down 30 enemy planes in a fierce series of battles over the Crimea, with Kochetov accounting for four personal victories and three more shares. Further combats over Poland, the Reich, and finally Berlin saw the pilots achieve 51 air victories to bring the total to 459 kills during 13,241 sorties.
Aces: A.V. Kochetov 27 of 34, A.D. Osadchiyev 26, S.I. Makovskij 23, S.A. Lebedev 22, V.I. Merkulov 21, N.V. Borodin 17, N.T. Konukoyev 15

44 IAP
Designated the 11 GIAP on 3-7-1942
Honorifics: Vyborgskij
Key commanders: Kap. S.P. Danilov (1938), Podpolk. V.G. Blagoveshchenskij, Podpolk. I.P. Neustroyev
Assignments: 7 IAK-PVO
Aircraft: LaGG-3s, La-5s
Battle honors: Leningrad Front 1941/43, Vyborg (Viipuri)
Aces: A.P. Savushkin 15

45 IAP
Activated in 1938
Designated the 100 GIAP on 6-18-1943
Full title: 100 Gvardejskij istrebitelnyj aviatsionnyj ordena Aleksandra Nevskogo Chenstokhovskij polk
Key commanders: Podpolk. I.M. Dzusov, Podpolk. S.I. Lukyanov (September, 1943-end of war)
Assignments: 216 SAD, 9 GIAD
Aircraft: Yak-1s, Kittyhawks, Airacobras
Battle honors: Kerch, Sevastopol, Mariupol, Crimea, Yassy, Lemberg-Sandomierz campaign, Breslau, Cottbus, Berlin

Combat record: During the fury of the Sevastopol air engagements the regiment excelled by claiming a total of 25 kills against great odds. On June 12, 1942, its Yak-1s reported the destruction of two Ju 88s, one He 111 and one Bf 109 for a single loss while engaged in escorting a formation of Il-2s to beat up ground targets in the vicinity of the Italian cemetery (Italyanskoye kladbishche). The following day two more Bf 109s were forced down, but two Yaks were lost and one pilot killed. The regiment was withdrawn in October, 1942 to convert to Kittyhawks and Airacobras for the Kuban fighting. Airacobras were assigned to 1st and 3rd Eskadrilya while Kittyhawks were assigned to the 2nd. A return to operations began on March 9, 1943, flying from Krasnodar. Strength at hand was 10 P-39D-2s, 11 P-39K-1a and 9 P-40Es. Here the unit quickly gained a high reputation for its fighting prowess, although an Airacobra failed to return from the first mission two days later, the first loss of a P-39D-2 in Russia. A big success was achieved on March 23, when eight Cobras chalked up 13 kills in a pitched battle with 30 enemy aircraft. Two pilots sacrificed their lives by purposely ramming Luftwaffe fighters: Serzhant N. Kudryashov and St.Lej. I. Shmatko. Boris Glinka, soon to be a top-scoring ace, was wounded when a shell exploded in his cockpit. April's series of fierce dogfights saw the regiment exact a heavy toll on opposing aircraft. Lej. I.I. Babak excelled with 14 fighters while runners-up were St.Lej. D.B. Glinka with five fighters and one bomber, Serzhant I. Kudrya with five resp. one, Lej. B.B. Glinka with three resp. two and Lej. N. Lavitskij with one resp. two. The Luftwaffe on the 15th exacted its revenge by downing D.B. Glinka, St.Serzhant V. Sapyan, St.Lej. M. Petrov and Serzhant Bezbabnov. Undoubtedly one of them fell to the guns of Erich Hartmann of 7./JG 52 who downed a P-39 near Taman that day to up his tally to seven – Hartmann was destined to become the greatest fighter ace of all time with 352 aerial victories. In two months combat over the Kuban, the regiment destroyed 118 aircraft in the air at the cost of seven P-39s and one P-40E in combat along with eight resp. one more damaged. During subsequent combat assignments the unit proved to be one of the most accomplished VVS fighter outfits, playing a big part in the heavy air battles across Russia and the Reich, finishing with a final bag of 502 air victories during 8,223 sorties and 975 encounters.
Aces: D.B. Glinka 50, I.I. Babak 37, B.B. Glinka 30, N.Ye. Lavitskij 26, P.I. Guchyok 20

46 IAP
Key commanders: Maj. I.D. Podgornyj (1941)
Assignments: 14 SAD, 235 IAD (1942)
Aircraft: I-16s, Hurricanes
Battle honors: Dubno, Kiev 1941, Leningrad 1941, Stalingrad

47 IAP
Key commanders: Maj. Ya.M. Kutikhin
Battle honors: Sevastopol 1941/42

49 IAP
Honorifics: Grodnenskij
Assignments: 309 IAD
Aircraft: La-5s
Battle honors: Stalingrad, Vitebsk, Polotsk, Grodno, Berlin
Combat record: The regiment was re-equipped with Lavochkin La-5 fighters in late 1942 and scored 16 victories during the next 180 sorties after taking these into action for the first time.
Aces: I.M. Astakhov 12

50 IAP
Key commanders: Podpolk. A.M. Vinokurov, Podpolk. A.M. Makarov
Assignments: 315 IAD
Aircraft: MiG-3s, La-5s
Battle honors: Kerch, Kursk-Orel, Bryansk, Gomel, Velikiye Luki, Idritsa, Riga, Courland

53 IAP
Key commanders: Maj. N.I. Bocharov (1939)

53 GIAP – see 512 IAP

54 IAP
It seems likely that the regiment was designated Guards, but this has not yet been substantiated.
Assignments: 1 GIAD
Battle honors: Kursk 1943

54 GIAP – see 237 IAP

55 IAP
Activated on 9-15-1939
Designated the 16 GIAP on 3-7-1942
Full title: 16 Gvardejskij istrebitelnyj aviatsionnyj ordena Aleksandra Nevskogo Sandomierskij polk
Key commanders: Podpolk. V.P. Ivanov (1941), Podpolk. N.V. Isayev (1942-1943), Maj. A.I. Pokryshkin (1943-1944), Maj. B.B. Glinka, Maj. G.A. Rechkalov (July, 1944-February, 1945), Kap. I.I. Babak (February-March, 1945)
Assignments: 20 SAD, 216 IAD, 9 GIAD
Aircraft: I-153s, Yak-1s, MiG-3s, Airacobras, La-7s
Battle honors: Donbas, Taganrog, Kuban, Mariupol, Taman, Cherkassy, Yassy-Kishinyov campaign, Lemberg-Sandomierz campaign, Breslau, Berlin, Prague
Combat record: The regiment was based at Beltsy, northeast of Kishinyov, on June 22, 1941, when it was caught in several Luftwaffe bombing raids. A number of MiG-3s were able to take to the air and intercepted 20 He 111s escorted by 18 Bf 109s. In the ensuing melee two bombers and one Messerschmitt were claimed destroyed, three MiGs being damaged in return. Later flight leader Mironov forced down an Hs 126 while A. Surov bagged a Ju 88. In all, the regiment reported the destruction of 10 enemy planes throughout the day, and there is a very

strong possibility that squadron leader F. Atrashkevich's victim was the Bf 109 flown by the famed Wolfgang Schellmann, Geschwaderkommodore of JG 27, although German records suggest that Schellmann was forced down into enemy territory after flying through the wreckage of an I-16 he had just shot down, being captured and shot by the NKVD two days later. The regiment later fought a very successful campaign in the Donbas, and in late 1942 re-equipped with the superb P-39 Airacobra fighters, and continued flying these until well into 1945. The regiment moved to Krasnodar on April 8, 1943 with 14 P-39L-1s, 7 P-39K-1s and 11 P-39D-2s on strength. The following day it began flying sorties over the Kuban. It was here that the unit won fame for achieving remarkable scores battling against the cream of the Luftwaffe including JG 52 and JG 3 "Udet." Claims for 79 enemy aircraft destroyed in the air were submitted durig the period of April 9-30, 1943 the Airacobras flying 289 sorties and encountering the enemy on 28 occasions. Most victories were against single-engine fighters, the most difficult opponents, with the breakdown being: 14 Bf 109Es, 12 Bf 109Fs, 45 Bf 109Gs, two Fw 190s, four Ju 88s and one each Do 217 and Ju 87. Topgun during the period was St.Lej. V.I. Fadeyev who racked up 12 kills. Also scoring high were Kap. A.I. Pokryshkin with 10 and St.Lej. G.A. Rechkalov with eight confirmed air victories. Eleven pilots were killed, along with eighteen Cobras lost in combat or failed to return, with two more losses due to accidents. The regiment subsequently established itself as one of the premier fighter outfits on the Eastern Front, and from it were to come some of the most talented fighter pilots of the VVS. It finished as the most famous Soviet fighter regiment, and was second only to the glorious 5 GIAP in air victories. By the time it flew its last mission in May, 1945, 697 enemy planes had fallen before its guns.
Aces: A.I. Pokryshkin 59, G.A. Rechkalov 56, A.F. Klubov 27 of 31, V.Ye. Bondarenko 24, A.I. Trud 24, K.V. Sukhov 22, V.A. Figichev 21, A.V. Fyodorov 20+ of 24, I. Grafin 19

55 GIAP – see 581 IAP

56 IAP
Key commanders: Maj. S.P. Danilov (7-17-1939/9-16-1939), Polk. T.F. Kutsevalov
Assignments: 194 IAD
Aircraft: I-16s (1939)
Battle honors: Khalkhin Gol 1939, Poland
Aces: S.P. Danilov 8

56 GIAP – see 520 IAP

57 GIAP – see 36 IAP

59 IAP
Battle honors: Russo-Finnish Winter War 1939/40

The battle is over for this Fw 190A-5 of an unknown Schlachtgeschwader. The aircraft still carries an SC-250 bomb on the fuselage centerline. During the final stages of the war many Fw 190 units were confined to the ground-attack role becoming meat on the table for the battle-hardened Red fighters. (Author's collection)

63 GIAP – see 169 IAP

64 GIAP – see 271 IAP

65 GIAP – see 653 IAP

66 IAP
Aircraft: Yak-1s
Battle honors: Moscow

66 GIAP – see 875 IAP

67 IAP
Key commanders: Maj. B.A. Rudakov
Aircraft: I-16s, Hurricanes (as of early 1942)
Battle honors: Bessarabia 1941, Moscow
Combat record: The regiment was out in force on June 22, 1941, to attack the mass of enemy aircraft striking Soviet airfields all along the front, claiming 13 kills. High scorer of the day was Starshij Lejtenant A.I. Moklyak, who forced down two Italian SM-81 bombers and was killed when he deliberately rammed a third. In all, the regiment submitted claims for 47 enemy planes in the air and four on the ground against six pilots KIA for the period June 22-July 10, 1941.

67 GIAP – see 436 IAP

68 IAP
Key commanders: Maj.V.V. Zelentsov
Aircraft: LaGG-3s
Battle honors: Russo-Finnish Winter War 1939/40, Kiev 1941
Combat record: The regiment fought during the Winter War, claiming 47 enemy planes destroyed in the air and on the ground to emerge as one of the more accomplished units of the conflict.
Aces: P.M. Petrov 10

68 GIAP – no trace to original unit
Assignments: 5 GIAD
Aircraft: Airacobras
Aces: I.N. Lagutenko 17, V.I. Kolyadin 16

69 IAP
Designated the 9 GIAP on 3-7-1942
Full title: 9 Gvardejskij istrebitelnyj aviatsionnyj Krasnoznamennyj Odesskij polk
Key commanders: Maj.L.L. Shestakov (as of August, 1941), Podpolk. A.A. Morozov (1943/KIA 6-18-1944), Maj. V.D. Lavrinenkov, Maj. A.V. Alelyukhin (1945)
Assignments: 234 IAD, 235 IAD, 303 IAD, 6 GIAD
Aircraft: I-16s, LaGG-3s, Hurricanes, Yak-1s, Airacobras(as of April, 1943), La-7s (as of June, 1944)
Battle honors: Kishinyov, Odessa, Kharkov, Stalingrad, Rostov, Batajsk, Kuban, Mius River, Taganrog, Melitopol, Dnyepropetrovsk, Sevastopol, Odessa, East Prussia, Berlin
Combat record: The regiment was to produce some of the most famous aces of the war, achieving remarkable scores against the Luftwaffe in the great aerial campaigns of the Eastern Front. It saw considerable fighting at Odessa, doing particularly well. On August 9, 1941, nine Bf 109s were claimed destroyed in action near Katarzhino, while on the 21st two more of these, together with a PZL-24, were shot down in separate tussles between Vygoda-Paliyevo-Karpovo for one pilot being wounded and four I-16s sustaining damage. Another PZL-24 fell to the regiment's guns in the Sukhoj Liman area on September 12 with a second victory near Groslinental being identified as either Spitfire or Hurricane. An I-16 fell victim to Bf 109s in the vicinity of Lenintal that same day, the pilot crashing to his death. Sixteen days later the regiment tore into a formation of Luftwaffe transports, claiming six Ju 52s at the cost of two I-16s and their pilots. By October 14, 1941, the bag had risen to 94 enemy aircraft in the air and 30 on the ground during the course of 6,608 sorties. The regiment then flew with great success during the Battle of Stalingrad, running up a string of 54 kills during 784 sorties. In October, 1942 the Soviet High Command ordered the concentration of notable pilots who tallied 10 or more kills within the 9 GIAP so as to establish a regiment of aces capable of defeating the enemy and establishing air supremacy, and from then on it was known throughout the VVS as "regiment of aces." As of October 25 the regiment boasted seven aces and would in time be receiving three notables of the 296 IAP and two of the 11 IAP. Thus major B.N. Yeremin, Kapitan M.D. Baranov, Starshij Lejtenants Amet-Khan Sultan, A.F. Kovachevich, Y.P. Dranishchev, Starshina V.D. Lavrinenkov, who had enjoyed considerable success while serving with other regiments, formed the nucleus of this remarkable outfit. On December 10 the regiment resumed operations after transitioning to Yak-1s. During 1942 the regiment received Hawker Hurricanes, which quickly proved most disappointing for operations on the Eastern Front. Here is how Podpolkovnik Morozov evaluated this machine: "We were punished with the Hurricane. The British discarded it from service in Africa and supplied it to us. It was underpowered and inadequately armed." The regiment had a big day on March 25, 1943, when it claimed 16 victories in the Rostov area. It later flew with great distinction over East Prussia, achieving 73 kills, and finished the war as the fourth highest scoring VVS regiment with a tally of 558 victories.

Podpolkovnik A.V. Alelyukhin, 69 IAP's top-scoring ace. (Author's collection)

Aces: A.V. Alelyukhin 40, V.D. Lavrinenkov 35, P.Ya. Golovachyov 31, S. Amet-Khan 30, A.N. Karasyov 30, I.G. Borisov 25, I.V. Timofeyenko 21, A.I. Cherevatenko 20, Ye.P. Dranishchev 20

69 GIAP – no trace to original unit
Full title: 69 Gvardejskij istrebitelnyj aviatsionnyj ordena Aleksandra Nevskogo Krakovskij polk
Key commanders: Podpolk. N.K. Krivyakov
Aircraft: Airacobras (as of September, 1943)
Assignments: 23 GIAD
Battle honors: Korsun-Shevchenkovskij campaign (1-24-1944/ 2-17-1944)
Aces: N.I. Proshenkov 19, V.I. Chizh 13

70 IAP
Key commanders: Kap. A.A. Zajtsev (1939), Maj. V.M. Zabaluyev
Aircraft: I-153s, I-16s
Battle honors: Khalkhin Gol 1939
Aces: N.P. Zherdev 14, A.A. Zajtsev 6

71 IAP-KBF
Activated in September, 1940
Designated the 10 GIAP-KBF on 5-31-1943
Full title: 10 Gvardejskij istrebitelnyj aviatsionnyj Krasnoznamennyj polk
Key commanders: Podpolk. A. Koronets (KIA April, 1942), Maj. K. Teplinskij (as of 4-20-1942), Podpolk. I.M. Rassudkov (as of 4-3-1943), Podpolk. T. Usychenko (as of 11-3-1943), Maj. D. Sharov (as of 1-18-1945)
Aircraft: I-153s, I-16s, La-5s (as of 1944)
Battle honors: Tallin, Kronshtadt, Lavansaari
Combat record: With twelve months of combat behind it the regiment claimed, at the end of June, 1942, 113 enemy planes destroyed in 742 air encounters. It had gained 18 kills over Kronshtadt between March 25 and April 5, 1942, and 11 in a three day period between March 27-29 in a burst of activity over the island of Sur-Sari (Hogland), east of Helsinki. By the close of war the unit had reached a total of 197 air victories plus 21 aircraft, 31 tanks, 737 motor vehicles, two locomotives, 58 rail cars and 40 armored vehicles destroyed in ground attacks during 20,000 sorties.
Aces: A.G. Baturin 18

72 IAP-SF
Activated in February, 1940
Designated the 2 GIAP-SF on 1-18-1942
Key commanders: Polk. G. Gubanov, Maj. I.K. Tumanov (as of January, 1942), Podpolk. B.F. Safonov (as of 3-20-1942), Kap. P.G. Sgibnev (as of November, 1942), Maj. M. Semenikhin (as of 5-5-1943), Podpolk. D. Marenko (as of 6-13-1943)
Aircraft: I-15bis, I-153s, I-16s, MiG-3s, Airacobras
Battle honors: Murmansk, Petsamo-Kirkenes campaign
Combat record: The regiment managed to put up a remarkable performance during the dark months of 1941, being credited with 140 enemy planes destroyed in the air and on the ground, Starshij Lejtenant B.F. Safonov drawing first blood on June 24 with an He 111 over the Kola Peninsula. Safonov was later to become a national hero and legendary figure in the VVS scoring 30 kills before being killed in action on May 30, 1942. The regiment's biggest day came on September 15, 1941, when it chalked up 10 kills without loss. The unit saw a further period of air fighting in 1944 when 56 enemy planes were shot down in 48 encounters.
Aces: P.L. Kolomoyets 18, Z.A. Sorokin 18, N.M. Didenko 17

72 GIAP – see 485 IAP

73 IAP – no trace

73 GIAP – see 296 IAP

83 GIAP – see 572 IAP

83 IAP
Designated the 85 GIAP, date not established
Assignments: 6 GIAD
Aircraft: Yak-1s (until late 1944)
Battle honors: Crimea 1944 including Kherson, Sevastopol; Hungary
Aces: M.S. Mazan 21, A.U. Konstantinov 19, A.P. Britikov 17

84 IAP
Designated the 101 GIAP, date not established
Honorifics: Shtetinskij
Key commanders: Maj. Ya.I. Antonov (KIA ? 8-25-1942), Podpolk. Pavlikov
Assignments: 229 IAD, 329 IAD
Aircraft: I-153s, I-16s, Airacobras
Battle honors: Caucasus, Kuban, Pomerania, including Stettin
Combat record: The Polikarpov I-153 biplane fighter soldiered on with the regiment alongside the I-16 until mid-1943 when it received Airacobras. On August 25, 1942, the regiment commander, Major Antonov, Hero of the Soviet Union and veteran of the Russo-Finnish Winter War, was leading a mission of eight of the regiment's I-153s and nine I-16s of the 88 IAP to attack the German airfield at Mozdok. In the target area they had a tussle with the famous JG 52, claiming four victories, but two I-153s including that of the commander were lost. This combat raises some problems, as is so often the case, accounts from both sides vary. The photo seen here was supplied through the courtesy of Herr Günther Rall, one of the leading Luftwaffe Experten and then Hauptmann and Kommandeur of III./JG 52. It, without any doubt, depicts Major Antonov after he had fallen into German hands. Günther Rall still remembers this combat vividly, telling the author that the Russian pilot had bailed out and landed safely in a field of sunflowers where he spiritedly had defended himself with his Tokarev before running out of ammunition. He later hesitatingly accepted tea and cigarettes during his interrogation before he was put in a Ju 52 to be taken to the prison camp. Strangely enough, the prisoner never arrived, recalls Günther Rall, and his subsequent fate unfortunately could not be traced. It is noteworthy that Herr Rall feels that the action rather occurred in late 1942 with no German losses being reported, but no simple explanation can be found and the date may be in error. Antonov officially was listed as killed in action, his place being taken by Kapitan Sereda, the experienced and very capable ace of the 88 IAP. Recent investigation has strongly suggested that Antonov was driven to forced labor in a factory and later was killed while trying to make a break or lost his life in a prison camp.
Aces: I.G. Pokhlebayev 18, A.M. Berkutov 15

84 GIAP – see 788 IAP

85 IAP
Battle honors: Sevastopol 1944

85 GIAP – see 83 IAP

86 GIAP – see 744 IAP

87 IAP
Key commanders: Maj. Suldin
Assignments: 16 SAD
Aircraft: I-16s, MiG-3s
Combat record: On the eve of the German attack the regiment was based at Buchach, 60 kilometers south of Ternopol, having 60 I-16s and four MiG-3s on strength. At 4:50 a.m. on June 22, 1941, a lone Ju 88 hit the airfield, destroying seven of 10 I-16s that were allotted to the 36 IAD. Vasilij Dmitriyev took off and immediately engaged the bomber, which fell from the sky in flames. At approximately 5:30 a.m. he attacked another, forcing it down west of Ternopol. In the same time frame P.A. Mikhajlyuk made a determined attack on a Do 217 that force-landed close to 86 SBAP's base near Terebov, its crew being captured while Ya.I. Moroz destroyed an He 111 over Ternopol for the fourth victory of the day.

88 IAP
Activated in 1940 from the 6 OAK
Designated the 159 GIAP in October, 1944
Honorifics: Novorossijskij
Key commanders: Maj. M.A. Bulgakov (1940), Maj. Ye.E. Markelov (as of June, 1941), Podpolk. V.I. Maksimenko (as of August, 1943)
Assignments: 44 IAD, 216 IAD, 229 IAD
Aircraft: I-16s, LaGG-3s (as of November, 1942), La-5s (as of May, 1944)
Battle honors: Vinnitsa, Kamenets-Podolsk, Rostov, Taganrog, Slavyansk, Izyum, Mozdok, Kuban, Novorossijsk, Taman, Kerch, Sevastopol, Byelorussia, East Prussia
Combat record: When the Germans knifed into Soviet Russia on June 22, 1941, the regiment was based near Vinnitsa, seeing action for the first time the following day. It soon became obvious that the I-16s lacked the performance to successfully intercept German bombers which outdistanced them so that they could not get close enough. Mladshij Lejtenant V. Knyazev, though, drew first blood that same day when he knocked down a Ju 88. On the next day the regiment moved to Shatava (Kamenets-Podolsk area), and by July the tally had already risen to some 20 kills while being occupied with armed reconnaissance. It was then engaged in heavy action, intercepting Luftwaffe strikes against Vinnitsa, Berdichev, and Zhmerinka. On July 27 four enemy planes were destroyed between Zhashkova-Tetiyeva-Gajsina-Teplika, a double by Mladshij Lejtenant N.M. Tregubov. The unit had a big day on August 14 while engaged in providing cover for the Dnyepr bridge at Kanev, claiming eight kills. Lejtenant V. Demenok was high scorer of the day with a triple, including a Messerschmitt that he destroyed by ramming being killed in the process. In mid-August the regiment moved to Chernobaj, northeast of Cherkassy, and on the 27th Starshij Lejtenant P.N. Maltsev successfully rammed an He 111 near Kamenka and safely force-landed in Soviet territory while the German pilot was captured.

This Major and Hero of the Soviet Union is tentatively identified as Ya.I. Antonov, commanding officer of the 84 IAP. He was shot down by JG 52 and became a prisoner but his subsequent fate remains a mystery. Antonov was born in the Novgorod area in 1908 and won the title of Hero of the Soviet Union for his efforts during the Russo-Finnish Winter War of 1939/40. (Günther Rall)

In early October the unit moved to Batajsk, and on the 30th to Shakhty (NE Rostov), seeing a good deal of action and claiming the destruction of five tanks, 129 motor vehicles, 10 anti-aircraft guns on the ground along with three victories in the air in November, all without loss. After more heavy fighting strength to hand by February, 1942 was down to eight I-16s. One squadron was disbanded while 1st Eskadrilya was assigned to the Barvenkovo area early next month with 2nd Eskadrilya moving to Bolshe-Krepinskaya to take an active part in the fighting for Taganrog. The regiment then saw considerable action at Slavyansk, Izyum, and Mozdok, and on August 25 nine I-16s joined up with eight I-153s of the 84 IAP to strafe the Luftwaffe airfield at Mozdok with Major Ya.I. Antonov, commander of the 84 IAP, leading the mission. Once over the target area they were immediately bounced by Bf 109s of JG 52, Kapitan Maksimenko being hit and wounded. He crash-landed close to the Russian lines and Lejtenant Shlyapkin landed in a nearby field to pull him from his blazing aircraft and carry him towards Russian infantry that was hurrying to the scene. Two I-153s were also lost with Major Antonov being listed as killed in action. It seems more likely that Antonov fell into German hands only to disappear on his way to a prison camp. The regiment had claims for six enemy planes in the air together with one more on the ground that day, although no

confirmation can be found from German records, and the date may be in error. In the fury of the North Caucasus air engagements the regiments lost 11 pilots killed and was then withdrawn in November, 1942 to reform and re-equip with LaGG-3s. In May, 1943 it was posted to the Kuban theater where it was engaged in very heavy fighting claiming some 40 kills. Outstanding pilots during this time were Afanasij Lukin with 6, Yevgenij Pylayev 5, Vasilij Knyazev and Vasilij Sobin 4 apiece. During September the regiment was occupied with Il-2 escorts to Novorossijsk and next flew sweeps out to Taman. Throughout the winter of 1943/44 it was greatly involved in the fighting at Kerch and on April 18, 1944, began combat operations over Sevastopol, running up 14 kills within three days. Lejtenant P.V. Seleznev claimed the honors accounting for three of these victories. In May Lavochkin La-5s arrived, and the unit began to progressively re-equip with this type. In June another move was made to take part in the smashing victory over Army Group Center in Byelorussia, and from November, 1944 it began to range deep into East Prussia. Between February-March, 1945 it was largely engaged in giving fighter cover against weakening Luftwaffe opposition over East Pomerania, including the cities of Danzig and Gdingen. On March 9 the regiment reported one of its last combat casualties when two La-5s were attacked by six Fw 190s while escorting several Il-2s out to the front. In turning for his life, Aleksej Bazunov managed to knock one of the attackers down, but his number two, Grigorij Shirshov, went in on fire and was killed. Soviet forces had now reached the Oder, and in a final burst of activity the regiment fought over Stettin prior to moving to its 85th base of war, Pasewalk airfield, 115 kilometers off Berlin, on April 30. The final score was 268 air victories, along with 48 enemy aircraft destroyed in ground attacks during 18,193 sorties.
Aces: V.A. Knyazev 29, Ye.A. Pylayev 20, P.S. Sereda 18, V.I. Maksimenko 17, V.V. Sobin 15, A.P. Lukin 14

88 GIAP – see 166 IAP

89 GIAP – no trace to original unit
Assignments: 7 GIAD
Aces: I.A. Gonchar 16

91 IAP
Key commanders: Maj. A.R. Kovalev, Maj. A.S. Romanenko (KIA 11-6-1943)
Assignments: 256 IAD
Aircraft: I-15s, I-153s, Yak-1s, Yak-9s, Yak-3s
Battle honors: Berdichev 1941, Kiev 1943
Aces: N.D. Miokov 22, A.S. Romanenko 21

91 GIAP – no trace to original unit
Assignments: 6 GIAD
Aces: I.A. Pishkan 16

92 IAP
Key commanders: Kap. I.I. Krasnoyurchenko, Maj. B. Solomatin
Assignments: 16 SAD, 44 IAD, 279 IAD
Aircraft: I-153s, I-16s, MiG-3s, Yak-1s, La-5s
Battle honors: Brod, Chernigov, Kharkov, Stalingrad, Kursk, Volkhov, Budapest
Aces: N.P. Logvinenko 20, Ye.M. Chistyakov 16, I.D. Sidorov 16

95 IAP
Key commanders: Polk. S.A. Pestov (1941)
Assignments: 6 IAK-PVO (as of 7-9-1941)
Battle honors: Moscow
Aircraft: Pe-3s (1941)

100 GIAP – see 45 IAP

101 GIAP – see 84 IAP

102 GIAP – see 124 IAP

103 GIAP – see 158 IAP

104 GIAP – see 298 IAP

105 GIAP – no trace to original unit
Full title: 105 Gvardejskij istrebitelnyj aviatsionnyj Krasnoznamennyj polk
Key commanders: Podpolk. V.A. Zajtsev

106 GIAP – see 814 IAP

107 GIAP - see 867 IAP

111 GIAP – see 13 IAP

112 GIAP – see 236 IAP

113 GIAP - see 437 IAP

115 GIAP - see 146 IAP

116 IAP
Key commanders: Maj. N.A. Najdenov
Assignments: 283 IAD, 295 IAD
Aircraft: I-16s, La-5s
Battle honors: Caucasus, Kursk-Byelgorod, Zaporozhye, Dnyepropetrovsk, Hungary
Aces: P.M. Dolgaryov 21, A.A. Pantelkin 21, V.V. Markov 20, I.S. Ulitin 17

116 GIAP - see 563 IAP

Yak-7s of the 12 GIAP at dispersal on the outskirts of Moscow. Note differently styled national insignias and markings. (Author's collection)

117 GIAP – see 975 IAP

120 IAP
Designated the 12 GIAP on 3-7-1942
Key commanders: Maj. A.S. Pisanko (1941), Maj. K.V. Marenkov
Aircraft: I-153s, I-16s, MiG-3s, Yak-7s, Yak-9s
Battle honors: Rzhev 1941, Mozhajsk 1942, Spas-Demensk, Vyazma

122 IAP
Honorifics: Budapeshtskij
Assignments: 11 SAD, 223 ShAD, 331 IAD
Aircraft: I-153s, I-16s, MiG-3s
Battle honors: Grodno, Moscow, 1st and 2nd Ukrainian Fronts
Combat record: The regiment was based at Novyj Dvor on June 22, 1941, with 68 I-16s and I-153s on strength, 15 of which were undergoing repair. Throughout the first day of the German attack, several pilots flew as many as 10 sorties, destroying their first enemy plane in the air. Mladshij Lejtenant Sergej Dolgushin, who was to become an ace with 17 kills, claimed a Bf 109, while the deputy regiment commander, Kapitan Ukhanev, got a Bf 110.

123 IAP
Designated the 27 GIAP on 11-22-1942
Honorifics: Vyborgskij
Key commanders: Maj.B.N. Surin (KIA 6-22-1941), Podpolk. F.M. Mishchenko, Podpolk. N.P. Mazhayev
Assignments: 10 SAD, 7 IAK-PVO
Aircraft: I-153s, Yak-1s, Tomahawks, Kittyhawks
Battle honors: Brest 1941, Leningrad, Kolpino, Tosno, Vyborg
Combat record: The regiment was based at Imenin on June 22, 1941, flying I-153 biplanes. In an outstanding effort 30 victories were claimed throughout that day (another source suggests 20+ victories), losing nine of their own in air combat. Pilots flew as many as 10-14 sorties, in one case even 17 sorties were reported that day! Ivan Kalabushkin excelled, claiming two Bf 109s, two Ju 88s and an He 111 while taking off three times.
Aces: A.T. Karpov 37, V.N. Kharitonov 26, I.D. Pidtykan 16

124 IAP
Designated the 102 GIAP on 7-7-1943
Honorifics: Vyborgskij
Key commanders: Podpolk. M.G. Trunov, Maj. A.G. Pronin
Assignments: 9 SAD
Aircraft: I-16s, MiG-3s, Spitfire IXs (until close of war)
Battle honors: Byelorussia 1941, Moscow, Leningrad, Vyborg
Combat record: The regiment made its mark against the Luftwaffe on June 22, 1941, when its deputy commander, Kapitan Kruglov, forced down an enemy aircraft at 4:15 a.m. Later that day D.V. Kokorev successfully rammed a Ju 88 with his MiG-3.

126 IAP-PVO
Key commanders: Maj. Yu.A. Nimtsov, Maj. V.M. Najdenko
Assignments: 9 SAD, 6 IAK-PVO
Aircraft: I-16s, MiG-3s, Tomahawks
Battle honors: Byelostok, Gomel, Moscow, Stalingrad
Combat record: At the outbreak of war the regiment was based at Dolubovo with MiG-3s and I-16s. It was in the forefront of action on the first day of the German attack, achieving six victories throughout that day. Lejtenant G. Alayev and V. Ushakov drew first blood, both pilots downing a Ju 88 each. The unit later converted to Tomahawks and was the first to introduce these to the Eastern Front on October 12, 1941, while fighting during the earlier stages of the Battle of Moscow. The dramatic battles saw the regiment claim a total of 29 kills, 17 with Tomahawks during 685 sorties between October 12 and November 15, 1941. It next moved to Stalingrad where it engaged in heavy action amassing 36 more kills.
Aces: S.G. Ridnyj 21, V.G. Kamenshchikov 12, V.M. Najdenko 12 of 22

127 IAP
Honorifics: Varshavskij
Key commanders: Podpolk. A. Gordiyenko, Podpolk. V.V. Puzyejkin
Assignments: 11 SAD, 282 IAD
Aircraft: I-153s, MiG-3s
Battle honors: Grodno, Leningrad, Kursk, Kiev, Poland, the Reich, Berlin
Combat record: The regiment went to war at dawn on June 22, 1941. Andrej Danilov was on patrol in his I-153 biplane between Grodno-Lida when he spotted a German bomber and shot it down on his first pass at approximately 10:00 a.m. With fuel getting low he turned for home and ran into nine Bf 110s, claiming to have shot down two and successfully rammed a third. Another successful ramming attack was performed by Lejtenant A.I. Pachin, who forced down a Ju 87 in this fashion near Grodno between 10:00-11:00 a.m.; Starshij Lejtenant P.A. Kuzmin claimed the regiment's third Luftwaffe aircraft destroyed by ramming that day over the village of Kamenka. For Kuzmin it was the second kill in his sixth sortie that day. In all, the regiment afforded as many as 180 sorties throughout the day, reporting the destruction of 20 enemy planes, Lejtenant S.Ya. Zhukovskij racking up four victories as did Starshij Politruk A.A. Artemyev. In fact, German losses had been quite low that day, amounting to perhaps a tenth of the total Soviet claims, the general chaos and heat of combat leading to some disproportionate overclaiming.
Aces: A.P. Savchenko 11

129 IAP
Designated the 5 GIAP on 12-6-1941
Key commanders: Maj. T.G. Vikhrov, Maj. Yu.M. Berkal (as of June, 1941), Polk. V.I. Zajtsev (September, 1942-April, 1944)
Assignments: 47 SAD, 9 SAD, 207 IAD, 11 GIAD

Kapitan V.V. Yefremov, deputy leader of the 1st Eskadrilya in the 5 GIAP, photographed on December 8, 1941. He earned the title of Hero of the Soviet Union for his efforts on Kalinin Front on May 5, 1942 and by the close of the war had destroyed at least 12 enemy planes in the air. (Author's collection)

Aircraft: I-153s, MiG-3s, LaGG-3s, La-5s (as of November, 1942), La-7s
Battle honors: Spas-Demensk, Smolensk, Kalinin, Kholm, Byelyj, Zubtsov, Stalingrad, Slavyansk, Kramatorsk, Byelgorod-Kharkov, Izyum, Zaporozhye, Dnyepropetrovsk, Nikopol, Krivoj Rog, Kovel, Breslau, Berlin
Combat record: The regiment was at its home base of Tarnovo with I-153s and MiG-3s when German forces knifed into Soviet Russia on June 22, 1941. Starshij Politruk A. Sokolov, flying a MiG-3, drew first blood with a Bf 109 while others brought the day's tally to six for the loss of only a single aircraft. Four days later the unit was withdrawn to Balbasovo and then to Shajkovka on West Front, eight kilometers south of Spas-Demensk. It came under operational control of the 47 SAD and became greatly involved in the fighting for Smolensk being occupied with escorting Il-2s of the 61 and 215 ShAPs and conduct-fighter sweeps out to Dukhovshchina, Yelnya, and Yartsevo. It had a big day on August 20 when nine enemy aircraft fell to its guns in the vicinity of Dukhovshchina (NE Smolensk). In late 1941 the regiment was posted to Kalinin Front, seeing some action around the city of Kalinin. A short time later it was awarded the Guards Banner for distinguishing itself in combat and in recognition of 62 enemy planes destroyed in the air and 20 on the ground during 1,793 sorties for 1,980 combat hours. In June, 1942 the regiment engaged in heavy action over Kholm and Byelyj, providing ground force cover

and flying escort for Il-2s and Pe-2s. Two months later it fought a hard battle against the Luftwaffe along the Vazuza and Osuga Rivers, at Zubtsov and Gnezdilovo. In early November it reassembled at Gorkij where it was re-equipped with Lavochkin La-5s, and after a working-up period was posted to the 207 IAD on December 15, 1942, to participate in the big air battles that broke loose along the Don when Southwest Front launched a massive offensive the following day to smash the German-Italian front in this area and to take part in the interdiction of the Stalingrad pocket. Starshij Lejtenant Igor Shardakov scored the first success in this theater by splashing a Bf 109 near Novaya Kalitva. In four weeks' combat the pilots claimed 45 kills, most of these being gained on fighter patrols instigated to catch the sluggish, almost defenseless transport aircraft that were thrown into the fray in desperate attempts to supply and evacuate the Stalingrad pocket. On December 29, 1942, the regiment flew in to an advanced airfield near Radchenkoye on the Don River, and on January 16, 1943, Major V.A. Zajtsev took off with eight fighters to strafe Gartmashevka airfield where great slaughter was done. On their first run Zajtsev, Ivan Kildyshev, Nikolaj Makarenko, and Aleksandr Masterkov all shot up single Ju 52s, while Dmitrij Shtokolov and Vitalij Popkov caught the alert flight of two Bf 109Fs from behind, claiming both destroyed in quick succession. In all, 10 Luftwaffe planes were destroyed on the ground without loss. February was to be a bright month with 39 victory claims being filed in the areas of Slavyansk-Kramatorsk, Zvanovka, Kremennaya, Lisichansk, Konstantinovka-Krasnoarmejskoye. On the 30th five La-5s with Kapitan Lavejkin in the lead stormed into a formation of 14 Ju-87s while providing ground force cover between Slavyansk-Kramatorsk, six of these being shot down by Sverlov (2), Lavejkin, Shtokolov, Lavrenko, and Yermolayev. Shortly afterward the regiment moved again, this time to Krasnyj Liman (SE Kharkov), from where Vasilij Zajtsev took six La-5s on a fighter sweep on March 10 out to the Yarovaya-Bannovskij-Prishib areas. They first spotted and shot down three of the elusive Fw 189 reconnaissance aircraft before engaging a flightof Ju 87s, the formation being dispersed and five being knocked down by Zajtsev (2), Kiyanchenko, Shtokolov, who had also claimed one Fw 189, and Karayev. Soon after a move was made to Polovinkino, from where the regiment saw some action at Starobyelsk, and on June 2 arrived in Shchenyachye to engage in heavy action over Kharkov, Byelgorod, and Izyum. On July 5 it was tasked with flying massive airfield strafes against Rogan, Sokolniki, Osnova, Barvenkovo, where about 11 enemy planes were destroyed in the air and on the ground. Mladshij Lejtenant Belyakov was hit and wounded by groundfire and made a force-landing in Soviet territory. Beginning in August, the unit was based at Nikolayevka and was fast becoming the top-scoring VVS fighter outfit. By August 27 the bag had risen to 495 air victories. The following day Lejtenant Sytov claimed two He 111s while another pilot added a Ju 88. On the 29th Vitalij Popkov, leading seven La-5s on a fighter sweep, racked up the regiment's 499th kill while to Mladshij Lejtenant Nikolaj Marisayev went the honor of destroying the 500th when he knocked down a Ju 88 soon after. A month later the regiment operated with distinction along the Dnyepr in the area of Zaporozhye. On October 15 eight La-5s tangled with 10 Bf 109s while prowling about in the frontline area, Konstantin Yevstratov, Vladimir Barabanov and Vladimir Ivashkevich all getting singles. Eight fighters with Dmitrij Shtokolov in the lead also had a tussle with Messerschmitts, three of these being forced down by Bayevskij, Voronchuk, and Vasilyev. On October 23 forces of 3rd Ukrainian Front launched the Dnyepropetrovsk campaign, an all-out assault to break out of the Dnyepr bridgehead and to penetrate into the western Ukraine with the 5 GIAP being continuously engaged. It next took an active part in the great battles for Nikopol and Krivoj Rog (January 30/February 29, 1944), and by June it was based at Razdelnaya, moving to Lutsk a short time later. In early July it would see very heavy combat when a main thrust by forces of 1st Ukrainian Front was initiated with overwhelming success, punching through the Kovel-Chertkov-Kolomyya frontline. During the same period the first of the new, powerful Lavochkin La-7s were beginning to arrive to replace the La-5s. The regiment transferred to Mogilno airfield on July 23 and then moved to Razlopy five days later. It soon began to take a heavy toll of the Luftwaffe during the subsequent Vistula campaign and was occupied with flying free hunt until December, 1944. On January 25, 1945, the war had reached its final phase when forces of the 1st Ukrainian Front reached the Oder River at Breslau and Glogau with the 5 GIAP being engaged in escorting Il-2 formations. Seven Fw 190s fell to the pilots' guns while operating on ground-support duty on February 14 and a short time later a move was made to Sprottau. On the 28th six fighters led by Bayevskij reported the destruction of seven Fw 190s and Bf 109s near Guben, Aleksandr Buzunkin, a young buck, being killed. In early March the regiment was operating in the Glogau area and next flew Il-2 escort and massive strafes around Arnsdorf. The task of covering 93 GShAP was accomplished with such good effect that during 500 Il-2 sorties throughout March no Shturmoviks

F.I. Mochalov, deputy leader of the 2nd Eskadrilya in the 5 GIAP, before starting off on a mission. The date is December 8, 1941. (Author's collection)

were lost to enemy fighter action. Between April 16-19 the regiment afforded 500 sorties on Il-2 and bomber escort to the Cottbus area with six Fw 190s being destroyed in air-to-air combat. On the 25th fighters of the 5 GIAP penetrated to Berlin for the first time and five days later, it concentrated on ground attack beating up everything that moved between Wendisch Buchholz and Halbe. The following day V.I. Popkov's 1st Eskadrilya mixed it with Fw 190s over the German capital claiming four victories with Popkov personally upping his tally to 41. The squadron, again led by Popkov, flew the last wartime mission of the 5th on May 8. In 46 months of combat, the accomplishments of the 5 GIAP had been varied and many. It finished as the top Soviet aerial scoring regiment of the war – 739 air victories, 1,832 motor vehicles and 283 artillery emplacements destroyed in ground attacks.
Aces: V.I. Popkov 41, I.N. Sytov 34, S.G. Glinkin 30, V.A. Zajtsev 30+ of 34, G.D. Onufriyenko – most of his score of 29, P.I. Peskov 26, I.P. Lavejkin 24, I.A. Shardakov 21, G.A. Bayevskij 19

129 GIAP – see 27 IAP

131 IAP
Designated the 40 GIAP on 2-8-1943
Full title: 40 Gvardejskij istrebitelnyj aviatsionnyj ordena Kutuzova Ternopolskij polk
Key commanders: Podpolk. L.A. Goncharov (KIA 10-31-1941), Podpolk. V.I. Davidkov, Maj. M.S. Tokarev (KIA 7-12-1943), Maj. M.V. Kartashov
Assignments: 20 SAD, 217 IAD, 8 GIAD
Aircraft: I-16s, LaGG-3s, La-5s
Battle honors: Donbas, Mozdok, Stavropol, Yejsk, Dnyepropetrovsk, Taganrog, Kursk-Orel
Combat record: The regiment reported 63 kills for 38 combat losses during 5,312 sorties, 1,493 of which were ground attack, for the period June to October, 1941. It operated with distinction at Rostov and Izyum in 1942 being credited with 90 enemy planes destroyed.
Aces: K.A. Novikov 29, V.I. Borodachyov 26, N.T. Kitayev 26, D.P. Nazarenko 24, M.S. Tokarev 22, V.I. Davidkov 20, I.I. Semenyuk 19, S.U. Kratinov 18, V.K. Kuleshov 16

133 IAP
Honorifics: Baranovichskij
Key commanders: Podpolk. K.A. Tovstashij
Assignments: 234 IAD
Aircraft: Yak-9s, Yak-3s
Battle honors: Kursk, Korsun, Uman, Batajsk, Baranovichi, VistulaOder campaign, East Prussia, Berlin
Aces: Ya.L. Ovodov 19, V.N. Yashin 16

133 GIAP – see 42 IAP

137 GIAP – see 160 IAP

V.I. Popkov, 5 GIAP's highest scoring ace. (Frunze House)

139 GIAP – see 20 IAP

144 IAP-PVO
Key commanders: Maj. N.A. Martynov
Battle honors: Kursk

145 IAP
Designated the 19 GIAP on 3-7-1942
Key commanders: Podpolk. G.A. Rejfshneider, Polk. P.S. Kutakhov
Aircraft: I-16s, LaGG-3s (as of July, 1941), MiG-3s, Hurricanes, Kittyhawks, Airacobras
Battle honors: Murmansk, Petrozavodsk, Karelia
Combat Record: The regiment saw some fighting during the Russo-Finnish Winter War of 1939-40 gaining five vicories but also losing five of their number. It next entered combat with the Luftwaffe flying I-16s and took part in the fierce fighting in the north, suffering fairly heavy casualties whilst operating LaGG-3s, MiG-3s and Hurricanes. In April, 1942 it withdrew to Afrikanda airfield to begin conversion to P-39 Airacobras and P-40E Kittyhawks. Combat was resumed with 16 Cobras and 10 Kittyhaks from Shonguj (south of Murmansk) on May 15, 19 GIAP thus becoming the first VVS regiment to introduce the P-39 to operational service. On June 15 six Co-

bras were able to bring down nine enemy aircraft without loss after running into six bombers escorted by 16 Bf 110s near Murmashi. By the close of 1942 14 Airacobras had been lost – 10 of these in combat, 1 missing in action, 1 in a flying accident and 2 to mechanical failure. By December 31, 1943 the record stood at 7,451 sorties for 5,410 hours of combat flying time, 171 air victories against 86 combat losses – 59 in air combat including 20 Cobras – three aircraft lost as a result of accidents and 46 pilots of whom 35 were lost in combat. Destroyed in the air were 56 Bf 109Es, 43 Bf 109Fs, 15 Bf 109Gs, one "He 113", 30 Bf 110s, 7 Ju 88s, 9 Ju 87s, one He 111, 2 Do 215s, 5 Hs 126s and one each Fi 156 and Fw 189.
Aces: L.A. Galchenko 24, G.F. Dmitryuk 18, P.S. Kutakhov 14, A.Zajtsev 14

145 GIAP – see 253 IAP

146 IAP
Designated the 115 GIAP on 9-2-1943
Full title: 115 Gvardejskij istrebitelnyj aviatsionnyj ordenov Aleksandra Nevskogo i Kutuzova Orshanskij polk
Key commanders: Maj. V.N. Buyanov, Podpolk. A. Koss (1945)
Assignments: 234 IAD, 7 GIAD
Aircraft: I-16s, MiG-3s, Yak-7Bs, Yak-3s
Battle honors: Odessa 1941, Kursk, Orsha, Vilnyus, Kaunas, Tilsit, Berlin
Combat record: The regiment was in the forefront of action during the period of June, 1941 to June, 1943, claiming 194 aerial victories. It next distinguished itself in the heavy air battles above Kursk by scoring 73 more kills during July, 1943. It later played a big part in the final clashes over Berlin, its fighters running up 48 victories during 1,215 sorties, 24 of these being claimed in a two day period between April 18-19.
Aces: K.V. Novosyolov 19, V.N. Buyanov 17

146 GIAP – see 487 IAP

147 IAP
Designated the 20 GIAP on 3-7-1942
Key commanders: Maj. P.Z. Shevel, Podpolk. M. Semyanistyj
Assignments: 1 SAD, 234 IAD
Aircraft: Kittyhawks, Airacobras, Kingcobras (as of 1946)
Battle honors: Murmansk, Karelia
Aces: V.F. Sizov 9, A.S. Khlobystov 7

147 GIAP – see 630 IAP

148 IAP
Honorifics: Rezhitskij
Key commanders: Podpolk. G.N. Zajtsev, Maj. M.P. Nekrasov
Assignments: 287 IAD, 185 IAD
Aircraft: Yak-9s
Battle honors: Stalingrad, Bryansk, Daugavpils (Dvinsk), Rezekne (Rezhitsa), Courland

Aeracobras of the 19 GIAP on a snow-covered Murmansk airfield. (Author's collection)

Aces: V.N. Buzinov 15, I.P. Rybin 12, M.Z. Teleshevskij 12

148 GIAP – see 910 IAP

149 IAP
Key commanders: Podpolk. N.T. Nikitin
Assignments: 16 SAD, 64 IAD, 216 IAD, 323 IAD
Aircraft: LaGG-3s, MiG-3s
Battle honors: Stanislau 1941, Izyum-Barvenkovo, Yelnya, Smolensk, Bobrujsk, Baranovichi, Poland, Breslau, Berlin
Combat record: The regiment experienced inordinate losses on June 22, 1941, when Luftwaffe strikes destroyed 21 of its MiG-3s on the ground whilst two more became the prey of German fighters in the air. Even though its pilots submitted claims for eight of the attackers, this certainly was not enough to offset the heavy losses.
Aces: P.P. Peresumkin 18, A.I. Morozov 13

149 GIAP – no trace to original unit
Key commanders: Maj. M.I. Zotov
Battle honors: Yassy-Kishinyov campaign

150 GIAP – see 427 IAP-PVO

151 GIAP – no trace to original unit
Assignments: 13 GIAD
Battle honors: Byelgorod-Kharkov, Poltava, Kremenchug, Yassy-Kishinyov campaign, Hungary, Austria, Czechoslovakia Aces: Ye.V. Vasilyevskij 21

152 IAP
Assignments: 103 SAD (1941)
Aircraft: Hurricanes

152 GIAP – see 270 IAP

153 IAP
Designated the 28 GIAP on 11-22-1942
Honorifics: Leningradskij, Volkhovskij (as of November, 1943)
Key commanders: Maj. S.I. Mironov, Podpolk. O.M. Rodionov (as of October, 1942)

Assignments: 5 SAD, 5 GIAD
Aircraft: I-153s, I-16s, Airacobras
Battle honors: Leningrad, Staraya Russa, Voronezh, Volkhov, Polotsk, East Prussia
Combat Record: In March, 1942 the regiment was withdrawn from the Leningrad Front becoming the first fighter unit to re-equip with Airacobra Is. On June 14 it moved to the Voronezh Front and resumed operations on the 30th marking the beginning of an impressive run of success. It later saw some fighting over Lipetsk and by September 25, 1942 the pilots had afforded 1,070 sorties for 1,162 combat hours knocking down 64 enemy planes during 259 air encounters. In aerial combat they had destroyed 39 Bf 109Fs, 15 Ju 88s, four MC.200s, one each Do 215, He 111, Fw 189, Bf 110 and Me 210 all while flying Airacobras. Losses in the same time frame totaled three pilots and eight aircraft in action along with one resp. two through accidents. Eight pilots led by Major O.M. Rodionov were detached to fight on West Front from Kubinka, Alferevo and Klimovo airfields claiming 13 kills with nine Ju 88s and four Bf 109Fs between August 8 and September 11, 1942, against combat losses of two pilots wounded and two aircraft in 167 sorties. Following reorganization at Ivanovo between October 1-27, 1942 the regiment tasted some action on Northwest Front submitting claims for four Bf 109Fs and one Ju 87 whilst operating from Lyubertsy and Vypolzovo airfields between October 31 and November 28 for two combat losses. It next saw heavy fighting during the period of December 1, 1942 and August 1, 1943 scoring 63 kills with the breakdown being: 23 Bf 109Fs, 23 Fw 190s, seven Fw 189s, six Ju 88s, and four Hs 126s. Fourteen Cobras were lost in combat, four were destroyed in air attacks and five were damaged in accidents, while 10 pilots were killed or failed to return. Transition to P-39Ns and Qs was accomplished by August 1, 1943.
Aces: A.S. Smirnov 34, L.A. Bykovets 19, F.M. Mazurin 18, A.V.Kislyakov 17

153 GIAP – see 516 IAP

154 IAP
Designated the 29 GIAP on 11-22-1942
Honorifics: Volkhovskij
Key commanders: Podpolk. A.A. Matveyev, Maj. P.A. Pilyutov
Assignments: 39 IAD, 275 IAD, 324 IAD
Aircraft: I-16s, Tomahawks (as of November, 1941), Kittyhawks, Yak-7Bs (as of January, 1943), Yak-9s (as of late 1943)
Battle honors: Leningrad, Volkhov, Narva, Tartu, Vyborg
Combat record: The regiment performed brilliantly during the darkest hours of the 1941 air war, claiming 118 kills, 16 on July 10, in a 45 day period between June and August, 1941. It next enjoyed considerable success in the hell of Leningrad, adding 159 more air victories to its bag.
Aces: F.M. Chubukov 34, I.S. Leonovich 28, N.A. Zelenov 24, P.D. Zyuzin 19, P.A. Pilyutov 17 of 23, K.I. Korshunov 15

Lejtenant I.I. Logvinov of the 153 IAP in front of his P-39. The photo is dated June 20, 1944 at which time Logvinov's score was 11 kills during 220 sorties. (Author's collection)

155 IAP
Designated the 3 GIAP on 12-6-1941
Honorifics: Rostovo-Donskij
Key commanders: Podpolk. D.S. Shpak, Podpolk. G.N. Prokopenko (KIA 6-14-1944)
Assignments: 235 IAD, 15 GIAD
Aircraft: La-5s
Battle honors: Petrozavodsk, Karelia, Volkhov, Leningrad, Stalingrad, Caucasus, Voronezh, Lemberg-Sandomierz campaign, Berlin
Combat record: The score at the end of the war was 400 in the air and on the ground.
Aces: G.N. Prokopenko 27, P.V. Bazanov 22, A.A. Murashov 22

156 IAP
Honorifics: Elbingskij
Key commanders: Podpolk. A.S. Yegorov (1943), Podpolk. S.F. Dolgushin (as of July, 1943)
Assignments: 215 IAD, 240 IAD
Aircraft: LaGG-3s (until late 1943), La-5s (as of July, 1943), La-7s

Battle honors: Stalingrad, Volkhov (April-July, 1943), Bobrujsk, Poland, Danzig
Aces: M.M. Zelyonkin 19

156 GIAP – see 247 IAP

157 IAP
Honorifics: Brestskij
Key commanders: Maj. V.N. Shtoff, Podpolk. V.F. Volkhov
Assignments: 273 IAD (1943), 234 IAD
Aircraft: Hurricanes, Yak-7Bs, Yak-9s, Yak-3s
Battle honors: Leningrad, Rzhev, Kholm, Kursk, Korsun-Shevchenkovskij, Uman, Bobrujsk, Baranovichi, Lemberg-Sandomierz campaign, Warsaw, Berlin
Combat record: The regiment had a big day on February 23, 1944, when 12 Yaks with Podpolkovnik Volkhov in the lead took on a formation of 30 bombers escorted by 12 fighters in the vicinity of Rogachyov, getting 12 kills.
Aces: M.S. Baranov 26, A.Ye. Borovykh c.25 of 32, I.V. Maslov 22

158 IAP
Designated the 103 GIAP on 7-7-1943
Key commanders: Podpolk. V.I. Matveyev (KIA 1-1-1942)
Assignments: 7 IAK-PVO, 2 GIAK-PVO
Aircraft: I-16s, Yak-1s, Kittyhawks, Airacobras, Yak-9s
Battle honors: Pskov 1941, Leningrad, Volkhov, Kolpino
Combat record: The regiment's final score was 245 air victories.
Aces: D.V. Dzhabidze 22, S.G. Litavrin 19, I.M. Shishkan 16, S.V. Demenkov 15

159 IAP
Honorifics: Tallinskij
Key commanders: Podpolk. P.A. Pokryshev (July, 1943-end of war)
Assignments: 275 IAD
Aircraft: I-16s, MiG-3s, Tomahawks (as of December, 1941), Kittyhawks, La-5s, La-7s
Battle honors: Leningrad, Novgorod, Volkhov, Narva, Pskov, Vyborg
Combat record: During the war the regiment destroyed 387 enemy planes in air combat.
Aces: V.G. Serov 39, V.A. Zotov 28, P.Ya. Likholetov 25, D.V. Yermakov 25, V.I. Vedeneyev 24, V.A. Zotov 17, A.D. Bulayev 15

159 GIAP – see 88 IAP

160 IAP
Designated the 137 GIAP, date not established
Full title: 137 Gvardejskij istrebitelnyj aviatsionnyj Krasnoznamennyj, ordena Suvorova III stepeni Minskij polk
Key commanders: Major Kostromin (1941), Podpolk. V.A. Yamanov
Assignments: 43 IAD, 3 GIAD
Aircraft: I-153s, I-16s, LaGG-3s, La-5s
Battle honors: Minsk, Bobrujsk, Mogilyov, Smolensk, Vyazma, Leningrad, Volkhov, Orel, Minsk, Courland, Berlin
Combat record: The regiment went to war in June, 1941 and saw a great deal of action at Minsk and over Bobrujsk, Smolensk and Vyazma, claiming 27 kills during 1,683 sorties until August 2, 1941.
Aces: A.I. Maksimenko 10

La-5 of the 159 IAP ready for combat, Karelian Isthmus, summer 1944. The regiment at that time was commanded by the legendary P.A. Pokryshev and eventually would boast some of the best fighter pilots in the VVS. Legend beneath the cockpit reads: "Eskadrilya Valerij Chkalov." Chkalov was chief test pilot of the Polikarpov Design Bureau, who crashed to his death in an I-180 prototype. Funds for the aircraft of the squadron were raised by the kolkhoz workers of the Gorkij area. (Author's collection)

161 IAP
Key commanders: Kap. Kulinich (1941), Podpolk. P.K. Moskovets
Assignments: 57 SAD, 43 IAD
Aircraft: I-16s
Battle honors: Minsk, Bobrujsk, Mogilyov, Smolensk, Vyazma, Staraya Russa, Leningrad, Demyansk
Combat record: In June, 1941 the regiment was based in the Minsk area with 62 I-16s. It was greatly involved in the dark months to follow, scoring 33 air victories during 1,192 sorties between June 22 and August 2, 1941.

162 IAP
Honorifics: Grodnenskij
Key commanders: Podpolk. Reznik (1941), Polk. P.I. Kolomin
Assignments: 43 IAD, 309 IAD
Aircraft: I-16s, MiG-3s, Yak-7Bs, Yak-3s
Battle honors: Minsk, Bobrujsk, Mogilyov, Smolensk, Vyazma, Kalinin Front, Smolensk, Mogilyov, Minsk, Grodno
Aces: Yu.I. Gorokhov 23, P.I. Kolomin 16, V.N. Kolomoyets 16, V.G. Shchegolev 16

163 IAP
Honorifics: Sedletskij
Key commanders: Maj. Lagutin (1941), Podpolk. P.A. Pologov (1943), Maj. V.M. Ukhanyev, Maj. P.K. Kozachenko
Assignments: 43 IAD, 273 IAD, 336 IAD
Aircraft: I-16s, Yak-1s, Yak-9s, La-5s
Battle honors: Minsk, Bobrujsk, Mogilyov, Smolensk, Vyazma, Karelia, Kursk, the Dnyepr, Gomel, Bobrujsk, Pinsk, Grodno, Poland
Combat record: At the outbreak of the war the regiment was flying I-16s with strength to hand being 59. It engaged in heavy action in the defense of Minsk claiming a record 21 kills on June 24, 1941, and saw further action over Byelorussia and at Smolensk adding 10 more air victories during 810 sorties until August 2.
Aces: N.S. Konyshev 18, P.A. Pologov 18, M.M. Kibkalov 17, V.M. Mankevich 17

163 GIAP – see 249 IAP

164 IAP
Assignments: 15 SAD, 295 IAD
Aircraft: MiG-3s, La-5s
Battle honors: Lemberg 1941, Kuban, Kursk, Kharkov, Dnyepropetrovsk, Yugoslavia, Hungary
Aces: A.I. Volodin 22, A.N. Belkin 17, V.M. Shevyrin 17, G.D. Oniskyevich 15

165 IAP
Honorifics: Varshavskij
Key commanders: Podpolk. N.V. Semyonov

Famous 159 IAP ace: V.G. Serov engaged in heavy action on Leningrad Front flying with the 159 IAP and became the top gun in that theater with 39 kills and eight fractional credits before losing his life in a Taran (ramming) attack on June 26, 1944. (Author's collection)

Assignments: 63 SAD, 44 IAD, 205 IAD, 286 IAD
Aircraft: La-5s
Battle honors: Proskurov 1941, Kursk, the Dnyepr, Gomel, Rogachyov, Bobrujsk, Poland, Berlin

166 IAP
Designated the 88 GIAP on 5-21-1943
Full title: 88 Gvardejskij istrebitelnyj aviatsionnyj ordena Bogdana Khmelnitskogo Krakovskij polk
Key commanders: Maj. S.S. Rimsha, Podpolk. I.S. Zlygostev
Assignments: 8 GIAD
Aircraft: LaGG-3s, La-5s
Battle honors: Caucasus, Kursk, Byelgorod, Poland
Combat record: The regiment entered combat on June 22, 1941, losing four aircraft with 10 more sustaining damage. It really came into its own in the contested air space above Kursk, the pilots being credited with 30 enemy planes in the air, with another three damaged for a loss of four pilots killed on July 5, 1943. The following day the bag was 26 together with one damaged. On this same day Aleksandr Gorovets set the all time record for victories in one day for Soviet aces when he blasted nine Ju 87s out of the sky between Vladimirovka-Olkhovatka before he was hit, crashing to his death.
Aces: V.S. Levitan 19, V.I. Mishustin 17, P.M. Nikonorov 17

168 IAP
Key commanders: Podpolk. S.D. Yaroslavtsev (1941/42), Maj. K.A. Pilshchikov, Podpolk. A.S. Danilov (as of June, 1943)
Assignments: 21 SAD, 45 SAD, 10 SAD, 303 IAD (as of 1943)
Aircraft: I-153s, I-16s, LaGG-3s (as of November, 1941), Yak-7Bs (as of February, 1943)
Battle honors: Moldavia 1941, Moscow, Karachyov, Kozelsk, Bryansk, Kursk, Spas-Demensk, Smolensk
Combat record: On July 12, 1941, three I-16s mixed it with four Fiat fighters and four Bf 109s while flying a frontline patrol in the Dnyestr River area. In the ensuing melee, Konstantin Pilshchikov and Pyotr Shurmin both bagged single Fiats, while Nikolaj Zadorozhnyj got a 109. Shurmin then was worked over by the Germans, however, crashing into the ground in a sheet of flame, while Pilshchikov made a forced landing. The regiment's big day came on March 7, 1942, when six LaGG-3s with Lejtenant V.G. Seregin leading engaged 12 Ju 87s escorted by Bf 109s near Yukhnov, where seven of the Stukas were shot down. On June 8, 1943, 1 VA flew massive airfield strafes at Borovsk, Seshcha, and Bryansk, but the Shturmovik units involved suffered particularly heavy losses. Among those punished for failing to furnish effective fighter cover was Major K.A. Pilshchikov, who was relieved from his command being sent to the air force reserves where he remained for the following three months.

168 GIAP – no trace to original unit
Full title: 168 Gvardejskij istrebitelnyj aviatsionnyj Krasnoznamennyj polk
Key commanders: Podpolk. I. Kalinin, Maj. F.F.Musatov (KIA 10-11-1944)
Assignments: 236 IAD
Battle honors: Lemberg-Sandomierz campaign, Yassy-Kishinyov campaign

169 IAP
Designated the 63 GIAP in March, 1943
Full title: 63 Gvardejskij istrebitelnyj aviatsionnyj ordena Kutuzova III stepeni Vilinskij polk
Key commanders: Maj. Ugrovatov (1941), Podpolk. N.P. Ivanov (June, 1942-August, 1943), Maj. A.A. Fedotov (KIA 12-15-1943), Maj. Ye.M. Gorbatyuk (as of February, 1944), Podpolk. A.M. Chislov
Assignments: 210 IAD, 3 GIAD
Aircraft: La-5s
Battle honors: Volkhov, Kalinin Front, Velikiye Luki, Demyansk, Kursk-Orel, Berlin
Combat record: The regiment fought a hard battle against the Luftwaffe in the Volkhov area, and by December, 1942 the scoreboard read 23 kills during 1,914 sorties. But the attrition rate was high, and it stood down for a rest and further training with Podpolkovnik Ivanov getting it into operational trim once more. The regiment had a field day on December 29, 1942, when its pilots submitted claims for 21 enemy aircraft destroyed. The final tally at the close of hostilities stood at 400 victories.
Aces: A.A. Fedotov 22, A.M. Chislov 21, P.A. Grazhdaninov 20, A.G. Voronko 17, A.V. Pashkevich 16, I.M. Beresutskij 15, N.P. Ivanov 15

170 IAP
Key commanders: Maj. Mishchenko (1941)
Assignments: 23 SAD, 43 IAD
Aircraft: I-16s, Yak-1s
Battle honors: Orsha, Mogilyov, Smolensk, Vyazma

171 IAP
Honorifics: Tulskij
Key commanders: Podpolk. S.I. Orlyakhin
Assignments: 125 IAD-PVO, 286 IAD, 315 IAD
Aircraft: MiG-3s, La-5s (as of early 1943), La-7s (as of February, 1945)
Battle honors: Tula 1941, Orel 1942, Mtsensk, Kursk-Orel, Karachyov, Bryansk, Gomel, Ostrov, Rezekne, Riga, Courland
Combat record: The regiment saw first success against the Luftwaffe during the fighting for Tula in 1941, claiming 16 victories in 47 encounters. It later flew with great distinction in the heavy air battles over Kursk, being credited with 63 kills between July 8-13, 1943, 21 of these coming on the 13th.
Aces: I.A. Vishnyakov 20, K.F. Sobolev 16, A.G. Shevtsov 15

172 IAP
Key commanders: Maj. I. Kukin, Podpolk. Samokhvalov
Assignments: 309 IAD
Aircraft: LaGG-3s, Yak-1s
Battle honors: Moscow, Mozhajsk, Smolensk
Aces: N.K. Spiridenko 15

173 IAP
Assignments: 256 IAD
Battle honors: Ukraine, Silesia

176 IAP
Honorifics: Berlinskij
Key commanders: Maj. G.P. Makarov (1941), Podpolk. V.N. Makarov
Assignments: 207 IAD, 283 IAD
Aircraft: Yak-1s, Yak-3s
Battle honors: Moscow, Stalingrad, Kursk, Bobrujsk, Baranovichi, Vistula-Oder campaign, Berlin
Combat record: The regiment participated in the Battle of Kursk and was able to run up 30 air victories between JulyAugust, 1943 to bring its score to 126. It was later greatly involved in the fighting for Berlin, and in an outstanding effort claimed a record 110 kills in April, 1945.

176 GIAP – see 19 IAP

177 IAP-PVO
Key commanders: Maj. M.I. Korolev (1941)
Assignments: 6 IAK-PVO
Aircraft: I-16s
Battle honors: Moscow
Aces: I.Z. Tyapin 8, V.V. Talalikhin 5 of 8

177 GIAP – see 193 IAP

178 IAP-PVO
Key commanders: Maj.R.I. Rakov (1941)
Assignments: 6 IAK-PVO
Aircraft: I-16s, LaGG-3s
Battle honors: Moscow, Kaluga, Podolsk
Aces: N.D. Dudnik 17, G.A. Grigoryev 17

178 GIAP – see 240 IAP

179 IAP
Assignments: 331 IAD

179 GIAP – see 297 IAP

180 IAP
Designated the 30 GIAP on 11-22-1942
Full title: 30 Gvardejskij istrebitelnyj aviatsionnyj Krasnoznamennyj, ordena Suvorova III stepeni Baranovichskij polk
Key commanders: Kap. A.P. Sergeyev (1941), Maj. I.M. Khluzovich
Assignments: 46 SAD, 235 IAD (1942), 1 GIAD, 273 IAD (1945)
Aircraft: I-16s, MiG-3s, Hurricanes (as of March, 1942), Airacobras, Yak-3s
Battle honors: Rzhev 1941, Kholm 1941, Kalinin Front, Stalingrad, Dmitrovsk, Kursk, Rogachyov, Minsk, Bobrujsk, Baranovichi, Poland, Berlin
Combat record: The regiment was extremely active during the early stages of the war and by January 7, 1943, the bag was 227 kills. In March, 1942 the unit converted to Hurricanes and became operational with 20 fighters on June 12, but suffered heavy losses. On July 20 it was withdrawn to re-equip with Airacobras, and flew these most successfully inflicting heavy losses. The unit subsequently had one of the highest kill rates

Right and below: Two shots of shattered and abandoned Luftwaffe aircraft discovered by advancing Soviet forces on an airfield in the Stalingrad area. This is believed to be Pitomnik, which was taken by Soviet forces on January 16, 1943. (Author's collection)

for the VVS, claiming 18 air victories on May 22, 1943, 10 for three combat losses on June 2, 1943, and 15 in the final clashes over Berlin on April 20, 1945.
Aces: M.P. Rents 20

181 IAP
Key commanders: Podpolk. N.D. Goryev
Assignments: 235 IAD
Aircraft: La-5s
Battle honors: Velikiye Luki, Stalingrad

181 GIAP – see 239 IAP
Assignments: 15 GIAD
Aces: L.D. Golyachkov 14

182 IAP-PVO
Key commanders: Maj. M.P. Noga
Assignments: 105 IAD-PVO
Aircraft: LaGG-3s
Battle honors: Mariupol, Rostov, Brody
Aces: S.K. Koblov 9, P.G. Ageyev 6

183 IAP
Assignments: 268 IAD, 269 IAD, 294 IAD
Aircraft: Yak-1s, Yak-7Bs
Battle honors: Donbas 1941, Stalingrad, Byelgorod-Kharkov, Korsun-Shevchenkovskij
Aces: M.D. Baranov 24, N.I. Leonov 20

184 IAP
Aircraft: I-15s, Yak-1s
Battle honors: Gomel 1941

184 GIAP – see 439 IAP

185 IAP
Key Commanders: Podpolk Vasin
Aircraft: Airacobras
Battle Honors: Leningrad Front

187 IAP – no trace

188 IAP
Aircraft: Yak-1s
Battle honors: Moscow

191 IAP
Key commanders: Podpolk. A.F. Radchenko, Maj. Grinko
Assignments: 257 SAD, 235 IAD, 7 IAK-PVO, 275 IAD
Aircraft: I-153s, I-16s, Hurricanes, Kittyhawks, Airacobras, La-5s
Battle honors: Leningrad, Stalingrad, Petsamo-Kirkenes campaign
Aces: T.A. Litvinenko 23, V.B. Mitrokhin 17, I.T. Tushev 15

Starshij Lejtenant I.T. Tushev, one of 191 IAP's most distinguished pilots, with his P-40 on Karelian Front in 1944. (Author's collection)

192 IAP
Key commanders: Kap. P.P. Kizilov
Assignments: 7 IAK-PVO, 279 IAD
Battle honors: Leningrad, Kursk, Yassy-Kishinyov campaign

193 IAP
Designated the 177 GIAP in August, 1944
Honorifics: Debretsenskij
Key commanders: Maj. I.F. Sukhoruchenko, Polk. G.M. Pyatakov (1944)
Assignments: 302 IAD, 14 GIAD
Aircraft: La-5s
Battle honors: Leningrad, Kursk-Byelgorod, Kremenchug, Krivoj Rog, Cherkassy, Yassy-Kishinyov campaign, Debrecen, Budapest, Austria
Aces: N.P. Belousov 23, N.I. Olkhovskij 19, N.S. Artamonov 18, I.G. Sklyarov 18, A.P. Blinov 17, A.M. Milovanov 17, A.D. Dogadajlo 16

194 IAP
Key commanders: Kap. M.I. Kuzmin
Battle honors: Leningrad

195 IAP
Key commanders: Maj. S.O. Sokolov
Aircraft: I-16s
Battle honors: Leningrad

196 IAP
Assignments: 324 IAD
Aircraft: Kittyhawks (as of January, 1943, obtaining these from the 29 GIAP), Airacobras
Aces: A.D. Bilyukin 22

197 IAP
Assignments: 178 IAD
Aces: V.V. Smaznov 18

208 IAP
Key commanders: Maj. I.Kibirin (1941)
Assignments: 6 IAK-PVO (as of July 9, 1941)
Aircraft: Pe-3 (1941)
Battle honors: Moscow

211 IAP
Assignments: 220 IAD (1942)
Aircraft: Yak-1s
Battle honors: Stalingrad

A.D. Bilyukin, top gun of the 196 IAP. (Author's collection)

211 GIAP – no trace to original unit
Full title: 211 Gvardejskij istrebitelnyj aviatsionnyj ordenov Suvorova i Kutuzova Yaroslavskij polk
Key commanders: Podpolk. S.I. Timofeyev

212 GIAP – see 438 IAP

213 GIAP – see 508 IAP

223 IAP – no trace

233 IAP
Honorifics: Minskij
Key commanders: Maj. K.A. Kuzmenko (1941), Podpolk. V.V. Kravtsov
Assignments: 286 IAD, 234 IAD
Aircraft: MiG-3s, Yak-3s
Battle honors: Moscow, Vyazma, Kursk, Kiev, Gomel, Bobrujsk, Minsk, Vistula-Oder campaign, Berlin
Combat record: Victories for the regiment came thick and fast during the Battle of Kursk, when it submitted claims for 79 enemy aircraft in the air between May 27 and August 14, 1943. It later continued to perform creditably over Pomerania, claiming nine kills without loss in a scrap with 10 Fw 190s and four Bf 109s in the Stargard area (SE Stettin) on February 19, 1945.
Aces: S.A. Kuznetsov 19, K.F. Zakharov 15, V.A. Shishov 14

234 IAP-PVO
Assignments: 105 IAD-PVO
Aircraft: LaGG-3s
Battle honors: Batajsk, Taganrog

236 IAP
Designated the 112 GIAP on 8-25-1943
Full title: 112 Gvardejskij istrebitelnyj aviatsionnyj Kamenets-Podolskij polk
Key commanders: Maj. S.M. Petukhov
Assignments: 201 IAD, 10 GIAD
Aircraft: Yak-1s
Battle honors: Moscow, Stalingrad, Salsk, Kharkov, Voronezh, Caucasus
Aces: L.V. Dema 17, V.A. Rogozhin 11, V.P. Tikhonov 11

237 IAP
Designated the 54 GIAP on 2-8-1943
Honorifics: Kerchenskij
Key commanders: Maj. A.B. Isayev, Maj. M.D. Mordvinov (KIA 10-21-1942), Podpolk. Ye.P. Melnikov (as of November, 1942)

Assignments: 220 IAD, 1 GIAD
Aircraft: Yak-1s, Yak-7Bs, Airacobras(as of September, 1943)
Battle honors: Moscow, Stalingrad, Kursk-Orel, the Dnyepr, Minsk, Poland, Berlin
Combat record: The unit enjoyed considerable success during the period of August 5, 1941, to December 31, 1942, chalking up 122 victories, as well as 38 aircraft damaged during 3,714 sorties and 863 encounters. September, 1942 proved to be a big month with 28 kills in the contested air space above Stalingrad. High-scorers of this battle were I. Balyuk and I. Rivkin with nine kills each, closely followed by Ya. Mikhajlik with seven and V. Limarenko with six. It next did particularly well at Kursk, where the pilots were credited with downing 22 Luftwaffe planes, together with 12 more damaged during 800 sorties, 304 of which were reconnaissance, 126 escorts, 126 patrols, and 84 scrambles. The Airacobra's introduction into combat came in Byelorussia in mid-1944, drawing first blood in their first aerial engagement on June 22, when they scored victories over three Fw 190s.
Aces: V.S. Batyaev 19, I.F. Balyuk 17 of 22, Ya.D. Mikhajlik 17

238 IAP
Key commanders: Podpolk. I.D. Zavrazhnov (later KIA as commander of the 72 RAP in August, 1943)
Aircraft: LaGG-3s
Battle honors: Demyansk

239 IAP
Designated the 181 GIAP, date not established
Key commanders: Maj. A.I. Kurochkin
Assignments: 235 IAD, 6 GIAD, 268 IAD
Aircraft: Yak-1s, La-5s
Battle honors: Velikiye Luki, Stalingrad, Zaporozhye, the Dnyepr, Crimea, Sevastopol
Aces: V.M. Dudnichenko 22, I.V. Lavronenko 15

240 IAP
Designated the 178 GIAP in August, 1944
Full title: 178 Gvardejskij istrebitelnyj aviatsionnyj Krasnoznamennyj, ordena Bogdana Khmelnitskogo polk
Key commanders: Kap. Andreyev, Kap. S.T. Rozhkov, Podpolk. S.I. Podorozhnyj (KIA January, 1944), Maj. I.S. Soldatenko, Podpolk. N.I. Olkhovskij, Podpolk. V.M. Makarov
Assignments: 8 SAD, 234 IAD (as of May, 1942), 302 IAD, 14 GIAD
Aircraft: I-15s, LaGG-3s (as of November, 1941), La-5s (as of mid1942), La-7s
Battle honors: Northwest, Leningrad, West and Southwest Fronts, Stalingrad, Byelgorod-Kharkov, Krivoj Rog, Korsun-Shevchenkovskij, Uman, Yassy-Kishinyov, Debrecen, Budapest, Austria
Combat record: The regiment began combat operations on Northwest Front having 13 I-15s on strength. 286 sorties were conducted in the defense of Leningrad from September 15 until November, 1941, with 12 kills in 15 air combats. Transition to LaGG-3s was accomplished a short time later, but it was not before May 29, 1942, that the unit was called back to action again, when Kap. Rozhkov led 20 fighters to join with the 234 IAD on West Front. 167 sorties were carried out before moving again, this time to Southwest Front on June 12, 1942, where it came under command of the 8th Air Army. After 150 sorties the first Lavochkin La-5s were beginning to arrive to replace the LaGG fighters. Under the leadership of Major Soldatenko the Lavochkins made their combat debut on Stalingrad Front in August, 1942. Between August 20-29 the regiment afforded 109 sorties, claiming 10 air victories in 58 encounters. After this modest start the regiment was stood down for further training, and a return to operations was made in early 1943. It began to realize its full potential at Kharkov in March and during the ordeal of Kursk. In the skies above Yassy the pilots chalked up 20 kills in a three day period between June 1-3, 1944. Kapitan Yevstigneyev racked up five kills during the same period to become the regiment's highest scoring ace with 44 confirmed victories, closely followed by Kapitan Kozhedub, who claimed the destruction of four Luftwaffe planes to bring his bag to 43. Mladshij Lejtenant Bryzgalov and Starshij Lejtenant Zhigulenkov bagged doubles each. In a flurry of action around Debrecen (October 6-28, 1944) the regiment scored 24 more victories for three pilots killed during 247 sorties. The total for the period March, 1943 to May, 1945 was 369 air victories during 5,619 sorties.
Aces: K.A. Yevstigneyev 53, I.N. Kozhedub 45 of 62, B.V. Zhigulenkov 20, P.A. Bryzgalov 19, V.F. Mukhin 19, V.F. Mudretsov 18, I.Ye. Sereda 17

246 IAP
Key commanders: Maj. T.I. Kochetkov
Battle honors: Krasnodar 1942
Combat record: The regiment fought a pitched battle with 16 Bf 109s in the vicinity of Navaginskaya on 10-7-1942, claiming six victories at the cost of two of its own.

247 IAP
Designated the 156 GIAP on 2-5-1944
Full title: 156 Gvardejskij istrebitelnyj aviatsionnyj Krasnoznamennyj, ordena Bogdana Khmelnitskogo Lvovskij polk
Key commanders: Maj. M.P. Fedoseyev (KIA 3-23-1942), Podpolk. Ya.M. Kutikhin, Podpolk. A.S. Yegorov, Maj. S.A. Karnach
Assignments: 240 IAD, 203 IAD, 12 GIAD
Aircraft: Yak-1s
Battle honors: Sevastopol 1942, Leningrad Front, Byelgorod-Kharkov, Poltava, Korsun-Shevchenkovskij, Yassy-Kishinyov, Poland, Germany, Czechoslovakia
Combat record: The regiment was very badly mauled by Luftwaffe strikes on June 22, 1941, 42 of its planes being de-

stroyed on the ground. It later fought at Sevastopol, and although outclassed by German fighters, managed to achieve 10 air victories.
Aces: A.Ye. Maksimov 22, N.V. Bykasov 20, A.A. Shokurov 18, S.A. Karnach 16, A.N. Pavlov 16, A.F. Shamanskij 16, A.I. Bezverkhij 15, M.A. Fedoseyev 13 of 20

248 IAP
Key commanders: Podpolk. V.S. Mukhin, Polk. Ye.Z. Tatanashvili
Assignments: 234 IAD
Aircraft: I-16s, Yak-7Bs, Yak-9s
Battle honors: Batajsk, Taganrog, Kharkov 1942, Kursk, the Dnyepr, Gomel, Bobrujsk, Vistula-Oder campaign, Pomerania, Berlin
Aces: D.G. Miroshnichenko 15

249 IAP
Designated the 163 GIAP, date not established
Full title: 163 Gvardejskij istrebitelnyj aviatsionnyj Krasnoznamennyj, ordena Suvorova III stepeni Feodosijskij polk
Key commanders: Kap. A.I. Khalutin (1941), Maj. P.K. Kozachenko
Assignments: 217 IAD
Aircraft: I-153s, LaGG-3s
Battle honors: Vinnitsa 1941, Berdichyov 1941, Caucasus, Kuban, Kerch
Combat record: In nine months of action the regiment between July, 1942 and March, 1943 destroyed 60 enemy aircraft in the air during 860 sorties and 63 engagements.
Aces: A.M. Kulagin 32, P.K. Babajlov 27, S.I. Kharlamov 17, N.M. Onopchenko 14

252 IAP
Key commanders: Maj. G.A.Trotskij (KIA 4-28-1942)

253 IAP
Designated the 145 GIAP on 10-9-1943
Key commanders: Maj. P.O. Petrov, Podpolk. G.T. Borovchenko
Assignments: 106 IAD-PVO
Aircraft: LaGG-3s
Battle honors: Rzhev, Demyansk
Aces: V.I. Afanasyev 14

254 IAP
Key commanders: Maj. Petrov, Maj. S. Mikhajlin
Assignments: 14 SAD, 36 IAD, 269 IAD
Aircraft: I-16s, La-5s
Battle honors: Kiev 1941, Volkhov, Novgorod, Estonia
Aces: V.K. Sidorenko 25, K.S. Nazimov 24

255 IAP-PVO
The regiment was activated in May, 1941 and assigned to the Kiev air defense zone. It suffered crippling losses while becoming engaged in the ferocious fighting on Southwest Front, but managed to gain 16 air victories during 815 sorties for the period June 22 to August 20, 1941. It was converted to LaGG-3s shortly after, but was then transferred to the RSVGK on March 20, 1942. On July 19, 1942, it was assigned to the Northern Fleet, enjoying considerable success while flying Airacobras.

Members of the 254 IAP standing at attention during an awards ceremony. Polkovnik Fyodorov confers decoration on Major Titov. (Author's collection)

The 254 IAP at Arzamas, south of Gorkij, on February 8, 1943 after reequipping with La-5s. (Author's collection)

262 IAP – no trace

263 IAP
Full title: 263 Istrebitelnyj aviatsionnyj ordena Suvorova Pomeranskij polk
Assignments: 215 IAD
Battle honors: Bobrujsk, Pomerania
Combat record: The regiment finished the war with a total score of 335 confirmed.

265 IAP
Assignments: 336 IAD
Battle honors: lst Byelorussian Front (Bobrujsk, Pinsk), 3rd and 1st Baltic Fronts
Aces: A.P. Bulgakov 18

266 IAP-PVO
Assignments: 105 IAD-PVO
Aircraft: I-16s
Battle honors: Batajsk, Rostov, Melitopol

267 IAP
Battle honors: Yassy-Kishinyov campaign

268 IAP-PVO
Key commanders: Maj. T.D. Kartuzov
Assignments: 310 IAD-PVO
Battle honors: Breslau

269 IAP
Assignments: 323 IAD
Aircraft: LaGG-3s, Yak-9s
Battle honors: Kuban, Kerch, Sevastopol, Baranovichi
Aces: P.M. Kamozin 35

Fighter leaders share a quiet moment. From left, they are: Major Titov, Polkovnik Fyodorov and an unknown Major. (Author's collection)

270 IAP
Designated the 152 GIAP on 2-5-1944
Full title: 152 Gvardejskij istrebitelnyj aviatsionnyj ordenov Bogdana Khmelnitskogo i Aleksandra Nevskogo Sandomirskij polk
Key commanders: Podpolk. V.A. Merkushev (POW 7-4-1944), Maj. S.D. Luganskij, Maj. V.M. Shevchuk (as of January, 1945)
Assignments: 203 IAD, 12 GIAD
Aircraft: LaGG-3s, Yak-1s, Yak-7Bs, Yak-9s
Battle honors: Stalingrad, Byelgorod-Kharkov, Poltava,

Cherkassy, Kirovograd, Lemberg-Sandomierz campaign, Breslau, Berlin, Prague
Combat record: During the war the regiment destroyed 245 enemy aircraft in air-to-air combat.
Aces: S.D. Luganskij 37, I.M. Korniyenko 24, N.K. Shutt 22, V.A. Merkushev c.21 of 29, N.P. Dunayev 20+ of 24, I.F. Kuzmichev 18, Ye.P. Menshutin 18

271 IAP
Designated the 64 GIAP in March, 1943
Full title: 64 Gvardejskij istrebitelnyj aviatsionnyj Krasnoznamennyj, ordena Aleksandra Nevskogo Orshanskij polk
Key commanders: Maj. A.M. Razsudkov
Assignments: 274 IAD, 4 GIAD
Aircraft: Yak-1s, Yak-7Bs, Yak-9s
Battle honors: Velikiye Luki, Demyansk, Kursk, Courland, Berlin
Aces: P.I. Muravyev 28, P.M. Vostrukhin 28, N.M. Alekseyev 21

272 IAP
Assignments: 203 IAD, 309 IAD
Aircraft: LaGG-3s
Battle honors: Mozhajsk, Kozelsk
Aces: A.A. Grachyov 16

273 IAP
Designated the 31 GIAP on 11-22-1942
Full title: 31 Gvardejskij istrebitelnyj aviatsionnyj Krasnoznamennyj Nikopolskij polk
Key commanders: Maj. N.V. Grinev (as of April, 1941), Maj. I.P. Suvorov, Maj. B.N. Yeremin (as of November, 1942), Maj. P.A. Matiyenko (KIFA 10-15-1944)
Assignments: 12 GIAD
Aircraft: I-16s, LaGG-3s, Yak-1s, Yak-7Bs
Battle honors: Caucasus, Moscow, Stalingrad, Byelgorod, Krasnograd, Poltava, Kremenchug, Dnyepropetrovsk, Kirovograd, Korsun-Shevchenkovskij, Uman, YassyKishinyov campaign, Lemberg-Sandomierz campaign, Breslau, Berlin
Aces: A.M. Reshetov 35, F.Ya. Morozov 21, N.Z. Vydrigan 16

274 IAP
Key commanders: Polk. P.A. Pologov
Assignments: 278 IAD
Aircraft: Yak-9K
Battle honors: Stalingrad, Nikopol, Kaunas, Vistula-Oder campaign
Aces: I.M. Kiselyov 14

279 IAP
Key commanders: Podpolk. A.M. Zhuravlev
Aircraft: La-5s
Battle honors: Pomerania

282 IAP
Key commanders: Maj. A.V.Minayev
Battle honors: Kharkov 1942
Combat record: By June 10, 1942, the score was 55 confirmed victories.

283 IAP
Honorifics: Vyborgskij
Key commanders: Podpolk. G.I. Kozachev
Battle honors: Karelia, Vyborg (Viipuri)

286 IAP
Key commanders: Maj. P.N. Baranov
Aircraft: I-16s
Battle honors: Leningrad Front

287 IAP
Assignments: 269 IAD
Battle honors: Akhtyrka, Rzhev, Novgorod, Volkhov, Tartu
Aces: V.D. Konyakhin 17, V.P. Lukin 16

291 IAP
Key commanders: Maj. G. Lapshin, Maj. S.L. Indyk (until June, 1943), Maj. V.I.Shishkin
Assignments: 220 IAD, 265 IAD
Aircraft: LaGG-3s, Yak-3s
Battle honors: Stalingrad, Nikopol, Melitopol, Kuban, Zaporozhye, Vistula-Oder campaign, Berlin
Aces: M.I. Kutsenko 23, A.F. Lavrenov 22, V.S. Konobayev 18, V.S. Baskov 15

293 IAP
Key commanders: Maj. A.I. Ketov
Assignments: 287 IAD, 185 IAD
Aircraft: Yak-1s, Yak-9s
Battle honors: Stalingrad, South, North Caucasus, Bryansk and 2nd Baltic Fronts
Aces: S.I. Safronov 27, V.S. Nagornyj 24, N.P. Logvinenko 20

296 IAP
Activated in June, 1941
Designated the 73 GIAP, on 5-3-1943
Honorifics: Stalingradskij
Key commanders: Podpolk. N.I. Baranov (KIA 5-6-1943), Maj. I. Golyshev, Podpolk. P.A. Mikhajlyuk
Assignments: 268 IAD, 6 GIAD
Aircraft: I-16s, MiG-1s, MiG-3s, Yak-1s (until the end of war), Yak-7Bs
Battle honors: Kirovograd, Stalingrad, Rostov, Batajsk, Mariupol, Kharkov, Debrecen, Budapest, Bratislava, Vienna, Brno
Combat record: The regiment reported the destruction of 17 enemy planes against four combat losses in the fighting for Kirovograd between July-September, 1941. In the skies above

Shattered carcasses of German aircraft at Danzig. This German port on the Baltic coast was trapped by superior forces of the 2nd Byelorussian Front and surrendered after vicious fighting on March 30, 1945. During this same month 4 VA went out to attack the city's airfields seven times totaling 232 bomber and Shturmovik sorties. They were covered by fighters of the 215 IAD under the leadership of Polkovnik M.N. Yakushin. Numerous Luftwaffe planes reportedly were left burning on the ground while "the remaining Focke-Wulfs and Messerschmitts were destroyed in the air by the escorts." (Author's collection)

Taganrog it was credited with 20 kills during 545 sorties for the period February to April, 1943.
Aces: I.I. Borisenko 23, A.F. Plekhanov 17

297 IAP
Designated the 179 GIAP in August, 1944
Honorifics: Transilvanskij
Key commanders: Maj. S.A. Matviyenko
Assignments: 302 IAD, 14 GIAD
Aircraft: La-5s, La-7s
Battle honors: Stalingrad, Kursk, Byelgorod-Kharkov, Sumy, Poltava, Yassy-Kishinyov campaign, Debrecen, Budapest, Austria, Prague
Combat record: The regiment had a big day on August 10, 1943, when 10 La-5 fighters ran into 80 enemy planes, 20 of these being shot down between Russkaya Lozovaya-Liptsy. While engaged in heavy action during the Yassy-Kishinyov campaign, 10 fighters with Major S.A. Matviyenko in the lead on August 20, 1944, destroyed five Ju 88s in breaking up the attack of 25 bombers on elements of 52nd Combined Arms Army.
Aces: A.A. Dyachkov 27, A.F. Ryazantsev 20, N.N. Kononenko 15

298 IAP
Designated the 104 GIAP, on 8-25-1943
Full title: 104 Gvardejskij istrebitelnyj aviatsionnyj ordena Aleksandra Nevskogo Krakovskij polk
Key commanders: Podpolk. I.A. Taranenko (until July, 1943); Maj. V.G. Semenishin (as of 7-18-1943)
Assignments: 219 BAD, 229 IAD, 9 GIAD (as of 8-21-1943)
Aircraft: I-16s, Airacobras (as of January, 1943)
Battle honors: Rostov, Taganrog, the Kuban, Mariupol, Melitopol, Yassy-Kishinyov campaign, Lemberg-Sandomierz campaign, Breslau, Krakau, Berlin, Prague
Combat record: The regiment fought with great success over the Kuban from Korenovskaya, claiming 167 kills with 29 more damaged during 1,625 sorties and 111 combats, while 30 Airacobras were lost and 11 damaged for the period March 17 to August 20, 1943.
Aces: M.S. Komelkov 32, V.M. Drygin 20, A.A. Vilyamson 18, M.S. Likhovid 16, A.S. Zakalyuk 16

309 IAP
Key commanders: Podpolk. A.G. Minov (1941)
Assignments: 6 IAK-PVO
Battle honors: Moscow, Ostashkov

347 IAP
Honorifics: Radomskij
Key commanders: Podpolk. P.B. Dankevich
Assignments: 273 IAD, 193 IAD
Aircraft: I-16s, Yak-9s
Battle honors: Kursk, Kiev, Gomel, Poland including Radom, Berlin
Combat record: The regiment was greatly involved in the air battles over the Vistula River, reporting the destruction of 15 Fw 190s for no losses in 13 air engagements throughout August, 1944.
Aces: V.M. Oganesov 23, L.K. Ryzhij 17

348 IAP-PVO
Assignments: 310 IAD-PVO
Aircraft: LaGG-3s
Battle honors: Kalinin Front, Breslau

352 IAP
Honorifics: Minskij
Key commanders: Podpolk. P.I. Khara
Battle honors: Bobrujsk, Minsk, Vistula-Oder campaign, including Breslau, Berlin
Combat record: The regiment's big day came on August 12, 1944, when 13 Luftwaffe planes were destroyed without loss in running battles over the Vistula River.

355 IAP
Key commanders: Podpolk. A.U. Yeremin
Aircraft: Yak-9s

368 IAP
Honorifics: Berlinskij
Key commanders: Maj. A.G. Zhulin

369 IAP – no trace

401 IAP
Activated in June, 1941
Key commanders: Podpolk. S.P. Suprun (KIA 7-4-1941), Maj. K.K. Kokkinaki
Assignments: 23 SAD
Aircraft: MiG-3s
Battle honors: Smolensk 1941, Vitebsk 1941
Combat record: By September, 1941, the score stood at 54 aerial victories

402 IAP
Honorifics: Sevastopolskij
Key commanders: Maj. P.M. Stefanovskij (1941), Maj. A.Ye. Rubakhin
Assignments: 57 SAD, 265 IAD
Aircraft: MiG-3s, Yak-1s (until late 1943), Yak-3s
Battle honors: Novgorod, Taganrog, Kuban, Nikopol, Sevastopol, Yassy-Kishinyov campaign, Vitebsk, Orsha, Minsk, Vistula-Oder campaign, East Pomerania, Berlin
Combat record: The regiment became heavily engaged in the early stages of the war, and by June, 1942 had reported the destruction of 224 enemy planes in the air and on the ground. On February 1, 1944, it flew a successful airfield strafe out to the Nikopol area where 10 Ju 52s were destroyed on the ground and two Bf 109s shot down in combat. The regiment emerged from World War II as one of the most accomplished VVS fighter outfits with a confirmed tally of 810 enemy planes in the air and on the ground.
Aces: N.S. Pavlushkin 35, V.A. Yegorovich 22, M.Ye. Pivovarov 21, A.Ye. Rubakhin 20, P.F. Gavrilin 19, K.A. Gruzdev 19

404 IAP-PVO
Honorifics: Tallinskij
Key commanders: Podpolk. M.I. Mukhin
Battle honors: Leningrad 1943, Tallin

423 IAP-PVO
Assignments: 142 IAD-PVO
Aircraft: I-16s, Yak-3s
Battle honors: Kiev 1941, Voronezh 1942, Yaroslavl 1943

427 IAP
Designated the 150 GIAP, date not established
Key commanders: Podpolk. A.A. Oboznenko, Podpolk. A.D. Yakimenko
Assignments: 13 GIAD
Aircraft: Yak-9s, Yak-3s
Battle honors: Leningrad, Stalingrad, Kursk, Yassy-Kishinyov campaign, Hungary, Austria

Scene of desolation at Danzig in 1945. (Author's collection)

Combat record: The regiment took an active part in the fighting on Kalinin Front, claiming 13 kills during the period of October 24, 1942, to January 10, 1943. It fought a very successful campaign at Kursk, where 60 air victories were chalked up in a six day period between July 5-10, 1943. It became greatly involved in the Yassy-Kishinyov campaign, and on August 20, 1944, 10 Yak-9s with Podpolkovnik Oboznenko in the lead were providing area cover between Yassy-Vulturul. They engaged 60 Ju 87s escorted by 20 fighters intent on attacking elements of 27th Combined Arms Army, shooting down seven Luftwaffe planes, three by the regiment commander.
Aces: Sh.N. Kiriya 22, I.F. Shamenkov 18, S.V. Nosov 15, N.S. Yegorov 15, V.M. Ivanov 13, A.D. Yakimenko 13, M.I. Zotov 13

429 IAP-PVO
Assignments: 220 IAD, 6 IAK-PVO
Aircraft: Yak-1s, Hurricanes
Battle honors: Kharkov 1942, Moscow 1943

431 IAP
Activated in 1941
Key commanders: Maj. A.A. Kukushkin, Podpolk. A.A. Zajtsev (February, 1944/May, 1945)
Assignments: 283 IAD (1942), 315 IAD
Aircraft: LaGG-3s, Yak-1s, Yak-7Bs, Yak-9s
Battle honors: Stalingrad, Kursk-Orel, Karachyov, Bryansk, Gomel, Velikiye Luki, Idritsa, Ostrov, Rezekne, Riga, Courland
Combat record: The regiment's bag for the period February 2, 1944, to May 9, 1945, was 23 air victories in 38 engagements, plus 26 aircraft, four locomotives, and 69 motor vehicles destroyed in ground attacks during 2,508 sorties.

434 IAP
Designated the 32 GIAP on 11-22-1942
Full title: 32 Gvardejskij istrebitelnyj aviatsionnyj ordenov Lenina i Kutuzova III stepeni Vilenskij polk
Key commanders: Maj. I.I. Kleshchyov (KIFA 12-31-1942), Maj. V.P. Babkov (1942/43), Podpolk. V.I. Davidkov (as of 7-17-1943), Podpolk. A.F. Semyonov (as of February, 1944), Maj. V.A. Lutskij (as of May, 1944)
Assignments: 210 IAD, 3 GIAD
Aircraft: LaGG-3s, Yak-1s, Hurricanes, Yak-7Bs, Yak-9s (as of September, 1942), La-5s (as of March, 1943), La-7s
Battle honors: Stalingrad, Staraya Russa, Velikiye Luki, Demyansk, Bryansk, Kursk, Vitebsk, Lemberg-Sandomierz campaign, Breslau, Berlin, Prague
Combat record: The regiment was in the center of the action at Stalingrad and took a heavy toll of the opposing Luftwaffe formations, but suffering staggering losses in so doing. In June, 1942 it claimed the destruction of 35 enemy planes in the air during 880 sorties and was withdrawn for a short period of rest the following month. It next took part in a series of tough battles over the city during the period of July 15 to August 3, running up 55 more kills in 827 sorties and 29 air combats. The unit's biggest day came on July 26 when it shot down 34 attackers at a cost of three aircraft (conceivably not including missing in action). Given only a short time again to recover and convert to Yak-7s and Yak-9s, the regiment returned to the struggle to score 74 air victories for 15 aircraft lost between September 16-28, 19 of which were turned in on the 18th with 15 more the following day for the loss of a single Yak-7B. By October 3, 1942, the score stood at 173 during 2,060 sorties. The regiment continued to prove its outstanding fighting qualities in the subsequent aerial campaigns, a battle near Velikiye Luki on January 6, 1943, resulting in claims for 17 enemy planes destroyed. In March, 1944 the pilots claimed 20 Luftwaffe planes, 14 of which were Ju 87s. It ranked highly amongst the top-scoring VVS fighter regiments when hostilities in Europe ceased in May, 1945.
Aces: A.Ya. Fyodorov 24, V.P. Babkov 23, V.A. Orekhov 19, M.A. Garam 19, Ya.V. Shishkin 18, A.G. Kotov 16, A.I. Markov 16, A.P. Shishkin 14

436 IAP
Designated the 67 GIAP in 1943
Honorifics: Baranovichskij
Key commanders: Polk. A.B. Panov (May, 1942 – KIA 9-12-1944)
Assignments: 1 GIAD, 235 IAD (1942), 273 IAD (1944)
Aircraft: I-16s, Kittyhawks, Airacobras, Yak-3s
Battle honors: Leningrad Front, Moscow, Demyansk, Stalingrad, Kursk, Korsun-Shevchenkovskij, Uman, Bobrujsk, Baranovichi, Warsaw, Berlin
Combat record: The regiment achieved a fair amount of success while flying the British Hurricane fighter, 20 enemy planes being destroyed within five days of combat in July, 1942. The total bag for the period May, 1942 to September, 1944 was 268 victories during 4,250 sorties. It had a field day on August 2, 1943, claiming 25.
Aces: S.M. Novichkov 24, V.A. Latyshev 17, I.A. Fyedorchuk 15

437 IAP
Designated the 113 GIAP on 8-25-1943
Full title: 113 Gvardejskij istrebitelnyj aviatsionnyj polk
Key commanders: Maj. B. Nikiforov
Battle honors: Stalingrad, Kuban

438 IAP
Designated the 212 GIAP, date not established
Full title: 212 Gvardejskij istrebitelnyj aviatsionnyj ordena Aleksandra Nevskogo Yaroslavskij polk
Key commanders: Podpolk. A.V. Oborin (August, 1942/KIA 8-7-1944), Maj. A.I. Ovchinnikov
Assignments: Hurricanes, Yak-7Bs
Battle honors: Rossosh, Starij Oskol, Stalingrad, Kursk-Byelgorod, Poltava, Kirovograd, Korsun-Shevchenkovskij,

YassyKishinyov campaign, Lemberg-Sandomierz campaign, Silesia, Berlin, Prague
Combat record: The regiment was in the forefront of action during 1942, sustaining very heavy losses. By December 28 strength to hand was down to four serviceable Hurricanes and seven pilots. It saw a great deal of action during the period of September, 1943 to January, 1944 when it was credited with downing 50 enemy planes during 840 combat sorties. In a flurry of action over Silesia, 18 kills were added to the tally during 355 sorties between March 16-31, 1945.
Aces: A.L. Kozhevnikov 27, A.A. Yegorov 26

439 IAP
Designated the 184 GIAP, date not established
Key commanders: Maj. S.I. Semyonov
Aircraft: MiG-3s
Battle honors: Stalingrad

440 IAP
Aircraft: LaGG-3s
Battle honors: Stalingrad

441 IAP
Assignments: 106 IAD-PVO
Battle honors: Kalinin Front 1942

445 IAP-PVO
Key commanders: Maj. V.P. Kruglov (1941)
Assignments: 6 IAK-PVO
Aircraft: I-16s, MiG-3s
Battle honors: Moscow, Kaluga
Combat record: The regiment was heavily engaged in the epic struggle for Moscow in 1941, claiming 20 air victories in the Kashira area in a very short time.
Aces: F.V. Mitrofanov 10+

482 IAP
Key commanders: Maj. G.V. Didenko
Assignments: 322 IAD
Aircraft: La-5s
Battle honors: Vitebsk, Minsk, Baltic, Silesia, Berlin, Dresden, Prague
Remarks: To prevent confusion between La-5s and Fw 190s, the nose rings of all regiment aircraft were finished red.
Aces: G.V. Didenko 22, V.I. Korolyov 21, F.M. Lebedev 17, P.A. Somov 17, P.M. Konyaev 16, I.I. Landik 16, V.V. Zajtsev 16

483 IAP
Assignments: 336 IAD
Battle honors: Bobrujsk, Pinsk
Aces: V.P. Nekrasov 21

484 IAP
Honorifics: Brestskij
Key commanders: Podpolk. P.D. Yegorov
Assignments: 323 IAD
Aircraft: Yak-1s
Battle honors: Bobrujsk, Baranovichi, Minsk, Brest

485 IAP
Designated the 72 GIAP on 3-18-1943
Key commanders: Maj. G.V. Zimin (March, 1942/April 13, 1943), Maj. P.F. Zavarukhin (as of April 13, 1943), Maj. I.D. Likhobabin
Assignments: 239 IAD (as of June, 1942)
Aircraft: Hurricanes, Yak-1s, Yak-7Bs, Airacobras
Battle honors: Leningrad Front, Staraya Russa, Demyansk, Riga
Combat record: The regiment saw a fair amount of action as part of the Moscow PVO between late July-late August, 1941 before being posted to Leningrad Front. It was withdrawn for a rest and reorganization after 650 sorties with three air victories in 12 encounters for the loss of four of their number. It converted to Hurricanes and moved to Northwest Front in March, 1942, deploying to Vypolzovo airfield, east of the Demyansk pocket, on April 2. It then took part in the fierce struggle at Staraya Russa, suffering heavy losses, though scoring some victories. By April 14 strength at hand was down to six serviceable Hurricanes. Four days later the pilots reported the destruction of six Bf 109s at the cost of one pilot KIA and two others making force-landings. On the 20th two more fighters were killed when six Hurricanes led by Kapitan Lazarev mixed it with German fighters while engaged in escorting Il-2s. In May the regiment enjoyed above-average success scoring 56 victories. On the 21st three Hurricanes with Major B.P. Kondratyev in the lead became involved in a melee with 10 Messerschmitts, six of these being claimed shot down without loss. Eight days later a flight successfully intercepted 20 Ju 52s headed for the Demyansk pocket destroying three and damaging six more. The following day another flight ran into 10 Ju 52s escorted by four Bf 109s claiming one transport and two fighters. The regiment next moved to Martyushino, southeast of the pocket, by which time two flights had been fully equipped with Yak-1s which were to be assigned to providing top cover for the Hurricane attack units. Some of the British fighters were modified by forward maintenance units to mount two 20mm ShVAK cannon and two 12.7mm machine guns instead of the inadequate original armament of eight 0.303in. (7.7mm) Brownings, and RS-82 82mm rocket projectiles were frequently carried. The regiment was to claim 13 kills with salvoes of RS-82s during subsequent encounters. On June 19 seven Hurricanes had a field when they attacked a formation of 12 Ju 87s escorted by 15 Bf 109s coming away with 10 kills against a single loss. Claimants on this occasion were Major Zimin, the regiment commander, who raised his tally to 11 with two Stukas and one 109, while Lejtenant Volkov got one each Ju 87 and Bf 109 to bring his score to 10, Starshij Lejtenant Loktionov

downed a Ju 87 to run his score to 7 and Starshij Lejtenant Yedkin knocked down a further fighter to become an ace with 5 victories. The regiment was then occupied with furnishing assault area cover in the Ostashkov area until February, 1943, by which time it had traded all Hurricanes for Yak-1s and Yak-7s. In late 1942 a third Eskadrilya had been formed around a nucleus of combat-seasoned pilots from the 402 IAP such as Kapitan I.D. Likhobabin, Starshij Lejtenant V.M. Ziborov. On February 18, 1943 the regiment drew first blood against the new Fw 190s of the III./JG 54, three of these falling to the guns of Lejtenant A. Smirnov's flight. In all, the regiment chalked up 111 kills in the tough battles fought over the Demyansk pocket in recognition being awarded the Guards banner on March 18, 1943. The final bag at the end of the war was 172 in 115 air encounters.
Aces: I.D. Likhobabin – the majority of his total of 30, V.M. Ziborov – the majority of his total of 22

486 IAP
Key commanders: Podpolk. D.A. Medvedev
Assignments: 279 IAD (1944)
Aircraft: I-16s
Battle honors: Vinnitsa, Dnyepropetrovsk, Kerch, Kursk-Orel, Yassy-Kishinyov campaign, Budapest
Combat record: The regiment's big day came on August 5, 1943, when 13 Luftwaffe planes were destroyed in the Orel area.
Aces: A.I. Girich 15, N.M. Gusarov 15

487 IAP
Designated the 146 GIAP on 10-9-1943
Key commanders: Maj. A.A.Zyuzya
Assignments: 101 IAD-PVO, 7 GIAD
Battle honors: Voronezh 1941, Voronezh 1943
Aces: G.I. Filatov 11

488 IAP
Aircraft: Hurricanes
Remarks: For want of parts, 16 of 18 Hurricanes in strength in the spring of 1942 had to be listed as out of commission.

494 IAP
Key Commanders: Maj. I.V. Belov
Assignments: 303 IAD (3-1-1943/11-30-1943)
Aircraft: Airacobras
Combat Record: Whilst operating with the 303 "Smolenskaya" IAD the regiment afforded 62 sorties for 44 combat hours and had claims for three enemy aircraft destroyed in air combat for the loss of one Airacobra and one pilot. It was posted to the 22 ZAP (Reserve Air Regiment) for reorganization on December 1, 1943.

495 IAP-PVO
Key commanders: Maj. I.V. Chernobayev
Assignments: 125 IAD-PVO
Battle honors: Tula, Kozelsk, Vyazma

508 IAP
Designated the 213 GIAP, date not established
Full title: 213 Gvardejskij istrebitelnyj aviatsionnyj ordenov Bogdana Khmelnitskogo i Aleksandra Nevskogo Oderskij polk
Key commanders: Maj. N.K. Diligej
Assignments: 205 IAD, 22 GIAD
Aircraft: Airacobras
Battle honors: Kursk, Byelgorod-Kharkov, Poltava, Kirovograd
Aces: V.P. Mikhalev 26, P.I. Chepinoga 22, N.K. Diligej c.16, N.V. Strojkov 14, A.I. Svistunov 14

512 IAP
Designated the 53 GIAP on 2-8-1943
Full title: 53 Gvardejskij istrebitelnyj aviatsionnyj ordenov Lenina i Aleksandra Nevskogo Stalingradskij polk
Key commanders: Maj. N.S. Gerasimov (1942), Maj. L.I. Binov (KIA 1-13-1943), Maj. I.P. Motornij, Maj. A.A. Platonov (1945)
Assignments: 268 IAD, 220 IAD (as of 7-30-1942), 1 GIAD
Aircraft: I-16s, LaGG-3s, Yak-1s, Yak-7Bs
Battle honors: Poltava 1941, Rostov, Stalingrad, Kursk-Kharkov, East Pomerania, Berlin
Combat record: The regiment had a considerable share in the successes achieved in the early stages of the war, claiming 52 kills during the period of October 10, 1941, to July 30, 1942. July 26, 1942, was a day of heavy dogfighting, and pilots were awarded with victories over six Bf 109s, three Bf 110s, and one each Fw 190, Ju 87, and Ju 88 for the loss of three Yak-1s and a single Yak-7B. The tough battles fought over Stalingrad saw the regiment chalk up 53 kills between October 9, 1942, and February 1, 1943.
Aces: V.N. Makarov 15+ of 30, I.P. Motornij 15+, Z.V. Semenyuk 14

513 IAP
Assignments: 224 ShAD
Battle honors: Moscow

515 IAP
Honorifics: Pomeranskij
Key commanders: Podpolk. G.V. Gromov
Assignments: 193 IAD
Aircraft: Yak-1s, Yak-9s, Yak-3s
Battle honors: Moscow, Stalingrad, Vistula-Oder campaign, East Pomerania, Berlin
Combat record: In a flurry of action between January 14, 1945, and February 3, 1945, the regiment was credited with downing 34 enemy planes. It finished the war with a confirmed score of 70.
Aces: M.N. Tyulkin 15, G.V. Gromov 13

516 IAP
Designated the 153 GIAP on 2-5-1944
Full title: 153 Gvardejskij istrebitelnyj aviatsionnyj ordenov Bogdana Khmelnitskogo i Aleksandra Nevskogo Sandomierskij polk

Key commanders: Maj. A.I. Mochalin, Maj. N.I. Loshak, Maj. P.A. Matiyenko
Assignments: 203 IAD, 12 GIAD
Aircraft: LaGG-3s, Yak-1s
Battle honors: South Front, Voronezh Front (March, 1943-July, 1943), Steppe Front (as of July, 1943), 2nd Ukrainian Front
Aces: I.F. Gnezdilov 24, I.F. Andrianov 23, M.K. Tokarenko 18, L.S. Chudbin 15

517 IAP
Assignments: 282 IAD
Battle honors: Kiev, Gomel, Poland, Berlin

518 IAP
Honorifics: Berlinskij
Key commanders: Maj. N.V. Grinev (1942), Podpolk. N.G. Khudokormov
Assignments: 193 IAD
Aircraft: Yak-1s, Yak-9s
Battle honors: Kuban 1942, Kalinin Front, Vistula-Oder campaign, Berlin

519 IAP
Key commanders: Podpolk. K.N. Murga
Assignments: 283 IAD
Aircraft: MiG-3s, LaGG-3s, Yak-7Bs
Battle honors: Moscow, Lipetsk, Kursk, Sumy, Vistula-Oder campaign, Berlin
Combat record: On May 16, 1943, 15 Yak-7Bs got into a scrap with 40 enemy planes in the Kursk area coming away with 10 kills.
Aces: I.A. Avekov 19, V.A. Bashkirov 19, S.K. Kolesnichenko 16

520 IAP
Designated the 56 GIAP on 2-8-1943
Honorifics: Altukhovskij
Key commanders: Podpolk. S.N. Chirva (1942), Maj. D.I. Rodin
Assignments: 283 IAD (1942)
Aircraft: Yak-1s, Yak-7Bs, Yak-9s
Battle honors: Stalingrad, Korsun-Shevchenkovskij, Uman, Bobrujsk, Baranovichi, Poland, Berlin
Combat record: The regiment took part in the epic struggle for Stalingrad with considerable success, 95 enemy planes being shot down in 125 air encounters plus 15 more being destroyed in ground attacks. On September 8, 1942, Major Chirva led 10 Yak-1s to attack a formation of 10 He 111s, five of these being claimed shot down. During the battle Kapitan A.A. Yefremov and Lejtenant N.V. Kharitonov excelled, both claiming between 11-12 kills each closely followed by Major D.I. Rodin and Starshina V.F. Vinogradov with 8-9 kills apiece.

521 IAP
Assignments: 209 IAD
Aircraft: Yak-1s
Battle honors: Kalinin Front
Aces: I.I. Kleshchyov 6 of 16

523 IAP
Honorifics: Orshanskij
Key commanders: Podpolk. A.Ye. Pilshchikov (POW 1944), Polk. I.A. Zamorin
Assignments: 234 IAD, 303 IAD
Aircraft: LaGG-3s, La-5s, Yak-9s
Battle honors: Pskov 1941, Smolensk, Vitebsk, Orsha, East Prussia
Combat record: The regiment destroyed 115 enemy planes during the course of the war, affording 8,285 sorties and entering 256 combats.

526 IAP
Designated the 2 GIAP on 12-6-1941
Full title: 2 Gvardejskij istrebitelnyj aviatsionnyj Krasnoznamennyj, ordena Suvorova Orshanskij polk
Key commanders: Podpolk. P.M. Metelkin (KIA 5-30-1942), Polk. Ye.F. Kondrat (until 3-28-1943), Podpolk. A.P. Sobolev (1944)
Assignments: 215 IAD (as of October, 1942), 322 IAD (as of 6-25-1943)
Aircraft: I-153s, MiG-3s, La-5s (as of October, 1942), La-7s (as of late 1944)
Battle honors: Southwest Front (as of July, 1941), Northwest Front (as of 10-1-1941), Kalinin Front (October, 1942/December, 1942), Leningrad (January, 1943/March, 1943), Orel-Bryansk, Byelorussia, East Prussia (August/September, 1944), Breslau, Berlin, Dresden, Prague
Combat record: The regiment first saw frontline action during the Russo-Finnish Winter War of 1939/40, following which it was transferred to the Kiev Military District. It joined combat with the Luftwaffe on June 22, 1941, the first day of Operation Barbarossa, flying a collection of I-153s and MiG-3s. It deployed to Southwest Front in mid-July where it was to see a great deal of action against great odds during the weeks to follow. After having scored 28 kills during some 800 sorties it was moved again, this time to Northwest Front. During the period of October 3 to November 18, 1941, the pilots reported the destruction of 16 more enemy planes in the air plus 356 motor vehicles and six tanks in ground attacks while affording 977 sorties. The regiment next was in the thick of the fighting on Volkhov Front where 48 kills were added to the bag during 2,500 sorties before being awarded the Guards Banner. On Kalinin Front they flew 351 sorties with four more kills and fought through the epic battles of Leningrad chalking up 43 air victories during 603 sorties. The battles of Orel-Bryansk were the stage for some of the fiercest aerial encounters, 215 La-5 sorties meeting a total of 417 enemy planes – 226 fighters, 121 bombers – on 33 occasions. In all, the regiment claimed 66 kills for the loss of nine pilots KIA. During the fighting in

Byelorussia 24 German planes were shot down in a number of highly successful combats. Over Berlin the regiment was engaged in some of the heaviest action for many months, coming away with claims for 17 Fw 190s between April 16-30, 1945. It finished the war as one of the VVS' high-scorers, with 327 kills during 8,474 sorties – 1,368 of which were strafing, 1,004 escorts, and 649 reconnaissance – entering into 399 combats.
Aces: A.I. Majorov 27, V.A. Savelyev 21, P.M. Nepryakhin 17, N.P. Pushkin c.17 of 19, M.Ye. Ryabtsev 15, A.P. Sobolev 15+

530 IAP
Assignments: 194 IAD
Aircraft: La-5s
Battle honors: Poland, Hungary

562 IAP
Honorifics: Kalininskij
Key commanders: Maj. A.I. Negoda
Assignments: 6 IAK-PVO
Aircraft: Yak-1s
Battle honors: Moscow, Kalinin Front

563 IAP
Designated the 116 GIAP on 9-2-1943
Honorifics: Radomskij
Key commanders: Podpolk. V.I. Nenashev (1942)
Assignments: 283 IAD (1942), 205 IAD
Aircraft: Yak-1s
Battle honors: Stalingrad, Kursk-Kharkov, Korsun-Shevchenkovskij campaign, Uman, Batajsk, Baranovichi
Aces: N.A. Najdyonov 29

564 IAP – no trace

572 IAP
Designated the 83 GIAP on 4-11-1943
Key commanders: Maj. V.A. Koryakin
Assignments: 102 IAD-PVO, 2 GIAD-PVO
Battle honors: Stalingrad

573 IAP-PVO
Assignments: 101 IAD-PVO, 310 IAD-PVO
Battle honors: Voronezh, Kharkov

579 IAP-PVO
Battle honors: Kursk

580 IAP
Assignments: 6 UAG (udarnaya aviatsionnaya gruppa – air attack group)
Aircraft: Yak-1s
Battle honors: Novgorod
Aces: A.N. Dekhtyarenko 10

581 IAP
Designated the 55 GIAP on 2-8-1943
Key commanders: Podpolk. V.I. Shishkin
Assignments: 220 IAD (1942)
Aircraft: Yak-1s
Battle honors: Stalingrad, Korsun-Shevchenkovskij campaign, Uman, Bobrujsk, Pomerania, Berlin

A Yak-7V, the two-seat trainer variant of the fighter, taxis along a frozen strip on Kalinin Front in early 1942. (Author's collection)

586 IAP
Key commanders: Maj. T.A. Kazarinova
Assignments: 144 IAD-PVO (as of 4-24-1942)
Aircraft: Yak-1s, Yak-7Bs
Battle honors: Stalingrad, Kursk, Korsun-Shevchenkovskij campaign, Rumania
Combat record: The famous all-women fighter regiment destroyed its first enemy plane in the air on September 24, 1942, when V. Khomyakova forced down a Ju 88. On March 18, 1943, a formation of 40 Luftwaffe bombers was engaged near Kastornoye (E Kursk) with Mladshij Lejtenanti T.U. Pamyatnykh and R.N. Surnachevskaya claiming the honors for achieving four kills between them. The regiment had a big day on December 19, 1943, when O.N. Yamshchikova led eight of her squadron to take on a large force of German bombers, seven of these being shot down in the Kiev area. The unit's final score was 38 confirmed during 4,419 sorties and 125 encounters.

590 IAP
Key commanders: Podpolk. A.D. Sokolov
Aircraft: I-15s, I-16s, LaGG-3s
Battle honors: Rostov 1941

591 IAP
Assignments: 36 IAD-PVO
Battle honors: Kholm

611 IAP
Key commanders: Maj. A.S. Chugunov (1943), Podpolk. N.F. Isayenko
Assignments: 236 IAD (1943), 288 IAD
Aircraft: I-153s (until 1943)
Battle honors: Caucasus, Kuban, Krasnodar, Akhtyrka, Rumania, Hungary
Aces: A.P. Churilin 17, M.F. Batarov 15, N.F. Isayenko 13

620 IAP
Battle honors: Kursk

627 IAP
Aircraft: I-16s
Battle honors: Moscow

628 IAP-PVO
Assignments: 102 IAD-PVO
Battle honors: Krasnodar 1943, Lemberg-Sandomierz campaign

629 IAP
Designated the 38 GIAP on 4-11-1943
Key commanders: Maj. S.Ya. Yavtushenko, Maj. V.S. Yezhov
Assignments: 102 IAD-PVO
Aircraft: I-153s, I-16s

Female warriors: G. Burdina, T. Pamyatnykh, V. Khomyakova, and V. Lisitsina of the 586 IAP confer. Autumn 1942. (Author's collection)

Battle honors: Stalingrad, Odessa 1944
Combat record: The regiment was in the center of the action at Stalingrad, emerging as one of the top-scoring Soviet fighter outfits of the battle with 104 air victories in 139 combats during 4,995 sorties. It had a big day on September 8, 1942, claiming 10 kills. Final bag not available.
Aces: Ye.A. Yevseyev 22

630 IAP
Designated the 147 GIAP on 10-9-1943
Key commanders: Podpolk. P.N. Novitskij
Assignments: 106 IAD-PVO, 240 IAD (as of April, 1943)
Aircraft: I-16s, Kittyhawks, Yak-7Bs, La-5s
Battle honors: Rostov 1941, Rostov 1942, Volkhov, Ladoga Lake
Combat record: The regiment saw a good deal of action between July 24, 1942, and October 6, 1942, claiming 24 air victories in 49 encounters for the loss of three pilots KIA and nine aircraft attributed to enemy planes. The Volkhov was the stage for some tough fighting in June, 1943, with the regiment enjoying great success. Between June 15-23, 58 enemy aircraft were claimed destroyed, including six at night. Major V.A. Shapochka excelled during this period by gaining four nocturnal kills.

631 IAP-PVO
Assignments: 141 IAD-PVO

651 IAP-PVO
Key commanders: Maj. I.Ye. Streblovskij
Assignments: 102 IAD-PVO
Battle honors: Stalingrad

652 IAP-PVO
Key commanders: Kap. I.Ye. Ashakov
Battle honors: Stalingrad

653 IAP
Designated the 65 GIAP, on 3-18-1943
Full title: 65 Gvardejskij istrebitelnyj aviatsionnyj Krasnoznamennyj, ordena Suvorova III stepeni Orshanskij polk
Key commanders: Podpolk. M.N. Zvorygin
Assignments: 274 IAD, 4 GIAD
Aircraft: Yak-1s, Yak-7Bs
Battle honors: Bryansk, 1st and 2nd Baltic, 3rd Byelorussian Fronts
Aces: V.N. Kubarev 46, A.G. Kuliyev 18, A.I. Popov 18, G.G. Guskov 14

659 IAP
Activated at Krasnoyarsk in November, 1941
Honorifics: Galatskij
Key commanders: Maj. G.A. Karaulov, Podpolk. V.M. Shmeshkov

V.I. Solomatin of the 653 IAP prepares for a mission. (Author's collection)

Assignments: 288 IAD
Aircraft: I-16s, Yak-1s, Yak-9s, Yak-3s
Battle honors: Stalingrad, Zaporozhye, Nikopol, Krivoj Rog, Dnyepropetrovsk, Yassy-Kishinyov campaign, Yugoslavia, Hungary
Combat record: On September 11, 1942, flight leader P. Dymchenko had a big scrap with his Yak-1 over the Kletsk bridgehead (SW Minsk), knocking down four Bf 109s and two Ju 87s before hits sent him crashing down to his death.
Aces: I.M. Pavlovskij 19, A.P. Frolov 13

721 IAP
Key commanders: Podpolk. N.M. Kosnikov, Podpolk. I.G. Trilyevich
Assignments: 216 IAD, 147 IAD-PVO, 286 IAD (1943)
Aircraft: La-5s, La-7s
Battle honors: Yaroslavl, Kursk, the Dnyepr, Gomel, Rogachyov, Bobrujsk, Poland, Berlin
Aces: A.S. Kobiskoj 16, I.S. Kozich 16, N.M. Tregubov 14

722 IAP
Aircraft: Yak-1s
Battle honors: Stalingrad
Aces: P.I. Shavurin 17

728 IAP
Activated in November, 1941 around a nucleus of pilot instructors of Kharkov military flying school
Full title: 728 Istrebitelnyj aviatsionnyj Krasnoznamennyj Shumsko-Kremenetskij polk
Key commanders: Polk. V.S. Vasilyaka
Assignments: 256 IAD
Aircraft: I-16s, Yak-7Bs (as of March, 1943), Yak-9s (as of October, 1943)
Battle honors: Kalinin Front, Kursk, Byelgorod-Kharkov, Poltava, Lemberg-Sandomierz campaign, Poland, Berlin, Czechoslovakia

Combat record: The regiment ranked highly amongst the top-scoring VVS fighter regiments with a confirmed score of 550 at the end of the war.
Aces: A.V. Vorozhejkin 46 of 52, M.I. Sachkov 25, A.A. Vakhlayev 24, A.I. Vybornov 20, S.I. Lazarev 15

729 IAP-PVO
Assignments: 104 IAD-PVO
Battle honors: Arkhangelsk

730 IAP-PVO
Assignments: 104 IAD-PVO
Battle honors: Arkhangelsk

731 IAP-PVO
Activated in October, 1941
Designated the 39 GIAP on 4-11-1943
Key commanders: Maj. D.K. Leshko
Assignments: 148 IAD-PVO
Battle honors: Stalingrad, Kursk, Kiev, Voronezh
Combat record: On September 3, 1942, the regiment claimed 10 air victories, and by October 16, 1944, the tally had risen to 96.

737 IAP
Key commanders: Polk. N.I. Varchuk (KIA 9-21-1943)
Assignments: 291 ShAD, 207 IAD
Battle honors: P.A. Pologov 18, N.I. Varchuk 14

738 IAP
Battle honors: Melitopol 1943, Dnyepropetrovsk 1944

739 IAP
Key commanders: Podpolk. V.F. Klimov, Maj. V.I. Popkov
Assignments: 220 IAD, 286 IAD (1943)
Aircraft: La-5s
Battle honors: Stalingrad, Kursk, Kiev, Gomel, Rogachyov, Bobrujsk, Vistula-Oder campaign, Berlin

740 IAP-PVO
Assignments: 148 IAD-PVO
Aircraft: MiG-3s
Battle honors: Leningrad

744 IAP
Designated the 86 GIAP on 5-1-1943
Honorifics: Borisovskij
Key commanders: Maj. Anashchenko, Podpolk. S.N. Najdenov (KIA September, 1943), Podpolk. V.A. Chistyakov (as of September, 1943)
Assignments: 282 IAD, 240 IAD
Aircraft: Yak-7Bs, Yak-9s (as of July, 1943), Yak-3s (as of October, 1944)
Battle honors: Northwest Front, Volkhov (April, 1943/July, 1943), Smolensk (September, 1943), Dukhovshchina (September, 1943), Nevel (October, 1943), Orsha (June, 1944), Borisov (June, 1944), Minsk (July, 1944), Kaunas (August, 1944), Gumbinnen (October, 1944), East Prussia, Berlin
Combat record: On May 27, 1943, Kapitani A.V. Zazayev and I.Ya. Popovich led 12 Yak-7Bs to attack 35 He 111s and 12 escorts in the Volkhov area, where six bombers and two Fw 190s were destroyed for the loss of two planes and one pilot KIA. By June, 1943, Mladshij Lejtenant D.I. Kudryavtsev had become the regiment's ranking ace with 11 air victories, runners-up being Starshij Lejtenant Dergach with 8, Mladshij Lejtenanti P.K. Lobas and V.P. Bojko with 6 apiece, and Mladshij Lejtenant I.K. Somov with 5. In a burst of energy and skill, Starshij Lejtenant N.A. Sergunin scored a string of 10 kills in the skies above Smolensk and Nevel between late August and mid-October, 1943, closely followed by Starshij Lejtenant I.A. Kulakov and Lejtenant N.I. Marchenko each getting 8.
Aces: P.K. Lobas 19, D.I. Kudryavtsev 16, M.F. Manulin 16, I.K. Somov 16

754 IAP – no trace

760 IAP
Assignments: 261 SAD
Aircraft: Hurricanes

761 IAP
Full title: 760 Istrebitelnyj aviatsionnyj ordenov Kutuzova i Suvorova Polotskij polk
Battle honors: Byelorussia, the Baltic, East Prussia

762 IAP – no trace

767 IAP-PVO
Activated in March, 1942
Assignments: 122 IAD-PVO
Battle honors: Murmansk

768 IAP-PVO
Activated in March, 1942
Assignments: 122 IAD-PVO
Aircraft: Kittyhawks
Battle honors: Murmansk

769 IAP-PVO
Activated in March, 1942
Assignments: 122 IAD-PVO
Aircraft: Hurricanes
Battle honors: Murmansk
Combat record: On March 24, 1942, four Hurricanes engaged a formation of eight Ju 87s escorted by 10 Bf 109s enroute to Murmansk claiming the destruction of two Stukas and forcing the rest to jettison their bombs.

774 IAP
Full title: 774 Istrebitelnyj aviatsionnyj ordenov Aleksandra Nevskogo i Suvorova Berlinskij polk
Key commanders: Maj. A.A. Makogon
Assignments: 282 IAD
Aircraft: Yak-1s
Battle honors: Stalingrad, Kursk, the Dnyepr, Gomel, Vistula-Oder campaign, Berlin
Aces: I.I. Romanenko 16, I.A. Manojlov 9

781 IAP
Assignments: 245 IAD
Aircraft: Kingcobras
Battle honors: Manchuria 1945

787 IAP-PVO
Assignments: 125 IAD-PVO
Aircraft: MiG-3s
Battle honors: Tula 1942

788 IAP-PVO
Designated the 84 GIAP on 4-11-1943
Key commanders: Maj. I.Ye. Steblovskij, Maj. I.Ye. Kapustin
Assignments: 102 IAD-PVO
Aircraft: Yak-1s
Battle honors: Stalingrad, Kursk, Kerch
Combat record: On August 4, 1942, ten fighters with Major Uvodenko in the lead engaged a Luftwaffe formation, submitting claims for five Ju 87s and four Bf 109s. During the arduous struggle for Stalingrad the regiment was joined by a number of Spanish volunteers including Juan Lario, Luis Negra, and Jose Santamaria, the latter reportedly winning a posthumous Order of Lenin for his bag of 14 personal kills.
Aces: G.K. Gultyaev 10+

790 IAP
Key commanders: Podpolk. I.G. Korolyov
Aircraft: LaGG-3s
Battle honors: Kuban, Kerch, Eltigen

791 IAP
Assignments: 220 IAD
Aircraft: LaGG-3s
Battle honors: Kharkov 1941

792 IAP
Assignments: 220 IAD
Aircraft: LaGG-3s
Battle honors: Kharkov 1941

805 IAP
Key commanders: Maj. V.A. Kolesnik (as of November, 1943)
Aircraft: Yak-1s, LaGG-3s, La-5s
Battle honors: Kuban, Novorossijsk, Kerch

812 IAP
Honorifics: Sevastopolskij
Key commanders: Maj. Lokhin (1942), Maj. Kornilov, Maj. N.G. Volchkov (KIA 3-26-1944), Maj. P.T. Tarasov (KIA 7-29-1944), Maj. S.P. Popov (KIFA December, 1944 while practicing instrument flying), Maj. M.V. Vlasov
Assignments: 220 IAD, Yak-7Bs (as of mid-1944), Yak-9Us (as of April, 1945)
Battle honors: Stalingrad, Kuban, Melitopol, Bolshoj Tokmak, Kherson, Vitebsk, Lepel, Uman, Vistula-Oder campaign, Berlin
Combat record: In October, 1942 the regiment chalked up 18 air victories over Stalingrad while becoming embroiled in 29 combats. It later deployed to the Kuban, but was very badly mauled by Bf 109s in its first scrap with enemy fighters in that theater on April 20, 1943, with six pilots being killed in action. Pilots learned how to deal with the Luftwaffe during the subsequent air fighting with some considerable success, achieving a total bag of 64 over the Kuban for the loss of 19 pilots KIA and 25 aircraft. The regiment later was doing well during the Vistula-Oder campaign and over the Oder bridgehead at Kustrin. On March 22, 1945, Lejtenant L.I. Sivko was successful in downing one of the vaunted Me 262 jets when he caught one of these at 18:20 hours in the Zechin area (NE Berlin). It seems possible that he shot down Feldwebel Franz Eichmer of 11./JG 7 who was reported killed by fighters in the Altdobern area (SE Berlin). In all, JG 7 lost three pilots killed and one wounded that day.
Aces: I.V. Fyodorov 36, P.T. Tarasov 24, A.T. Tishchenko 21, A.M. Mashenkin 18, Ye.Ye. Ankudinov 15

813 IAP
Assignments: 215 IAD
Battle honors: Bobrujsk, East Prussia
Aircraft: La-7s

814 IAP
Designated the 106 GIAP on 8-25-1943
Full title: 106 Gvardejskij istrebitelnyj aviatsionnyj ordenov Kutuzova i Aleksandra Nevskogo Vislenskij polk
Key commanders: Podpolk. M.V. Kuznetsov (1942/end of war)
Assignments: 207 IAD, 11 GIAD
Aircraft: MiG-3s, Yak-1s, Yak-3s
Battle honors: Leningrad, Kharkov, Dnyepropetrovsk, Krivoj Rog, Lemberg-Sandomierz campaign, Vistula-Oder campaign, Berlin
Combat record: By the close of hostilities the regiment had destroyed 299 enemy planes in the air.
Aces: M.V. Kuznetsov 22, N.S. Putko 21, Ye.P. Savelyev 20, N.S. Kiyanchenko 17, A.I. Voloshin 16, N.V. Zabyrin 15

821 IAP – no trace

822 IAP
Assignments: 126 IAD-PVO

831 IAP
Assignments: 126 IAD-PVO

832 IAP
Key commanders: Podpolk. V.A.Sokolov
Assignments: 126 IAD-PVO, 315 IAD
Aircraft: Yak-1s, Yak-7Bs, Yak-9s
Battle honors: Velikiye Luki, Riga, Idritsa, Rezekne

833 IAP
Assignments: 126 IAD-PVO
Battle honors: Melitopol 1943

845 IAP
Assignments: 269 IAD
Aircraft: Yak-1s, Yak-7Bs, Yak-9s
Battle honors: 3rd Baltic Front
Aces: A.S. Gutsalov 18, S.V. Bitsayev 16, V.F. Polunovskij 13

848 IAP —no trace

862 IAP
Assignments: 217 IAD

863 IAP
Aircraft: LaGG-3s
Battle honors: Kuban

866 IAP
Honorifics: Izmailskij
Key commanders: Maj. P.M. Ivanov (KIA 11-28-1943), Podpolk. S.N. Kuzin (as of November, 1943), Podpolk. Chugunov
Assignments: 288 IAD
Aircraft: Yak-1s, Yak-7Bs, Yak-3s
Battle honors: Stalingrad, Voronezh, Kursk, Izyum, Zaporozhye, Krivoj Rog, Yassy-Kishinyov campaign, Hungary, Austria
Aces: A.I. Koldunov 46, I.I. Chuchvaga 20, N.G. Surnev 18, S.A. Burnazyan 17 of 22, P.M. Ivanov 17, D.D. Syrtsov 16, A.A. Bondar 15

867 IAP
Designated the 107 GIAP on 8-25-1943
Full title: 107 Gvardejskij istrebitelnyj aviatsionnyj ordena Aleksandra Nevskogo Oderskij polk
Key commanders: Podpolk. S.L. Indyk (as of June, 1943)
Assignments: 220 IAD (1942), 207 IAD, 11 GIAD
Aicraft: Yak-1s
Battle honors: Stalingrad, Voronezh, Kursk, Izyum, Lemberg-Sandomierz campaign, Vistula-Oder campaign, Berlin
Combat record: Under the leadership of Podpolkovnik Indyk the regiment was credited with downing 120 enemy planes during 4,266 sorties between June, 1943 and May, 1945. On April 30, 1945, Starshij Lejtenant Kuznetsov and Lejtenant Trofimov teamed to destroy a Me 262 jet southeast of Cottbus, the first such aircraft to be claimed by 2 VA. The jet was almost certainly one of I./KG(J)54's aircraft, which reported the loss of one through Soviet groundfire on this same day.
Aces: N.S. Sivtsov 22, P.D. Khudov 18, L.M. Sokolov 17

875 IAP
Designated the 66 GIAP on 3-18-1943
Full title: 66 Gvardejskij istrebitelnyj aviatsionnyj Krasnoznamennyj, ordena Suvorova III stepeni Vilenskij polk
Key commanders: Kap. A.R. Kovalev
Assignments: 274 IAD, 4 GIAD
Aicraft: Yak-1s, Yak-7Bs, Yak-9s, Yak-3s
Battle honors: Velikiye Luki, Demyansk, Kursk-Orel, Courland, Berlin
Combat record: The regiment had a big day on March 16, 1943, claiming 20 victories in running battles over the Lovat River.
Aces: I.P. Vitkovskij 22, A.P. Kondrashev 15, S.V. Syromyatnikov 15

886 IAP – no trace

888 IAP
Assignments: 128 SAD
Aircraft: Kingcobras (as of July, 1945)
Battle honors: Kurile Islands (1945)

894 IAP
Assignments: 101 IAD-PVO
Battle honors: Southwest, West, Stalingrad, Ist Ukrainian Fronts
Aces: N.I. Abramchuk 16

896 IAP
Assignments: 286 IAD (1943)
Aircraft: Yak-1s, La-5s
Battle honors: Kursk, Gomel, Bobrujsk
Combat record: The regiment started flying combat in August, 1942 claiming 21 kills for the loss of 18 Yak-1s until late 1942. It next built up a respectable score with 17 more victories for a single loss during the period of January 27 to February 12, 1943.

897 IAP
Honorifics: Kishinyovskij
Key commanders: Maj. A.M. Markov
Assignments: 288 IAD
Aircraft: Yak-9s
Battle honors: Stalingrad, Kharkov, Zaporozhye, Nikopol, Krivoj Rog, Odessa, Yassy-Kishinyov campaign, Yugoslavia, Hungary, Austria
Aces: V.A. Merenkov 22, V.A. Lozovskij 19, D.G. Barchenkov 16, P.P. Karavaj 16, V.V. Mikryukov 16, V.K. Chugunov 15

900 IAP
Honorifics: Orshanskij
Key commanders: Maj. A.F. Khotinskij (KIFA 1-17-1945 colliding with an Il-2)
Assignments: 209 IAD, 240 IAD (as of 7-19-1943)
Aircraft: Yak-9Ts
Battle honors: Stalingrad, Bryansk Front, Smolensk (September, 1943), Dukhovshchina (September, 1943), Nevel (October, 1943), Orsha (June, 1944), Borisov (June, 1944), Minsk (July, 1944), Molodechno (July, 1944), Kaunas (August, 1944), Gumbinnen (October, 1944), East Prussia, Berlin
Combat record: On October 7, 1943, a squadron led by Lejtenant G. Lisetskij took on a formation of 40 enemy planes claiming to have forced down nine bombers and two escorts in the action that followed. High-scorers during the period of August to mid October, 1943 were Starshij Lejtenant I.Ye. Klimov and Lejtenant N.A. Duman with three kills each in the skies above Smolensk and Nevel.

907 IAP
Key commanders: Maj. N.A. Kozlov (September, 1943/end of war)
Assignments: 101 IAD-PVO, 148 IAD-PVO
Aircraft: La-5s
Battle honors: Kursk, Dnyepropetrovsk, Korsun-Shevchenkovskij campaign, Berlin
Combat record: Under the leadership of Major Kozlov the regiment racked up 119 air victories between July, 1943 and May, 1945.
Aces: K.D. Garkusha 9

909 IAP – no trace

910 IAP
Designated the 148 GIAP on 10-9-1943
Key commanders: Podpolk. A.A. Tereshkin, Podpolk. A.N. Maltsev
Assignments: 101 IAD-PVO, 148 IAD-PVO
Aircraft: Yak-7Bs, Yak-9s
Battle honors: Stalingrad, Kursk, Korsun-Shevchenkovskij campaign, Berlin
Aces: S.G. Ivanov 22, N.L. Chasnyk 19, V.P. Ivanov 14, Ye.F. Trofimov 14

926 IAP
Key commanders: Kap. V.A. Emirov (KIA 9-10-1942)
Assignments: 219 BAD
Aircraft: I-16s, LaGG-3s
Battle honors: Caucasus
Combat record: August, 1942 was a bright month for the regiment when it was credited with downing 43 enemy planes while entering into 88 group and 90 individual encounters. On September 5, 1942, the LaGGs reported the destruction of 10 Luftwaffe planes in the air.
Aces: V.A. Emirov 7

927 IAP
Assignments: 8 GIAD
Aircraft: La-5s
Battle honors: Kursk
Aces: V.B. Provorikhin 12

933 IAP-PVO
Assignments: 144 IAD-PVO
Aircraft: Hurricanes (until 1944)

937 IAP
Full title: 937 Istrebitelnyj aviatsionnyj Krasnoznamennyj Nemanskij polk
Key commanders: Maj. A.I. Koltsov (KIA 9-2-1943), Podpolk. F.M. Kosolapov
Assignments: 322 IAD
Aircraft: La-5s, La-7s
Battle honors: Kursk, Byelorussia, Silesia, Berlin, Dresden, Prague
Combat record: The regiment was in the forefront of action at Kursk, claiming 69 air victories during 667 sorties between July 12 and August 10, 1943.
Aces: A.I. Koltsov 14

940 IAP
Assignments: 245 IAD
Aircraft: Kingcobras
Battle honors: Manchuria 1945

948 IAP – no trace

960 IAP-PVO
Assignments: 328 IAD-PVO
Aircraft: La-5s
Battle honors: Tula, Smolensk, Orsha

961 IAP-PVO
Battle honors: Batajsk 1943, Ternopol 1944

964 IAP-PVO
Aircraft: Tomahawks (as of late 1942), Hurricanes
Battle honors: Leningrad Front, Tikhvin, Ladoga Lake

975 IAP
Designated the 117 GIAP on 9-2-1943
Key commanders: Podpolk. G. Grokhovetskij
Assignments: 236 IAD
Aircraft: I-153s, I-16s
Battle honors: Krasnodar 1941, Caucasus, North Caucasus, South, 1st, 3rd and 4th Ukrainian Fronts including Lemberg-Sandomierz campaign, Yassy-Kishinyov campaign
Aces: G.A. Shadrin 14

976 IAP
Key commanders: Maj. S. Tereshchenko
Assignments: 259 IAD
Battle honors: Stalingrad, East Prussia
Aces: D.V. Gudkov 19, V.F. Semyonov 16

979 IAP
Full title: 979 Istrebitelnyj aviatsionnyj Krasnoznamennyj, ordena Suvorova III stepeni Volkhovskij polk
Key commanders: Maj. G.I. Romantsov
Assignments: 230 ShAD
Aircraft: LaGG-3s, MiG-3s, La-5s
Battle honors: Byelostok, Stalingrad, Volkhov, Kuban, Crimea, Byelorussia
Aces: V.I. Fyodorenko 18

1007 IAP-PVO
Key commanders: Maj. B.Ya. Ternovoj
Assignments: 9 IAK-PVO
Aces: B.Ya. Ternovoj 11

Major Vladimir Semyonovich Kulyov of the 976 IAP, photographed with a Yak on March 3, 1944. With six confirmed victories during 112 sorties Kulyov was one of the unit's more successful pilots of this time. (Author's collection)

APPENDICES

Appendix I
THE ACES (AERIAL VICTORY LIST)

The following list is a partial list with some 900 entries. As of this date, it is the most comprehensive and detailed list available. Official Russian estimates indicate that some 800 pilots in World War II became aces with 15 or more air victories. A large number of these notables was in continuous action from the first until the last days of the war, initially meeting opponents who enjoyed superior equipment, more experience and effective leadership. Although they amassed numerous missions with prolonged aerial fighting, it is interesting to note that a majority of the top-scoring Russian aces survived the attrition.

As it never was Soviet practice to encourage adulation of individuals, no comprehensive personal kill lists have ever been prepared with the result that figures vary from source to source. As a matter of fact, Soviet sources frequently do not differentiate between final scores and victory tallies that qualified a pilot for the award of the title of Hero of the Soviet Union, or do not divide claims between individual and group victories.

A word concerning the corroboration of victory claims may be helpful. Soviet criteria for establishing victory credits as a rule were rigid and strict, and recent evidence confirms that the normal claims procedures were applied throughout the war, rendering Soviet figures as reliable as those of any western air force. The guidelines were as follows:

1. Written combat report giving a description of the aerial victory and pinpointing its location;
2. written testimony of one or more air and ground observers;
3. report of a search party or civil authorities that the wreckage of the enemy plane was recovered.

If an enemy aircraft was shot down in enemy territory, the downing usually was credited to the unit rather than to an individual. Gun camera film also was accepted as evidence when these became available later in the war. Without a witness, however, a claim was not filed.

More contentious were some of the combat claims that were submitted during the Russo-Finnish Winter War and the early stages of the Great Patriotic War, though these would rather appear to reflect the situation of the time, with crushing defeats and disorderly retreats, than any dishonesty. It needs to be pointed out that it is difficult to ascertain which of the claims quoted in this study from Soviet accounts to describe certain aerial encounters or battles, failed to become credits. All individual totals quoted here though represent officially confirmed tallies only. A case in point is A.I. Vybornov, who claimed 28 kills during his World War II career, only 20 of which though were officially allowed; Sasha Pokryshkin, the second ranking ace, had a total of 13 more unconfirmed victories, all of which occured over enemy territory.

Each pilot had his own logbook for personal record-keeping, entering all relevant data immediately after a combat mission. However, only the confirmed kills received verification through the regiment commander's signature.

Throughout World War II the Soviet air forces reported the destruction of 43,000 enemy planes in aerial encounters with 19,000 more being shot down by groundfire and 13,000 destroyed in ground attacks. Even allowing for a normal overclaiming of one third, this still represents a tremendous score.

The order in which the aces are listed is as follows:

Line 1 : surname, given name, father's name – personal score (lichno) plus fractional credits (v gruppa) – number of sorties – number of air encounters
Line 2 : rank (latest wartime ratings) – combat units – remarks

Some of the most notable pilots produced by the VVS during the war pose for a 1949 photograph in Moscow. First row, from left, they are: V.I. Mykhlik (566 ShAP), A.N. Yefimov (62 ShAP), Fomichyov (unknown), D.B. Glinka (100 GIAP), V.I. Popkov (5 GIAP), A.I. Koldunov (866 IAP); second row: S.G. Litavrin (158 IAP), A.N. Medvedev (122 GBAP), unknown, unknown, unknown, I.I. Kindyushev (26 GAP-ADD); third row: M.A. Zuyev (73 GIAP), G.G. Golubev (16 GIAP), unknown, V.M. Vishenkov (8 ODRAP), unknown. (Author's collection)

KOZHEDUB, Ivan Nikitovich Maj., 240 IAP, 176 GIAP	62	330	120
POKRYSHKIN, Aleksandr Ivanovich Polk., 55 IAP, 16 GIAP, 9 GIAD; 48 V on P-39s	59	560	156
GULAYEV, Nikolaj Dmitriyevich Kap., 27 IAP, 129 GIAP; 5 V 3-5-1944	57 +3	248	69
RECHKALOV, Grigorij Andreyevich Maj., 55 IAP, 16 GIAP; 44 V on P-39s	56 +5	450	122
YEVSTIGNEYEV, Kirill Alekseyevich Maj., 240 IAP, 178 GIAP; 5 V 10-7-1944	53 +3	283	109
VOROZHEJKIN, Arsenij Vasilyevich Polk., 22 IAP, 728 IAP, 32 GIAP; 6 V Khalkhin Gol	52 +13	300	90
GLINKA, Dmitrij Borisovich Podpolk., 45 IAP, 100 GIAP; c. 40 V on P-39s	50	300	90
KOLDUNOV, Aleksandr Ivanovich Kap., 866 IAP; 3 USAAF P-38s	46	358	96
KUBAREV, Vasilij Nikolayevich Maj., 65 GIAP	46		
SKOMOROKHOV, Nikolaj Mikhajlovich Maj., 31 IAP; plus 3 e/a ground	46 +8	605	143
BOBROV, Vladimir Ivanovich Polk., 129 GIAP; 13 V Spain; plus 2 Me 262s ground 4-18-1945	43 +24		112
GRITSEVETS, Sergej Ivanovich Maj., 22 IAP; KIFA 9-16-1939; 30 V Spain	42		
POPKOV, Vitalij Ivanovich Maj., 5 GIAP, 739 IAP; 1 aerial ramming; plus 3 V Korea 1950-53	41 +1	300+	117
ALELYUKHIN, Aleksej Vasilyevich Maj., 69 IAP, 9 GIAP; 12 V Taganrog	40 +17	601	258

SEROV, Vladimir Georgiyevich St.Lej., 159 IAP; KIA 6-26-1944	39 +8		104
LUGANSKIJ, Sergej Danilovich Maj., 162 IAP, 270 IAP; 2 aerial rammings	37 +6	417	200
BABAK, Ivan Ilyich Maj., 45 IAP, 100 GIAP; POW 3-16-1945; 4 V 7-16-1944	37 +4	330	103
FYODOROV, Ivan Vasilyevich St.Lej., 812 IAP; plus 9 e/a ground	36 +9	416	104
KUZNETSOV, Nikolaj Fyodorovich Maj., 191 IAP, 436 IAP, 30 GIAP	36 +12	400	
KAMOZIN, Pavel Mikhajlovich Kap., 269 IAP	35 +13	131	56
LAVRINENKOV, Vladimir Dmitriyevich Maj., 4 IAP, 9 GIAP; 9 V Stalingrad	35 +11	448	134
PAVLUSHKIN, Nikolaj Sazonovich Kap., 402 IAP	35		
RESHETOV, Aleksej Mikhajlovich Maj., 31 GIAP; 11 V Stalingrad	35 +8	821	200
CHUBUKOV, Fyodor Mikhajlovich Kap., 154 IAP, 29 GIAP	34 +5	300+	
GNIDO, Pyotr Andreyevich Maj., 13 IAP, 111 GIAP	34	300+	
KOCHETOV, Aleksandr Vasilyevich Kap., 629 IAP, 43 IAP	34 +8	450	
SMIRNOV, Aleksej Semyonovich Maj., 153 IAP, 28 GIAP	34 +15	457	72
SYTOV, Ivan Nikitovich St.Lej., 5 GIAP; KIA 10-16-1943	34		
ZAJTSEV, Vasilij Aleksandrovich Polk., 129 IAP, 5 GIAP, 11 GIAD, 105 GIAP	34 +19	427	163
STEPANENKO, Ivan Nikiforovich Maj., 4 IAP	33 +8	414	118
BOROVYKH, Andrej Yegorovich Maj., 157 IAP, 728 IAP	32 +14	424	104
KOMELKOV, Mikhail Sergeyevich Kap., 104 GIAP	32 +7	321	75
KRASNOV, Nikolaj Fyodorovich Maj., 402 IAP, 31 IAP, 116 IAP; KIA 1-29-1945	32 +10	300	
KULAGIN, Andrej Mikhajlovich Kap., 249 IAP; 7 NF V	32 +7	762	142
RYAZANOV, Aleksej Konstantinovich Maj., 736 IAP, 4 IAP	32 +16	551	97
GOLOVACHYOV, Pavel Yakovlevich Kap., 9 GIAP; 1 aerial ramming	31 +1	457	125
KLUBOV, Aleksandr Fyodorovich Kap., 10 IAP, 16 GIAP; KIFA 11-1-1944; 27 V on P-39s	31 +19	467	95
KUMANICHKIN, Aleksandr Sergeyevich Maj., 41 GIAP, 176 GIAP	31 +4		
AMET-KHAN, Sultan Maj., 4 IAP, 9 GIAP; 1 aerial ramming	30 +19	603	130
ARKHIPENKO, Fyodor Fyodorovich Maj., 129 GIAP	30 +14	467	102
DENISENKO, Vladimir Guryevich Lej., 32 IAP; KIA 4-26-1945	30	300	
GLINKA, Boris Borisovich Kap., 45 IAP, 100 GIAP; all V on P-39s	30	200	
GLINKIN, Sergej Grigoryevich St.Lej., 5 GIAP; 1 aerial ramming	30	200+	
KARASYOV, Aleksandr Nikitovich Kap., 9 GIAP	30 +11	380	112
LIKHOBABIN, Ivan Dmitriyevich Maj., 402 IAP, 485 IAP, 72 GIAP	30 +9	321	
MAKAROV, Valentin Nikolayevich Podpolk., 512 IAP, 176 IAP	30 +9	638	150
SAFONOV, Boris Feoktistovich Podpolk., 72 SAP-SF, 78 IAP-SF, 2 GIAP-SF; KIA 5-30-1942	30 +3	234	34
CHIRKOV, Andrej Vasilyevich Maj., 29 GIAP, 196 IAP; 1 aerial ramming	29 +9	400	78
KNYAZEV, Vasilij Aleksandrovich Kap., 12 IAP, 88 IAP	29	1,088	139

MERKUSHEV, Vasilij Afanasyevich Maj., 270 IAP; POW 7-4-1944	29	418	
NAJDYONOV, Nikolaj Alekseyevich Kap., 563 IAP, 116 GIAP	29		
NOVIKOV, Konstantin Afanasyevich Kap., 131 IAP, 40 GIAP	29		
ONUFRIYENKO, Grigorij Denisovich Polk., 129 IAP, 5 GIAP, 31 IAP	29	405	
POGORELOV, Mikhail Savelyevich Kap., 4 IAP; 1 aerial ramming	29		
IGNATYEV, Mikhail Trofimovich Kap., 13 IAP, 5 GIAP	28		
KOVZAN, Boris Ivanovich Kap., 42 IAP, 744 IAP, 184 IAP; 4 aerial rammings	28	360	127
LEONOVICH, Ivan Semyonovich St.Lej., 29 GIAP; 6 V 1-x-1944	28	340	51
MURAVYEV, Pavel Ignatyevich Kap., 271 IAP	28		
TRESHCHEV, Konstantin Mikhajlovich Kap., 127 IAP, inspektor IA-VVS	28	569	
VOSTRUKHIN, Pyotr Mikhajlovich St.Lej., 271 IAP; KIA 7-23-1943; 4 V 5-1-1943	28		
ZOTOV, Viktor Alekseyevich Kap., 159 IAP	28 +10	416	
BABAJLOV, Pavel Konstantinovich Kap., 163 GIAP; KIA 10-14-1944; 2 aerial rammings	27 +4	417	75
DYACHKOV, Aleksandr Alekseyevich St.Lej., 179 GIAP; KIA 3-31-1945	27 +1	217	54
GRISHCHENKO, Pyotr Lukyanovich Kap., 32 IAP	27	380	78
KARPOV, Aleksandr Terentyevich Kap., 27 GIAP; KIA 10-20-1944	27 +10	519	130
KLIMOV, Vasilij Vladimirovich Maj., 15 IAP	27	303	89
KOZHEVNIKOV, Anatolij Leonidovich Maj., 438 IAP, 212 GIAP	27	300	69
MAJOROV, Aleksandr Ivanovich Maj., 2 GIAP	27	460	68
MORGUNOV, Sergej Nikolayevich Kap., 15 IAP; 4 V Berlin 4-18-1945	27 +16		
SAFRONOV, Sergej Ivanovich Kap., 293 IAP	27 +4	147	
BARANOV, Mikhail Semyonovich Kap., 157 IAP	26 +9		85
BORODACHYOV, Viktor Ivanovich Kap., 40 GIAP	26 +5	552	116
KHARITONOV, Vasilij Nikolayevich Kap., 123 IAP-PVO; 2 aerial rammings	26	395	88
KHOLODOV, Ivan Mikhajlovich Podpolk., 28 IAP-PVO, 32 GIAP, 111 GIAP	26	480	
KITAYEV, Nikolaj Trofimovich Kap., 40 GIAP	26		
LAVITSKIJ, Nikolaj Yefimovich Kap., 45 IAP, 100 GIAP; KIA 3-10-1944	26		
LOBANOV, Aleksandr Vasilyevich St.Lej., 41 GIAP	26 +14	811	83
MIKHALEV, Vasilij Pavovich St.Lej., 508 IAP	26		
MOTUZ, Ivan Fomich Kap., 20 IAP, 744 IAP; plus 5 e/a ground	26	400	89
OSADCHIYEV, Aleksandr Dmitriyevich St.Lej., 274 IAP, 43 IAP	26	250	100
PESKOV, Pavel Ilyich Kap., 5 GIAP	26	326	
YEGOROV, Aleksej Aleksandrovich Kap., 212 GIAP	26 +7	370	70
BORISOV, Ivan Grigoryevich Lej., 4 IAP, 9 GIAP; plus 4 e/a ground	25 +8		
GUBANOV, Aleksej Alekseyevich Kap., 13 IAP	25		

LIKHOLETOV, Pyotr Yakovlevich Kap., 159 IAP; DOW 7-13-1945	25 +5	382	78
SACHKOV, Mikhail Ivanovich Kap., 728 IAP	25	68	
SIDORENKOV, Vasilij Kuzmich St.Lej., 254 IAP	25	350	
SUVIROV, Viktor Ivanovich Maj., 15 IAP; plus 10 e/a ground; 3 V Khalkhin Gol	25 +7	200	50
YERMAKOV, Dmitrij Vasilyevich St.Lej., 123 IAP, 159 IAP	25	247	64
BARANOV, Mikhail Dmitriyevich Kap., 183 IAP, 9 GIAP; KIFA 1-17-1943 ; plus 6 e/a ground	24 +28	285	85
BONDARENKO, Vasilij Yefimovich St.Lej., 16 GIAP	24	324	68
DUNAYEV, Nikolaj Panteleyevich Maj., 16 IAP, 270 IAP; 6 V Byelgorod	24 +9	500	
FYODOROV, Aleksandr Yakovlevich Kap., 32 GIAP	24		
FYODOROV, Arkadij Vasilyevich Kap., 131 IAP, 16 GIAP	24 +18	554	183
GALCHENKO, Leonid Akimovich Maj., 145 IAP, 19 GIAP, 609 IAP	24 +12	410	90
GNEZDILOV, Ivan Fyodorovich St.Lej., 153 GIAP	24	376	120
GORBUNOV, Ivan Mikhajlovich Kap., 42 GIAP	24		
GORELOV, Sergej Dmitriyevich Kap., 111 GIAP	24 +1	214	47
GREBENYOV, Arkadij Dmitriyevich Kap., 111 GIAP	24		
KORNIYENKO, Ivan Mikheyevich Kap., 270 IAP; 11 V Byelgorod-Kharkov	24		
LAVEJKIN, Ivan Pavlovich Maj., 5 GIAP	24 +15	498	106
MOROZOV, Anatolij Afanasyevich Podpolk., 4 IAP, 9 GIAP; KIA 6-18-1944	24 +8	400	
NAGORNIJ, Viktor Sergeyevich Kap., 293 IAP	24		
NAZARENKO, Dmitrij Pavlovich Maj., 131 IAP	24 +8	500	120
NAZIMOV, Konstantin Savelyevich Kap., 254 IAP; KIA 12-23-1944	24		
NOVICHKOV, Stepan Matveyevich St.Lej., 67 GIAP	24	173	
TARASOV, Pavel Timofeyevich Maj., 812 IAP; KIA 7-29-1944	24	235	81
TRUD, Andrej Ivanovich Kap., 16 GIAP; 14 V Kuban	24 +1	420	120
VAKHLAYEV, Aleksandr Alekseyevich Kap., 728 IAP	24	195	
VEDENEYEV, Valentin Ivanovich St.Lej., 159 IAP; 6 V 4-21/22-1944	24	182	52
ZELENOV, Nikolaj Andrianovich Kap., 154 IAP, 29 GIAP; KIA 6-29-1944	24 +9		
ANDRIANOV, Ilya Filippovich Kap., 273 IAP, 153 GIAP	23		
BABKOV, Vasilij Petrovich Maj., 434 IAP, 32 GIAP; 7 V Kursk	23	450	
BELOUSOV, Nikolaj Petrovich Lej., 193 IAP	23	265	50
BORISENKO, Ivan Ivanovich Kap., 73 GIAP	23 +2	245	63
GERMAN, Grigorij Ivanovich St.Lej., 42 IAP	23 (+)		
GOROKHOV, Yurij Ivanovich Kap., 162 IAP; KIA 1-1-1944	23 +10	307	57
KOZLOV, Nikolaj Aleksandrovich Podpolk., 788 IAP, 907 IAP; 2 aerial rammings	23	620	130
KUTSENKO, Mikhail I. Kap., 291 IAP; 12 V Kuban	23		

LITVINENKO, Trofim Afanasyevich	23	519	
Maj., 191 IAP			
MAKOVSKIJ, Spartak Iosifovich	23 +2	218	79
Maj., 165 IAP, 43 IAP; plus 5 e/a ground; 1 aerial ramming			
NEUSTRUYEV, Ivan Pavlovich	23 +6	400	85
Podpolk., 195 IAP, 11 GIAP			
OGANESOV, Vozgen Mikhajlovich	23	324	
St.Lej., 347 IAP			
PILYUTOV, Pyotr Andreyevich	23	1,945	76
Podpolk., 154 IAP, 29 GIAP			
POKRYSHEV, Pyotr Afanasyevich	23 +7	300	72
Podpolk., 7 IAP, 154 IAP, 159 IAP; 2 V Russo-Finnish Winter War			
SEMENISHIN, Vladimir Grigoryevich	23 +13		
Maj., 131 IAP, 298 IAP; KIA 9-29-1943; 4 V 5-27-1943			
SHESTAKOV, Lev Lvovich	23 +44	400	
Polk., 69 IAP, 9 GIAP; KIA 3-13-1944; 11+31 V Spain			
SHMELEV, Ilya Vasilyevich	23		
Maj., 4 IAP; 15 V Kuban			
YAKUBOVSKIJ, Pyotr Grigoryevich	23 +20	523	120
Kap., 31 IAP			
YEREMIN, Boris Nikolayevich	23	342	60
Podpolk., 296 IAP, 239 IAP, 31 GIAP, 6 GIAD			
BALYUK, Ivan Fyodorovich	22 +16	247	98
Maj., 38 IAP, 237 IAP, 54 GIAP; 9 V Stalingrad			
BARSUKOV, Vasilij Nikolayevich	22 +6	360	70
Kap., 18 GIAP; 7 V East Prussia			
BAZANOV, Pyotr Vasilyevich	22 +6	320	60
Kap., 3 GIAP			
BILYUKIN, Aleksandr Vasilyevich	22 +1	418	35
Kap., 196 IAP; 4 V 8-1-1943			
BURNAZYAN, Sergej Avdeyevich	22 +2	224	
St.Lej., 629 IAP, 866 IAP; KIA 4-15-1943			
CHEPINOGA, Pavel Iosifovich	22 +1	100	37
Kap., 508 IAP			
DIDENKO, Gavriil Vlasovich	22 +37	365	80
Maj., 482 IAP			
DUDNICHENKO, Viktor Markovich	22	180	40
St.Lej., 239 IAP			
DZHABIDZE, David Vasilyevich	22	274	64
Kap., 158 IAP, 812 IAP; 1 aerial ramming			
FEDOTOV, Andrej Andreyevich	22		
Maj., 169 IAP, 63 GIAP; KIA 12-15-1943			
IVANOV, Stepan Gavrilovich	22	463	
Maj., 148 GIAP-PVO			
KIRILYUK, Viktor Vasilyevich	22 +9	448	95
Lej., 31 IAP			
KIRIYA, Shalva Nesterovich	22 +1	189	57
Maj., 427 IAP			
KUZNETSOV, Mikhail Vasilyevich	22 +6	345	72
Maj., 814 IAP, 106 GIAP			
LAVRENOV, Aleksandr Filippovich	22	150	
Lej., 291 IAP; KIA 3-26-1944; 17 V Kuban			
LEBEDEV, Semyon Andrianovich	22 +2	220	55
Maj., 43 IAP			
MAKSIMOV, Aleksandr Yefimovich	22	440	68
Maj., 156 GIAP			
MANUKYAN, Akop Balabekovich	22	207	55
Kap., 402 IAP			
MASLOV, Ivan Vasilyevich	22	285	60
St.Lej., 157 IAP			
MERENKOV, Viktor Alekseyevich	22	166	39
St.Lcj., 897 IAP			
MIOKOV, Nikolaj Dmitriyevich	22	226	54
Maj., 91 IAP			
MURASHOV, Aleksej Andrianovich	22 +9	450	125
Polk., 3 GIAP			
NAJDENKO, Vasilij Mikhajlovich	22 +57	550	350
Podpolk., 126 IAP; fought in four wars			
NOGA, Mitrofan Petrovich	22		
Polk., 70 IAP, 256 IAD, 322 IAD; 9 V Khalkhin Gol			

PINCHUK, Nikolaj Grigoryevich	22	+2	307	68
Maj., 18 GIAP; 1 aerial ramming; 5 V Smolensk				
SAVITSKIJ, Yevgenij Yakovlevich	22	+2	216	81
Gen.Lej., 29 IAP, 205 IAD, 3 IAK				
SHUTT, Nikolaj Konstantinovich	22		444	120
Maj., 270 IAP				
SIVTSOV, Nikolaj Stepanovich	22		78	34
St.Lej., 867 IAP; KIA 9-23-1943				
SUKHOV, Konstantin Vasilyevich	22		297	68
St.Lej., 16 GIAP				
TOKAREV, Moisej Stepanovich	22			
Maj., 862 IAP, 40 GIAP; KIA 7-8-1943; 4 V 7-8-1943				
VITKOVSKIJ, Ivan Petrovich	22		357	148
Maj., 66 GIAP				
VOLODIN, Anatolij Ivanovich	22		397	76
Kap., 164 IAP				
YEGOROVICH, Vladimir Alekseyevich	22		248	71
Kap., 402 IAP				
YEVSEYEV, Yevgenij Arkhipovich	22			
Lej., 629 IAP-PVO				
ZIBOROV, Vasilij Mikhajlovich	22			
St.Lej., 402 IAP, 485 IAP, 72 GIAP				
ALEKSEYEV, Nikolaj Mikhajlovich	21		102	35
Ml.Lej., 64 GIAP; KIA 7-12-1943; 1 aerial ramming				
CHISLOV, Aleksandr Mikhajlovich	21	+13	333	
Podpolk., 63 GIAP				
DOLGARYOV, Pavel Mikhajlovich	21	+7	152	42
Lej., 116 IAP; plus 1 e/a ground; 12 V Budapest				
FADEYEV, Vadim Ivanovich	21	+1	394	48
Kap., 446 SAP, 630 IAP, 16 GIAP; KIA 5-5-1943				
FIGICHEV, Valentin Alekseyevich	21			
Kap., 16 GIAP				
KOROLYOV, Konstantin Ivanovich	21	+10	435	97
Maj., 482 IAP				
KOVALYOV, Konstantin Fyodotovich	21	+13		
St.Lej., 13 IAP-KBF				
KRASAVIN, Konstantin Alekseyevich	21	+4	376	106
Maj., 485 IAP, 150 GIAP				
KUZMIN, Georgij Pavlovich	21	+7	280	
Maj., 161 IAP, 239 IAP, 9 GIAP; KIA 8-18-1943; 1 aerial ramming				
MAZAN, Mikhail Semyonovich	21		440	91
Kap., 85 GIAP; KIA 12-12-1944				
MERKULOV, Vladimir Ivanovich	21			
Kap., 43 IAP				
MOROZOV, Fotij Yakovlevich	21			
Kap., 31 GIAP				
NEKRASOV, Vladimir Petrovich	21			
St.Lej., 483 IAP				
PANTELKIN, Anatolij Aleksandrovich	21		300	
Kap., 116 IAP; KIA 3-14-1945				
PIVOVAROV, Mikhail Yevdokimovich	21		269	69
St.Lej., 402 IAP; 11 V Byelorussia				
PUTKO, Nikolaj Savelyevich	21		450	
St.Lej., 106 GIAP				
RIDNYJ, Stepan Grigoryevich	21		100	60
St.Lej., 126 IAP; KIFA 2-17-1942				
ROMANENKO, Aleksandr Sergeyevich	21	+5	220	150
Maj., 91 IAP; KIA 11-6-1943				
RUDENKO, Nikolaj Sergeyevich	21	+2	186	38
St.Lej., 176 GIAP				
SAVELYEV, Vasilij Antonovich	21			
St.Lej., 2 GIAP				
SHARDAKOV, Igor Aleksandrovich	21		483	
St.Lej., 5 GIAP				
STARIKOV, Dmitrij Aleksandrovich	21	+6	479	51
St.Lej., 32 IAP-ChF, 11 GIAP-ChF; 4 V 11-6-1943				
TIMOFEYENKO, Ivan Vasilyevich	21	+6	436	107
Maj., 9 GIAP				
TISHCHENKO, Aleksandr Trofimovich	21	+3	397	83
Kap., 812 IAP				

VASILYEVSKIJ, Yegor Vasilyevich Kap., 151 GIAP	21		296	
BYKASOV, Nikolaj Vladimirovich St.Lej., 156 GIAP	20	+1	325	69
CHEREVATENKO, Aleksej Tikhonovich Maj., 69 IAP, 9 GIAP	20			
CHUCHVAGA, Ivan Ivanovich Kap., 651 IAP, 866 IAP; KIA 3-12-1943	20		250	80
DAVIDKOV, Viktor Iosifovich Polk., 131 IAP, 8 GIAD	20	+2	434	
DRANISHCHEV, Yevgenij Petrovich St.Lej., 9 GIAP; KIA 8-20-1943; 9 V Stalingrad	20			
DRYGIN, Vasilij Mikhajlovich Kap., 298 IAP; 10+5 V Kuban	20			
FEDOSEYEV, Mikhail Andreyevich Podpolk., 6 OAE, 88 IAP, 247 IAP; KIA 3-22-1942; 7 V Spain	20		329	67
GRAZHDANINOV, Pavel Aleksandrovich St.Lej., 169 IAP; KIA 3-5-1943; 1 aerial ramming	20			
GUCHYOK, Pyotr Iosifovich St.Lej., 100 GIAP; KIA 4-18-1945	20	+3	209	56
KANKOSHEV, Akhmet-Khan Tallovich Lej., 42 GIAP; KIA 12-28-1943	20		200	100
KRAVCHENKO, Grigorij Panteleyevich Podpolk., 22 IAP, 11 SAD, 215 IAD; KIA 2-23-1943	20			
LAUKHIN, Aleksandr Kirillovich St.Lej., 1 GIAP	20			
LEONOV, Nikolaj Ivanovich St.Lej., 183 IAP	20			
LOGVINENKO, Nikolaj Pavlovich Maj., 92 IAP, 293 IAP	20	+6		
MARKOV, Vasilij Vasilyevich St.Lej., 116 IAP	20		225	67
NIKIFOROV, Pyotr Pavlovich Kap., 129 GIAP	20		297	69
PECHYONY, Nikolaj Nikolayevich Maj., 42 GIAP	20	+3	219	88
RENTS, Mikhail Petrovich Maj., 30 GIAP; 5 V Berlin	20	+5	294	56
RUBAKHIN, Anatolij Yermolayevich Maj., 402 IAP	20			
RYAZANTSEV, Aleksej Fyodorovich Maj., 179 GIAP	20		150	50
SMIRNOV, Oleg Nikolayevich St.Lej., 31 IAP	20	+7	404	120
VISHNYAKOV, Ivan Alekseyevich Maj., 296 IAP, 171 IAP	20	+3	296	100
VYBORNOV, Aleksandr Ivanovich St.Lej., 728 IAP	20		190	42
ZHIGULENKOV, Boris Vasilyevich St.Lej., 240 IAP, 178 GIAP; KIA 2-7-1945	20		200	50
AVEKOV, Ivan Avdeyevich Kap., 519 IAP; KIA 4-17-1943; plus 23 e/a ground	19	+6	178	
BASHKIROV, Viktor Andreyevich Maj., 519 IAP; 4 V 11-3-1943	19		281	35
BATYAEV, Vasilij Sergeyevich Kap., 88 IAP, 54 IAP	19	+7	639	234
BAYEVSKIJ, Georgij Arturovich St.Lej., 5 GIAP	19		232	52
BRYZGALOV, Pavel Aleksandrovich St.Lej., 178 GIAP; plus 1 e/a ground	19		248	61
BYKOVETS, Leonid Aleksandrovich St.Lej., 28 GIAP	19		274	50
CHASNYK, Nikolaj Leontyevich St.Lej., 630 IAP, 148 GIAP-PVO; POW 7-7-1944	19	+8	685	46
DZYUBA, Pyotr Petrovich Maj., 2 GIAP, 85 GIAP	19	+16	319	
GAVRILIN, Pavel Fyodorovich Lej., 402 IAP	19		244	54
GRAFIN, Iosif St.Lej., 16 GIAP; KIA 4-28-1945	19			

GRUZDEV, Konstantin Afanasyevich Major., 402 IAP; 416 IAP; KIFA 2-2-1943	19		
GUDKOV, Dmitrij Vasilyevich Maj., 976 IAP; 1 aerial ramming	19	314	28
GUGNIN, Nikolaj Pavlovich Maj., 122 IAP	19		
KARLOV, Valentin Andreyevich St.Lej., 129 GIAP	19 +7	246	71
KARMIN, Aleksandr Leontyevich Kap., 129 GIAP	19 +14	221	31
KHUDYAKOV, Nikolaj Vasilyevich Maj., 32 IAP, 5 GIAP	19	308	65
KOMARDINKIN, Konstantin Petrovich Kap., 274 IAP; KIA 4-17-1944; plus 3 e/a ground	19		
KOMOSA, Anatolij Savelyevich Maj., Inspektor-lyotchik 2 VA	19 +4	383	
KONSTANTINOV, Anatolij Ustinovich Kap., 85 GIAP	19	294	90
KUZNETSOV, Sergej Alekseyevich Maj., 233 IAP	19 +8	227	52
LEVITAN, Vladimir Samojlovich Kap., 88 GIAP	19 +4	291	64
LITAVRIN, Sergej Gavrilovich Kap., 158 IAP	19 +5	462	90
LOBAS, Pyotr Kalinikovich Kap., 86 GIAP; 4 V East Prussia	19 +3	160	
LOBOV, Georgij Ageyevich Gen.Maj., 322 IAD, 7 GIAD; plus 4 V Korean War 1950-53	19 +8	346	
LOZOVSKIJ, Viktor Artemyevich Kap., 897 IAP	19	327	42
LUSTO, Mikhail Vasilyevich St.Lej., 129 GIAP	19 +1	251	49
MARIINSKIJ, Yevgenij Pakhomovich Lej., 129 GIAP	19		
MUKHIN, Vasilij Filippovich St.Lej., 178 GIAP	19	340	
NOVOSYOLOV, Kuzma Vasilyevich St.Lej., 115 GIAP	19 +5	235	
OLKHOVSKIJ, Nikolaj Ivanovich Podpolk., 193 IAP, 178 GIAP	19	128	
OREKHOV, Vladimir Aleksandrovich St.Lej., 434 IAP, 32 GIAP; plus 4 e/a ground	19 +2		
OVODOV, Yakov Leontyevich Maj., 133 IAP	19		
PAVLOVSKIJ, Ilya Mikhajlovich Kap., 659 IAP	19 +8	375	95
POZDNYAKOV, Yakov Mironovich Rank or unit not established	19	400	
PROSHENKOV, Nikolaj Ivanovich Maj., 69 GIAP	19 +4	375	86
PUSHKIN, Nikolaj Petrovich Kap., 2 GIAP	19 +8	380	52
SEMENTSOV, Mikhail Ivanovich Kap., 41 GIAP; KIA 2-12-1945; 2 aerial rammings	19 +12	363	83
SEMENYUK, Ivan Ivanovich Kap., 40 GIAP	19 +8	430	125
SEMYONOV, Aleksandr Fyodorovich Polk., 7 IAP, 180 IAP, 434 IAP, 322 IAD	19 +12	315	70
SGIBNEV, Pyotr Georgiyevich Kap., 78 IAP-SF; KIA 5-3-1943	19	318	38
SLIZEN, Leonid Nikolayevich Maj., 15 IAP	19 +2	222	95
ZELYONKIN, Mikhail Mikhajlovich St.Lej., 156 IAP	19 +3	218	
ZIMIN, Georgij Vasilyevich Gen.Maj., 53 IAP, 42 IAP, 485 IAP, 240 IAD	19 +20	249	69
ZYUZIN, Pyotr Dmitriyevich Lej., 29 GIAP	19 211	41	
ARTAMONOV, Nikolaj Semyonovich St.Lej., 32 IAP, 193 IAP, 177 GIAP; KIA 3-26-1945; plus 19 e/a ground	18 +8	165	42

BASHKIROV, Vyacheslav Filippovich Politruk, 788 IAP, 907 IAP; 6 V Stalingrad	18	312	
BATURIN, Aleksandr Gerasimovich St.Lej., 71 IAP-KBF, 10 GIAP-KBF	18 +12	543	84
BEKASHONOK, Mikhail Vasilyevich Kap., 129 GIAP	18 +4	170	50
BULGAKOV, Andrej Panteleyevich St.Lej., 265 IAP	18	182	39
DMITRYUK, Grigorij Fedoseyevich Kap., 19 GIAP	18	206	37
FYODORENKO, Vasilij Ivanovich Kap., 979 IAP; KIA 9-22-1943	18 +2	169	52
GUTSALOV, Aleksandr Semyonovich Kap., 691 SAP, 845 IAP; plus 7 e/a ground	18 +3	494	52
ISTRASHKIN, Vladimir Ivanovich Maj., 446 SAP, 979 IAP	18 +6	525	100
KARAYEV, Aleksandr Akimovich St.Lej., 176 GIAP; 5 V Berlin	18	373	75
KHUDOV, Pyotr Dmitriyevich Maj., 867 IAP	18	235	107
KOLOMIYETS, Pyotr Leontyevich Kap., 2 GIAP-SF	18	400	
KONOBAYEV, Vasilij Sergeyevich Ml.Lej., 291 IAP; KIA 9-18-1943; 17 V Kuban	18 +2		
KONYSHEV, Nikolaj Sergeyevich Maj., 163 IAP	18	287	41
KOROLEV, Ivan Georgiyevich Lej., 69 IAP, 9 GIAP; plus 19 e/a ground	18 +11	c.500	
KRATINOV, Semyon Ustinovich Kap., 40 GIAP	18 +3	321	64
KULIYEV, Adil Gusejnovich Kap., 65 GIAP	18	265	64
KUZMICHEV, Ivan Fyodorovich Maj., 152 GIAP	18 +36	402	
LITVINCHUK, Boris Mikhajlovich Kap., 11 GIAP-ChF	18 +9	459	44
MASHENKIN, Aleksej M. St.Lej., 812 IAP; plus 7 e/a ground	18	200	
MASTERKOV, Aleksandr Borisovich St.Lej., 5 GIAP; KIA 3-23-1945; 1 aerial ramming	18	195	40
MAZURIN, Fyodor Makarovich Kap., 28 GIAP	18 +2	222	50
MENSHUTIN, Yevgenij Petrovich Lej., 152 GIAP	18	427	
MUDRETSOV, Valentin Fyodorovich St.Lej., 240 IAP, 178 GIAP	18 +1	350	70
MUKHIN, Anatolij Fyodorovich St.Lej., 177 GIAP; plus 2 e/a ground	18	230	45
NARZIIIMSKIJ, Vladimir Aleksandrovich Kap., 2 GIAP-SF, 11 GIAP-ChF	18	404	
OLEJNIK, Grigorij Nikitovich Kap., 293 IAP	18 +2	296	67
PERESUMKIN, Pyotr Petrovich Kap., 149 IAP; plus 2 e/a ground	18 +2	113	38
POKHLEBAYEV, Ivan Grigoryevich St.Lej., 101 GIAP	18	138	42
POLOGOV, Pavel Andreyevich Maj., 737 IAP	18 +12	365	90
POPOV, Andrej Ivanovich St.Lej., 65 GIAP; MIA 6-23-1944	18	126	40
SEREDA, Pyotr Seliverstovich Kap., 88 IAP	18	500	
SHAMENKOV, Ivan Frolovich St.Lej., 150 GIAP	18	200	
SHISHKIN, Yakov Vasilyevich Kap., 32 GIAP	18	244	36
SHMELKOV, Nikolaj Ivanovich Polk., 1 SAD, 234 IAD; 13 V Spain	18		
SHOKUROV, Aleksandr Alekseyevich St.Lej., 156 GIAP	18	460	58

SINCHUK, Vasilij Prokofyevich	18		305	
Kap., 22 IAP, 662 SAP, 254 IAP; KIA 2-1-1944; 4 V 10-25-1942				
SKLYAROV, Ivan Grigoryevich	18		135	28
St.Lej., 193 IAP				
SMAZNOV, Viktor Viktorovich	18	+1	162	42
St.Lej., 197 IAP				
SOROKIN, Zakhar Artyomovich	18			
Kap., 72 IAP-SF, 2 GIAP-SF; 1 aerial ramming				
SURNEV, Nikolaj Grigoryevich	18		177	53
St.Lej., 866 IAP				
TOKARENKO, Mikhail Kuzmich	18		332	47
Kap., 153 GIAP				
VILYAMSON, Aleksandr Aleksandrovich	18	+6	382	66
Kap., 104 GIAP				
YEREMIN, Aleksej Ustinovich	18		93	
Podpolk., 355 IAP				
AVDEYEV, Mikhail Vasilyevich	17		498	141
Podpolk., 8 IAP-ChF, 6 GIAP-ChF				
BALALUYEV, Aleksej Andreyevich	17	+5	345	52
Maj., Lyotchik-inspektor USP-VVS				
BELKIN, Aleksandr Nikitich	17	+1	173	54
St.Lej., 164 IAP				
BLINOV, Aleksej Pavlovich	17		100	
Kap., 177 GIAP				
BORODIN, Nikolaj Vasilyevich	17		239	75
St.Lej., 43 IAP; plus 2 e/a ground				
BRITIKOV, Aleksej Petrovich	17	+4	492	
Kap., 85 GIAP				
BUYANOV, Viktor Nikolayevich	17		309	127
Maj., 146 IAP				
CHURILIN, Aleksej Pavlovich	17		273	83
Maj., 611 IAP; plus 21 e/a ground				
DEMA, Leonid Vasilyevich	17	+5	273	38
Kap., 112 GIAP; 1 aerial ramming				
DIDENKO, Nikolaj Matveyevich	17		378	
St.Lej., 2 GIAP-SF				
DOLGUSHIN, Sergej Fyodorovich	17	+11	500	
Podpolk., 122 IAP, 180 IAP, 434 IAP, 32 GIAP, 30 GIAP, 156 IAP				
DUDNIK, Nikolaj Denisovich	17			
St.Lej., 178 IAP-PVO				
GLAZOV, Nikolaj Yelizarovich	17	+7	537	70
St.Lej., 111 IAP, 31 GIAP; KIA 7-30-1943; 8 V Moscow				
GRIGORYEV, Gerasim Afanasyevich	17		300	18
Kap., 178 IAP-PVO				
GRINKO, Nikolaj Ivanovich	17			
St.Lej., 13 IAP; KIA 4-21-1943				
ISAYEV, Vasilij Vasilyevich	17	+5	241	
Kap., 42 GIAP				
IVANOV, Pyotr Mikheyevich	17		299	80
Maj., 866 IAP; KIA 11-28-1943				
KHARLAMOV, Semyon Ilyich	17	+6	755	147
St.Lej., 163 GIAP				
KIBKALOV, Mikhail Moiseyevich	17		276	38
St.Lej., 163 IAP				
KISLYAKOV, Anatolij Vasilyevich	17		539	
Kap., 28 GIAP; plus 15 e/a ground				
KIYANCHENKO, Nikolaj Stepanovich	17	+4	360	46
Maj., 106 GIAP				
KLIMANOV, Ivan Kirillovich	17	+5	284	63
Kap., 272 IAP, 49 IAP				
KOSOLAPOV, Filipp Markevich	17	(+)		
Podpolk., 2 GIAP, 937 IAP				
KONYAKHIN, Vasilij Dmitriyevich	17	+2	227	28
St.Lej., 287 IAP				
LAGUTENKO, Ivan Nikitovich	17	+3	288	79
Maj., 68 GIAP				
LATYSHEV, Vladimir Aleksandrovich	17		232	
St.Lej., 67 GIAP				
LEBEDEV, Fyodor Mikhajlovich	17	+2	351	36
Maj., 482 IAP				

MAKSIMENKO, Vasilij Ivanovich Podpolk., 88 IAP	17 +8	516	
MANKEVICH, Viktor Mikhajlovich Maj., 163 IAP	17 +5	240	58
MARKIN, Nikolaj Vasilyevich St.Lej., 274 IAP; KIA 9-28-1943	17	220	42
MARTYNOV, Aleksandr Vasilyevich St.Lej., 296 IAP	17 +16		
MIKHAJLIK, Yakov Danilovich St.Lej., 211 IAP, 237 IAP, 54 GIAP; 7 V Stalingrad	17 +6	316	73
MILOVANOV, Aleksej Mikhajlovich Kap., 193 IAP; KIA 3-6-1944	17 +5	215	30
MISHUSTIN, Vasilij Ivanovich Maj., 88 GIAP; 1 aerial ramming	17 +8	388	68
MITROKHIN, Vasilij Borisovich Kap., 191 IAP	17	174	36
NEPRYAKHIN, Pavel Markovich St.Lej., 2 GIAP; 5 V 8-6-1943	17	149	28
NIKONOROV, Pyotr Mikhajlovich Lej., 88 GIAP	17 +5	167	44
OSIPENKO, Aleksandr Stepanovich Gen.Lej., 20 SAD, 8 IAK; all V Spain	17 +34	360	
PLEKHANOV, Andrej Filippovich Kap., 73 GIAP	17	621	
RYZHIJ, Leonid Kirillovich Kap., 347 IAP	17	250	89
SEREDA, Igor Yemelyanovich Lej., 240 IAP, 178 GIAP	17	159	27
SHAVURIN, Pyotr Ivanovich St.Lej., 722 IAP, 2 aerial rammings	17	350	
SHEVYRIN, Valentin Mikhajlovich St.Lej., 164 IAP	17	298	84
SOKOLOV, Leonid Mikhajlovich Maj., 107 GIAP	17 +6	230	62
SOMOV, Pyotr Arsentyevich St.Lej., 482 IAP	17 +1	102	24
ULITIN, Ivan Semyonovich Lej., 116 IAP; KIA 5-20-1944	17	202	64
VORONKO, Aleksandr Grigoryevich Maj., 63 GIAP	17	133	
ZALEVSKIJ, Vladimir Nikolayevich Kap., 157 IAP; KIA 7-5-1943; 1 aerial ramming	17 +23		
ABRAMCHUK, Nikolaj Ivanovich Kap., 894 IAP-PVO	16	300	
ADONKIN, Vasilij Semyonovich Maj., 78 IAP-SF, 255 IAP-SF; KIA 3-17-1944	16 +6	365	42
BARCHENKOV, Daniil Gavrilovich Kap., 897 IAP	16	230	39
BITSAYEV, Sergej Vladimirovich Lej., 845 IAP	16	263	
CHISTYAKOV, Yevgenij Mikhajlovich Ml.Lej., 92 IAP	16		
DANILENKO, Nikolaj Nikitovich Kap., 18 GIAP; 5 V Smolensk	16 +1	256	49
DILIGEJ, Nikolaj Kupriyanovich Maj., 9 IAP, 508 IAP, 213 GIAP	16 +3	200	30
DOGADAJLO, Aleksej Dmitriyevich St.Lej., 177 GIAP	16	220	43
GLOTOV, Nikolaj Ivanovich Ml.Lej., 129 GIAP	16 +8	334	
GOLUBEV, Vasilij Fyodorovich Podpolk., 13 IAP-KBF, 4 GIAP-KBF	16 +23	546	133
GONCHAR, Ivan Alekseyevich St.Lej., 89 GIAP; KIA 4-20-1945	16	87	28
GORBACHEVSKIJ, Aleksandr Ivanovich Kap., 29 GIAP	16 +7	386	78
GRACHYOV, Anatolij Aleksandrovich St.Lej., 272 IAP	16 +6	210	54
GROMAKOVSKIJ, Vladimir Aleksandrovich St.Lej., 176 GIAP	16	186	29

ISKRIN, Nikolaj Mikhajlovich St.Lej., 16 GIAP	16	297	80
KALSIN, Pyotr Terentyevich Lej., 5 GIAP; KIA 12-20-1943	16		
KARAVAJ, Pavel Petrovich Kap., 897 IAP	16 +7	145	27
KARNACH, Stepan Andreyevich Kap., 247 IAP	16 +4	346	84
KHARITONOV, Nikolaj Vasilyevich Kap., 520 IAP	16	300	100
KHOLODNYJ, Georgij Stepanovich Kap., 157 IAP	16 +1	169	38
KHRAMOV, Nikolaj Ivanovich Podpolk., St.lyotchik-inspektor	16 +4	327	113
KLESHCHYOV, Ivan Ivanovich Maj., 521 IAP, 434 IAP; KIFA 12-31-1942	16 +32		
KOBISKOJ, Aleksandr Sergeyevich St.Lej., 721 IAP	16	314	47
KOLESNICHENKO, Stepan Kalinovich St.Lej., 519 IAP; KIA 8-30-1943	16 +4	114	24
KOLOMIN, Pyotr Ivanovich Podpolk., 162 IAP	16 +7	326	75
KOLOMOYETS, Vasilij Nikolayevich Kap., 49 IAP, 162 IAP	16 +1	365	67
KOLYADIN, Viktor Ivanovich St.Lej., 68 GIAP	16	685	
KONYAEV, Pyotr Mikhajlovich St.Lej., 482 IAP	16 +1	165	35
KOTOV, Aleksandr Grigoryevich St.Lej., 32 GIAP	16	250	88
KOZICH, Ivan Semyonovich Starshina, 721 IAP	16 +4	423	31
KUDRYAVTSEV, D.I. Lej., 86 GIAP; KIA Oct., 1943; 11 V Leningrad Front	16		
KULESHOV, Vladimir Kuzmich St.Lej., 40 GIAP; KIA 11-3-1943; plus 4 e/a ground	16 +6	351	73
LAKEYEV, Ivan Alekseyevich Gen.Maj., 107 Eskadrilya, 15 GIAD; 12 V Spain	16 +20	312	50
LANDIK, Ivan Ivanovich Kap., 482 IAP; KIA 4-18-1945	16	160	38
LIKHOVID, Mikhail Stepanovich St.Lej., 298 IAP, 104 GIAP; KIA 8-12-1944; plus 6 e/a ground	16 +11	208	44
LUKIN, Vasilij Petrovich Kap., 287 IAP	16 +2	349	48
MANULIN, Mitrofan F. Lej., 86 GIAP; KIA Oct., 1943; 5 Fw 190s 10-x-1943	16		
MARKOV, Aleksej Ivanovich St.Lej., 32 GIAP	16	255	
MATSIYEVICH, Vasilij Antonovich Kap., 26 IAP-PVO	16 +6	196	44
MIKRYUKOV, Vitalij Vasilyevich Kap., 897 IAP; DOW 4-4-1945	16	226	34
MURASHKIN, Yakov Andreyevich Kap., 111 GIAP	16	214	40
PANKRATOV, Sergej Stepanovich Maj., 66 IAP	16 +9	264	52
PASHKEVICH, Aleksej Vasilyevich Maj., 63 GIAP; 4 V 9-19-1944	16	115	
PAVLOV, Aleksej Nikolayevich St.Lej., 156 GIAP	16	224	40
PISHKAN, Ivan Anikeyevich Kap., 91 GIAP	16 +35	421	
PYLAYEV, Yevgenij Alekseyevich Kap., 88 IAP, 159 GIAP; 5 V Kuban	16 +4	285	94
ROMANENKO, Ivan Ivanovich Kap., 774 IAP; 3 V 7-7-1943	16 +1	85	23
SELYUTIN, Arkadij Mikhajlovich Lej., 4 GIAP-KBF	16	222	25
SEMYONOV, Vladimir Fyodorovich St.Lej., 976 IAP	16	220	

SEREGIN, Vasilij Georgiyevich	16 +8	332	35
Maj., 168 IAP, 303 IAD			
SHAMANSKIJ, Anatolij Fyodorovich	16 +1	253	61
St.Lej., 156 GIAP			
SHCHEGOLEV, Vladimir Georgiyevich	16	346	52
Kap., 162 IAP; KIA 7-29-1944			
SHEMENDYUK, Pyotr Semyonovich	16 +8		
Kap., 158 IAP, 157 IAP			
SHISHKAN, Ilya Minovich	16		
St.Lej., 158 IAP; KIA 6-21-1943			
SHMAGAJLO, Vladimir Grigoryevich	16		
Rank or unit not established			
SHMAN, Valerij	16		
St.Lej., 4 IAP			
SHUMILOV, Ivan Petrovich	16	565	
Lej., 16 IAP; 1 aerial ramming			
SIDOROV, Ivan Dmitriyevich	16 +7	400	130
Kap., 92 IAP; KIA 7-5-1943			
SIDOROV, Nikolaj Grigoryevich	16 +3	334	59
Maj., 329 IAD			
SOBOLEV, Konstantin Fyodorovich	16 +3	168	93
Maj., 171 IAP			
SOMOV, Ivan Konstantinovich	16 +3	276	35
Lej., 86 GIAP			
SYRTSOV, Dmitrij Dmitriyevich	16	343	120
Maj., 866 IAP			
TATARENKO, Dmitrij Mitrofanovich	16	598	
Kap., 3 GIAP-KBF			
TIKHONOV, Nikolaj Viktorovich	16 +1	229	53
Kap., 42 IAP; KIA 9-10-1943			
TVELENEV, Mikhail Stepanovich	16 +28	290	110
St.Lej., 9 GIAP			
VOLOSHIN, Aleksandr Iovich	16 +4	293	65
St.Lej., 106 GIAP; 1 aerial ramming			
VYDRIGAN, Nikolaj Zakharovich	16 +2	629	57
St.Lej., 31 GIAP			
YAREMENKO, Yevgenij Mikhajlovich	16 +1	183	
Kap., 5 GIAP			
YASHIN, Viktor Nikolayevich	16	184	42
Kap., 133 IAP			
ZABEGAJLO, Ivan Ignatyevich	16 +6	326	99
St.Lej., 1 GIAP			
ZAJTSEV, Vasilij Vladimirovich	16	448	42
Maj., 482 IAP; 3 V 3-2-1944			
ZAKALYUK, Aleksej Semyonovich	16	594	90
Kap., 298 IAP, 104 GIAP			
ZHIDOV, Georgij Nikanorovich	16 +13		
Kap., 123 IAP-PVO, 27 GIAP			
ALEKSANDRYUK, Viktor Ilyich	15 +4	252	69
Lej., 171 IAP, 176 GIAP			
AMELIN, Aleksej Stepanovich	15	216	70
St.Lej., 240 IAP			
ANKUDINOV, Yegor Yefremovich	15	250	
Maj., 812 IAP; plus 4 e/a ground			
AZAROV, Yevgenij Aleksandrovich	15	339	101
Maj., 19 IAP; 1 aerial ramming			
BAJKOV, Georgij Ivanovich	15 +5	244	50
St.Lej., 9 GIAP			
BALANDIN, Vladimir Aleksandrovich	15 +1	228	30
St.Lej., 18 GIAP; KIA 12-30-1944; 7 V Smolensk			
BALASHOV, Georgij Sergeyevich	15	103	37
Kap., 402 IAP			
BASKOV, Vladimir Sergeyevich	15	293	88
Maj., 291 IAP			
BATAROV, Mikhail Fyodorovich	15 +1	322	72
Maj., 611 IAP			
BELIKOV, Oleg Stepanovich	15 +14	635	114
Kap., 19 IAP, 176 GIAP; 4 V 7-5-1943			
BEREZUTSKIJ, Ivan Mikhajlovich	15	223	73
Maj., 63 GIAP			

BERKUTOV, Aleksandr Maksimovich Podpolk., 101 GIAP	15	332	68
BEZVERKHIJ, Aleksej Ignatyevich St.Lej., 156 GIAP	15 +1	333	47
BONDAR, Aleksandr Alekseyevich St.Lej., 866 IAP	15	252	48
BRINKO, Pyotr Antonovich Kap., 13 IAP-KBF; KIA 9-14-1941; 2 aerial rammings	15		
BULAYEV, Aleksandr Dmitriyevich Maj., 159 IAP; KIA 5-17-1943	15 +8	269	
BUZINOV, Vadim Nikolayevich Kap., 148 IAP; plus 1 e/a ground	15	160	22
CHUDBIN, Leonid Sergeyevich St.Lej., 153 GIAP	15	274	45
CHUGUNOV, Viktor Konstantinovich Kap., 897 IAP; KIA 2-15-1945	15 +4	218	32
DEMENKOV, Sergej Vasilyevich St.Lej., 103 GIAP	15	358	78
DMITRIYEV, Nikolaj Pavlovich Maj., 5 GIAP	15	415	75
DOLNIKOV, Grigorij Ustinovich Rank not established, 100 GIAP	15 +1	160	42
DRANKO, Pyotr Aleksandrovich Maj., 1 GIAP, 89 GIAP	15	277	59
FYEDORCHUK, Igor Aleksandrovich Lej., 191 IAP, 67 GIAP	15	136	
GIRICH, Andrej Ivanovich Maj., 486 IAP	15 +7	479	
GOREGLYAD, Leonid Ivanovich Polk., 22 GIAD	15 +6	146	53
GORBUNOV, Nikolaj Ivanovich Kap., 31 IAP; KIA 10-12-1944	15	196	40
GRIB, Mikhail Ivanovich St.Lej., 6 GIAP-ChF	15	500	
GUSAROV, Nikolaj Mikhajlovich Maj., 486 IAP; 1 aerial ramming	15 +14	432	69
IVANOV, Nikolaj Pavlovich Podpolk., 63 GIAP; KIA 8-7-1943	15	50	
KALABUSHKIN, Ivan Nikolayevich Kap., 123 IAP, 562 IAP	15		
KOBYLETSKIJ, Ivan Ivanovich Maj., 43 IAP, 53 GIAP	15 +9	465	95
KONDRASHEV, Aleksandr Petrovich Kap., 66 GIAP	15	100	35
KONONENKO, Nikita Nikiforovich Kap., 297 IAP, 179 GIAP	15 +9	169	52
KONOVALOV, Sergej Ivanovich St.Lej., 150 GIAP	15 +1	161	26
KONUKOYEV, Nazir Tituyevich Podpolk., 43 IAP; plus 15 e/a ground	15	229	
KONYAEV, Arkadij Nikolayevich St.Lej., 32 IAP	15	150	49
KORSHUNOV, Konstantin Ionovich St.Lej., 29 GIAP	15 +3	508	91
KOSSA, Mikhail Ilyich St.Lej., 42 GIAP	15	375	
KOSTIKOV, Fyodor Mikhajlovich St.Lej., 43 IAP	15 +11	233	67
KRAVTSOV, Ivan Savelyevich St.Lej., 3 GIAP-KBF	15 +4	315	85
KRUPSKIJ, Viktor Iosifovich St.Lej., 760 IAP	15		
LAVRONENKO, Ivan Vasilyevich St.Lej., 239 IAP; KIA 6-6-1944	15	167	32
LAZAREV, Sergej Ivanovich St.Lej., 728 IAP; KIA 3-1-1945	15 +3	131	48
LUKYANOV, Sergej Ivanovich Maj., 16 GIAP, 100 GIAP; plus 2 e/a ground	15 +19	361	70
LYUSIN, Vladimir Nikolayevich St.Lej., 85 GIAP	15	205	

MALTSEV, Konstantin Savelyevich Kap., 177 GIAP	15	+1	180	32
MANOSHIN, Konstantin Vasilyevich Maj., 64 GIAP	15		132	38
MATVEYEV, Aleksandr Andreyevich Polk., 154 IAP, 275 IAD	15			
MIROSHNICHENKO, Dmitrij Grigoryevich St.Lej., 248 IAP	15		108	26
MOTORNIJ, Ivan Porfiryevich Kap., 512 IAP	15		435	117
NOSOV, Savelij Vasilyevich Lej., 150 GIAP	15	+1	101	31
ONISKYEVICH, Grigorij Demyanovich St.Lej., 164 IAP	15	+8	372	57
PASKO, Nikolaj Fyodorovich St.Lej., 28 GIAP	15		265	32
PETROV, Georgij Georgiyevich Kap., 154 IAP; KIA 6-13-1944	15	+9		
RYABCHEVSKIJ, Mikhail Fyodorovich Maj., 807 ShAP	15		192	
RYABTSEV, Mikhail Yevseyevich St.Lej., 2 GIAP	15		147	
SAVUSHKIN, Aleksandr Petrovich Kap., 11 GIAP; KIFA 5-17-1943; 4 V 9-29-1942	15		373	49
SEREDIN, Vladimir Alekseyevich Kap., 866 IAP; KIFA 4-6-1945; 1 aerial ramming	15		195	76
SHCHERBAKOV, Ivan Ivanovich Kap., 176 GIAP	15		123	20
SHEVTSOV, Aleksandr Grigoryevich Maj., 171 IAP	15		270	52
SHPUNYAKOV, Sergej Pavlovich St.Lej., 402 IAP; plus 5 e/a ground	15		335	51
SIROTIN, Vyacheslav Fyodorovich Kap., 17 IAP	15		233	
SITKOVSKIJ, Aleksandr Nikolayevich St.Lej., 15 IAP	15		105	40
SOBIN, Vasilij Vasilyevich St.Lej., 88 IAP, 159 GIAP; DOW 2-8-1944; 4 V Kuban	15		379	122
SOBOLEV, Afanasij Petrovich Podpolk., 2 GIAP	15	+9		
SPIRIDENKO, Nikolaj Kuzmich Maj., 172 IAP	15	+6	337	85
STARCHIKOV, Nikolaj Alekseyevich Kap., 16 GIAP	15	+1	389	72
SVITENKO, Nikolaj Ivanovich Podpolk., 7 IAP	15			
SYROMYATNIKOV, Sergej Vasilyevich Lej., 875 IAP, 66 GIAP; KIA 3-19-1943	15	+5	122	65
TSAPOV, Ivan Ivanovich Kap., 3 GIAP-KBF	15		530	58
TSYKIN, Mikhail Dmitriyevich Lej., 31 IAP	15	+6	437	68
TUSHEV, Ivan Timofeyevich Kap., 191 IAP	15	+1	534	45
TYULKIN, Mikhail Nikolayevich Maj., 515 IAP	15		254	64
UTSIN, A.N. Maj., 137 GIAP	15			
VASKO, Aleksandr Fyodorovich Lej., 176 GIAP	15		303	49
VOLKOV, Viktor Fyodorovich Maj., 157 IAP	15	+8	236	59
YEDKIN, Viktor Dmitriyevich Maj., 485 IAP, 72 GIAP	15	+3	294	53
YEGOROV, Nikolaj Sergeyevich St.Lej., 150 GIAP	15	+1	109	22
YELIZAROV, Sergej Mikhajlovich St.Lej., 9 GIAP	15	+3	200	70
ZABYRIN, Nikolaj Vladimirovich Lej., 106 GIAP	15		315	67

ZAJTSEV, Aleksandr Andreyevich	15			
Podpolk., 19 IAP, 70 IAP, 431 IAP; 8 V Spain				
ZAKHAROV, Konstantin Fyodorovich	15	+1	190	41
Kap., 233 IAP; KIA 1-13-1944				
ZELENIN, Ivan Maksimovich	15	+6		
Rank or unit not established				
AFANASYEV, Vladimir Ilyich	14	+3	260	
St.Lej., 145 GIAP				
AGANTSEV, Aleksandr Nikolayevich	14			
Rank or unit not established				
CHUPIKOV, Pavel Fyodorovich	14	+6	400	77
Polk., 40 IAP, 19 IAP, 176 GIAP				
DUGIN, Nikolaj Dmitriyevich	14		325	77
Kap., 402 IAP; KIA 5-2-1945; plus 6 e/a ground				
GOLUBIN, Ivan Filippovich	14			
Lej., 16 IAP-PVO; KIA 11-1-1942; 4 V 10-29-1941				
GOLUBOV, Anatolij Yemelyanovich	14		355	43
Podpolk., 18 GIAP, 303 IAD				
GOLYACHKOV, Leonid Dmitriyevich	14		281	43
Maj., 181 GIAP				
GUSKOV, Gavriil Gavriilovich	14		105	35
Ml.Lej., 65 GIAP; KIA 7-17-1943				
IGNATYEV, Nikolaj Petrovich	14	+15	365	63
Kap., 728 IAP				
ISHCHENKO, Vasilij Kalenikovich	14	+4	310	66
Maj., 1 GIAP				
IVANOV, Viktor Pavlovich	14	+4	556	33
Kap., 148 GIAP-PVO				
KATRICH, Aleksej Nikolayevich	14		250	
Lej., 27 IAP, 12 GIAP; 2 aerial rammings				
KISELYOV, Ivan Mikhajlovich	14	+2	156	25
St.Lej., 274 IAP				
KISELYOV, Sergej Ivanovich	14		225	38
Kap., 162 IAP; KIA 2-4-1945				
KOLTSOV, Aleksej Ivanovich	14	+6	222	60
Maj., 937 IAP; KIA 11-7-1943				
KONYEV, Georgij Nikolayevich	14	+18	312	98
Podpolk., 21 GIAP; KIA 12-30-1942				
KOZLOV, Aleksej Vasilyevich	14		304	
St.Lej., 118 ODRAE				
KUTAKHOV, Pavel Stepanovich	14	+28	367	79
Polk., 20 IAP, 19 GIAP				
KUZNETSOV, Nikolaj Aleksandrovich	14	+12	375	35
Maj., 191 IAP, 760 IAP				
LUKIN, Afanasij Petrovich	14	+4	325	120
Kap., 88 IAP, 159 GIAP; 6 V Kuban				
MASHKOVSKIJ, Stepan Filippovich	14	+17	280	
St.Lej., 32 IAP; 4 V Khalkhin Gol; 1 aerial ramming				
MEDVEDEV, Dmitrij Aleksandrovich	14	+15	298	
Podpolk., 486 IAP				
MOSKOVENKO, Vasilij Ivanovich	14	+3	175	37
St.Lej., 1 GIAP				
MURGA, Kirill Nikitich	14	+4		
Podpolk., 153 GIAP; 519 IAP				
NIKITIN, Aleksej Ivanovich	14			
Lej., 153 IAP				
NIKOLAYEV, Dmitrij Semyonovich	14		370	58
St.Lej., 27 GIAP-PVO				
ONOPCHENKO, Nikolaj Markovich	14		642	87
St.Lej., 163 GIAP; plus 1 e/a ground				
ORLOV, Aleksandr Ivanovich	14	+8	629	56
St.Lej., 5 GIAP				
ORLOV, Viktor Nikolayevich	14	+4	148	66
Kap., 133 GIAP; KIA 12-9-1943				
OSKALENKO, Dmitrij Yefimovich	14			
Kap., 26 IAP; KIA 9-26-1942; all V on I-16s				
PANOV, Aleksej Borisovich	14		241	41
Podpolk., 185 IAP, 67 GIAP; KIA 9-12-1944; 1 aerial ramming				
PCHYOLKIN, Aleksandr Ivanovich	14	+2	387	61
St.Lej., 5 GIAP				

RUDENKO, Anatolij Vladimirovich Rank not established, 28 IAP	14	350	
SEMENYUK, Zakhar Vladimirovich Maj., 512 IAP, 220 IAD	14 +4	357	95
SERZHANTOV, Ivan Yakovlevich Lej., 9 GIAP; DOW 4-29-1943	14 +8	258	85
SHADRIN, Gennadij Alekseyevich Maj., 177 GIAP	14	503	76
SHEVCHUK, Vasilij Mikhajlovich Maj., 247 IAP, 152 GIAP	14 +1	194	42
SHISHKIN, Aleksandr Pavlovich Maj., 434 IAP, 32 GIAP	14	132	67
SHISHOV, Vladimir Aleksandrovich Kap., 233 IAP	14	300	
SHVAREV, Aleksandr Yefimovich Rank not established, 201 IAD	14	445	
SIBIRIN, Semyon Alekseyevich Maj., 18 GIAP; 6 V Smolensk	14 +1	246	36
STROJKOV, Nikolaj Vasilyevich St.Lej., 213 GIAP	14 +21	245	66
SVISTUNOV, Anatolij Ivanovich Kap., 213 GIAP	14 +21	274	
TREGUBOV, Nikolaj Mikhajlovich Kap., 721 IAP; 6 V 7-6-1943	14 +3	411	58
TROFIMOV, Nikolaj Leontyevich Kap., 16 GIAP	14 +11	341	72
TROFIMOV, Yevgenij Fyodorovich Kap., 148 GIAP	14 +3		20
TSYGANOV, Yevgenij Terentyevich Kap., 13 IAP-KBF, 4 GIAP-KBF	14	492	65
UGLYANSKIJ, Pyotr St.Lej., 28 GIAP	14		
VARCHUK, Nikolaj Izotovich Maj., 737 IAP; KIA 9-21-1943	14 +9		
VERNIKOV, Yakov Ilyich Kap., 234 IAP, 147 GIAP	14 +1	302	64
ZAJTSEV, Aleksandr Petrovich Maj., 145 IAP; KIFA 5-30-1942	14 +21	200	
ZHERDEV, Nikolaj Prokofyevich Maj., 70 IAP, 821 IAP; KIA 11-15-1942	14	105 (+)	
ZUB, Ivan Andreyevich St.Lej., 111 GIAP	14		
ZYUZIN, Dmitrij Vasilyevich St.Lej., 11 GIAP-ChF	14	535	51
BAKLAN, Andrej Yakovlevich St.Lej., 434 IAP	13 +23	400	
BASULIN, Yevgenij Dmitriyevich Kap., 239 IAP	13 +1	88	25
BERKO, Aleksandr Maj., 42 IAP	13 +16		
BOBKOV, Valentin Vasilyevich Kap., 88 IAP, 812 IAP, 106 GIAP	13 +4	400	80
BOKIJ, Nikolaj Andreyevich Ml.Lej., 2 GIAP-SF, 11 GIAP-ChF	13	400	40
CHIZH, Vasilij Ivanovich Kap., 69 GIAP	13	232	53
DENCHIK, Nikolaj Fyodorovich St.Lej., 64 GIAP	13 +3	63	18
DENISOV, Konstantin Dmitriyevich Podpolk., 8 IAP-ChF, 7 IAP-ChF	13 +6	536	
FROLOV, Aleksandr Pavlovich Kap., 659 IAP	13 +7	475	
GARAM, Mikhail Aleksandrovich St.Lej., 434 IAP, 32 GIAP; DOW 6-28-1944; 1 aerial ramming	13	185	
GRISHIN, Aleksej Nikolayevich Kap., 153 GIAP	13	378	49
GROMOV, Georgij Vasilyevich Podpolk., 15 IAP	13	400	64
ISAYENKO, N.F. Rank not established, 611 IAP	13		

IVANOV, Vasilij Mitrofanovich Ml.Lej., 427 IAP	13	101	38
KARASYOV, Boris Ivanovich Kap., 88 IAP	13	509	
KHIMICH, Fyodor Vasilyevich Maj., 127 IAP, 282 IAD	13 +4	535	
KOVACHEVICH, Arkadij Fyodorovich St.Lej., 9 GIAP	13 +6	356	58
KOVALENKO, Aleksandr Andreyevich Kap., 2 GIAP-SF	13 +6	207	38
KRAVTSOV, Dmitrij Stepanovich Maj., 31 IAP	13 +8	430	80
LESHCHENKO, Vyacheslav Sergeyevich Lej., 4 IAP	13 +10	285	45
MAKAROV, Arkadij Sergeyevich St.Lej., 32 GIAP	13	132	51
MATIYENKO, Pyotr Andreyevich Maj., 270 IAP, 153 GIAP; KIFA 10-15-1944	13 +1	259	41
MATVEYEV, Vladimir Ivanovich Kap., 154 IAP; KIA 1-1-1942; 1 aerial ramming	13		
MERKVILADZE, Garri Aleksandrovich St.Lej., 152 GIAP	13 +2	386	87
MOROZOV, Arsenij Ivanovich St.Lej., 149 IAP; KIA 7-24-1944	13 +9	271	33
NAUMCHIK, Nikolaj Kuzmich Kap., 42 GIAP	13 +9	319	54
NOVOZHILOV, Ivan Vasilyevich Kap., 13 IAP	13 +7		
OBORIN, Aleksandr Vasilyevich Podpolk., 563 IAP, 438 IAP; KIA 8-7-1944; 2 aerial rammings	13 +13	283	119
PANIN, Pavel Alekseyevich Maj., 255 IAP-SF; KIA 8-26-1943	13	114	18
PILSHCHIKOV, Konstantin Aleksandrovich Maj., 168 IAP, 523 IAP	13	260	
POLUNOVSKIJ, Valerij Fyodorovich St.Lej., 845 IAP; KIA 3-27-1944; 1 aerial ramming	13		
RYZHOV, Yefgraf Mikhajlovich Maj., 32 IAP-ChF, 7 IAP-ChF; 1 aerial ramming	13 +6	250	54
SAVELYEV, Yevgenij Petrovich St.Lej., 106 GIAP	13 +3	244	47
SAVIN, V.I. St.Lej., 291 IAP; all V Kuban	13 +1		
SENCHENKO, Vladimir Petrovich Kap., 1 GIAP	13 +5	224	
SHAROV, Dmitrij Mikhajlovich Maj., 13 IAP-KBF	13 +4	274	46
SHEVELEV, Pavel Fyodorovich Kap., 67 GIAP	13 +2	189	
TIMOSHENKO, Afanasij Ivanovich Maj., 106 GIAP; KIA 3-3-1945	13	250	67
VOJTENKO, Stefan Yefimovich Maj., 6 GIAP-ChF; 1 V Winter War; plus 3 e/a ground	13	336	
YAKIMENKO, Anton Dmitriyevich Maj., 22 IAP, 67 IAP, 427 IAP, 150 GIAP; plus 3 V Khalkhin Gol	13 +35	241	29
ZAVARUKHIN, Pavel Filippovich Podpolk., 72 GIAP	13 +4	480	
ZOTOV, Matvej Ivanovich Maj., 427 IAP, 149 GIAP	13	163	52
ABDRASHITOV, Shamil Munasypovich Lej., 402 IAP; KIA 5-4-1944	12	155	17
ARKHIPOV, Vasilij St.Lej., 18 GIAP; KIA 6-8-1944	12		
ASTAKHOV, Ivan Mikhajlovich Kap., 49 IAP, 168 IAP; KIA 3-3-1944	12 +7	283	63
BAZAROV, Ivan Fyodorovich Kap., 247 IAP; KIA 11-22-1943	12	342	69
BENDELIANI, Chichiko Kajsarovich Maj., 43 IAP, 54 GIAP; KIA 7-20-1944; 1 aerial ramming	12 +20	400	72
BEREZKIN, Vyacheslav St.Lej., 16 GIAP	12		

BLAGOVESHCHENSKIJ, Aleksej Sergeyevich	12 +25	73	
Gen.Lej., 27 SAD, 2 IAK; all V Khasan 1938			
BOGOMAZOV, Grigorij Ivanovich	12 .+4	350	50
St.Lej., 158 IAP			
BURMATOV, Vladimir Aleksandrovich	12 +1	191	43
St.Lej., 255 IAP-SF			
CHERNYENKO, Vasilij Ivanovich	12 +8	235	37
St.Lej., 3 GIAP-KBF			
DUBENOK, Gennadij Sergeyevich	12 +11	372	
Kap., 53 GIAP			
FYODOROV, Fyodor Fyodorovich	12		
St.Lej., 629 IAP-PVO; 9 V Stalingrad			
GOLUBEV, Georgij Gordeyevich	12	252	56
St.Lej., 16 GIAP			
KAMENSHCHIKOV, Vladimir Grigoryevich	12 +37		
Lej., 126 IAP; KIA 5-22-1943			
KHOLZUNOV, Aleksej Ivanovich	12	265	87
St.Lej., 32 GIAP; KIA 3-7-1943; 7 V Stalingrad			
KISLYAK, Nikolaj Aleksandrovich	12	302	50
Kap., 11 GIAP-ChF			
KOZLOVSKIJ, Vasilij Ivanovich	12		50
Kap., 810 ShAP; plus 16 e/a ground			
KRETOV, Stepan Ivanovich	12		
Maj., 278 IAD			
KURZENKOV, Sergej Georgiyevich	12	225	
Kap., 78 IAP-SF			
LITVYAK, Lidiya Vladimirovna	12 +4	168	
Ml.Lej., 586 IAP, 437 IAP, 73 GIAP; KIA 8-1-1943			
LUTSKIJ, Vladimir Aleksandrovich	12	185	
Maj., 32 GIAP			
MIRONENKO, Aleksandr Alekseyevich	12 +4	629	32
Maj., 13 IAP-KBF			
NAUMOV, Pyotr Izotovich	12 +5	215	40
Maj., 201 IAD			
ODINTSOV, Mikhail Petrovich	12	215	
Maj., 820 ShAP, 155 GShAP			
POKROVSKIJ, Vladimir Pavlovich	12 +6	350	60
Kap., 2 GIAP-SF			
PROKOPENKO, Georgij Nikolayevich	12 +15	217	
Polk., 3 GIAP; KIA 7-14-1944			
PROVORIKHIN, Vladimir Borisovich	12	300	
St.Lej., 927 IAP			
RASSADKIN, Pyotr Alekseyevich	12	190	
Kap., 255 IAP-SF			
RIVKIN, Boris Mironovich	12 +7	176	95
Kap., 54 GIAP			
RYBIN, Ivan Petrovich	12	168	30
Maj., 148 IAP; KIA 4-26-1943			
SHAPIRO, Valentin Yefimovich	12	590	48
St.Lej., 31 GIAP			
SHARENKO, Vasilij Denisovich	12 +4	223	51
Maj., 45 IAP, 100 GIAP; KIA 7-30-1944			
SIDORENKO, Rostislav Ivanovich	12 +4	137	30
Kap., 897 IAP			
SKOBARIKHIN, Vitt Fyodorovich	12	169	23
Maj., 22 IAP, 10 GIAD; 5+6 V Khakhin Gol			
SNESARYOV, Vladimir Semyonovich	12 +4	302	32
St.Lej., 11 GIAP-ChF; 6 V Tuapse			
SOLOMATIN, Aleksej Frolovich	12 +15	266	108
Kap., 296 IAP; KIA 5-21-1943			
TELESHEVSKIJ, Mikhail Zakharovich	12	146	28
Kap., 148 IAP; MIA 5-7-1943			
YAKHNOV, Gennadij Mikhajlovich	12 +5	572	112
Maj., 33 IAP-PVO			
YEFREMOV, Vasilij Vasilyevich	12		
Kap., 5 GIAP; 5 V Russo-Finnish Winter War			
YUDIN, Aleksej Sergeyevich	12 +7	202	53
Maj., 183 IAP; KIA 1-8-1944			
ZABOLOTNYJ, Ivan Nikolayevich	12	110	20
St.Lej., 16 IAP-PVO; KIA 1-4-1942; 1 aerial ramming			

ZAMORIN, Ivan Aleksandrovich Polk., 523 IAP, 18 GIAP; 6 V Smolensk	12 +14		
ZHERDEV, Viktor Ivanovich Kap., 16 GIAP; KIA 1-13-1945	12		
ZUYEV, Mikhail Aleksandrovich Kap., 73 GIAD	12 +4	335	63
ARKHIPOV, Nikolaj Arsentyevich Kap., 32 IAP, 265 IAP; 5 V Byelorussia	11 +8	275	134
BAKHULENKOV, Ivan Petrovich St.Lej., 177 GIAP, 178 GIAP	11	346	
BLOKHIN, Ivan Ivanovich Maj., 239 IAP	11 +10	240	80
BUDANOVA, Yekaterina Vasilyevna St.Lej., 296 IAP, 73 GIAP; KIA 5-6-1943	11		
BURYAK, Nikolaj Vasilyevich St.Lej., 247 IAP	11 +1	254	84
CHAPCHAKHOV, Lazar Sergeyevich Maj., 38 IAP; KIA 4-13-1942; 5 V on I-153s	11 +19	268	59
CHERNOBAJ, Andrej Petrovich Lej., 875 IAP	11 +27	90	40
CHUVIN, Nikolaj Ivanovich St.Lej., 2 GShAP	11		
DANILOV, Stepan Pavlovich Gen.Maj., 56 IAP, 44 IAP, 7 IAK-PVO, 5 SAD, 287 IAD, 14 IAK	11	172 (+)	
DERGACH, Aleksej Nikolayevich Maj., 86 GIAP	11 +14	273	24
FILATOV, Grigorij Ivanovich St.Lej., 146 GIAP	11 +3	128	
FLEJSHMAN, Aleksej Dementyevich St.Lej., 4 IAP	11 +14	306	57
GORBATYUK, Yevgenij Mikhajlovich Maj., 28 IAP-PVO, 63 GIAP	11	347	
GORODNICHEV, Nikolaj Pavlovich Maj., 5 GIAP; KIA 3-1-1943	11	180	27
GOROVETS, Aleksandr Konstantinovich St.Lej., 166 IAP, 88 GIAP; KIA 7-6-1943; 9 V 7-6-1943	11 +6	74	11
KALARASH, Dmitrij Leontyevich Podpolk., 236 IAD; KIA 10-29-1942	11 +6	242	
KHIMUSHIN, Nikolaj Fyodorovich Lej., 106 GIAP; KIA 7-27-1943	11	192	49
KHLUD, Boris Alekseyevich Kap., 146 IAP	11 +1	327	52
KOSTYLEV, Georgij Dmitriyevich Kap., 3 GIAP-KBF	11 +32	418	112
KRAMARENKO, Sergej Makarovich St.Lej., 176 GIAP	11		
KUZENOV, Ivan Petrovich Ml.Lej., 66 GIAP	11	70	
LEGCHAKOV, Aleksandr M. Maj., 42 IAP, 133 GIAP	11 +2	274	
MARESYEV, Aleksej Petrovich Kap., 580 IAP, 63 GIAP; 7 V with artificial legs	11	86	
MOSHIN, Aleksandr Fyodorovich Kap., 56 IAP, 402 IAP, 32 GIAP; KIA 7-13-1943; 1 aerial ramming	11	299	29
NESTERENKO, Aleksej Markovich St.Lej., 171 IAP; KIA 8-26-1944	11		
NOVIKOV, Aleksej Ivanovich Kap., 17 IAP	11	242	34
NOVIKOV, Yegor Pavlovich Ml.Lej., 191 IAP; KIA 9-17-1941; 1 aerial ramming	11 +6	60	
ORLOV, Pavel Ivanovich Kap., 2 GIAP-SF; KIA 3-15-1943	11	276	24
PAVLOV, Grigorij Rodionovich St.Lej., 42 GIAP; plus 4 e/a ground	11 +5	378	60
PETRENKO, Yevgenij Vasilyevich Kap., 20 IAP-SF	11 +1	261	69
PIDTYKAN, Ivan Dmitriyevich St.Lej., 123 IAP-PVO; KIA 8-2-1942	11 +5	217	58
PLEKHANOV, Ivan Yefimovich Kap., 158 IAP	11 +2	244	34

RATNIKOV, Pyotr Petrovich Lej., 512 IAP, 53 GIAP; KIA 7-24-1943	11	+4	220	85
ROGOZHIN, Vasilij Aleksandrovich Ml.Lej., 236 IAP; KIA 10-25-1943	11	+5	124	
SAVCHENKO, Aleksandr Petrovich Kap., 127 IAP	11	+15	424	64
SELDYAKOV, Yurij Sergeyevich St.Lej., 34 IAP	11			
SHCHERBAKOV, Viktor Ivanovich St.Lej., 11 GIAP-ChF	11	+7	359	35
SHCHERBINA, Nikolaj Gavrilovich Kap., 26 GIAP; 3 NF V; plus 12 e/a ground	11		424	51
SHIPOV, Aleksandr Pavlovich Kap., 20 IAP-SF	11		68	21
SIDORENKO, Mark Lukyanovich Lej., 66 GIAP; KIA 3-27-1945	11		50	
SKRYABIN, Viktor Ivanovich St.Lej., 40 GIAP; KIA 4-12-1943	11	+3	198	33
SLEPENKOV, Yakov Zakharovich Podpolk., 21 IAP-KBF	11		90	10
STOLYAROV, Ivan St.Lej., 18 GIAP; KIA 10-14-1943	11			
SVEZHENTSEV, Fyodor Rank not established, 812 IAP; KIA 5-5-1943; 1 aerial ramming	11			
TARANENKO, Ivan Andreyevich Polk., 298 IAP, 294 IAD	11		265	50
TASHCHIYEV, Suren Kap., 11 GIAP-ChF; KIA 1944	11		400	
TERNOVOJ, Boris Yakovlevich Maj., 1007 IAP	11	+8		
TIKHONOV, Viktor Pavlovich Ml.Lej., 236 IAP; KIA 8-15-1943	11	+4	140	48
VLASOV, Nikolaj Ivanovich Podpolk., 42 IAP; KIA 1-27-1945; 1 aerial ramming	11		220	27
YEGOROV, Vasilij Vasilyevich St.Lej., 21 IAP	11	+1	315	16
YELDYSHEV, Anatolij Alekseyevich Lej., 910 IAP-PVO	11	+7	272	17
ZENKOVICH, Nikolaj Yakovlevich Kap., 2 GIAP	11		237	37
ZHUCHKOV, Tikhon Sviridovich St.Lej., 3 GIAP-KBF	11	+12	257	37
ALEKSEYEV, Konstantin Stepanovich Maj., 6 GIAP-ChF, 8 IAP-ChF, 25 IAP-ChF; 8 NF V	10		272	110
ALKIDOV, Vladimir Yakovlevich Lej., 434 IAP, 529 IAP	10		300	
ANISKIN, Aleksandr Dmitriyevich St.Lej., 32 GIAP; KIA 2-20-1943	10		295	105
ANTONENKO, Aleksej Kasyanovich Kap., 13 IAP-KBF, 5 IAP-KBF; KIA 7-26-1941	10			
BERESTNEV, Pavel Maksimovich St.Lej., 45 IAP, 100 GIAP	10	+2	131	32
DEKHTYARENKO, Andrej Nikolayevich St.Lej., 580 IAP; KIA 7-11-1942; plus 2 e/a ground	10		39	
GLOBIN, Nikolaj Ivanovich St.Lej., 525 ShAP	10		180	
GLUKHIKH, Ivan Mikhajlovich Kap., 271 IAP; plus 11 e/a ground	10	+4	141	38
GULTYAEV, Grigorij Kapitonovich Lej., 788 IAP	10	+5		
KULAGIN, Fyodor Zakharovich Lej., 42 GIAP	10	+3	252	56
KARNACHENOK, Nikolaj Aleksandrovich St.Lej., 434 IAP; KIA 9-22-1942	10		349	
KHARCHISTOV, Viktor Vladimirovich Kap., 153 GIAP	10		367	50
KHASIN, Viktor Yakovlevich Maj., 271 IAP; KIA 1-14-1944; plus 8 e/a ground	10	+5	656	257
KHRYAEV, Vasilij Ilyich Kap., 9 IAP-ChF; KIA 7-16-1943	10		201	56

KIRYANOV, Konstantin Andrianovich St.Lej., 875 IAP; KIA 8-27-1943	10	297	59
KOLOGRIVOV, Mikhail Mikhajlovich Kap., 6 GIAP-ChF	10 +2	583	130
KOMAROV, Viktor Stepanovich Maj., 630 IAP-PVO; KIFA 9-9-1945	10 +2	209	26
KOVAL, Dmitrij Ivanovich Lej., 45 IAP, 100 GIAP; KIA 5-8-1943	10 +3	127	26
KRYUCHKOV, Vasilij Yegorovich Kap., 163 IAP	10	572	117
KUCHERENKO, Pyotr St.Lej., 240 IAP; KIA 1943	10		
KUDRYA, Nikolaj Danilovich Ml.Lej., 45 IAP, 100 GIAP; KIA 5-26-1943	10	53	24
KUZNETSOV, Georgij Dmitriyevich Kap., 16 GIAP	10 +12	350	
KUZNETSOV, Ivan Aleksandrovich St.Lej., 107 GIAP	10	219	59
LOGINOV, Boris Aleksandrovich Lej., 29 GIAP	10 +2	172	32
LYUBIMOV, Ivan Stepanovich Polk., 32 IAP-ChF, 11 GIAP-ChF, 4 IAD-ChF	10		
MACHABELI, Mikhail Zakharovich St.Lej., 10 GIAP-KBF; POW 4-4-1944	10	204	
MAKARENKO, Nikolaj Fyodorovich Maj., 153 IAP	10	320	
MAKAROV, Sergej Vasilyevich Lej., 180 IAP; KIA 2-10-1942	10 +13	260	35
MAKSIMENKO, Aleksej Iosifovich Lej., 160 IAP	10 +11		
MASNEV, Aleksej Nikanorovich Kap., 13 IAP	10 +7	356	70
MIKHAJLICHENKO, Ivan Kharlampovich St.Lej., 667 ShAP, 141 GShAP	10	179	
MITROFANOV, Fyodor Vasilyevich Maj., 445 IAP, 562 IAP, 813 IAP; KIA 2-4-1945	10 +3	250	18
MOLODCHININ, Aleksej Yegorovich Kap., 1 GIAP	10 +7	163	27
MURAVITSKIJ, Luka Zakharovich St.Lej., 29 IAP; KIA 11-30-1941	10 +37		
MUSATOV, Fyodor Frolovich Maj., 168 GIAP; KIA 10-11-1944	10	284	
OBUKHOV, Timofej Petrovich Maj., 12 IAP	10 +2	263	
PARSHIN, Georgij Mikhajlovich Maj., 943 ShAP	10	253	
PAVLOV, Aleksandr Georgiyevich Kap., 41 GIAP	10 +16	392	83
PAVLOV, Pavel Ilyich Kap., 21 IAP-KBF	10 +3	557	40
PAVLOV, Pavel Ivanovich Podpolk., 21 IAP-KBF	10 +5	454	44
PETROV, Pyotr Mikhajlovich Kap., 68 IAP; KIA 11-23-1943	10		
PILIPENKO, Ivan Markovich Kap., 40 IAP; KIA 10-2-1942 ; plus 3 e/a ground	10 +29	520	82
POPOV, Georgij Timofeyevich St.Lej., 47 ShAP-KBF	10	150	
SAJKO, Aleksej N. Rank or unit not established	10	339	
SEMYONOV, V.G. St.Lej., 721 IAP	10	228	
SEREBRENNIKOV, Gennadij St.Lej., 148 IAP; KIA 7-12-1944	10		66
SERGOV, Aleksej Ivanovich Maj., 508 IAP	10 +17	331	
SHEVELEV, Sergej Nikolayevich Kap., 249 IAP	10 +2	135	34
SHPYNOV, Aleksandr St.Lej., 240 IAP	10	218	

SOKOLOV, A.F.	10 +4		
Kap., 2 GIAP			
SURAVESHKIN, Aleksej Semyonovich	10 +6		
St.Lej., 431 IAP			
TARASOV, Aleksej Kondratyevich	10	213	48
Kap., 20 IAP-SF			
VISHNEVETSKIJ, Konstantin Grigoryevich	10 +13	123	39
Kap., 298 IAP; KIA 7-30-1944			
YAKUBOV, Ilya Fomich	10	68	23
Lej., 653 IAP			
YEVTEYEV, Mikhail Ivanovich	10 +6	285	65
Kap., 11 GIAP			
ZAKHAROV, Georgij Nefyodovich	10	153	48
Gen.Maj., 43 IAD, 303 IAD; plus 6 V Spain			
BAKHIREV, Vasilij Andreyevich	9 +5	310	57
St.Lej., 162 IAP			
BELYASNIK, Pyotr Nikiforovich	9 +17	250	78
Kap., 126 IAP-PVO			
BYKOVSKIJ, Yevgenij Vlasovich	9	100	
Ml.Lej., 5 GIAP; KIA 4-27-1943			
CHULKOV, Ivan Denisovich	9 +2	187	
St.Lej., 41 IAP; KIA 2-2-1942			
DEVYATAYEV, Mikhail Petrovich	9	180	35
St.Lej., 104 GIAP			
DOGAYEV, Vladimir Ivanovich	9	105	
St.Lej., 622 ShAP			
DZYUBA, Ivan Mikhajlovich	9 +12	238	
Maj., 12 IAP			
GARKUSHA, Kuzma Dmitriyevich	9 +5	320	30
St.Lej., 907 IAP; plus 25 e/a ground			
GRACHYOV, Ivan'Petrovich	9 +4	102	
Ml.Lej., 191 IAP; KIA 9-14-1944			
ISAYEV, Nikolaj Vasilyevich	9 +4	280	38
Polk., 273 IAD			
KLIMOV, Pavel Dmitriyevich	9 +18	306	33
Kap., 2 GIAP-SF			
KOBLOV, Sergej Konstantinovich	9		17
St.Lej., 182 IAP-PVO			
KULAGIN, Vladimir Tarasovich	9		20
Lej., 248 IAP; KIA March, 1942; 2 aerial rammings			
LIPILIN, Aleksandr Alekseyevich	9	112	
St.Lej., 41 IAP			
MANOJLOV, Ivan Antonovich	9	190	
St.Lej., 774 IAP; KIA 12-17-1942			
OSETROV, Nikolaj Nikolayevich	9	118	35
Rank or unit not established			
PROKOPENKO, Fyodor Fyodorovich	9	126	
St.Lej., 32 GIAP			
SAKHAROV, Pavel Ivanovich	9	157	18
Kap., 78 IAP-SF			
SAMOKHVALOV, Nikolaj Stepanovich	9 +10	309	46
St.Lej., 126 IAP-PVO; KIA 8-14-1944			
SIGOV, Dmitrij Ivanovich	9 +6	123	52
Kap., 131 IAP; KIA 10-26-1942			
VASILYEV, Boris Mikhajlovich	9		35
St.Politruk, 44 IAD			
YEFIMOV, Matvej Andreyevich	9 +29	350	106
St.Lej., 3 GIAP-KBF; KIA 1-7-1943			
ZHUKOV, Mikhail Petrovich	9 +5	286	66
Ml.Lej., 158 IAP; KIA 1-12-1943; 1 aerial ramming			
ZINOVYEV, Ivan Ivanovich	9	102	
Kap., 108 GShAP; plus 87 e/a ground			
ZUDILOV, Ivan Sergeyevich	9 +3	125	19
Ml.Lej., 163 IAP			
ACHKASOV, Sergej Vasilyevich	8 +2	160	17
Lej., 16 IAP, 176 IAP; KIA 3-14-1943; 2 aerial rammings			
AFANASYEV, Boris Mikhajlovich	8 +1	367	23
St.Lej., 21 IAP			
BELOZEROV, Ivan Pavlovich	8	300	34
St.Lej., 6 GIAP-ChF			

BOCHKOV, Ivan Vasilyevich	8 +31	308	45
Kap., 19 GIAP; KIA 4-4-1943			
DEMENOK, Vasilij	8	48	18
Lej., 88 IAP; KIA 8-14-1941; 1 aerial ramming			
FOMCHENKOV, Konstantin Fyodorovich	8 +26	320	37
Maj., 145 IAP, 19 GIAP-; KIA 2-24-1944			
GORGOLYUK, Aleksandr Ivanovich	8 +5	376	48
St.Lej., 30 GIAP			
GORIN, Vasilij Alekseyevich	8 +9	310	
Lej., 15 ORAP-KBF			
GUBENKO, Anton Alekseyevich	8		
Polk., Unit not established; KIA 3-31-1939			
IGNATYEV, N.I.	8		
Lej., 27 IAP-SF; KIA 12-3-1943			
INDYK, Semyon Leontyevich	8	93	21
Podpolk., 194 IAP, 291 IAP, 107 GIAP			
KABEROV, Igor Aleksandrovich	8 +18	397	92
Kap., 3 GIAP-KBF			
KILDYSHEV, Ivan	8		
Rank not established, 5 GIAP; KIA 5-15-1943			
KLEPIKOV, Nikolaj Fyodorovich	8 +32	600	117
Kap., 41 GIAP; MIA 9-5-1943			
KOLESNIK, Vasilij Artemyovich	8 +13	462	106
Maj., 88 IAP, 805 IAP			
KRASNOYURCHENKO, Ivan Ivanovich	8 +16	111	55
Polk., 22 IAP, 43 IAP, 92 IAP, 102 IAD-PVO, 147 IAD-PVO, 9 IAK-PVO			
KUZNETSOV, Anatolij Ivanovich	8	270	60
Kap., 4 GIAP-KBF; KIA 2- 19-1943; plus 1 e/a ground			
LYSENKO, Nikolaj Kalistratovich	8	250	60
Podpolk., 218 ShAP, 74 GShAP			
MIKHAJLOV, Vladimir Aleksandrovich	8 +4	690	113
St.Lej., 163 GIAP			
NIKOLAYENKOV, Aleksandr Ignatyevich	8 +23	229	28
St.Lej., 126 IAP, 760 IAP; KIA 7-7-1943			
POSHIVALNIKOV, Stepan D.	8	138	27
Kap., 800 ShAP; KIA August, 1944			
PRIKAZCHIKOV, Aleksej Lukich	8 +12		49
Kap., 42 GIAP			
RAKHOV, Viktor Georgiyevich	8 +6	68	
St.Lej., 22 IAP; DOW 8-25-1939			
SEMYONOV, Fyodor Georgiyevich	8 +4	340	
Kap., 240 IAP; KIA 10-19-1944; plus 3 e/a ground			
SHCHAPOV, Boris Dmitriyevich	8	133	53
Ml.Lej., 144 GShAP; KIA 5-30-1944			
SILANTYEV, Aleksandr Petrovich	8	359	35
St.Lej., 160 IAP; plus 16 e/a ground			
SILIN, Pavel N.	8	218	48
Maj., 2 GIAP			
SIROSHTAN, Vasilij Vasilyevich	8 +1	421	
Rank not established, 512 IAP			
SOKOLOV, Anatolij Mikhajlovich	8	148	37
Batalyonnyj Komissar, 5 GIAP; KIA 1-25-1942			
STOLYAROV, Nikolaj Georgiyevich	8	185	
Kap., 667 ShAP, 141 GShAP			
STOROZHAKOV, Aleksej Nikolayevich	8 +3	152	25
St.Lej., 154 IAP; KIA 9-10-1941			
TALALIKHIN, Viktor Vasilyevich	8		
Ml.Lej., 177 IAP-PVO; KIA 10-27-1941; 1 nocturnal aerial ramming			
TRISHKIN, Aleksej V.	8		
St.Lej., 2 GIAP; KIA 1942			
TRUBACHENKO, Vasilij Petrovich	8	120	50
Kap., 22 IAP, 182 IAP; KIA 9-16-1941; all V Khalkhin Gol			
TYAPIN, Ivan Zakharovich	8	270	
Rank not established, 177 IAP-PVO			
YERSHOV, L.I.	8		
Rank not established, 629 IAP			
ZHIDOV, Georgij Nikonovich	8 +13	266	40
Kap., 123 IAP-PVO			
AZAROV, Sergej Semyonovich	7 +8	324	47
St.Lej., 57 GIAP; DOW 5-10-1943			

BAJSULTANOV, Alim Yusufovich Kap., 4 GIAP-KBF; KIA 9-28-1943	7	277	45
BAKHAREV, Yakov Lej., 485 IAP; KIA	7 +5		
BEGELDINOV, Talgat Yakupbekovich St.Lej., 144 GShAP	7	305	
CHABROV, Mikhail Stepanovich Kap., 111 GIAP	7		
EMIROV, Valentin Allakhiyarovich Kap., 926 IAP; KIA 9-10-1942; 1 aerial ramming	7	169	
FEOKTISTOV, Sergej Alekseyevich Kap., 568 ShAP, 187 GShAP	7 +4	146	
KALUZHNYJ, Pavel Pavlovich Maj., 146 GIAP-PVO	7 +9	200	40
KARDANOV, Kubati Lokmanovich Kap., 88 IAP	7 +12	550	90
KHITRIN, Vasilij Alekseyevich St.Lej., 29 IAP; KIA 10-18-1941	7	173	10
KHLOBYSTOV, Aleksej Stepanovich Kap., 147 IAP, 20 GIAP; KIA 12-13-1943; 3 aerial rammings	7 +24	335	
KOVATS, Pyotr Semyonovich St.Lej., 129 IAP; KIA 8-20-1941; 3 V Khalkhin Gol	7	78	26
KRIVOV, Dmitrij Ml.Lej., 240 IAP, 156 IAP	7	131	
KUSTOV,Igor Yefremovich St.Serzhant, 728 IAP; KIA 12-22-1943	7 +12	71	
LOMAKIN, Anatolij Georgiyevich St.Lej., 21 IAP-KBF; KIA 1-25-1944	7 +19	452	49
MARIN, Nikolaj G. Kap., 2 GIAP	7		
NESTERENKO, Grigorij Karpovich Lej., 291 IAP; KIA 10-21-1943	7 +1	55	23
POSTNOV, Aleksej Alekseyevich St.Lej., 88 GIAP	7 +3	457	136
REZNIKOV, Nikolaj M. Kap., 2 GIAP	7		
SAVENKOV, Nikolaj Konstantinovich St.Lej., 511 ORAP	7		
SHARONOV, Mikhail Fyodorovich St.Lej., 191 IAP; KIA 1-16-1944	7		
SOROKIN, Yevgenij St.Lej., 5 GIAP	7		
STETSENKO, Andrej Rank not established, 176 GIAP	7		
TAVADZE, David Elizbarovich Kap., 190 ShAP	7	109	
YELDYSHEV, Anatolij Petrovich Kap., 995 ShAP	7	160	
ZAJTSEV, Sergej Fomich Lej., 43 IAP; KIA 9-2-1941	7		
ZHIGARIN, Fyodor Aleksandrovich St.Lej., 299 ShAP	7	61	
ZHULOV, Fyodor Yegorovich Ml.Lej., 235 ShAP; KIA 4-23-1944; plus 8 e/a ground	7	108	
AGEYEV, Pyotr Grigoryevich St.Lej., 182 IAP	6 +1	160	
ANUFRIYEV, Mitrofan Alekseyevich Maj., 523 IAP	6 +2	487	42
BUTKO, Aleksandr Sergeyevich St.Lej., 667 ShAP	6	118	
DZUSOV, Ibragim Magometovich Gen.Maj., 45 IAP, 216 IAD, 6 IAK	6	89	11
FYODOROV, Konstantin Feofilaktovich Maj., 18 GIAP	6	150	
GAJDAYENKO, I.D. Kap., 19 GIAP	6 +23		
GERMAN, Ivan Moiseyevich Maj., 74 GShAP, 70 GShAP; plus 30 e/a ground	6	91	27
GODOVIKOV, Aleksej Nikolayevich Politruk, 740 IAP; KIA 2-7-1942; 1 aerial ramming	6	170	

GOSHKO, S. Rank not established, 11 IAP	6 +8		
KALACHEV, Vladimir Nikolayevich Maj., 22 IAP, 35 IAP, 15 IAP; KIA 6-28-1942; 2 V Khalkhin Gol	6 +2		
KARPOV, Aleksandr Aleksandrovich St.Lej., 806 ShAP	6	127	
KOZACHENKO, Pyotr Konstantinovich Maj., 249 IAP; KIA 3-18-1945	6	155	26
KOZHANOV, Pyotr Pavlovich Kap., 4 GIAP-KBF; KIA 4-22-1943	6 +3	386	59
KRYUKOV, Pavel Pavlovich Maj., 16 GIAP	6 +1	415	40
KUNITSA, Semyon Andreyevich St.Politruk, 69 IAP; KIA 8-28-1941	6		
LIKHACHEV, Viktor Kirillovich Lej., 106 GIAP	6	181	15
LVOV, Semyon Ivanovich Kap., 3 GIAP-KBF	6 +22	280	98
MARCHENKO, Ivan Timofeyevich Kap., 30 ORAP-ChF	6	417	
MARIN, Viktor Aleksandrovich St.Lej., 294 IAD	6 +6	160	
MATAKOV, Vasilij Nikolayevich St.Lej., 27 IAP-PVO	6	163	
MAKSIMOV, Nikolaj Vasilyevich Kap., 624 ShAP; plus 9 e/a ground	6 +12	131	
ORLOV, M.I. St.Lej., 213 GIAP	6 +3		
SELIFONOV, Ivan Ivanovich St Lej., 106 GIAP	6 +2	110	
SMIRNOV, Viktor Petrovich Starshina, 629 IAP; KIA 10-2-1942	6	129	37
STOLYAROV, Nikolaj Ivanovich Lej., 629 IAP; all V Stalingrad	6 +4	310	67
STRELNIKOV, Vasilij Polikarpovich Kap., 78 IAP-SF	6	150	14
TARAKANCHIKOV, N.Ye. Lej., 34 IAP-PVO	6 +9		
TSOKOLAYEV, Gennadij Dmitriyevich St.Lej., 4 GIAP-KBF	6 +11	309	38
USKOV, Vasilij Mikhajlovich Kap., 234 IAP	6	36	
VOROBYOV, Ivan Alekseyevich Maj., 76 GShAP; plus 12 e/a ground	6 +6	388	
VORONIN, Viktor Fyodorovich Maj., 190 ShAP; KIA 7-12-1944; plus 16 e/a ground	6	81	
YEMELYANOV, Ivan Alekseyevich Maj., 622 ShAP; plus 24 e/a ground	6	71	
ZUYEV, Gavril Prokofyevich Kap., 427 IAP	6 +2	46	
ABRAMOV, Vladimir Fyodorovich Kap., 10 GIAP-KBF	5 +15	287	57
BAKHCHIVANDZHI, Grigorij Yakovlevich Kap., 402 IAP; KIFA 3-27-1943	5 +10	65	26
BATYREV, Pyotr Mikhajlovich Kap., 163 GIAP; KIA 9-30-1944	5 +1	330	52
BUSLOV, Fyodor Vasilyevich St.Lej., 136 GShAP; plus 7 e/a ground	5	183	56
CHECHELASHVILI, Otari Grigoryevich Kap., 141 GShAP	5 +10	220	43
DANILOV, Grigorij Semyonovich St.Serzhant, 807 ShAP	5	58	
DRACHENKO, Ivan Grigoryevich Ml.Lej., 140 GShAP; plus 9 e/a ground	5	178	24
DYAKOV, Pyotr Mikhajlovich St.Lej., 683 ShAP; KIA 2-16-1945	5	130	22
GALKIN, Mikhail Petrovich Lej., 4 IAP; KIA 7-21-1942	5	58	18
GARANIN, Vladimir Ivanovich Ml.Lej., 254 IAP	5 +1	130	

GEJBO, Iosif Ivanovich	5	177	
Polk., 6 GIAD			
GES, Grigorij Ivanovich	5	21	20
Kap., Unit not established; plus 9 V Korea 1950-53			
GOPNIK, Khaskel Moiseyevich	5	122	
Maj., 948 ShAP			
GRIGORYEV, Ivan Ivanovich	5	155	31
St.Lej., 93 GShAP; KIA 5-8-1945			
KANAYEV, Aleksej Fyodorovich	5	120	
St.Lej., 451 ShAP			
KARMANOV, Afanasij G.	5		
Kap., 4 IAP; KIA 7-21-1941			
KOKOREV, Dmitrij Vasilyevich	5	100	
Ml.Lej., 124 IAP; KIA 10-12-1941; 1 aerial ramming			
KONDAKOV, Viktor Aleksandrovich	5	149	
Maj., 136 GShAP; DOW 10-13-1944			
KONDRAT, Yemelyan Filaretovich	5		
Polk., 2 GIAP			
KOVTYLEV, Dmitrij Filippovich	5 +7	141	44
Ml.Lej., 518 IAP			
KRIVOSHEYEV, Yefim Avtonomovich	5 +15	96	29
Lej., 19 GIAP; KIA 9-9-1942			
KRYUKOV, Konstantin Alekseyevich	5 +10	297	24
St.Lej., 27 IAP, 12 GIAP; KIA 12-9-1943			
LEONOV, Ivan Dmitriyevich	5 +4	267	
Kap., 85 GIAP; KIA 5-30-1944			
MESHCHERYAKOV, Ivan Ivanovich	5	135	15
Kap., 5 GIAP; KIA 2-8-1942			
MIGUNOV, Vasilij Vasilyevich	5	170	
St.Lej., 29 IAP; KIA 3-31-1942			
MIKHAJLOV, Yevgenij Vitalyevich	5	92	22
Lej., 32 GIAP; KIA 3-17-1944			
MIRONOV, Viktor Petrovich	5	127	25
St.Lej., 145 IAP, 19 GIAP; KIFA 2-16-1943			
MOSHKOV, Boris Nikolayevich	5	106	
St.Lej., 431 ShAP			
NEGRIYENKO, Boris Alekseyevich	5 +1	191	25
St.Lej., 3 GIAP-KBF; all V Fw 190s			
OSIPOV, Mikhail Mikhajlovich	5 +3	127	26
Lej., 8 IAP; MIA 5-26-1943			
PANFILOV, Yevgenij	5	275	30
St.Lej., 126 IAP, 148 IAP; KIA 8-12-1942			
PETROV, Nikolaj Stepanovich	5 +6	170	
Lej., 141 GShAP			
PIROZHKOV, Boris Grigoryevich	5	242	
St.Lej., 787 IAP; DOW 9-4-1942; 2 aerial rammings			
REPNIKOV, Nikolaj Fyodorovich	5	51	
St.Lej., 152 IAP; KIA 12-4-1941; 1 aerial ramming			
RODIONOV, Mikhail Aleksandrovich	5	242	
Ml.Lej., 562 IAP; KIA 6-3-1942; 1 aerial ramming			
RYABOSHAPKO, Vasilij Ya.	5		
St.Serzhant, 299 ShAP			
SELIVERSTOV, Kuzma Yegorovich	5 +2	132	
Lej., 55 IAP; KIA 10-15-1941			
SHLEPOV, Viktor Petrovich	5 +16	685	122
Kap., 41 GIAP			
SOLOVYOV, Konstantin Vladimirovich	5 +10	427	65
Maj., 71 IAP-KBF; KIA 12-27-1942; 1 He 111 at night on I-153			
TARANENKO, Vasilij	5 +3		
Starshina, 485 IAP; KIA			
URSUL, Sergej Grigoryevich	5	94	
Lej., 157 IAP			

Appendix II
TOPS AND FIRSTS

Top-scoring Soviet ace of WW II
I.N. Kozhedub (62 victories)

Top-scoring Soviet Navy ace of WW II
B.F. Safonov (30 victories)

Top-scoring Soviet ace of Spanish Civil War (1936/39)
S.I. Gritsevets (30 victories)

Top-scoring Soviet ace of Khalkhin Gol conflict (1939)
S.I. Gritsevets (12 victories)

Top-scoring Soviet ace of Russo-Finnish Winter War (1939/40)
V.V. Yefremov (5 victories)

Top-scoring woman fighter pilot
L.V. Litvyak (12 victories)

Top-scoring Shturmovik ace
M.F. Ryabchevskij (15 victories)

Top-scoring strafing ace
I.I. Zinovyev (87 ground kills)

Most kills in a single sortie
A.K. Gorovets (9 victories on 7-6-1943)

Most aerial rammings
B.I. Kovzan (4)

Most fractional credits
V.M. Najdenko (57)

Most aerial encounters
V.M. Najdenko (350)

Most sorties
P.A. Pilyutov (1,945)

First regiment to reach 500 kills
5 GIAP (8-29-1943)

Top-scoring fighter regiment
5 GIAP (739 victories)

Top-scoring Soviet ace of Korean War (1950/53)
N.V. Sutyagin (22 victories)

First Soviet jet-ace of Korean War
S.I. Naumenko (scored his 5th kill on 12-24-1950)

First Soviet ace of Korean War to down 5 jets
F.A. Shabanov (5-20-1951)

Most jet-kills in a single day
M.S. Ponomarev (4 on 9-11-1951)

Most jet-kills in a single sortie
A.N. Karasyov (3 F-84s on 9-19-1950)

Appendix III
EQUIVALENT RANKS

VVS	Luftwaffe	USAAF
General Polkovnik	Generaloberst	Colonel General
General Lejtenant	Generalleutnant	Lieutenant General
General Major	Generalmajor	Major General
Polkovnik	Oberst	Colonel
Podpolkovnik	Oberstleutnant	Lieutenant Colonel
Major	Major	Major
Kapitan	Hauptmann	Captain
Starshij Lejtenant	Oberleutnant	Lieutenant
Lejtenant	Leutnant	2nd Lieutenant
Mladshij Lejtenant	–	Flight Officer
Starshina	Oberfeldwebel	Staff Sergeant
Serzhant	Feldwebel	–
Mladshij Serzhant	Unteroffizier	–
–	Obergefreiter	
Yefrejtor	Gefreiter	
Lyotchik	Flieger	

Appendix IV
USAAF REPORT ON AERIAL ENCOUNTER WITH RUSSIAN AIRCRAFT

On November 7, 1944, Yaks under the leadership of Hero of the Soviet Union A.I. Koldunov became inadvertantly engaged in combat with 15th USAAF P-38s over Yugoslavia, with several of the the Lightnings being shot down. The following material relating to this incident was supplied through the courtesy of the Air Force Historical Research Agency, Maxwell AFB, Alabama.

HEADQUARTERS
82ND FIGHTER GROUP
Office of the Intelligence Officer

A-3 Tactics

7 November 1944.

MISSION NO. 829 95th, 96th, 97th Squadrons. Sjenica, Novi Pazar, Raska,
NARRATIVE REPORT Mitrovica, Yugoslavia.

1. MISSION AND TARGET: To strafe M/T on roads from Sjenica to Novi Pazar, to Raska, to Mitrovica, Yugoslavia.

2. AIRCRAFT AND CHRONOLOGY: 60 P-38's took off by 0857 hours; 2 returned early (mechanical); 16 P-38's strafed between Sjenica and Novi Pazar between 1015 and 1040 hours; 21 P-38's strafed between Maglic, Raska, Mitrovica, and Pristina between 1020 and 1130 hours; 21 P-38's provided top cover from 1015 to 1130 hours; 2 P-38's lost; 1 P-38 missing; 55 P-38's down by 1305 hours.

	Took off	Early returns	Target	Missing	Down
95th	25	0	25	2	23
96th	17	1	16	1	15
97th	18	1	17	0	17
	60	2	58	3	55

3. ROUTE: 95th and 97th Squadrons - Base to Bijelo Polje for 250 miles; to 15 miles north of Raska for 55 miles; to Maglic for 10 miles; to Raska for 25 miles; to Mitrovica for 30 miles; to Pristina for 25 miles; to base for 305 miles. 96th Squadron - Base to Bijelo Polje for 250 miles; to Sjenica for 15 miles; to Novi Pazar for 30 miles; to Ibar River between Raska and Mitrovica for 15 miles; to Pristina for 30 miles; to base for 310 miles. Total mileage: 700 miles.

4. FORMATION AND ASSAULT: 95th led with 97th on left and 96th on right on route out at 12,000 feet. 96th started down at Bijelo Polje and strafed on deck along road between Sjenica to Novi Pazar. 95th and 97th continued at 12,000 feet to point 15 miles north of Raska where 95th spiraled down towards the deck. On the way down a locomotive was seen near Maglic. 95th turned north, went to the deck and destroyed the locomotive; it then turned south and strafed M/T along road between Maglic, Raska, Mitrovica, and Pristina. Mitrovica and Pristina were not definitely identified by all pilots as 95th was attacked between these points by fighters later identified as Russian. 97th flew top cover at 14,000 feet and one flight of the 95th Squadron stayed up and did not strafe.

5. RESULTS OF BOMBING: None.

6. STRAFING: Totals - Destroyed 3 oil trucks, 28 trucks, 4 staff cars, 1 warehouse, 2 locomotives, 1 cart. Damaged 22 trucks, 25 railroad cars, 1 radio station.

Individual results:
95th Squadron:
Col. Edminson - 1 locomotive destroyed, 2 oil trucks (burned), 2 staff cars destroyed, 2 six wheel and 4 cargo trucks burned.

1.

47C

destroyed

Lt. Olsen - 2 trucks, 1 damaged
Lt. Col. Wray - 1 warehouse destroyed; 10 RR cars damaged
Lt. Blurock - 2 trucks and 1 staff car strafed; 1 radio station strafe
Lt. Tough - 1 cart destroyed
Lt. Black - 2 trucks strafed
Lt. Small - 1 staff car (blue) destroyed; 3 trucks damaged
Lt. Carr - 3 trucks destroyed (1 pulling cannon); 2 trucks damaged
Lt. Kennedy - 3 trucks destroyed (burned); 1 damaged
Lt. Hardy - strafed trucks
Lt. Blumer - Strafed 2 trucks and 1 train
Lt. Wilson - 1 locomotive and 1 six wheel German truck full of troops; destroyed; strafed 15 railroad cars
Lt. Anderson - strafed 1 truck
Capt. Coffelt - destroyed 1 six wheel German truck with troops; strafed 1 truck and 1 trailer
Lt. Brookman - destroyed 1 gas truck (burned); strafed 2 trucks
Lt. Stakem - destroyed 1 truck (burned)
Lt. Hague - damaged 2 trucks
Lt. Armstrong - strafed 1 recon car and 1 van truck

96th Squadron:

Lt. Loehr - 4 trucks strafed
Lt. Sprague - made 3 passes at truck convoy
Lt. Sides - strafed 4 - 5 trucks.
Lt. gustafson - strafed 4 - 5 trucks - 1 destroyed (burned)
Lt. Malojki - destroyed 1 truck (burned)
Lt. Jelke - strafed trucks - no claims
Lt. Burgess - strafed 2 trucks
Lt. Bardwell - strafed 1 truck
Lt. Noel - destroyed 1 truck (burned)
Lt. Kielar - destroyed 3 turcks ((burned)
Capt King - 3 passes on 15/20 truck convoy - 3 seen to burn
Lt. Howard - strafed 15/20 truck convoy - 1 destroyed (burned)
Lt. Barrier - destroyed 1 truck (burned); strafed 2 additional
Lt. Leszczynski - strafed 1 truck
Lt. Spiegal - strafed 2 trucks
Lt. Andrews - strafed 5 trucks

7. ENEMY AERIAL ACTIVITY: None.

As the P-38's were pulling up from the deck, the top cover reported that 8/8 aircraft were taking off from a field immediately in front of them. A s the leading P-38's peeled up and away a Yak pulled his nose up immediately after take off and shot one P-38 down. It is thought that this was Lt. Brewer. One Yak crossed below Lt. Urton and broke into him and a general dogfight started in which 4 P-38's and 6 Yaks were engaged. Lt. Urton recognized one plane that he was shooting at as a Yak and called to his flight that they were friendly. Just then someone called to Lt. Urton to break and he looked back to see a Yak on his tail shooting at him at close range. Lt. Blumer shot this Yak down in flames. The other Yaks continued to press the attack and a second one was hit and went spiraling down smoking. A third was hit while on a P-38's tail and left the fight. Lt. Coulson was last seen in this fight and was probably one of the P-38's seen to crash and burn by each pilot in the fight. This dogfight finally separated and when Lt. Urton waggled his

2.

CONFIDENTIAL

wings the Yaks did the same and allowed the P-38's to withdraw.

Col. Edwinson's flight pulled up near the A/D and saw three s/e fighters taking off. At the same time one at about 2,000 feet made a head on pass at them firing. The P-38's broke into him and after two or three passes Lt. Blurock got on his tail and saw hits. This plane's wheels dropped part way down and he started pouring smoke. After this fight was over a s/e that appeared to be a Spit 9 gave the wing signals from a distance and was answered by Col. Edwinson. Lt. Katschke was flying at about 7,000 feet as part of the top cover when he saw a s/e a/c take off from the L/G and then pull up and shoot a P-38 down in flames as the P-38 was peeling up. Lt. Katschke was unable to identify the plane but supposed it was an enemy and dived on it and shot it down from 3,000 to 4,000 feet. He saw the red star on the aircraft as it spun in and crashed.

En route to the target the 96th Squadron saw 4 T/E unidentified A/C about 10 miles west of Sjenica flying at 1,500 feet headed northwest. These were seen from 2,500 feet and were thought to be FE 2's.

8. FLAK: Intense accurate light flak and small arms fire from M/T on roads and from all towns in target area was encountered; also 20 and 40 mm. fire on hills along road; moderate inaccurate heavy flak from Raska and from unidentified A/D; intense accurate light and heavy from Mitrovica. 1 plane lost to flak; 5 ships holed.

9. SIGNIFICANT OBSERVATIONS: (a) Trucks were spaced at 50' intervals from Sjenica to Novi Pazar.
(b) Pilots report blue uniforms on personnel.

10. WEATHER: Clear but hazy.

11. AIR SEA RESCUE: None.

12. RADIO SECURITY: Satisfactory.

13. FRIENDLY A/C IN TROUBLE: None.

14. ENEMY A/C DESTROYED BY OTHER GROUPS: None.

15. VICTORIES AND LOSSES:
Lt. Katschke - destroyed 1 Yak. Lt. Blumer - destroyed 1 Yak.
Lt. Blurock - probably destroyed 1 Yak. Lt. Urton - probably destroyed 1 Yak. damaged 1 Yak.

Losses: 3 P-38's.
Capt. King - hit by flak and crash landed with both engines on fire against side of a mountain near Sjenica.
Lt. Brewer - shot down by Yak about ½ mile north of an unidentified airdrome.
Lt. Coulson - last seen at beginning of encounter with Yaks - probably 1 of 2 P-38's seen to crash.

Damage to our planes: 5 P-38's holed by flak.

16. SORTIES: 60 aircraft sorties; 2 non effective sorties; 58 effective sorties; 57 pilot mission credits.

3.

17. FORMATION AND FLIGHT LEADERS: 95th - Col. Edwinson (formation leader), Lts. F. C. Kennedy, Tough, Wilson, Urton, and Stakem. 96th - Lts. Loehr, Malejki, Noel, Barrier. 97th - Lts. Durell, Sims, Phillips, and Davis.

18. COMMENTS: None.

19. CORRECTIONS TO TELEPHONIC REPORT: None.

HENRY E. COLLINS,
1st Lt., Air Corps,
Intelligence Officer.

WAR DEPARTMENT
CLASSIFIED MESSAGE CENTER
INCOMING CLASSIFIED MESSAGE

TOP SECRET

URGENT

Col Geyer copy

From: Allied Force Headquarters, Caserta, Italy

To: War Department

Nr: F 57991 25 November 1944

Reur WX 65531. F 57991 for Marshall from Eaker signed McNarney. T[redacted]T.

Following text of release scheduled for November 29 if Deane agrees. Have sent complete text to Deane to obtain his concurrence.

"Early this month, a squadron of 15th AAF Lightnings, flying always less than 50 feet from the ground through mountain passes of Yugoslavia at more than 200 miles per hour, often under sharp attack from light flak, missed their assigned target through navigational error and strafed a column of Red Army Troops. Russian Yak fighters, protecting the column, attacked the US Lightnings and shot down two of them.

Before the leaders of the groups of Allied fighters could establish recognition, two Yaks were shot down by US Lightnings. The Russian leader then courageously closed with the American leader and flew formation until identities were clearly confirmed and all fighters immediately broke off combat. Among those killed by the strafing was Russian Lieutenant General Kotov.

At the direction of Lieutenant General Ira C. Eaker, Commander in Chief, Mediterranean Allied Air Forces, there was an immediate investigation of the tragic incident. All facts were submitted to the Combined Chiefs of Staff in

CM-IN-24936 (25 Nov 44)

GEN. LOOTZENHEISER:
Be sure Col Rex Smith's office sees – should discuss with Gen. F Smith
L.S.K.

MC7967

COPY NO. 10

WAR DEPARTMENT
CLASSIFIED MESSAGE CENTER
INCOMING CLASSIFIED MESSAGE

URGENT

Page 2.

From: Allied Force Headquarters, Caserta, Italy

Nr: F 57991 25 November 1944

Washington. After careful examination of all the evidence, it was decided that the sole reason was navigational error on the part of the leader of the strafing squadron, a group commander with more than 4,000 flying hours of experience, both in this theater and in Alaska.

The request for the strafing came through Balkan Air Force, based on the needs for air effort to trap and destroy the Germans trying to move north through Yugoslavia. Two groups of P 38's of the 15th AAF were assigned to the strafing; all squadrons except one strafed the assigned areas.

This was no new type of mission for the 15th AAF; between the 18th of August and the date of this incident, bombers and fighters of the 15th had carried out 37 missions in direct support of the forces of the Red Army and Marshal Tito in Hungary and Yugoslavia. On these missions, 621 German aircraft were destroyed and 306 damaged by the fighters and bombers of the 15th. Many enemy trucks and tanks and railroad cars were also destroyed on these support operations. On none of them was there any incident of damage to other than enemy objective, with the exception of the strafing mission of this single squadron on November 7th.

The following message concerning this incident has been sent to the Red Army General Staff by the Joint Chiefs of Staff:

CM-IN-24936 (25 Nov 44)

COPY NO. 10

THE MAKING OF AN EXACT COPY OF THIS MESSAGE IS FORBIDDEN

WAR DEPARTMENT
CLASSIFIED MESSAGE CENTER
INCOMING CLASSIFIED MESSAGE

TOP SECRET

URGENT

Page 3.

From: Allied Force Headquarters, Caserta, Italy

Nr: F 57991 25 November 1944

"The attack by US Lightnings on a Soviet column in Yugoslavia on November 7 has been completely investigated.

This investigation indicates that the strafing between Nis and Aleksinac was carried out by one squadron of a group which had been sent to attack enemy columns and rail movements between Sjenica, Novi Pazar, Raska and Mitrovica. Upon the split up of the group, this squadron headed for its assigned section of the target, flying at tree top level. Upon arrival at what the leader believed to be Novi Pazar, heavy traffic was observed and the column was immediately strafed.

Upon completion of the strafing run, this squadron was justifiably attacked by Soviet fighters defending their column, and in the first clash one Lightning was shop down. The US leader then recognized the Soviet markings, but before he could disengage his unit from the ensuing air fight, another Lightning and two or three Soviet fighters were shot down. The Soviet Flight Leader courageously closed into formation with the US Flight Leader and mutual identification was confirmed.

The squadron which made the strafing run was personnally led by a Group Commander who was an experienced combat pilot, having flown more than 4,000 hours. The group had been briefed carefully on its assigned target. A navigational error by the leader, together with striking similarity between the map appearance of the target briefed

CM-IN-24936 (25 Nov 44)

COPY NO. 10

THE MAKING OF AN EXACT COPY OF THIS MESSAGE IS FORBIDDEN

WAR DEPARTMENT
CLASSIFIED MESSAGE CENTER
INCOMING CLASSIFIED MESSAGE

SECRET

URGENT

Page 4.

From: Allied Force Headquarters, Caserta, Italy

Nr: F 57991 25 November 1944

and the target actually attacked, made the leader feel positive as to the identifications of the communication lines he was attacking. All personnel of the mission were equally sure that this was the correct target until gun camera film was developed which established positively that the wrong road had been strafed. The two roads are approximately 45 miles, or less than 10 minutes flying time, apart.

After careful analysis we find that this regrettable incident has resulted from a type of error which has occured in all theaters of war and which we have been unable to eliminate entirely even with the exercise of the greatest care and foresight. In our experience, it has been demonstrated that the best method of preventing such incidents is to maintain close liaison between the air and ground forces involved. This is particularly true in fast offensive operations, such as our break through in France. Between August 18 and November 11 the 15th Air Force has flown 37 bombing and strafing missions near Soviet lines in Yugoslavia and Hungary against the escape routes of retreating Nazi columns. In these missions 621 enemy aircraft have been destroyed, 306 others damaged, as well as large numbers of railway rolling stock, vehicles and Germans destroyed. The incident of November 7 is the only known error which has occurred.

NO (LSK)

The Group Commander who led the attacking squadron has been relieved of his command. Additional restrictions have now been imposed in this theater which normally prohibit

NO! (LSK)

CM-IN-24936 (25 Nov 44)

10

COPY NO.

WAR DEPARTMENT
CLASSIFIED MESSAGE CENTER
INCOMING CLASSIFIED MESSAGE

SECRET

URGENT

Page 5.

From: Allied Force Headquarters, Caserta, Italy

Nr: F 57991 25 November 1944

tactical air operations closer than 80 miles from known Soviet positions. Exceptions to these restrictions will be made only by agreement and after special briefing.

The Joint Chiefs of Staff again express deep regret at the occurence of such an incident. We feel that we must continue our efforts to develop a system of close liaison between operational headquarters with a view to eliminating the possibility of mistakes, while at the same time continuing the large contribution to the destruction of the common enemy which can be attained through close cooperation of our air and ground forces in the field" and this message was sent by General Wilson, Supreme Allied Commander Mediterranean:

NO (LSK)

"I learn with sincere regret of the unfortunate encounter between United States elements of the Mediterranean Allied Air Forces and Red Army and Air Force elements on 7 November. Washington further advised of the tragic death of Lieutenant General Kotov and others as a result of the incident.

The United States Flight Leader had been directed to attack columns of German troops expected to be moving northward on roads nearer the Adriatic Coast, my investigation reveals. The column of Red troops was attacked by Flight Leader through a navigational error in the belief that it was the column of German troops which he had been directed to attack and so the unfortunate chain of events started. Apparently seeing the column which he was bound to protect

CM-IN-24936 (25 Nov 44)

COPY NO. 10

WAR DEPARTMENT
CLASSIFIED MESSAGE CENTER
INCOMING CLASSIFIED MESSAGE

SECRET

URGENT

Page 6.

From: Allied Force Headquarters, Caserta, Italy

Nr: F 57991 25 November 1944

under air attack, the Soviet Flight Leader engaged the attackers. Two United States fighters were shot down in the ensuing battle as well as two Red fighters before identification could be established. To Captain Koldunov of the Red Air Force high tribute must be paid in this connection for his courage and quick thinking by exposing himself in order to identify his flight as friendly and so terminate the engagement.

In view of the strenuous efforts of our respective forces to destroy the maximum number of the German invaders, it is especially regrettable that an incident of this kind should occur. This happening is, I know, a direct result of that zealousness to advance the cause of the war against our common enemy.

The Air Forces are studying the extension of means to prevent a repetition of this event and it will be the subject of further signals.

My admiration for the magnificent accomplishments of the Red Army and Air Force and my hope for their further successes let me take this occasion to express" the Commander in Chief of Mediterranean Allied Air Forces, Lieutenant General Ira C. Eaker, sent this message

"I am most grieved to hear of the unfortunate incident whereby fighters of this Command inadvertently strafed a Red Army column and clashed with Red Air Force fighters. The knowledge of the death of your distinguished

CM-IN-24936 (25 Nov 44)

COPY No. 10

THE MAKING OF AN EXACT COPY OF THIS MESSAGE IS FORBIDDEN

WAR DEPARTMENT
CLASSIFIED MESSAGE CENTER
INCOMING CLASSIFIED MESSAGE

TOP SECRET

URGENT

Page 7.

From: Allied Force Headquarters, Caserta, Italy

Nr: F 57991 25 November 1944

Lieutenant General Kotov particularly shocked me. My investigation reveals this incident to have been a result of a navigational error on the part of the United States Flight Leader. Please accept my heartfelt regrets for the incident, and be assured that every precaution has been taken to prevent such errors in the future."

End

ACTION: General Hull

INFORMATION: General Arnold
General Bissell
General Surles
CofS

CM-IN-24936 (25Nov 44) 2308Z bjm

COPY NO. 10

WAR DEPARTMENT
CLASSIFIED MESSAGE CENTER

OUTGOING MESSAGE

TOP SECRET

Joint Chiefs of Staff
77500

19 November 1944

U.S. Military Mission
Moscow, Russia

Commanding General
Allied Force Headquarters
Caserta, Italy

Commanding General
Mediterranean Allied Air Forces
Caserta, Italy

Number WARX 65545

[illegible] to Deane for action to McNarney and Eaker for information from the Joint Chief of Staff.

You should present the following to the Red Army General Staff from the Joint Chiefs of Staff:

"Detailed investigation of the attack by United States Lightnings on a Soviet Column in Yugoslavia on 7 November has been completed. The results of this investigation show that the strafing between Nis and Aleksinac was carried out by one squadron of a group which had been dispatched to attack enemy columns and rail movements between Sjenica, Novi Pazar, Raska and Mitrovica. After group split-up, this squadron headed for its assigned portion of the target at treetop level. Arriving at what the leader thought to be Novi Pazar, heavy traffic was observed and the column was immediately strafed. At the completion of the strafing run, squadron was justifiably attacked by Soviet fighters defending their column and one lightning was shot down in the first clash. The U.S. leader then recognized the Soviet markings, but before he could disengage his unit from the ensuing air fight, another Lightning and two or three Soviet fighters were shot down. The Soviet Flight Leader courageously closed into formation with the U. S. flight leader and mutual identification was confirmed.

CM-OUT 65545 (19 Nov 44)

MC7839

COPY No. 35

THE MAKING OF AN EX[illegible]Y OF THIS MESSAGE IS FORBIDDEN

WAR DEPARTMENT
CLASSIFIED MESSAGE CENTER

OUTGOING MESSAGE

Number WARX 65545 - 2 - 19 November 1944

The Group Commander who personally led the squadron which made the strafing run was an experienced combat pilot, having flown more than 4,000 hours. The group was carefully briefed on their assigned target. A navigational error by the leader, together with striking similarity between the map appearance of the target briefed and the target actually attacked, caused the leader to feel positive as to the identification of the communication lines he was attacking. All personnel on the mission were equally certain that this was the correct target until gun camera film was developed which positively established that the wrong road had been attacked. The respective roads are approximately 45 miles, or less than ten minutes flying time, apart. After careful analysis, we find that this regrettable incident has resulted from a type of error which has occurred in all theaters of war and which we have been unable to eliminate entirely, even with the exercise of the greatest care and foresight. In our experience, it has been demonstrated that the best way to prevent such indicents is to maintain close liaison between air and ground forces involved. This is particularly true in fast offinsive operations, such as our breakthrough in France.

Between 18 August and 11 November, the Fifteenth Air Force has flown 37 bombing and strafing missions near Soviet lines in Yugoslavia and Hungary against the escape route of retreating Nazi columns. These missions have resulted in the destruction of 621 enemy aircraft and damage to 306 others, as well as destruction of large numbers of railway rolling stock, vehicles and Germans. The incident of 7 November is the only known error that has occurred.

The Group Commander who led the attacking squadron has been relieved of his command. Additional restrictions have now been applied in this theater normally prohibiting tactical air operations closer than 80 miles from known Soviet positions. Exceptions to these restrictions will be made only by agreement and after special briefing.

CM-OUT 65545 (19 Nov 44)

COPY No. 35

THE MAKING OF AN EXACT COPY OF THIS MESSAGE IS FORBIDDEN

WAR DEPARTMENT
CLASSIFIED MESSAGE CENTER

OUTGOING MESSAGE

TOP SECRET

Number WARX 65545 - 3 - 19 November 1944

The Joint Chiefs of Staff again express their deep regret that such an incident has occurred. We feel that we must continue our efforts to develop a system of close liaison between operational headquarters with a view to eliminating the possibility of mistakes while at the same time retaining the material contribution to the destruction of the common enemy that can be attained through close cooperation of our air and ground forces in the field."

In MX-36696, November 10 and MX-37011, November 13, both from Eaker, you now have copies of all available information on the results of the investigation of this incident. Copies of the detailed report referred to in the latter message will be forwarded to you by courier.

End

ORIGINATOR: JCS

INFORMATION: ADM. LEAHY
GEN. ARNOLD
GEN. HULL
GEN. BISSELL
ADM. KING
C of S

CM-OUT 65545 (19 Nov 44) 1958Z om

THE MAKING OF AN EXACT COPY OF THIS MESSAGE IS FORBIDDEN 35

24-75724

GLOSSARY

ChF	CHERNOMORSKIJ FLOT. The Black Sea Fleet
e/a	enemy aircraft
eskadrilya	squadron
free hunt	in Russian: SVOBODNAYA OKHOTA. A fighter sweep for the purpose of destroying targets of opportunity
Guards	certain military units and naval vessels were designated Guards by virtue of having distinguished themselves in combat. The first such titles were awarded on September 18, 1941.
GIAD	GVARDEJSKAYA ISTREBITELNAYA AVIATSIONNAYA DIVIZIYA. Guards Fighter Air Division
GIAP	GVARDEJSKIJ ISTREBITELNYJ AVIATSIONNYJ POLK. Guards Fighter Air Regiment.
GShAD	GVARDEJSKAYA SHTURMOVAYA AVIATSIONNAYA DIVIZIYA. Guards Ground-attack Air Division
GShAP	GVARDEJSKIJ SHTURMOVOJ AVIATSIONNYJ POLK. Guards Ground-attack air Regiment
Honorifics	Honorary titles awarded to units which had distinguished themselves in particular battles or campaigns
IAD	ISTREBITELNAYA AVIATSIONNAYA DIVIZIYA. Fighter Air Division
IAP	ISTREBITELNYJ AVIATSIONNYJ POLK. Fighter Air Regiment
Il-2, Il-10	The excellent ground-attack planes evolved by the aircraft designer Ilyushin
I-16	Soviet single-seat fighter monoplane evolved by the Polikarpov design bureau
I-153	Soviet fighter biplane evolved by Polikarpov. Dubbed CHAJKA (gull) by Russian pilots.
KBF	KRASNOZNAMENNYJ BALTIJSKIJ FLOT. The Red Banner Baltic Fleet
Khudoj	literally: skinny or scrawny. Soviet service slang for the Bf 109 fighter
KIA	killed in action
KIFA	killed in flying accident
komissar	A Soviet political officer attached to headquarters of all units above the size of a battalion for political indoctrination
LaGG-3	Soviet fighter plane evolved by the experimental design bureau of Lavochkin, Gorbunov and Gudkov
La-5, La-7	Soviet fighter planes evolved by S.A. Lavochkin. German and Finnish pilots incorrectly called them LaGG-5s resp. LaGG-7s
Lapot or Lapotnik	literally: "bast shoe." Soviet service slang for the Junkers Ju 87. The appellation resulted from the aircraft's mainwheels resembling the traditional Russian bast shoes.
Letayushchij tank	literally: flying tank. Unofficial appellation for the Il-2 ground-attack plane
Messer	a popular Russian abbreviation for the Messerschmitt Bf 109 and Bf 110
MIA	missing in action
Mushka	literally: fly. Nickname for the I-16
ORAP	OTDELNYJ RAZVEDYVATELNYJ AVIATSIONNYJ POLK. Independent Reconnaissance Aviation Regiment
para	a two-plane formation. The smallest tactical element in the VVS
politruk	abbreviation for POLITICHESKIJ RUKOVODITEL. Literally: political leader. A Soviet political officer attached to the headquarters of all units smaller than a battalion for the purpose of political indoctrination and supervision
PVO	PROTIVOVOZDUSHNAYA OBORONA. The Soviet air defense forces
RVGK	REZERV VERKHOVNOGO GLAVNOGO KOMANDOVANIYA. Reserves of the Supreme High Command
Samolyot soldat	literally: "soldier airplane." Nickname for the Il-2 ground-attack plane
ShAD	SHTURMOVAYA AVIATSIONNAYA DIVIZIYA. Ground-attack Aviation Division
ShAP	SHTURMOVOJ AVIATSIONNYJ POLK. Ground-attack Aviation Regiment
shturman	navigator
SF	SEVERNYJ FLOT. The Northern Fleet
ShKAS	Soviet machine guns designed by B.G. Shpitalnyj and I.A. Komaritskij
ShVAK	Soviet cannon designed by B.G. Shpitalnyj and S.V. Vladimirov:
SMERSH	Short for Smert Shpionam (death to the spies). A counter-intelligence unit subordinate to the NKVD, devoted to the protection of information against espionage, personnel against subversion and installations against sabotage.
STAVKA	also: STAVKA VERKHOVNOGO GLAVNOGO KOMANDOVANIYA. The supreme high command general headquarters
taran	the deliberate ramming of an enemy aircraft
VA	VOZDUSHNAYA ARMIYA. Air army
VMF	VOYENNO-MORSKOJ FLOT. Soviet Navy
VVS	VOYENNO-VOZDUSHNYE SILY. The Soviet Air Force
VYa	Soviet cannon designed by A.A. Volkov and S.A. Yartsev
Yastreb	literally: hawk. Nichname for the I-16
Yastrebok	literally: little hawk. Nickname for the I-16
zveno	flight, a four-plane formation

BIBLIOGRAPHY

MAGAZINES

Aviatsiya i kosmonavtika
Krylya rodinu
Morskoj sbornik
Sovyetskij voin
Voenno-istoricheskij zhurnal
As – aviatsionnyj zhurnal
Mir aviatsii

ENCYCLOPAEDIAS

Soobshcheniya Sovyetskogo Informbyuro, Moscow, 1944-45, 8 vols.

Sovyetskaya voennaya entsiklopediya, Moscow, 1976-80, 8 vols.

Velikaya Otechestvennaya voina 1941-1945. Slovar-spravochnik. Moscow, 1985

Grif sekretnosti snyat. Poteri vooruzhennykh sil SSSR v vojoakh, boevikh dejstviyakh i voennykh konfliktakh, Moscow, 1993

SOVIET REPUBLICS AND MILITARY DISTRICTS

Sovyetskaya Armeniya v gody Velikoj Otechestvennoj Vojny, Erevan, 1975

Krasnoznamennyj Byelorusskij voennyj okrug Minsk, 1973

Istoriya ordena Lenina Leningradskogo voennogo okruga, Moscow, 1974

Istoriya ordena Lenina Leningradskogo voennogo okruga, Moscow, 1988

Krasnoznamennyj Severo-Kavkazkij, Moscow, 1990

Krasnoznamennyj Turkestanskij, Moscow, 1988

Chuvashskaya ASSR v period Velikoj Otechestvennoj voiny, Cheboksary, 1975

Gorkovchane v Velikoj Otechestvennoj voine, Gorkij, 1970

Khersonskaya oblast v gody Velikoj Otechestvennoj vojny, Odessa, 1968

Moldavskaya SSR v Velikoj Otechestvennoj Vojne Sovyetskogo Soyuza, Kishinyov, 1975-76, 2 vols.

Ordena Lenina Moskovskij Voennyj okrug, Moscow, 1977

Ordena Lenina Zabajkalskij Moscow, 1980

Zakavkazkij front Velikoj Otechestvennoj Vojny, Tbilisi, 1971

V plameni i slave. Ocherki istorii Sibirskogo voennogo okruga, Novosibirsk, 1969

STUDIES OF MAJOR BATTLES AND CAMPAIGNS

Na Byelgorodskom napravlenii, Byelgorod, 1963

Poslednij shturm. Berlinskaya operatsiya, Moscow, 1970

P.S. Belan: Kazakhstantsy v boyakh za osvobozhdeniye Byelorussii Sovyetskoj Pribaltiki, Alma Ata, 1988

A.A. Kiselev: Murmansk-gorod geroj, Moscow, 1988

N.G. Andronikov, et al.: Bitva pod Moskvoj, Moscow, 1989

Narodnyj podvig v bitve za Kavkaz Moscow, 1981

Khalkhin Gol, Moscow, 1990

Leto 1941 Ukraina, Kiev, 1991

Za oevobozhdeniya Chekhoslovakii, Moscow, 1965

Tvoi osvoboditeli, Donbas, Donetsk, 1976

B.S. Venkov: Geroi Karpat, Uzhgorod, 1972

V ogne Kurskoj bitvy, Kursk, 1963

Na ognennoj duge, Moscow, 1963

Kurskaya bitva, Moscow, 1970

My iz Kronshtadta, Leningrad, 1975

Slavnaya pobeda pod Leningradom, Leningrad, 1975

V ognennom koltse, Moscow, 1963

V.I. Dmitriyev: Salyut Leningrada 1941-1944, Moscow, 1959

Oborona Leningrada 1941-1944, Leningrad, 1968

A.V. Burov: Blokada den za dnyem, Leningrad, 1979

Dorogoj muzhestva, Leningrad, 1964

Geroi osvobozhdeniya Prikarpatya, Uzhgorod, 1970

Dvesti ognennykh dnej, Moscow, 1968

A.D. Kolesnik: O tekh, kto zashchishchal Stalingrad, Moscow, 1973

Na Severo-Zapadnom fronte 1941-1943, Moscow, 1969

Slava bessmertna. O geroyakh Sovyetskogo Soyuza, uchastnikakh razgroma Gitlerovtsev v Vostochnoj Prussi, Kaliningrad, 1963

Yassko-Kishinyovskiye kanny, Moscow, 1964

SOVIET AIR FORCE

M.I. Golyshev: Sertsa krylatykh, Moscow, 1961

N.M. Skomorokhov et al.: Voenno-vozdushnaya akademiya imeni Yu.A.Gagarina Moscow, 1984

A.I. Shakhurin: Krylya pobedy, Moscow, 1990

A.N. Ponomarev: Sovyetskiye aviatsionnye konstroktury Moscow, 1990

Ye.Ye. Smirnov: Vybirayu aviatsiyu, Moscow, 1989

V.S. Shumikhin et al.: Vozdushnaya moshch Rodiny Moscow, 1988

M.N. Kozhevnikov: Komandovaniye i shtab VVS Sovyetskoj armii v Velikoj Otechestvennoj vojne 1941-1945gg Moscow, 1977

V nebe – lyotchiki baltiki, Tallin, 1974

I.V. Timokhovich: Operativnoye iskusstvo Sovyetskikh VVS v Velikoj Otechestvennoj voine Moscow, 1976

Aviatsiya i kosmonavtika SSSR, Moscow, 1968

I.N. Berezovoj: Tak srazhalis gvardejtsy Moscow, 1960

A.G. Fyodorov: Aviatsiya v bitve pod Moskvoj Moscow, 1975

N.A. Shmelev: Ogon s neba, Yaroslavl, 1972

N. Shtuchkin: Groznoye nebo Moskvy, Moscow, 1972

S.V. Chernousov: V nebe Donskom, Rostov-on-Don, 1974

Ya.A. Sukhorukov: Zhivaya pamyat, Moscow, 1967

Sokoly – ocherki o lyotchikakh, srazhavshikhsya za Leningrad Leningrad, 1971

Za chistoye nebo, Leningrad, 1978
Krylatye bogatyri, Leningrad, 1965
P.N.Ivanov: Krylya nad morem, Moscow, 1973

SOVIET FIGHTER ARM
V.F. Tolubko: Na grani vozmozhnogo, Moscow, 1990
A.P. Kalinin: Istrebiteli nad "Goluboj liniej" Moscow, 1963
V. Rylnikov: Na krylyakh muzhestva, Moscow, 1973
I.P. Byelozerov: V nebe Tavrii, Simferopol, 1975
A. Kuliyev: Do vstrechi v Berline, Baku, 1975
G.A. Pshenyanik: V nebe Severnogo Kavkaza Nalchik, 1975
F.A. Vazhin: Vozdushnyj taran, Moscow, 1962
M.V. Novikov: Molnii pod krylom, Moscow, 1973

UNIT HISTORIES

GENERAL
V. Achkasov/B.Vajner: Krasnoznamennyj Baltijskij flot v Velikoj Otechestvennoj vojne, Moscow, 1957
B. Vajner: Severnyj flot v Velikoj Otechestvennoj vojne Moscow, 1964
Vojska PVO strany v Velikoj Otechestvennoj Vojne 1941-1945/ kratkaya khronika, Moscow, 1981
Dvazhdy Krasnoznamennyj Baltijskij flot, Moscow, 1990
P.P. Bochkarev, N.I.Parygin: Gody v ognennom nebe. Aviatsiya dalnego dejstviya, Moscow, 1991

VARIOUS UNITS
(1 GIAP) G.Kh.Dyachenko: Nasledniki Nesterova, Moscow, 1963
(1 GIAD) G.A.Chechelnitskij: Srazhalis lyotchiki istrebiteli, Moscow, 1964
(1 GIAK) F-A. Kostenko: Korpus krylatoj gvardii – boevoj put 1-go Gvardejskogo
istrebitelnogo aviatsionnogo Minskogo Krasnoznamennogo korpusa 19421945gg, Moscow, 1974
(2 GIAP) A. Semyonov/B. Dashtseren: Eskadrilya "Mongolskij arat", Moscow, 1978
(2 VA) 2-ye vozdushnaya armiya v boyakh za Rodinu, Monino, 1965
(4 VA) K.A. Vershinin: Chetvertaya vozdushnaya, Moscow, 1975
(5 GIAP) N.G. Ilyin/V.P. Rulin: Gvardejtsy v vozdukhe, Moscow, 1973
(5 VA) S.M. Davtyan: Pyataya vozdushnaya, Moscow, 1990
(6 IAK) 6-j Istrebitelnyj aviatsionnyj korpus PVO v bitve pod Moskvoj, Moscow, 1974
(6 VA) F.P. Polynin: Boevye marshruty, Moscow, 1981
(8 VA) B.A. Gubin/V.A.Kiselyov: Vosmaya vozdushnaya, Moscow, 1986
(9 GIAD) Yu. Zhukov: Odin MiG iz tysyachi, Moscow, 1963
(15 VA) G.A. Chechelnitskij: Lyotchiki na vojne – voenno istoricheskij ocherk o boevom puti 15-j Vozdushnoj armii, Moscow, 1974
(16 VA) G.K. Prussakov et al.: 16-ya Vozdushnaya – voenno istoricheskij ocherk o boevom puti 16-j Vozdushnoj armii, Moscow, 1973
(17 VA) 17-ya Vozdushnaya armiya v boyakh ot Stalingrada do Veny, Moscow, 1977
(18 GIAP) F.S. Gnezdilov: Na vysotakh muzhestva Minsk, 1987
(88 IAP) G.A. Pshenyachik: Doletim do Odera Moscow, 1985
(586 IAP) Z. Seidmamedova: Zapiski lyotchitsy Baku, 1969
(761 IAP) , I. Kurguzov: Zvezdy nad Pribaltikoj Moscow, 1973

MEMOIRS
A.N. Bibijchuk: Chelovek, nebo, kosmos, Moscow, 1979
K.D. Denisov: Pod nami – Chernoye more, Moscow, 1989
M.P. Devyatayev: Pobed iz ada, Saransk, 1974
G.G. Golubev: V pare s "Sotym", Moscow, 1978
I.N. Kozhedub: Vernost otchizne, Moscow, 1975
A.L. Kozhevnikov: Zapiski istrebitelya, Moscow, 1959
A.L. Kozhevnikov: Startuyet muzhestvo, Moscow, 1966
S.A. Krasovskij: Zhizn v aviatsii, Moscow, 1960
S.G. Kurzenkov: Pod nami zemlya i more, Moscow, 1967
V.D. Lavrinenkov: Vozvrashcheniye v nebo, Moscow, 1974
S.D. Luganskij: Na glubokikh virazhakh, Alma Ata, 1966
Ya.D. Mikhajlik: Sokolinaya semya, Moscow, 1971
A.I. Pokryshkin: Krylya istrebitelya, Moscow, 1948
A.I. Pokryshkin: Nebo vojny, Moscow, 1975
A.I. Pokryshkin: Poznat sebya v boyu, Moscow, 1993
I.A. Prachik: Frontovoye nebo, Moscow, 1984
I.I. Pstygo: Na boevom kurse, Moscow, 1989
G.A. Rechkalov: Dymnoye nebo vojny, Sverdlovsk, 1968
G.A. Rechkalov: V nebe Moldavii, Kishinyov, 1967
S.I. Rudenko: Krylya pobedy, Moscow, 1976
Ye.Ya. Savitskij: Polveka s nebom, Moscow, 1988
A.F. Semyonov: Na vzlete, Moscow, 1969
V.M. Shevchuk: Komandir atakuyet pervym, Moscow, 1980
N.S. Skripko: Po tselyam blizhnim i dalnim, Moscow, 1981
Z. Sorokin: V nebe Zapolyarya, Moscow, 1960
B.A. Smirnov: Nebo, moej molodosti, Moscow, 1990
A.T. Tishchenko: Vedomye "Drakona", Moscow, 1966
I.A. Vishnyakov: Na krutykh virazhakh, Moscow, 1973
A.V. Vorozhejkin: Rassvet nad Kievom, Moscow, 1966
A.V. Vorozhejkin: Nad Kurskoj dugoj, Moscow, 1962
A.V. Vorozhejkin: Pod nami Berlin Gorkij, 1970
A.V. Vorozhejkin: Istrebiteli, Moscow, 1961
K.A. Yevstigneyev: Krylataya gvardiya, Moscow, 1982
G.V. Zimin: Istrebiteli, Moscow, 1988

BIOGRAPHIES
Lyudi bessmertnogo podviga, Moscow, 1961, 2 vols.
Kniga o geroyakh, Moscow, 1963, 1958, 1968
S.S. Smirnov: Rasskazy o neizvestoykh geroyakh, Moscow, 1964
I.G. Pukhaev: Vernost otchizne v boyakh dokazali, Tskhinvali, 1990
A.M. Kucherov et al.: Geroi i podvigi, Moscow, 1986
A.N. Kulakov: Lyudi bolshoj sudby, Moscow, 1987
Geroi Sovyetskogo Soyuza – voiny Karelskogo fronta, Petrozavodsk, 1970
N.M. Rumyantsev: Geroi Khalkhin Gola, Moscow, 1989
Lyotchiki.Sbornik, Moscow, 1981
A.V. Burov: Tvoi geroi, Leningrad, Leningrad, 1970
Dvazhdi Geroi Sovyetskogo Soyaza. Albom, Moscow, 1973
Geroi Sovyetskogo Soyaza. Kratkij biograficheskij slovar, Moscow, 1987-1988, 2 vols.
(Ames-Khan) B. Butaev: Amet-Khan Sultan, Moscow, 1990
(V.I. Fadeyev) V.I. Pogrebnoj: Chelovek iz legendy, Moscow, 1963
(A.K. Gorovets) G. Men: Istoriya odnogo podviga, Moscow, 1961
(A.F. Klubov) M. Bukhanov: Bessmertiye, Vologda, 1971
(P.P. Kozhanov) V.F. Golubev: Vperedi komissar, Moscow, 1988
(S.D. Luganskij) N. Kuzmin: Sergej Luganskij, Alma Ata, 1968
(A.A. Novikov) A.M. Khorobrykh: Glavoyj marshal aviatsii A.N.Novikov, Moscow, 1989
(A.I. Pokryshkin) M.K. Pokryshkina: Zhizn, otdannaya neby, Moscow, 1989
(B.F. Safonov) S.G. Kurzenkov: Vozdushnyj as, Moscow, 1966
(B.F. Safonov) M.I. Khametov: V nebe Zapolyarya, Moscow, 1987
(Ye.Ya. Savitskij) G.A. Somov: Marshal aviatsii, Moscow, 1990
(A.K. Serov) Z.Chalaya: Anatolij Serov, Sverdlovsk, 1970
(Z.A.Sorokin) M. Vodopyanov: Sibirskij kharakter, Moscow, 1958

HEROES OF VARIOUS DISTRICTS
(Amur)
A. Sergiyenko: Amurtsy – Geroi Velikoj Otechestvennoj vojne, Blagoveshchensk, 1970
(Astrakhan)
Sozvezdiye slavy, Volgograd, 1968
(Bashkir)
Slavnye syny Bashkirii, Ufa, 1966
(Bashkir)
Litsom na Zapad, Ufa, 1972
(Byelgorod)
Geroi – Byelgorodtsy, Voronezh, 1965
(Byelorussia)
Navechno v serdtse narodnom, Minsk, 1977
(Cheboksary)
Nashi zemlyaki – Geroi Sovyetskogo Soyuza, Cheboksary, 1968
(Chechen-Ingus)
Zolotye zvezdy Checheno-Ingushetii, Groznyj, 1964
(Crimea)
Zvezdy nemerknushchej slavy, Simferopol, 1975
(Dagestan)
Otvashnye syny gor, Makhachkala, 1968
(Dnyepropetrovsk)
Zolotye zvezdy, Dnyepropetrovsk, 1967
(Gorkij)
Za otchizny, svobody i chest!, Gorkij, 1975
(Irkutsk)
I.I. Kuznetsov: Zashchishaya otechestva, Irkutsk, 1968
(Irkutsk)
I.I. Kuznetsov: Zolotye zvezdy Irkutyan, Irkutsk, 1982
(Izhevsk)
I.G. Kulemin: Geroyev nashikh imena, Izhevsk, 1966
(Kazakhstan)
Geroi Sovyetskogo Soyuza – Kazakhstantsy, Alma Ata, 1968, 2 vols.
(Kharkov)
I.T. Grichenko/N.M.Golovin: Podvig, Kharkov, 1977
(Kharkov)
Podvigi vo imya otchizny, Kharkov, 1974
(Kherson)
Voshedshiye v bessmertiye, Simferopol, 1974
(Kherson)
Medal za boj, medal za trud, Simferopol, 1990
(Kiev)
Boevye zvezdy Kievlyan, Kiev, 1968
(Kirov)
Geroi Sovyetskogo Soyuza – Kirovchane, Kirov, 1973
(Komi)
A.I. Usov: Serdtsa i zvezdy, Syktyvkar, 1966
(Kursk)
Zolotye zvezdy, Voronezh, 1966
(Leningrad)
A.V. Burov: Tvoi geroi, Leningrada, Leningrad, 1965
(Lipetsk)
Dorogoj slavy i bessmertiya, Voronezh, 1966
(Moscow)
Geroi ognennykh let Moscow, 1975-1976, 2 vols.
(NW RSFSR)
Zolotye zvezdy Severyan, Arkhangelsk, 1967
(Novgorod)
Geroi zemli Novgorodskoj, Leningrad, 1965
(Novgorod)
V.Ivanov: Tridtsat otvazhnykh, Novgorod, 1958
(Omsk)
Omichi v boyakh za Rodinu, Omsk, 1963
(Orel)
Za zemlyu Rodnuyu, Orel, 1963
(Orenburg)
Rasskazy o geroyakh, Orenburg, 1960
(Pavlodar)
Pobedivshiye smert, Pavlodar, 1967
(Penza)
Geroi i podvigi, Saratov, 1966
(Perm)
Otchizny vernye syny, Perm, 1964
(Petrozavodsk)
Geroyam Rodiny slave!, Petrozavodsk, 1970
(Ryazan)
Vsegda v stroyu, Ryazan, 1963
(Saratov)
Radi zhizhni na zemle, Saratov, 1965
(Saratov)
Shagnuvshiye v bessmertiye, Saratov, 1971
(Simferopol)
Zvezdy nemerknushchej slavy, Simferopol, 1967
(Southern Urals')
A.Kislitsyn: Yuzhnouraltsy – Geroi Sovyetskogo Soyuza, Chelyabinsk, 1960
(Stavropol)
Oni proslavili Stavropol, Stavropol, 1962
(Sverdlovsk)
Zolotye zvezdy Sverdlovchan, Sverdlovsk, 1970
(Tambov)
L.G. Dyachkov: Geroi Sovyetskogo Soyuza – Tambovtsy, Voronezh, 1974
(Tambov)
L.G. Dyachkov: Nasha gordost i slave, Voronezh, 1963
(Tatary)
L. Khanin: Geroi Sovyetskogo Soyuza – syny Tatarii, Kazan, 1963
(Tula)
Tulyaki – Geroi Sovyetskogo Soyuza, Tula, 1967
(Turkmenistan)
Imi gorditsya Turkmenistan, Ashkhabad, 1973
(Uzbekistan)
Bessmertiye, Tashkent, 1975
(Volgograd)
Geroi Volgogradtsy, Volgograd, 1967
(Vologda)
Vologzhanye – Geroi Sovyetskogo Soyuza, Vologda, 1959
(Voronezh)
A.Grinko/G.Ulayev: Bogatyri zemli Voronezhskoj, Voronezh, 1965
(Yakutsk)
D.D. Izbekov: Yakutyane v nebe frontovom, Yakutsk, 1970
(Yaroslavl)
Geroi ognennykhlet, Yaroslavl, 1968
(Yoshkar-Ola)
Nashi geroi, Yoshkar-Ola, 1963
(Zaporozhye)
Podvigom slavny tvoi zemlyaki, Zaporozhye, 1962

AIRCRAFT
Istrebitel P-39 Aeracobra, Moscow, 1990
K. Kosminkov/D. Grinyuk: Samolyoti Stalininskikh sokolov Sankt-Peterburg, 1992
V. Voronin/P.Kolesnikov: Sovyetskiye Istrebiteli Velikoj Otechestvennoj vojny Moscow, 1986

Lavochkin La-7 "27" in the livery of I.N. Kozhedub, the Allied ace of aces, when he was fighting with the 176 GIAP in the latter stages of the war. Kozhedub gained 17 kills while flying this particular aircraft.

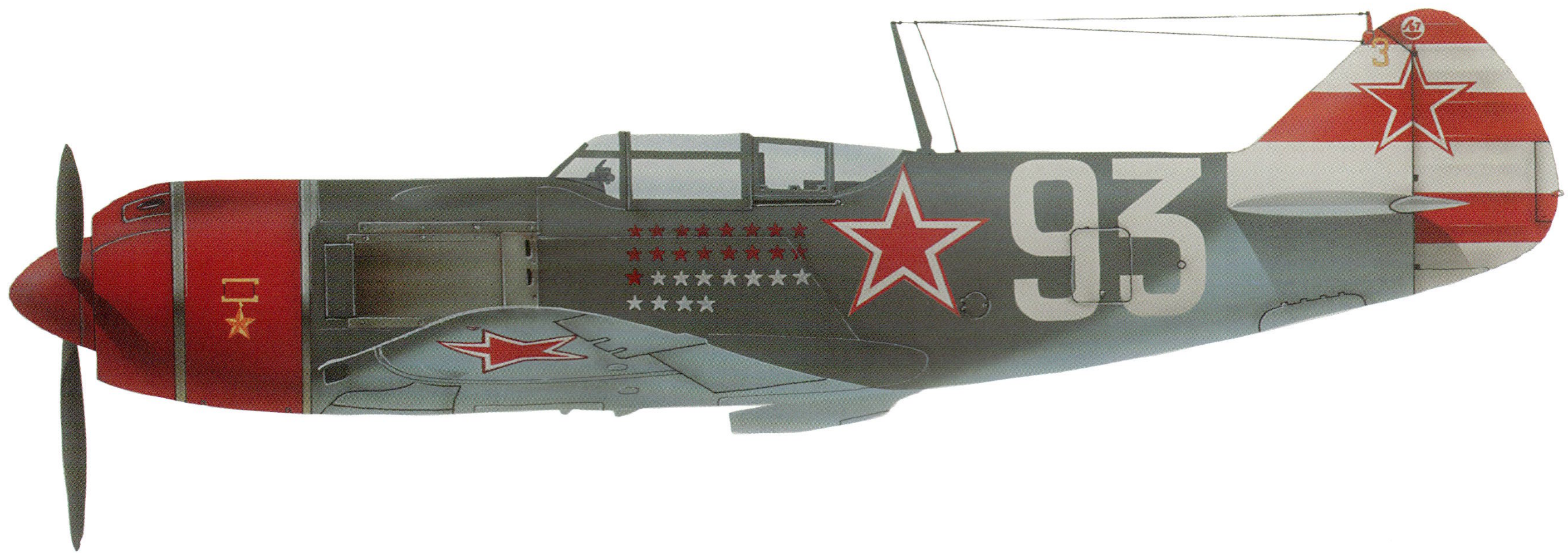

Lavochkin La-7 "93" flown by Podpolkovnik S.F. Dolgushin, the last wartime commander of the 156 IAP. A Gold Star medal, token of Hero of the Soviet Union, graced the nose of his aircraft. Seventeen red and eleven white stars beneath the cockpit denote his final official tally of personal kills, resp. fractional credits. Red spinner and nose were distinctive 8 IAK markings, while the 156 IAP applied three alternating red and white tail stripes to its aircraft. The plane wears an overall gray-skyblue finish with skyblue undersurfaces.

Lavochkin La-5 "Yellow 01" flown by twice Hero of the Soviet Union V.I. Popkov carrying the pilot's rather unique and striking markings as of 1944. Popkov finished as 5 GIAP's top-scoring ace with 41 personal kills.

Bell P-39N Airacobra "100" assigned to the second ranking Allied ace of World War II, A.I. Pokryshkin.

This Bell P-39Q was G.A. Rechkalov's personal mount when he scored most of his kills. Cyrillic three-letter code "RGA" denote his initials.

Yakovlev Yak-1 "White 1" flown by 183 IAP's famous ace, M.D. Baranov, on Stalingrad Front in 1942. The inscription on the rear fuselage reads, "Terror to the Fascists - M.D. Baranov."

Yakovlev Yak-1 liberally adorned with V.P. Pokrovskij's personal artwork. He was a 12-victory ace flying this aircraft with the Northern Fleet's 2 GIAP in 1945. Eighteen victories shown on the Yak's tail possibly constitute his final bag of personal kills and fractional credits.

Yakovlev Yak-7B "33" flown by twice Hero of the Soviet Union P.A. Pokryshev when he was serving with the 29 GIAP. This particular aircraft formed one of the exhibits of the Museum of Defense of Leningrad in 1945 sporting 20 red and 10 yellow victory stars; this bag would appear to be incorrect as his final tally was more than likely 23 individual kills with 7 fractional credits.

Yakovlev Yak-9D "White 38" flown by A.I. Vybornov, high-scoring 728 IAP ace, in Poland late 1944. Inscription on the fuselage reads, "To A.I. Vybornov from the school-children of Kashira" (who transferred the sum of 72,000 rubles for the construction of this aircraft).

Lavochkin-Gorbunov-Gudkov LaGG-3 flown by Lejtenant Yurij Shchipov, who became an ace flying with the Black Sea Fleet's 9 IAP in 1944. The aircraft sported the standard 1943/45 color scheme.

A Mikoyan-Guryevich MiG-3 produced by Moscow's Aircraft Factory No.1 in winter finish, February, 1942. The inscription reads, "For the Bolshevik Party."

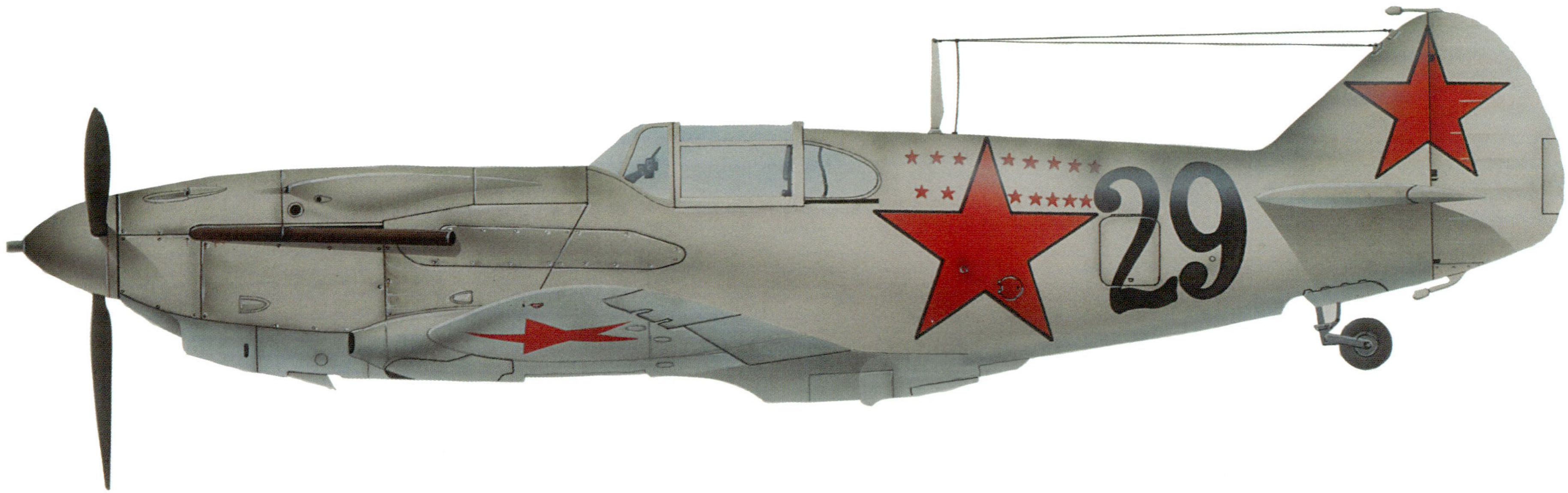

Lavochkin-Gorbunov-Gudkov LaGG-3 "Black 29" in winter finish flown by Kapitan G.A. Grigoryev, a notable 178 IAP pilot of the epic battle for Moscow, winter 1942/43.

Curtiss P-40K "White 23" flown by 36-victory ace N.F. Kuznetsov when he was flying with the 436 IAP at Staraya Russa in 1942.

Curtiss P-40E "White 10" flown by legendary B.F. Safonov, commander of Northern Fleet's 2 GIAP, and the aircraft in which he was lost on May 30, 1942.

Ilyushin Il-2 assigned to the top Allied tank hunter of World War II, A.N. Yefimov, when he was a Starshij Lejtenant in the 198 ShAP and leader of the 2nd Eskadrilya, Byelorussia 1944. His gunner at this time was Lejtenant I.A. Nechiporenko.

Mikoyan-Gurevich MiG-15bis "925" was the personal mount of Ye.G. Pepelyaev, second ranking jet ace of all time, in the early stages of the Korean war. The aircraft wears standard North Korean markings, i.e. a red star in a red circle, surrounded by a blue circle. Kill markings were only applied in the latter stages of the war.